FWS4995

SOFTWARE ENGINEERING
Design, Reliability, and Management

McGraw-Hill Computer Science Series

SOFTWARE ENGINEERING
Design, Reliability, and Management

Martin L. Shooman

Professor of Electrical Engineering and Computer Science
Polytechnic Institute of New York

McGraw-Hill Book Company

New York   St. Louis   San Francisco   Auckland   Bogotá   Hamburg
Johannesburg   London   Madrid   Mexico   Montreal   New Delhi
Panama   Paris   São Paulo   Singapore   Sydney   Tokyo   Toronto

This book was set in Times Roman by Science Typographers, Inc.
The editors were James E. Vastyan and Scott Amerman;
the production supervisor was Leroy A. Young.
The drawings were done by ECL Art Associates, Inc.
Halliday Lithograph Corporation was printer and binder.

SOFTWARE ENGINEERING
Design, Reliability, and Management

234567890 HALHAL 89876543

ISBN 0-07-057021-3

Library of Congress Cataloging in Publication Data

Shooman, Martin L.
    Software engineering.

    (McGraw-Hill computer science series)
    Bibliography: p.
    Includes indexes.
    1. System design. 2. Computer programs—Relia-
bility. 3. Computer programming management.
I. Title. II. Series.
QA76.9.S88S56 1983   001.64'25   82-9943
ISBN 0-07-057021-3   AACR2

To Sylvia, Andrew, and Alice

CONTENTS

PREFACE

OBJECTIVES

This book presents software engineering methodologies for the development of quality, cost-effective, schedule-meeting software. This approach serves a diverse audience: (a) upper-level undergraduates or graduates studying computer science, electrical engineering, mathematics, operations research, or industrial management, and (b) programmers, system analysts, software engineers, digital system engineers, engineering managers, or quality and reliability engineers in industry and government.

CONTENTS

Chapter 1 addresses the reader who has little previous software development experience. It focuses on the source of software costs, the technical and managerial problems of software development, and the techniques for designing high-quality software at a reasonable cost. This orientation is especially important to those without experience in the pressures and realities of an industrial project involving many programmers.

Chapter 2 focuses on modern software-design methods such as modularity, structured programming, top-down design, and defensive programming. A variety of design representations including pseudo-code, HIPO diagrams, high-level flowcharts, and control flowgraphs are discussed. The emphasis is on approach and philosophy rather than on implementation details.

Chapter 3 develops complexity measures related to development cost and the number of program errors. Traditional measures such as the number of lines of code are compared with newer methods involving operator-operand counts, program information content (entropy), and control graph cyclomatic number.

Chapter 4 treats testing as the prime method of revealing and pinpointing residual program errors which must be reduced in number to improve the software. The various levels of testing are described (module, integration, functional, and simulation) and several kinds of tests (code reading, path testing, and exhaustive testing) are introduced. Algorithms are developed for computing and enumerating the number of paths in a program.

Chapter 5 explains reliability concepts and develops models for predicting and measuring software errors, reliability, and availability. Several proven software reliability models are presented, and techniques are introduced for estimating the model parameters based upon observations during software testing.

Chapter 6 deals with the basic principles of software management. Four main themes are stressed: (1) using formal and well-defined requirements, specifications, and carefully planned reviews; (2) estimating development costs and times, and planning and controlling the monthly expenditures of these resources; (3) monitoring the development process using both reliability and complexity models; (4) controlling quality by applying standards to the entire software life cycle.

Appendixes A, B, and C contain background mathematics for study or review of the probability, reliability, and graph theory concepts utilized in the text.

APPROACH

The scope of software engineering is broad and encompasses many topics. This book selects those portions of the subject which present a logical and coherent body of knowledge for classroom presentation or self-study. The emphasis is on quantitative methods, tools, and analytical techniques which aid the manager, programmer, and engineer in carrying out the difficult task of software development.

The book presents material of interest to both the experienced programmer and the neophyte. The professional will find that much of the material in the text is reinforced by his own experience. Practical examples and case studies are included for the reader who has not been exposed to a large-scale software development.

Important features for self-study or classroom use are: (a) the large number of problems given in the text along with selected solutions, (b) the comprehensive reference list and frequent citations throughout the text, and (c) the selected set of introductory references following Chapter 1.

ORGANIZATION FOR CLASSROOM STUDY

The subject matter of this book is broad and has been divided into six chapters; each chapter covers a large number of topics. Individual chapters and major subsections are written in modular fashion, which will aid an instructor who wishes either to use a different approach or to supplement and replace portions of the text with material of his own choosing.

More than enough material for a one-semester junior or senior course or first year graduate course is included. An alternative structure is having a two-semester course with students engaged in term projects during the second semester.

For use in the former type of course I suggest: Chap. 1; Chap. 2 (omit Secs. 2.5, 2.6); Chap 3 (omit Secs. 3.2.6, 3.2.9, 3.2.10, 3.3, 3.4); Chap. 4 (omit Secs. 4.6.5, 4.7.1, 4.7.2, 4.9, 4.10); Chap. 5 (omit Secs. 5.4, 5.5, 5.6.4, 5.6.5, 5.7.7, 5.7.8, 5.8, 5.9); Chap. 6 (omit Secs. 6.3 to 6.7).

At the Polytechnic Institute of New York I offer this material as a two-term graduate sequence. The first term covers the material listed above but also includes all sections of Chaps. 3 and 4. The second semester covers all remaining sections of Chaps. 5 and 6 and focuses on a design project. The students are organized into 3 to 5 person groups, and topics are chosen during the first three weeks of the semester. About one-third of the course sessions are reserved for class design reviews given by each group. Reviews are held on the specifications, the preliminary design, and the management plan. Many other approaches to the organization and presentation of the text material are possible.

OTHER FEATURES

A teacher's manual has been prepared which contains suggestions on how the material can be presented in various classroom settings. Discussions are included regarding how projects can be chosen and directed for undergraduate- and graduate-level students. Typical examinations and solutions are given. Copies of the manual are available to instructors through the publisher.

A set of videotapes of the author's course lectures has been recorded, and further details can be obtained from the Director of Educational Development at the Polytechnic Institute of New York.

Many short courses (from one to five days) have been given on various phases of this material, and information on such courses is available through the author.

ACKNOWLEDGMENTS

The author wishes to thank the Office of Naval Research and the Rome Air Development Center who provided support for much of the research material incorporated in this book under Office of Naval Research contracts Nos. N00014-67-A-0438-0013 and N00014-75-C-0858 and Air Force contracts Nos. F30602-74-0294 and F30602-78-C-0057. Additional support during the early phases of this work was provided by NASA under contract No. NAS 9-4065 via subcontract No. 438 with the MIT Draper Laboratory.

The author accepts full responsibility for any omissions or errors in the text; however, he wishes to thank the reviewers for their many helpful suggestions and guidance, especially: Prof. Frank L. Friedman, Prof. Henry Ruston, and Mr. John D. Musa. In addition, the author's students provided many helpful suggestions as the manuscript was being prepared and class-tested.

He also wishes to thank Mrs. Betty Johnson who carefully typed the manuscript and inserted the corrections throughout the revision process.

The author wishes to specially thank his family for their general encouragement—specifically to Sylvia Shooman who read the manuscript for style and clarity and Andrew and Alice Shooman who aided in the final proofreading.

Martin L. Shooman

INTRODUCTION

1.1 WHAT IS THE PROBLEM?

Some of the most fundamental forces which have shaped the twentieth century are technological in origin and relate to transportation, communication, energy, and manufacturing technology. Advances in these areas are linked to the invention and widespread use of automobiles and airplanes; radio, television, and radar; nuclear and solar energy; and the assembly line and automated manufacturing. Two other developments interact with and magnify the impact of all the above-mentioned colossal inventions, namely, electronics and the computer. Furthermore, the last two are inseparably linked, since our modern computers are electronic, digital devices.

We may subdivide a computer system into its input-output and memory systems (readers, printers, terminals, and disk and tape storage units), its central processing unit (the thinking and calculating portion), and its software (the programs, input and output data, and operating instructions). This book deals with the engineering techniques, methods, and theories which allow us to plan, design, develop, and maintain the software for modern computer systems.

The purpose of this chapter is to convey to the reader the problems of designing software for complex systems, the pervasiveness and impact of program errors, and how one designs software in a cost-effective manner when faced by such problems. The experienced practitioner knows these problems well and may wish to skim this chapter and begin reading Chap. 2.

1.1.1 The Seeming Infinite Power of the Computer

There are two phrases I have never heard used to describe computer projects: *I don't think we can do it* and *I'm not sure it's worthwhile doing*. This seems strange, since every engineer and scientist knows that there are periods in our technological development when state-of-the-art limitations or economic constraints restrict what we can do. However, when it comes to the computer we are all, even professionals in the field, somewhat overawed by the power of the device. We are now using the computer in the solution of problems which less than 25 years ago appeared in adventure comic strips and science fiction magazines.

In the majority of these cases, we have been successful, and this has led to leaps of technological advance which stagger the imagination. What is often not told is that in a number of cases we have let our unbridled enthusiasm specify systems whose sophistication has led to huge costs, and to a level of unreliability which outweighs the benefits. In some cases we have unwisely replaced "people functions" by lower-cost but error-prone "computer functions." Often a more modest goal or more thorough study, planning, and engineering would have led to a much less costly implementation, which achieved most, if not all, of the intended benefits. One need not look to the experts in the field for examples; the media are full of them:

1. A recent newspaper article reports that "partial failure of a computer that tracks planes coming into New York and Philadelphia airports led to delays of more than two hours for at least 100 incoming flights; ...the failure may have been caused by a new program installed [yesterday]...."[1] More serious is this excerpt from an official report by an air traffic controller. "On the 8 to 4 shift...my radar [screen] went completely blank twice. I was left with no indication of how many airplanes were under my control, where they...were, how high they were, what direction they were traveling. Nothing. Just blank."[2]
2. A magazine story gave 11 examples of computer errors. The most unusual concerned a major hotel in Chicago which ordered a form letter sent to past customers to stimulate future business. Unfortunately the printer's computer was erroneously loaded with a different mailing list. Thus, hundreds of Chicago housewives opened letters from the hotel thanking their husbands for their patronage. The hotel was soon swamped by calls from the irate husbands demanding an explanation for their wives, many of whom were threatening divorce.[3]
3. A recent newspaper feature article[4] entitled "When a Computer Makes an Error, Who Pays?" quoted three hypothetical but not fanciful situations posed by the vice chairman of the American Bar Association's Computer Law

---

[1] *Newsday*, Garden City, Long Island, N.Y., Sept. 7, 1978.
[2] *Newsday*, Feb. 16, 1976.
[3] *U.S. News & World Report*, May 2, 1977, pp. 61, 62.
[4] Reprinted on Sept. 7, 1978, in *Newsday* from a *Washington Post* article.

Section:
a. An air traffic controller, relying on information from his computer console, directs two Boeing 747s onto intersecting paths. The jets collide and burst into flame, and all aboard perish.
b. A hospital minicomputer, monitoring a patient recovering from surgery, fails to alert hospital staff that the patient is having a stroke. The patient dies.
c. A company discovers that its computer has mangled valuable and sensitive information beyond recovery. The loss gravely weakens the company's market position.

Many of the above problems stem from an unrealistic view of what it takes to construct the set of programs—the computer software—which is required to instruct the computer hardware in performing the necessary computations. In order to improve the record to date, we must better understand the software development process and learn how to estimate and trade off the time, manpower,

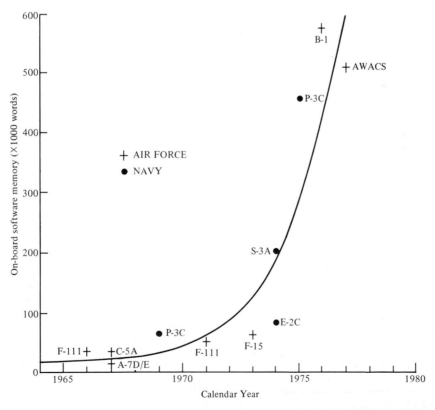

Figure 1.1 Exponential growth of computer memory requirements for planned or actual military aircraft. *(Boehm, 1976a)*

and dollars needed to produce software. An important goal is to learn how to initially estimate and subsequently measure the quality, reliability, and cost of the end product.

Some of the most avid proponents of computer systems are military organizations, which deal with increasingly huge and complex technological problems. A graphic illustration of such trends is given in the graph compiled by Barry Boehm and shown in Fig. 1.1. In this figure, we see the size of airborne computer memories growing at an exponential rate as a function of calendar years over the period from 1970 through 1978, and we infer that the programs stored in these memories are also growing exponentially.

In Sec. 1.1.2 we comment on the rapid decreases in cost, volume, weight, and power requirements resulting from the rapid advances in digital electronics; however, of vital importance is the question whether these advances will keep up with the growth trends depicted in Fig. 1.1.

Two curve-fitting programs were run on the data shown in Fig. 1.1. The raw-data points and the fitted power and exponential models are given in Table 1.1. Extrapolating into the future using the better-fitting exponential curve, we expect that, by the year 1985, on-board airborne computer memory sizes will exceed 4 million words for the largest projects. The implications of these predictions are contrasted with the advances in integrated-circuit and bubble memories in Sec. 1.1.2. In Sec. 1.2 we examine whether it is feasible to write, in a cost-effective manner, so big a program.

Table 1.1 Mathematical fit to Boehm's curve in Fig. 1.1

Year	Distance from base year 1960	Words of memory from Fig. 1.1	Power curve* $M = 199.3(Y - 1960)^{2.63}$	Exponential curve† $M = 4080\,e^{0.28(Y - 1960)}$
1965	5	25,000	13,705	16,588
1967	7	30,000	22,188	29,070
1969	9	35,000	64,251	50,945
1971	11	55,000	108,884	89,281
1973	13	180,000	168,915	156,465
1975	15	290,000	246,052	274,203
1977	17	600,000	341,909	480,540
1980	20	....	524,129	1,114,846
1985	25	....	946,432	4,474,263

Note: M = words of memory and Y = calendar year.

* Using Texas Instruments SR-52 Statistics Library Program ST 1-09, "Power Curve Fit." (Note: Correlation coefficient = 0.84.)

† Using Program ST 1-10, "Exponential Curve Fit" (Texas Instruments SR-52). (Note: Correlation coefficient = 0.93.) For further discussion of this program and the accuracy of the fitted curve, see Prob. 1.3.

1.1.2 The Dynamic Growth of Digital Electronics

Technology in the twentieth century has created the wondrous world of electronics. The vacuum tube, which made possible some of the remarkable technological advances prior to and during World War II, gave way to the transistor immediately following the close of the war.[1] During the early 1950s the size, cost, and power drain of all electronic circuits were dramatically lowered as the transistor came into its own. The decreased failure of a transistor, and the manyfold reduction in cooling requirements, gave rise to much more reliable computers.[2] In more recent years the integrated-circuit and microprocessor revolutions have resulted in further drops in the cost, size, failure rate,[3] and power requirements of a computer and have created entirely new markets for these devices.

Other ways of gauging more quantitatively the integrated-circuit revolution and its impact on computer hardware are given in Figs. 1.2 and 1.3. Figure 1.2 illustrates the yearly increase in computing power (bits processed per second) per dollar. In Fig. 1.3 the decreasing cost of computer memory per binary digit (bit) is illustrated versus calendar year. These curves will be used again in Prob. 1.5 to illustrate how computing costs are changing.

Now that we have discussed the counteracting effects of program size and memory cost, we turn to the human role in the next section.

1.1.3 Is the Programmer a Scientist, an Engineer, or an Artist?

A symptom of some of the problems in the software business is the confusion in everyone's mind, whether teacher, student, practitioner, or manager, about what role the programmer should play; also, what the role is of a system analyst, software engineer, software manager, or whatever. Many of these questions are indigenous to any large, complex development project—as is the key problem of defining the interfaces between various segments of the design which must be integrated during the design process. To shed some light on these problems, let us see what the roles of the scientist and the engineer are in the development of, say, an electrical or mechanical system.

First, we could probably all agree that the role of scientists belongs in the research and advanced development areas, creating new technology and techniques which allow others to do the development effort in better fashion. Sometimes, they are assigned to development projects, almost as consultants, to tap to advantage some of their superior skills. At the other end of the spectrum, we have the designer, whose prime function is to take a design (first built in the form of a model), show that it is feasible, and then transform the initial design

---

[1] Braun and MacDonald (1978).
[2] Thornton (1970), pp. 20, 21.
[3] Schnable et al. (1978), pp. 6–13.

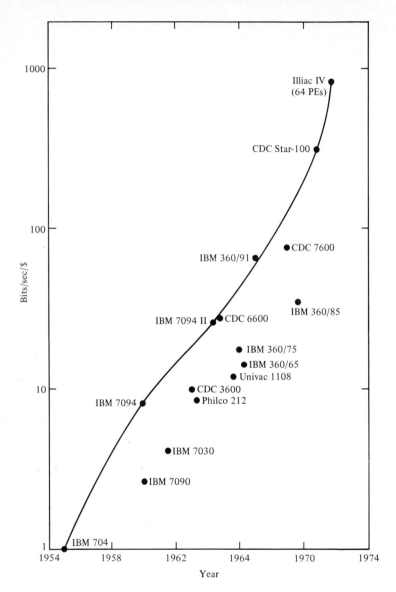

Figure 1.2 Cost-effectiveness of general-application computer hardware. *(Turn, 1974, p. 55)*

into a finished product which can be manufactured, meets environmental specifications, utilizes standard parts in manufacturing techniques, etc.

The bulk of the creative work lies in conjuring up a feasible design, verifying that it meets specifications, and making initial cost estimates. This work falls upon the shoulders of the engineer, who stays with the project until the model has been built and tested and then passes the responsibility to the designer (or

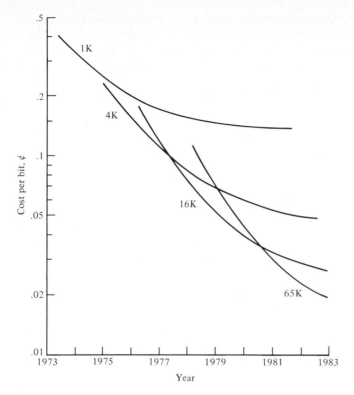

Figure 1.3 Decrease in memory cost with calendar year. Each curve is for a different package bit density. The transfer from one curve to another represents a step change in package bit density. *(Noyce, 1977. Copyright © 1977 Scientific American, Inc. All rights reserved.)*

manufacturing engineer). Of course the boundary line between engineering and design is not clear-cut.

Let us contrast this with the state of affairs in the software area. For many years, programmers thought of themselves as artists, and some still do. This term is perhaps appropriate for a small number of people who excel at their craft to an extraordinary degree. However, there are all too few such people present in the software field. Supposedly, if we were to have a piece of software created by such an artist, we would supply him or her with a description of the task and with all the information we had, disappear, and 2 years later ask to see the completed masterpiece.

Perhaps this is satisfactory with someone with as much talent as Michelangelo. However, there are very few programmers whose skills, genius, and lasting impression on their craft will in sum total equal Michelangelo's. Furthermore, the frescoes in the Sistine Chapel took 5 years to complete, and if we may believe the popular movie characterization of Michelangelo's life, Pope Julius II spent a good portion of his time wandering into the chapel looking up at Michelangelo on his scaffolding and asking, "Is it done yet?"

At the other end of the programming spectrum, we have *computer science*, the name of the degree program under which a great many software people have studied which represents the theoretical end of the business. Most of the ideas studied here help one to formulate, conceptualize, and understand what programming and computer solutions are about; yet, they often do little to help us actually produce software. Again the largest portion of the task falls upon someone who performs the function of software engineer and software designer. The dilemma is that there are too few such people who perform these latter functions well, and the universities are still struggling with curricula for software engineering training.

1.1.4 Lack of Program Engineering and Design Techniques

The technique of design in most engineering fields is not one of synthesis, but one of iteration. An approximate design is conceptualized and then analyzed to see if it meets the specifications; if not, the design is modified. This process is iterated a number of times to yield a satisfactory design. Thus, inherent in the design process is an ability to analyze the design and then compare the results of the analysis with the desired specifications. It is this very point—its lack of adequate analysis techniques—in which software engineering is the weakest.

As a means of analogy, we may look at other engineering techniques. In mechanical engineering, for example, one has a host of techniques based upon static and dynamic analysis of freebody diagrams, thermodynamic theory, and stress-strain calculations. If we borrow terms from the area of kinematics of motion, we can speak of *static* and *dynamic analysis* of a program.

Static analysis pertains to how inputs, initial conditions, and the software transform the program variables from their initial states to their final states when control passes through and leaves the single module of code under study. There are a number of techniques which help us to do such analysis. For example, we can study the data structure that exists in the input and within the storage of the program and manually process one set of data through the program, examining the role each instruction plays in the data transformations.

Dynamic analysis is a much more difficult situation. By dynamic analysis we mean a study of the complete history of data transformation in a program as a path is traversed and control is passed from one module to another, driven by new input. The lack of such tools makes the design process harder, and prevents us from clearly illustrating or documenting the full evolution of data during problem solution.

1.1.5 Management Thinking Is Rooted in the Computer Hardware

If we assume that most upper-level managers are in their mid-fifties and their formal training period terminated sometime during their mid-twenties, then it follows that they have been involved in industry for, perhaps, the past 30 years. This means that their college training was completed in the 1950s, before digital computers were widely used. If during the rise to their present position they became involved on a working level with a project requiring a computer, they absorbed some of the flavor and details of programming and software development. More likely, most of their computer experience is relatively recent (coming after they had already achieved a fairly high position) and has been with systems hardware. Some middle-level managers may fall into the same category; however, many more will have participated in projects involving software and will have had firsthand experience with software problems. Understanding is the first step, but management tools and experience are needed to deal with and control software problems.

For many years it has been common during project reviews for hardware people to present such things as schedule charts, block diagrams of the system, and lists of specific problems still to be solved. Such quantitative information is understandable to upper-level management and is useful for judging whether the project is doing well, is on schedule, or is being properly supervised. We contrast this with the presentations which were frequently made in the past by the software counterpart: "Rely on me! We have good programmers! The programs will be done well and will be ready on time!" What happened all too often in the past was that all the program modules[1] were written and individually tested while the lengthy and difficult task of interconnecting (integrating) these modules and removing all the ensuing errors was only partially completed. Extension of this period beyond the planned date by many weeks or months generally involved huge schedule delays, cost overruns, and generally a bad and distressing situation internally and externally.[2]

The software situation has significantly changed for the better. Modern design techniques produce top-down modular designs, which are easier to explain and much easier to integrate. Various design representation techniques, such as HIPO diagrams, pseudo-code, and structured flowcharts, allow the presentation of design ideas in a form which upper-level management can absorb. Yet the problems and mistakes of the past linger and often impede management from appreciating and supporting the improvements which have evolved over the years. In fact, getting upper management (and many practitioners) to realize that major changes have occurred and obtaining their acceptance and support is a continuing problem, which is discussed in Chap. 6.

To place matters in perspective, it is generally true that large projects traditionally have time and cost overruns (some of which are covered if management has included a "safety factor" in the original estimate). The advantage for hardware is that these overruns can often be anticipated during the course of the project by using existing management tools and experience. In the software area we are just beginning to develop and apply equivalent tools, skills, and insight.

---

[1] The term *module* is used to describe a largely self-contained section of the program which performs a specific function or subfunction.

[2] "The typical 200–300% cost overrun is no longer tolerable when the cost is measured in millions of dollars and the most optimistic schedule expectation is three years or more" (Putnam and Wolverton, 1977, p. i).

Now that we have uncovered the nature of the problem (the curse of complexity, the ready availability of low-cost hardware, the lack of adequate design tools, and managerial and design-personnel naiveté), we attempt to measure the size of the problem.

1.2 THE ALARMING SIZE OF THE PROBLEM

1.2.1 The High Cost of Software

The computer business is widely recognized as a large and important fragment of our national economy. However, how many readers realize that in the government fiscal year 1980 approximately $57 billion was spent on computer systems![1] What is even more startling is that $32 billion (56 percent of the total) was spent on computer software. Gradually, people are beginning to realize that some of the largest costs in the development of a new computer system, or in the modification of an existing system, are those associated with development of the system software.

If it can be assumed that advances in technology continue to drive down (inflation-corrected) hardware costs, designers will continue to utilize more and more powerful computers in wider and wider ranges of applications. It is quite possible that the effects of increased complexity and the decrease in component costs will cancel so that the total hardware cost of new computer equipment may stay relatively constant. Software costs, however, will continue to rise for many reasons: (1) each new application means new programs, (2) new computers replacing older, existing ones often mean either new software or modifications of existing software, and (3) programming is a highly labor-intensive skill, strongly affected by inflation. Although we have some new techniques which increase software productivity, it is unlikely that these gains will offset the large additional workloads of the future.

We can obtain insight into software costs by examining how the annual cost of software can be estimated. In Fig. 1.4, we see a trend curve of the split between hardware and software costs in Air Force computer systems. (Beyond 1972, the curve is an extrapolation.) In Table 1.2, we have utilized these data along with federal budget data for 1980. Air Force automatic data processing costs are 9 percent of the budget, and 80 percent of these costs are software (RAND Corporation study chaired by Barry Boehm, U.S. Air Force, 1972). The same percentages are assumed for the entire military budget, and corresponding percentages for the other two categories are the author's estimates. Since software costs represent over 7 percent of the yearly military budget, compared with 0.5 percent for the nongovernmental economy, it is clear why the military has spearheaded the drive for reduction of software costs.

---

[1] For comparison purposes, we note that annual sales of 9 million automobiles at an average cost of $8000 each represents $72 billion.

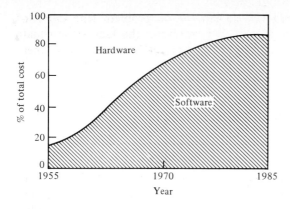

Figure 1.4 Hardware and software cost trends. *(U.S. Air Force, 1972)*

Table 1.2 Estimates of automatic data processing and software costs in the United States

Sector of economy	Budget or GNP, $ billions*	Total computer costs, % of budget	Software costs, % of total computer costs	Estimated software costs, $ billions	Estimated hardware costs, $ billions
National defense budget	125.8	9	80	9.1	2.3
Remainder of U.S. budget	405.8	5	50	10.1	10.1
Gross national product of U.S.	2565	1	50	12.8	12.8
Total				32.0	25.2

* "Carter Faces Problems in Achieving His [1980] Budget Goals," *Wall Street Journal*, Tuesday, Jan. 23, 1979, pp. 4, 5.

Other, similar cost estimates corroborate the computation in Table 1.2:

1. Boehm[1] estimated that software costs $16 billion per year based on 450,000 programmers in the United States in 1974 and an average yearly salary with overhead of $35,000.
2. A computation paralleling that of Table 1.2 using 1975 data yielded $19 billion per year in software costs.[2]
3. Arthur D. Little conducted a survey for *Datamation* magazine which showed total computer sales were above $30 billion and sales of one-of-a-kind software were $3 billion to $4 billion. Excluded from the computation were military

[1]1975, (p. 4).
[2]Shooman (1978).

Table 1.3 Exponential curve fit to McClure's data for software growth*

Year	Year − 1950	Memory words	
		McClure's data (machine instructions)	Exponential curve†$M = 951e^{0.43(Y-1950)}$
1954	4	5,000	5,414
1956	6	20,000	12,919
1959	9	35,000	47,628
1961	11	100,000	113,657
1964	14	350,000	418,983
1966	16	1,000,000	999,838
1967	17	2,000,000	1,544,532
1970	20	....	5,693,740
1980	30	....	440,622,966
1985	35	....	3,268,228,800

* Data on amount of machine language code provided as support with standard computer products versus year of release, prepared by McClure in Naur et al. (1976).

† Using Program ST 1-10, "Exponential Curve Fit" (Texas Instruments SR-52). (Note: Correlation coefficient = 0.986.) See Prob. 1.3.

software, company supplied software, and software written by the customers themselves.[1]

4. A wealth of detailed data on computer hardware and software costs appears in Phister (1979).

Another estimate of software growth can be obtained from the amount of software (machine instructions) provided by computer manufacturers (see Table 1.3). Note that an exponential growth is clearly displayed over the 1954–1967 range. Extrapolating to 1970 yields a believable 5.7 million memory words, but extrapolation to 3.3 billion in 1985 is unreasonable. Great increases in productivity will be needed to control the costs of such huge software sizes (see Probs. 1.5 to 1.10 at end of this chapter).

1.2.2 The Impact of Software Errors

Software errors,[2] which surface during system operation, result in two costs: (1) the harm which ensues and (2) the effort of subsequent correction. For example, consider an electronic-funds-transfer banking system. Suppose an error occurs (in the rare case) when a person creates a new account and closes out the account *that same day*. Assume that the system successfully creates but never deletes the

[1] Rothenbuescher (1978), p. 85–110.

[2] In Chap. 5 a software error is defined as a problem in the external operation of the system (system failure) due to an internal software error (fault). The colloquial term *bug* is often used loosely when a precise definition is unnecessary.

account. Then, clearly, an overpayment can occur. A bank manager has four different options when confronted by such an error:

1. Such a case hardly ever happens, and someone will probably detect the error by normal accounting methods. The probability that someone will utilize such an error for theft is small; therefore, it can be forgotten.
2. Because of the high cost of correction and the small probability of occurrence, the software will not be changed. However, *all responsible individuals will be notified to watch for such an abnormality*.
3. The *error will be corrected* when convenient, e.g., in the new release of the software planned in several months.
4. A software designer will be assigned *immediately* to the diagnosis, redesign, test, and installation of a correction to eliminate the error.

Clearly, approach 2 or 3 seems to fit this situation (and will fit most cases). Approaches 1 and 4 are rarely appropriate and cost-effective. The expected losses relate to the possible theft[1] via the mistake and the time required to watch for this error. Using the techniques of Chap. 6, we can estimate the cost of correcting such a problem.

Prior to discussing costs, we should clarify what steps are included in the process of software development. The so-called womb-to-tomb cycle shown in Table 1.4 is a generic list of phases which hold for any large project. In the case of software, a few comments are in order. First, the design process in Table 1.4 includes software design and program writing (coding). Software generally does not have an equivalent prototype-manufacturing (breadboard, scale-model) phase. However, in Chap. 6, we will discuss some management techniques involving a two-step design process in which the first stage can be considered a prototype. Second, somewhere between step 6 and step 8 each of the relevant functions or processes which the software must perform (called modules or units) are individually written and module-tested before the system-integration phase (testing the modules together). Last, the production phase is merely the duplication of computer tapes, disks, or read-only memories (ROMs).[2] We now discuss how total effort is distributed throughout the development cycle.

If we examine Table 1.5, which was compiled by Boehm, we see that about 40 percent of the effort on programming projects is devoted to testing to detect errors (bugs) and correcting (redesigning) the software to eliminate those which are found. If we could guarantee that a program would be initially coded without error, then the significant error-removal costs could be saved. Modern programming techniques (structured programming; top-down design) will produce significantly fewer errors; however, there are still some bugs, and we cannot reduce the

---

[1] The harm associated with the error need not involve potential theft. Suppose that the system actually closed out a different account held in the bank by the same (or a different) customer. The effort on the customer's part to correct the error would be substantial.

[2] Some people call software stored in ROM, *firmware*.

Table 1.4 List of project phases for the development of a large system

1. Initial conception
2. Requirements analysis
3. Specification
4. Initial design
5. Verification and test of design
6. Redesign
7. Prototype manufacturing
8. Assembly and system-integration tests
9. Acceptance tests (validation of design)
10. Production (if several systems are required)
11. Field (operational) trial and debugging
12. Field maintenance
13. Design and installation of added features
14. System discard (i.e., the death of a system) or
    complete system redesign

amount of testing to zero. In fact, unless we are experienced with a low-bug-content design technique, or unless we can *measure* the bug content to judge the quality of the software, we may not be willing to trust the method (take a chance) and reduce the amount of program testing. Quantitative estimates of software quality are important in judging progress during the development cycle. Thus, the reliability and error-content measures discussed in Chap. 5 also should be viewed

Table 1.5 Software effort distribution by activity

	Analysis and design*	Coding and auditing†	Test and integration*
Command-control (SAGE, NTDS)	35%	17%	48%
Command-control (TRW)	46%	20%	34%
Spaceborne (Gemini, Saturn)	34%	20%	46%
GP executive (OS/360)	33%	17%	50%
Scientific (TRW)	44%	26%	30%
Business (Raytheon)	44%	28%	28%

Source: Boehm (1975), p. 7.

* Documentation costs (estimated as an additional 10 percent) are not included.

† Auditing involves reading of the code and study of the design (desk checking) to find errors before a module is machine-tested.

as quantitative measures to sell management when enough testing has been done and the product is ready for release.

Until now we have been speaking mainly about development errors. However, a much more costly class of errors consists of those which are detected in the field. An interesting study of the relative cost of removing computer errors, by phase of development, is given in Fig. 1.5. Many of the reasons for increases in error-removal costs as a project progresses are:

1. Testing becomes more complex and costly.
2. Documentation of changes becomes more widespread and costly.
3. Communication of problems and changes involves many people.
4. Repeating of previous tests (regression testing) becomes costly.
5. Once operation is begun, the development team is disbanded and reassigned.

Additional funds spent on extra checking and testing at the beginning of a program pay off handsomely later on by reducing the number of costly after-deployment computer errors. The tremendous cost of correcting errors during operation is discussed further in Sec. 1.2.3.

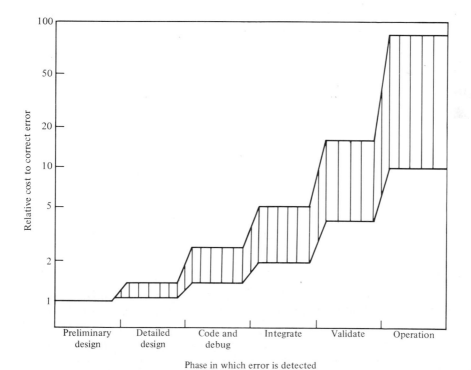

Figure 1.5 The relative cost of fixing errors versus phase of development. The data sources were IBM-SDD, TRW, GTE, and BELL LABS programs. The upper and lower curves represent a 95 percent confidence interval. *(Boehm, 1976b)*

1.2.3 The Problem of Software Modification and Maintenance

As we begin to study data in the area of software engineering, we find that as large as the development costs are, the maintenance expenses of software are even larger. A careful definition of maintenance costs is necessary since there is often confusion in this area. The term *maintenance cost* refers to the sum needed to fix errors in software that has been officially released and placed in operation. In addition, almost every large software system which has been deployed for a number of years has been modified in one way or another. The efforts associated with such changes, which we will call *redesign* (enhancement, added features), are very large and can approach or exceed the initial cost of the software. Some of the sources cited in Chap. 5 indicate that 30 to 80 percent of data processing budgets are spent on redesign and software maintenance. Note that in many cases a careful breakdown cannot be made between redesign and maintenance efforts because the costs are lumped together.

Considering economics, it would be wise to pay, say, 10 percent more for the development of reliable software with proper documentation. This will more than pay for itself in the long run through reduced maintenance and ease of redesign. The problem is that development and maintenance are generally separate budgets managed by different groups. Thus, it is difficult for the development group to negotiate a 10 percent price increase even if it will represent a 20 percent price decrease later on in the maintenance budget. It is important in the initial planning of a system to deal with total life-cycle costs. In hardware design we commonly use standardized parts. Section 1.2.4 considers whether this is feasible in software design.

1.2.4 Can We Standardize Software?

One of the phenomena evident in software is the "reinventing-the-wheel" syndrome. People are constantly designing many programs or large parts of programs over and over again. An obvious area, that of searching and sorting, has long been recognized, and in *Fortran-77*, searching and sorting facilities were provided as built-in functions for the user. Also, in mathematical software, there are numerous programs which perform matrix computations, statistical analyses, and plotting functions. These are designed over and over again. In fact, it is the developers of mathematical software who have championed the cause of "certified" software.[1]

Certified software is supposed to be approved by some standardizing agency, much in the same way Underwriters Laboratories tests and approves certain electrical products. Such software would meet fixed standards, be clearly described, be periodically (or occasionally) maintained, have flexible and well-defined interfaces, and in general be available for inclusion in other projects or for use as a stand-alone product. Some of the developments in the areas of certified

---

[1] Cowell (1972).

software are described in the following references:

1. IBM scientific subroutine packages in Fortran and PL/1[1]
2. Conferences on certified software[2]
3. British standard software projects[3]

Progress in software standardization has been slow for several reasons. The most important reason is the great effort needed to accomplish the work and to overcome the partisan narrowness and quibbles that occur in all standardization efforts. Some of the early history of language standardization efforts for Fortran, Algol, Cobol, and PL/1 appear in Rosen (1967, Pt. 2, pp. 29–36).[4] More recent standardization efforts on Fortran, and the U.S. Department of Defense language Ada, will be discussed in Chap. 2. The IEEE Computer Society Standards Office and ANSI took the initiative to standardize Pascal in 1979. We hope that new and substantial efforts in the certification of software will soon be forthcoming.

1.2.5 The Computer Business in the Last Quarter of the Twentieth Century

We now try our hand as pundits to predict the nature of the field during the remaining two decades of this century and the impacts on the software development process. Most probably developments in the field will be evolutionary rather than revolutionary. Many of these comments are mere extrapolations of items which have already been discussed. However, collecting them in a single list may better illustrate their interrelationships and present a composite picture. During this time period we would expect that:

1. The cost of computer central processing units will continue to decrease.
2. The cost of computer memory will continue to decrease.
3. The power of microprocessors available on a single integrated-circuit chip will continue to increase.
4. The cost of peripheral equipment such as card readers, disks, printers, and tape units will decrease more slowly than that of central processing units and memory.[5]
5. In the decade of the 1980s the computer business will overtake the automobile business as the largest single element in the United States economy.[6]

---

[1] IBM scientific subroutine packages for System 360 in Fortran and PL/1 (360A-CM-074).

[2] Cowell (1972).

[3] Numerical Algorithms Group, Ltd., NAG Central Office, 13 Banbury Road, Oxford, OX26NN, United Kingdom (a cooperative British universities project).

[4] See also "Cobol 1961."

[5] Disk subsystems may drop more rapidly. A 600-megabyte unit is expected to drop from $39,000 in 1981 to under $3000 in 1989 (see Isaacson, 1979).

[6] If we study Phister's data, we see in 1975 that passenger car sales were above $24 billion and have been rising roughly linearly since 1945. Computer shipments and revenues have been rising exponentially since 1955 and reached $5 billion in 1965 and $20 billion in 1975. (See Phister, 1974, Figs. 1.1.5 and 1.20.2.)

6. There will be an intensive effort during the 1980s and 1990s to employ some of the newer programming methods and force more and more programmers to use them in a desperate attempt to reduce software costs.
7. There will be both an increased understanding of the dynamic operation of the computer and better theories of program organization.
8. More and better software-engineering design techniques will be developed.
9. The manufacturers will offer software-engineering design tools as part of the regular software supplied with computers.
10. Military, industrial, and standards organizations will move more rapidly into the area of certifying standard software as a means of controlling the product and spreading the usage, thereby decreasing the unit costs to each user.
11. The small cost, size, and power requirements of microprocessors will vastly expand the number of high-volume products that include a computer. (At present this list is really only pocket calculators and digital watches.)
12. The microprocessor will invade the home products area and will be present in such diverse products as the automobile, television, stereo equipment, radio, audio and video recorders, major home appliances, the telephone, heating and cooling systems, and home security systems.
13. In the business area rapid progress is under way. Word processors are replacing typewriters, electronic funds transfer is rapidly changing the banking field, and only a spoken-word-to-printed-text machine eludes our grasp.
14. With the spread of cable TV, the future prospects of a home information system using the cable as input, the TV screen as output, and a microprocessor control box seem bright.

All the above forces indicate that our software problems will continue through the next two decades, but in somewhat changed form. The available new design and development techniques will establish more order and control to the development process. On the other hand, each of these new applications will require new software, and a succession of improved products and modified applications will continue to expand the amount of modified software which must be written. Overall it is clear that the amount and dollar volume of software will increase.

The most significant new factor will be the large number of dedicated microprocessors (embedded in another product, such as an automobile or a videotape recorder). Almost all these devices will operate with a prewritten program stored in read-only memory. Thus, the number of dollars spent for hardware for such products will overshadow the software costs as production runs increase. This might lead us to the conclusion that software will play a role of diminishing importance in such products. This will not be the case for the more sophisticated microprocessors, and furthermore, the cost of a software error multiplied over so many units can truly become horrendous. Think of the microprocessor with read-only memory which controls an automobile fuel and ignition system. Suppose the system also provides facilities for recording trip mileage and calculating gasoline miles per gallon. We now postulate a truly catastrophic software error: clearing (under certain conditions) the miles per gallon computation causes an error which advances the throttle! If this happens on five automobiles and causes accidents, injury, and death, the National Highway Traffic Safety Agency may recall the ROM that controls that program! The cost of that error might be measured in terms of millions of replacements and hundreds of lawsuits and the consequences would be appalling. In such cases we will have to utilize test methods on commercial products that are now used only on crucial military and aerospace projects. Many of the checking procedures discussed in Sec. 2.7.4 may be required.

1.3 HOW ARE WE DEALING WITH THE PROBLEM?

One hopes that the answers to such a question would be (1) application of all available engineering and management techniques to the development process in a cost-effective manner, (2) invention of imperfect but adequate ad hoc techniques where none presently exist, and (3) implementation of a vigorous and broad research program. Unfortunately this is not the truth. In some cases it seems that whenever software problems exist, we throw money at them until they go away, and that only a vibrant, growing industry like the computer business can sustain such waste. Although both extremes have been used, most projects fall somewhere between the sublime and the ridiculous. Obviously, the desire of this author and the other workers in the field of software engineering is to continue to push, at the greatest speed possible, toward the former solution.

1.3.1 Awareness of the Problem

The solution of any major problem requires many steps:

1. Awareness of the problem[1]
2. Diagnosis of the problem
3. Study and development of methods for treating the causes or alleviating the consequences
4. Application of the solution

[1] The first large-scale management report documenting the kind of present and future problems of software was a study prepared by the Rand Corporation for the U.S. Air Force, under the direction of Dr. Barry Boehm. (See U.S. Air Force, 1972.) The author's initiation into the field came during lunch on Apr. 24, 1970, at a conference of the Northern New Jersey Section of the American Society for Quality Control. His friend and mentor, Mr. George Levenbach, then head of system reliability at Bell Laboratories, mentioned that the author and/or some of his students should look into the pressing problems of software reliability. This comment was followed by a query from the author, "What's that, George?"; laughter by both parties; and the comment by Levenbach, "That's just why we think it's important for some people to look into it."

5. Verification that the problem is being removed, or alleviated in some way
6. Decision about what should be done in the future (ranging from documentation of the problem to a return to step 3)

Opinions will vary about our present state of progress in the software area; however, this author feels that we have progressed through stages 1 and 2 and are well into stages 3 and 4.

1.3.2 New Methods and Technology

One of the major accomplishments in the area of software engineering is the widening acceptance of the fact that most programming should be done in a higher-level language rather than in assembly language. During the 1960s the art of programming grew, and nearly all the sophisticated practitioners utilized assembly languages in their programming. Gradually people came to accept the fact that higher-level languages were superior vehicles for applications programming. However, many still maintained that for system programming only assembly languages gave the required efficiency in terms of computing time and memory requirements. In the 1970s more and more people were made to realize that these supposed advantages of assembly languages over higher-level languages were not always present. Even when the advantage was present, it might represent only 10 or 20 percent savings in general, and a number of large projects have been done successfully in higher-level languages.[1] In addition, sizable increases in programming productivity (amounts of code written, tested, rewritten, and verified per man-hour) could be shown for higher-level-language versus assembly language programming. In fact, the Department of Defense has a formal position against the use of assembly language. In a directive concerning software (DOD Directive No. 5000.29, April 1976) one section essentially said you must program in an approved higher-level language unless you can prove that assembler would be more effective *over the system life cycle*.

In a subsequent directive (DOD Directive No. 5000.31, November 1976) an interim list of seven languages was approved.[2] An obvious exception is that if one is writing an assembler, an interpreter, or a compiler for a new computer, one must use assembly and machine language programming techniques.[3] Also, in a few cases a small amount (5 to 10 percent of total) of assembly code may be

---

[1] The Bell Laboratories UNIX System is a compact, powerful timesharing system designed for the Digital Equipment Corporation's line of PDP-11 computers; see Thompson and Ritchie (1974). The MIT-Honeywell Multiplexed Information and Computing Service (MULTICS) was originally begun as an MIT-GE-Bell Labs Project, using PL/1 and the GE 645 Computer, see Corbató and Vyssotsky (in Rosen, 1967, pp. 714–728).

[2] The languages were Fortran, Cobol, and five traditional triservice languages: Tacpol, CMS-2, SPL/1, Jovial J3, and J73 (see *Datamation*, July 1979, p. 143).

[3] Of course if the machine directly executes a higher-level language, as is the case in some Pascal and Ada machines, even this is unnecessary.

warranted:

1. Input and output operations
2. Timing loops in real-time systems
3. Programming a microprocessor with a very small memory
4. Small sections of high-use code

However, the number of such cases in which one can truthfully show the superiority of assembly language programming is rapidly dwindling to a small, readily identifiable hard core of applications. In many of these cases the intelligent approach is to use a powerful macro assembler language or a few carefully written assembly language subroutines callable from a main program which is written in higher-level language. The new Department of Defense language Ada (available in the early 1980s) will join Fortran and Cobol as the only acceptable languages (see Sec. 2.8).

By far, the most important development in software design in recent years is the evolution of structured programming techniques. Basically, structured programming involves the use of three single-input and single-output control structures: SEQUENCE, IF THEN ELSE, and DO WHILE. Although there is still a minority viewpoint, and inertia on the part of many, the overwhelming bulk of opinion and collected evidence endorses the utility of structured programming and indicates significant gains in productivity.

The most important management advance has been the almost universal adoption of software configuration control on large projects and the requirements that the *design* be documented adequately. Such design documentation generally uses one or a mixture of design representation methods as vehicles. Typical methods such as HIPO charts, pseudo-code, flowcharts, and Warnier-Orr diagrams are studied in Chap. 2. At present there is a diversity of design descriptions and a loose characterization of many of these. It would be nice to standardize on one design characterization and stick with that. However, this is as unlikely as are standardizations on one spoken language throughout the world, or the use of just a single computer language. We will probably have to content ourselves with the coexistence of several design representations. The important point here is that the design be reduced to paper, and not merely maintained in the minds of a few of the designers.

One of the great needs in software engineering is for a group of meaningful quantitative measures of the goodness of software. Some substantial progress has been made in this area, and a number of software reliability models have been formulated (several of which have been tested and shown to work reasonably well).[1] Presently, many of the larger computer projects sponsored by the Department of Defense include separate requirements that the hardware and software meet specified mean time between failures (MTBF). Although some programmers

---

[1] Musa (1975).

cling to a deterministic view of programming and the programming process, an increasing number are endorsing the idea that there is more than one approach to the achievement of reliable programs. A designer may say (and rightly so) that no matter how many calculations you make, the reliability of the program will only be changed by more or better initial design, testing, and redesign. On the other hand, the analyst points out that unless we have a technique for measuring the level of reliability achieved, we will have no quantitative tools for comparing the efficacy of various designs or design techniques. Also, we will not be able to quantitatively predict when we have tested and redesigned enough to raise the software to an acceptable level. Thus, only intuition and good luck can save us from the penalties of overexpenditure or underexpenditure of resources.

Section 1.4 explores what improvements we may hope for in the future.

1.4 THE HOPES OF THE FUTURE

1.4.1 Improved Languages and Tools

A pattern seems to be developing in the industry for the standardization of our wide range of different computer languages into a practical working set of 5 to 10 languages. All will eventually be standardized, and gradually their range of features and areas of use will narrow. Also, the matching compilers will incorporate a wide range of debugging features to aid the programmer.

Within the last 4 or 5 years program developers have found it increasingly necessary to develop various programming tools to aid them in the development process.[1] These tools can be divided into several broad classes:

1. Program editing and storage
2. Program processors and preprocessors
3. Program configuration control and data collection
4. Testing and debugging programs

As better and better tools are evolved over the forthcoming years, these will be standardized and written into readily available packages which mesh with the standardized languages.[2]

1.4.2 Increased Use of New Development Methods

If we play the role of the eternal optimist, we may predict that sometime within the next decade or two some new developments or design concepts will be evolved which will revolutionize program development. However, even if we take a more

[1]Kernighan and Plauger (1976).
[2]UNIX (1976) pp. 164–189.

pessimistic view and discount such a possibility, great progress can be made as more practitioners adopt the design techniques which now exist along with their predictable extensions. Such developments will enforce a greater uniformity on the design process and produce a few different, well-defined, competitive design procedures. We will then have the opportunity to collect a sizable sample of reliability and productivity data for each of the procedures. Given a statistically significant sample, we can then study them, compare and contrast them, and learn about their good and bad features.

1.4.3 Program Proofs and Automatic Programming

The eventual future of program proofs and automatic programming techniques is more speculative than the other concepts which we have discussed in this chapter. Program-proof techniques utilize various logical methods to prove the validity of program segments. Automatic program techniques involve either (1) a dialogue between the designer and the computer to integrate available modules and subroutines to rapidly obtain a reliable, moderately efficient program or (2) the use of high-level requirements language which can be read and "compiled" into a conventional high-level programming language. There is some possibility that some of these techniques will not emerge from the research stage for a long time (if ever). However, should they be perfected, they would provide a most spectacular set of tools for program development. Program-proof techniques, even if not 100 percent perfect, would greatly decrease the number of program errors and give us greater peace of mind regarding how many residual ones might still be lurking in the software. Some of the presently practical approaches to program proofs are briefly discussed in Chap. 2.

One approach to automatic programming requires that the programmer sit at a console and build a new program by interacting in a conversational mode with the computer, first specifying the main program and some of its major component functions. The known subprograms would automatically be interfaced to the main programs via subroutine calls, and any subprograms not available in the system library would be newly created by the programmer in a consistent form with well-defined interfaces. Once such subroutines were perfected, they would be stored and available for further use. The advantage of such a programming system would be that each stored module could be written, tested, and perfected by experts and used by ordinary programmers. Of course, the main program and custom subroutines would not be of "expert quality." Such a technique would have maximum utility in a narrowly defined applications field, such as business data processing, for example, where a new program is largely a customized collection or integration of old subroutines and program functions. Should such a scheme be perfected, it would raise the skill level of many application programmers and change the development of a 10,000-word program into, say, the integration of 8000 words of existing code, the creation of a new subprogram 1000 words long, and the creation of a new 1000-word control structure. Thus, only about 2000 words of new code would have to be written.

Another approach to automatic programming begins with the definition of a high-level requirements language which can be used for the stating of the system requirements. Once these requirements were checked, the language would be compiled to yield a program. The resulting program would then be tested and debugged in conventional fashion. The advantage of such a procedure would be that variations between specifications and code would be eliminated.

We all hope that someday such techniques will pass from the research stage to operational use by all programmers.

1.5 SUMMARY OF THE CHAPTERS

1.5.1 Design

The top-down and bottom-up approaches have evolved as two schools of software design. However, if we reflect on the philosophies a bit, we see that the concepts are really not peculiar to software, but are valid for a wide range of engineering and organizational tasks. It is even convenient for us to utilize these terms to describe the organization of this textbook.

To begin with, we must start top-down and explain and illustrate the approach, content, and scope of software engineering. That is the purpose of this introductory chapter, and it is hoped that by now the reader has a good feel for the material that will be exposed in the subsequent chapters of this book. When we begin to study the details concerning each topic, we find the top-down approach not as appropriate for expository material as the bottom-up approach. A top-down approach may be quite appropriate for some areas of mathematics teaching; however, it is difficult to think of any engineering area (with the exception of the few areas where *synthesis* techniques are available) where we can stay in a top-down mode. Design, which is the heart of engineering, is almost always an iterative process in which the focus switches from top-down to bottom-up many times in the course of the design.

If we desire good software, it is imperative that the design be well done. The design stage includes not only initial coding, but also the preceding algorithm-formulation and specifications phases, and the subsequent test planning stage. Chapter 2 is concerned with software architecture in general and embraces the philosophy that the software will be good if it is initially well constructed. The concepts of top-down, structured, and modular design are introduced early in the chapter. In addition to these broad principles, some more definitive techniques such as defensive programming and redundant programming are explored. The effect of language on the end result is then discussed. It is clear to most workers in this field that one can almost always recommend a higher-level language in preference to assembly language. However, given a certain project, a computer with both a good Fortran and a good PL/1 compiler, and enough competent programmers who know both languages, which one should you choose? The chapter then explores and summarizes some specific design tools which are presently available.

We then switch to a brief discussion of two topics which are still largely in the research stages: automatic programming and program proofs. Although few commercial developers are presently using these techniques, the potential, should they become practical, is vast. In fact, if program proofs should become practical, Chaps. 4 and 5 of this book would really be of diminished importance, and a major chapter on program proofs would be substituted. Since this is not yet the case, and many doubt that it ever will be, Chaps. 4 and 5 are in many ways the most important portion of this book.

1.5.2 Complexity

Chapter 3 aims to codify and reduce to analysis, experiment, or quantitative estimate (albeit crude in some cases) these important software quality measures: the complexity of the problem, the required algorithm, the processing time, and the data-representation and memory requirements. These must be considered at the earliest design stages. We have numerous examples in the history of programming where a software manager, anxious to win a big contract, ignored warning signs that the problem was too complex for the budgeted resources. The resultant mess was severely damaging to both contractor and contractee. Estimates of complexity are most useful to us in the early and middle design stages. Since some complexity models focus on the testability of a program as the desired measure, these may continue to be useful into the design phase.

In a similar fashion, estimates of the processing time and storage are well understood (though not always well defined) and are of importance during the early contracting stages. In fact, processing-time estimates are especially important in embedded real-time computer systems. Most of this is due to the difficulty in dealing with time-critical portions of the software. Unless one has the foresight to provide safety margins in time-critical loops, the problems will remain with the programmer throughout most of the project.

Estimates of memory size must begin at the early stages of contracting and continue to be verified and refined as the project progresses.[1] In fact, one might view a case in which a marginal design feature was eliminated in order to conserve memory space as a mature and wise design trade-off.

1.5.3 Testing

At present the most important weapon in our arsenal for attacking software bugs is testing. In Chap. 4 we summarize the conventional techniques presently used to test software, analyze some of the proposed advanced techniques, and discuss and model test effectiveness. Clearly, a set of models allows one to plan on how to deploy testing resources (man-months and computer hours) in order to achieve the most error-free programs. At the outset of the chapter we discuss the relative advantages of code reading versus machine testing for the purpose of uncovering

---

[1]In some situations the rapidly decreasing size, cost, and power drain of integrated-circuit and bubble memories make memory size of secondary importance.

errors. The chapter then makes the well-known point that exhaustive testing is impossible. However, it defines an exhaustive test and shows how to approach in a logical fashion a series of practical tests of increasing thoroughness. The use of the computer as an aid in planning and developing tests is then discussed in the sections on automatic test generation and test tools. The chapter concludes with a discussion of the broader implications of testing, acceptance, validation, and verification.

It is not sufficient to merely remove the bugs from the program; we must prove to all concerned that the program satisfies the problem specifications. Further, we must also prove that the specifications do in fact solve the problem. All this adds up to a tremendous amount of testing which is open-ended unless we agree in the contract to an acceptance test which defines on what basis we will accept or reject the software. Lastly, the concept of certification is explored; it deals with the production of standard (efficient, documented, tested, and verified) software programs or subroutines which can be incorporated in subsequent problems.

1.5.4 Reliability

The subject of reliability (and availability) discussed in Chap. 5 is, in the last analysis, one of the most important factors in software quality, sometimes transcending the importance of the performance parameters. Since reliability is so important, we must be able to define, control, and measure the reliability of a program. Accordingly, Chap. 5 begins by defining reliability and the types of errors which occur in software. Some of the basic data in the literature are described, and error models are developed. The operational reliability of software is related to these error models, and techniques are developed to measure the parameters of the reliability and error models. Examples in which the models have been used with success in practice are discussed. The concluding section focuses on how one should plan and collect data which can be used to estimate the proposed model parameters and to explore future refined models. Clearly, reliability should be estimated at the outset of software development, and recomputed and refined as the development progresses. Further uses are to measure the present quality and rate of design improvement throughout development, and to indicate when enough testing has been done that the product can be released.

1.5.5 Management

In the concluding chapter, Chap. 6, on management techniques, we return to a top-down view of our subject. The concepts developed in Chaps. 2 through 5 are reviewed and discussed in terms of where they fit in the development of a project from initial concept stages to discard. In each case the impact on program schedule and cost will be discussed. A certain technique may be too expensive on a small project; but it may be the best investment a manager can possibly make on a larger project. The chapter concentrates on organization and personnel, as well as program control and documentation measures. It also continues with a discussion of computer software and cost estimation.

The last section of the book contains brief descriptions of five successful systems, three commercial and two military ones, which typify many of the issues which have been discussed. The systems we have chosen are the SAGE Air Defense System, the SAFEGUARD Antiballistic Missile System, the American Airlines SABER Airlines Reservation System, the Bell Laboratories UNIX Time Sharing System, and the Bell-GE-MIT-Honeywell MULTICS Time Sharing System.

Cost estimates, complexity management, reliability, processing time, storage time, and development time are the key items which differentiate project success from project failure. Chapter 6 tells us what to do and when to do it to achieve good programs. However, before we can proceed, we must absorb the details of how it can be done, which are contained in Chaps. 2 to 5.

PROBLEMS

1.1 The most dramatic story of a software error comes from the popular American science fiction movie *2001: A Space Odyssey*.[1] The dialogue occurs between Mission Commander David Bowman and the computer HAL while the spaceship controlled by HAL is on its way to the planet Jupiter. HAL detects and Bowman replaces a faulty component. Bowman orders, "HAL, carry out fault prediction tests" (on the removed module). "Circuit fully operational," reports HAL after only 10 seconds.

But Mission Control, following these actions, has its own interpretation. " . . . This is mission control . . . there is another possibility. Your computer may have made an error in predicting the fault. Both our own HAL computers agree in suggesting this. . . ."

Bowman drums his fingers on the console. "HAL . . . is something bothering you—something which might account for this problem?"

"Look, Dave, I know you are trying to be helpful. But my information processing is normal; . . . check my record; you will find it completely free from error."

"I know about your service record, but . . . anyone can make mistakes."

"I don't want to insist, Dave, but I am incapable of making an error. . . ."

"Hello, this is Mission Control. We have completed analysis of your AE-35 difficulty, and both our HAL computers are in agreement. The trouble lies in the prediction circuits, and we believe that it indicates a programming conflict which we can only resolve if you disconnect your HAL computer and switch to Earth mode control."

As Bowman began to switch off the computer, HAL fought back, and Bowman only gained control of his spaceship by dismantling the computer's memory.

Our software problems haven't gone this far yet, *or have they*?

(*a*) How could Bowman have diagnosed the onset of "insanity" in HAL without the help of Mission Control?

(*b*) How should HAL have been designed to avoid this problem?

[1]Arthur C. Clarke, *2001: A Space Odyssey*, based on the MGM film screenplay of the same name, Signet, New York, 1968, pp. 119–1157.

1.2 The evolution of the Digital Equipment Corporation PDP-8 and PDP-11 minicomputer lines provides a graphic example of how the electronics revolution has rapidly decreased the cost of computer equipment.

In 1965 the Polytechnic Institute of New York acquired its first PDP-8 computer, with 4000 words of memory at a cost of $18,000. It was approximately $1\frac{1}{2}$ times the size of the standard two-drawer office filing cabinet. Three or four years later an integrated-circuit version called the PDP-8I was designed. The cost dropped to $10,000, and the size was reduced to that of a small overnight suitcase. By the early 1970s, although the cost of the new PDP-8 models continued to drop, a new, more powerful minicomputer, the PDP-11, was announced at the price (for the main processor plus 4000 words of memory) of $11,000. As sales for the PDP-11 grew, manufacturing costs were cut, and despite inflation, there was a gradual decrease in price of the computer. However, by the mid-1970s large-scale integrated-circuit versions of the PDP-11 computer were designed, and in 1977 a kit version of this computer appeared on the market at a cost of about $1400.[1]

(*a*) Sketch cost versus calendar year for the above example.

(*b*) Do you believe this trend will continue? Explain

(*c*) Compare the above example with Fig. 1.2. Assume that (1) an average 12-bit-long PDP-8 instruction took 3 μs to process and (2) an average 16-bit-long PDP-11 instruction takes 1 μs to process.

(*d*) Scan the literature and use your own experiences to compare more modern machines with the data in Fig. 1.2.

1.3 The Texas Instruments SR-52 exponential curve-fitting program uses a common stratagem for simplifying the job of exponential curve fitting.[2] The direct approach is more difficult and is described first.

Suppose we wish to fit the functions $y = ae^{bx}$ to a set of n data which we suspect to be an exponential curve. Our data are a set of n pairs, $(y_1, x_1), (y_2, x_2), \ldots, (y_n, x_n)$. We wish to determine the values of a and b which best fit the data (in a least-squares sense).

At each point we calculate an error

$$g_i(a, b) = \left(y_i - ae^{bx_i} \right)^2$$

The sum of all these errors

$$G(a, b) = \sum_{i=1}^{n} g_i(a, b) = \sum_{i=1}^{n} \left(y_i - ae^{bx_i} \right)^2$$

is the quantity to be minimized.

(*a*) Find the optimum values of a and b computing $\partial G/\partial a$ and $\partial G/\partial b$ and setting these to zero. The resulting equations are called *normal equations*.

(*b*) How easy is it to solve the pair of normal equations for the values of a and b which best fit the data of Table 1.1?

The simplifying stratagem is to first take the natural log of both sides of the equation. Thus,

$$\ln y = \ln a + bx$$

---

[1] Bell et al. (1978). See Chaps. 1–3 and pp. 195, 200.

[2] The author is indebted to Professor Harold Stone of the University of Massachusetts at Amherst for calling this to his attention.

This has transformed the exponential curve-fitting problem into an equivalent linear one, where we use $\ln y_i$ and x_i as the data pairs. The solution of the transformed problem for a and b yields values which are close to but are not exactly the least-squares fit parameters.[1]

(c) Evaluate how close these two methods are by solving numerically the normal equations derived in part (b), using the values in Table 1.1 as starting values and plotting the two resulting curves. (Note that the values of a and b given in the table are rounded to three decimal places.)

(d) What is the software engineering lesson to be learned from the fact that the author did not investigate the accuracy of the curve-fitting method? From the fact that Texas Instruments made no mention of it?

1.4 *Fortune* publishes lists of the top 500 and second 500 industrial companies in two different spring issues of the magazine. The companies are also classified as to industry. Locate data from several previous years and plot the percentage of computer companies in the *Fortune* 500 (1000) list versus calendar year. How does this growth rate compare with other indicators, such as the ratio of IBM revenue to gross national product?

1.5 We can compare the projected cost of future computer hardware and software if we make certain assumptions:

(a) Show that Table 1.1 corresponds to a growth in the memory size of airborne computers according to the formula $M = 4080\,e^{0.28(Y-1960)}$.

(b) The cost of memory will decrease according to the formula derived by Bell[2]

$$\text{¢/bit} = 0.3 \times 0.72^{Y-1974}$$

If our computer word length is 16 bits,

$$\text{\$/word} = 0.048 \times 0.72^{Y-1974}$$

Do you agree with Bell's formula? Does it agree with Fig. 1.3?

(c) Assume that the year is 1985. What will the size of memory be? What is the hardware cost of this memory if each word is 16 bits long?

(d) Assume that in 1985 a programmer can develop programs at a rate of 10 instructions per day. Assume a reasonable salary (including 100 percent overhead) and calculate the cost to fill the memory with instructions.

1.6 Assume that, in 1974, twenty debugged instructions were written per man-month[3] and that the salary of an experienced programmer was $4000 per month, including overhead. What is the cost per instruction?

Assume that over the period 1974 to 1984 modern programming methods will decrease instruction costs exponentially to $20 per instruction in 1984. Show that if we fit an exponential curve through these two points we obtain $200\,e^{-0.23(Y-1974)}$ dollars per instruction.

1.7 Compare the data in Tables 1.1 and 1.3, comment, and explain why these are so different.

1.8 We wish to estimate the growth in cost of military aircraft with calendar year. We will base this calculation on Fig. 1.1.

(a) Assume the same programming cost model as in Prob. 1.5d and calculate the software costs.

(b) Using the cost model of Prob. 1.5b, calculate the hardware costs.

---

[1]Hoel (1954), pp. 134–136; Crow et al. (1960), p. 184.
[2]Bell et al. (1978), p. 34. Curve was fitted by Bell to the data of Fig. 1.3.
[3]Based on 1000 man-months of effort for a 20,000-word program. See Putnam and Wolverton (1977), p. 216.

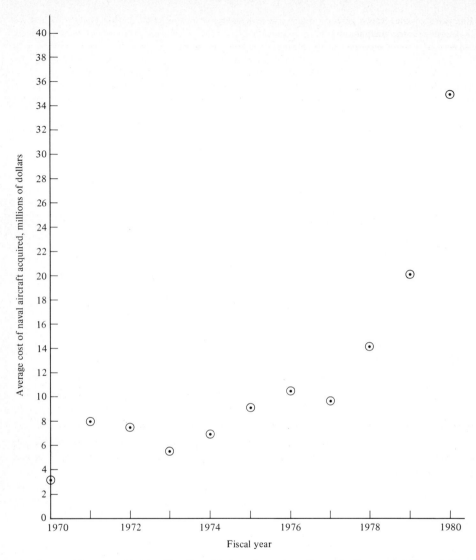

Source: Data provided by Dr. Tom Varley, Operations Research Program, Office of Naval Research, Washington, D.C.

(*c*) How does this ratio compare with Fig. 1.4?

(*d*) Calculate the total computer cost and see what fraction this represents of the total aircraft cost shown in the accompanying figure.

1.9 Combine the information developed in Probs. 1.5 and 1.6 and verify the results shown in the accompanying table.

Estimates of the growth of the program size, memory cost, and programming cost for a typical real-time airborne computer system

Year	Memory size, words $\times 10^3$	Unit memory cost, $/word	Unit programming cost, $/instruction	Memory cost per system, $	Programming cost for project, $ millions
1974	206	0.048	200	9900	41
1976	360	0.025	126	9000	45
1978	630	0.013	80	8100	50
1980	1103	0.0067	50	7400	55
1982	1932	0.0035	32	6700	62
1984	3382	0.0018	20	6100	68

1.10 Assume an application program is to be developed in Fortran to run on a VAX 750 computer (1982 hardware cost = $125,000). If we can develop the program at an average rate of five Fortran instructions per day and our length estimate is 5000 Fortran instructions,
- (a) How many man-days will this take?
- (b) Compute the total software costs.
- (c) What is the ratio of software to total cost?
- (d) Using the data in Table 1.5, estimate the costs per phase.

SELECTED REFERENCES

A worker entering a new field often desires to survey the literature and gauge the scope and broad aspects of the subject. The following list of selected references should provide the reader with a general overview of software engineering. These publications should be available in any major research library. No attempt has been made to be complete; a more comprehensive list of references appears at the end of the book.

Textbooks

Boehm, Barry W., et. al.: *Characteristics of Software Quality*, 1978.
Boehm, Barry: *Software Engineering Economics*, 1981a.
Brandon, Dick H., and Sidney Seligstein: *Data Processing Contracts: Structure, Contents, and Negotiations*, 1976.
Brooks, Fredrick P., Jr.: *The Mythical Man-Month*, 1975.
Buxton, J. N., Peter Naur, and B. Randell: *Report on Software Engineering Techniques*, 1976.
Coutinho, John de S.: *Advanced Systems Development Management*, 1977.
Data and Analysis Center for Software: *A Bibliography of Software Engineering Terms*, 1979.
Freiberger, Walter, ed.: *Statistical Computer Performance Evaluation*, 1972.
Frielink, A. B., ed.: *Proceedings of the International Symposium on Economics of Automatic Data Processing*, 1965.
Gilb, Tom: *Software Metrics*, 1977.
Glass, Robert L.: *Software Reliability Guidebook*, 1979.

Goos, G. and Hartmanis, J.: *Advanced Course on Software Engineering*, 1973.

Halstead, Maurice H.: *Elements of Software Science*, 1977.

Hetzel, Willian C., ed.: *Program Test Methods*, 1973.

Horowitz, Ellis, et. al.: *Practical Strategies for Developing Large Software Systems*, 1975.

IEEE Computer Society Committee on Software Engineering: *Software Engineering Terminology*, 1979.

IEEE Computer Society Tutorial Notes (Various Topics).

Jackson, Michael A.: *Principles of Program Design*, 1975.

Jensen, Randell W., and Charles C. Tonies: *Software Engineering*, 1979.

Katzen, Harry, Jr.: *Systems Design and Documentation*, 1976.

Kernighan, Brian W., and P. J. Plauger: *Software Tools*, 1976.

Kernighan, Brian W., and P. J. Plauger: *The Elements of Programming Style*, 1978.

Kreitzberg, C. B., and Ben Shneiderman: *The Elements of Fortran Style*, 1972.

Linger, R., H. Mills, and B. Witt: *Structured Programming Theory and Practice*, 1979.

Myers, Glenford J.: *Software Reliability Principles and Practice*, 1976.

Myers, Glenford J.: *The Art of Software Testing*, 1979.

Nauer, Peter, et. al.: *Software Engineering Concepts and Techniques*, 1976.

Perlis, Alan J., et. al.: *Software Metrics*, 1981.

Phister, Montgomery, Jr.: *Data Processing Technology and Economics*, 1979.

Putnam, Lawrence H. and Ray W. Wolverton: *Quantitative Management: Software Cost Estimating*, 1977.

Pyle, I. C.: *The ADA Programming Language*, 1981.

Shneiderman, Ben: *Software Psychology*, 1980.

Shooman, Martin L.: *Probabilistic Reliability*, 1968.

Shooman, Martin L.: Software Reliability, Chap. 9 in T. Anderson and B. Randell, eds., *Computing Systems Reliability*, 1979.

Tauseworthe, Robert C.: *Standardized Development of Computer Software*, Part I 1977, Part II 1979.

Thayer, Thomas A., et. al.: *Software Reliability*, 1978.

Warnier, Jean D.: *Logical Construction of Programs*, 1976.

Wegner, Peter: *Programming with Ada*, 1980.

Weinberg, Gerald M.: *The Psychology of Computer Programming*, 1971.

Wooldridge, Susan: *Systems and Programming Standards*, 1977.

Yourdon, Edward: *Techniques of Program Structure and Design*, 1975.

Yourdon, Edward, and Larry L. Constantine: *Structured Design*, 1979.

Zelkowitz, Marvin V., et. al.: *Principles of Software Engineering and Design*, 1979.

Journals and Magazines:

BIT.

Bell System Technical Journal.

BYTE Magazine.

Communications of the ACM.

Computer Magazine.

IBM Systems Journal.

IEEE Transactions on Reliability.

IEEE Transactions on Software Engineering.

Symposia and Conference Proceedings

Digest of Papers, COMPCON, IEEE, fall and spring.

National Computer Conference, annually.

Proceedings of the Annual Reliability and Maintainability Symposium, IEEE, annually.

Proceedings COMPSAC, IEEE, annually.

Proceedings of IFIP Congress, American Federation of Information Processing Societies, *triennial.*

Record 1973 IEEE Symposium on Computer Software Reliability, April 30, 1973.

Proceedings of the 1975 International Conference on Reliable Software, IEEE, April, 1975.

Proceedings of the Symposium on Computer Software Engineering, Polytechnic Press, New York, April, 1976.

Proceedings of the Software Quality and Assurance Workshop, ACM SIGMETRICS, Nov. 1978.

Proceedings of Specifications of Reliable Software, IEEE, 1979.

Proceedings Workshop on Quantitative Software Models for Reliability, Complexity, and Cost: An *Assessment of the State of the Art*, IEEE, Oct. 9–11, 1979.

Proceedings 1981 ACM Workshop/Symposium on Measurement and Evaluation of Software Quality, ACM SIGMETRICS, March 25–27, 1981.

Proceedings of the First [–Sixth] International Conference[s] on Software Engineering, IEEE. Conference dates: Sept. 1975, Oct. 1976, May 1978, Sept. 1979, Sept. 1981, Sept. 1982.

TWO

PROGRAM DESIGN TOOLS AND TECHNIQUES

2.1 INTRODUCTION

The heart of any large engineering project is the design. This is especially true when we are dealing with a large work force assigned to individual portions of the problem. The design philosophy (along with inspired management) is essentially the glue that holds the project together. Thus, a large portion of this chapter treats design techniques.

Many professionals do not focus on the fact that in order for their designs to be implemented, the program must be read by two different entities. The computer with the help of its associated system software must read and execute the program. The designer's colleagues who are working on the program while it is being designed, or who will work on future modifications, must read and understand the program. The only way to succeed in making the program readable to the latter is to document, circulate, and review the design via clear and concise design charts and high-level notational languages. The reader will find that design representations play a key role in this chapter.

A significant amount of detail work and documentation is needed to carry out a large design. It is evident that we should try to lessen this burden by providing the designer with automated facilities (tools) which can be of assistance in this task. A standardized and concise but powerful and flexible programming language aids the designer. The compatibility of popular languages with modern design philosophies is discussed.

The end goal is to produce a cost-effective design which satisfies its intended use. It is almost assumed that a corollary of this goal is to produce a design with low residual error content. In certain high-reliability applications this is not sufficient, and various techniques for self-checking and limiting the effect of an error (defensive programming) must be built into the design.

Based on the discussion of the last paragraph, there could have been several logical choices as to which topic should appear in Chap. 2. The topic of design was chosen as the best way to get the reader rapidly immersed in the philosophy and details of software engineering so that the remaining chapters would have a base upon which to build. Furthermore, design is an interactive process, and one must repeatedly use the complexity and reliability measures of Chaps. 3 and 5 to evaluate the progress of the design. Similarly, design, testing, and redesign form a repetitive cycle.

2.1.1 The Nature of the Design Process

The reader who has studied some of the material on program design which has appeared over the last decade may come away with an unsatisfied feeling. Most of the material uses programming terms now considered salutary, such as *structured*, *modular*, and *top-down*. In some cases, evolution of these techniques is based purely upon written discussions, while in other cases specific examples are used to develop the ideas. Other authors use certain design representations such as structured flowcharts or indented pseudo-code. After reading such a presentation, it is generally quite easy to comprehend the main idea and philosophy behind the design; however, it is difficult to pin down specific details and to abstract a generalized design procedure.

A little reflection by the reader should lead to the conclusion that this is not too unusual in any kind of engineering design. Design is a very personalized and highly interactive process in which the analyst uses a mixture of knowledge and intuition to generate initial approaches or configurations. He then applies any known design tools to analyze those approaches, compares them with the specifications, and iterates if the solution does not meet the specifications. Actually, the process of design is more complex than this.

At the outset, we often wish to explore a number of different designs to choose those that are "optimum" or most cost-effective. Thus, it is particularly important for us to have principles, theorems, or experience which shows that, for example, a design of type A is seldom a wise approach in a problem of type X. This sometimes allows us to rule out designs at a very early stage if they do not appear feasible. Such choices, however, should be made formally and be stated in a short paragraph or two in a written memorandum. This is very important because, as we all know, the specifications often are stated imprecisely and as the design evolves, "ground rules" sometimes change. It is possible that a change in rules may make quite feasible a design approach which was originally eliminated.

Standardized and generalized approaches are important to counteract the fact that individual designers establish their own personal style and use certain local jargon, which may be fully understood only within their own circle of associates. They also may use tools which are available only at their own company and which they, in fact, may themselves have invented or helped to invent. Although these tools may perform essentially the same function as other tools available elsewhere, designers prefer to use their own since they are familiar with them.

Before we begin our discussion of the elements of software design, it is useful to comment further on the concept of the design process in general. The design process includes analysis, synthesis, conceptualization, and trial and error. The beginning of any design is the specification (discussed in Chap. 6), and the end is the product which meets the specification. Sometimes in the design process we can show that the specification is mathematically impossible or beyond the present state of the art, or that none of the most creative people who are presented with the problem can evolve a design which meets the specifications. If such is the case, a change in specifications is needed and the design process must be started over again. Clearly, part of the design process involves testing the specifications for feasibility.

2.1.2 Synthesis versus Iteration

Assuming that our specifications are valid, many people would claim that the ideal design is one which involves a synthesis. In synthesis, we use a clear-cut and straightforward algorithm to evolve a design which exactly meets the specifications. Unfortunately, synthesis is seldom possible in practical engineering designs. One notable exception occurs in the area of network theory. Someone who wishes to design a filter (analog or digital) with certain frequency-response characteristics can specify a transmission pattern and then proceed in a step-by-step mathematical process to obtain a network (or program) with these characteristics. In general, synthesis is not possible and we are forced to evolve our design via a trial-and-error process.

We begin the iterative design process by assuming that an analysis technique exists. We then propose intuitively some hypothetical design and subject it to analysis. If the result of the analysis shows that the hypothetical design meets the system specifications, then our job is done. In most cases it will meet several of the specifications and fail the rest. At that point we either produce a new conceptual design or, by study of the features which fail to meet specifications, evolve an improved version of the original design. This new conceptualized or evolved design is then subjected to analysis and tested against the system requirements. This process continues until either a satisfactory design is found or the designer concludes that the design is impossible for certain particular reasons. The iterative process is shown graphically in Fig. 2.1 and is contrasted with synthesis. In theory, a true synthesis procedure is a "one-shot," open-loop design. However, because we are always on guard for human error, we check the design. An iterative design is generally checked several times.

2.1.3 Modern Design Techniques

Many of the concepts in design which we will discuss, such as those given in Table 2.1, are often spoken of as concepts of *modern* programming design. Actually, few of them are new, and examples could be found in the early days of

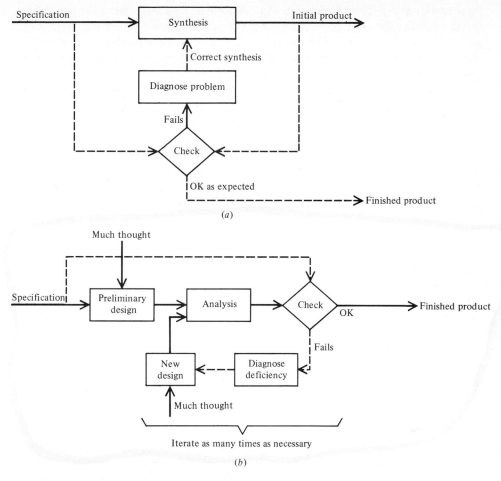

Figure 2.1 Comparison of a synthesis procedure (*a*) vs an iterative design procedure (*b*). Solid lines represent design and dotted lines represent checking.

Table 2.1 Topics in modern software design

1. Top-down design, top-down implementation (programming)
2. Bottom-up design, bottom-up implementation (programming)
3. Modular design and programming
4. Structured design and programming
5. Defensive design and programming
6. Redundant design and programming
7. Automatic programming
8. Design representations
9. Design and programming tools
10. Program proofs

programming in which a programmer intuitively followed these design rules. What is new is the explicit recognition that following many of these design rules generally leads to good code while the reverse often results in poor code. Nevertheless, we may not be able to give a set of principles which can turn every programmer into a magnificent designer. At the other extreme, these new rules and techniques may have little or marginal effect on improving a truly poor programmer. We can, however, give ordinary programmers a set of rules and techniques to follow which should measurably improve their code. Such knowledge and sets of rules can also decrease the length of time it takes to turn an inexperienced programmer and designer into a seasoned one, thereby shortening the "apprentice" phase. These concepts also afford a better way of monitoring the development of a programming project, through improved insight into the design process.

The design representations which have been developed to document programming design are also useful in program management. Notations and tools such as pseudo-code, structured flowcharts, HIPO diagrams, and other techniques can be used to provide quantitative measures which are useful in assessing design progress.

Sections 2.2 to 2.6 seemingly present distinct techniques; however, upon study of these approaches and comparison of the similarities and differences, we find a great amount of overlap. The basic thrust is that software must not be designed in a helter-skelter fashion, but must proceed with a very definite plan and approach in mind. One must introduce discipline in evolving that approach. In achieving the discipline, it is necessary to introduce certain formal steps in the procedure.

Providing discipline is, of course, a two-edged sword. We wish our designers to exercise initiative, inject new ideas and solutions, and, in general, be creative. Yet, we specify that they must do it all under certain established guidelines. Some flexibility and choice are the key to choosing a proper middle ground between these two extremes which fits the styles of most of the programmers working on the project, but insists that within the general guidelines the programmers follow each step in the procedure.

The concluding sections of this chapter discuss topics such as language effects and development tools, which impinge on program design but are not really classifiable or attributable to any of the known "schools" of design. They are therefore discussed as separate issues which in many ways cut across all the different design approaches. We begin our discussion of the philosophy of design by introducing the concepts of top-down and bottom-up design.

2.2 TOP-DOWN AND BOTTOM-UP DESIGN

2.2.1 Introduction

The two terms *top-down* and *bottom-up* have been absorbed into the terminology of software design over the last decade. These terms appear to describe many different areas of organizational behavior and have also been applied recently to hardware design and project management. In fact, these descriptors were used in Sec. 1.5 to discuss the organization of ideas within the chapters of this book.

At the outset we should emphasize that the term *design* is used in this chapter in a broad sense. It begins with the specification phase (which is covered in more detail in Chap. 6) and continues with the evolution of the design. Design is followed by coding and then by the test (discussed in Chap. 4), debug, and redesign-correction phases.

We focus our discussion on the design and coding phases in this chapter, but other phases which relate to subsequent chapters will also be discussed. Correspondingly, the reader will find that top-down and bottom-up testing and problem specifications are discussed respectively in Chaps. 4 and 6.

2.2.2 Design Philosophy and Principles

Top-down design is basically a decomposition process which focuses on the flow of control or on the control structure of the program; at later stages it concerns itself with code production. The first step is to study the overall aspects of the task at hand and to break it into a number (perhaps 3 to 10) of independent constituent functions or modules. This is the first step in the decomposition. The second step is to break each one of these modules further into independent submodules. The process is repeated until one obtains modules which are small enough to grasp mentally and to code at one sitting in a straightforward, uncomplicated manner. Clearly, one module of the structure may extend to a lower level than the next.

One important feature of top-down design is that at each level the details of the design at lower levels are *hidden*. Only the necessary data and control which must be passed back and forth over the interface are defined. Furthermore, if a data structure is contained wholly within a lower-level module, it need not be specified until that level is reached in the design process. However, if data must be shared by several modules at some level, then the data structure must be chosen before progressing to a lower level. The design will include both the data structure and the means of data access for each involved module.

If we also decide to employ top-down programming (coding), then we will begin to detail a control structure at the first level of decomposition and to produce the necessary code. Similarly, the control code for each lower-level module will be written, and the last code to be written will be that for the lowest-level modules.

It is difficult to quantify just when a module is small enough and should no longer be decomposed. Some people have defined this as one page of printed output (about 50 lines). The concept as presented by Harlan Mills[1] is to make a module small enough that it is within a programmer's intellectual span of control. By this, Mills means that the listing can be spread upon one's desk, read,

[1]Mills (1976), p. 79.

discussed, and considered as one entity, without the need to decompose it further into submodules because it is too complex or cumbersome to keep in one's mind.

In a bottom-up design one first visualizes a typical system design and decides by experience, intuition, or perhaps simple, quick analysis which part or parts of the design are the most difficult or limiting ones. These crucial parts are investigated first, and necessary design decisions are made. The remainder of the design is tailored to fit around the designs already chosen for the crucial parts.

In some ways a bottom-up design vaguely represents a synthesis. The specifications of the key parts are given, and the design is formulated for these key parts. If the design is not feasible under the given specifications and constraints, the requirements are changed and the design proceeds.

One strong point of the top-down method is that it postpones details of decisions until the last stages of the design. This allows one to accommodate easily small design changes or improvements of technology partway through the design. There is also a concomitant danger that the specifications will be incompatible or unrealizable and that this will not be discovered until late in the design process. By contrast, the bottom-up process first focuses on the crucial parts, so the feasibility of the design is tested at an early stage. However, the control structure which is fitted around these key parts may in extreme cases be horrendous.

If each module is coded as soon as its design is fixed, then the approach is called *bottom-up coding*. It is possible to have a top-down design and bottom-up coding, and vice versa. In fact, in most complex problems there are several layers of design: preliminary, prototype, and final. Thus, it is not uncommon to have mixtures of top-down and bottom-up design and coding used in a project (see Fig. 4.7).

In mixing top-down and bottom-up design, it often appears that we start in the middle of the problem and work our way both up and down from there. This is sometimes called *middle-out* design. In a complex problem, it is often difficult to decide how to modularize the first level (or, in a huge problem, the second level of some module). In such cases, one might consider a list of the system inputs and decide what functions are necessary to process these inputs. The name *back-to-front* design is sometimes applied to this approach. Similarly, one can start with the required outputs and work backward, evolving a so-called *front-to-back* design. In some cases, the data structures are crucial to the solution and the term *data-directed design* is appropriate.

A simple example which illustrates some of the differences between top-down and bottom-up design is given in Fig. 2.2. The program is to solve for and classify the roots of the cubic equation $Ax^3 + Bx^2 + Cx + D = 0$.

The top-down solution does not commit the design to a specific approach at the first decomposition level. This will come when we go to the second level of detail, where the singular cases and the roots modules appear. In the case of the bottom-up approach, the algorithm is already specified; we use Newton's method for one root and the quadratic formula for the other roots. It is obvious from inspection of Fig. 2.2 that a change in the algorithm to be used will change the

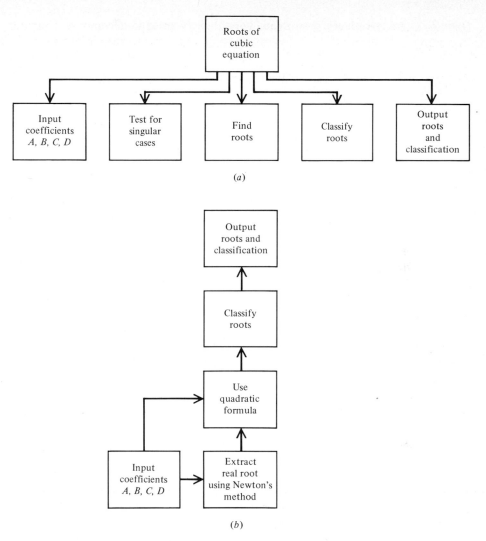

Figure 2.2 Block diagram comparison of a top-down and a bottom-up solution for finding and classifying the roots of a cubic equation. (*a*) First decomposition level for a top-down design. (*b*) Major functions in a bottom-up design.

entire structure of the bottom-up design, whereas in the top-down design, the main (perhaps sole) change is in the Find Roots module.

A comparison of other features of the top-down and bottom-up approaches is given in Table 2.2. A cost comparison of the two design methods appears in Chap. 6. A more comprehensive example is given in Sec. 2.2.3 to illustrate the role of specifications and to continue our comparison of top-down and bottom-up design.

Table 2.2 Comparison of top-down and bottom-up programming

Feature	Top-down	Bottom-up
1. Specifications	Requires well-defined specifications and definition of environment from outset.	Work can begin based on detailed specifications only for the crucial module(s).
2. Design mistakes	If made at a high level and not found until later, they can necessitate major rewriting. If made at a low level, the impact will be small. Only a single small module will be affected.	More tolerant of early errors since they only represent redesign and recoding of a single module in most cases.
3. Testing	Top-down testing requires test stubs but not test drivers* (see Chap. 4).	Bottom-up testing requires test drivers but no test stubs* (see Chap. 4).
4. Standardization	Where appropriate, standardized structure can be developed for a particular application area.	Standardized modules can be devised for critical functions which are often used.
5. Data structures	One can delay details of data structures wholly contained in lower levels during the initial stages of design.	One must decide on all data structures which the module interfaces with before proceeding.
6. Crucial storage problems	We must use both bottom-up and top-down approaches in this case.	Best philosophy is to begin bottom-up design only on crucial storage-related problems in parallel with top-down design for other portions of software.
7. Critical real-time problems	Same as item 6.	Same as item 6; i.e., crucial real-time (often input-output) function is tackled bottom-up.
8. Impact on existing personnel	Requires a different approach from that previously used. Can pose a threat to the less skilled.	Comfortable, with no surprises (with no intellectual challenges in many cases).
9. Impact on new personnel	Many are now trained this way in college. If not, the novelty appeals to them.	As long as they aren't "computer enthusiasts" who revel in bit juggling and assembly language tricks, the illogic of poorly chosen bottom-up designs will be clear to them.
10. Management acceptance	It may take some time to educate top-level managers about what to expect at various stages. Structured flowcharts or pseudo-code for all levels of design are completed first before code is written.	It is easy to convince top-level management that you are making good progress if you cite the percentage of code completed. The best way to display rapid progress in this regard is to code bottom-up.

Table 2.2 *(continued).*

Feature	Top-down	Bottom-up
11. Module size	Limited to 1 page, say, 50 lines of code or less. If a function takes more code, it is divided into subfunctions.	Size is set by the function being coded. May be very large or small.
12. Integration-test problems	Usually no serious surprises occur to interrupt the integration phase, because the interfaces are already designed.	Surprises sometimes occur as integration progresses because testing reveals interface incompatibility.
13. Feasibility	If others have completed similar problems, feasibility is proved and top-down design is recommended.	If feasibility is in question, a two-stage design is recommended: bottom-up to prove feasibility, then top-down for final design.
14. Added features	Easy to include because they generally represent added modules or redesign of a few modules, but same control structure. If they can be anticipated, the interface plus test stubs can be coded and left in for future use.	May cause major redesign if interfaces are no longer compatible. This problem can be alleviated somewhat if additions are anticipated.

* A test driver is a program which provides control and input data for testing a module when the remainder of the code has not yet been written. A test stub is a dummy program (often a print statement) inserted in place of code not as yet written, to indicate that the right point in the program has been reached.

2.2.3 Example: A Word-Processing System

The difference in evolution of a top-down and a bottom-up design is best illustrated by an example. Let us suppose that we wish to produce a word-processing system[1] for a technical university. The big problem with technical word processing is that a large portion of the effort goes into typing equations and special symbols and preparing graphs. Over the years, such material is continually changed and updated, e.g., as material progresses from rough-draft notes to a technical paper to a section in a book chapter. We wish to have a system in which the images of the previous typing can be stored on some medium such as magnetic tape or disk. There must then be a simple, rapid procedure for editing

[1] This term has come to mean an automated input-edit-output system for typing, generally employing a computer as the heart of the system. The most sophisticated versions of commercially available word-processing systems include input of already printed or typed data via optical character readers, remote input via telecopiers or computer-computer communications, and book-quality output using masters prepared on a phototypesetting device. For an illustration of operational and proposed systems, see (1) Kernighan (1979), (2) Knuth (1978), and (3) Leeman (1978).

and updating the material. Finally, there must be a high-quality output device which will produce a master copy of the edited material, including mathematical and technical symbols. Obviously, the old version might be retained on one storage medium and a new version created, or the old version might be erased and only the new version maintained.

Before continuing with the design, a detailed specification must be written for the problem. We can approach the specification problem by considering the major inputs and outputs of the system. The inputs to the system will be:

1. Handwritten drafts of material
2. Typed rough drafts or initial drafts of manuscripts with hand corrections
3. Dictated material stored on magnetic tape, belts, etc.
4. Corrections to previous versions of typed material which are submitted along with a stored copy or file number of the previously recorded material

Inputs from optical character readers or computer telecommunications are not needed now, but may be required in the future.

The outputs of this system will be:

1. Material typed in various formats on $8\frac{1}{2}$- by 11-in standard bond paper
2. Material typed on various-sized model paper used for oversized masters, which are photographically reduced for conference and journal proceedings
3. Ordinary business letters typed on letterhead
4. Technical research reports (similar to item 1; however, a cover page with artwork is generally required)
5. Typing of figure captions, figure legends, etc. (figures are prepared separately by the art department, for insertion in outputs 2 and 4)
6. Short-term computer storage of any of the above items
7. Long-term storage on secondary storage material (magnetic tapes, diskettes, etc.) of any of the above material
8. Typing and formatting of bond-paper masters from which 35-mm slides are prepared by a photographer or the art department.
9. Typing and formatting of bond masters from which overhead transparencies are prepared on a copy machine
10. Preparations of miscellaneous notices, posters, etc., which require special typing of one sort or another
11. Occasional typing of ditto masters, mimeograph masters, etc.

The next stage in drafting a set of specifications is to consider how the human author, human typist, computer input equipment, computer hardware and software, and computer output equipment will interact. Similarly, we identify the type of input, editing, and output functions that are required of the system. Last, specifications for the computer hardware and software portions of the system are written.

A top-down design for this problem might begin by considering all input, output, and storage functions as major modules. In addition, the major processing functions of editing and formatting will be separate modules. The design corresponding to this approach is shown in Fig. 2.3. (The hierarchy diagram depicted in the figure essentially uses the same technique as the block diagram shown in Fig. 2.2*a* and is discussed further in Sec. 2.3.4.)

When the top-down design is completed, one has a choice of coding the system in either a top-down or a bottom-up fashion. The top-down coding starts by specifying which available operating system is to be used for the chosen computer. Then the appropriate techniques for initialization and loading phases are determined and a control program designed. Major software modules are then identified and stubs written for these major modules. The control program is first tested with the stubs that have been written or any of the major modules of the program that have been completed. In the case where bottom-up coding follows a top-down design, one might focus on the fact that the heart of the system is the text editor and immediately begin to code and test the text editor. Later, we would code the existing control program design and hope it is still compatible with the text editor program.

If the same problem is approached using bottom-up design, the first focus will be on the critical components of this system. Without analyzing the problem in great depth, one would assume that the two critical portions of the design are the secondary storage system (cassette, diskette, etc.), which is mainly a hardware problem, and the ease and utility (for the operator) of the editor program, which is a software problem. On the software side, we begin by investigating whether

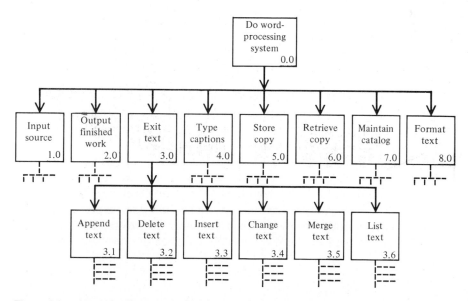

Figure 2.3 A hierarchy diagram (H diagram) for word-processing system.

existing editor programs can be used or modified for use. Once we have decided upon the secondary storage medium, the computer and operating system to be used, and the editor program, large portions of the design will have been completed. It is possible, once we have completed our design, to begin coding in a top-down manner, i.e., to start with the control program, specify the interfaces to the editor and other major functional programs, and then finally code in a modular fashion those other programs. More likely, as soon as one completes the specifications for the editor, one or two good programmers will begin to code the editor while the remainder of the team works on the design of the other modules. Final testing is accomplished by integrating all the modules into the system after they have been tested as modules in a bottom-up fashion. Thus, it is most common that if one begins a bottom-up design, one also codes and tests the system in the bottom-up fashion.

Harlan Mills (1976) has recently pointed out another very important aspect of system design: the principle of interacting with the user in a feedback mode during the early stages of the design. In many cases, the user does not understand fully the characteristics of the desired system. Thus, the original specification document may not really delineate the kind of system that is actually wanted. It may be just a good first attempt at specifying what is required. Thus, if the contractor builds a system which exactly meets that specification, the contract may be satisfied even though the customer is left with a partially unsatisfactory system.

This is especially true where the system involves heavy interaction with human operators or users, or where it is the customer's first effort at computerization in a particular field. In such a case, it is particularly important to do a two-stage design. The first stage is to rapidly put together a rough approximation of the final product as envisioned by specifications. This will probably require using existing software, i.e., making the choice of: an editor which exists and is similar to the one you want; a rapidly designed control program which does some of the things you want; one or two available input-output terminals that will interface with the software; and an available computer.

The next step is to put the system together rapidly into a working entity.[1] In doing such an initial design, you may find that you are using combinations of the top-down and bottom-up methods. The design should be carried out in a modular fashion so that successful modules can be reused in the final design. Give the user ample time to experiment with this preliminary system. Make sure that there is ample feedback and interaction between the user and the developer. At the end of this trial period, rework the specifications on the basis of your experiences. (This step must be delayed until the user has had sufficient time to try out the system with actual operators and has received feedback.) Once the new specification is

---

[1] A contractor who has done many similar problems in the past may be able to complete the first-stage prototype rapidly using modules from past systems. This is especially true if the past systems were developed top-down with similar control structures.

written, do the second design. Wherever possible, use modular pieces of the first design; however, do not hesitate to discard all the modules and start from scratch, where necessary. Remember, the coding of modules requires only a small portion of the total development time. Thus, what we are really advising is that the design be developed in two stages. The first stage is a preliminary design, which is discarded, and the second stage is the real design, which is utilized. This is the philosophy urged by Fred Brooks in his book. "Hence, plan to throw one away; you will, anyhow" (1975, p. 116).

In summary, most practical designs are neither totally bottom-up nor totally top-down. On the basis of the consensus which has developed in the literature, we should strive to:

1. Do a two-stage design
2. Discard the first design (the prototype) and develop the second design after considering the feedback from the trial use of the first design
3. Try to do both the first and second design in as much a top-down fashion as possible
4. Try to code and test the design in a top-down fashion, if possible (see Chap. 4 for a discussion of top-down versus bottom-up testing)
5. Find out where really crucial problems exist, and use bottom-up design and possibly bottom-up coding to prove feasibility for these particular modules in the first design

2.3 DESIGN REPRESENTATIONS

2.3.1 Introduction

In any design process an important milestone occurs when the conceptual design is first reduced to memorandum form, including diagrams, charts, drawings, series of equations or algorithms, etc. In general, we refer to this as *documenting* the initial design in terms of a representational scheme. Such a design representation becomes even more important when we progress to the details of the intermediate or final design process.

Unfortunately, the design of many software projects is never documented on paper but only resides in the minds and memories of the designers. In such a case if one asks for a copy of the software design for a project, one is handed a listing of the program which is 10 to 20 in thick and contains several hundred thousand lines of source code. A hardware analog of such a situation would be the receipt of 100 to 200 large schematic diagrams as the design documentation for a radar system. In both cases considerable additional information is needed to supplement and act as a guide to the overwhelming detail of the total design.

As an example of proper documentation for a smaller hardware design, consider the contents of the 87-page service manual for a black-and-white television receiver:[1]

1. Thirty-seven tables of component information (part numbers, ratings, location, replacement cost)
2. Twenty-six schematic diagrams (circuit diagrams of entire circuit subcircuits, test circuits)
3. Eighteen pictorial diagrams (part locations, cables and connectors, test points, controls, adjustments)
4. Eighteen photographs (test waveforms, test equipment)
5. Thirteen pages of text (operation, alignment, test procedures)
6. Eleven signal-path diagrams (paths of sound circuit, composite video, vertical circuit, horizontal circuit, and intermediate frequency)

If we treat each of the above items as a separate documentation element, then the 26 schematics represent only 20 percent of the total. No doubt the set of *design documents* for the line of receivers contains the above information plus many more descriptive pages of text and test results.

Software design has suffered from the fact that there is no single design-representation scheme or group of schemes commonly used. In fact, in two summary papers which describe the design process and representational schemes, 18 different models were described.[2] A listing of these 18 techniques appears in Table 2.3, along with several others. We will discuss a few of these design representations, and will recommend a combined approach using more than one scheme. Additional techniques are discussed in Sec. 2.9.

2.3.2 Flowcharts

The flowchart method[3] is the oldest, most controversial,[4] most widely used, and most misunderstood tool of program design. It is almost certain that each reader will have used flowcharts and have formed an opinion about them. We will begin by defining what a flowchart is and showing how it can be used as a design and documentation tool. In our discussion we will try to highlight its advantages, its disadvantages, and its proper use.

The standard symbols generally employed in flowcharting are given in Fig. 2.4. As an example, flowcharts are used to design a program to compute the heading-angle response of a ship to a step input of left rudder, followed by an equal step input of right rudder (see Fig. 2.5*a* and *b*). The associated program

---

[1] Zenith (1966).

[2] Fairley (1976), pp. 111–131; Peters and Tripp (1976), pp. 31–56.

[3] Ruston (1978), pp. 6–13.

[4] John Beidler, in *Datamation* Readers Forum, January 1977, pp. 200–202. "Chartae Fluxus Consilii Requiescant in Pace" (Beidler's translation, with the help of two clergymen is: Program Flow Charts, May They Rest in Peace). After reading his comments, I think his real title is "Program Flow Charts Can Go to the Devil."

Table 2.3 Design representation schemes

Scheme	Comments
1. Code listing	A universally available technique
2. Table of attributes	A table of data types; listed by PL/1 and some other compilers
3. Pseudo-code	A shorthand version of a programming language
4. Flowchart	A diagram generally drawn by hand or by a program reading the code after the fact
5. Structured flowchart	A modified flowchart customized for structured programming
6. Control graph	A graph of only the control structure of the program
7. Softech approach	A technique depicting blocks, nodes, and nesting
8. Dill-Hopson-Dixon	A modification of the flowchart to highlight a loop: range, entry, exit
9. Hamilton-Zeldin	A flowchart modified to highlight control flow
10. Widerman-Rawson scheme	A flowchart modified to highlight control flow
11. Structure chart	A hierarchy block diagram
12. HIPO (hierarchy plus input-process-output)	A structure chart H plus an IPO chart
13. Design tree and control graph	A technique similar to a hierarchy diagram and control graph
14. Nassi-Shneiderman	A block diagram with pseudo-code to detail control and computation (see item 23)
15. Scat	A block diagram with pseudo-code to detail control and computation
16. Transaction diagram	A block diagram with pseudo-code to detail control and computation
17. Decision table	A tabular representation of logic
18. Data-structure charts	A method that defines relationships among data only
19. Cause-effect diagrams	An attempt to mimic digital-logic diagrams[a]
20. Warnier-Orr diagram	A horizontal hierarchy chart using braces instead of blocks[b]
21. BELLFLOW	A program developed by Bell Labs which includes special comment (control) cards to produce higher-level flowcharts[c]
22. Dimensional flowcharting	A technique tied in with the stepwise refinement method which involves flowcharts which can be drawn and syntax to be checked by machine[d]
23. Chapin charts	A technique which seems to bridge conventional (ANSI) flowcharts and HIPO diagrams[e]
24. Process design language (PDL)	An open-ended mixture of natural language, pseudo-code, and mathematics[f]

Source: Fairley (1976); Peters and Tripp (1976).
[a] Elmendorf (1973).
[b] Higgins (1977b); Warnier (1976).
[c] Repsher (1971).
[d] Witty (1977).
[e] Chapin (1974); Ruston (1978), pp. 156–161.
[f] Linger, Mills, and Witt (1979), Chap. 3.

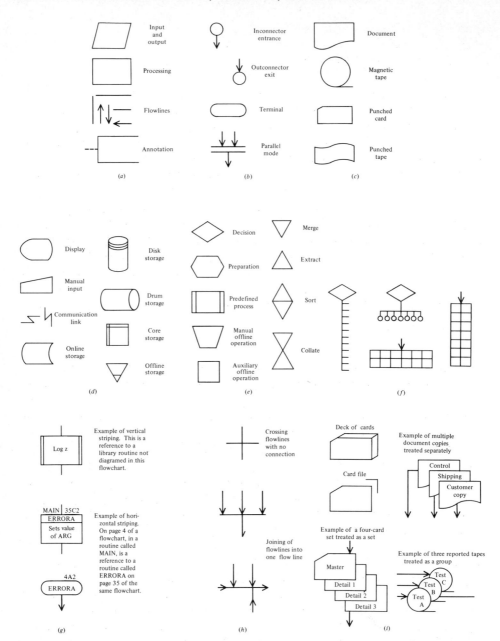

Figure 2.4 The symbols used in ANSI standard flowcharting: (*a*) basic outlines; (*b*) additional outlines; (*c*) specialized outlines for media; (*d*) specialized outlines for equipment; (*e*) specialized outlines for processing; (*f*) outlines for large numbers of decisions; (*g*) conventions for striping and references; (*h*) conventions for flowlines; (*i*) multiple-symbol conventions. (See Chapin, 1970.)

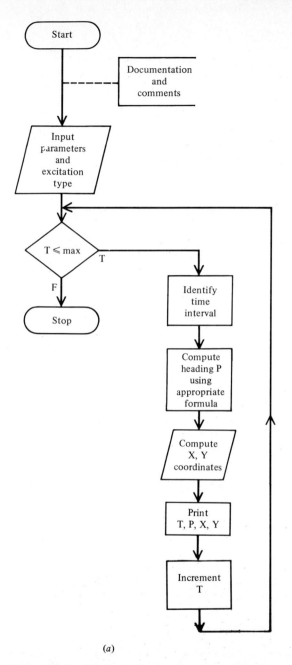

(a)

Figure 2.5 Flow chart of ship's heading angle response (see Table 2.4). (*a*) Higher-level flowchart. (*b*) Detailed flowchart. (*Note*: The numbers in parentheses correspond to the statements in Table 2.4.)

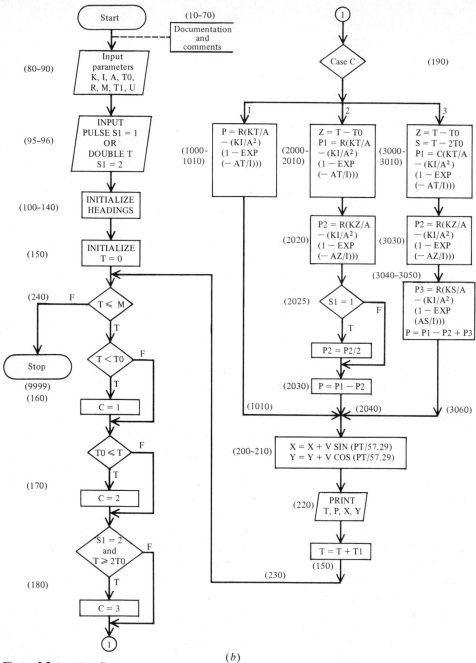

Figure 2.5 (*continued*).

(b)

written in the Basic language is given in Table 2.4. The program is simply the evaluation of one of two different formulas which are valid over three different time ranges, along with some trigonometry to compute the associated x and y coordinates. This was a small program, and we now must consider how these techniques apply to large programs, because it is there that one really needs design-representation tools.

First of all we must differentiate between a high-level, macro flowchart and a detailed, micro flowchart.[1] In a detailed flowchart, the object is to produce a diagram such that there is a one-to-one correspondence between each symbol on the diagram and each line of code in the program (note the numbers in parentheses in Fig. 2.5b). Such representations are often offered along with the listing of a program as an aid to documentation. In general a flowchart with 10,000 symbols occupying several hundred pages is as cumbersome as a listing of the program occupying about 200 pages of standard printer output. Then why should anyone ever want to produce detailed flowcharts? The answer is that they are required as contract deliverables (end items) in many military and civilian contracts. This is because we have not yet standardized documentation tools. Thus, lacking other universally used tools, customers have included the flowchart along with the program listing as a contract deliverable.

Since many programmers choose not to use flowcharts, almost all large companies have automatic flowcharting programs. These accept as input the program source statements and produce a flowchart on the printer with each program statement neatly inserted in the appropriate symbol. The author chooses to call such flowcharting programs *dumb* flowcharters, because they really don't increase our information or understanding. There have been some attempts to produce smart flowcharters,[2] which read the statements and comments and abstract the ideas to a higher level, producing a simplified, higher-level flowchart. More research is needed in this area.[3]

Without smart flowcharters, the use of flowcharting as an after-the-fact documentation tool is impractical; however, it can be used as a before-the-fact design representation. This is precisely the use to which it should be put, and the way it is used by its proponents. Once the design is adequately described verbally, a very-high-level flowchart is drawn indicating which modules or subprograms are to carry out which functions. Individual high-level flowcharts are then drawn for each major module and subroutine. *At no time are detailed flowcharts drawn.* By use of the very-high-level flowchart, the control structure for the program is coded. Each individual module is coded using its respective high-level flowchart.

If we follow the order just described, we are performing a top-down design. If we reverse the order, we have a bottom-up design. Suppose that the designer

---

[1]Shneiderman et al. (1977).

[2]Repsher (1971) and Witty (1977); also references in "Historical Development" section of Chapin (1970).

[3]Becerril et al. (1980).

Table 2.4 Listing of a Basic program which computes the transient response of a ship's heading when subjected to particular rudder input signals

READY
#LIST

```
0010   REM***SHPRSP***BY MARTIN L. SHOOMAN 2/7/78
0020   REM COMPUTES SHIP RESPONSE TO PULSE TYPE INPUTS DESIGNED TO PRODUCE
0030   REM HEADING OR LATERAL POSITION CORRECTIONS. TRANSFER FUNCTION OF
0035   REM SHIP'S HEADING
0040   REM PSI(S)/DELTA(S) = (KS/IZ)/S(S + A/IZ)
0045   REM PULSE INPUT GIVEN BY DELTA(T) = ALPHA(U(T) − U(T − T0))
0050   REM APPROXIMATE DOUBLET INPUT IS GIVEN BY: DELTA (T) = ALPHA (V(T) −
0060   REM 2V(T − T0) + V(T − 2T0)). VARIABLES: KS = K, IZ = I, A = A, PSI = P, T = T, T0 = T0,
0070   REM ALPHA = R, TMAX = M, TIME INTERVAL = T1, VELOCITY = V.
0080   PRINT "INPUT VALUES FOR: K, I, A, T0, R, M, T1, V."
0090   INPUT K, I, A, T0, R, M, T1, V
0095   PRINT "DO YOU WANT PULSE INPUT(1) OR DOUBLET INPUT(2)";
0096   INPUT S1
0100   LET X = 0
0110   LET Y = 0
0120   PRINT
0130   PRINT "TIME", "HEADING", "X", "Y"
0140   PRINT "(SECS.)", "(DEGREES)", "(FT.)", "(FT.)"
0150   FOR T = 0 TO M STEP T1
0160   IF T < T0 THEN LET C = 1
1070   IF T > T0 THEN IF T < (2*T0) THEN LET C = 2
0180   IF S1 = 2 THEN IF T > = (2*T0) THEN LET C = 3
0190   ON C GOSUB 1000, 2000, 3000
0200   LET X = X + (V*SIN(P/57.2958)*T)
0210   LET Y = Y + (V*COS(P/57.2958)*T)
0220   PRINT T, P, X, Y
0230   NEXT T
0240   GOTO 9999
1000   LET P = R*((K*T/A) ≡ (K*I/A^2)*(1 − EXP(−A*T/I)))
1010   RETURN
2000   LET Z = T − T0
2010   LET P1 = R*((K*T/A) − (K*I/A^2)*(1 − EXP(−A*T/I)))
2020   LET P2 = 2*R*((K*Z/A) − (K*I/A^2)*(1 − EXP(−A*Z/I)))
2025   IF S1 = 1 THEN LET P2 = P2/2
2030   LET P = P1 − P2
2040   RETURN
3000   LET Z = T ≡ T0
3010   LET S = T − 2*T0
3020   LET P1 = R*((K*T/1) − (K*I/A^2)*(1 − EXP(−A*T/I)))
3030   LET P2 = 2*R*((K*Z/A) − (K*I/A^2)*(1 − EXP(−A*Z/I)))
3040   LET P3 = R*((K*S/A) − (K*I/A^2)*(1 − EXP(−A*S/I)))
3050   LET P = P1 − P2 + P3
3060   RETURN
9999   END
```

Note: The correspondence between Fig. 2.5 and this table is discussed in Probs. 2.23 and 2.24.

decides to write a very-high-level flowchart, but not the set of high-level flowcharts, and begins the coding immediately. There arises the question of whether there is any need to draw the high-level flowcharts at all in such a situation. In actuality, we have oversimplified the program design process. First of all, in Sec. 2.2.3 we discussed the fact that most large designs will be done twice. Second, the design process will be made up of specification, initial design, design review, final design, and testing. At each one of these interfaces documentation will be needed. Even if the programmer involved does not prefer flowcharts, one or more of the other workers involved in the project may find them helpful. Furthermore, if the programmer uses a different design representation as a primary tool, it will be useful to produce high-level flowcharts for use as a checking tool. Thus, intelligent use of high-level flowcharts is a valid design representation.

One of the legitimate problems with using flowcharts is that when the code is changed, we often have to change the flowchart as well. If we abstain—as was recommended—from dealing with detailed flowcharts, then not all the changes in code will necessitate changes in the flowchart. All those code changes which impact the higher-level flowchart, however, will necessitate redrawing. This is analogous to the situation of the mechanical or electrical designer who has to change the mechanical drawing or electrical schematic whenever a significant change is made. All such changes are laborious, but are a necessity, and there has been some success in computerizing the drafting function.[1] The field of software design would be similarly aided if we had smart flowcharting programs at our disposal.

High-level flowcharts which contain only control constructs used in structured programming are called *structured* flowcharts; they are discussed in Sec. 2.4.

2.3.3 Pseudo-code

Suppose we were faced with the task of writing a 25-page instruction manual describing the use of a text-editing system. We would start the design with an outline. Then, we could begin to write specific sections immediately; however, a better plan would be to annotate the outline with a few brief sentences or a list of topics contained in each section. These notes could be written in standard English sentences, or abbreviated to just a few words, phrases, and mathematical symbols. The programming analog of the outline is the very-high-level flowgraph, described in Sec. 2.3.2, or the hierarchy chart, to be described in Sec. 2.3.4. The detailed subsections of the hierarchy charts and the notes on their contents represent the analogous high-level flowcharts or pseudo-code.

Pseudo-code (sometimes called *metacode*) is a shorthand notation for the control structures and certain other elements of a programming language.[2] Comments are liberally inserted, and often words substitute for expressions. For example, a DO loop in PL/1 might read: DO I = 1 TO N;...;...;...END;. The

---

[1]Pferd and Ramachandran (1979).
[2]Fairley (1976), pp. 23–24; Linger and Mills (1975).

same loop in pseudo-code might be written: DO (for each element)...END. Generally, control structures are indented to show nesting of control. A designer who is best versed in a particular programming language will probably write pseudo-code that is an abbreviated version of that language; however, it should still be possible to implement the design in any language desired. Thus, if we are doing the same program in Fortran and Pascal, we should be able to use the same pseudo-code as the starting point for final coding in each language. An example of the pseudo-code for a program which reads text records, identifies different words, counts the frequency of occurrence, and prints out a table of this information is given in Table 2.5.

The process design language (PDL) listed as one of the entries in Table 2.3 represents a formal pseudo-code. An interesting technique is used to indicate the end of each control structure by spelling the keyword backwards. Thus a DO loop would appear as DO...OD. Similarly an IF clause would be ended by FI. The various program levels are represented by a decimal label for each statement. An example of PDL pseudo-code is given in Table 2.6.

In some ways pseudo-code is more flexible than a flowchart. One can easily increase the level of detail in pseudo-code whenever more details are needed to prevent confusion. For example, when we see a loop in a flowchart we often can't

Table 2.5 Pseudo-code for a word-frequency counting program

INITIALIZE THE PROGRAM
READ THE FIRST TEXT RECORD
DO WHILE THERE ARE MORE WORDS IN THE TEXT RECORD
    DO WHILE THERE ARE MORE WORDS IN THE TEXT RECORD
        EXTRACT THE NEXT TEXT WORD
        SEARCH THE WORD-TABLE FOR THE EXTRACTED WORD
        IF THE EXTRACTED WORD IS FOUND
            INCREMENT THE WORD'S OCCURRENCE COUNT
        ELSE
            INSERT THE EXTRACTED WORD INTO THE TABLE
        END IF
        INCREMENT THE WORDS-PROCESSED COUNT
    END DO AT THE END OF THE TEXT RECORD
    READ THE NEXT TEXT RECORD
END DO WHEN ALL TEXT RECORDS HAVE BEEN READ
PRINT THE TABLE AND SUMMARY INFORMATION
TERMINATE THE PROGRAM

Source: Fairley (1976), p. 24.
See also discussion regarding possible errors in this pseudo-code in Prob. 2.22.

Table 2.6 A fragment of tax computation code

```
             . . .
m.1          do [if necessary, compute tax payment or refund
                for next record from tax file]
   2.1           read next record from tax file
     2.1         if
       2             tax due not equal to withholding
       3         then
         4.1         if
           2             tax due greater than withholding
           3         then
           4             compute tax payment
           5         else
           6             compute tax refund
           7         fi
       5         fi
   3         until
   4             all  tax records processed
   5         od
             . . .
```

Source: Linger, Mills, and Witt (1979), p. 63.

tell whether the loop is formed by (1) a DO I = 1 TO MAX...END DO; (2) an L:IF T > MAX THEN STOP...GO TO L; or (3) a WHILE T ≤ MAX...END WHILE. Of course, the pseudo-code or annotation on the flowchart would immediately clarify the issue. A Chapin chart or any other annotated flowchart notation would also clarify this ambiguity.

Another major advantage of pseudo-code is that it can be created, modified, controlled, and reproduced with ease by use of a terminal, a text editor, a number-date convention, and a printer associated with a modern interactive computer system.

2.3.4 HIPO Diagrams

Flowcharts, a graphical design tool, give the programmer a picture to which he or she can relate the design. In this section we will describe HIPO (Hierarchy plus Input-Process-Output), which uses block diagrams and tabular charts.[1]

HIPO diagrams are useful at a number of different stages in the development process: initial design, detailed design, design reviews, testing, and maintenance. The complete set of diagrams consists of (1) one hierarchy diagram, which presents in block form the relationships among major functions, minor functions, and modules in the program; (2) the overview IPO diagram, which provides in essence lists of input variables, process functions, and output variables for the

---

[1]IBM (1974); IBM (1975); Katzan (1976). The acronym is usually pronounced "hypo," the same as the familiar photographic fixing chemical.

highest level of the H diagram; and (3) a set of detailed (lower-level) IPO diagrams, which give the specifics of the design. The use of HIPOs in the design process is best illustrated by example.

We return to the word-processing system example. The information necessary to construct the HIPO diagrams was provided in Sec. 2.2.3. The H diagram was shown in Fig. 2.3. Note that we have called the top level 0.0 and that the functions on the second level are numbered successively from 1.0 to 8.0. Because of space and time, we have expanded only the Edit Text function to third level; however, the dotted lines in the figure indicate that the other second-level functions must also be expanded, and a fourth level of Text Edit may be required.

In constructing an H diagram, several practical questions arise; for example, how many functions should be represented at each level? This is a matter of judgment; however, if there are fewer than three functions at each level below the top, the hierarchy descends very slowly. (Sometimes a breakdown into two functions makes sense at the second or last level.) If a level contains more than 10 functions, it becomes complex and unwieldy. Thus, 3 to 10 functions per level is a good rule of thumb.

Another important question is, To what level down does one continue the composition? The answer is to as low a level as one wishes, but not below the code module level (say, 50 lines of higher-level source code). Since some of the functions will be more complex than others, not all branches of the diagram need to terminate at the same level.

In essence, the H diagram serves as a table of contents for the design. Note that the structure of Fig. 2.3 almost implies a top-down approach and the control structure is essentially the program which relates the level-1 task to the level-2 functions. But what if we decide to do a bottom-up development for good and appropriate reasons: how should we draw the H diagram? There is no discussion of this question in any of the sources. Thus, this author recommends that the H diagram be drawn in an inverted fashion for bottom-up development. We begin with the lowest level at the bottom and insert branches reaching up (see Fig. 2.2).

The IPO diagram is first drawn at an overview level, generally level 1. Most of the information for the IPO diagram at this level was already discussed in Sec. 2.2.3 and appears in Fig. 2.6. Note that the process part of the IPO is mostly verbs and the input and output sections, nouns. In fact, in the previously cited IBM memo (1975), it is suggested that the verbs be chosen from the list given in Table 2.7. Solid arrows are used in the diagram to indicate flow of control, and clear arrows represent data movement.

In addition to the overview IPO, there are detailed IPO diagrams for each block on the H diagram. An example of one such detailed IPO is shown in Fig. 2.7. Notice that pieces of pseudo-code are beginning to creep into the process block at this stage. Also, the nouns which are used should now begin to correspond to program variables.

HIPO diagrams have been successfully used on many projects; however, on a large project the amount of detail on documents and graphs becomes difficult to manage. As an example, consider a 250,000-object instruction program with 1000

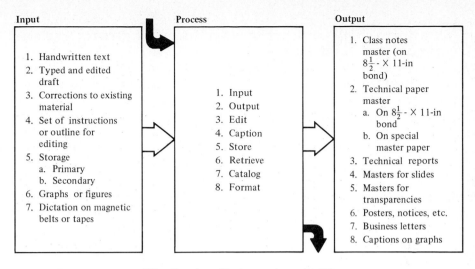

Title: Overview of text-processing system 0.0

Figure 2.6 Overview-level IPO diagram for the word-processing system.

Table 2.7 Verbs for HIPO

accept	delete	get	perform	select
add	dequeue	handle	place	set
allocate	detach	identify	position	specify
alter	determine	increment	post	start
analyze	display	initialize	process	stop
assign	do until	insert	provide	store
begin	do while	issue	purge	supply
build	edit	locate	put	suspend
calculate	encode	link	queue	switch
check	enqueue	load	read	terminate
clear	enter	look up	record	test
close	establish	maintain	reinstate	transfer
complete	examine	make	release	translate
construct	execute	merge	resolve	update
control	exit	modify	restore	use
convert	extract	monitor	return	validate
copy	find	move	scan	verify
create	fix	obtain	schedule	write
decrement	format	open	search	

Source: IBM (1975), Fig. 63.

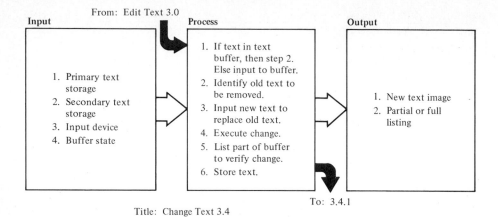

Figure 2.7 An IPO (input-process-output) diagram for the change text function.

modules. This represents potentially 1000 detailed IPO diagrams plus the overall IPO and the H diagram. Neglecting the H diagram and the overall IPO, and assuming that we are using 1-ft square sheets, we need 1000 ft^2 of wall space to display all these diagrams. These would more than fill all the wall space of a room with 8-foot ceilings and a perimeter of 120 ft (a room 30 ft $\times$ 30 ft). In fact, the author was shown just such a room of diagrams at RCA some time ago which represented all the block diagrams for the hardware and software of a large military system. The wall space had been augmented by many swinging panels like the ones used to display prints in museum print shops. An attempt was made to computerize the process but the effort was abandoned because of schedule deadlines and the size of the task. The room of documentation was maintained by a full-time engineer and two part-time student draftsmen.[1]

To avoid such problems of size and upkeep complexity, most projects draw HIPO diagrams only down to a certain level. In most cases this is still too high a level to begin coding, and either flowcharts or pseudo-code is then used as an intermediate step before code writing.

2.3.5 The Warnier-Orr Diagram

A technique which has become popular in recent years was begun by Warnier,[2] continued by Orr,[3] and popularized in journal and magazine articles.[4] The

---

[1] An important question arises in the case of paper documentation such as that in this example. What happens in case of a fire? An obvious defense is to keep a duplicate set of documents in a locked, fireproof file cabinet in another building. Even in the case of a computerized documentation data base, backup copies on tape in a locked, fireproof safe are still needed.

Most appliance manufacturers store schematics, drawings, and parts lists on indexed microfiche. It is surprising that no editor, graphics, or photographic system has been invented to serve this need.

[2] Warnier, (1976).

[3] Orr (1978).

[4] Higgins (1977a; 1978); Rudkin and Sphere (1979).

technique utilizes nested sets of braces, some pseudo-code, and logic symbols to indicate the system structure. The main feature of the technique can be appreciated by considering an example.

A high-level flowchart for our illustrative program is shown in Fig. 2.8. A pseudo-code representation of this program is given in Fig. 2.9. Note that a set of arrows has been added to the pseudo-code to indicate the nesting and hierarchy of the program. (The author feels this is a useful addition to pseudo-code representation.) A Warnier-Orr diagram for the example is given in Fig. 2.10. Note that the braces play the same role as the arrows in Fig. 2.9, and that the EXCLUSIVE OR symbol, ⊕, replaces the THEN ELSE structure of the pseudo-code. The numbers in parentheses represent the number of times each structure is executed.

In general, pseudo-code is a little more compact than a flowchart, and a Warnier-Orr Diagram is the most compact of the three. Thus, the Warnier-Orr technique may save 25 percent on documentation, which is helpful but not that significant. A study of Figs. 2.9 and 2.10 shows that the addition of arrows and indention to pseudo-code results in a pseudo-code structure which looks much like a Warnier-Orr diagram.

In each of the design representations, elements S1 to S11 and A to J may represent modules with many sequential statements or nested control structures. Thus, the example may represent the entire structure of a modest-sized problem or the upper-level structure of a very large problem.

The following section discusses the author's personal preferences regarding the use of design-representation techniques.

2.3.6 Recommended Design-Representation Techniques

A large number of design-representation techniques exist, and many of these have been mentioned in this section. Four techniques, high-level flowcharts, HIPO diagrams, pseudo-code, and Warnier-Orr diagrams, were described in some detail. In the author's opinion, no one technique dominates over the others either in utility or pervasiveness of use.

More important than which technique should be used is the necessity for using *some* design technique. Without proper management controls (see Chap. 6), there will always be a certain percentage of projects and individual software designers who will use virtually *no* design representation and will keep all the design in their heads. The real problem is ensuring that the design is documented adequately using some technique(s), and the choice of an optimum technique is a second-order consideration—actually a matter of personal preference. A summary of the benefits and drawbacks of the four design representations is given in Table 2.8.

The author's own personal preferences are for a composite method:

1. An H diagram is drawn and major subprograms are identified.
2. High-level flowcharts are drawn for the control structure and each major subprogram (the set of flowcharts can be omitted in a small program).

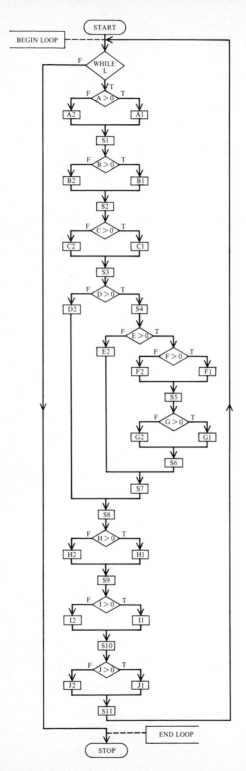

Figure 2.8 High-level flowchart for a program containing one DO WHILE and 10 IF THEN ELSE control structures.

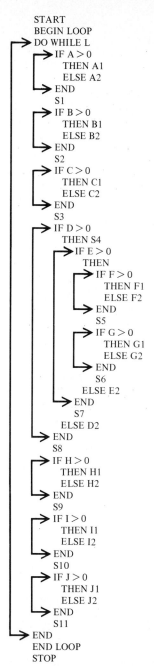

```
START
BEGIN LOOP
DO WHILE L
    IF A > 0
        THEN A1
        ELSE A2
    END
    S1
    IF B > 0
        THEN B1
        ELSE B2
    END
    S2
    IF C > 0
        THEN C1
        ELSE C2
    END
    S3
    IF D > 0
        THEN S4
            IF E > 0
            THEN
                IF F > 0
                    THEN F1
                    ELSE F2
                END
                S5
                IF G > 0
                    THEN G1
                    ELSE G2
                END
                S6
            ELSE E2
            END
            S7
        ELSE D2
    END
    S8
    IF H > 0
        THEN H1
        ELSE H2
    END
    S9
    IF I > 0
        THEN I1
        ELSE I2
    END
    S10
    IF J > 0
        THEN J1
        ELSE J2
    END
    S11
END
END LOOP
STOP
```

Figure 2.9 The pseudo-code for the program of Fig. 2.8.

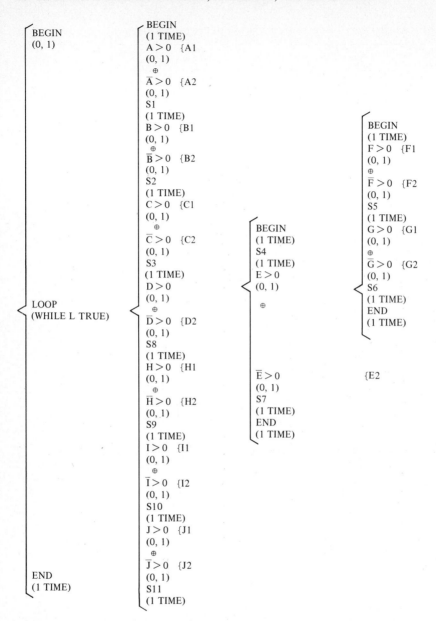

Figure 2.10 The Warnier-Orr diagram for the program of Fig. 2.8.

Table 2.8 Comparison of four design-representation techniques

Technique	Advantages	Disadvantages
A. Flowcharts	1. Universally known 2. Pictorial representation 3. Most easily understood by people without training in programming	1. Requires much space 2. Clumsy for depicting subroutines, interrupts 3. Laborious to make structural changes
B. Pseudo-code	1. Easy to learn 2. Very flexible since English instructions can be interspersed 3. Portions carry over to code with little or no modification 4. More compact than flowcharts 5. Easily stored in a computer 6. Easier to update than other methods	1. Not pictorial, except for indention (and arrow groupings) 2. Not standardized
C. HIPO diagrams	1. H chart fits in well with top-down design 2. Highlights inputs and outputs 3. H chart easily understood by people without training in programming	1. If implemented for entire design, requires much space 2. Requires some practice to learn the method 3. Laborious to make structural changes
D. Warnier-Orr	1. Easy to learn 2. Standardized 3. Slightly more compact than pseudo-code	1. Not pictorial, except for indention (and bracket groupings) 2. Requires more practice to learn than pseudo-code

3. Pseudo-code is written for each flowchart.
4. The program (code) is written in the source language.

Such a procedure has the advantage that at least some phase of the design should be in a form familiar to all interested participants. After a few hours of study, all participants should obtain a working knowledge of each different representation. As a check, one can write pseudo-code for step 2 and high-level flowcharts for step 3; such a procedure will provide variety as an aid in preventing the repetition during checking of the same mistakes made during design.

2.4 STRUCTURED PROGRAMMING

2.4.1 Introduction

The digital computer was born in the 1940s and became a tool of widespread use in business, government, and universities during the 1950s.[1] Extensive use of higher-level language began with Fortran, which was initially proposed in 1954 but did not reach popularity until the end of the decade.[2] Initially, the main focus of programming was to learn machine or assembly language and write some sort of program that worked. Gradually the emphasis became programming cleverness in which tricks or convoluted logic was used to write a more concise or faster program. This helped to minimize memory and compensate for slow execution speeds. The developers of higher-level languages catered to such a concept of superior programming and incorporated great flexibility into new languages. Only in the late 1960s and early 1970s did the consequences of such an approach become clear. Many of the programs were unreadable, incomprehensible, and unmodifiable. The average computer programmer was believed to be a master architect the worth of Sir Christopher Wren.[3] A more realistic comparison would be with the architect responsible for the design of a modern high-rise office building. Thus, in retrospect the 1970s might be described as "back to programming basics"; however, professionals were still unsure what the basics of programming really were.

In studying what was wrong with contemporary programming, it was observed that program control structure was often vastly complicated by GO TO statements.[4] The problem was that indiscriminate use of GO TO statements generally led to an unduly complicated control structure. One way to correct this problem was to eliminate GO TO statements completely, and to rely on a single decision structure and a single repetition (looping) structure. Bohm showed that any program control structure could be synthesized in terms of IF (exp) THEN ELSE and DO WHILE (exp) control structures.[5] This became the basic philosophy behind structured programming, which has to a large part been developed and popularized in this country by Mills.[6]

2.4.2 Rules of Structured Programming

The structured programming philosophy aims to provide a well-defined, clear, and simple approach to program design. Such a method should be easier to

[1] Sackman (1967), p. 29. In 1950 there were 20 computer installations in the United States; by 1960 there were 6000.

[2] Backus et al. (1964). The author explains that the Fortran programming project started in 1954 and took $2\frac{1}{2}$ calendar years and 18 man-years to complete. Also see pp. 29–47 in Rosen (1967).

[3] Famous British architect (1632–1723) who built seven major structures in London, most of which are now standing and are architectural gems.

[4] Dijkstra (1968).

[5] Bohm and Jacopini (1966).

[6] Mills (1972).

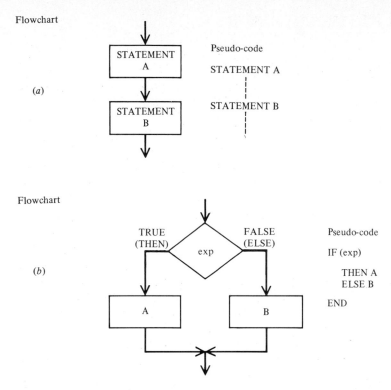

Figure 2.11 The three classical structured programming constructs: (*a*) SEQUENCE; (*b*) IF THEN ELSE; (*c*) DO WHILE. *Note*: (1) The notation "exp" can mean any legal expression in the language in question; (2) sometimes the THEN branch is shown on the right and the ELSE branch on the left in part *b*; (3) both orientations of the DO WHILE flowchart are used; (4) the flowcharts given (sometimes called *structured* flowcharts) are composed of decision symbols, processing symbols, and joinings of flowlines (merges) as given in Fig. 2.4 *a*, *e*, and *h*.

understand, evaluate, and modify than any arbitrary method conceived by the designers on the spur of the moment. Structured programming requires the use of single-entry and single-exit control structures. The classical technique used to implement these principles is to restrict all control constructs to one of the three statements shown in Fig. 2.11 above and on the following page.

The first structure, the SEQUENCE (Fig. 2.11*a*), merely indicates that if there is no intervening control structure, the flow of control naturally passes from one instruction to the next in sequence. This author knows of no modern higher-level language which does not possess this feature.[1]

The second control structure, the IF THEN ELSE (Fig. 2.11*b*), is a two-way selector common in a number of modern programming languages (PL/1, Algol, Pascal, etc.). Whenever the expression (exp) is true, THEN branch of the

[1]For examples of experimental three address computers having assembly languages without the sequence property see British ACE (1953), American MIDA (1956), and Russian STRELA (1959) (Bell and Newell, 1971, Chaps. 11, 14, and 15).

Flowchart

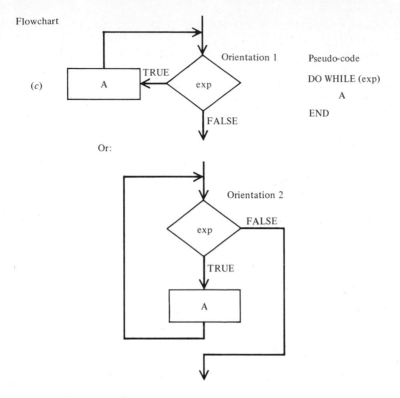

(c)

Figure 2.11 (*continued*).

statement is executed. When the expression is false, the ELSE branch of the statement is executed. In either case control is transferred subsequently to the statement following the END statement. In some cases (if the programmer desires, and if the language permits) the expression may itself be very complex, or may be preceded by a complex assignment statement which sets the value of the expression. In general, one may omit the ELSE statement, which is equivalent to inserting a null statement for B. In some languages the entities A and B can be either single executable statements or groups of statements. In other languages (PL/1, for example) if we wish A or B to be a group of statements, we must enclose them by a "parenthesizing type" of structure such as a BEGIN END block or a DO GROUP.[1]

The third basic control structure is the DO WHILE (Fig. 2.11c), which controls repetition (looping). The expression is tested, and if it is true, the body of the structure, A, is performed. As soon as the expression becomes false, repeated performance of A is terminated, and control transfers to the instruction following the END statement. As before, the entity A can be either a single instruction or a

---

[1]Although, in general, BEGIN END and DO GROUP constructs affect control, they are considered special cases of the SEQUENCE structure, as are procedure and subroutine calls.

group of instructions. Note that if the expression in the DO WHILE is initially false, then entity A is not performed even once.

It is clear that the structured programming restriction of a single entry of control into the beginning of a module and a single exit of control from the end of the module fits in very well with top-down design principles. The novice may have to practice program design using the three basic control structures given in Fig. 2.11 before agreeing that loss of the GO TO instruction does not excessively handicap creativity. Before we begin any structured design examples, it is useful to outline some of the issues regarding structured programming which are treated in subsequent sections of this chapter.

Some of the questions which arise when one begins to consider the implications of structured programming are:

1. Can we express any algorithmic solution to a problem as a structured program?
2. Should we use any control structures in addition to the classical ones given in Fig. 2.11?
3. What sort of approach or techniques should be used in writing a structured program?

After some thought and experience with the technique, additional questions will be generated:

4. How efficient in terms of time and space are structured programs?
5. What are the other advantages of structured programs?
6. Will people use structured programming?
7. How can I convert nonstructured programs to structured programs?
8. How can I write structured programs in a language which does not have all the constructs of Fig. 2.11?

These and other questions will be answered in the following sections.

2.4.3. Examples of Structured Design

Some of the differences between structured and nonstructured programs will be better appreciated if we consider a few introductory examples.

The flowchart and PL/1 listing of a simple number-counting program taken from Ruston are given in Fig. 2.12. The program specification is as follows:

> Given a list of numbers, obtain (1) the count of positive numbers, (2) the count of negative numbers, and (3) the sum of all positive numbers. The program is to stop if either (1) we encounter the number 0 or (2) the sum of positive numbers exceeds 1000.

Inspection of the program listing (Fig. 2.12a) reveals three GO TO statements; thus clearly this is not a classical structured program. Furthermore, if we study

```
COUNTS:     PROCEDURE OPTIONS (MAIN);
            /* THIS PROGRAM COUNTS POSITIVE NUMBERS,              */
            /* NEGATIVE NUMBERS, AND SUMS POSITIVE NUMBERS.       */
            /* IT STOPS IF EITHER INPUT IS ZERO OR IF THE         */
            /* SUM EXCEEDS 1000.                                  */

            K = 0; L = 0; TOTAL = 0;          /*K COUNTS POSITIVE NUMBERS    */
                                              /*L COUNTS NEGATIVE NUMBERS    */
REPEAT:     GET LIST (A);
            IF A = 0 THEN GO TO PRINT;        /*IF A = 0 WE ARE FINISHED     */
            IF A > 0 THEN GO TO UPDATE;       /*FOR A POSITIVE A WE MUST     */
                                              /*INCREASE K AND TOTAL         */
            L = L + 1;                        /*INCREASE NEGATIVE COUNT      */
            GO TO REPEAT;
UPDATE:     K = K + 1;
            TOTAL = TOTAL + A;
            IF TOTAL < = 1000 THEN GO TO REPEAT;  /*REPEAT IF NOT DONE       */
PRINT:      PUT LIST (K, L, TOTAL);           /*RESULTS OF THE PROGRAM       */
            END COUNTS;
```

Figure 2.12 Unstructured design for a number-counting program: (*a*) Program listing; (*b*) Program flowchart. *(From Ruston, 1978, pp.29–30)*

the flowchart (Fig. 2.12*b*), we also see two exits from the main program loop (GET A, A = 0, A > 0, L = L + 1, GET A,...). The first exit is if A = 0 and the second is if TOTAL > 1000. Thus, the single-entry and single-exit criteria of classical structured programs are also violated. We can easily design a structured solution to this problem by using IF THEN ELSE and DO WHILE, as shown in Fig. 2.13, instead of GO TOs. The flowchart of Fig. 2.13 has only a single exit from the main loop, i.e., the false condition of the DO WHILE. Since the program uses only the three allowed control structures and has only single entries to and single exits from each control structure, it is a classical structured program.

Examination of the flowcharts of Figs. 2.12 and 2.13 reveals a simpler topology for the structured program, obviously a benefit. On the negative side, the structured program requires an extra initial GET A and a compound expression in the DO WHILE, resulting in perhaps a 5 percent penalty in speed and storage.

As a second example consider the Fortran program from Kernighan and Plauger that appears in Table 2.9. The program is an implementation of Newton's method of solving for the square root B of an input value X. The flowchart for this program is given in Fig. 2.14. The program is nonstructured because of the two GO TO control statements. In Fig. 2.15 we have redesigned the flowchart as a classical structured program using a DO WHILE control structure and have simplified the program through use of the absolute-value operator. In terms of the flowcharts, the complexity has been reduced from 11 boxes to 9 boxes. In Kernighan and Plauger's book it is pointed out that many other things are wrong

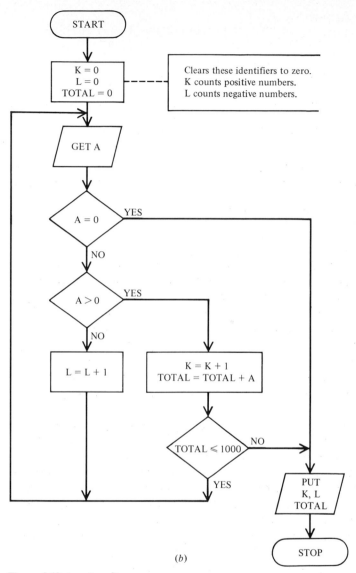

Figure 2.12 (*continued*).

with this program:

1. Sometimes Newton's method doesn't converge, and the program doesn't test for that.
2. The square root of 0 is not 0.
3. A relative rather than an absolute convergence criterion is better for very large or small values of X.

```
COUNTS:  PROC OPTIONS (MAIN);
         K, L, TOTAL = 0;          /* K COUNTS POS NUMBERS, L NEG NUMBERS     */
         GET LIST (A);
         DO WHILE (TOTAL < = 1000 & A ¬ = 0);
            IF A > 0 THEN DO;
                              TOTAL = TOTAL + A;
                              K = K + 1;
                           END;
                    ELSE L = L + 1;
            GET LIST(A);
         END;
         PUT LIST (K, L, TOTAL);
         END COUNTS;
```

(a)

Figure 2.13 Structured design for a number-counting program: (a) Program listing; (b) Program flowchart. *(From Ruston, 1978, p. 127)*

In changing the program of Fig. 2.14 into a structured one, a DO WHILE statement was needed. Because in a DO WHILE the test is made before the first iteration begins, this construct must be preceded with an initialization program segment. In the initialization segment both A and B must be initially calculated. Sometimes a programmer would prefer a control construct with a loop repetition test after the first iteration. Such a construct is the DO UNTIL control structure. Use of a DO UNTIL in Fig. 2.16 simplifies initialization and eliminates precomputation of A before entering the loop. The reader can verify the equivalence of the slightly different solutions given in Figs. 2.15 and 2.16 by substituting typical values for X and hand-processing the resulting values. It is interesting to note that the algorithm will find the root of 4 exactly in one trial. Some purists deny the use of DO UNTIL in classical structured programming and advise the use of the DO WHILE instead.

Let us consider a final example. In performing a payroll computation, the rules for the withholding for city, state, and federal tax differ in the percentage withheld for varying numbers of dependents. If we let D be the number of dependents, and if the tax categories change for $D < 2, 2 \leq D < 4, 4 \leq D < 6$, and $D \geq 6$, then we might write a subprogram similar to that shown in Fig. 2.17. The structure is clear; however, we have had to make four successive decisions which were nearly the same. Note that in the first test we included the possibility that $D = 0$, and this case should not be overlooked. It is not too uncommon for a wage earner with outside income to claim 0 dependents to increase his or her withholding so that no additional tax has to be paid at the end of the year. (Of course, it is better economics to put the extra money in the bank, where it will draw interest until tax time. However, some people view this as forced savings.) Structures such as those that appear in Fig. 2.17 have led language designers to invent a multiple-alternative-decision construct known as a DO CASE structure. The program is redesigned using a DO CASE structure in Fig. 2.18. The DO CASE structure is essentially a selector switch with many positions.

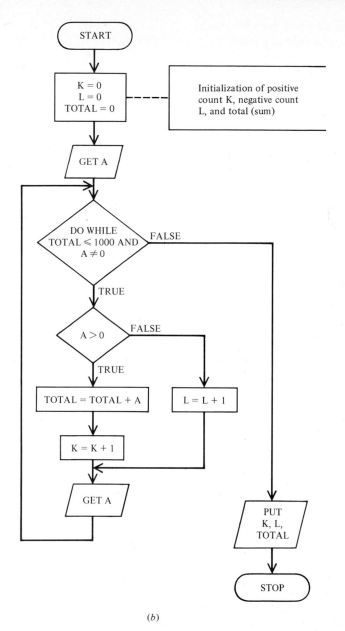

(b)

Figure 2.13 (*continued*).

Table 2.9 A Fortran program which uses Newton's method to solve for the square root of a number

The following is a typical program to evaluate the square root (B) of a number (X):

```
        READ (5, 1)X
1       FORMAT (F10.5)
        A = X/2
2       B = (X/A + A)/2
        C = B − A
        IF (C.LT.0)C = −C
        IF (C.LT.10.E-6)GOTO 3
        A = B
        GOTO 2
3       WRITE (6, 1)B
        STOP
        END
```

Source: Kernighan and Plauger (1974), p. 3.

Some practitioners consider the three control structures given in Fig. 2.11 to be the classical control elements of structured programming and recommend that only these be used. The majority of users extend the canonical set of structured programming control constructs to also include the DO UNTIL and the DO CASE structures shown in Fig. 2.19.

Before we leave the example of Fig. 2.17, we have more to learn from it. First of all, we have not treated the case of what happens when $D > 6$. In order to know how to proceed, we should first find out what happens if the value of I is outside the range of cases supplied. (This is much like the problem of an array reference in which the subscript value falls outside the declared range for the array.) The action taken by the DO CASE expression in such a case depends on the language implementation.[1]

---

[1]In the case of Pascal the answer is clear—the result is difficult to predict. "The value of the CASE expression must be one of the case-labels listed in the body of statement. If it is not, the result of executing the CASE statement is 'undefined'—that is, there is just no telling what PASCAL will do. (It may be more-or-less reasonable, but you are not supposed to count on it.) To avoid this embarrassment [disaster?], it is a good idea to make sure the value of the expression is proper before executing the CASE statement" (Conway et al., 1976, p. 71).

In the case of Algol 60, "if a switch designator occurs outside the scope of a quantity entering into a designator expression in the switch list, and an evaluation of this switch designator selects this designational expression, then the conflicts between the identifiers for the quantities in this expression and the identifiers whose declarations are valid at the place of the switch designator will be avoided through suitable systematic changes of the latter identifiers" (Naur, 1967, p. 109). Any reader who understands this statement will know how to proceed; however, one who shares the author's puzzlement had better obviate the problem just as in Pascal.

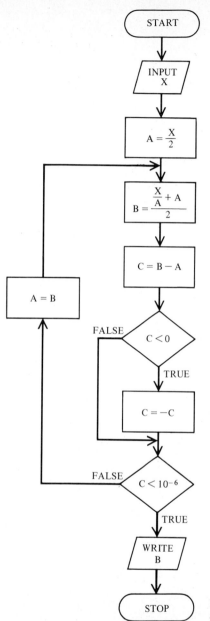

Figure 2.14 Flowchart for the nonstructured program of Table 2.9 (containing two GO TO structures).

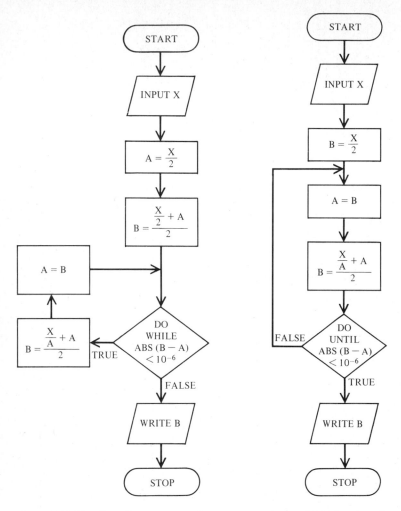

Figure 2.15 Flowchart for a structured version of the program of Table 2.9, using a DO WHILE structure.

Figure 2.16 Flowchart for a structured version of the program of Table 2.9, using a DO UNTIL control structure.

However, for our purposes we can assume that such a situation is undesirable, and we should protect against it. In Fig. 2.18, the single DO CASE construct has replaced four IF THEN structures in Fig. 2.17 and the number of assignment statement blocks has increased from 5 to 9. It is easy to simplify the number of cases in Fig. 2.18 by using an expression to define I in terms of D. The technique used (divide by 2 and take the rounded values) simplifies the program somewhat. Both these improvements are incorporated in the design of Fig. 2.20.

We may use our example of Fig. 2.17 to introduce yet another control construct which sometimes is suggested as an addition to the extended canonical

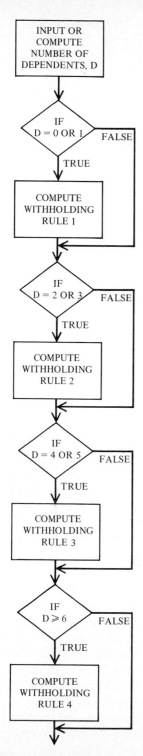

Figure 2.17 A withholding tax subprogram.

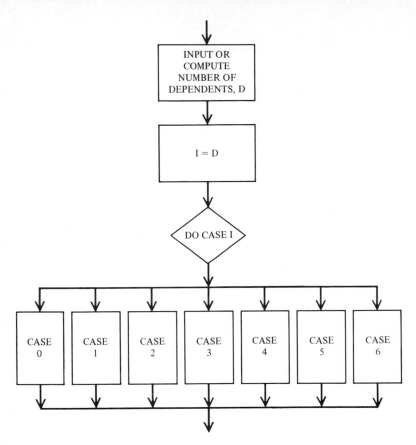

Figure 2.18 The program of Fig. 2.17 redesigned using a DO CASE construction.

set. Suppose in our example that $D = -10$. One obvious reply is that it is physically impossible for the number of dependents to be negative so why worry about such an impossible case. This is a poor viewpoint to take, and is antithetical to one of the major axioms of software engineering: no matter how hard we try, errors will occur, and thus we must plan for them. One obvious way for a negative value of D to enter the data base is via an input error initially or during a correction. There are also other, more mysterious (at least until they are explained) ways in which such a condition could occur. Techniques for dealing with such potential problems are generally called *defensive programming*.

One technique of defensive programming is to check all input data for validity upon entry. If this is done, it is unlikely that a value such as $D = -10$ could occur. However, if the variable D is corrupted in some way after data entry, it will not be detected. Thus we may wish to check D only before the DO CASE statement or in both places. Some programmers argue that the checks required in defensive programming result in additional memory usage and slow the running time of the program. In most cases, this is a small penalty to pay for such

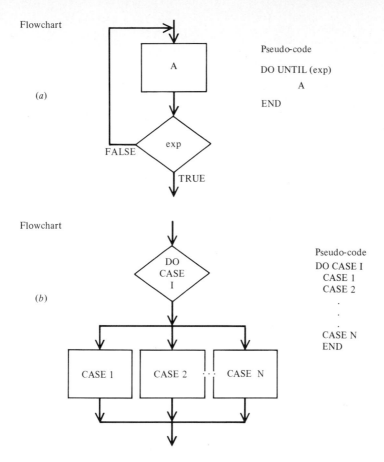

Flowchart

(a)

Pseudo-code

DO UNTIL (exp)

A

END

Flowchart

(b)

Pseudo-code

DO CASE I
   CASE 1
   CASE 2
      .
      .
      .
   CASE N
END

Figure 2.19 (*a*) DO UNTIL and (*b*) DO CASE constructs.

significant benefits. Let us assume we will test D for validity before the DO CASE statement. This is easy to do with a simple IF D < 0 THEN (statement) preceding the IF D > 5 statement in Fig. 2.20. The question is, What should we do if the D < 0 test fails? The simplest way to handle such a situation is to use a GO TO INVALID-D or CALL INVALID-D( ) statement. Then any error message or recovery procedure will be at label INVALID-D or in the subroutine of the same name. The objection to these two procedures is that either violates one of the principles of structured programming, since both create two exits from a loop. If this will occur only once or twice in an entire program, then perhaps it is best to leave it this way since it will cause little confusion (a little bit of sin isn't too harmful?). An alternate technique is to raise an error condition by setting a flag and allowing the loop to complete its repetition.[1] Upon exit from the loop, the flag can be tested, and if it is set, appropriate action can be taken.

[1]An example of the use of a flag is given in Fig. 2.24 and is discussed later in this section.

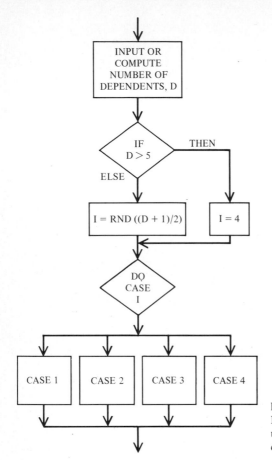

Figure 2.20 Improvement of the design of Fig. 2.18 by handling the case $D > 5$ and utilizing the rounding function to group the cases efficiently.

Clearly, using a flag does not violate any structured programming principles. However, it has the disadvantage that we must wait for normal completion of the current loop repetition. This is a waste of time and may also damage a data base or complicate recovery. To handle such a case, some programmers use the LEAVE construction, which terminates all loops immediately and transfers control to the outermost END statement. The LEAVE (label) instruction is implemented in several versions of PL/1 and allows one to leave a single loop, many loops, or all of a nested set of loops by specifying the appropriate label.[1] The BREAK instruction implemented in the C language operates like the LEAVE instruction but terminates only a single loop.[2] An example of a LEAVE instruction is given in Fig. 2.21. Inspection of the figure shows that the instruction LEAVE LOOP 2 behaves in all respects as if it were GO TO LABEL 2. Thus,

[1] Conway (1978), pp. 110, 111.
[2] Kernighan and Ritchie (1978), pp. 61–62.

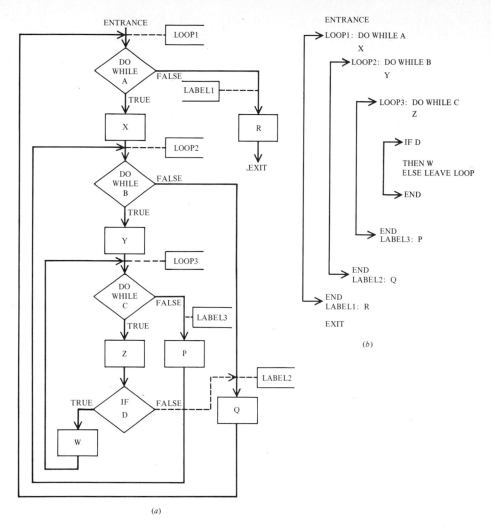

Figure 2.21 Illustration of a LEAVE statement situated within an inner program loop: (*a*) flowchart; (*b*) pseudo-code.

BREAK and LEAVE instructions are just restricted GO TOs in which the transfer point can only be the instruction following a loop END statement.

Clearly, we can go on inventing all kinds of extensions to structured programming to cover special cases. This is much like the weekly group of card players who decide to vary their rules for the game of poker and name special wild cards. The group should expect confusion when a stranger is invited to join their group one night. Furthermore, if this card group were to try to suggest their special local rules to other card groups, they might meet with resistance or derision or both. The author feels that special structured programming rules are even worse, since

Table 2.10 A nomenclature for the popular structured-programming variants

	SEQUENCE IF THEN ELSE DO WHILE	DO UNTIL DO CASE	BREAK LEAVE	GO TO	Single entry and single exit
1. Classical structured programming	Yes	No	No	No	Yes
2. Extended structured programming	Yes	Yes	No	No	Yes
3. Modified structured programming	Yes	Yes	Yes	No	Yes (except for BREAK and LEAVE)
4. Structured programming with GO TOs	Yes	Yes	Yes	Yes (a few carefully chosen ones)	(Occasional multiple exits, no multiple entries)
5. Unstructured programming	Yes	Yes	Yes	Yes (many used at will)	Frequent multiple exits and entries

programming is not a game but a business and a very serious and expensive one at that.

It is useful to provide a standard nomenclature for the variations of structured programming which have already been discussed. Such a notation is given in Table 2.10. The use of only the basic three constructs is called *classical* structured programming, and the addition of DO CASE and DO UNTIL is named *extended* structured programming. If we also allow BREAK or LEAVE statements, the term *modified* structured programming is used, since two exit points are created. If GO TOs are used extensively and indiscriminately, then a nonstructured program ensues. In some cases the use of GO TOs in a carefully controlled fashion can be used to achieve modified structured programming.[1] This is further discussed in Sec. 2.4.6.

2.4.4 Techniques of Structured Programming

The best approach to writing a structured program is to begin with a high-level program plan. Any loop repetitions and decisions which appear at this level are realized in the design by using DO WHILE (plus DO UNTIL) and IF THEN ELSE (plus DO CASE). Each major section of the design can then be expanded in a similar manner. Such a technique is generally referred to as *stepwise refinement*.[2]

[1] Knuth (1974).
[2] Wirth (1976).

On first consideration, it is difficult to differentiate between the design philosophy just described and top-down design. Top-down design is a technique for decomposing a problem and is independent of which control structures will be used. Thus, a top-down design could be implemented in either a nonstructured or a structured fashion. The term *stepwise refinement* is applied to the successive decomposition of a structured program. This results in lower-level structures which are a succession of cascaded and nested repetition and decision constructs. If a top-down design is to be implemented as a structured program, the distinctions between the methods become very small. The upper levels of the design involving H diagrams, high-level flowcharts, and pseudo-code would be called a top-down design. Once the design descended to the code level (or low-level pseudo-code), we would speak of it as a structured program developed via stepwise refinement. We now elaborate on the question of what kind of programs can be realized as structured programs.

The basic proof that a large class of programs can be realized by the three classical structured programming constructs is due to Bohm and Jacopini (1976). The proof has been further developed by Mills,[1] who also gives a constructive algorithm showing how nonstructured programs can be converted to structured ones. A different technique has been developed by Ashcroft and Manna.[2] The fact that Mills and Ashcroft-Manna have algorithms for converting a nonstructured program to a structured one is essentially a sufficiency proof. To enhance our insight into structured programming, we will examine the assumptions required in Mills' proof.

Mills' method utilizes the concepts of *nesting* (expansion) of flowcharts and employs the classical structured constructs given in Fig. 2.11. The result is an algorithm which specifies how to produce a structured program from any *proper* nonstructured program. A proper program is one which has the following properties:

1. The program must be such that a flowchart can be drawn using only processing blocks, flowlines, decision symbols, and merges (joining of flowlines) (Fig. 2.4*a*, *l*, and *h*).
2. Each control structure must have only one entry and one exit.
3. Each flowchart element must be reachable from the starting point of the program.

Clearly a SEQUENCE structure satisfies properties 1 and 2, as do the two decision structures given in Fig. 2.11. The only programs which violate property 3 are incorrect ones where some lines of code are not executable. The concept of nesting essentially means that a process block can be expanded by stepwise refinement generating lower-level structured elements within. Thus, the details of the program evolve by refining the process blocks as many times as required.

---

[1] Mills (1972). Also see Linger, Mills, and Witt (1979).
[2] Ashcroft and Manna (1972).

Note that the iterative DO GROUP (for example, DO I = 1 to 20 BY 1,..., END), which we have not discussed so far, is a loop control structure (essentially a special case of a DO WHILE) and thus satisfies properties 1, 2, and 3. Similarly, we can examine the legality of including subroutine calls as an element in structured programs. Clearly, a subprogram call will satisfy properties 1, 2, and 3 because after the subprogram completes its task, the control returns to the statement immediately following the call statement; the subroutine itself must obviously be structured. On the flowchart, we can represent the subprogram as a process and include a separate flowchart for the subprogram.

At this point we might ask if there are any practical programs which are not proper programs. Any program which contains one or more of the following features is an improper program:[1]

1. Interrupt and trap instructions in assembly language
2. Fortran-type end-of-file conditions
3. PL/1-type on conditions
4. Fixed overflow and underflow conditions
5. DO CASE, BREAK/LEAVE instructions
6. Self-modifying code if it can become nonstructured

In the case of category 6, self-modifying code is generally very confusing, and the best procedure is to religiously avoid it. As far as category 5 is concerned, we sanction a small amount of nonstructured code if it *really* helps. Further discussion of the Ashcroft-Manna constructive technique appears in Prob. 2.48 at the end of the chapter.

Often the question arises whether we can convert a nonstructured program into a structured program. Before we discuss the details of this question, we might inquire why anyone would want to do this. Often the question is posed as a theoretical one related to a constructive proof for which problems can be realized as structured programs. This latter question was just discussed; however, it is academic unless there is some practical object to such a conversion. If a program is running properly, it should be left alone, no matter how convoluted the logic or structure is. Some practical reasons that may exist for wanting to convert a nonstructured program into a structured program are:

1. There are major problems with the logic or structure of the program and some rewriting or redesign is probably necessary. Converting to a structured version should be an aid in redesign.

---

[1]Hardware failures may be added to the list if we have redundant processors and a recovery technique, parallel processing, multiprocessing, or other similarly configured programs or systems. The way to deal with programs which contain constructs in categories 1 to 4 is to allow that at the operating system level the program may be nonstructured; however, at all inner levels it is structured.
Tausworthe (1977, Sec. 5.5) proposes special program structures for improper programs.

2. An existing program is to be modified. Although the program works well, the structure is very difficult to understand, thus a structured version will be a better starting point for the new design.
3. As a standard measure to enforce uniformity, all new programs will be written in structured fashion, and in addition all existing programs will be converted for documentation purposes to an equivalent structured form.

Details of how to convert an unstructured into a structured program are contained in the constructive proofs just discussed; however, some of the techniques used are useful in designing structured programs and will now be discussed.

Sometimes the initial approach to a design contains a little nonstructured logic, and it is easier to transform those sections to structured logic than to invent an entirely new approach. As a first example, we consider the unstructured flowchart of Fig. 2.22*a* and its structured equivalent in Fig. 2.22*b*. Note that the

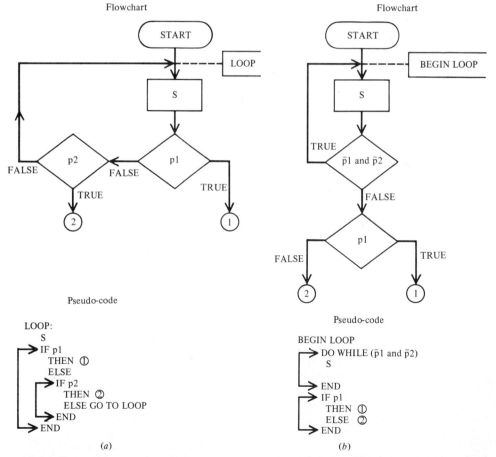

Figure 2.22 A nonstructured program (*a*) and its structured equivalent (*b*). (*From Nicholls, 1975, Fig. 10.2, p. 371*)

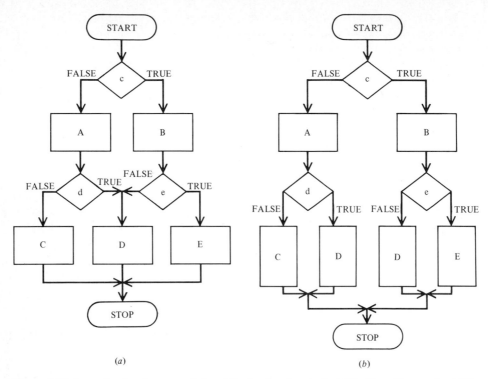

Figure 2.23 A nonstructured program (*a*) and its structured equivalent (*b*). *(From Tausworthe, 1977, Fig. 5-21, p. 128)*

compound decision p1 AND p2 is used in the structured version.[1] One can also rewrite the nonstructured flowchart as a structured flowchart using only simple decisions if S is repeated. This is explored in problems 2.30 and 2.43 at the end of the chapter.

Another example is given in Fig. 2.23, where the nonstructured flowchart is given in part *a* and its structured equivalent in part *b*. Duplication of element D was all that was required; however, the structured version involves more elements, 11 versus 10, than the nonstructured counterpart. If D is such a large program that duplication is undesirable, it can be written as a subprogram and accessed via two subprogram calls.

As a last example, we consider the use of flags as a technique for converting a nonstructured flowchart into a structured one. A flag is a variable which "remembers" whether a previous decision was true or false, and retains this information for use later in the program. A nonstructured flowchart is shown in Fig. 2.24*a*. Blocks A and B in general represent other flowcharts and may or may not be structured; however, the object at this point is to eliminate one of the two loop exits from the THEN and ELSE clauses of Fig. 2.24*a*. This can be accomplished

---

[1]The notation $\bar{p}1$ is used to denote the *complement* of p1, that is, NOT p1.

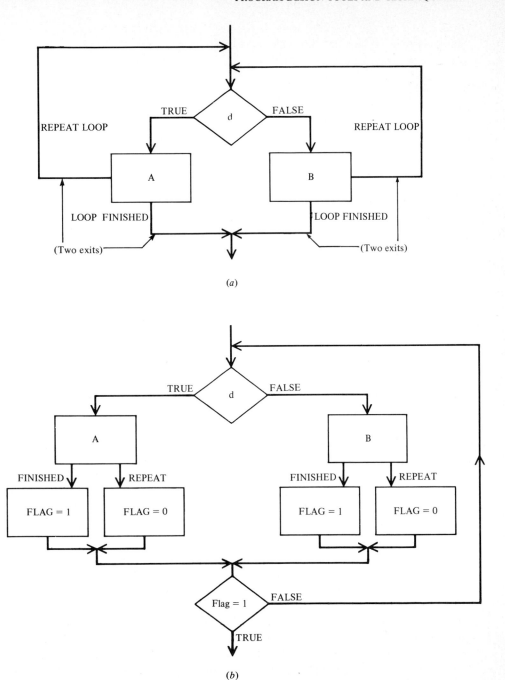

Figure 2.24 Transformation of unstructured loops (*a*) to equivalent structured loops (*b*). In part *a*, the loops are unstructured and either or both (or neither) of flowcharts A and B may be unstructured. In part *b* there may still be nonstructured elements in flowcharts A and B, but the loops are structured.

by one flag storage variable, four flag assignment statements, and one flag test. This may seem to be a considerable increase in program size; however, if A and B are large programs, the impact may be negligible. Also, we could always start over and redesign the program from the beginning as a structured program.

The example given in Fig. 2.24 is one of the steps in Mills' constructive proof of structured programming (see also Tausworthe, 1977).

2.4.5 Advantages and Disadvantages of Structured Programming

Now that we have completed the basic exposition and examples of structured programming, it is appropriate to discuss the pros and cons of the technique, which are listed in Table 2.11. We will try to focus our discussion on objective items without excessive optimism or pessimism.

The most important advantage of structured programming is its clarity. Much of the huge cost and difficulty of programming lies in the complexity of the problems we attempt and the chore of explaining our ideas to others. A structured design clearly presents the control structure of the program and fits in well with either top-down or bottom-up programming techniques. (Obviously, a poorly

Table 2.11 Pros and cons of structured programming

Advantages	Disadvantages
1. Clarity: Structured programs generally have a clarity and logical pattern to their control structure which is a tremendous advantage throughout the design process.	1. Reactionary attitudes: There are many programmers and managers who hesitate to learn new techniques they view as unproven.
2. Productivity: Programmers who use structured techniques show a significant increase in instructions coded per man-hour of work. Similar advantages are claimed for the test phase.	2. Inefficiency: In some cases it can be clearly shown that structured programs require somewhat more memory or running time than their nonstructured counterparts.
3. Fixed style: Structured programming tends to limit the coding to a few straightforward design approaches. This aids the designer and the designer's associates and successors in understanding the design.	3. Nonstructured languages: Many present-day languages do not have all the control concepts needed for structured programming and thus require some additional effort to simulate missing constructs.
4. Maintenance: The clarity and modularity of a structured design is of great help in localizing an error and redesigning the offending section of code.	
5. Redesign: Most large software products are subject to occasional redesign (often called enhancement). The clarity and modularity of structured design maximizes the amount of code which can be reused.	

done structured program is of no advantage; however, we are comparing average structured programs with average unstructured ones.)

As a direct result of the increase in clarity, or because of other independent factors, many people have observed significant increases in programming productivity when structured programming is used. An analysis of typical gains in productivity is given in Chap. 6; however, from Table 2.11 (items 1, 4, and 5 in the left-hand column) we see that structured programming reduces costs in both the acquisition and maintenance phases.

The fact that structured programming constrains one's style is viewed as a disadvantage by some, but as a large advantage by others. To fix the style of a creative artist is anathema; however, to standardize an engineering technique is a great accomplishment. Since the author considers that increasing the amount of engineering in programming is a consummation devoutly to be wished, he feels that reduction to a standard (and good) style is a benefit! One might envision one programmer saying before reading another's code, "Do you use DO CASE and LEAVE in your programming or just the three classical structures?" This communicates much information to the other programmer rapidly, just as two friends playing bridge together for the first time might ask, "Do you use the Goren point count system of bidding? How about the short club convention?" It also aids us in composing prose descriptions of how a program works, because the internal control structures all have defined names, and just a handful at that.

The primary disadvantage of structured programming is the reluctance of many programmers to learn and use the technique. This is rapidly changing, since all new graduates are taught the method, many practitioners know or are learning the technique, and few who learn structured programming later reject it. This matter is discussed further in Chap. 6.

It is often claimed, with some justification, that structured programs take more memory than nonstructured ones. Suppose two paths in a program must use the same code. If they can't be merged just before the code block is encountered, then there are three alternatives: (1) put the code block in both paths; (2) make the code block a subroutine and call it from both paths; and (3) put the code block in one path and add a GO TO (beginning of code block) in the other path, and an IF statement with another GO TO for return. The first two are structured solutions and the last nonstructured. In most cases the use of a callable subroutine will only add a small (and acceptable) amount of overhead to the problem, usually little more than the third solution. Even if we decide to totally duplicate the code block, unless this block represents a significant portion of the program, the percentage increase in program size will be small. Furthermore, because of the rapid decreases in electronic memory costs in recent years, 10 to 20 percent more memory may not cost that much in terms of dollars, weight, size, or power.

Similarly, the slower running times of structured programs are often cited as a drawback. These slower running times are attributable to the so-called slower execution times of the structured-programming control constructs and the slow exiting of such programs from a nested inner loop (see problem 2.44 at end of this chapter). This issue is explored in more detail in Sec. 3.4.3; however, the basic question to be answered is, How much slower? In many cases, the long running time of programs is due to lack of analysis on a global level of the predicted running times of proposed designs. The analysis techniques of Sec. 3.4 can often be used to speed up a program much more than the amount of any small slowdown due to structuring. It has been estimated that structuring increases memory and processing time by perhaps only 10 to 20 percent. In addition, if we allow some nonstructuring in a problem and it is done clearly, we can probably improve the efficiency of the one or two problem areas that are the major source of inefficiency.

Not all languages contain the control constructs normally used by a designer of structured programs. Thus, the ability to use structured programming is somewhat compromised in certain languages. This topic is addressed in detail in the next section, where it is shown that ample techniques exist to circumvent this problem.

2.4.6 Structured Programming in Various Languages

In order to begin our discussion of the suitability of various languages for structured programming we classify the 10 programming languages in Table 2.12 in the four categories shown. Since among the languages in Table 2.12 only the first four are well suited to structured programming, one might conclude that structured programming, should be attempted only when one of these languages has been chosen. Similarly, one might adopt the corollary: If one wishes to do structured programming, one should insist that one of the languages in the first group be chosen. Neither of these conclusions is valid, and we shall shortly show that one can perform structured programming in all the languages of Table 2.12 except APL by keeping to a fixed style and using preprocessing techniques.

Table 2.12 Basic suitability of various languages for structured programming

Language	Suitability
Algol PL/1 Pascal Bell Labs C	Most structures available
Fortran* Cobol Basic*	Some structures available
Assembler languages Programmable calculator languages	Lacking important structures
APL	Not well suited

*Fortran-77 and Basic-plus rank along with Algol, PL/1, etc.

One might also adopt the attitude that we should wait for the millennium, when the Ideal Programming Language is defined and designed and its ideal translator (compiler or interpreter) is written. If one studies the history of programming languages, and the organizational and financial forces which have sired them, one finds such an attitude most impractical. The cost of developing a new computer language at this point in the history of the computer field is too great for any except the largest organizations to contemplate. In fact we might make the observation that PL/1 and the C language would not have come into being and continued to grow if they had not received the corporate support of IBM and Bell Labs, respectively. Furthermore, the existence of the C language and its spread and future are closely bound to the popularity of Digital Equipment Corporation's PDP-11 computer and the captivating UNIX operating system which Bell Labs has written.

The record of the Pascal language is equally instructive.[1] This language, devised by Professor Niklaus Wirth, has won the admiration of many university language experts both in Europe and in the United States. At present many compilers and interpreters are available for popular machines, and as soon as manufacturers write supported versions, the use of Pascal in commercial and governmental environments will increase.[2]

Since each of the languages given in Table 2.12 has its constituency, literature, and capital investment in existing programs, it is unlikely that any of them will disappear in the near future. In fact, the trend has been to standardize these languages and allow slow evolution via successive updates.[3] All the new language standards include the addition of most of the missing structured-programming constructs.

At present the author knows of only one major project involving the development of a new programming language, the language being Ada, which is described in Sec. 2.8.2.[4]

We now turn to the question of how to write structured programs in a language in which not all of the structured-programming control structures exist. The answer is that one carries out the design using pseudo-code and/or structured flowcharts and faces the implementation problem only at the end step, where the pseudo-code or flowcharts are implemented in the chosen programming language. It is true that we may have to use GO TO constructs to "simulate" the missing structured control elements. However, this violates only the letter of the "don't use GO TOs" edict, but certainly not the spirit. Thus, an IF THEN ELSE can be implemented in, say, Basic by using a certain *fixed* configuration of

---

[1] Jensen and Wirth (1974).

[2] Fletcher (1979) and Shillington (1979).

[3] *FOR-WORD: Fortran Newsletter*, Loren P. Meissner, ed., Applied Mathematics Department, Lawrence Berkeley Laboratory, University of California, Berkeley, CA 94720. The American National Standards Institute (ANSI) has published: X3.9 = 1966 (*Fortran*), X3.10 = 1966 (*Basic Fortran*), and X3J3 (*Fortran 77*) (published in 1978); and the X3J3 committee began work in 1978 on *Fortran 82*.

[4] *U.S. Department of Defense Language Effort.* Other relevant documents include *Requirements for Revised "IRONMAN"* and *Requirements for "STEELMAN."* See also U.S. Department of Defense (1980), Wegner (1980), Pyle (1981), and Freedman (1982).

GO TOs each time.[1] The final translation can be done by a software pre-processor[2] or manually. The latter technique is illustrated in the examples which follow.

In order to assess the particulars of coding a structured design in a variety of languages, we can study Table 2.13. This table is not meant to define the syntax of the statements, but only to indicate (1) whether the structure exists in the language (in the common, least advanced version unless otherwise stated); (2) the name of the structure; and (3) (if it does not exist) how it can be simulated. The reader who is not familiar with a particular language will have to consult a book or manual for details. In order to cover a variety of languages, we will discuss structured-programming examples using a powerful higher-order language (HOL), PL/1; a simpler HOL, Basic; and two primitive assembly languages, PAL-3 (the assembly language for the Digital Equipment Corporation's PDP-8 minicomputer) and the language of the Texas Instruments SR-52 programmable calculator.

In Table 2.14 we see five different implementations of the IF THEN ELSE statement. The PL/1 version is the cleanest, since the language contains the basic construct. In case *b*, through the liberal use of comments and indenting, we have made the center column of the program identical to the PL/1 program. The comments, the keyword, and the necessary GO TOs are pushed to the left and right, respectively. However, if we don't mind repeating the IF statement twice, the very compact form of case *c* can be used. Obviously the PAL-3 and SR-52 versions are much longer. In addition the only comments we can put in the SR-52 program are handwritten ones on the coding sheet.

A similar set of examples is given in Table 2.15 for the DO WHILE structure. The particular set of constructs which one uses to realize the two control structures is not too important, but the constructs must be clear and consistent.

In all likelihood the necessity for preprocessing either by machine or by hand will soon fade (except for assembly and calculator languages) as present-day languages acquire structured statements via evolution.

2.4.7 Program Proofs

Since programs are generally based on mathematical algorithms, it is natural to inquire whether one can prove the validity or correctness of a program by proof of the underlying algorithm. Much effort has been expended on (1) the theoretical basis of such a method; (2) developing formal techniques of proof; and (3) developing a practical methodology. This subject is frequently discussed along with structured programming, since structured control and iterative refinement are key features upon which the method builds.[3]

Even an introduction to program-proof techniques requires considerable mathematical rigor and development beyond the scope of this book. (Program

---

[1] Koffman and Friedman (1979).
[2] The most popular preprocessors are Fortran ones. See Kernighan and Plauger (1976) and Elliott (1976).
[3] Linger, Mills, and Witt (1979), Berg (1982).

Table 2.13 Comparison of structured programming in various languages

Language	Sequence	Structured programming control structures				
		IF THEN ELSE	DO WHILE	DO UNTIL	DO CASE	LEAVE
Algol	Standard control mode for all languages	IF THEN ELSE	WHILE DO	FOR UNTIL	SWITCH	GO TO(label)
PL/1		IF THEN ELSE	DO WHILE	DO UNTIL[a]	SELECT[a]	LEAVE[a]
Pascal		IF THEN ELSE	WHILE DO	REPEAT UNTIL	CASE OF	GO TO(label)
Ada[b]		IF THEN (ELSE IF THEN) ELSE	WHILE LOOP	FOR LOOP THEN	CASE WHEN	EXIT (loop) WHEN (condition)
C		IF ELSE	WHILE	Use WHILE	SWITCH	BREAK
Fortran		IF THEN ELSE[c,d]	WHILE DO[c] DO WHILE[d]	IF THEN DO[c] DO REPEAT UNTIL[d]	TEST[d]	GO TO(label)[c] EXIT[d] CYCLE[d]
Cobol		IF THEN ELSE	Use PERFORM UNTIL	PERFORM UNTIL	GO TO DEPENDING	GO TO(label)
Basic		Use two IF THENs	Use GO TOs	Use GO TOs	IF GO TO[e] ON GO TO[e]	GO TO(label)
		IF THEN ELSE[f]	FOR WHILE[f]	FOR UNTIL[f]	ON GO-SUB[e]	
PAL-3 assembler	Not available, thus control structures such as JMP (GO TO), JMS (GO SUB), SPA, SZA, etc. (skip on positive, negative. etc. accumulator), must be used.					
SR-52 programmable calculator	Not available; thus, unconditional transfers such as GTO (GO TO), SBR (GO SUB), or conditional transfers IF (flag, error, register) GO TO, must be used.					
APL	(?)[g]					

[a] Available in PL/CS and optimizing compiler.
[b] See U.S. Department of Defense (1980).
[c] WATF IV.
[d] Fortran-77.
[e] Some versions have computed GO TO.
[f] Basic-plus.
[g] Geller and Freedman (1976): "Perhaps, in closing, we should mention something about the mysterious phrase "Structured Programming; which appears in the title, but nowhere else. ... We prefer to think of it as an attitude rather than a collection of techniques..." (p. 282, Epilogue).

Table 2.14 IF THEN ELSE structures in different languages

a. PL/1

```
IF  A = B
    THEN   X = 2;
    ELSE   X = 1;
```

b. Basic (method 1)

```
100 IF A = B   THEN 130
110            GO TO 150
120 REM  THEN
130 LET  X = 2
140            GO TO 170
150 REM  ELSE
160 LET  X = 1
170 REM  END
```

c. Basic (method 2)

```
100 IF A = B     THEN X = 2
110 IF A < > B   THEN X = 1
```

d. PAL-3

```
/IF A = B
    CLA        /Clear Accumulator(AC = 0)
    TAD A      /Add A(AC = A)
    CIA        /Complement AC(AC = Ā + 1)
    TAD B      /Add B(AC = B + Ā + 1)
    SZA        /Skip (next instruction if AC = 0)
    JMP E      /Jump to Else Clause
/THEN CLAUSE
T,  CLA        /(AC = 0)
    TAD TWO    /(AC = 2)
    DCA X      /Deposit AC in X, CLA AC   (X = AC )
                                          (AC = 0)
    JMP END/GO TO END
/ELSE CLAUSE
E,  CLA        /(AC = 0)
    TAD ONE    /(AC = 1)
    DCA X          (/X = AC)
                   ( AC = 0)
END,           /End of Program
A,             /Numerical value of A stored here
B,             /Numerical value of B stored here
ONE,  1        /Storage location for constant 1
TWO,  2        /Storage location for constant 2
X,    0        /Storage location for variable X
```

e. SR-52 calculator language

```
000 A
001 –
002 B
003 =
004 IF ZRO   (if the display register is 0)
005 0        (transfer to 3-digit address)
006 1
007 6
008 1
009 STO      (store 1 in register)
010 0
011 0        (number 00)    (R00 = 1)
012 GTO      (GO TO)
013 0
014 2        (End location)
015 0
016 2
017 STO
018 0
019 0        (R00 = 2)
020 ...       (End location)
```

Table 2.15 DO WHILE structures in different languages

a. PL/1

```
Z = Z0;
SUM = 0;
X = X0;
DO WHILE Z > 0;
    SUM = SUM + 1;
    Z = Z - X;
END;
```

b. Basic

```
100 LET   Z = Z0
110 LET   S = 0
120 LET   X = X0
130 REM   DO WHILE Z > 0
140                      IF Z < = 0 THEN 180
150 LET   S = S + 1
160 LET   Z = Z - X
170                      GO TO 130
180 REM   END
```

c. PAL-3

```
/DO WHILE   Z > 0
LOOP,       CLA
            TAD Z
            SPA
            JMP END

            CLA
            TAD SUM
            TAD ONE
            DCA SUM (SUM = SUM + 1)
            TAD X
            CIA
            TAD Z
            DCA Z (Z = Z - X)
            GO TO LOOP
END,
```

d. SR-52 calculator language

```
000  ⎫      (as many digits
001  ⎬ ZO    as needed; 3
002  ⎭      shown here)
003 STO
004 0
005 0      (R00 = Z0)
006 0
007 STO
008 0
009 1      (R01 = S = 0)
010  ⎫
011  ⎬ XO
012  ⎭
013 STO
014 0
015 2      (R02 = X0)
016 RCL
017 0
018 0
019 INV
020 IFPOS  (if display register
021 0          not positive GO TO)
022 5
023 2      (address of END)
024 IF ZRO
025 0
026 5
027 2
028 RCL
029 0
030 1
031 +
032 1
033 =
034 STO
035 0
036 1
037 RCL
038 0
039 0
040 −
041 RCL
042 0
043 2
044 =
045 STO
046 0
047 0
048 GTO
049 0
050 1
051 6
052 ...(End location)
```

proofs have not as yet become an engineering technique but are still in the research phase.) A brief example of a program proof follows to introduce the reader to the essence of the method.

A simple example of a program proof given in Linger, Mills, and Witt (1979, Sec. 1.1.4) will be used to demonstrate the method. The problem specification is:

Find a result y which is the integer part of the square root of a given integer x.

The problem is simple enough that a solution and associated proof can be developed intuitively, without developing a formalized proof technique. The flowchart of a solution to the problem is given in Fig. 2.25. Several statements (conditions, assertions) about the initial, final, and intermediate states of the program variables are given in Fig. 2.25. The systematic proof of these assertions constitutes the program proof.

A necessary assumption is that $x \geq 0$. A formal statement of the properties of the solution is: x unchanged and $y^2 \leq x < (y + 1)^2$. The five-step proof given in Linger, Mills, and Witt (1979, pp. 6–7) is reproduced as follows:

The program will correctly compute values for x and y that satisfy the *out* condition, the specification of the program. The proof will consist of a subproof for each condition except *in*:$[x \geq 0]$, which is assumed. The sequence of subproofs is immaterial. It is sufficient to ensure that every condition is ultimately proved, assuming the truth of the immediately prior conditions in the flowchart. Thus, we state each condition followed by a proof argument:

1. *init*:$[x \geq 0$ and $y = 0]$
   The entry condition *in*:$[x \geq 0]$ gives the first part, and y has just been set to zero, giving the second part. Therefore, *init*:$[x \geq 0$ and $y = 0]$ is satisfied.

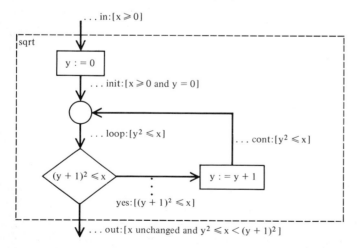

Figure 2.25 A flowchart solution for the square root example. *(From Linger, Mills, and Witt, 1979, p. 6)*

Table 2.16 Fallibility of mathematical proofs

1. Over 130 errors have been committed since antiquity by mathematicians of the first and second rank.

2. A previous editor of *Mathematical Reviews* estimates that about half of all published mathematical papers contain errors.

3. Several hundred errors were found in the *Handbook of Mathematical Functions.*

Source: Davis (1972).

2. *loop*:$[y^2 \leq x]$
   The condition *loop* is entered either from *init*:$[x \geq 0$ and $y = 0]$ in which case *loop* is satisfied directly, or from the condition *cont*:$[y^2 \leq x]$, which is identical to *loop*. Therefore, *loop*:$[y^2 \leq x]$ is satisfied in either case.
3. *cont*:$[y^2 \leq x]$
   The condition *cont* is the exit condition when y is set to $y + 1$ with entry condition *yes*:$[(y + 1)^2 \leq x]$, so $y^2 \leq x$ (after y is set to $y + 1$), and *cont*:$[y^2 \leq x]$ is satisfied.
4. *yes*:$[(y + 1)^2 \leq x]$
   The test $(y + 1)^2 \leq x$ has just been passed successfully.
5. *out*:$[x$ unchanged and $y^2 \leq x < (y + 1)^2]$
   First, an examination of the entire program shows that x is reset nowhere, and must therefore be unchanged. Second, the test $(y + 1)^2 \leq x$ has just failed, so therefore $(y + 1)^2 > x$. Finally, the entry condition *loop*:$[y^2 \leq x]$ for the test must still hold. The last two conditions can be combined into $y^2 \leq x < (y + 1)^2$. Therefore, condition *out* is satisfied.

The reader is referred to the above mentioned text for further details about this example and a thorough and lucid introduction to the methods of program proofs.

Before we leave this subject, we should include one further comment for proper perspective. Even if the millennium of practical program proofs were here, we could not guarantee error-free programs. After all, mathematical proofs also contain errors! (See Table 2.16.) Even if program proofs could only reduce the probability of program error to $1/10$ or $1/100$ of that of the best techniques we now have, it would still be a boon.

2.5 DATA-DIRECTED DESIGN TECHNIQUES

2.5.1 Introduction

Many of our ideas concerning what constitutes program design are very much colored by our experiences. Someone who deals with mathematical software almost exclusively tends to focus on the algorithm needed to solve a specific problem. Such a programmer may perform a large part of the design by writing sets of equations or steps in a procedure. A design-representation scheme such as HIPO, flowcharts, or pseudo-code is still useful for detailing and properly documenting the design, but the heart is in the algorithm.

Similarly, designers dealing with data communications may find that their real problems are the control of the process. In this case, the HIPO diagrams, pseudo-code, and flowcharts are the essence of the problem. Once these are devised, the choice of appropriate algorithms is relatively straightforward.

There is still a third major class of design problems, which we have slighted until now, those whose function is to create data bases and to transform them into output data and reports. Many business data systems fall into this class. For such systems the input, storage, and output data structures, as well as the transformations relating them, are the most important aspects of the design. In such a case, once the data are designed the choice of algorithm and control structure is relatively simple.

Thus, we can characterize classes of design problems by whether the design of the data structure, the algorithm, or the control is hard or easy. Such a comparison is made for six different classes of problems in Table 2.17. Obviously, these are broad generalizations, and in any specific system, the conclusions may change; however, consideration of such factors is an important part of the first stages of design.[1]

The remainder of this section discusses representation tools and techniques which focus on data structures and transformations. These will prove useful in all designs, especially for problems in which data are the critical factor.

2.5.2 Data Flowgraphs

Many problems reduce to data storage and transformation, and so the designer will focus on the data and file structure before proceeding with further details of the design. A designer who thinks in terms of design representation schemes will probably make a list of files instead of an H diagram, and additional lists detailing the organization of the files instead of IPO diagrams. The last step might be to write pseudo-code or draw flowcharts.

As an example of a data-directed design, we will study the organization of a payroll program. We make the tacit assumption that the structure depicted in the documentation was actually used in the development of the program and was not merely an afterthought. In the book *Payroll with Cost Accounting* (Poole and Borchers, 1977), the authors begin with a two-page overview describing the 34 different programs which the software system contains. The next 22 pages list in tabular form the 13 data files (see Table 2.18) and include detailed tables of from half a page to five pages giving the variables, field descriptions, size, and comments for each of the files. Flowcharts do not appear until page 41 of the book. The authors feel that it is necessary to include two prior pages describing flowchart notation but assume that the notation used in the tables detailing the file structure is self-explanatory! A very useful matrix does appear on page 25 to indicate the interrelations between the files and the programs (see Table 2.19).

---

[1] Many programmers would add a seventh class consisting of "the problems which are assigned to me," which they would no doubt classify as hard-hard-hard!

Table 2.17 A comparison of the difficulties by type for various kinds of software projects

Kind of problem	Data structure	Algorithm*	Control[†]
1. Business data (accounting-type) processing	Hard	Easy	Easy
2. Scientific and engineering computations and simulation	Easy	Hard	Easy
3. Voice, written-word, and data communications	Easy	Easy	Hard
4. Real-time (embedded) computer system	Easy	Hard	Hard
5. Information retrieval: searching and sorting	Hard	Hard	Easy
6. Operating systems, compilers, and other support software	Hard	Easy	Hard

* In cases 2 and 4, where the algorithms are difficult, one frequently finds that a prior scientific study is available which has already solved the problem.

[†] If a significant amount of exception handling is required, the control structure may be difficult even in cases 1, 2, and 5.

Table 2.18 List of data files for a payroll program

Number	Description
1	Employee Master
2	Employee History
3	Deduction/Misc. Pay
4	Transaction Entry
5	Transaction Summary
6	Federal Tax
7	State Tax
8	General Information
9	Employee Activity Sort
10	Job
11	Job Posting
12	Temporary Work
13	CRT Mask

Source: Poole and Borchers (1977), p. 6.

Table 2.19 Program–data file cross reference

Data file

1. Employee Master
2. Employee History
3. Deduction/Misc. Pay
4. Transaction Entry
5. Transaction Summary
6. Federal Tax
7. State Tax
8. General Information
9. Employee Activity Sort
10. Job
11. Job Posting
12. Temporary Work
13. CRT Mask

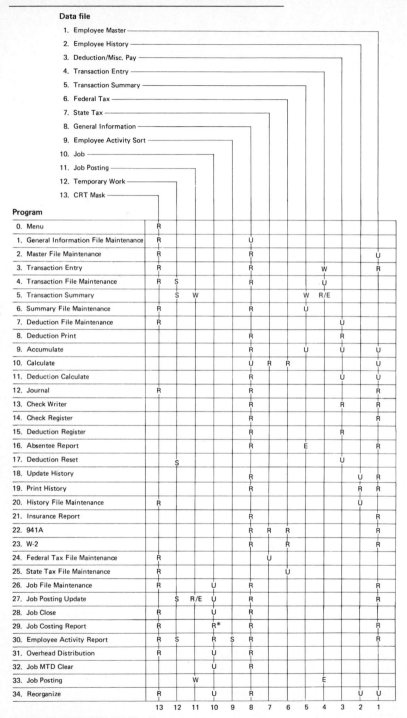

Program	13	12	11	10	9	8	7	6	5	4	3	2	1
0. Menu	R												
1. General Information File Maintenance	R					U							
2. Master File Maintenance	R					R							U
3. Transaction Entry	R					R			W				R
4. Transaction File Maintenance	R	S				R				U			
5. Transaction Summary		S	W						W	R/E			
6. Summary File Maintenance	R					R			U				
7. Deduction File Maintenance	R										U		
8. Deduction Print						R					R		
9. Accumulate						R		U			U		U
10. Calculate					U	R	R						U
11. Deduction Calculate						R					U		U
12. Journal	R					R							R
13. Check Writer						R					R		R
14. Check Register						R							R
15. Deduction Register						R					R		
16. Absentee Report						R		E					R
17. Deduction Reset		S									U		
18. Update History						R						U	R
19. Print History						R						R	R
20. History File Maintenance	R											U	
21. Insurance Report						R							R
22. 941A						R	R	R					R
23. W-2						R		R					R
24. Federal Tax File Maintenance	R						U						
25. State Tax File Maintenance	R							U					
26. Job File Maintenance	R			U		R							R
27. Job Posting Update		S	R/E	U		R							R
28. Job Close	R			U		R							
29. Job Costing Report	R			R*		R							R
30. Employee Activity Report	R	S		R	S	R							R
31. Overhead Distribution	R			U		R							
32. Job MTD Clear				U		R							
33. Job Posting			W							E			
34. Reorganize	R			U		R						U	U

Source: Poole and Borchers (1977), Table 2-A, p. 25.

*Job records may optionally be selectively deleted.

R	Read	W	Write	S	Sort (W/R/E)
E	Erase	U	Update (R/W)		

Although the authors do a good job of documentation, a design representation other than a tabular listing of the file organizations would have been of help to the reader and, initially, of even more help to the designer. The most popular representation for problems of this type is the data flowgraph.

A data flow diagram (data flowgraph) essentially performs the same function as a HIPO diagram. The input to and output from a data flowgraph are considered to be a file or some other data structure. A composite flow diagram for a system is made up of individual flow-diagram elements with one or more inputs, one or more outputs, and an associated transform (function, process). In the case of more than one input or output, logic relationships (AND, OR, etc.) between the inputs and/or between the outputs are added.

The seven basic data flowgraph symbols are given in Fig. 2.26. This author has added the OR (inclusive OR) function (in entries 4 and 5), whereas most

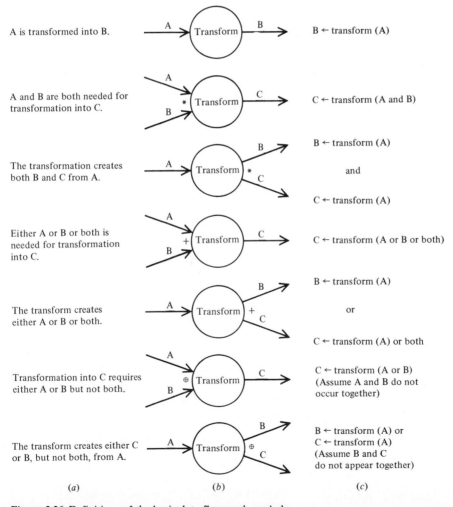

Figure 2.26 Definitions of the basic data flowgraph symbols.

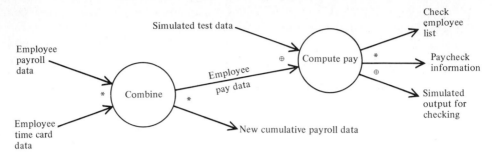

Figure 2.27 Data flowgraph for two typical functions in a payroll program. *(From Yourdon and Constantine, 1979, p. 44)*

authors[1] only use the EXOR (exclusive OR) function (entries 6 and 7). The reason for the inclusion of both types of OR functions will be discussed shortly. Although only one or two outputs and inputs are shown in Fig. 2.26, the technique allows as many as are required. Also, the logic operations among three or more inputs or outputs may be either homogeneous or mixed logic.

In Fig. 2.27, we see individual data flowgraphs for two payroll functions combined to form a composite data flowgraph. The verbal description of Fig. 2.27 would read: Employee payroll data and employee time card data are combined to yield both the employee pay and a new cumulative payroll number. The employee pay data (or, in a test mode, the simulated data) are used to compute the pay, which is checked against a master employee list, as a safeguard; and paycheck information (or simulated output for checking) is produced.

One of the features of the data flowgraph which is useful in top-down design is the principle of *hiding*. Not only is the mechanism hidden whereby functions are to be performed, but also details of the control flow are suppressed. In Fig. 2.28 we show data flowgraphs and their associated flowcharts in order to illustrate the differences for two examples. In the first example we wish to change a decimal pay amount into the number of dollars and the rounded number of cents. In the data flowgraph, we simply define the transformation. (The details of the transformation may appear in a more detailed, lower-level data flowgraph.) However, in the flowchart we focus on the control and often work out detailed procedures. Normally, the two techniques are used in a complementary fashion, rather than as competitors.

In the second example of Fig. 2.28, we see the reason why the author introduced both types of OR logic. As shown in the diagram, if the salary amount seems unreasonable, a paycheck is printed anyway, but a message appears on the printer to check it manually. If we had used the EXCLUSIVE OR symbol, then no paycheck would have been produced had the check failed, and the manual step would have had to include further checking as well as manual production of a

---

[1] For example, Yourdon and Constantine (1979), Sec. 3.5, and Weinberg (1978), Chap. 4.

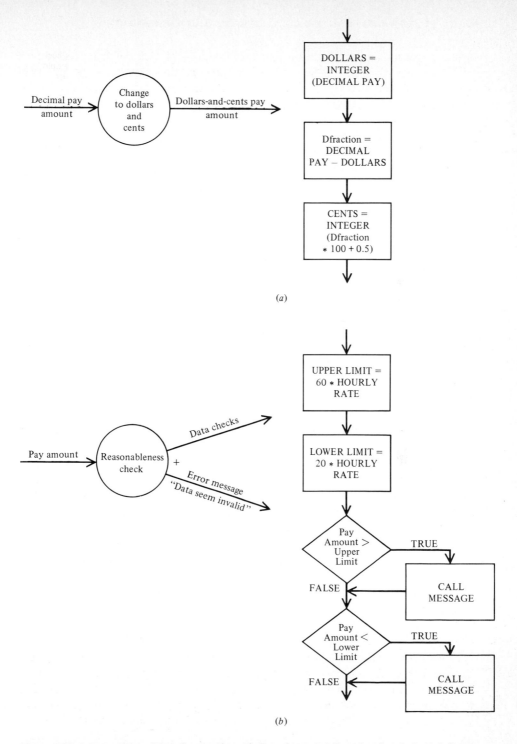

Figure 2.28 A comparison of data flowgraphs with flow charts. (*a*) Transforming decimal dollars to dollars and cents. (*b*) Checking pay data for reasonableness.

correct paycheck after verification. The ramifications of such defensive techniques will be further discussed in Sec. 2.7.4. For those readers familiar with statistical terms used in quality control, a trade-off of the benefits and costs of such checking procedures is essentially a case of employee's risk versus employer's risk.

2.5.3 Example: Data Flowgraphs for a Payroll Program

The use of data flowgraphs can be best illustrated by applying the concept to a particular problem. We consider as an example an abbreviated version of the payroll program outlined in Table 2.19. Assume that we have devised a simplified version which uses only 5 of the 13 data files (Employee Master, Transaction Entry, Federal Tax, State Tax, and General Information), and 5 of the 34 programs (Menu, Transaction Entry, Accumulate, Calculate, and Check Writer). The Menu program is the main program from which we call all other programs. Once a program is called and in operation, we may leave the called program in two ways: (1) by waiting until the program finishes, or (2) by issuing an exit command, which immediately returns us to Menu. If we issue the exit command

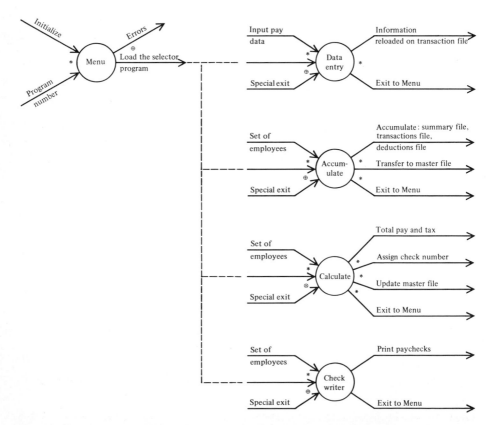

Figure 2.29 Overview data flowgraph for abbreviated version of payroll program.

either inadvertently or after discovering an error, then some or all of the program results are lost.

A data flowgraph showing the overall structure of the problem is given in Fig. 2.29. Only the basic ideas are presented, and all details are suppressed. Detailed data flowgraphs for each program are presented in Fig. 2.30. Note that the Data Entry program is the most complex, and its data flowgraph is split into the three parts shown in Fig. 2.30. Just as in the case of HIPO diagrams, we continue to make more and more detailed diagrams until we have sufficient detail to code from them. Alternately, we might substitute an intermediate step in which we write pseudo-code or flowcharts before coding. In fact, in examining the second part of Fig. 2.30*b*, we see that no logic symbols have been used to specify whether all the data inputs are required or whether just some of them are needed. The choice depends upon the work type and job type; thus at least one more level of detail is needed before we can code the Data Entry program.

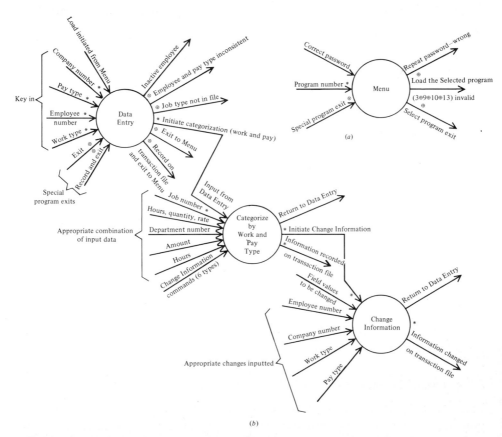

Figure 2.30 Detailed data flowgraphs for payroll program: (*a*) Menu program; (*b*) Data Entry program; (*c*) Accumulate program; (*d*) Calculate program; (*e*) Check Writer.

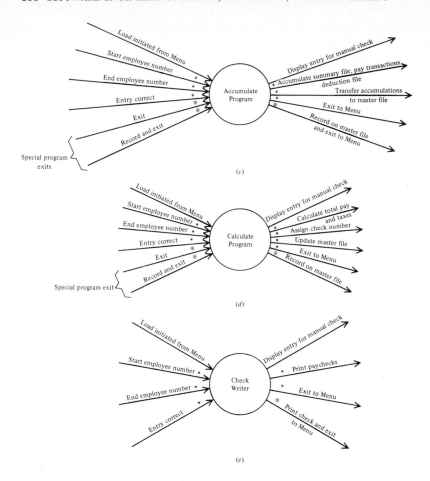

Figure 2.30 (*continued*).

Just as in the case of HIPO diagrams, data flowgraphs serve as an easily explained and understood vehicle for the system designer to use in meetings with the customer (for example, to explain the initial design, and to determine whether it satisfies the customer's requirements). In fact, data flowgraphs have been introduced as a representation technique for data-driven problems; however, if the designer or analyst prefers them, they can also be used with other types of programs as well.

2.5.4 Other Techniques

Many authors have recognized the need for design representations and design philosophies which aid the design of data-driven problems. Some techniques and approaches similar to those discussed in this section are program-structure charts (Yourdon and Constantine, 1979; Weinberg, 1978), data-structure diagrams

(Jackson, 1975), and to a certain extent cause-effect graphs (Myers, 1976), which are also used in testing. As was stated in Sec. 2.3, the urgent thing is not the specific *method* one uses—most practitioners will have a favorite; it is crucial that *some method* be used to reduce "thought waves" to something easier to study, describe, and discuss than pages of typewritten prose. It is noteworthy that almost all of these techniques produce some type of diagram, and as more and more usage and standardization occur, we will have program tools which automatically or interactively produce such diagrams.

2.6 MODULAR DESIGN

2.6.1 Introduction

Thus far in this text, we have used the term *module* so many times that the reader should now be familiar with the concept. However, we have not precisely defined what a module is. Basically it is a modest-sized subprogram which performs independently one specific function. A module is self-contained and its removal from a system should only disable the unique function performed by the module, nothing else. Similarly, if we substitute a new module of different design for an old one and maintain the same specifications on input and output variables, then the system should work with little or no change. If we design software based on these principles, the design is called a modular design. Although there is no requirement that a modular design be top-down or structured, it is clear that a top-down design invariably results in a modular design as well. Furthermore, if we require that the program be structured, then the single-entry and single-exit property helps to make the functions independent of one another.

The size of a module is another important criterion. Many people have defined module size in terms of hardware memory package sizes, such as 4096 words, or 512 bytes. Other choices seem to be related to company traditions or standards of one sort or another. In recent years, people have focused on the fact that one should be able to find the code for a module on one printed computer page and read it without turning to another page. Some have described this as trying to keep the program small enough that it is within one's "intellectual span of control." Assuming that a standard printer page is 50 to 60 lines long and a one-to-one correspondence exists between assembly language and machine language, then an assembly language module will be about 50 memory words long. Similarly, if we assume that an average line of PL/1 expands into seven lines of machine code, then such a module will be about 350 or 400 memory words long. Other restrictions on module size related to the control complexity are discussed in Chaps. 3 and 4 (see especially Sec. 3.2).

In carrying out a modular design, one should initially select modules as independent functions and then subdivide any which are too large. If any function is a self-contained entity smaller than 50 lines, we accept its smaller size and do not try to combine smaller modules into a larger one. At the other extreme, if a module is, say, $1\frac{1}{2}$ pages long but is clear and simple and represents only one function, then there is no sense subdividing it just to meet the chosen criteria. In no event should one produce a modular program in the manner cited by Yourdon:[1]

> A programmer claimed it was easy for him to fix the module size. He just wrote the program without any regard to size as one monolithic block. When done, he arbitrarily chopped the program into *n* sections so that each section met his module size requirement. This is certainly not the way to write modular programs!

2.6.2 Module Coupling and Module Strength

One of the difficulties with modular programming is that everyone easily grasps the concept, yet it is difficult to implement. The problem is, How do we avoid coupling among the modules, i.e., make them independent? Myers (1978) has classified seven levels of dependency, listed in the order of decreasing desirability, which serve as a guide to minimizing coupling:

1. No direct coupling (best)
2. Data coupling
3. Stamp coupling
4. Control coupling
5. External coupling
6. Common coupling
7. Content coupling (worst)

Two modules are said to be content-coupled if one directly references the interior of the other, e.g., if a module branches to rather than calls another module. Common coupling occurs when two or more modules reference the same global data structure. External coupling is possible in some languages (e.g., PL/1) where we can control the variable coupling and limit it to those variables which are formally declared as external. Control coupling occurs when one module passes switch, flag, or module-name information from one module to another. If the language (e.g., PL/1) has conditions which can be raised, these can also lead to control coupling.

Myers gives the name *stamp coupling* to the situation in which a data structure is shared among two or more modules, not by common coupling, which is a global technique, but via passing the data structure by using module call and return parameters. Data coupling occurs when the data between two modules mentioned in the input-output interface are the same, i.e., when rather than passing an entire data structure across the interface, only the required subset is passed.

---

[1]1975, p. 95.

No direct coupling occurs when two modules do not in any way relate to each other but each independently relates only to the main program (the control or calling program).

Clearly, Myers' scale of coupling is only relative, and many situations will occur where coupling between the two modules is of a mixed type. Although, as a general rule, we may wish to aim for no direct coupling, sometimes one of the other types of moderate coupling may be used because of other desirable features. For example if we had to include four types of error messages in our program, we might include them in the modules in which they occur and eliminate any coupling. Another alternative is to put all four messages in the same module and to call the message module and pass the error type over the interface. This would represent control coupling, and in this example it might eliminate duplicate messages, standardize all message formats, and allow the designer to focus on the design of efficient and clear error messages. Thus, the choice of what type of coupling to use is really a design trade-off.

Until now we have been discussing the coupling between two called modules (brothers or sisters), but now we turn to the relationship between each module and the main or control program (the parent). Myers (1978) uses the term *module strength* to refer to the relationship between the control program and its modules, and again creates a scale of ranking with seven levels:

1. Functional strength (best)
2. Informational strength
3. Communicational strength
4. Procedural strength
5. Classical strength
6. Logical strength
7. Coincidental strength (worst)

The worst situation, of lowest strength, is where a module performs a function which cannot be easily defined, or where it performs several unrelated functions. This situation is called *coincidental strength*. Somewhat better is logical strength, where the module performs a set of related functions individually activated by a selection parameter which is passed to the module. The next highest, but still somewhat low on the scale, is classical strength, where the module performs several sequentially but weakly related functions. Good examples of such modules are initialization modules, where each initialization seems more strongly related to the module containing the variables (functions, files) to be initialized than to other initializations in the module.

A procedural-strength module is a classical-strength module in which the sequential relationship among the functions is implied by the problem or application statement. A communicational-strength module is similar to a procedural-strength module; however, there is, in addition, a data relationship among the sequential functions. The highest level in the ranking is functional strength, where the module performs a single specific function.

Myers introduces the concept of informational strength because sometimes one encounters functional-strength modules related by a common data structure, concept, or resource. An informational-strength module is a package of all such modules combined into a bigger one so that the common data structure or other linking element is hidden within.

Just as in the case of coupling, module strengths of more than one type can occur in a module, and use of only the highest-strength modules need not be the best design objective.

The concepts of module coupling and module strength are really more a matter of point of view than totally separate concepts. For example, if modules A and B each exhibit logical strength with respect to the main program, then they may exhibit control coupling with respect to each other. The reader is referred to Myers and to Probs. 2.36 and 2.37 at the end of this chapter for more details.

2.6.3 Advantages and Disadvantages of Modular Programming

To a certain extent, our discussion should not focus on whether or not to use modularization, but how much and how. Most large programming problems are too complex to approach as an entity, and the only way we can deal with such

Table 2.20 Advantages and disadvantages of modular programming

Advantages	Disadvantages
1. It is easier and less costly to change features, add features, or correct errors after deployment.	1. Because there are few formal design techniques, it is difficult to learn, although the principles are clear.
2. It is easier to write and debug the program.	2. Modular programming requires more design effort and care.
3. It is easier to manage since more difficult modules can be given to more skilled programmers and easy modules to junior programmers.	3. Many programmers are reluctant to try new things, including modular design.
4. One can divide a large, complex problem into a number of modules each of manageable complexity .	4. Modular programming may require slightly more memory space and run time.
5. The modular concept fits in well with top-down design.	5. To avoid slow processing, in some operating systems one may have to ensure that modules that call each other frequently are in the same machine page.
6. Formal module interface definition may be especially helpful in "organizing" a bottom-up design, or a two-stage design, first bottom-up, and then top-down.	6. Although modular programming probably is a help in managing a project organized along conventional lines, if group programming is employed, it may be disadvantageous to associate one programmer's name with each module.

complexity is to divide the larger problem into a number of constituent parts. Thus, in this sense we can call all large programs modular. Clearly, we are dealing with two competing effects. If it is very difficult to program large modules, then the initial coding time and the test and debugging times will decrease rapidly as we modularize a program. If we divide the program into k modules, then the average cost of writing each module must decrease faster than $1/k$ if we are to realize an advantage through modularization. On the other hand, there is additional work in programming each interface, and this cost grows with k. Thus, we are implying that minimum programming costs will be achieved if we pick the optimum module size.

Although we have already discussed some of the advantages and disadvantages of modular programming, we collect the factors already stressed along with some others in Tables 2.20 and 2.21.

Another feature of modular programming which has not been discussed yet is the advantage of reusing standard program modules. Theoretically we buy much, since portions of our program don't have to be written, but can be borrowed. This concept is discussed in Sec. 2.7.1 as a form of automatic programming.

Table 2.21 Reported experiences with modular programming

The benefits of modular programming

Benefit	Users reporting benefit
Easier maintenance and amendment	89%
Better program design	85%
Easier program testing	78%
Easier progress recording	70%
More accurate project control	67%
Higher programmer productivity	64%
More reliable programs	64%
More likely to meet target dates	63%
Easier resource allocation	61%

The disadvantages of modular programming

Disadvantage	Users reporting disadvantage
More computer time required during development	28%
Less efficient final programs	27%
More difficult to train programmers	19%
More difficult documentation	13%

These statistics and other information on modular programming appear in Central Computer Agency Guide (1973).

2.6.4 Module Interface Specifications

At the outset of this section we stated that most workers understand the concept of modular programming; however, the details and application are hard to grasp. The work by Myers on defining cohesion- and strength-ranking levels does much to help quantify modular-programming techniques. In this section we will discuss the methods evolved by Parnas (1972) for producing quantitative specifications for modular interfaces. This takes us an additional step closer to a theory of modular design.

Parnas considers all modules to be functions in the most general sense and to belong to one of two classes, one class stored-data-dependent and the other only input-data-dependent. Functions which depend on stored data hide from the user not only the details of the computation but also the stored data. For example, if we were constructing a program which prints out a sequence of prime numbers, then we would probably have a module which checks a newly suggested number to see if it possesses the properties of a prime number. Conventionally this module would maintain a table of prime numbers and divide the new input (candidate) by each prime less than the square root of the candidate. The candidate would be prime only if all divisions resulted in a remainder. Thus, this module is dependent on stored data and an algorithm.

An input-data-dependent module, on the other hand, merely transforms the input data into the output data. As an example, suppose we wished to transform rectangular coordinates into polar coordinates. In this case the module would in no way depend on data stored in the module, but only on the input rectangular coordinates and the transformation equations.

In Parnas' scheme, a module specification contains four items:

1. The set of possible input values and their attributes and ranges
2. The initial values of each input
3. The parameters associated with each input value
4. The effect the function produces (the task it accomplishes)

Each of these four items must be considered for each module, and in some cases the specification will state that certain items are undefined or not applicable. The attributes of the input values will be integer, real, complex, boolean, character, etc. In specifying the effect, it will generally be convenient to use mathematical equations and pseudo-code where appropriate, for brevity and lack of ambiguity.

Some examples of typical module specifications are given in Table 2.22, which is adapted from Parnas (1972). Note that these specifications focus on input and output specifications and "hide" the details from the calling routine. In fact the specifications in Table 2.22 are really incomplete. They contain the *implied* but not *explicit* assumption that the reader knows what a stack data structure is and how the data are processed internally for multiple pushes or pops. Thus, there should be a prose statement of the purpose of these functions which precedes the detailed specifications. The statement and specifications must be carefully written so that together they are complete and state even the obvious.

Table 2.22 Examples of module specifications†
Four functions that can be used to create and manipulate a stack

Purpose	Specification	Comments
1. Function PUSH(a)	Input values: a is an integer between 0 and p_2. Output values: None. Effect: *Call* ERR1 if $a > p_2$ or a <0 or 'DEPTH' $= p_1$. *Else* VAL $= a$; DEPTH $=$ 'DEPTH' $+ 1$.	Adds a new value to top of stack with a maximum depth p_1. ERR1 indicates a is out of range. 'DEPTH' is the old stack depth, and DEPTH is the new value. VAL is the quantity stored on top of stack.
2. Function POP(b)	Input values: None. Output values: b is an integer between 0 and p_2. Effect: *Call* ERR2 if 'DEPTH' $= 0$. *Else* b $=$ VAL; DEPTH $=$ 'DEPTH' $- 1$.	Removes the value stored on the top of the stack. ERR2 indicates a call to an empty stack. Note: The sequence PUSH(a), POP(b) has no effect unless error calls occur.‡
3. Function VAL(c)	Input values: None. Output values: c is an integer between 0 and p_2. Effect: *Call* ERR2 if 'DEPTH' $= 0$. *Else* c $=$ VAL.	Reads the value stored on the top of the stack without disturbing the stack. ERR2 indicates a call to an empty stack.‡
4. Function DEPTH(d)	Input values: None. Output values: c is an integer between 0 and p_1; the initial value of 'DEPTH' is 0. Effect: d $=$ DEPTH.‡	Returns the depth of the stack without disturbing the stack.

†After Parnas (1972).
‡For a discussion of additional error checking see Sec. 2.7.4.

Note that in the module specifications, VAL is checked only to see if it is in range for the PUSH function. The matter of whether range checks should be made for the other three functions is discussed in Sec. 2.7.4.

2.7 APPROACHES TO PROGRAMMING

2.7.1 Automatic Programming

One of the eternal hopes of the theoreticians of computer science is to devise a program that will write another program. Generally such concepts are classified under the general title of automatic programming. Two approaches to this problem have been taken. Carl Hewitt[1] has devised a language called Planner, wherein problems are expressed in terms of a series of goals and associated

[1]Project MAC (1973).

concepts. Another approach to this problem is essentially a glorification of the concepts of modular programming.[1] The idea is to accumulate a large group of subroutines with good, self-contained documentation, flexible and well-defined interfaces, and a main program-building code. The user would interact in a question-and-answer fashion with the building code to establish the proper sequences and calls to the existing modules. If the construction of the desired program involved the writing of nonexisting modules (preferably only 10 to 25 percent of the program), then these would be constructed in the same general fashion and incorporated into the program library for future use.

If such a system could be made practical, the advantages would be cheaper and quicker writing of programs, availability of highly reliable and optimized subprograms prepared by experts for use by the less skilled, and all the other, concomitant benefits of modular programming given in Tables 2.20 and 2.21. If one considers the wide variety of programs which must be written in a "general programming shop," it is difficult to see how such an approach can succeed. However, if one limits the scope to business (accounting) types of programs, there is a good chance that one can define enough commonly used modules to make such an approach viable. One hopes to see some of these techniques emerge in the future from the research stage to practical implementation.

2.7.2 Redundant Programming

An important technique for improving the reliability of a system is redundancy. In the case of hardware, one provides extra components or systems which operate in parallel with the primary system. In some cases the connection is such that all elements operate in parallel and if one fails, it "drops out" and the redundant components maintain system operation. In other cases, only the online (primary) element is operating, so that when a failure occurs, a detecting circuit (sometimes a human) switches in one of the standby elements. The former system philosophy is often called *parallel* redundancy and the latter *standby* redundancy. (The terms *hot* and *cold standby* or *active* and *passive redundancy* are also used.)

We can illustrate the numerical gains of redundancy by considering a simple example of two parallel elements. If the reliability of a single element is .9 for 1000 h of operation, then the probability of failure in the same interval is .1. If we have two parallel elements, then the system fails only if both elements fail. If they are independent, this probability is $.1 \times .1 = .01$. Thus, the reliability of the parallel system is .99.

In the case of software, some of these concepts are the same, yet others must be changed. If we attempt to implement software redundancy by utilizing two

---

[1]Project Calico, in Project MAC (1973), pp. 119–123; also Petrick (1975). Two generator programs for some computers have a similar design: *C.O.R.P.*, Maromaty and Scotto Software Corp., P. O. Box 610, Floral Park, N. Y. 11004; *The Last One*, D. J. 'AI' Systems Ltd., Ilminster, Somerset, TA 19 9BQ, England.

computers with identical versions of the same program, then we have redundant hardware, but not redundant software.[1] If the program is the same on both computers, then any error in the software will cause identical failures in both computers. What we must do if we want redundant software is to devise two different programs with different algorithms, designs, and programmers which implement the same computation. For example, if we wish to compute the real roots of a quadratic equation, we might use the quadratic formula in one program, and the Newton-Raphson numerical approximation in the second one. If the two answers agreed within a predetermined "computational difference," then we could use either answer, or the average of the two, to print out the solution. In the case of disagreement, we would detect an error, but would not know which answer was incorrect. Hence we could print out a message to the operator and take other corrective action. Such a system is called an *error-detecting system*. If we have three or more independent computations, then we can use the answer of the majority, and our system will be error-correcting for a single error and error-detecting for one or two identical errors (and also error-detecting for three errors if at least two differ). Since the comparison element tends to side with the majority opinion, such a technique is called *majority logic* or *majority voting*.

At the outset, it may appear that the development cost of two redundant copies of a program should be twice the cost of a single version. Actually, the cost is probably less than 1.5 times, because the cost of specification, some of the design costs, and most of the testing and documentation costs can be shared by the two versions. The additional costs of redundant programming are the increased memory space of the two or more versions and the lengthened running time. This is not surprising, since in most engineering situations, improvements come only at a cost and a trade-off must be made. One could minimize some of these costs by using a mass-storage device and overlay techniques and only calling in the redundant computation at selected, key intervals.

For a further discussion of this subject, the reader is referred to the literature on the theory of error correction and detection,[2] reliability gains through voting logic,[3] and the advantages of implementing redundancy at the subroutine or instruction level[4] and the means of doing so.[5]

---

[1] The author has heard of a case in which two redundant computers with the same program *occasionally* experience a software failure on one computer but not on the other. The users attribute this to the fact that the two computations are not always synchronized and thus one computer sometimes leads the other. Consequently, for some computations, the outside real-time data may produce a different internal state for the two computers. For a detailed discussion of such effects, see "Space Shuttle Software" (1978), also see Garman (1981).

[2] Kohavi (1970), pp. 14–21.

[3] Shooman (1968), pp. 298–305.

[4] Ibid., pp. 281–283.

[5] Miller (1967) and Hassett and Miller (1966).

2.7.3 Programming Style

Many authors have commented on the similarities between the writing of programs and the writing of natural-language prose. Just as one who studies literature becomes familiar with a specific author's style, one who reads other people's programs finds that they also follow a certain style. Numerous authors have written style manuals in order to improve the quality of written English, and a favorite one is William Strunk, Jr.'s *Elements of Style*, originally published in 1918.[1] Other authors have taken their lead from Strunk and have written similar manuals of style for computer programmers.[2]

In each of the above-mentioned manuals, the authors focus on a number of principles both positive and negative. Each of the do's and dont's is illustrated by an example and commentary. Although it is difficult to distill the wisdom offered in some of these manuals, we can at least indicate their scope by listing the summary of the 77 rules discussed in Kernighan and Plauger's excellent 160-page manual. (See Table 2.23.) The reader is referred to the references for further study, however, he may wish to use Table 2.23 as a check list, from time to time, when he reviews his own programming style, or comments on another's programs. (This table is also suggested as a vehicle for a design review in Chap. 6.)

2.7.4 Defensive Programming

If one adopts the philosophy that programs can be written without error, it makes little sense to build checks into the software. Conversely, if one believes that there will always be residual software errors, then built-in error checking is an important strategy.[3] Defensive programming techniques can be classified as active or passive. A passive technique checks information at an appropriate point in a computer program when the checking code is reached. For example, the section of an air traffic control program that processes radar input data should check that the target azimuth angle is between 0 and 360° and that the slant range is between zero and the maximum radar range.

An active defensive technique is one that searches throughout the program or data base periodically or during slack periods looking for unusual conditions. For example, in the same radar data processing already mentioned, each acquired target might have its own file in the data base. Certain areas in each file would be designated as storage for an alphanumeric descriptor of the flight identity, and

---

[1] See Strunk and White, 3d ed. (1979).

[2] Kreitzberg and Shneiderman (1972); Ledgard (1975); Kernighan and Plauger (1974) and 2d ed. (1978). The authors of all three books agree about variable names:"...The name should indicate the variable's mode and value" (Kreitzberg and Shniederman, p. 90); "Use good mnemonic names" (Ledgard, p. 27); "Use variable names that mean something" (Kernighan and Plauger, 1974, p. 121); "Choose variable names that won't be confused" (Kernighan and Plauger, 1978, p. 15). However, Parnas (1972, p. 153) says, "If one [uses] names with a high mnemonic value, both reader and writer tend to become sloppy." The author sides with the majority.

[3] Most experienced engineers believe Murphy's law always holds: "Whatever can go wrong, will!" See Bloch (1977).

Table 2.23 A summary of the elements of programming style

Write clearly—don't be too clever.

Say what you mean, simply and directly.
Use library functions.
Avoid temporary variables.
Write clearly—don't sacrifice clarity for "efficiency."
Let the machine do the dirty work.
Replace repetitive expressions by calls to a common function.
Parenthesize to avoid ambiguity.
Choose variable names that won't be confused.
Avoid the Fortran arithmetic IF.
Avoid unnecessary branches.
Use the good features of a language; avoid the bad ones.
Don't use conditional branches as a substitute for a logical expression.
Use the "telephone test" for readability.

Use DO-END and indenting to delimit groups of statements.
Use IF-ELSE to emphasize that only one of two actions is to be performed.
Use DO and DO-WHILE to emphasize the presence of loops.
Make your programs read from top to bottom.
Use IF ... ELSE IF ... ELSE IF ... ELSE ... to implement multi-way branches.
Use the fundamental control flow constructs.
Write first in an easy-to-understand pseudo-language; then translate into whatever
    language you have to use.
Avoid THEN-IF and null ELSE.
Avoid ELSE GOTO and ELSE RETURN.
Follow each decision as closely as possible with its associated action.
Use data arrays to avoid repetitive control sequences.
Choose a data representation that makes the program simple.
Don't stop with your first draft.

Modularize. Use subroutines.
Make the coupling between modules visible.
Each module should do one thing well.
Make sure every module hides something.
Let the data structure the program.
Don't patch bad code—rewrite it.
Write and test a big program in small pieces.
Use recursive procedures for recursively-defined data structures.
Test input for validity and plausibility.
Make sure input cannot violate the limits of the program.
Terminate input by end-of-file or marker, not by count.
Identify bad input; recover if possible.
Treat end of file conditions in a uniform manner.
Make input easy to prepare and output self-explanatory.
Use uniform input formats.
Make input easy to proofread.
Use free-form input when possible.
Use self-identifying input. Allow defaults. Echo both on output.
Localize input and output in subroutines.

Make sure all variables are initialized before use.
Don't stop at one bug.
Use debugging compilers.

Table 2.23 (*continued*).

Initialize constants with DATA statements or INITIAL attributes; initialize variables
    with executable code.
Watch out for off-by-one errors.
Take care to branch the right way on equality.

Avoid multiple exits from loops.
Make sure your code "does nothing" gracefully.
Test programs at their boundary values.
Program defensively.
10.0 times 0.1 is hardly ever 1.0.
Don't compare floating point numbers just for equality.

Make it right before you make it faster.
Keep it right when you make it faster.
Make it clear before you make it faster.
Don't sacrifice clarity for small gains in "efficiency."
Let your compiler do the simple optimizations.
Don't strain to re-use code; reorganize instead.
Make sure special cases are truly special.
Keep it simple to make it faster.
Don't diddle code to make it faster—find a better algorithm.
Instrument your programs. Measure before making "efficiency" changes.

Make sure comments and code agree.
Don't just echo the code with comments—make every comment count.
Don't comment bad code—rewrite it.
Use variable names that mean something.
Use statement labels that mean something.
Format a program to help the reader understand it.
Indent to show the logical structure of a program.
Document your data layouts.
Don't over-comment.

Source: Kernighan and Plauger (1978), pp. 159–161. Used by permission.

other portions would be for numeric information on the target's position. We
might actively check to see that no character information appears in the position
portion of the data base.

There are many excuses programmers give for avoiding defensive programming:

1. "Our code has very few, if any, errors; thus defensive programming is not
   needed."
2. "It is not *fair* to ask me to include checks in *my* program to detect errors that
   are coming from the outside, that is, from *someone else's* program." (Anything
   that helps is fair in love, war, and engineering!)
3. "Error checking slows down a computer system, and requires extra memory."
4. "Error checking takes too much programming time."
5. "I'll put it in but remove it as soon as we finish our testing."

The response to all these objections is directly or indirectly related to the number of errors anticipated in a program and their potential effect. If we believe that a significant number of post-release errors are inevitable, we must plan accordingly by using defensive programming. If such a defense is helpful during the testing phases of a program, we certainly must include it during operational use as well. If one accepts the fact that errors will occur, it is more important to find them and mitigate their effect than to assess blame for their occurrence. Again the objections based on running time, memory space, and programming cost are only significant if the additional resources added to a design by defensive programming are sizable.

There are few cases where such additional resources are so large that defensive programming must be discarded without consideration. Yourdon (1975) also makes a good point about including defensive coding early in the design process. The size of most designs grows to fill the available memory rapidly during the course of the design process. If we attempt to introduce defensive code toward the end of the design process, there is sure to be no remaining space, and a powerful objection will be raised to removing anything else from the design to make room. If we incorporate defensive programming from the beginning, there is a much better chance that it will get a fair shake and that much of it will survive any design trade-off that must be made to include as yet unincorporated features.

An important consideration is what to check. Clearly, if we try to check everything in our computation, essentially we are implementing redundant programming, yet in fact we can go beyond this concept and check an unreasonable number of items. In arriving at a decision as to what to check, the author suggests that the designer prepare the following set of tables to help in reaching an intelligent decision: a list of possible checks along with their estimated costs in programming time, running time, and memory requirements; and a list of the expected frequency of error occurrence, by type and by the estimated consequences of each type. In the reliability area, tables of such information are often called *failure mode effect and criticality analysis* (FMECA). Study of this information should aid one in arriving at a good decision. Typical items which need checking are listed in Table 2.24.

The technique to be used in checking depends largely on the problem; however, we can suggest certain methods which are often used. In business programs, bookkeeping, whether manual or computerized, allows cross-totals to be made. Other techniques involving audit trails are often used. In the case of scientific programs, there are many checks that we can make. Whenever a program is written to solve an equation, we can always substitute the solution obtained into the original equation to see if it is satisfied. In the case of probability computations, we know they must all fall between zero and unity. Additional checks were discussed in the radar processing problem examined in this section, and in the payroll program in Sec. 2.5.3.

All defensive techniques discussed so far are classified as passive techniques, since we must await the appearance of an input to begin checking. Other techniques, classified as active, can be applied either during the processing of

Table 2.24 Typical items to be checked in defensive programming

1. Input data from peripheral devices (range, attributes)
2. Data provided by other programs
3. Data base (arrays, files, structures, records)
4. Operator inputs (nature, sequence)
5. Stack depth
6. Range of I in DO CASE I (also computed GO TO)
7. Array bounds
8. Possibility of a zero divisor in expressions
9. Whether the desired version of the program is being run (date of last system reconfiguration)
10. Output to other programs or peripheral devices

input signals or while the system is idling, awaiting the next input.[1] Examples of active redundancy techniques are:

1. Memory-range check. If we store only certain types and ranges of data in certain blocks of memory, then we can check these conditions from time to time.
2. Flag verifications. If flags are used to indicate the state of the system, often they can be independently checked.
3. Reverse translation. If data or variable values must be translated from one code or system to another, then we can utilize an inverse transformation to check with the original values.
4. State checks. In many cases a complex system has many states of operation, which may be indicated by certain stored values. If such states can be independently verified, a check can be made.
5. Linkage checks. If linked list structures are used, the linkages can be checked.
6. Time-out checks (sometimes called *watchdog timers*). If a certain computation is known to take a certain maximum time, the timer can be set to monitor this computation.
7. Other techniques. Often careful consideration of the data structures used, the sequence and timing of operations, and the function of the program suggest other active checks which can be performed.

2.8 INFLUENCE OF THE IMPLEMENTATION LANGUAGE

2.8.1 Introduction

Until now we have tried to express our designs and principles in terms of various design representations that are essentially language-independent. Obviously, the

---

[1]Chang (1977), pp. 188–190; Myers (1978), Chap. 7; Kettlen et al. (1970).

final design must be written in one (or more) language(s) to run on one (or more) computer(s). In this section we address some of the salient points in the extensive literature that has been written on the subject of programming languages.

It is indicative of the viewpoint taken in this book that consideration of specific languages has been delayed to this point. Much of the discussion that ensues focuses upon two points: whether to use assembly language or a higher-level language, and, once such a choice has been made, which language to choose. The reader must also realize that the discussion proceeds from two viewpoints: What should we do on project Z for which I have just been made responsible, and what do we do in the best of all possible worlds?

Clearly, we must consider the latter question if the field is to evolve; however, we must be cognizant that practitioners generally have to make decisions based upon very difficult and often conflicting constraints. Suppose all the designers agree that a job should be done in a higher-level language but that the computer has already been chosen and an assembly language exists for the machine, but not a higher-level language. Only the very largest of projects contain sufficient resources to write an interpreter or complier for the machine along with the project. When one is forced into using assembly language, the least one can do is to recognize the problems associated with assembly languages in general and the language in question in particular and to plan to avoid the difficulties.

It is useful to review briefly at this point a few important points in the development of programming languages.[1] The first computers were developed in the period from 1937 to 1945. All programming was done in machine language. The concept of storing and automatically executing a computer program was first suggested by John von Neumann in 1946.[2] Between 1946 and 1955, there were so many rapid changes in computer hardware that one computer tended to become obsolete before any significant optimization of the software was attempted. In 1955, the IBM 650 computer became the first commercial success; it utilized the Symbolic Optimizer and Assembly Program (SOAP). The first higher-level language for a commercial machine was Fortran, an acronym for Formula Translation language; it was developed for the IBM 704 computer between 1957 and 1959. During about the same period, the language Algol (Algorithmically Oriented Language) was developed under the joint sponsorship of the American Association for Computing Machinery (ACM) and the European professional association of computer specialists, GAMM.

Among the myriad lists of other programming languages[3] we will cite a few additional ones: Cobol (COmmon Business-Oriented Language), 1959–1960; PL/1, 1963–1964; Basic (Beginners All-purpose Symbolic Instruction Code), 1963; APL (A Programming Language), 1966; Pascal, 1971–1973; the programming languages for the Hewlett-Packard HP-35 and the Texas Instruments TI-52 pocket programmable calculators, developed in the early 1970s; and the Intel

---

[1] Maisel (1969), Chap. 2.
[2] Bell and Newell (1971), Chap. 4, is a reprint of the paper "Preliminary Discussion of the Logical Design of an Electronic Computing Instrument," by Burks, Goldstein, and vonNeumann.
[3] Sammet (1969); Rosen (1967); Nicholls (1975).

8008 microprocessor assembly language, 1971. In addition, there are a host of specialized, problem-oriented languages whose input structure and nomenclature follow closely the problem area, such as ECAP,[1] CSMP,[2] GPSS,[3] numerical machine control languages, process control languages, etc.

Thus, it is more than two decades since the introduction of the first higher-level languages, and years since a new major language has been introduced (except for the Department of Defense language Ada, which we shall discuss[4]). If higher-level languages are really so good, why do people still program in assembly code?

2.8.2 Higher-Level versus Assembly Language Programming

At first glance, the pros and cons of higher-level (higher-order) language (HLL or HOL) versus assembly language appear clear. Higher-level-language programming is usually quicker and less error-prone (see Table 2.25). In addition, HOL programs are generally easier to understand and modify; thus the productivity, in lines of code per man-day, is higher. The main reason for this is that researchers have found that a programmer codes about the same number of instructions per day whether in assembly or HOL and an HOL program is 3 to 7 times smaller. (For more details see Chap. 6.) On the other hand, higher-level languages run more slowly and require more memory space than equivalent assembly languages.

Of course, the complete analysis involves a deeper study: How much more productivity? How much more memory? and How much more time? We must determine, for the particular application in question, the best trade-off among the competing factors. Some modern optimizing compilers are as efficient as all but the very best assembly language programmers on many problems. In addition, there are ways to try to combine the best of both worlds.

We begin our evaluation by focusing on the area in which most practitioners agree that assembly language should be used: systems software. Although there have been some computers whose machine language is simply the binary code for a higher-level language such as Fortran or Pascal, or for an intermediate-level translator language, most present-day computers, excepting some micro-programmed machines, have a binary machine language which deals with register operations, peripheral-device flags, etc. When a new computer is designed, one of the first pieces of software written is an assembly language translator (assembler). Thus, every new computer must have at least one or two assembly language programmers assigned during the development phase to produce the assembler.

[1] IBM Applications Program, "Electronic Circuit Analysis Program" (1965).
[2] IBM Applications Program, "1130 Continuous System Modeling Program" (1967).
[3] IBM Applications Program "General Purpose Simulation System/360" (1967).
[4] The Higher Level Language Working Group of the Department of Defense Advanced Research Projects Agency began work in 1975 on a higher-level language for embedded real-time computer systems. In 1979, the language was named Ada in honor of Augusta Ada Byron, Lady Lovelace, Babbage's first "programmer" (see Randell, 1975, p. 11). Details of the features of Ada are contained in U.S. Department of Defense (1980) and Wegner (1980). See also *Computer*, vol. 14, no. 6, special issue on Ada, June 1981, Pyle (1981), and Freeman (1982).

Table 2.25 A list of common errors which occur in assembly language programming but do not or are less likely to occur in higher-level-language programming.

1. Array overwrite
2. Stack overflow
3. Off by 1 in indexing or shifting
4. Wrong flag bit
5. Complement arithmetic problems
6. Floating-point arithmetic problems
7. Double-precision arithmetic problems
8. Initialization
9. Pointer problems
10. Wrong transfer of control
11. Indirect address problems
12. Iterated DO LOOP problems

Source: Shooman (1972*b*).

In most cases, this is just the beginning of an entire set of systems software. The next pieces of system software to be developed are some sort of higher-level-language translator (interpreter or compiler) and an operating system. Most of the higher-level-language interpreters and compilers and the operating systems now in use were written in assembly language; however, this situation is changing.

Two often-quoted examples of operating systems written in a higher-level language are the MIT-Honeywell MULTICS[1] and the Bell Labs UNIX[2] time-sharing systems. The former was written in PL/1 and the latter in the C programming language (developed at Bell Laboratories).[3] Most sections of these systems, except for a few crucial input-output modules, were written in the higher-level language.

Of course, the production of system software, while highly glamorous and intellectually exciting, is essentially the task of a small number of experts. The largest use of software is in applications programming, and we should inquire what percentage of this programming is done in assembler and what percentage in higher-level language. In 1968, one author estimated that in scientific programming 98 percent was in higher-order language, in business data processing 50 percent was in HOL and the proportion was growing, and in real-time systems 5 percent was in HOL and the proportion was holding steady.[4] At present, the use of higher-level languages in business data processing must be over 90 percent, and clearly, there is greater than a 5 percent HOL usage in real-time programming. Furthermore, with the introduction of Ada, this percentage will grow.

[1]Corbató and Vyssotsky (1967).
[2]Ritchie and Thompson (1974).
[3]Kernighan and Ritchie (1978).
[4]Opler (1968).

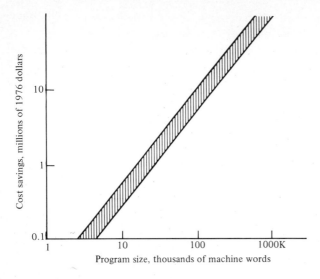

Figure 2.31 Program size versus estimated cost savings through the use of a higher-level language instead of an assembly language (assuming a compiler is already written). *(Adapted from Premo 1976)*

Cost savings, millions of 1976 dollars

Program size, thousands of machine words

The proponents of assembly language also believe that critical input-output requirements force the programmer to write real-time system software in assembly language. However, even real-time software can be largely written in HOL. As an example, we consider the SAFEGUARD antiballistic missile system, which had the equivalent of over 2 million assembly language instructions: 789,000 real-time software, 632,000 support software, and 840,000 (hardware) maintenance and installation instructions.[1] Although equivalent software size is stated in terms of equivalent assembly language instructions, the real-time software was written in a PL/1-like special language developed for the project. Also, most of the support software was in PL/1, and only the maintenance and installation instructions and a small amount of support software were in assembly language.

We can report on the cost benefits of using HOL in *large* real-time software projects. GTE Automatic Electric Laboratories cites a 20 percent reduction in total development effort when it used a HOL and a good compiler to develop real-time programs.[2] In Figs. 2.31 and 2.32 a rough estimate of the cost advantages of HOL over assembly language is shown to be about $5 million for a 100,000-word (machine code) project if the cost of a compiler ($5 million) is subtracted, or $10 million if a compiler is already available. These 1976 estimates must be adjusted for inflation, as discussed in Chap. 6.

As another example, Intel coded the 8008 assembler for its Intelec 8 developmental system in its PL/M higher-level language in 100 man-hours, requiring 6000 bytes of memory. Intel estimated a 5 : 1 saving through the use of PL/M instead of assembly language.[3]

---

[1] Stephenson (1977).
[2] Daly (1977).
[3] Kidall (1975). It was also estimated that if the program had been coded in assembly language, there would have been little or no reduction in the memory space required.

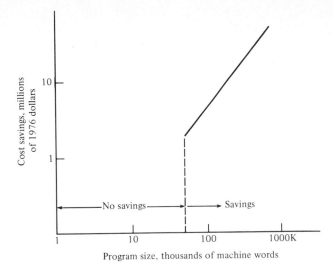

Figure 2.32 Program size versus estimated cost savings through the use of a higher-level language instead of an assembly language (assuming no complier is available and the project must pay for its development). *(Premo, 1976)*

The newest factor accelerating the use of HOL in real-time systems is the development of Ada. For many years the U.S. Department of Defense (DOD) has been working toward the standardization of programming languages as a means of reducing cost. The military role in supporting the development of Cobol exemplifies DOD's effectiveness. In 1975 the High Order Language Working Group (HOLWG) was established.[1] The steps taken by HOLWG included the following:[2]

1. It was affirmed that Cobol should receive continued support as the standard language of the financial management community.
2. It was affirmed that Fortran should receive continued support as the standard language of the scientific computational community.
3. It was decided that DOD-approved higher-order languages must be used exclusively (no assembly language) on embedded[3] computer systems, unless a *strong case* could be made against their being cost-effective *over the entire system life cycle.*
4. HOLWG would work toward the establishment of a single HOL for embedded software. The working title DOD-1 was chosen.
5. As an interim measure the list of approved DOD HOLs for embedded software would be Cobol, Fortran, Tacpol, CMS-2, SPL/1, Jovial J3, and J73.

[1]Glass (1979).

[2]Items 1 to 6 are contained in U.S. Department of Defense (1976*b*) and U.S. Department of Defense (1976*a*), and the remaining items are discussed in *U.S. Department of Defense Language Effort* and in Amoroso et al. (1977).

[3]An embedded computer system is one which includes a dedicated processor, generally operates in real-time, and performs commands, control, communications, or similar tasks.

6. A single HOL for embedded software was deemed feasible, but no existing language or modified existing language would do.
7. An evolving set of increasingly more refined specifications for the new language appeared under the names of Strawman, Woodenman, Tinman, Ironman, Steelman, and Pebbleman.[1]
8. A large-scale evaluation was conducted of 23 HOL candidates as to their suitability for DOD-1.
9. The possible base languages chosen were Pascal, PL/1, and Algol 68.
10. Four contracts were awarded to companies to create a design based on one of the three languages in item 9; however, all four competitors chose Pascal as their base.
11. The four preliminary efforts were narrowed to two; however, the efforts have been described at software conferences as Pascal-like in syntax but PL/1-like in size!
12. The name Ada was chosen for the language.
13. A simulator was written to use as a learning tool prior to the appearance of a compiler or interpreter.
14. Additional steps in the project now in progress include test and evaluation of the resulting language, production of compilers and allied tools for software development and maintenance, control of the language, and validation of the compilers.

Although DOD software accounts for perhaps only one-third of all software dollars spent in the United States (see Table 1.2) and embedded software is only a fraction of that, it is clear that such a well-organized (and we hope successful) effort is bound to have a lasting impact on software development. We now turn to the topic of how to write HOL programs for microprocessor systems.

As was stated in Chap. 1, the advent of the microprocessor revolution will bring with it a plethora of devices and systems containing a microprocessor and 500 to 4000 bytes of memory. In addition, there will be many minicomputers used in real-time applications which are based on essentially the same or a similar microprocessor with varying peripheral devices and memory sizes.[2]

In considering the prospects that a higher-level language will exist for such machines, we should note that all the popular microprocessors have assemblers. These are made available free or at nominal cost by the manufacturer. An example is the PL/1-like language PL/M, illustrated in Table 2.26. Even when design requirements do not allow more than 500 to 1000 bytes, one can run the software on a larger-memory development system and prepare the binary code for loading into the actual product memory. In fact, in most cases, one would use the

---

[1]The military uses the term *strawman* to mean a proposed working paper or a model of a project used to critically focus discussion. A strawman may be demolished or may survive as a modified, stronger woodenman. Will the sequence continue with Silverman, Goldman, and Platinumman? If so, we hope it will be figurative and not literal.

[2]Modern technology now allows up to 64k and more of fast electronic memory, and floppy and winchester disk technologies allow millions of bytes of magnetic storage.

Table 2.26 Example of a PL/M program called Serial Sender

To print a short message on a teletypewriter, this routine in PL/M transmits 11 pulses at 9.1-ms intervals for each character in the message, stopping after the last one. The pulse train consists of one start pulse, eight data pulses, and two stop pulses.[†]

Line	Statement
1	DECLARE MESSAGE DATA ('WALLA WALLA WASH'),
2	(CHAR, I, J, SENDBIT) BYTE;
3	
4	/* SEND EACH CHARACTER FROM MESSAGE VECTOR TO TELEPRINTER */
5	DO I = 0 TO LAST(MESSAGE);
6	CHAR = MESSAGE(I);
7	SENDBIT = 0;
8	
9	/* SEND EACH BIT FROM CHAR TO TELEPRINTER */
10	DO J = 1 TO 11;
11	OUTPUT(0) = SENDBIT:
12	CALL TIME (91); /* WATTS 9.1 MS */
13	SENDBIT = CHAR AND 1;
14	/* ROTATE CHAR FOR NEXT ITERATION */
15	CHAR = ROR (CHAR OR 1, 1)
16	END;
17	END;

[†]Kidall (1975); McCracken (1978).

development machine to prepare a program and load it into ROM to create *firmware*, i.e., a program residing in read-only memory.

Sometimes a cross-assembler (an assembly program residing on and written in the language of a larger computer, which performs the assembler operation) is used with many interesting advantages. Because of the large machine size and high speed, many users can share a cross-assembler effectively. Also, if required, there is plenty of room in memory to add special features. Furthermore, if a new hardware machine is being developed, often a prototype cross-assembler can be written before the first hardware prototype is available, so that experimentation with the programming can parallel or lead the hardware development.

Higher-level languages exist for many microprocessors.[1] Both compilers and interpreters are available. The reader is referred to the literature for a detailed description of the languages available (for example, PL/Z for the Z-80, PL/65 for the M6800, and a universal PLMX).[2] However, we will discuss some of the evidence that through the use of a proper mix of techniques, the memory and running time increases of an HOL over assembly language may be made small.

[1]Hilbing (1977); Fergerson and Gibbons (1977); Lewis and Saunders (1977); Cohen and Francis (1977); and Brown (1977).
[2]"Speaking of Chip Shortages" (1980).

Thus it is probably advantageous to use an HLL in many real-time systems, even with their "tight" memory and speed specifications.[1]

Maples and Fisher (1977) describe a Basic compiler that fits in a 5-kilobyte PROM (programmable read-only memory) and is used along with an interpreter and an optimizing cross-compiler. One sample problem involving an ideal gas law computation took 4 to 5 days to write in 8080 assembler and 1 hour in Basic. The assembler program took 100 bytes, and the Basic program, 29 instructions, 16 of which were comment statements. The Basic program took more storage; however, neither the size of storage nor the comparative run times are stated in the reference. In another example, a simple assembly language program is written which does two additions, one subtraction, one multiplication, and one division in conjunction with the floating-point arithmetic package. The assembly language program ran 12 percent faster than the equivalent compiled Basic version.

Holthouse and Cohen (1977) start with a high-level language (characteristics are not given) and use an interpretative technique. This uses about half the memory that a compiler would take, but of course an interpreter runs more slowly than a compiler by a factor of 4, as estimated by the authors. In order to speed up the program, they take frequency counts[2] of instruction execution to document those areas slowing down the program. Then by analyzing the occurrence frequencies and execution times they are able to estimate the increase in speed that would be achieved if selected portions were coded in assembly language. The authors estimate that the speed increase factor averages 6. The amount of the code that one has to replace to obtain significant speedup is really quite small. In one example, recoding 5 percent of the program reduced execution time by one-third. An average speedup factor of 4 could be obtained for the four examples if 12 percent of the HOL code were replaced by assembly code. Such an improvement matched the speed of a compiled version. In fact, by replacing the slowest 25 percent of the HOL code with carefully coded assembly language, they could obtain a speedup factor of about 5, thus outperforming a compiler. A summary of the suggested techniques which should be employed to speed up a program that is executing too slowly is given in Table 2.27.

Before we leave the subject of how to minimize the amount of assembly language programming on a microprocessor, we should consider one other possibility. Perhaps we can raise the level of the assembler in order to improve programming productivity. One can certainly add an efficient floating point arithmetic package (generally standard) and put it in a ROM for convenience. The addition of macro facilities provides many of the benefits of HOL subprograms without measurably degrading efficiency. One could also add some of the control statements needed for structured programming, such as IF THEN ELSE and DO WHILE. Such features are included in the Super Assembler for the General Instruments 16-bit CP1600 microprocessor, which is a very powerful

---

[1] Holthouse and Cohen (1977); Maples and Fisher (1976).
[2] Knuth and Stevenson (1973).

Table 2.27 Techniques for redesigning HOL software which executes too slowly

1. Use frequency-counting techniques to pinpoint the major sections of the program responsible for most of the processing time. Redesign and recode these sections using efficient HOL techniques to speed up the program.

2. Search for an algorithm that executes faster than the one chosen.

3. Look for a different solution (design) for the problem which will run faster.

4. Same as item 1, except recode the slow sections in assembly language.

5. If an interpreter is used, use a compiler for the entire program or at least for the key sections.

machine and in many ways resembles a PDP-11. Additional material on the design of microcomputer software appears in the literature.[1]

2.8.3 Comparison of Language Features That Affect Reliability and Productivity

As we stated in the introduction, one is seldom free to choose an ideal language for the task at hand. Only occasionally do the computers under consideration support two or more suitable higher-level languages. Generally, the choice is among a few computers, each of which supports one or two suitable languages, and the trade-off involves balancing the hardware advantages and disadvantages of each of the computers. However, it would be a useful guide for present decisions as well as future developments to know how to evaluate language suitability for a given task.

If one searches the literature, there is little comparative information on how the various available languages perform with respect to error rate and productivity. In fact, if one consults textbooks on programming languages (see Sammet, 1969, and Nicholls, 1975) the word *reliability* does not even appear in the index. Furthermore, the word *error* is found only in Nicholls' book, and the discussions refer to error messages and syntax errors. In software engineering circles, most people agree that we don't even start counting and recording errors until after the first successful (no error messages which inhibit execution) compilation or interpretation. Clearly much research remains to be done in this area.

Results of research studies in this area have just begun to appear in the literature.[2] Most of these efforts are introductory and not definitive, partly because of the high cost of running a realistic programming experiment.[3] For

[1] McIntire (1978); Ogdin (1978); Digital Equipment Corporation (1972*a*); Digital Equipment Corporation (1972*b*). Also the following, all printed in *IEEE Microcomputer '77 Conf. Rec.*: Holthouse and Cohen (1977); Chien and Dreizen (1977); Williams and Smith (1977).

[2] Goodenough and Ross (1973); Gannon and Horning (1975); Gannon (1976); Hilburn and Julich (1976), Chap. 5.

[3] Sackman (1967), Chap. 9; Sackman (1970).

example, suppose that we wish to investigate productivity and the errors which occur in the use of Fortran as opposed to PL/1 or Pascal. We will require problems from a variety of applications to balance out any special features of one language which make it especially suitable to one particular problem class. Also, we will need several programmers to average out the level of experience with each language and differences in programming ability. If we choose three problems which each take 3 months to design, code, test, debug, and document and employ five programmers, then we have a total of $3 \times 3 \times 5 = 45$ man-months. Assuming that a programmer's salary plus 100 percent overhead is $4000 per month, we arrive at an estimated cost of $180,000 for this limited experiment, to which we must add the cost of direction, analysis, and documentation of the results by the investigator. Unfortunately, few organizations would be capable of or interested in funding such an experiment.

2.8.4 Language Standards

Programming language standards are a subset of the software engineering standards discussed in Chap. 6 and are an important feature in the development of software.[1] Their utility has been succinctly stated by Hecht: "Software standards can help the developer, the user, and regulatory agencies in facilitating communications, in extending software life, in broadening the applicability of programs, and in reducing the personnel and organizational reorientation required in transitioning from one project to another" (1978). Unfortunately, the establishment of standards is a long, drawn-out, and costly process. In order to get universal enough agreement to issue a standard, a broad class of users must be involved. This leads to large committees, often with conflicting needs and opinions; and to reach a consensus takes a long time, and an able chairman with skill and persistence. The old joke that a committee is where one substitutes the enjoyment of conversation for the dreariness of work and the loneliness of thought doesn't apply to standards committees. They are hard work and at times exasperating. Most large companies write their own standards where no nationally accepted ones exist, and though these are more manageable than a national or an international standard, the same difficulties are experienced.

Most of the programming language standards work in the United States revolves around three organizations: the American National Standards Institute (ANSI),[2] the Institute of Electrical and Electronic Engineers (IEEE Standards Office),[3] and the various technical committees on specific programming languages of the Association for Computing Machinery Special Interest Group on Programming Languages (ACM-SIGPLAN).[4]

[1] Woolridge (1977).
[2] 1430 Broadway, New York, NY 10018.
[3] Standards Office, Institute of Electrical and Electronic Engineers, Engineering Societies Building, 345 E. 47th St., New York, NY 10017.
[4] Association for Computing Machinery, 1133 Avenue of the Americas, New York, NY 10036.

Table 2.28 Programming language standards currently used in the United States*

Basic Fortran ANSI X3.10-1966

ANS Fortran ANSI X3.9-1976 (also ANSI X3.9-1966)

ANS Fortran X3.9-1978 (Fortran 77)

Programming language APT ANSI X3.37-1974

Programming language Cobol ANSI X3.23-1974

Programming language PL/1 ANSI X3.53-1976

Minimal Basic ANSI X3.60-1976

Programming language Minimal Cobol ANSI X3.65-1977

Programming language IEEE/ARINC, standard Atlas test language,
   IEEE standard 416-1976

* At present three organizations are working on a Pascal language standard: the IEEE Standards Office, the ANSI X3J9 Committee, and the British Standards Institute.

A partial list of the language standards used at present in the United States is given in Table 2.28. Other activities of interest are the *Fortran Newsletter*[1] and the Ada language development already discussed. In addition, any language which receives extensive support from a manufacturer over a number of years generally becomes a de facto standard of sorts.

2.9 SOFTWARE TOOLS

2.9.1 Introduction

As people began to study the various steps of the program development process, it became clear that all the skilled practitioners used a set of programs which aided them in their tasks. Any skilled worker needs tools, and these are the tools of the programming trade. Some typical tools are program editors, sorting programs, binary dumps, disk space utilities, peripheral interchanges, debuggers, test-case generators, and text processors. A more complete list of tools appears in Table 2.29, and Rauch-Hinden (1982).

It is clearly wasteful for each programmer to develop a personal set of tools. Brooks (1975) suggests that each large project have a tool builder who is responsible for choosing and maintaining any existing tools, and for building any others which are necessary for the particular project in question. Since the construction of good tools is costly, there is considerable economy in the central development of such tools. This can be done by a manufacturer who offers such tools to all customers, a government organization that places the tools in the public domain, a vendor of software who builds and sells such tools, or an in-house development of a large software supplier.[2]

[1] Quarterly *FOR-WORD: Fortran Newsletter*, Loren P. Meissner, ed., 50B 3239, Lawrence Berkeley Laboratory, Berkeley, CA 94720. Published under a U.S. Department of Energy contract.

[2] Kernighan and Plaugert (1981).

Table 2.29 A comprehensive list of program-development tools and techniques

Tool or technique	Simu-lation	Devel-opment	Test and evalua-tion	Opera-tions and mainte-nance	Perfor-mance measure-ment	Program-ming support
1. Accuracy study processor			X			
2. Analytical modeling	X					
3. Analyzer		X	X	X	X	
4. Automated test generator			X	X		
5. Automated verification systems			X	X		
6. Bootstrap loader						X
7. Comparator			X	X		
8. Compiler		X	X	X	X	
9. Compiler building system		X				
10. Compiler validation system			X			
11. Consistency checker		X	X			
12. Correctness proofs			X			
13. Cross-assembler		X				
14. Cross-reference program			X	X		
15. Data base analyzer		X	X	X		
16. Data description language		X				
17. Decompiler			X	X		
18. Design language processor		X				
19. Diagnostics/debug aids			X			
20. Driver			X			
21. Dynamic simulator	X		X			
22. Editor			X	X		
23. Engineering scientific simulations	X		X			
24. Environment simulator	X		X			
25. Emulation		X	X		X	
26. Extensible language processor		X				
27. Flowcharter						X
28. Generator			X			
29. Instruction simulator	X	X	X	X		
30. Instruction trace			X	X		
31. Interface checker			X			
32. Interpreter		X				
33. Interrupt analyzer			X			
34. Language processor		X				
35. Library						X
36. Linkage editor		X				
37. Linking loader						X
38. Relocatable loader						X
39. Logic-equation generator			X	X		
40. Macroprocessor		X				
41. Map program			X			
42. Modular programming		X	X	X		
43. Overlay program		X	X			
44. Postprocessor			X			
45. Preprocessor			X			
46. Process construction		X	X			
47. Production libraries						X

Table 2.29 (*continued*)

Tool or technique	Simu-lation	Devel-opment	Test and evalua-tion	Opera-tions and mainte-nance	Perfor-mance measure-ment	Program-ming support
48. Program flow analyzer			X			
49. Program sequencer			X	X		
50. Record generator						X
51. Report generator						X
52. Requirements language processor		X				
53. Requirements tracer		X	X			
54. Restructuring program				X		
55. Simulator	X				X	
56. Snap Generator			X	X		
57. Software monitor					X	
58. Standards enforcer			X			
59. Structure analyzer			X	X		
60. Structured programming		X	X	X		
61. System simulations	X					
62. Test beds			X	X		
63. Test drivers, scripts, data-generators			X			
64. Test-result processor			X			
65. Text editor						X
66. Timing analyzer	X	X	X	X	X	X
67. Top-down programming		X				
68. Trace program		X	X			
69. Translator		X		X		
70. Utilities						X

Source: Reifer and Trattner (1977).

In discussing a computer system development in which a new computer is being designed, we might include the operating system, assemblers, interpreters, compilers, simulators, and maintenance programs as software tools. Generally these are called *support software* or *software utilities*; however, this is really just a matter of semantics. Certainly, one would classify a preprocessor designed to change structured control statements into their equivalents in unstructured Fortran[1] as a development tool. Similarly, a postprocessor that indented the program code to clearly indicate levels of nesting of control structures would be a tool. A compiler that gave one execution frequency counts to aid in minimizing processing time would be equally handy whether one called it a tool or just a compiler with useful features.[2]

[1] Kernighan and Plauger (1976).
[2] An entire additional class of tools consists of those associated with formal software requirements and specifications languages (see Chap. 6). Two important references are Teichroew (1977) and Teichroew (1976).

Table 2.30 Comparison of the advantages and disadvantages of a program-development facility (PDF)

Advantages	Disadvantages
1. The needs of a program *developer* and those of a *user* differ. Thus, they can be separately optimized.	1. More hardware and communications equipment are needed. We now have both a target machine and (a) PDF machine(s).
2. A small machine can be used to develop software for a large one, or vice versa, depending on the relative advantages, availability, costs, etc.	2. If the PDF is used for many projects, any downtime becomes tremendously disruptive. To minimize this effect, redundancy and partial operating modes are recommended.
3. In many cases the tools can be made independent of the target machine, and the required development costs and user learning costs can be spread over many projects.	3. If data have to be transmitted between target and PDF computers, the communications lines must be able to handle the load.
4. A separate PDF provides early programming start-up in a new project and cushions the disruption of any major changes in software or hardware during the system life cycle.	4. Incompatible character sets between the target and PDF machine can cause problems.
5. The program-development team need not be housed in the immediate proximity of the development computer.	5. A small machine may not be able to simulate all actions of a larger machine.
6. An efficient timesharing-based PDF system can be used to develop a batch system.	6. If, as is likely, several copies of the system software are needed, they must all be updated and controlled so that they are identical.
	7. The PDF may not be able to adequately model the running time or timing problems of the target machine.

2.9.2 Software-Development Facilities

A number of large software-development facilities have been developed or are in various stages of construction.[1] A study of the various objectives and accomplishments of such systems yields a list of advantages and disadvantages (see Table 2.30). Clearly the proponents of such systems view the advantages as far outweighing the disadvantages. Some of the facilities provided by the UNIX program-development system are described in Table 2.31.

---

[1]Dolotta and Mashey (1976); Mashey (1976); Mashey and Smith (1976); Dolotta et al. (1976); Knudsen (1976); Bianchi and Wood (1976); Robinson (1976); Straeter et al. (1977); Robinson (1977); Conrad et al. (1977); Blum and Richeson (1977); Stenning et al. (1981); Hamilton and Zeldin (1979); Higher Order Systems (1981); Rauch-Hinden (1982).

Table 2.31 Facilities provided by the UNIX Programmer's Workbench (PWB)

1. The UNIX timesharing operating system is used as the starting point.
2. A flexible remote job entry facility is provided.
3. A source-code control system stores all official versions of the software and provides lists of changes between versions.
4. A modification-request control system manages change requests, error reporting, and debugging progress.
5. A wide variety of documentation tools are supported.
6. Two test drivers simulate different types of terminal load.

2.10 SUMMARY

The lessons of this chapter are not difficult to grasp, but many have found them hard to implement. The difficulty lies in the necessity of changing work habits and approaches which are intuitive and comfortable, and replacing them with a different and disciplined set of principles. The basis of any good software product is a design both well conceived and well executed. The major approaches to good software design that were developed in this chapter are listed as follows:

1. A consistent and comprehensive set of requirements and specifications is the foundation of any design. The properties of a good requirements document are introduced in more detail in Chap. 6.
2. The designer must take a studied and consistent approach to design. The methods of top-down, bottom-up, and two-stage design have been found to be of great help in defining and directing the design process.
3. It is necessary to document the design to aid in its review and improvement throughout the iterative steps of the design process, and during subsequent maintenance and enhancement activities. High-level flowcharts, pseudo-code, HIPO diagrams, and data flowgraphs were introduced as examples of popular and effective design-representation techniques.
4. As the design progresses toward lower levels, one must adopt an implementation philosophy before coding begins. The techniques of structured programming and modular programming are widely employed to organize the structure of the program code.
5. A number of other issues impinge on these four design steps:
   a. The use of defensive programming improves the design.
   b. Wide use of higher-order languages increases productivity and decreases errors.
   c. The use of pseudo-code preprocessing (either manually or via machine translator) aids one in implementing a structured design in an ill-suited language.
   d. Software-development tools help to relieve some of the drudgery of software design and coding and encourage good practices.

If during the future evolution of software engineering, the design process ever reaches a stage of near perfection, then the material on testing in Chap. 4 will become superfluous. Similarly, the prediction and measurement of software reliability discussed in Chap. 5 would be an idle task if designs consistently produced nearly error-free code. At present, software design is far from perfect. Thus, all the aforementioned elements must be employed with vigor to assure that a high-quality product is delivered. The responsibilities of management in initiating, enforcing, and documenting the engineering of software during product development are covered in Chap. 6.

In the preceding paragraphs we have identified how all the remaining book chapters, except for Chap. 3, relate to software design and development. If the topics of Chaps. 2 and 3 were introduced in this book in the same sequence as they occur in a development project, then Chaps. 2 and 3 would change places. Chapter 3 deals with methods of estimating problem complexity and its relationship to design cost, running time, and memory requirements. Such estimates are useful during preliminary design; however, the author chose to discuss design first for pedagogical reasons. It is difficult to appreciate much of the material in Chaps. 3 through 6 unless the design process is well understood. Using our newly acquired vocabulary, we can describe the design of this book in the following fashion:

1. Chapter 1 is a statement of the requirements and specifications.
2. A bottom-up approach was chosen, and the most critical topic—design—appears in Chap. 2.
3. Once the design process is understood, we revert as closely as possible to a top-down approach, in Chaps. 3 to 5.
4. After completing our first description of software engineering in Chaps. 1 to 5, we present a second description of the process in Chap. 6, using a top-down approach and stressing the management viewpoint.

PROBLEMS

2.1 You are to choose some computer application with which you are at least moderately familiar. This can be a problem you have studied at work or in some other class, or one you have read or heard about.

(a) Describe the important features of the problem in about one page of text.
(b) Draw an H diagram for the problem.
(c) Draw a top-level IPO diagram for the problem.
(d) Compare the advantages and disadvantages of a top-down and a bottom-up design for this problem.
(e) Design the control structure for the problem using a structured programming implementation. Your design should be in terms of structured flowcharts and pseudo-code.

2.2 This problem discusses the design of a payroll-adjustment program, via flowcharts, HIPO diagrams, or pseudo-code
(a) Write a requirements document.
(b) Write a specifications document.

(*c*) Write a top-down design for the payroll-adjustment problem.

(*d*) Write a bottom-up design for the payroll-adjustment problem.

Statement of the payroll-adjustment problem

Glen Cove University, which employs 200 faculty members, has just signed a new faculty union contract. All salaries of $26,000 or higher are to remain unchanged. Any faculty member who earns less than $26,000 per year is to receive a pay raise according to the following formula: The employee will receive $100 per year additional for each dependent (including himself or herself), plus $50 per year for each year of employment. In no case may the new salary exceed $26,000 per year.

The personnel data on all faculty members are stored on magnetic tape in the business office and include present annual salary, number of dependents, date of hire, and other information. The problem is to write a program which computes and prints out the list of faculty members along with their old and new salary.

2.3 You are now asked to repeat Prob. 2.2 after having specified the problem in more detail.

Detailed specification of the payroll-adjustment problem

Glen Cove University, which employs 200 faculty members, has just signed a new faculty union contract. All salaries of $26,000 or higher are to remain unchanged. Any faculty member who earns less that $26,000 per year is to receive a pay raise according to the following formula: The employee will receive $100 per year additional for each dependent (including himself or herself), plus $50 per year for each year of employment. In no case may the new salary exceed $26,000 per year.

The personnel data on all faculty members are stored on magnetic tape in the business office and include present annual salary, number of dependents, date of hire, and other information. The problem is to write a program which computes and prints out the list of faculty members along with their old and new salary.

Assume that the business office will give you a set of cards with the data for each person on one card. Assume the following arrays will store the input data for your program:

NAME (200):	Contains a name of up to 30 characters
DEPEND (200):	Contains number of dependents in two decimal digits
DHIRE (200):	Contains a string of 10 characters, 2 digits for month, a blank, 2 digits for day, a blank, and 4 digits for year
PRES SAL (200):	Contains five digits with yearly salary in rounded dollars

(*a*) Does the detailed specification affect the design given in Prob. 2.2? Explain.

(*b*) Approaches (compare the two approaches):

(i) Search the list of names for those making less than $26,000 per year, compute the new salary, check for the $26,000 limit, store the new salary, print output.

(ii) Sort the list by salary from lowest to highest, stop when $26,000 is exceeded, compute the new salary, check for the $26,000 limit, store the new salary, print output.

(*c*) Language and computer: Student should choose the language and the computer and state the reasons for the choice.

2.4 Repeat Prob. 2.1 for the following problem statement:

Roots of a cubic equation

(*a*) Statement of the problem:

The polynomial equation $a_3 x^3 + a_2 x^2 + a_1 x + a_0 = 0$ is to be solved for its three roots. A general solution is desired which will work for any finite real values of $a_3, a_2, a_1,$ and a_0. The values of $a_3, a_2, a_1,$ and a_0 are to be acquired as floating (single-precision) input data at the beginning of each run. Write your program with a loop so it reads any number of data cards and terminates on the last data card.

(b) Approaches (compare the two approaches):

(i) The general formula (i.e., Cardamo's formula) for the solution of a cubic equation (see part d) is to be used to compute the roots.

(ii) An iterative solution for a single real root is to be obtained. Once the real root is removed, the quadratic formula is to be used to solve for the other two roots.

(c) Language and computer: Student should choose and specify the language and computer.

(d) Cardamo's formula for cubic equations: A cubic equation, $y^3 + py^2 + qy + r = 0$ may be reduced to the form

$$x^3 + ax + b = 0$$

by substituting for y the value $x - (p/3)$. Here

$$a = \tfrac{1}{3}(3q - p^2) \text{ and } b = \tfrac{1}{27}(2p^3 - 9pq + 27r)$$

For solution, let

$$A = \sqrt[3]{-\frac{b}{2} + \sqrt{\frac{b^2}{4} + \frac{a^3}{27}}} \qquad B = \sqrt[3]{-\frac{b}{2} - \sqrt{\frac{b^2}{4} + \frac{a^3}{27}}} \,,$$

Then the values of x will be given by

$$A + B \qquad -\frac{A+B}{2} + \frac{A-B}{2}\sqrt{-3} \qquad -\frac{A+B}{2} - \frac{A-B}{2}\sqrt{-3}$$

If

$$\frac{b^2}{4} + \frac{a^3}{27} > 0$$

there will be one real root and two conjugate imaginary roots. If

$$\frac{b^2}{4} + \frac{a^3}{27} = 0$$

there will be three real roots of which at least two are equal. If

$$\frac{b^2}{4} + \frac{a^3}{27} < 0$$

there will be three real and unequal roots.

In the last case a trigonometric solution is useful. Compute the value of the angle ϕ in the expression

$$\cos \phi = -\frac{b}{2} \div \sqrt{-\frac{a^3}{27}}$$

Then x will have the following values:

$$2\sqrt{-\frac{a}{3}} \cos\frac{\phi}{3} \qquad 2\sqrt{-\frac{a}{3}} \cos\left(\frac{\phi}{3} + 120°\right)$$

$$2\sqrt{-\frac{a}{3}} \cos\left(\frac{\phi}{3} + 240°\right)$$

2.5 Repeat Prob. 2.1 for the following problem statement:

Manipulation of a file of research reports

(*a*) Statement of the problem:

At present the Reliability, Safety, and Software Engineering Group at the Polytechnic has about 1000 reports, papers, books, and journal proceedings in its library. Each item is entered on an index card in a file box. It is anticipated that the library may eventually grow to 10,000 items in the future. In the near future, two punched cards will be created for each of the items in the library and we wish to create a program to perform various searches, sorts, and listings.

(*b*) Data structures:

Assume that each punched card contains four fixed-column character fields. The first field is 30 characters wide and contains the name(s) of the author(s). The second field is 50 characters wide and contains the full or abbreviated title. (No *important words* in the title are to be abbreviated.) The second card contains field 3, which is 50 characters wide and contains keywords (or abbreviated keywords) in the item. The last field is 30 characters wide and contains the source (journal, issue, book publisher, proceedings, etc.) of the item.

(*c*) Specified functions:

The program must be able to perform the following tasks, and the selection (and possibly sequence) of tasks to be performed must be controlled by the first data card, which will serve as a program control card. Provide a means of performing multiple tasks on the same run.

(i) Read in a variable-length stack of item cards and store them.

(ii) Alphabetize the data by first author.

(iii) Print out the list of items.

(iv) Create a list of keywords (from field 3), eliminate duplicates, alphabetize, and print out.

(v) Search the author field for a given author's name, and print out the list of items he or she has written.

(vi) Search the keyword field for items which contain the intersection (the AND) of one, two, or three chosen keywords.

(vii) Provide the same search facility as in item vi on words in the title field.

(*d*) Approaches:

Students should provide their own approaches.

(*e*) Language and computer:

Students should choose the language and computer, and state reasons for their choice.

2.6 Repeat Prob. 2.5 assuming that the data entry and search will be done on a terminal.

2.7 Suppose you were to design the research-report information system of Prob. 2.5 using (*a*) a powerful text editor on a medium-size machine such as UNIX (on the PDP-11 or VAX) or TECO (on the DEC 10), or (*b*) a simpler microcomputer text editor such as Pencil or Scripsit (on the TRS-80). How would your design change? Explain.

2.8 Repeat Prob. 2.1 for the following problem statement:

Specifications for a ballot-counting procedure

Terms: An *election* consists of sets of *ballots* to elect persons for various committees. Each set of ballots is called a *committee election*. There may be up to 10 committee elections for an election.

All ballots for a particular committee have the name of the committee punched in columns 61 to 80 and contain the names of the candidates to that committee. There are up to 25 nominees for each committee.

When a person votes for a candidate, an "11" punch (i.e., a minus sign) is punched in the ballot in the field consisting of columns 21 to 45, corresponding to candidates 1 to 25. Such a punch is a *mark*. A particular ballot may have more than one mark, since a particular committee may have more than one vacant position (i.e., there may be more than one vote allowed to each voter on each ballot).

An *election package* consists of one ballot for each committee. Each eligible voter receives one and only one election package, which is to be marked and returned for counting.

Specifications: Prior to counting the ballots, the program must read certain preliminary information concerning the election. For each committee election the program must be informed as to:

1. The name of the committee
2. The number of candidates
3. The number of marks permitted (i.e., "vote for three" means three marks are allowed)

A rough flowchart is:

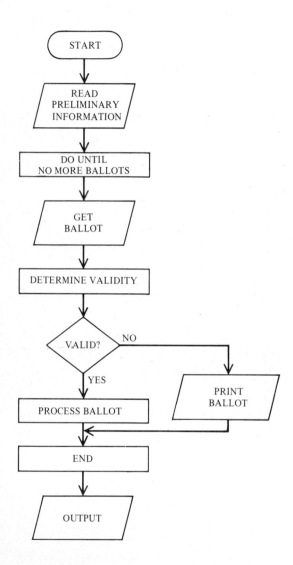

DETERMINE VALIDITY:

1. Check election name (columns 61 to 80). If name is found, then go to step 2.
2. Check all marks (columns 21 to 45) to see if all are either a minus sign or an empty space. If OK, then go to step 3.

3. Check that no mark occurs after the last candidate. If OK then go to step 4.
4. Count the number of marks. If the total is less than or equal to the number of marks permitted, then the ballot is valid.

If any test fails, then the ballot is invalid.

PROCESS BALLOT: This consists of tallying the marks in some sort of array, probably 25 × 10.

OUTPUT: This consists of printing the tallies.

Typical output for three committees named PPC, SAB, TENURE

CANDIDATE

NUMBER	PPC	SAB	TENURE
1	5	3	9
2	2	2	2
3	6	8	3
4	7	7	5
5	9	1	8
6	1	0	7
7		4	2
8		0	5
9		0	
10		8	

THERE WERE 50 VALID BALLOTS

THERE WERE 4 INVALID BALLOTS AND THESE ARE REPRINTED
ON PREVIOUS PAGE

If there are no invalid ballots, then the last line can be left unprinted. The sample output has 10 rows of tallies, since SAB has 10 candidates. Provision should be made for printing any number of rows from a minimum of 2 to a maximum of 25 depending on the maximum number of candidates for any committee.

2.9 The student must *draw a HIPO diagram* for the following problem:

The following set of rules defines a two-player card game (similar to three-card poker). You are to design a computer program which (1) deals two hands (using a random-number generator), (2) determines the winner and class of hand, and (3) computes the estimated probability of winning or ties for each class of hand assuming N simulated games.

Rules for card game

1. There are two players, A and B.
2. The deck contains 52 cards in 4 suits—diamonds, clubs, hearts, and spades—numbered $2, 3, \ldots, 10, J, K, A$ in ascending order.
3. Each player is dealt three cards face up, and the winner is determined.
4. The highest first class of hand is a FLUSH, which is three cards all of the same suit. The highest FLUSH is Q, K, A all of the same suit.
5. The second class of hand is a STRAIGHT, which is any three cards in sequence. The highest STRAIGHT is Q, K, A not all of the same suit.
6. The third class of hand is 3-OF-A-KIND, which is all three cards of the same number. The highest 3-OF-A-KIND hand is A, A, A.
7. The fourth class of hand is a PAIR, which is two cards of the same number. The highest PAIR is A, A, K.
8. The fifth class of hand is NOPAIR, which is all hands not in classes 1 to 4. The highest NOPAIR hand is A, K, J.
9. If players have different-class hands, the highest class wins. If the classes are equal, the higher hand wins, but equal hands represent a tie.

2.10 Draw a high-level flowchart for Prob. 2.9.

2.11 Write a pseudo-code version of Prob. 2.9.

2.12 The concept of "hiding" is one of the important beneficial properties of a top-down design. By hiding we mean that the implementation of a task specified at a higher level is not determined, i.e., it is hidden, until the task is encountered at a lower level in the design. Give three examples of this concept and explain.

2.13 For the program designs given in the accompanying illustration,

    (*a*) If the given design is a control-structure graph, write the equivalent pseudo-code.

    (*b*) If the given design is pseudo-code, draw the equivalent graph.

    (*c*) State whether the design is structured and explain why or why not.

    (*d*) Is there a unique transformation from pseudo-code to flowgraphs and vice versa? Explain.

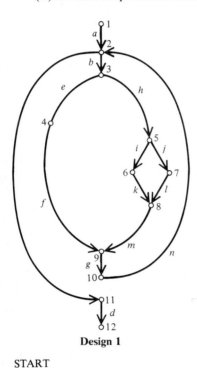

Design 1

Design 3

```
START
INPUT X, N
DIMENSION A(N), F(N)
DO I = 1 TO N
    INPUT F(I)
END
K = 0
DO WHILE K < N
    A(K) = 0
    DO J = 1 TO N − KA
    (K) = A(K) + F(J)*F(J + K)/(N − K + 1)
    END
    PRINT (K * X, A(K))
    K = K + 1
END
STOP
```

Design 2

2.14 Draw a control graph for the following pseudo-code structures and discuss the result.

Structure 1	Structure 2	Structure 3
DO I = 1 to 100	DO WHILE Z > 0	I = 0
. . . .	. . . .	LOOP:
. . . .	. . . .	. . . .
. . . .	. . . .	. . . .
END DO	END DO	. . . .
		I = I + 1
		IF I > 10
		THEN GO TO END
		ELSE GO TO LOOP
		END IF
		END:

2.15 Write a data flowgraph for the following examples;
   (*a*) Problem 2.1   (*b*) Problem 2.3
   (*c*) Problem 2.4   (*d*) Problem 2.5
   (*e*) Problem 2.8   (*f*) Problem 2.9
   (*g*) Problem 2.13

2.16 Compare the advantages and disadvantages of using data flowgraphs, HIPO diagrams, high-level flowcharts, and pseudo-code as the design-representation technique for the example studied in Prob. 2.15.

2.17 The documentation for a large software design can become voluminous. One can estimate the size of such documentation if the HIPO method is to be used, on the basis of the following assumptions:
1. Let N be the number of higher-level-language instructions.
2. Assume that one H diagram is to be drawn for the entire system and one IPO diagram for every rectangle in the H diagram, yielding a total of D diagrams.
3. Let M be the number of modules, and fix the average module size at 50 statements.
4. Plot M versus N.
5. The average number of levels (the depth) of the H diagram is denoted by L.
6. Assume as a lower bound that each level of the H diagram has on the average three rectangles, and plot D versus N.
7. Assume as an upper bound that each level of the H diagram has 10 rectangles on the average, and plot D versus N.
   Comment on the results.

2.18 A decision has been made to include a microprocessor to adjust the electronic ignition system of an automobile as an aid in improving the gas mileage. Since the basic processor will be present, we wish to design as an accessory package the following additional functions:
1. Antiskid braking and brake monitoring
2. Vehicle and passenger security—doors and seatbelts
3. Safety and performance monitoring—lights; fuel; water temperature; oil pressure and temperature; electrical system voltage and current; and gas, water, and oil level
4. Convenience items—digital calendar, alarm, clock, trip mileage, speed monitors, speed controls, miles-per-gallon meter and computation, and calculator
   (*a*) Draw a top- (first-) level H diagram for the full system (including ignition function, as well as functions 1 to 4.
   (*b*) Draw a set of second-level H diagrams for the functions of part *a*.
   (*c*) Draw an input-process-output diagram for the electronic ignition function of the system.
   (*d*) Repeat part *c* for the vehicle and passenger security module.

2.19 Assume that one has only SEQUENCE and DO WHILE control structures. How would one use these to perform an IF THEN ELSE operation?

2.20 Assume that one has only SEQUENCE and IF THEN ELSE control structures. How would one use these to perform a DO WHILE operation?

2.21 Consider how you can apply the principles of defensive programming to a specific example. Prepare a list of specific features you would include for the examples of:

(*a*) Problem 2.3
(*b*) Problem 2.4
(*c*) Problem 2.18

2.22 Careful reading of the pseudo-code given in Table 2.5 reveals an error. Can you find it? Since Table 2.5 is an exact replica of the example given in Fairley (1976), how do you think the error occurred?

2.23 Do the flowchart of Fig. 2.5*b* and the listing of Table 2.4 agree? If not, what is the difference? Does it matter? What should be changed (if anything), and how?

2.24 Notice that in order to set the value of C in the flowchart of Fig. 2.5*b* we have used three consecutive IF statements. Is there any way to set the value of C via a single expression? If so, explain how. Is it advisable to change the design, or to leave it as given in Fig. 2.5*b* and Table 2.4?

2.25 You are faced with the following hypothetical (but only partially unrealistic) choice. You must make significant modifications to an existing piece of software. You are offered *only two* of the three following items: (1) the program specification, (2) the detailed program design (prose description plus some kind of design representation), and (3) a listing of the source code including a modest number of comments. Which two would you choose? Why? How would you proceed? Does any situation similar to this ever happen in practice?

2.26 Compare at least four languages from the following viewpoints:

(*a*) Ease of structured programming
(*b*) Portability of the language
(*c*) Ease of learning the language
(*d*) Special language features

Typical languages to choose from include Pascal, PL/1, Ada, Fortran 77, C, Modula 2, Ratfor, and Extended Basic.

2.27 Take a program fragment that can be written equally well in assembly language (AL) or a higher-level language (HLL). Write the AL and HLL versions.

(*a*) Analyze and compare the object-code versions of both programs.
(*b*) Compare the memory size of both programs.
(*c*) Test the running time of both programs.

2.28 Repeat Prob. 2.27 for an example in which an AL program is significantly smaller or runs faster than an HLL program. Can the methods given in Table 2.25 be used to speed up the HLL version?

2.29 Draw a flowchart for the following two pseudo-code programs:

(*a*) Program 1:
```
START
IF P THEN
        WHILE q DO
                F
        END DO
    ELSE
        BLOCK
            g
            n
        END BLOCK
END IF
STOP
```
(*b*) Program 2: Use the pseudo-code given in Table 2.5.

2.30 (Taken from Mills, 1976)

The accompanying flowchart represents a nonstructured program:

(*a*) Explain why it is nonstructured.

(*b*) Devise an equivalent structured program.

(*c*) Did you use "flags" in part *b*? If not, redesign with flags; if so, redesign without flags.

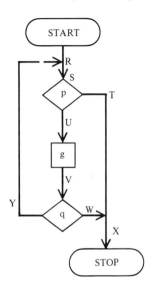

2.31 The student is to select a problem, write a set of specifications (prose), and design the program (HIPO and/or flowchart and/or pseudo-code). Devise a design change and *estimate* how difficult the change will be. Do not carry out the design change.

2.32 Each student is to exchange the problem, specification, design, and design change prepared for Prob. 2.31 with a neighboring student. Each student is then to change the design according to the design change and rate the quality of the design documentation. Discuss the results as a group without involving individual egos. (The instructor may also wish to do Prob. 2.31 and join with the class in the exchange of programs. The student who receives the instructor's program may then start the discussion.)

2.33 Each student is to design a program for a problem the instructor specifies. Pairs of students will then exchange programs and evaluate their fellow students' programs for clarity and design quality. Each two students will discuss the results. A group discussion will follow.

2.34 Make a survey of the programming tools available to you in your work environment. Tabulate the name of each tool and what it does, estimate how long it takes to learn, and describe its usefulness. Which tools do you presently use? Which do you plan to learn? What kind of tools do you lack?

2.35 Study the proof from Linger, Mills, and Witt in Sec. 2.4.7 and explain it.

2.36 Give an example of each type of module coupling defined in Sec. 2.6.2.

2.37 Give an example of each type of module strength defined in Sec. 2.6.2.

2.38 Comment critically on the following software systems and explain whether you would use a top-down or bottom-up design for each. Include in your evaluation factors of cost and risk, difficult portions of the task, time to first working model, etc.

(*a*) An upgraded air traffic control system for Kennedy Airport

(*b*) A Pascal compiler for an M6800 minicomputer system

(*c*) An expanded payroll system for an IBM 360/65 computer

(*d*) An advanced graphics editor to create special effects for an experimental three-dimensional, holographic version of the movie *Star Wars II*

2.39 The following pseudo-code program is to be studied; (see Yourdon, 1975, Prob. 27, p. 189):

LOOP: Set I to (START + FINISH)/2.
                If TABLE (I) = ITEM go to FOUND.
                If TABLE (I) < ITEM set START to (I + 1).
                If TABLE (I) > ITEM set FINISH to (I − 1).
                If (FINISH − START) > 1 go to LOOP.
                If TABLE (START) = ITEM go to FOUND.
                If TABLE (FINISH) = ITEM go to FOUND.
                Set variable FLAG to 0.
                Go to DONE.
FOUND: Set variable FLAG to 1.
DONE: Exit.

(*a*) Draw a structured flowchart.
(*b*) Is the program structured? Explain.
(*c*) If it is unstructured, draw a flowchart of a structured redesign.
(*d*) What does the program do?

2.40 Take one of your previous programs and evaluate it to see how well it follows the rules given in Table 2.23.

2.41 Write the pseudo-code for the following structured programs:

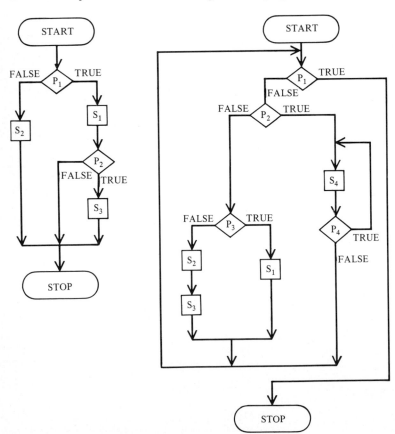

2.42 Write the pseudo-code for the programs of Figs. 2.14, 2.15, and 2.16.

2.43 (See Nicholls, 1975, p. 301)

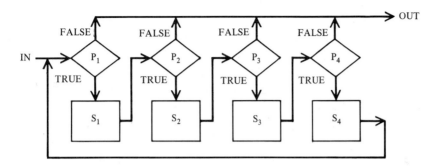

(*a*) Write the pseudo-code for accompanying flowchart.

(*b*) Redesign the program as a structured one and give the flowchart and pseudo-code.

(*c*) Repeat part *b* using a different technique.

(*d*) Compare and contrast the clarity and efficiency of the pseudo-codes and flowcharts of the designs in parts *a*, *b*, and *c*.

2.44 The following program structure written in pseudo-code contains two nested DO loops and a GO TO transfer out of the middle of the inner loop. The program as given is unstructured.

```
A: DO WHILE p = 0
      B: DO WHILE q = 0
            . . .
            . . .
            . . .
            IF R = 0 THEN GO TO C
            . . .
            . . .
            . . .
      END B
END A
      W = · · ·
      X = · · ·
C: Y = · · ·
      Z = · · ·
```

(*a*) Why is the pseudo-code unstructured?

(*b*) Give an equivalent structured design using flags.

(*c*) Give another design which uses BREAKs to replace the GO TO.

(*d*) Give another design which uses LEAVEs to replace the GO TO.

(*e*) Can you think of another structured design?

(*f*) Comment on the various designs with respect to clarity, length of the resulting compiled object program measured in machine language instructions, running time of the program, ease of coding, and ease of testing.

2.45 Your job is to be the software expert on a team designing a microprocessor-controlled home entertainment center. The center will include AM, FM, TV, records, microphones and TV cameras, an electric scanner which converts optically projected slide and movie images into "electronic images," an audio tape recorder, a videotape recorder, and video disks. The functions include play only, playback only, record only, play and record, timer for delayed playback or recording, a search mode, and an edit mode.

(*a*) Would you design the system top-down or bottom-up? Two-stage? What information would you need to make your decision?

(*b*) Would you make the timer function software or hardware? Explain.

(*c*) Draw an H diagram for this design.

(*d*) Draw an overview high-level IPO diagram for this design.

(*e*) Would you add a home computer option to the package? Explain.

2.46 (*a*) Draw a flowchart for the accompanying program written in pseudo-code.

(*b*) Is the given program structured or nonstructured? Explain why.

(*c*) If it is nonstructured,

(i) Show how to make it structured by using only three basic elements.

(ii) Write pseudo-code for the structured design.

(iii) Draw a flowchart for the structured design.

(*d*) There seems to be an obvious error (typographical?) in the logic of this problem which can be detected by thinking about how such a search program should work. Find the error, correct it, and repeat parts *a*, *b*, and *c*.

```
COMMENT:     PROGRAM SEARCHES FOR FIRST N REFERENCES TO A TOPIC IN AN
             INFORMATION RETRIEVAL SYSTEM WITH T TOTAL ENTRIES

             INPUT N
             INPUT KEYWORD(S) FOR TOPIC
             I = 0
             MATCH = 0
             DO WHILE I ≤ T
                   I = I + 1
                   IF WORD = KEYWORD
                         THEN MATCH = MATCH + 1
                         STORE IN BUFFER
                   END
                   IF MATCH = N
                         THEN GO TO OUTPUT
                   END
             END
             IF N = 0
                   THEN PRINT "NO MATCH"
OUTPUT:              ELSE CALL SUBROUTINE TO PRINT BUFFER INFORMATION
             END
```

2.47 In Prob. 2.46 problems can occur if unreasonable or bad values for N and KEYWORD are entered.

(*a*) Give examples of unreasonable values of these variables.

(*b*) What effects would these values have on the program?

(*c*) Show how to insert some defensive programming in the program to protect against such problems.

2.48 The Ashcroft-Manna technique can be used to convert nonstructured programs to structured programs. From the example given in the figure, which is a structured version of the flowchart given in Fig. 2.23(*a*), can you guess how the technique works? Explain. (See Tauseworthe, 1977, p. 140)

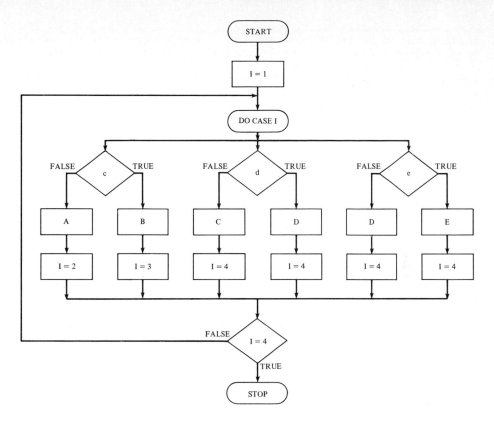

THREE

COMPLEXITY, STORAGE, AND PROCESSING-TIME ANALYSES

3.1 INTRODUCTION

The main thrust of the initial design phase is to propose one or more designs which seem to meet the project requirements and preliminary specifications. If few or no specifications exist, then preliminary ones must be formulated or augmented. In order to help evaluate the proposed preliminary design or to choose among multiple alternatives, we must answer some hard questions. Is the design feasible? Is it practical? Is it needed? What resources are required to complete the project? Should our organization actively pursue, reluctantly pursue, or simply participate in this project? What price should we charge?

The purpose of this chapter is to describe techniques which can be used to analyze preliminary designs and provide technical guidance for the managerial decisions which must be made. All these activities are an integral part of the preliminary design process.

One of the best definitions of software complexity this author is aware of is based upon expenditure of resources.[1] The following is a modified version:

> Complexity is a measure of the resources which must be expended in developing, maintaining, or using a software product. A large share of the resources are used to find errors, debug, and retest; thus, an associated measure of complexity is the number of software errors.

[1]Basili (1979).

In cataloging the needed resources, we must take a broad viewpoint. When the software interacts with the computer during operation, it utilizes both running time and memory space. Similarly, time and memory are expended during the testing phases of development. The management and engineering of the project require man-hours of time to supervise, comprehend, design, code, test, maintain, and change the software. Other items which must be considered are (1) the number of interfaces; (2) the scope of support software;[1] (3) the amount of reused code modules; (4) the required travel expenses; (5) the extent of secretarial and technical publications support; and (6) other environmental and overhead factors relating to support of personnel and system hardware.

The dynamics of software development and the concomitant resource expenditures are difficult to analyze and quantify. Only a few of the resource requirements discussed above have been sufficiently well studied for quantitative metrics to exist. We will focus our attention on those areas for which analysis and estimation techniques exist, namely, development man-hours, program running time, and storage requirements. Estimates of the number of test hours needed during development will be treated in Chap. 4, and more detailed estimation of man-hours is discussed in Chap. 6. Few formal analytical techniques exist for estimation of program running time and storage requirements. Experimental measurements and ad hoc analysis methods are used in practice and will be discussed in Secs. 3.3 and 3.4.

3.1.1 Analysis versus Software-Development Stage

The various phases of the software-development cycle have been defined in Chaps. 1 and 2 (see Table 1.4 and Fig. 2.1). They are repeated in Fig. 3.1 in a different format and in more detail. This development cycle was portrayed as the typical one for a large hardware-software (-operator) system which is to be used by the buyer and produced under contract by the seller. In many large military or industrial organizations, the situation is even more complex in that the buyer is not the end user but only the agent for the end user. Another important difference is that many in-house development projects do not go through a formal contracting phase. However, there are planning conferences, decision meetings, definition memos, management decisions, etc., which play a similar role. Also, in many small development projects, several steps are combined and the development process is more streamlined.

Consideration of storage, complexity, and processing time may or may not enter into the conceptualization phase. Suppose we were exploring the possibility of entering the entire contents of the Library of Congress into a computer data base for use in a large information retrieval system. Clearly the first question that would occur is, Can it all fit in a reasonable storage area? Thus, a preliminary

---

[1]Support software includes assemblers, interpreters, compilers, operating systems, maintenance programs, editors, debuggers, and other utility software.

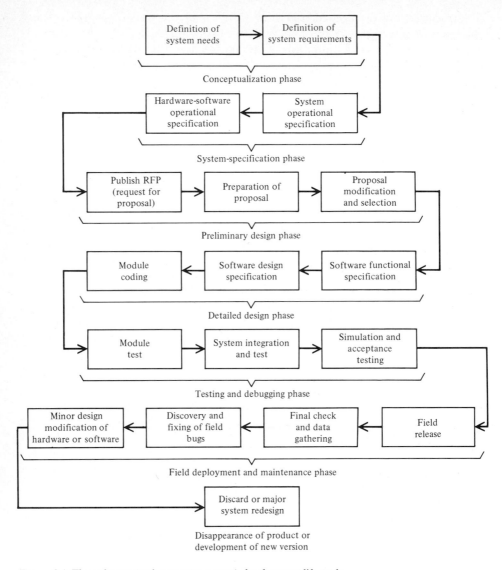

Figure 3.1 The software (and computer system) development life cycle.

storage analysis would be a key feature of the conceptualization phase. Conversely, imagine that we were considering the design of an information retrieval system for a research library containing 10,000 books and reports. If we knew of other, similar-sized systems which had been implemented in the past on medium-sized computer systems without major problems, then an analysis of storage requirements would probably wait until the system-specification phase. Actually, implicit in this latter example is an analysis and comparison of complexity. The analyst observes that the proposed system is of the same order of complexity as other, previous systems and thus concludes that it can be implemented with roughly the same kind of resources that the previous designs have required.

Complexity, storage, and processing time must be specified in both the preliminary and detailed design phases. In the testing and debugging phases we have an opportunity to observe and measure the storage and processing times which are being achieved, and to compare them with the initial estimates. Gross disagreements between predictions and measurements might be due to mistakes or inaccuracies of the estimation procedure, more or fewer design problems than expected, or large deviations from the design philosophy. In all such cases the reasons for the discrepancy should be studied and resolved in order to improve the analysis technique so it is more accurate in the future, or to correct the design step which has gone astray.

During simulation testing and field deployment we can continue our comparisons of predicted memory size and processing time with the actual measured quantities. This is the first time we will be able to observe whether these estimates have been reasonable. If we have made too low an estimate of the problem complexity, then the field-deployed system may experience a shortage of memory or too long a processing time in certain modes.

Another important measure of operational performance is the operational availability of the software, which is discussed in Chap. 5.

3.1.2 Need for Quantitative Measures

Complexity measures are generally intermediate values which are ultimately multiplied by appropriate conversion factors to yield the desired quantities (e.g., man-hours, seconds, bytes, etc.). Thus, it is unlikely that we will see a specification with regard to the complexity of a system. However, one of the first steps in preliminary design is to form an intuitive feeling for the complexity of the problem and how it compares with other problems for which the analyst may have some data. In most cases we will also compute complexity in the design phase and compare the calculation with the initial intuitive estimate.

In the discussions above we have implied that complexity is to be calculated, appropriate multiplication factors applied, and the results compared to see if we meet specifications. This is, of course, an important use of these techniques. However, in other cases we are evaluating competitive designs and are most interested in ranking the different designs with respect to several attributes and variables prior to a trade-off study. In such a case, we also need a quantitative analysis procedure; however, it need not correlate exactly with desired end results. What it must do is accurately rank the competitive designs and give a good estimate of the relative "distance" between the rankings.

Other uses of complexity measures are:

1. As a rank of the difficulty of various software modules to be used along with other factors in the assignment of personnel
2. In the case of module complexity, as a guide to judge whether subdivision of a complex module is warranted

3. As a direct measure of progress and an indirect measure of quality during the various phases of development
4. As an aid in normalizing data used in retrospective studies of past development projects.

Section 3.2 discusses complexity measures which relate to development man-hours and initial and final error content. Sections 3.3 and 3.4 treat estimates of processing time and storage requirements.

3.2 COMPLEXITY MEASURES

3.2.1 Types of Complexity Measures

Whenever one is introduced to a computer systems problem, as with most other large-scale problems, one of the first steps in the solution is to gauge its complexity. Generally this is done in some sort of "gestalt" (overall) way by comparing and contrasting the given problem with others which have been solved or were abandoned because of special difficulty. One tries to judge whether this is a task for a single designer for 1 day, 1 week, 1 month, or 1 year. Perhaps it is a team task which will involve many man-years. Other questions to be asked concern what kind and size of computer will be needed; what the most appropriate programming language might be; what memory size is required (for instructions and data); and, given the computer speed, what processing time will be required. An analyst's success in performing a gestalt estimate depends on how well the problem can be described quantitatively, its similarity to other problems in past experience, the analyst's power of insight and intuition, and luck.

In actuality, we are interested in not just one measure of complexity but several. Clearly, some problems are more complex than others because of sheer physical bulk, or intricacy and sophistication, or a combination of these. Next, the algorithm chosen for solution of the problem will have its own inherent complexity. In a small problem the statement of the algorithm is essentially the design of the problem. However, in a large or challenging problem, the same algorithm can be implemented in more than one way, and we should consider the design complexity. We may be free to choose the language during design, or more often, because of the nature of the problem and the computer, we may have only one logical language choice. If, on the other hand, more than one language appears feasible, we will wish to consider the effect on complexity caused by language choice. Last, the end result of all these elements is software with a composite complexity.

Although we are really interested in the composite complexity, we desire an analytical procedure which will allow us to relate composite complexity to problem, algorithm, design, and language complexity. Furthermore, in a really complex problem, we will wish to decompose the problem into subproblems, functions, modules, etc., so as to aid in the analysis. If this is done, then it is important that the complexity measures for the subparts of the problem be amenable to a tractable combinatorial analysis to yield the entire system measure.

Unfortunately, complexity theory has not yet advanced to the stage where measures for each of the various types of complexity exist. Furthermore, there is no common basis for the various metrics, much less any combinatorial technique to relate them. The best we can do in the remainder of this chapter is to focus on *program* complexity and its correlation with resource utilization (and also running-time and storage requirements analyses). The reader must appreciate that there is still much research in progress in this area. Also, the techniques which are discussed in the later sections of this chapter are relatively new to the field. A recent survey article on complexity lists over 60 techniques which have appeared in the literature.[1] Belady, in his survey, classified methods as being informal (which we call *heuristic*) methods, counts, probabilistic methods, and empirical methods. We will discuss a few examples of each method and focus in depth on the probabilistic method.

3.2.2 Heuristic Measures of Complexity

Whenever one is faced with a difficult analytical problem, it is useful to explore what is known about the problem on the basis of experience or intuition. We should also ponder what kind of analysis is required and what practical uses such computations serve. Often such an approach will suggest approximate techniques of analysis. Such approximations may not be wholly satisfactory, but will provide a starting point for later work and may serve as an initial approach.

One of the first problems one encounters when trying to analyze complexity is how to deal with the notions of bulk and sophistication. For example, a program might have huge arrays, which increase vastly the necessary storage. However, does the size of these arrays also influence the processing, the design, and the coding time? In the case of processing time, the effect of a large array is dependent on its use in the program (and perhaps on the processor architecture).

If we are performing a mathematical computation, such as the inversion of a matrix (and the array is the matrix), then clearly the processing time is related to the size of the matrix. The processing time is easily predictable on the basis of the matrix-inversion algorithm to be used. Similarly, if the array is a list to be searched, then the search time is a function of the type of search used—a well-studied problem in the computer literature.

Last, we consider a large file containing data about many individuals. Suppose the data for a single individual have to be retrieved and processed. In such a case the size of the array will affect the search time but have little effect on the processing time.

The conclusion is that the effect of bulk on processing time may vary considerably, but is usually calculable via analysis of the algorithm used. The effect of bulk on complexity is somewhat more difficult to describe.

---

[1]Belady (1979).

As an example, let us return to the problem of inverting a matrix. Clearly, both the processing time and storage are functions of the size of the array which contains the matrix; however, does complexity also vary with array size?

We now consider some of the quantities for which complexity serves as an intermediate measure: development man-hours, number of errors, and number of tests. Continuing with our example, array size will not affect the number of design man-hours. Processing of the array will be handled by program loops, and array size is merely the upper limit of the loop variable. However, the number of errors and the test time will be related to the number of array coefficients.

The above examples were chosen purposely to correspond to situations where intuition immediately suggests analysis techniques. We now explore an approach to complexity classification based upon our knowledge of natural languages (e.g., English, Dutch, or Hebrew).

In discussing the various types of complexity which are important in program development, the literary analogy given in Table 3.1 is useful. The lowest level of complexity relates to the length or bulk of the work. At the next level we focus on the complexity of language and syntax the author uses. In the following sections of this chapter, we will relate this level of program complexity to the operator-plus-operand count. The structural complexity of a program will be studied by constructing a control graph of the program and utilizing a formula from graph theory that calculates the graph cyclomatic complexity. Last, a summary of some of the results that have been obtained in the literature on algorithmic complexity will conclude our discussion.

3.2.3 Instruction Counts

The classical technique used to estimate program complexity is that of instruction counts. This technique is widely employed, but is often not as good a measure of complexity as we would like. Furthermore, it is often difficult to estimate accurately the number of instructions at the beginning of a design. Instruction counts are widely used to predict development man-hours, and the latter are used to predict development costs. This subject is treated in depth in Chap. 6.

Table 3.1 Types of Complexity

Type	Literary measure	Software measure
1. Size or bulk	Number of book pages	Number of instructions
2. Difficulty of text	Author's style (e.g., James Joyce vs. Winston Churchill)	Operators plus operands
3. Structural	Flashbacks and mingled subplots	Graph properties of control structure
4. Intellectual	Subject matter (e.g., relativity vs. woodworking)	Algorithmic difficulty

Table 3.2 Expansion of higher-level language instructions

Source language	Object language	Expansion factor
Simple assembly language	Machine language	1:1
Advanced macro assembler	Machine language	1.2:1 to 1.5:1
Fortran	Machine language	4:1 to 6:1
PL/1	Machine language	4:1 to 10:1

Initially, one might suppose that instruction counts are primarily a measure of bulk. If the count is in terms of the number of higher-level-language instructions, this is essentially true. However, suppose we choose to state the instruction count in terms of the number of machine language instructions. If most machine language instructions for the machine in question consist of one operator and one operand, then the count is related to the operator-operand count.

In carrying out instruction counts, it is often useful to know how many machine language instructions a line of higher-level language will produce when compiled. Of course, this depends on the programmer and the problem. One can always take data on previous programs and obtain an accurate estimate. As a working tool, the conversion factor given in Table 3.2 will be used in this book.

3.2.4 A Statistical Approach to Program Complexity

Introduction In the early 1970s investigators began to take a statistical approach to program complexity. The pioneering work in this area was that of the late Professor Maurice Halstead of Purdue University. He focused on the total number of operators and operands in a program as the measure of complexity, developed estimator formulas for program complexity, and related his results to the number of man-hours and errors. Halstead's early writing used the term *software physics* to describe his work, but this was later changed to *software science*[1] to avoid confusion with another author's use of the same title for work on computer system performance metrics. Many of Halstead's students and colleagues independently corroborated his work;[2] however, much of his mathematical development was motivated by intuition.

Subsequently, Professor Arthur Laemmel of the Polytechnic Institute of New York and the author were successful in showing that Halstead's work was related to more basic ideas rooted in statistical communication theory, namely, Zipf's laws of natural languages and Shannon's information theory.[3] Laemmel and Shooman developed improved estimator formulas and showed that two different probabilistic models for program generation also lead to their results. The narrative and mathematical development which follow interweave the various

---

[1] Halstead (1977*a*).
[2] Halstead (1977*a*), p. xii.
[3] Shooman and Laemmel (1977); Laemmel and Shooman (1977); and Shooman (1979*a*).

work in this area, and the reader who wishes to trace individual contributions is referred to the cited references.

Operator-operand length The statistical approach is based on the viewpoint that the complexity of the program is related to the number of operators and operands. *Operators* are syntactical elements such as $+, -, >, <$, IF THEN ELSE, DO WHILE, etc. *Operands* are the quantities which receive the action of the operators, namely, variables and constants. (Note: Comments, declarations, and other nonexecutable statements are not counted.) Of course, once we have a program, it is simple but time-consuming to count the operators and operands (manually or with a "parserlike" program). Thus, this technique might be useful for retrospective studies of the features of past programs; however, it will not help us in estimating program complexity at the early design stages.

However, if we look further into the matter, we find that we can derive simple estimation formulas if we concentrate on the number of distinct occurrences (*types*) of operators and operands rather than their total count. For example, in the short Fortran program given in Table 2.9 we have:

1. Thirteen distinct operators (operator types): READ, FORMAT, $=$, $/, ( )$, $+$, $-$, .LT., IF, GO TO, WRITE, STOP, and END.
2. Twenty-four total operators: five $=$; three $/$; two each of $( )$, $-$, .LT., IF, and GO TO; and one each of the other six.
3. Eleven distinct operands (operand types): X, F10.5, A, 2, B, C, 10.E $-$ 6, 0, and the labels 1, 2, and 3.
4. Twenty-five total operands: five each of A and C; four B; three X; two 2; and one each of the other six.

The program contains examples of most operator and operand classes, except for character strings. Character-string variables must also be counted, as must character-string constants (see Table 2.4, lines 80 and 95, each of which contains one string constant, and lines 130 and 140, which contain four string constants).

Our initial objective is to learn how to estimate the number of operator and operand types during the preliminary design stage and, via an estimator formula (to be derived shortly), to predict the total program operator-operand length.

Upon further reflection, we can state that the number of operand types is simply the sum of the number of input variables, the number of output variables, the number of intermediate variables, and the number of constants. Thus, from an initial analysis of the requirements, preliminary specifications, and early design, we should be able to estimate the number of operand types.

Similarly, the number of operator types can be estimated. In PL/1, for example, the number of operator types is the sum of the number of arithmetic operators, the number of comparison operators, the number of built-in functions, and the number of keywords. Not every programmer knows or uses all the PL/1 keywords, but we can still estimate the number of operator types that might be used, on the basis of the initial design and anticipated algorithms.

It is a remarkable fact that there are statistical laws which relate the total number of occurrences of operators and operands to the number of distinct operator and operand types. Such laws allow us to estimate the total operator-plus-operand length on the basis of an estimate of the number of distinct types. Laws of this nature were first studied by Zipf in the 1930s in connection with natural languages.[1]

3.2.5 Zipf's Laws of Natural Language

Introduction Many investigators have studied ways of describing the structure of computer languages. The task is a formidable one on account of the seemingly infinite variety of programs we can write with a computer language. Much can be learned about this problem by studying the analogous and even more complex problem of describing the structure of a written or spoken natural language. A set of analogies between the elements of natural and computer languages is given in Table 3.3.

Inspection of Table 3.3 shows that there is overall agreement between natural and computer languages in that they are built up from elements according to rules of construction. An exact analogy exists if we describe the natural language by using Chomsky's grammar[2] and the computer language by using BNF form,[3] which is essentially an adaptation of Chomsky's work. However, it will not be necessary for us to use such formal methods. We need only consider words, statements, operators, and operands in the derivation of length formulas, and each of these terms is easy to define and deal with.

The reader may comment that like apples and oranges, natural and computer languages are really different things that cannot be compared. The following hypothetical situation can be used to refute this argument. Suppose we consider a programmer who understands a particular computer language and give him or her a complete listing, with comments and documentation, of a computer program. We instruct our programmer to study the computer program to the point where it is understood and then to write a memorandum documenting the program. The memorandum is to be in good English containing paragraphs, complete sentences, and algorithms expressed as sequences of steps without mathematical notation. This will produce a report that another programmer can read and hand-process (perhaps with the aid of a nonprogrammable calculator) to produce an output. In principle, the report and the computer program will be equivalent. Thus, any studies one might make of the elements of the computer program will have to bear a close resemblance to the equivalent elements of the report.

Much of our effort will be centered on the counting of the number of times, n_r, particular types occur in a sample of n tokens. We have used the subscript r because in our comparison of word types we will order the types in terms of their

---

[1] Zipf (1965); Zipf (1949).
[2] Chomsky (1965).
[3] Donovan (1972), Chap. 7.

Table 3.3 Analogies between elements of natural and computer languages

Natural literature (or dialog)	Computer programs (software)
Book, magazine, or speech	Software system
Chapter, article, conversation	Program
Paragraph, section	Subprogram, module
(?)	Loop
Sentence	Statement
Phrase, clause	Expression
Subject	(?)
Predicate	(?)
Word	Keyword or symbol
Noun	Operand
Adjective, adverb	(?)
Verb	Operator
Auxiliary verb	(?)
Preposition, conjunction	(?)
Pronoun	(?)
Article	(?)

occurrence frequency and assign ranks. The most frequently occurring type will be assigned rank 1, the second most frequent type rank 2, etc. If we assume there are t word types in our sample of n tokens, then clearly

$$\sum_{r=1}^{t} n_r = n \tag{3.1}$$

The absolute frequency of occurrence for type r is n_r; however, the relative frequency of occurrence f_r is simply n_r/n.

Zipf studied the relationship between frequency of occurrence n_r and rank r for words from English, Chinese, and the Latin of Plautus. The resulting data are given in Fig. 3.2, where Zipf plotted the logarithm to base 10 of n_r on the abcissa and the logarithm of r on the ordinate. Note that the data for English are an excellent fit to a straight line, as are the data for Latin for ranks larger than 10. If we had plotted log f_r on the abcissa in Fig. 3.2, we would have obtained the same result shifted by the scale factor n. The straightness of such plots on log-log paper is an empirical justification (we shall later discuss theoretical justifications) for the relationship

$$f_r r^a = \text{constant} = c \tag{3.2}$$

Careful study of Zipf's data and those of others shows that the constant a (the slope on log-log paper) is approximately 1. Thus, we arrive at the simple relationship generally called Zipf's first law:

$$f_r r = c \tag{3.3}$$

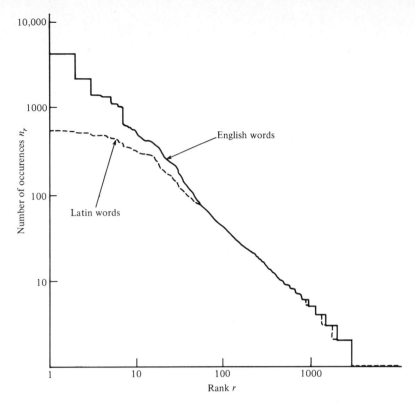

Figure 3.2 Occurrence frequency versus rank for English and Latin words. *(From Zipf, 1965, Plate IV)*

which can also be written in the form

$$n_r = \frac{cn}{r} \tag{3.4}$$

Inspection of Eq. (3.4) reveals that the constant c can be interpreted as the relative frequency of the rank-1 word type. There are some theoretical and practical problems with this obvious interpretation. In a practical sense, if we use the ratio of n_1/n to determine the constant c, we will probably obtain a poorer estimate of c than could be obtained from the y axis intercept of the straight line fitted to the data on log-log paper. This is so because Zipf's law holds less well at times for the lowest ranks.

We now examine the frequency distribution to see if we can interpret it as a probability distribution, p_r. If we compute the sum of the individual p_r terms, we obtain

$$\sum_{r=1}^{t} p_r = \sum_{r=1}^{t} f_r = \sum_{r=1}^{t} \frac{n_r}{n} \tag{3.5}$$

Substituting Eq. (3.1) into Eq. (3.5) yields

$$\sum_{r=1}^{t} p_r = 1 \tag{3.6}$$

as of course it should (cf. the fundamental definition of probability).

Derivation of length equation We can obtain other fundamental relations via the summation of Zipf's first law. If we sum both sides of Eq. (3.4) we get a helpful result:

$$\sum_{r=1}^{t} n_r = cn \sum_{r=1}^{t} \frac{1}{r} \tag{3.7}$$

The summation of the series $1/r$ is given as follows:[1]

$$\sum_{r=1}^{t} \frac{1}{r} = 0.5772 + \ln t + \frac{1}{2t} - \frac{1}{12t(t+1)} \cdots \tag{3.8}$$

Substitution of Eqs. (3.1) and (3.8) (retaining only two terms for modest-sized t) into Eq. (3.7) and rearrangement yields an expression for the constant c in terms of t.

$$c \approx \frac{1}{0.5772 + \ln t} \tag{3.9}$$

If we know the number of types, t, we can use Eq. (3.9) to estimate c.

We notice in Eq. (3.9) that as t increases, c decreases. From Eq. (3.4) $f_1 = c$; thus, the frequency of the first rank (and all the other ranks) changes with c, which in turn varies with t. Normally we would expect t to increase with n. However, if we think of our statistics as a sample and apply the relative-frequency interpretation of probability, we will expect f_r to approach finite values as the sample size (number of tokens, n) approaches infinity. The concept that p_1 is a function of sample size is contradictory if we assume random statistically independent tokens or if the n tokens represent an arbitrary slice from a larger work. However, if we require that the n tokens represent some cohesive unit (e.g., abstract, paragraph, chapter, or paper), then it is reasonable that the author's style and word probabilities will change with length.[2]

---

[1] Jolley (1961), p. 36, note 200, and p. 14, note 70. Note that the constant 0.5772 is called *Euler's constant.* See Courant (1951), vol. 1, pp. 381, 420.

[2] The theoretical problems lie in the application of the frequency definition of probability. This definition requires that probabilities of particular events approach a limit as the sample size becomes infinite. In the case of Zipf's law, as the token length of the sample increases, t increases and the distribution changes. Perhaps we can avoid this anomaly if we issue a written vocabulary sheet of t words and ask someone to write m articles, each n tokens long using only the issued vocabulary sheet. We then construct our sample with length m_n as the concatenation of all the articles. The resulting Zipf-law distribution should approach a stable limit as m_n goes to infinity. See also Pierce (1965), p. 245.

We can derive a different equation relating t and c by considering the behavior of Eq. (3.4) for the smallest rank, where $r_{max} = t$ (e.g., if there are 100 types, then the largest rank is obviously 100). In most cases the rarest type (largest rank) will occur only once; thus we assume $n_{r_{max}} = 1$. Substituting these values in Eq. (3.4) yields another interpretation for the constant c, that is, the ratio of types to tokens:[1]

$$c = \frac{t}{n} \qquad (3.10)$$

Equating Eq. (3.9) to Eq. (3.10) and solving for n yields the fundamental equation relating token length to number of types:

$$n = t(0.5772 + \ln t) \qquad (3.11)$$

We can illustrate the utility of Eq. (3.11) with the following example. Suppose we are told that a certain newspaper article contains 100 different word types. We can use Eq. (3.11) to estimate the length of the article. Substitution yields

$$n = 100(0.5772 + \ln 100) = 518 \text{ words long}$$

We will use this same equation and similar techniques to estimate program operator-operand length, later in this chapter. However, we must first continue our theoretical development of Zipf's laws and also prove that computer programs follow Zipf's laws.

Zipf's second law We can derive a second form of Zipf's law from the first form by making other assumptions about word behavior in the region where r is large.[2] We compute the derivative of n_r with respect to r for Eq. (3.4) and take its magnitude:

$$\left| \frac{dn_r}{dr} \right| = \left| \frac{-nc}{r^2} \right| = \frac{cn}{r^2} \qquad (3.12)$$

Eliminating r by substitution from Eq. (3.4) into Eq. (3.12) yields

$$\left| \frac{dn_r}{dr} \right| = \frac{n_r^2}{cn} \qquad (3.13)$$

In the tail of Zipf's law, there are generally several identical n_r values; thus there is a plateau of t_k types, each with the same n_r value, denoted by k, which are tied for the same rank. The curve becomes a staircase function, and we define the slope as the vertical decrement (r to $r + 1 = 1$) divided by the horizontal width t_k of the plateau of ties; thus

$$\left| \frac{dn_r}{dr} \right| = \frac{1}{t_k} \qquad (3.14)$$

In the tail we assume that $n_{r_{max}} = 1$ and $k = 1$, $n_{r_{max-1}} = 2$ and $k = 2$; thus in this

---

[1] Miller (1951); Pierce (1980).
[2] Laemmel and Rudner (1969), p. 4-4; Parker-Rhodes and Joyce (1956), p. 1308.

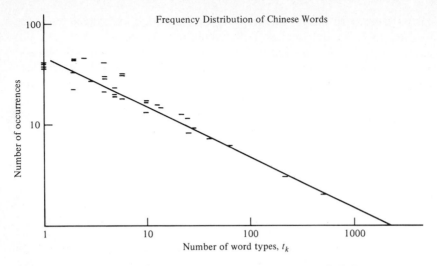

Figure 3.3 Experimental verification of Zipf's second law. *(From Zipf, 1965)*

region $n_r = k$ and substitution of $n_r = k$ into Eqs. (3.13) and (3.14) yields the second form of Zipf's law,

$$t_k = \frac{cn}{k^2} \qquad (3.15)$$

Experimental verification of Zipf's second law is given in Fig. 3.3, where the plot of $\log k$ versus $\log t_k$ yields a straight line with a slope of $-\frac{1}{2}$.

Derivation of the alternate length equation We can also derive a second set of basic equations by using the second law. Summing Eq. (3.15), we obtain the following:[1]

$$t = \sum_{k=1}^{n} \frac{cn}{k^2} \approx \sum_{k=1}^{\infty} \frac{cn}{k^2} = \frac{\pi^2}{6} cn \qquad (3.16)$$

Combining Eqs. (3.9) and (3.16) yields

$$n = \frac{6}{\pi^2}(0.5772 + \ln t)t \qquad (3.17)$$

Note that except for a factor of $6/\pi^2$ the results given in Eqs. (3.11) and (3.17) are identical. The occurrence of either $6/\pi^2 = 0.6079$ or unity as a coefficient in these equations arises because of the slightly different assumptions made concerning the behavior of Zipf's law for small ranks in the two derivations. The relative accuracy of the two equations will be discussed in Sec. 3.2.8.

---

[1]See the discussion of the Riemann zeta function in National Bureau of Standards (1964), p. 804.

Zipf-type laws applied to other phenomena Zipf's law (or Zipf-type laws) have been shown to apply to a wide variety of different phenomena:[1]

1. The population of the larger cities (even more, that of metropolitan districts) for every United States census since 1790 follows a Zipf-type law; also all cities of Europe (but not Great Britain, for unknown reasons).
2. If the constant a is equal to $1/2$, the law holds for the income of people in the United States (this is called Pareto's law).
3. The number of students attending a university (the data studied were for Harvard, MIT, and Princeton) from any state times the distance from the state is proportional to the population of the state.
4. The same law as in item 3 applies to the number of charge accounts at Jordan Marsh of Boston in various cities and towns of New England.
5. The "interchange" between the cities is proportional to the product of the populations divided by the distance between them. This applies to telephone calls, rail express packages, truck and passenger trips, and many other items.
6. Many different languages and language elements obey Zipf's law.

Thus, Zipf's law seems to hold for a wide variety of "organized" behavior, of both humans and machines.

3.2.6 Generalized Zipf Laws

Zipf's law in its simple form closely describes many different phenomena and leads to the rather simple and powerful theory developed in the preceding sections. In some cases, the experimental fit to Zipf's first law is only approximate and the ensuing theory can be thought of as a gross approximation. In such cases, two generalized forms of Zipf's laws can be used to yield a better fit between theory and data. The algebraic expressions and computations become more cumbersome; however, a computer program can be used to solve the computational problem. Parametric studies provide sensitivity information on how the results change as parameters vary, and the simple Zipf theory can still be used to provide insight into the results.

A generalized form of Zipf's law (suggested by Zipf and other authors) is of the form

$$p_r = \frac{n_r}{n} = \frac{C}{(r + A)^B} \tag{3.18}$$

We can easily see the role which the constants play in Eq. (3.18) by taking logarithms of both sides of the equation:

$$\ln p_r = \ln C - B \ln (r + A) \tag{3.19}$$

Clearly if $A = 0$ and $B = 1$ we obtain Zipf's first law. The constant B represents

---

[1] Zipf (1941); Zipf (1949); Goode and Machol (1957).

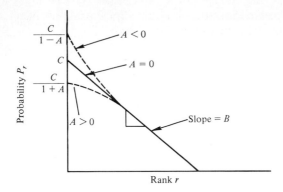

Figure 3.4 Role of coefficients A, B, and C in Eq. (3.18).

the slope of a straight line on log-log paper, and A is a "shift" parameter. For convenience we will call this the slope-shift form of Zipf's first law. The role of A can be illustrated if we set $B = 1$ and $r = 1$:

$$\ln p_1 = \ln C - \ln(1 + A) = \ln \frac{C}{1 + A} \tag{3.20}$$

If $A = 0$, then C is the frequency of the first rank, i.e., the y axis intercept. If $A = 0.1$, the intercept is about $0.9C$, and if $A = -0.1$ the intercept is about $1.1C$. Examination of Eq. (3.19) shows that for large r, the effect of A is negligible. These results are illustrated in Fig. 3.4, where we see that B allows us to match a slope other than unity and A adjusts for derivations from straight-line behavior for the initial ranks.

The physical meanings of the constants A, B, and C have been studied in linguistics,[1] and the following observations have been noted:

1. Values of B greater than unity occur in individuals who possess a limited vocabulary, such as young children.
2. Values of B less than unity are associated with large vocabularies, as, for example, in the writings of James Joyce or collections of writings by various authors in a newspaper of anthology.
3. Values of A greater than zero occur if the probability of the first-rank word is small, as is the case in English of words following *the*, or in a highly inflected language.
4. Values of A less than zero occur if the probability of the first word is large, as in the case of words following *of* (*the* being very frequent here).

In order to derive the modified basic equations for the slope-rank-shift form of the law, we will apply Eq. (3.6) to Eq. (3.18):

$$n = \sum_{r=1}^{t} n_r = Cn \sum_{r=1}^{t} \frac{1}{(r + A)^B} \tag{3.21}$$

[1]Miller (1951).

We can sum the series in Eq. (3.21) with the aid of the Euler-Maclaurin formula,[1] which relates a finite sum of a function to the integral of the function:[2]

$$
n = \left[\frac{12}{B^2 + 7B + 12} \right]^B
$$
$$
\times t^B \left[\frac{12A^2 + 6(B + 3)A + B^2 + 5B + 6}{12(B - 1)(A + 1)^{B+1}} \right. \tag{3.21a}
$$
$$
\left. - \frac{1}{(B - 1)(t + A)^{B-1}} \right]
$$

For the special case where $B \to 1$,

$$
n \to \frac{3}{5} t \left[\ln(t + A) - \ln(A + 1) + \frac{6A + 7}{12(A + 1)^2} \right] \tag{3.21b}
$$

and where $A = 0$

$$
n = \left[\frac{12}{B^2 + 7B + 12} \right]^B t^B \left[\frac{B^2 + 5B + 6}{12(B - 1)} - \frac{1}{(B - 1)t^{B-1}} \right] \tag{3.21c}
$$

Similarly one can show that

$$
cn = \left[\frac{12t}{B^2 + 7B + 12} \right]^B \tag{3.21d}
$$

$$
t_k = \frac{cn^{1/B}}{Bk^{(1+1/B)}} \tag{3.21e}
$$

$$
t = \frac{(B^2 + 7B + 12)(cn)^{1/B}}{12} \tag{3.21f}
$$

$$
\frac{t_k}{t} = \frac{12}{(B^2 + 7B + 12)k^{(1+1/B)}} \tag{3.21g}
$$

When we plot Zipf-law data, sometimes we find experimental results on log-log paper which look like straight-line segments with different slopes. (The reader who is familiar with the control system literature will notice the analogy with Bode plots.) Limiting our model to two piecewise linear segments (see Fig. 3.5), we obtain

$$
n_r = \begin{cases} \dfrac{C_1}{r^{B_1}} & 1 \le r \le D \\[2mm] \dfrac{C_2}{r^{B_2}} & D \le r \le t \end{cases} \tag{3.22}
$$

[1] Franklin (1964), p. 322.
[2] Laemmel and Shooman (1977).

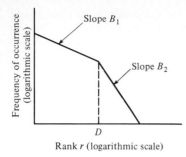

Figure 3.5 A two-slope, piecewise-linear generalization of Zipf's law.

and at the boundary the two expressions must match; thus

$$\frac{C_1}{D^{B_1}} = \frac{C_2}{D^{B_2}}$$

Again, by using the low-order terms in the Euler-Maclaurin formula, for the two segments we obtain each of the following:

$$n = \left(\frac{12t}{B_2^2 + 7B_2 + 12}\right)^{B_2}$$

$$\times \left[\frac{B_1^2 + 5B_1 + 6}{12(B_1 - 1)D^{B_2 - B_1}} - \frac{B_2 - B_1}{(B_1 - 1)(B_2 - 1)D^{B_2 - 1}} \right. \qquad (3.22a)$$

$$\left. - \frac{1}{(B_2 - 1)t^{B_2 - 1}} \right]$$

$$t_0 = \frac{12t}{B_2^2 + 7B_2 + 12} \qquad (3.23)$$

$$C_2 = t_0^{B_2} \qquad (3.24)$$

$$C_1 = n_1 = C_2/D^{B_2 - B_1} \qquad (3.25)$$

$$n_D = C_2/D^{B_2} \qquad (3.26)$$

Constructive models leading to Zipf's law In Sec. 3.2.5, we introduced Zipf's law as an experimental law based upon observation and heuristics. Many authors, notably Mandelbrot, have been able to derive Zipf's laws by assuming a model of how words are built up from letters and by applying a minimum-effort approach to the word lengths and frequencies.[1]

Another approach is to define a branching probabilistic process. The resulting linear graph model[2] can be used to derive a binomial distribution with one configuration, and a Zipf-law model with a different configuration.

[1] Mandelbrot (1954); Mandelbrot (1961); Cherry (1970); Good (1965), p. 70.
[2] Laemmel (1975); Laemmel and Shooman (1977).

For the details of these derivations, the reader is directed to the cited references. The importance of these results to our development is that the validity of Zipf's law is strengthened by these constructive models beyond the experimental evidence, which is strong enough in its own right.

3.2.7 Zipf's Laws Applied to Computer Languages

Introduction In Section 3.2.5 we began our discussion of the analogies between natural language and computer language. In essence, the analogy is close enough that we suspect at the outset that computer languages will obey one of the original or generalized forms of Zipf's law. Other convincing evidence would be the development of a stochastic model which generates computer programs and satisfies Zipf's law along the lines of Mandelbrot's work. In the final analysis, proof is dependent on how well the experimental data plotted on log-log paper fit Zipf's law and on the prediction accuracy of any formulas developed in the analysis. We explore each type of evidence in succession.

Experimental evidence We have examined a number of computer programs and always find that some form of Zipf's law seems to fit the data reasonably well. The types of programs studied[1] are listed in Table 3.4, and the Zipf plots for programs 1 and 3 in the table are given in Figs. 3.6 to 3.9. The Fibonacci program is now studied in more detail.

The listing of the PL/1 Fibonacci number program is given in Table 3.5.[2] The analysis of the number of operators and operands and their combined total is given in Tables 3.6 to 3.8. We have followed Halstead generally in our definition of operators and operands.[3] Basically, in PL/1, operators include keywords, comparison operators, comma, and colon. The operands include numerical and character-string variables and constants. Excluded from both lists are declare statements and comments. Labels are considered part of the GO TO statement; i.e., GO TO Label 1 is an operator. Labels which are not used are ignored, as are comments. Note that in this example a simple Zipf law fits operators and operands well (see Figs. 3.6 and 3.7); however, the combination of operators and operands is better fitted by the slope-shift form of Zipf's law (see Fig. 3.8), because of the curvature for small ranks.

The MIKBUG is an assembly language program that provides interfacing to a terminal and simple debugging for the M6800 microprocessor. Figure 3.9 shows the relations between the rank and the counts of operators (op codes) and operands (variable names and statement labels) and their total. In Fig. 3.9 the upper part of the operand plot is flattened, and the lower part of the operator

---

[1] Laemmel and Shooman (1977). Also see Fig. 1 in Zweiben and Halstead (1979), (Commemorative issue in memory of Dr. Maurice Halstead).

[2] The Fibonacci numbers $(F_0, F_1, \ldots, F_k)$ are defined so that each number is the sum of the preceding two, or $F_n = F_{n-1} + F_{n-2}$, where $F_0 \equiv 0, F_1 \equiv 1$.

[3] Halstead (1975).

Table 3.4 Experimental data on computer programs and Zipf's laws

Program	Distinct types	Total tokens
1. PL/1 Fibonacci numbers program—11 lines long		
a. Operators	12	31
b. Operands	9	24
c. Operators plus operands	21	55
2. PL/1 student grades program—27 lines long		
d. Operators	20	117
e. Operands	31	105
f. Operators plus operands	51	222
3. MIKBUG—executive program for the M6800 microprocessor		
g. Operators	25	190
h. Operands	62	132
i. Operators plus operands	87	322
4. PDP-11 assembly language programs		
j. Operators	39	1572
5. Variable names in three PL/1 programs		
k. Names, program X	50	370
l. Names, program Y	24	238
m. Names, program Z	34	239
6. Fortran statement types		
n. Sample M	40	200 K (statements)
o. Sample V	40	10 K (statements)

plot drops off more rapidly than the upper part. These two effects compensate each other, and the sum of the two is a better fit to Zipf's law than either one separately.

Conclusions On the basis of the data just discussed, studies of the other programs listed in Table 3.4, and our previously drawn analogies between computer and natural languages, we conclude that computer programs do follow Zipf's law and its extensions. More research is needed to draw detailed conclusions on whether there are any major exceptions or classes of programs which fit particular forms

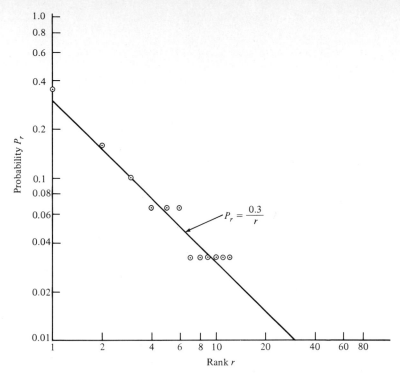

Figure 3.6 Zipf-law plot for operators of the PL/1 Fibonacci program.

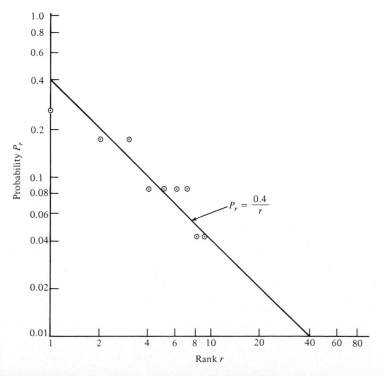

Figure 3.7 Zipf-law plot for operands of the PL/1 Fibonacci program.

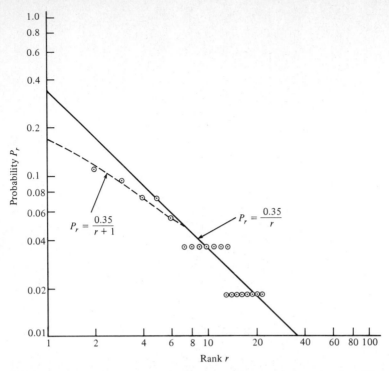

Figure 3.8 Zipf-law plot for combined operators and operands of the PL/1 Fibonacci program.

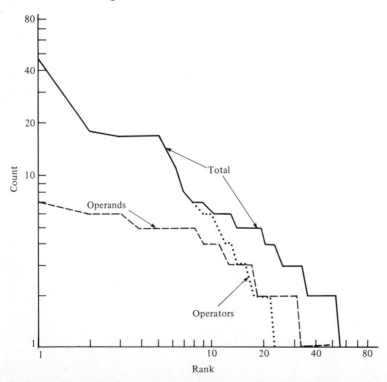

Figure 3.9 Relation between the rank and counts of operators, operands, and operators plus operands for the MIKBUG program.

Table 3.5 Listing of Fibonacci numbers: PL/1 program

FIBONACCI:	PROCEDURE; N = 2; GET LIST (PREV__F, LAST__F, LIMIT); PUT LIST (PREV__F, LAST__F);
REPEAT:	TEMP = LAST__F; LAST__F = LAST__F + PREV__F; PREV__F = TEMP; PUT LIST (LAST__F); N = N + 1; IF N < LIMIT THEN GOTO REPEAT; END FIBONACCI;

Source: Neuhold and Lawson (1971), p. 81.

Table 3.6 Rank-probability data for operators of the program given in Table 3.5

Rank r	Probability p_r	Symbol	Count
1	.35	;	11
2	.16	=	5
3	.10	,	3
4	.065	:	2
5	.065	PUT LIST	2
6	.065	+	2
7	.032	PROCEDURE	1
8	.032	GET LIST	1
9	.032	IF THEN	1
10	.032	<	1
11	.032	GO TO	1
12	.032	END	1
Total			31

Table 3.7 Rank-probability data for operands of the program given in Table 3.5

Rank r	Probability p_r	Symbol	Count
1	.25	LAST__F	6
2	.17	N	4
3	.17	PREV__F	4
4	.083	FIBONACCI	2
5	.083	LIMIT	2
6	.083	REPEAT	2
7	.083	TEMP	2
8	.042	2	1
9	.042	1	1
Total			24

Table 3.8 Rank-probability data for combined operators and operands of the program given in Table 3.5

Rank r	Probability p_r	Symbol	Count
1	.20	;	11
2	.11	LAST__F	6
3	.091	=	5
4	.073	N	4
5	.073	PREV__F	4
6	.055	,	3
7	.036	:	2
8	.036	PUT LIST	2
9	.036	+	2
10	.036	FIBONACCI	2
11	.036	LIMIT	2
12	.036	REPEAT	2
13	.036	TEMP	2
14	.018	PROCEDURE	1
15	.018	GET LIST	1
16	.018	IF THEN	1
17	.018	<	1
18	.018	GO TO	1
19	.018	END	1
20	.018	2	1
21	.018	1	1
Total			55

of the model. However, we can explore the accuracy of the equations for the constant c and the token length—see Eqs. (3.9) and (3.11)—using the data in Table 3.4 for program $1a$, b, and c and program $2f$.

In Table 3.9 a comparison is made for the four examples between the calculated value of c, the ratio n_1/n, and the abscissa intercept of the Zipf graph. The results are shown in the table. We can compare the variability of the three estimates of c by computing the standard deviation and dividing by the mean. The variabilities for $1a$, b, and c and $2f$ are 7.7 percent, 23 percent, 27 percent, and 21.8 percent.

Similarly, we can calculate the value of token length from the equation and compare it with the actual value. The agreement between the values for the four examples is 18.3 percent, 4.2 percent, 38.2 percent, and 3.6 percent.

The numerical agreement of these above examples is about 25 percent overall, which is quite reasonable and certainly accurate enough for estimation purposes during proposal and early design phases.

We conclude our discussion with two theoretical models that further show that Zipf's law describes the probability distribution of operators and operands in a computer language. The first theoretical model is that of a binary palindrome generator.

Table 3.9 Comparison of calculated versus experimental values of c and n

Data	t	Constant c			Length n	
		Calculated $\dfrac{1}{0.5772 + \ln t}$	$c = p_1 = \dfrac{n_1}{n}$	Graph Intercept	Calculated $t(0.5772 + \ln t)$	Data n
$1a$	12	0.33	0.35	0.3	36.7	31
$1b$	9	0.36	0.25	0.4	25	24
$1c$	21	0.28	0.20	0.35	76	55
$2f$	51	0.22	0.16	0.25	230	222

Laemmel has shown that one can model certain probability processes as branching graphs.[1] One example he uses is that of a binary palindrome generator.[2] He assumes a set of formal production rules from the theory of context-free languages and shows that the palindromes satisfy Zipf's law.

The second example, a probabilistic model for a program which leads to Zipf's law, which was first suggested by Halstead and Bayer and is discussed in Sec. 3.2.9, in the context of Halstead's work.

3.2.8 Estimation of Token Length at the Beginning of Design

The evolving field of software engineering has a great need for theoretical concepts, especially quantitative ones. Thus, a complexity theory such as the operator-operand length developed in the preceding sections is of considerable use as a tool for theoretical studies. However, it can play an even more important role if it can be used for estimation of program complexity early in the design process. Such a technique is described in this section.

One method of initially estimating program length[3] (number of tokens) is to estimate the number of types. We assume that the analyst initially has a complete description of the problem (requirements) and that a partial analysis and choice of key algorithms have been made (initial specifications and preliminary design). An elementary approach might be to estimate the token size by

1. Estimating the number of operator types in the programming language which will be used by the programmers

---

[1]Laemmel and Shooman (1977).

[2]A palindrome in natural languages is a word or phrase which is the same spelled backward or forward, e.g., "madam," "Ana," or the famous sentence attributed to Napoleon: "Able was I ere I saw Elba." A binary palindrome is a sequence of digits which is the same when read backward or forward, such as 1001 or 01110.

[3]The reader should remember that we do not include in our token count certain nonexecutable code such as comments, declares, assembler directives, etc.

Table 3.10 Estimation of program length for several examples

Type of Program	Language	Instruction length	Estimated token length	Actual token length
1. QUADRAC Given coefficients A, B, C as inputs, program solves and classifies roots of quadratic equation (Brown, 1976, p. 877).	Basic	53	171	177
2. PLOT Plots 6 different functions of a single variable simultaneously (Brown, 1977, p. 486).	Basic	110	258	306
3. Case study 3 Current in a series *RLC* circuit (McCracken, 1961, p. 65).	Fortran	18	140	111
4. Servo frequency response The frequency response of a second-order transfer function is to be evaluated at a number of points (McCracken, 1961, p. 68).	Fortran	17	90	88
5. Subroutine RTF Calculating the roots of a given function by three different methods (IBM, 1969, p. 159).	PL/1	119	275	409

2. Estimating the number of distinct operands by counting input variables, output variables, intermediate variables, and constants which will be needed
3. Summing the estimates of steps 1 and 2 to obtain the value of t and substituting in Eq. (3.11)

An estimation experiment along these lines was carried out on five different programs.[1] The results appear in Table 3.10. The reader will note that the estimated token lengths (obtained by reading the algorithm and applying the above three steps) differ from the actual lengths (obtained by count from the program) by −3.4 percent, −15.7 percent, +26.1 percent, +2.3 percent, and −32.8 percent, respectively.

Some individuals have criticized this method as impractical on the ground that in many projects the design is started long before adequate requirements and specifications are available. The response is obvious. Any final or even intermediate design built on partial or rapidly changing requirements and specifications is headed for high development costs and possibly failure. As requirements and specifications change in an *ordered manner* over the lifetime of the project, the initial estimate of token length can be revised periodically.

[1] Shooman and Laemmel (1977).

Additional examples of this technique of estimation appear in the problems at the end of the chapter.

3.2.9 Relationship to "Software Physics"

Introduction At the beginning of Sec. 3.2.4, we introduced the work of Professor Maurice Halstead. We now present some of his work in summary form and show how it parallels the work in the previous sections on Zipf's law. In fact, we will take the position that Zipf's law plus other developments based on Shannon's information theory serve as basic points of departure in this area and complement Halstead's work.

Halstead uses many of the same terms we have developed in the preceding sections; however, different notation is used. In order to avoid confusion, since we will be using both sets of symbols, a brief glossary of terms to be used in this section is given in Table 3.11.

Halstead early in his work arrives at a formula for program length based on a combinatorial argument on how operators and operands can be combined to form a program:[1]

$$N = \eta_1 \log_2 \eta_1 + \eta_2 \log_2 \eta_2 \tag{3.27}$$

where N = program length (total operators plus operands)
η_1 = number of operator types
η_2 = number of operand types

Note that Eq. (3.27) and Eqs. (3.11) and (3.17) are of similar form. In fact substitution of $t = \eta_1 + \eta_2$ and $n = N$ into Eq. (3.11) allows direct comparison:

$$N = (\eta_1 + \eta_2)[0.5772 + \ln(\eta_1 + \eta_2)] \tag{3.28}$$

Comparison of Halstead and Zipf length We begin our comparison of Eqs. (3.27) and (3.28) by investigating certain limiting cases and then using a direct numerical comparison for a number of examples. In the case where $\eta_1 \gg \eta_2$, Eq. (3.28) reduces to

$$N = \eta_1(0.5772 + \ln \eta_1)$$

A similar result is obtained if $\eta_2 \gg \eta_1$. Furthermore, if the dominating η term is large, the constant 0.5772 can be ignored and the two equations will differ by the ratio

$$\frac{\ln \eta_1}{\log_2 \eta_1} = \frac{1}{\log_2 e} = \ln 2 = 0.693$$

[1]1975; 1977a. For computation it is convenient to remember that
$$\log_2 x = (\log_{10} x)/(\log_{10} 2) = 3.3219 \log_{10} x$$
$$\log_2 x = (\ln x)/(\ln 2) = 1.4427 \ln x$$

Table 3.11 Comparison of equivalent terms

Laemmel-Shooman development		Halstead development	
Symbol	Terminology	Symbol	Terminology
t_1	Number of operator types	η_1	Number of unique or distinct operators
t_2	Number of operand types	η_2	Number of unique or distinct operands
t	Total operator-operand types $t = t_1 + t_2$	η	Vocabulary $\eta = \eta_1 + \eta_2$
n_1	Number of operator tokens	N_1	Total usage of all the operators
n_2	Number of operand tokens	N_2	Total usage of all the operands
n	Token length $n = n_1 + n_2$	N	Length $N = N_1 + N_2$

Thus, the Zipf length in such a case is about 30 percent smaller than the Halstead length. For a moderate size of the dominating η term, the constant 0.5772 tends to "boost" the Zipf length, reducing the difference.

We now consider the special case where the number of operator types is equal to the number of operand types, or $\eta_1 = \eta_2 = \eta$. The ratio of Zipf length to Halstead length then becomes

$$\frac{0.5772 + \ln 2\eta}{\log_2 \eta} = \frac{1.27 + 0.693\log_2\eta}{\log_2\eta}$$

Again, for large η the two measures differ by only $\ln 2$, and for moderate values of η the compensating constant is 1.27, which should narrow the difference even more than before.

A direct numerical comparison can be made between the three length formulas (Eqs. (3.27), (3.11), and (3.17)) for 3 of the examples given in Table 3.4 and 14 examples in Halstead's book (1977, p. 12). Such a comparison is made in Table 3.12.

After detailed study of Table 3.12, no clear pattern emerges in the comparison of estimates 1 and 2. It is clear, however, that estimate 3 is inferior to the other two. In some cases, the estimates are optimistic, and in other cases they are pessimistic. The overall performance of the estimates is compared in the last two lines of the table by computing the average error for the 17 examples, both the algebraic average and the average of the absolute values. The averages for the Halstead measure are somewhat closer. However, we must have data on significant-sized real-world programs, rather than "tutorial examples," to draw a definitive conclusion.

Table 3.12 Comparison of length-estimation formulas

Sample source and type	Actual number of tokens n	Halstead		Laemmel-Shooman			
		Estimate 1		Estimate 2		Estimate 3	
		Eq. (3.27)	% error	Eq. (3.11)	% Error	Eq. (3.17)	% error
Neuhold, 11-statement PL/1	55	72	+30	76	+38	46	−16
Neuhold, 27-statement PL/1	222	240	+8	230	+4	140	−37
MIKBUG—M6800 microprocessor executive	322	485	+51	439	+36	267	−17
CACM 1*	104	104	0	105	+1	66	−36
CACM 2	82	77	−6	81	−2	49	−40
CACM 3	453	300	−34	280	−38	170	−62
CACM 4	132	139	+5	140	+6	84	−36
CACM 5	123	123	0	124	+1	76	−39
CACM 6	98	101	+3	105	+7	64	−35
CACM 7	59	62	+5	67	+13	40	−31
CACM 8	131	117	−10	119	−9	72	−45
CACM 9	314	288	−8	269	−11	164	−48
CACM 10	46	53	+14	58	+26	35	−23
CACM 11	53	53	−1	58	+9	35	−33
CACM 12	59	62	+5	67	+13	41	−31
CACM 13	59	57	−3	62	+6	38	−36
CACM 14	186	163	−12	160	−14	97	−48
Average error	...	...	+2.8	...	+4.9	...	−36
Average magnitude error	...	...	11	...	13.9	...	36

*From the series of standard algorithms published in Comm. ACM. See Halstead (1977), p. 12, and SIGPLAN Notices, February 1972, p. 22.

The most striking result is that these formulas estimate length within less than 14 percent of error. When we estimated the number of operators and operands from preliminary design information in Table 3.10, the average magnitude of error for the five examples was 16 percent. Thus, we may conclude that most of the errors in the examples in Table 3.10 are due to the length formula. In any case, this is excellent accuracy for an early estimate. In addition, accuracy can be improved as the design progresses and more detailed information becomes available.

Derivation of the Halstead length formula In the previous section we stated the formula for the Halstead length, Eq. (3.27), without any development. In this section we repeat one of Halstead's original derivations and show that a slight modification leads to the Zipf-law length, Eq. (3.28). This development is especially appealing for three reasons:

1. It provides a single derivation which leads to either the Halstead- or the Zipf-length equation, depending on the assumption made.
2. It is based on a probabilistic model of how a program can be constructed by alternating operators and operands.
3. It provides another theoretical model that leads to Zipf's laws.

We begin by assuming the following model for a program.[1]

A program is viewed as a sequence of symbols, made up of alternating operator and operand symbols, chosen from "alphabets" of η_1 and η_2 symbols, respectively. The program contains exactly η_1 and η_2 operator and operand symbol types, and we consider the program to be generated by a stochastic process. The character string which represents the program is generated by choosing at random from the alphabet of operators, then choosing at random from the alphabet of operands, and continuing the alternation process. The program generation stops when the last unused operator or operand is chosen for the first time.

The length of the character string is calculated by formulating the probability distribution of operator and operand lengths and then computing the expected length (mean length). For simplicity we focus on a single character string composed of an alphabet of η symbols. We observe that as our character-string generator proceeds, it generates many substrings made up of k symbols, where $k \leq \eta$. We denote the substring lengths as SL_k. By a substring length we mean the number of new symbols generated before a new alphabet type is encountered. Clearly, the length of the string which uses up all η symbol types is just the sum of the lengths of its constituent substrings:

$$\mathrm{SL}_\eta = \sum_{k=1}^{\eta} \mathrm{SL}_k \tag{3.29}$$

The expected-value operator is written as $E(\ )$, and the expected value of a sum of independent random variables is the sum of the expected values.[2] Thus,

$$E(\mathrm{SL}_\eta) = E\left(\sum_{k=1}^{\eta} \mathrm{SL}_k \right) = \sum_{k=1}^{\eta} E(\mathrm{SL}_k) \tag{3.30}$$

The probability that substring k has exactly s symbols is given by the probability that the first $s-1$ symbols are generated from $k-1$ alphabet types

[1] Halstead and Bayer (1973), p. 126.
[2] See Shooman (1968), p. 404, or most probability texts.

followed by a single letter[1] generated from the remaining alphabet types. If $k = 7$, then there are 6 alphabet types out of η symbols which have already appeared. Thus for $k = 7$, the probability of a substring sequence of length s is given by the equation

$$P(\text{SL}_7) = \left(\frac{6}{\eta}\right)^{s-1}\left(1 - \frac{6}{\eta}\right) \tag{3.31}$$

In general, for any value of k, the probability of a substring sequence of length s is given by the equation

$$P(\text{SL}_{k+1}) = \left(\frac{k}{\eta}\right)^{s-1}\left(1 - \frac{k}{\eta}\right) \tag{3.32}$$

and the expected value of substring length (see App. A, Eq. (A.34)) is as follows:

$$E(\text{SL}_{k+1}) = \sum_{s=1}^{\infty} s\left(\frac{k}{\eta}\right)^{s-1}\left(1 - \frac{k}{\eta}\right) \tag{3.33}$$

Equation (3.33) can be simplified if we notice that the last term is independent of the summation index and the first two terms generate a known series:

$$\sum_{i=1}^{\infty} ix^{i-1} = \frac{1}{(1-x)^2} \tag{3.34}$$

Thus, Eq. (3.33) simplifies to

$$E(\text{SL}_{k+1}) = \frac{1}{1 - k/\eta} = \frac{\eta}{\eta - k} \tag{3.35}$$

Substitution of Eq. (3.35) into Eq. (3.30) yields an expression for the sequence length:

$$E(\text{SL}_{\eta}) = \eta \sum_{k=1}^{\eta} \frac{1}{\eta - k + 1} \tag{3.36}$$

A term-by-term inspection of Eq. (3.36) shows that it is a sum of a descending sequence of terms, $1/\eta, 1/(\eta - 1), \ldots, 1/1$, which is equivalent to the ascending sequence

$$E(\text{SL}_{\eta}) = \eta \sum_{i=1}^{\eta} \frac{1}{i} \tag{3.37}$$

Had Halstead and Bayer desired, at this point in their derivation they could have used Eq. (3.8) and obtained

$$E(\text{SL}_{\eta}) \approx \eta(0.5772 + \ln \eta) \tag{3.38}$$

However, Halstead and Bayer chose to bound Eq. (3.37) by transforming the

---

[1] This means that the last substring is generated when the last unused symbol is picked (i.e., used once). Note the similarity between this assumption and those accompanying Zipf's law.

summation. Let

$$i = 2^j$$

Then

$$j = \log_2 i$$

and for $i = \eta$, the last equation becomes $j = \log_2 \eta$ and for $i = 1$, $j = \log_2 1 = 0$. Using these substitutions, the summation in Eq. (3.37) becomes as follows:[1]

$$E(\mathrm{SL}_\eta) = \eta \sum_{j=0}^{\log_2 \eta} \frac{1}{2^j} \tag{3.39}$$

The leading terms in the summation of Eq. (3.39) are $1 + 1/2 + 1/4 + \cdots$. If we recognize that each term is always smaller than unity, then we can bound Eq. (3.39) by assuming that each term $1/2^j \le 1$ and thus

$$E(\mathrm{SL}_\eta) \le \eta \log_2 \eta \tag{3.40}$$

If we return to our previously stated program model and impose the constraint that operators and operands must alternate, then the expected length is the sum of the expected operator and operand lengths. Thus Eq. (3.40) leads directly to Eq. (3.27), which is the Halstead-length equation.

If we remove the restriction that operators and operands must alternate, then $\eta = \eta_1 + \eta_2$, and substitution into Eq. (3.38) yields the Zipf length (cf. Eq. (3.28)). If we had still retained the restriction that operators and operands alternate and substituted into Eq. (3.38), we would have obtained another length equation (which must surely give nearly the same numerical answers), namely,

$$L = \eta_1(0.5772 + \ln \eta_1) + \eta_2(0.5772 + \ln \eta_2) \tag{3.41}$$

Information content of a program One of the most fundamental results of statistical communication theory is Shannon's information theory. By ignoring the meaning of messages and focusing on the probability of choosing any one message out of a set of i messages, Shannon was able to establish an entropy function H which measured the statistical information content. We will find that we are able to apply some of Shannon's concepts to programs and calculate the information content of a program. Again we will find that program information content is nearly identical with Halstead's concept of program volume. Before we summarize a few of the mathematical results of Shannon's development, a few motivating examples are discussed.

Let us consider a well-known message from America's Revolutionary history. The famous artisan and patriot Paul Revere learned that the British were planning to march on Concord, Massachusetts, where ammunition was stored for the colonial minutemen. His comrades waited in Boston to see if the British

---

[1]Strictly speaking, the upper limit of the summation must still be an integer and so is really the largest integer smaller than $\log_2(\eta + 1)$.

would come by land or by sea. On April 18, 1775, Revere readied himself for the prearranged signal—one if the British moved by land and two if by sea. As the clock struck 11 p.m., his comrades displayed two lanterns in the tower of the Old North Church in Boston. Thus informed, Paul Revere began his famous midnight ride. The information contained in this signal concerned which of the two messages was correct.

Suppose other information reached Revere that day, e.g., reports that supplies were being loaded on British ships in Boston Harbor. In such a case, the probability of two lanterns would be not .5 but perhaps .75, and the information contained in the final message would be less. After all, Revere would be fairly sure of the result and would only be waiting for confirmation. Suppose in the extreme case that another comrade rode up to Revere at 10:35 p.m. and breathlessly reported seeing the British ships, loaded with troops, sailing from the harbor. In such a case, the message would carry no information, since the probability of two lanterns was now 1.0, and in fact, Revere would have left early and not waited for the signal. Thus, the amount of information carried by a message is a function of the number of different possible messages and the probability that each message will be sent.

As a second example, let us consider the classical problem of sending standard telegram greetings. The telegraph company knows that many of the messages are birthday and anniversary greetings or wedding, birth, or other announcements. It makes up perhaps 64 different standard messages to be shown as samples to the sender. If the customer selects number 27, then the company transmits information on the sender and the addressee, plus number 27. The receiving telegraph office composes the telegram after referring to the standard list. A customized message could be sent, at a higher cost. Assuming that each message is equiprobable, each message will occur with frequency 1/64. If we decided to represent the message number by a binary code, we would need 6 bits to transmit any of the $2^6 = 64$ messages. In such a case, the bit length is a measure of the information content. Note that in no case have we considered how many words are in the message or what the message contains in defining information content. We now summarize the results we will need from information theory.[1]

The central formula in Shannon's information theory defines the information content (also known as the entropy H), which uses bits as units. If we have a message that is selected from a set of i messages, each with a probability of occurrence p_i, then the entropy is given by the equation

$$H = - \sum_{j=1}^{i} p_j \log_2 p_j = \sum_{j=1}^{i} p_j \log_2 \frac{1}{p_j} \qquad (3.42)$$

[1]For a detailed development, the reader is referred to Schwartz (1959), Chap. 1, or Shannon and Weaver (1975). A shorter, less mathematical, but equally authoritative presentation is contained in either Pierce (1980) or Cherry (1970).

If all the messages are equiprobable, then $p_j = 1/i$, and Eq. 3.42 becomes

$$H = \log_2 i \qquad (3.43)$$

For illustration, suppose that our family of messages is the 16 different binary numbers we can express with a 4-digit binary number. In this case $i = 16$, and if we assume $p_i = 1/16$, then Eq. (3.43) yields $H = 4$ bits. This example illustrates the appropriateness of bits as the unit for H.

As a second example, let us again consider that our messages are the 16 different binary 4-digit numbers, but we now assume that $p_i = 1/2$, $p_2 = p_3 = 1/4$, and P_4 to p_{15} equal 0. Substitution of these values into Eq. (3.42) yields

$$H = \tfrac{1}{2}\log_2 2 + \tfrac{1}{4}\log_2 4 + \tfrac{1}{4}\log_2 4 + 0 + \cdots = 1.5 \text{ bits}$$

In general, one can show that H is maximized when all the p_i's are equal (see the problems at the end of the chapter).

If we use the program model of the preceding section but drop the restriction that operators and operands must alternate, then we can view a program as a sequence of N symbols (operators or operands). If the probabilities of each symbol are *equal*, then $p_j = 1/(\eta_1 + \eta_2)$, and the entropy is given as follows:[1]

$$H = N \log_2(\eta_1 + \eta_2) \qquad (3.44)$$

We now return to our Zipf-law model of a program and assume that the probabilities p_j *are not equiprobable* but are given by Zipf's law (Eq. (3.3), with f_r defined as p_j). It can be shown that the use of the Euller-Maclaurin series allows one to express the summation obtained by substitution in Eq. (3.42) as follows:[2]

$$H = \frac{N}{\ln 2}\left[\frac{(\ln t)^2}{2(\ln t + 7/12)} + \ln\left(\ln t + \frac{7}{12}\right)\right] \qquad (3.45)$$

For $t > 100$, say, we can neglect the $7/12$ terms; and since $\ln t = \ln 2 \log_2 t$, Eq. (3.45) can be simplified to give

$$H \approx N \log_2\left(\sqrt{t} + \ln t\right) \qquad (3.46)$$

For large t, $\sqrt{t} \gg \ln t$, and we obtain

$$H \approx \frac{N}{2}\log_2 t \qquad (3.47)$$

Note that since $t = \eta_1 + \eta_2$, Eq. (3.47) gives one-half the entropy of Eq. (3.44). This is because the Zipf-law distribution of probabilities has reduced to one-half the maximum value of H that the equiprobable distribution yielded.

Minimum information content As we stated in Sec. 3.2.1, we should consider not only program complexity but also problem complexity. If we use the same units of measure, and if we can compute problem complexity, then the efficiency of the

---

[1] In his work on software physics (1975), Halstead defines a quantity called volume, denoted by V, which has this same formula.

[2] Laemmel (1976).

solution will be related to the ratio of problem complexity to program complexity. To pursue this concept, we must first define problem complexity.

Returning to information theory concepts, we can define problem complexity as the minimum amount of information needed to solve the problem. If we are to compute minimum H, we must be able to define the set of possible results out of which our problem solution is chosen. This task may be difficult, but we will begin our discussion with a well-defined problem.

Consider the famous logic puzzle: You are given 12 coins of the same denomination. Eleven of the coins are identical and are of the same weight. One coin looks identical to the others but is either lighter or heavier than the rest. You are given a balance scale and three weighings in which to pick out the maverick coin and to determine whether it is heavier or lighter. The information needed to solve the problem is the sum of the information needed to isolate the maverick coin (see Eq. (3.43)),

$$M = \log_2 12 = 3.59 \text{ bits}$$

and the information needed to determine whether it is heavier or lighter,

$$M = \log_2 2 = 1 \text{ bit}$$

Thus, the total information requirement is 4.59 bits.

To solve the problem, we break the coins into 3 groups of 4 each, A, B, and C. Group A is placed on one side of the scale and group B on the other for trial 1. We assume the scale balances. Each of the eight coins has a probability of 1 in 12 of being the maverick coin; thus Eq. (3.43) yields

$$M = \sum_{i=1}^{8} \frac{1}{12} \log_2 12 = \frac{8}{12} \log_2 12 = 2.39 \text{ bits}$$

We now know that the maverick coin is among the four in group C, and we place three of these on one side of the scale and three of the normal coins from group A on the other side. Each of the three coins from group C has a 1-out-of-4 chance of being the maverick; thus

$$M = \sum_{i=1}^{3} \frac{1}{4} \log_2 4 = \frac{3}{4} \log_2 4 = 1.5$$

Thus, the total information content of the first two weighings is 3.89 bits, which is less than 4.59 bits. Assume the scale balances, then we know that the remaining coin in group C is the maverick, and we compare it on our third weighing with one of the other normal coins to determine whether it is heavy or light. This last weighing has two possible outcomes, heavy and light; thus

$$M = \sum_{i=1}^{2} \frac{1}{2} \log_2 2 = \log_2 2 = 1$$

The three weighings accumulate 4.89 bits, which is greater than 4.59, and the problem is solved. Similar computations can be made for the other possible outcomes to show that all possible outcomes will lead to enough information to solve the problem (see problems 3.25–3.27).

Use of this technique requires the identification of the possible outcomes at each step in the problem solution and a computation of the associated probabilities. Halstead has developed a different and simple approach.

Halstead proposes that if Eq. (3.44)—or Eq. (3.43)—represents the information content (volume) of a program, then the minimum value of H, denoted by H^*, is obtained if the minimum values of η_1, η_2, and N, η_1^*, η_2^*, and N^* are used. He defines the minimum number of operators to be 2, and he uses a function which does all the work of the program, $f(\ )$, and an assignment symbol (the equal sign). Alternately we could consider the two operators as PRINT $(f(\ ))$. The minimum number of operands is the sum of the required input and output variables.[1] Since we use each operator and operand only once, $N_1 = \eta_1$ and $N_2 = \eta_2$; thus

$$\text{Min } \eta_1 = \eta_1^* = 2 \tag{3.48}$$

$$\text{Min } \eta_2 = \eta_2^* = \text{sum of input and output variables} \tag{3.49}$$

$$\text{Min } N = \eta_1 + \eta_2 \tag{3.50}$$

Substitutions of Eqs. (3.48) to (3.50) into Eqs. (3.44) and (3.47) gives

$$V^* = (2 + \eta_2^*)\log_2(2 + \eta_2^*) \tag{3.51}$$

$$H^* = V^*/2 \tag{3.52}$$

Expressed in this form, the information content (potential volume) should be independent of the program language. In fact, if we have a very-high-level language with a primitive operator that solves our problem at hand, then the information content of the program written in this language should equal the minimum information content.

A direct extension of the concept of minimum information content or volume is to define the level l of a program as the ratio of minimum volume to actual volume:

$$l = \frac{V^*}{V} = \frac{H^*}{H} \tag{3.53}$$

Thus, the highest-level program language approaches or reaches the level of unity, and lower-level program languages rate between unity and zero on the scale that has been created. Problems 3.30 and 3.31 at the end of this chapter explore the levels that are reached for various practical programs.

Effect of modularity on information content If we partition a program into M modules, we will affect the length and information content by affecting the value

---

[1]A practical case which comes close to this minimum situation is the matrix-inversion operator MAT(B) = INV(A). Of course, we still have to input the elements of A (unless they are stored), output the elements of B, and dimension A and B. See Digital Equipment Corporation (1978), Sec. 7-6, "Matrix Manipulation."

of t. Assume that an unpartitioned program has t token types and each module has t/m of these types. Assume that we must also add one type for the subroutine call-return (CALL ATAN...RETURN FROM ATAN), and $\bar{\alpha}M$ interface variables. The parameter $\bar{\alpha}$ is the average number of interface variables per subroutine call. Suppose the language we are using does not have an arctan function. If we write a subroutine to compute $y = \arctan x$, then $\alpha = 2$, that is, x and y. On the other hand, if we write a subroutine to convert from rectangular coordinates x and y to polar coordinates R and θ, then $\alpha = 4$. Thus, the number of token types for each module is given by the equation

$$t_m = \frac{t}{M} + 1 + \bar{\alpha}M \tag{3.54}$$

and from Eqs. (3.11) and (3.47), for each module

$$n = t_m(0.5772 + \ln t_m) \tag{3.55}$$

$$h = \frac{n}{2}\log_2 t_m \tag{3.56}$$

For the entire modularized program,

$$N = Mn \tag{3.57}$$

$$H = Mh \tag{3.58}$$

Combining Eqs. (3.54) to (3.58) yields

$$N = n\left(\frac{t}{M} + 1 + \bar{\alpha}M\right)\left[0.5772 + \ln\left(\frac{t}{M} + 1 + \bar{\alpha}M\right)\right] \tag{3.59}$$

$$H = \frac{Mn}{2}\log_2\left(\frac{t}{M} + 1 + \bar{\alpha}M\right) \tag{3.60}$$

A comparison of Eq. (3.59) with Eq. (3.11) and Eq. (3.60) with Eq. (3.47) for given values of t and $\bar{\alpha}$ will yield the values of M that minimize N and H. These computations are explored in the problems at the end of the chapter and are compared with Halstead's work on modularization (Halstead, 1977, Chap. 12).

Effort measure Halstead proposes an effort measure E that is the number of mental discriminations needed to develop a program. He postulates that this measure should be proportional to the program volume and inversely proportional to the level; thus

$$E = \frac{V}{l} \tag{3.61}$$

Using Eq. (3.53) and the fact that $H = V/2$ (for a Zipf-law distribution), we obtain alternate expressions for E:

$$E = \frac{V^2}{V^*} = \frac{2H^2}{H^*} \tag{3.62}$$

and substitution of Eqs. (3.11) and (3.47), (3.51), and (3.52) into Eq. (3.62) yields

$$E = \frac{[t(0.5772 + \ln t)\log_2 t]^2}{(2 + \eta_2^*)\log_2(2 + \eta_2^*)} \tag{3.63}$$

In the next section we investigate the correlation between the number of program errors or man-months of development time and:

1. The token length
2. The volume or entropy
3. The effort metric E

3.2.10 Complexity versus Number of Errors and Development Time

The complexity measures developed in the preceding sections are useful in two ways: (1) they provide metrics which allow comparison of the relative complexity of two different designs or algorithms; and (2) when multiplied by an appropriate proportionality constant, they should provide estimates and predictions for the number of errors and the manpower required for software development.

Number of errors versus complexity We begin by discussing the relationship between the number of errors and our measures of complexity. In Chap. 5, we will present several sets of data from the literature on the number of errors removed from a number of large and small programs during development. In the reliability model developed in Chap. 5, the assumption is made and proof is given that the number of errors is proportional to the number of program instructions. We examine this hypothesis in this section and again in Chaps. 5 and 6. Unfortunately, there are only a few sets of complete error data in the literature. We use the set of data collected by Akiyama[1] for the correlation studies which follow. Akiyama's machine language program was about 25,000 assembly language instructions long and contained the nine modules shown in Table 3.13. The number of bugs (errors) found in each module during development is given in the third column of the table.

The data collected by Akiyama are sufficiently complete to warrant detailed exploration, and four different hypotheses will be tested:

1. *Length hypothesis.* The number of bugs is proportional to the number of machine language statements. Since each machine language statement contains one operator and one operand, the number of machine statements is just one-half the number of tokens (operators plus operands). Thus, a study of bugs versus machine language statements and one of bugs versus token length are equivalent since the two lengths are directly proportional to one another.
2. *Information hypothesis.* The number of bugs is proportional to the information content of the program, where information content (or Halstead volume) is

[1]Akiyama (1971).

Table 3.13 Raw data from Akiyama (1971)

Module	Machine language statements	Bugs	Decisions	Calls	Decision plus calls
MA	4032	102	372	283	655
MB	1329	18	215	44	249
MC	5453	93 (146)*	552	362	914
MD	1674	26	111	130	241
ME	2051	71	315	197	512
MF	2513	37	217	186	403
MG	699	16	104	32	136
MH	3792	50	233	110	343
MX	3412	80	416	230	646

*Two values were stated in Akiyama.

calculated from (3.44) or (3.47). (The two equations are identical except for the factor of $1/2$, which will be absorbed in the experimentally determined constant of proportionality.)

3. *Halstead effort measure*. The number of bugs is proportional to effort in programming, E. This hypothesis was explored in Funami and Halstead (1976).

4. *Akiyama's hypothesis*. The number of bugs is proportional to the number of decisions plus subroutine calls.

Use of Akiyama's data for correlating errors and complexity measures Akiyama's raw data given in Table 3.13 provide us with the appropriate quantities to test the length hypothesis and Akiyama's hypothesis. In order to calculate H and E so as to test the other two hypotheses, we must make some assumptions. First we assume that each machine language statement contains one operator and one operand and thus N equals twice the number of statements (see the second column of Table 3.14). To compute the number of unique operators, η_1, Halstead assumed that it was equal to the sum of the number of machine language instruction types, the number of program calls, and the number of *unique* program decisions. He guessed that there were 64 types of machine language instructions and that only one-third of the decisions were unique, and he arrived at the following formula:[1]

$$\eta_1 = \text{decisions}/3 + \text{calls} + 64 \tag{3.64}$$

The third column of Table 3.14 is calculated by using Eq. (3.64). Knowing η_1 and N, we are able to calculate η_2 by substitution in Eq. (3.27). This provides the data necessary for computation of H (see Table 3.14). The computation of E in Halstead's paper was done by using Eq. (3.61) and an alternate estimator formula

---

[1]Funami and Halstead (1976).

Table 3.14 Values derived from Akiyama's data in Table 3.13

Module	N = twice the number of machine language statements	η_1 (Eq. (3.64))	η_2 (Eq. (3.27))	H (Eq. (3.44)), thousands	E, millions
MA	8,064	471	442	79.3	170.3
MB	2,658	180	176	22.5	15.3
MC	10,906	610	574	111.3	322.6
MD	3,348	231	201	29.3	28.2
ME	4,102	366	138	36.8	100.2
MF	5,026	322	287	46.5	65.5
MG	1,398	131	76	10.8	6.5
MH	7,584	252	603	73.9	58.5
MX	6,824	433	357	65.7	135.9

for l:

$$l = \frac{2\eta_2}{\eta_1 N_2} \tag{3.65}$$

(See Halstead, 1977, p. 27, and Funami and Halstead, 1976, p. 135.)

The four hypotheses are tested in Figs. 3.10 to 3.13. Clearly, the first two hypotheses fit the data fairly well, but the third and fourth hypotheses yield better fits. In fact, Halstead's effort measure yields an excellent fit except for the MC module. (Note: Since Akiyama speaks of two values for MC we plot one as MC and the other as MC'.)

There is a question of the usefulness of Eqs. (3.64) and (3.65) in these computations. Estes (1981) has reanalyzed these data using the Zipf-law formulation to compute η_2, H, and E. (See Eqs. (3.28), (3.44), (3.51), and (3.53).) He

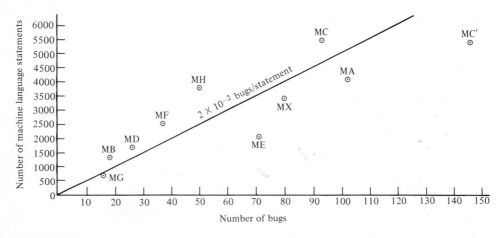

Figure 3.10 Number of bugs versus number of machine language statements.

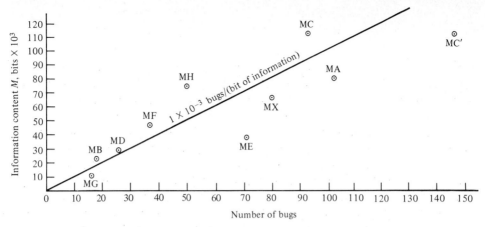

Figure 3.11 Number of bugs versus information content in bits.

made the further assumption that η_2^* is equal to $0.05\eta_2$. The numerical results were different, but the correlation was about the same.

The correlation between Akiyama's data and the four different hypotheses is explored in greater detail in Table 3.15. A least-squares straight line ($y = Mx + b$) was fitted to the data for each of the four hypotheses. Both error values MC = 93 and MC = 146 were used in the data analysis. The correlation coefficients ρ for each set of data are given in the second column of Table 3.15 and confirm the conclusions reached about goodness of fit by visual inspection of Figs. 3.10 to 3.13.

The straight lines which appear on Figs. 3.10 to 3.13 are not the least-squares fits but were chosen by eye: (1) to pass through the origin; (2) to have a slope

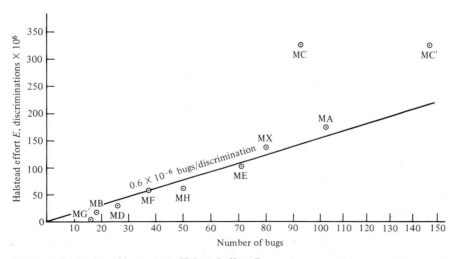

Figure 3.12 Number of bugs versus Halstead effort E.

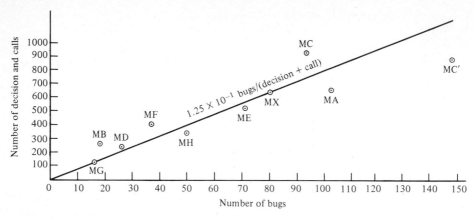

Figure 3.13 Number of bugs versus Akiyama's measure.

(actually the reciprocal of the slope is given), which is an "even" number; and (3) to fit the data points reasonably well. Thus, in Fig. 3.10 the value of 2×10^{-2} bugs per statement is equal to 50 statements per bug, which is somewhat larger than the least-squares value of $M = 38.5$ or 31.2, given in Table 3.15.

We can compare the various proportionality constants obtained from Figs. 3.10 to 3.13 if we normalize all values in terms of per token quantities. This is done in Table 3.16.

Table 3.15 Least-squares fit of a straight line for the four hypotheses

Hypothesis	Correlation coefficient ρ	Slope m	Intercept b
1. Bugs proportional to machine language instructions			
MC = 93	0.832	38.5	666
MC′ = 146	0.896	31.2	879
2. Bugs proportional to information content			
MC = 93	0.828	811	8,487
MC′ = 146	0.900	665	12,572
3. Bugs proportional to effort E			
MC = 93	0.853	2,595,000	−41,835,000
MC′ = 146	0.982	2,251,000	−36,251,000
4. Bugs proportional to calls plus decisions			
MC = 93	0.923	7	72
MC′ = 146	0.976	5.58	116.9

Table 3.16 Comparison of proportionality constants

1 statement = 2 tokens

2×10^{-2} bugs/statement $\div$ 2 tokens/statement = 1×10^{-2} bugs/token

1×10^{-2} bug/token $\div$ 1×10^{-3} bug/bit = 10 bits/token

1×10^{-2} bug/token $\div$ 0.67×10^{-6} bug/discrimination = 1.5×10^{4} discriminations/token

1×10^{-2} bug/token $\div$ 1.25×10^{-1} bug/(decision + call) = 8×10^{-2} (decision + call)/token

Further study of additional data is needed to choose among the hypotheses; however, use of one or more of these measures with the appropriate proportionality constant should yield a rough initial estimate of the number of program errors.

Complexity versus man-months We now turn to the problem of relating programming time (man-months) to program complexity measures. In Chap. 6 we shall present and discuss a number of cost-estimation techniques for evaluating program productivity, i.e., lines of code per man-month. The range in productivity roughly extends from 1 to 100 instructions per man-day. Some of the reasons for the vast range are the large differences observed in individuals, problem complexity, language level, and definitions. Since initial coding of a problem constitutes only 15 to 20 percent of the total effort, the productivity data for coding only should be higher by a factor of 5 to 8 than that for all phases of the development effort. It is not clear exactly how programming is defined for the data presented in the literature.

Again we turn to Akiyama's data for evaluation of the proposed hypotheses. We restate the four hypotheses previously given by merely exchanging the words *the programming effort in man-days* for the phrase *the number of bugs*. From Akiyama's data we find that his 25,000-step machine language program (there is some confusion between the total length and the sum of module lengths in Tables 1 and 2 of his paper) took 100 man-months to produce. This time represented the entire development cycle, and extended from the initial phase of checking the specification to the final phase of field testing. Assuming that the 25,000-step program (actually 24,955) represents 50,000 tokens, we obtain a productivity rate of 500 tokens per man-month. Assuming an average of 20 working days per month, this becomes 25 tokens per day. (This is equivalent to 12.5 instructions per day, which coincides well with some of the data given in Chap. 6.) Since we do not have the individual man-months per module, we cannot correlate productivity data with the various complexity metrics, as was done in Figs. 3.10 to 3.13. However, we can relate the total productivity for the program to the various metrics through use of the 100 man-month figure, as is done in Table 3.17.

We cannot comment further on the accuracy of the predictions of programming effort based on the constants calculated in Table 3.17 without further data. It is to be hoped these techniques will be applied on new projects to see if they yield reasonable predictions, or that a few sets of retrospective data will be unearthed and studied in detail.

Table 3.17 Coefficients of productivity
Totals from tables 3.13 and 3.14

Hypothesis	Total	Per man-month	Per man-day
Length, tokens	50,000	500	25
Information, bits	4.76×10^5	4.76×10^3	2.38×10^2
Effort, discriminations	9.03×10^8	9.03×10^6	4.52×10^5
Decisions plus calls	4.10×10^3	4.10×10^1	2.05×10^{-1}

Before we leave this topic we will summarize some work done by Halstead in attempting to develop a method for calculating the effort coefficient, which he defines as discriminations per man-day. His approach is to relate the total number of discriminations to the human information-processing rate for "similar" tasks. In evaluating this hypothesis, we will examine some of the work done by psychologists in relating the human processing rate to the information content H of the task.

Human performance and information theory An excellent summary of information theory applied to psychology appears in Chap. XII of Pierce (1980). In the discussion, Pierce introduces many experiments that have been performed. Some of these experiments show that human response time in performing a task is proportional to the information content of the task. Other experiments show little or no increase with H. Some of the experiments involve human memory capacity. The following results are cited:

1. A subject was placed in front of a panel with eight lights, and each light was labeled with a monosyllabic "name." The subject was told to speak the name of the light as soon as possible when it flashed. The response time was measured for cases ranging from only one light ($H = 0$) to the case of all eight lights ($H = 3$). The response time rose linearly with H, and the equation $T = 0.2 + 0.15H$ provided a good fit to the data. The equivalent processing rate dH/dT was $1/0.15 \approx 7$ bits per second.
2. Other experiments patterned along the same lines as these have shown that a subject who has had much practice learns to respond more quickly and there is little increase in response time with H. Also, if the lights are replaced by vibrating keys underneath the fingers and the response consists of depressing the vibrating key, then even without learning there is little change in response time with H.
3. Experiments involving the reading of sentences constructed from various vocabulary sizes gave results that showed initial time dependence on H for small H, little dependence for moderate H, and considerable dependence for large H. Processing rates varied between 30 and 44 bits per second.

4. In studies of the human memory capacity a tachistoscope (an apparatus that flashes images on a screen for a fraction of a second) is used, and the subjects of the experiment are queried as to what they saw. Miller has found that one can remember 7 ± 2 objects.[1] One can correctly identify the number (from 0 to 9) of black beans flashed on a screen. ($H = \log_2 10 = 3.3$ bits.) One can also remember a sequence up to 7 binary bits. ($H = \log_2 2^7 = 7$.) A subject who is shown letters can remember as many as 4 or 5. ($H = 5 \log_2 26 = 23$.) A subject can remember only 3 or 4 short, common words. (If these are chosen from the 500 most common words, $H = 3 \log_2 500 = 27$ bits.)

5. It seems that there is both a short- and long-term memory. If 16 to 18 letters are tachistoscopically projected and followed immediately by a randomly chosen pointer, the subject can repeat the pointed-to letter; however, the subject cannot recall all 18 letters a few seconds later (the long-term memory). Thus the short-term memory can store about $H = 18 \log_2 18 = 75$ bits. The transfer rate from the short-term memory to the longer one is about 1 item per 0.01 s. The long-term memory has the smaller capacity, and this probably relates to Miller's 7 ± 2 figure.[2]

6. In an Air Force study of a human's processing rate, a number of colored lights were displayed and the human was asked to flip a switch corresponding to the light that came on. The reaction time was found to follow the curve $T = 0.2 + 0.067H$.[3] The equivalent processing rate dH/dT was approximately 15 bits per second.

7. The author remembers an undergraduate experimental psychology laboratory experiment (circa 1955, directed by Professor J. C. R. Lickleider) which measured the error rate in tracing paths on a simulated oscilloscope screen (a simplified model of the air traffic controller problem). The results showed that the error rate was related to the logarithm of the number of paths, which would predict an error rate proportional to H.

8. Stroud estimates that the number of basic discriminations per unit of time for the human brain lies "between 5 and 20 or a little less" per second.[4]

The basic conclusion is that modeling human performance is by no means a simple task, even for flashing lights, black beans, and monosyllables. Clearly, the human task of writing a computer program is much more complex, and additional work needs to be done in the psychological area before we will better understand this process.

Notwithstanding the caveats of the previous sentence, we will summarize Halstead's approach to relating discriminations to man-days. Basically he quotes Stroud's paper (1966) and uses a figure of 18 mental discriminations per second. This is converted to 1.08×10^3 discriminations per minute, 6.48×10^4 discriminations per hour, and 5.18×10^5 discriminations per 8-hour day. If we

[1] Miller (1956).
[2] For further data also see Miller (1951), Chap. 10.
[3] Shooman (1968), pp. 455–456.
[4] Stroud (1966), pp. 623–631.

apply this technique to Akiyama's data, we divide the 9.03×10^8 discriminations (see Table 3.17) by the daily discrimination processing rate (5.18×10^5) and obtain 1.74×10^3 man-days. For a 20-day month this reduces to 87 man-months. This agrees remarkably well with Akiyama's statement that the project took 100 man-months to complete. However, before we become too jubilant at this result, we should consider several factors:

1. The human processing rates cited in the preceding pages varied from 3 to 83 bits. Clearly, choices at the extremes of this range would have resulted in a predicted productivity range between 15 and 400 man-months for Akiyama's project.
2. Perhaps these information-processing rates can model the initial code-production phase, if the coder sits at a desk and writes the code on a code pad. However, can the single discriminations per second rate account for typing of the program and data (keypunch or terminal, coder or professional typer), debugging, correction, and resubmittal of programs?
3. Since initial coding of the data comprises only 15 to 20 percent of the development effort, perhaps we should be comparing our predictions with 15 to 20 man-months rather than 100 man-months. Clearly, more study is needed in this area, and the reader is referred to the literature.[1]

3.2.11 Graph Theoretic Complexity Measures

Introduction The complexity models developed in the previous section related to the length and difficulty of individual program statements. As described in Table 3.11, this did not account for the interrelationships among the instructions, i.e., the structural intricacy. In this section we will introduce some recent work on the structural complexity of a computer program related to certain program graph topological measures. We will focus on cyclomatic complexity and knot complexity. We will treat polynomial complexity in Sec. 4.6.4.

In this section we assume that the reader has some knowledge of graph theory and include only a brief explanation of the required concepts. A short summary of the pertinent features of graph theory appears in App. C.

Graph properties Graph theory can be applied to a wide variety of problems in science and engineering; however, we will focus only on graphs applied to computer programs. We can introduce succinctly the concept of a program graph by considering it as a limiting form of the flowgraph for the program. A program graph is obtained if we shrink each processing and decision symbol in a flowgraph to a point, yielding a diagram composed of points (called *vertices* or *nodes*) and lines (called *arcs* or *branches*). If no directional arrows appear on the arcs, then the diagram is an ordinary graph, or bidirectional graph. If arc

---

[1]Halstead (1977*b*).

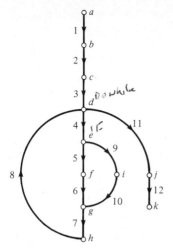

Figure 3.14 A digraph corresponding to the program flowchart given in Fig. 2.13*b*.

directions are important, as they are in a computer program, then each arc has an associated flow direction (arrow) and the diagram is called a *directed graph* or *digraph*. In Fig. 3.14, a diagram is given which corresponds to the flowchart of Fig. 2.13*b*. Nodes *a* and *k* correspond to the start and stop nodes, respectively. Similarly, node *c* corresponds to GET A, node *i* corresponds to $L = L + 1$, etc. The cycle or loop in the program is easily seen to be composed of branches 4, 5, 6, 7, and 8. Similarly, an IF THEN ELSE structure appears as the two parallel paths created by branches 5 and 6 and branches 9 and 10. If the graph were nondirected, the arrows would be removed, and two loops—(4, 5, 6, 7, 8) and (5, 6, 10, 9)—would appear. In the case of a nondirected graph, a loop is also called a *chain*.

Cyclomatic number of a graph In the development of the theory of graphs, a very interesting formula emerges for the complexity of the graph as a function of the number of branches and nodes. An alternate formula for this same graph complexity is based on the number of loops (cycles) in the graph. Thus, the name *cyclomatic number* is given to this complexity metric. The intuitive appeal of this measure is strengthened by subjective comparisons between high cyclomatic complexities and error-prone programs. We begin by introducing the formula for cyclomatic numbers.

The cyclomatic number of a digraph which is *strongly connected* is given by the following formula:

$$v(G) = m - n + p \tag{3.66}$$

where
$v(G)$ = the cyclomatic number for graph G

m = the number of branches (arcs) in graph G

n = the number of nodes (vertices) in graph G

p = the number of separate parts in graph G

A graph has more than one part if there are one or more collections of nodes and branches which are disconnected from the rest of the graph, i.e., if a circle can be drawn enclosing the part so as not to cut any branches of the graph. For the moment, we assume that all the graphs of interest to us will consist of only one part and so $p = 1$. We now consider the meaning of the term *strongly connected*, which has not as yet been defined. A strongly connected graph is one in which *each* node in the graph can be reached from *any other* node. In the case of a strongly connected *digraph* there must be a directed path from each node to all other nodes. If we consider the graph shown in Fig. 3.14, we see that it is *not* strongly connected, since many nodes cannot be reached from others; e.g., we cannot reach node *b* from node *j* (even though the converse is true). If the reader can visualize removing nodes *a*, *b*, *c*, *j*, and *k* and branches 1, 2, 3, 11, and 12 from the graph, then the new graph which results is strongly connected. We now consider how the cyclomatic number formula applies to computer programs.

Cyclomatic complexity of a computer program We begin by considering some of the properties of a graph for a computer program.[1] The program graph is the control structure of the program, and the first node encountered is the start node. The last node in the graph is the stop node. A single branch leads from the start node to the first processing node in the program, which we call the entry node. Similarly, a single branch leads from the last processing node in the program, called the exit node, to the stop node (see Fig. 3.15). If the program is properly constructed, then we should be able to reach each node in the program from the entry node. (An unreachable node represents unreachable code, and therefore an obvious design or coding error which must be corrected.) In general the program graph is not strongly connected, since it is impossible to reach upper nodes in the graph from lower ones. However, if the program structure has an outer loop enclosing the entire program, then an exit-to-entry branch exists from the exit node to the entry node. This branch makes the graph strongly connected because (1) we can always reach any node in the graph from the entry node, (2) we can always reach the exit node from any node in the graph, and (3) we can reach the entry node from the exit node via the exit-to-entry branch. In the case of a program which does not have an exit-to-entry branch, we add a phantom branch to the graph to ensure that it is strongly connected and that Eq. (3.66) is valid.

We now compute the cyclomatic complexity of the graph in Fig. 3.14. Since the graph is not strongly connected, we must add a phantom branch from node *j* to node *b*, as shown in Fig. 3.16. The number of nodes (*a* to *k*) is 11, and the number of branches is 13. Substitution in Eq. (3.66) yields a cyclomatic complexity of 3:

$$v(G) = 13 - 11 + 1 = 3$$

There are two other techniques for computing cyclomatic complexity based on the associated nondirected graph (the digraph with arrows removed). The

[1]McCabe (1976), p. 308.

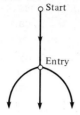

Start

Entry

(Remainder of graph)

Exit

Stop

Figure 3.15 Definitions of start, stop, entry, and exit nodes in a program graph model.

cyclomatic complexity is equal to the number of branches which must be removed from the network to interrupt all loops and still yield a tree (a subgraph with all nodes connected and no loops). In Fig. 3.16 we can form a tree by removing branches 11, 6, and 10 or 2, 4, and 5, or many other combinations of three branches. In the special case of a planar graph (one which can be drawn on a sheet of paper with no crossing branches), we can compute the cyclomatic

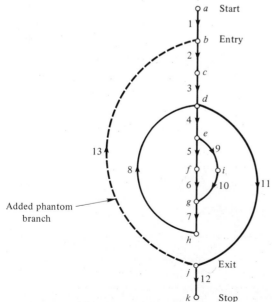

Added phantom branch

Figure 3.16 Transformation of Fig. 3.14 into a strongly connected graph through addition of a phantom branch.

number by counting the number of independent loops (also called *meshes* or *faces*).

In the case of Fig. 3.16, there are three meshes: $(b, c, d, j, b), (d, e, f, g, h, d)$, and (e, i, g, f, e). These two alternate computation schemes, as well as other material relating structured programs and cyclomatic complexity, are discussed in App. C and in the problems at the end of this chapter.

In some programs there are several entry points. One example is a programmable calculator that allows a program to be initiated at any labeled statement by a GO TO LABEL X command. Similarly, many computers have operating systems which allow similar multiple entries in a higher-level language. Also, at the assembly or machine language level breakpoints, interrupts, continue commands, and other control features result in multiple entry points. In such cases we must consider the entry node shown in Fig. 3.15 to be connected by a set of branches to each such entry point. In many programs, one also encounters multiple stop instructions, in which each stop instruction is assumed to connect to the exit node. These manipulations ensure that we can still draw our graph in the form given in Fig. 3.15. In other cases, such as program calls to the operating system, e.g., ON CONDITIONS in PL/1, we have more difficulties.

Experience with the cyclomatic complexity measure As was previously stated, not only must cyclomatic complexity make intuitive sense, but the measure must be useful as well. McCabe has put the index to two uses. The first use is to assume that $v(G)$ is a good measure of complexity and to specify that all modules in a top-down structured design have a complexity of, say, $v(G) = 10$ or less. This would replace our normal rule of thumb of one page of code (that it should be about 50 to 60 lines). Secondly, McCabe has written a program which displays the graph of a program on a CRT and computes $v(G)$. He has used this to study many programs and has found that those which have a complex graph and a large $v(G)$ are often the trouble-prone programs.

Myers (1977) has pointed out that if one has a multiple decision such as

$$\text{IF A} = 0 \quad \& \quad \begin{array}{c} \text{B} = 1 \\ \text{THEN} \end{array}$$

we can treat the compound statement as a single decision (one node) or a multiple decision (two nodes). The second interpretation yields a cyclomatic number larger by 1 than the former interpretation.

There are also relationships between the cyclomatic complexity and the number of test cases, which are explored in Chap. 4.

We now turn our attention to two other topological approaches to program complexity, the knot count and the polynomial complexity.

Figure 3.17 Three examples of knot complexity calculations from Woodward et al. (1977) based on programs from Brown and Nelson (1977). (*a*) Routine with 4 knots. (*b*) Routine having 9 knots. It has 2 branch-creating statements, and so $v(G) = 2 + 1 = 3$. (*c*) Rewritten version of routine in (*b*) having no phantom paths and 3 knots. It still has 2 branch-creating statements and so $v(G) = 2 + 1 = 3$.

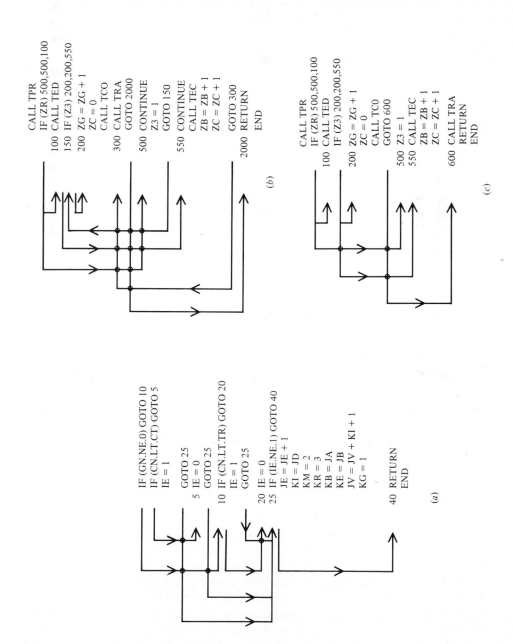

(b)

```
        CALL TPR
        IF (ZR) 500,500,100
100     CALL TED
150     IF (Z3) 200,200,550
200     ZG = ZG + 1
        ZC = 0
        CALL TCO
300     CALL TRA
        GOTO 2000
500     CONTINUE
        Z3 = 1
        GOTO 150
550     CONTINUE
        CALL TEC
        ZB = ZB + 1
        ZC = ZC + 1
        GOTO 300
2000    RETURN
        END
```

(c)

```
        CALL TPR
        IF (ZR) 500,500,100
100     CALL TED
        IF (Z3) 200,200,550
200     ZG = ZG + 1
        ZC = 0
        CALL TC0
        GOTO 600
500     Z3 = 1
550     CALL TEC
        ZB = ZB + 1
        ZC = ZC + 1
600     CALL TRA
        RETURN
        END
```

(a)

```
        IF (GN.NE.0) GOTO 10
        IF (CN.LT.CT) GOTO 5
        IE = 1
        GOTO 25
5       IE = 0
        GOTO 25
10      IF (CN.LT.TR) GOTO 20
        IE = 1
        GOTO 25
20      IE = 0
25      IF (IE.NE.1) GOTO 40
        JE = JE + 1
        KI = JD
        KM = 2
        KR = 3
        KB = JA
        KE = JB
        JV = JV + KI + 1
        KG = 1
40      RETURN
        END
```

Table 3.18 Table of metrics for a sample of 26 Fortran subroutines from a numerical algorithms library

Routine	Lines	GOTOs	IFs	$v(G)$	Knots
A	3	0	0	1	0
B	7	1	1	3	0
C	8	0	1	2	0
D	16	1	1	3	0
E	17	2	3	7	0
F	21	2	5	5	3
G	21	1	1	7	0
H	24	2	3	8	0
I	39	0	0	6	0
J	43	7	9	17	0
K	47	4	10	10	11
L	50	11	11	14	9
M	51	4	4	13	1
N	55	9	7	13	2
O	58	6	8	19	3
P	59	5	15	17	12
Q	68	7	2	7	2
R	69	4	18	19	27
S	74	7	7	22	1
T	77	12	12	18	7
U	93	13	13	22	5
V	95	11	19	27	83
W	112	15	14	24	15
X	210	52	42	62	30
Y	249	23	32	62	42
Z	310	59	54	85	33

Source: Woodward et al. (1977).

Knot complexity Another topological measure which has been suggested in the research literature is knot complexity.[1] Essentially the technique relates to the number of crossings of flow or control lines added to a listing of program code or pseudo-code. In Fig. 2.9 we depicted the pseudo-code of a program with control lines added. Since there are no crossings of control lines, the knot complexity is zero. Three examples of knot complexities of 4, 9, and 3 are shown in Fig. 3.17*a*, *b*, and *c*. (Note that the cyclomatic complexities $v(G)$ of the examples in Fig. 3.17*b* and *c* are given in the figure captions.) Woodward compares the knot complexity of 26 numerical algorithms with the program length (in lines) and the cyclomatic complexity, as shown in Table 3.18. For the 26 examples chosen, the correlation between program complexity and statement length was .98. If this correlation is true in general, then there is no advantage in computing $v(G)$ instead of the simpler program length. Since all the programs studied were of one

[1]Woodward et al. (1977).

type, one should not form any general conclusions about cyclomatic complexity without further study.

Other complexity measures Among the many other complexity measures in the literature (see Belady, 1979), we will mention two others.

In Chap. 4 we shall discuss various methods of computing the number of paths in a computer program. One of the techniques introduced in Chap. 4 for determining the number of paths in a computer program can also be viewed as a complexity measure. This is discussed further in Sec. 4.6.4 in the subsection "Polynomial Complexity."

Another interesting study[1] compares several different intuitive measures of complexity—number of calls, GO TOs, etc.—for a number of examples. The reader is referred to the paper for details.

3.3 MEMORY REQUIREMENTS

3.3.1 Introduction

The term *storage* is generally understood; however, it applies to many collections of data and several physical devices in a computer system. A typical memory hierarchy is shown in Fig. 3.18. The archives can be composed of information in many forms; however, they can be categorized among several basic types: books, journals, reports, data tables, and magazines. These may be in hard-copy form (paper) or in microfiche (microfilm). Microfiche obviously provides a great decrease in physical size. We assume that a sheet of microfiche is the same width and half the height of a book, and that each microfiche sheet can store 100 frames (1 frame = 1 book page). Thus, a "page" of microfiche stores 200 book pages. We assume that 200 book pages require a centimeter of storage space. If we can file 20 microfiche sheets per centimeter, then 4000 microfiche book-page images can be stored in the same space as a 1-cm-thick book containing 200 pages. Thus, the reduction factor is 20 : 1.

The other storage media in the figure correspond to the well-known magnetic and electronic technologies. The data in Fig. 3.18 correspond to typical values achieved in the period 1971 to 1974, and future projections appear in Figs. 3.19 and 3.20.

It is difficult to formulate any overall technique for storage analysis, since such an analysis is so intimately related to the problem details: the data structures and language chosen and the design approach. The approach taken here is to separately consider the problem, the program which solves the problem, and the data storage associated with the program. An analysis of the problem leads to an approach, a list of variables, possible algorithms, and input and output data

[1]Zolnowski and Simmons (1977).

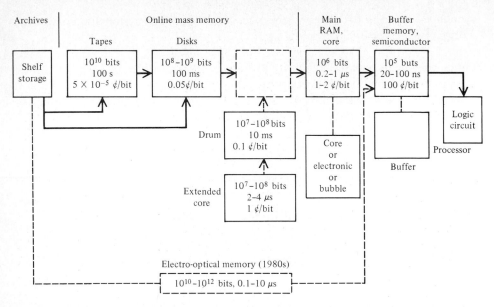

Figure 3.18 Typical memory hierarchy, 1971–1975. (*Note:* Costs and processing time are circa mid-1970's.) *(From Turn, 1974, p. 68)*

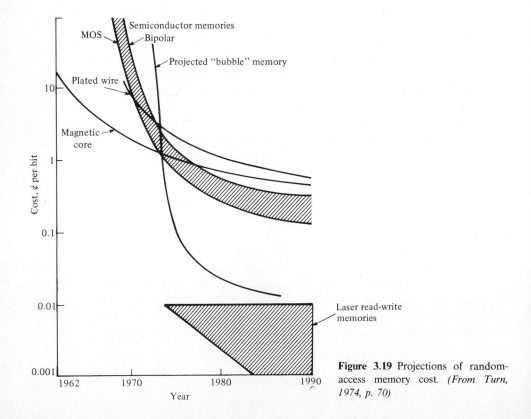

Figure 3.19 Projections of random-access memory cost. *(From Turn, 1974, p. 70)*

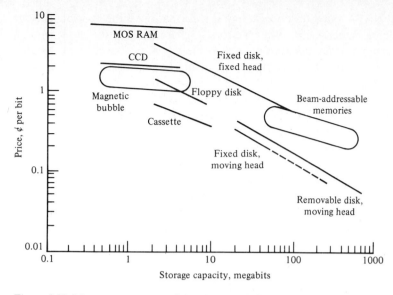

Figure 3.20 Memory storage capacity versus cost. MOS RAMs and magnetic bubbles have the same basic storage capacity, but bubbles are almost a factor of 10 cheaper. Floppy, fixed, and removable disk memories have greater storage capacities at a lower cost per bit by several orders of magnitude. Also see Bernard (1980, pp.30–33). He projects that in 1985 costs of bubble memory will be 1–3 millicents/bit. *(From Hnatek, 1979, p. 69)*

requirements. On the basis of the problem analysis, we can use the methods of Sec. 3.2.8 to estimate the operator-operand length. The analyst then considers the language, computer system, and storage media and:

1. Converts program length in terms of operators and operands into memory locations
2. Estimates the amount of input, intermediate, and output memory storage required and converts this into memory locations

The initial storage analysis is completed when the program and data storage needs are summed and apportioned among the various long- and short-term storage devices.

We focus on the problem-analysis phase and present two problems as case studies to illustrate memory analysis. The first example is that of the collection, storage, and display of the data gathered by a NASA satellite. The data appear in the Sec. 3.3.2. The second example is the planning of a software reliability data repository, involving many storage media, which is discussed in Sec. 5.9.7.

3.3.2 Storage Analysis for a Data-Limited Example

A data processing application in which the limiting factors are data storage and data transfer rate is in the collection, transmission, and processing of satellite data. Typically NASA satellites collect digital information, either periodically or continuously, from cameras and other sensors. Generally the data can be transmitted only during certain portions of the orbit when the satellite is roughly above the ground station. Thus, during each orbit the on-board computer must store data collected over most of the orbit, transmit them as a very high rate during the pass over the ground station, and reset itself for the next orbit.

Let us assume that the satellite is in a 100-mi-high orbit which takes 90 min to traverse. A simple construction from plane geometry reveals that the satellite just comes into sight over the horizon when the tangent constructed at the ground station (4000 miles above the earth's center) intersects the orbit, which is 4100 miles above the earth's center. When the satellite first comes into view the angle between the ground station–earth center and the earth center–satellite lines is about 12.5°. By symmetry, the total viewing angle of the satellite from the ground station is about 25°. Since the satellite traverses 360° in 90 min and, in a circular orbit, its rate is constant, it is in view above the ground station for about 6 min.

Typical satellite missions now planned by NASA[1] will collect between 10^{12} and 10^{14} bits of data per day. For a 90-min orbit this reduces to 6.25×10^{10} to 6.25×10^{12} bits per orbit. This means that in the 6-min pass, assuming the smaller data-collection rate, the satellite must beam data to the ground station at 10^{10} bits per minute, or 174 megabits per second. The higher data collection rate is 100 times greater! The smaller storage requirement of 6.25×10^{10} bits should be compared with conventional minicomputer memory device capacities such as a cassette tape (0.75 megabits) and a disk (20 to 80 megabits).[2] Thus each pass would fill 1000 disks with 62.5-megabit capacity! Is it any wonder that NASA is in the forefront of new research and rapid application of new developments in memory systems and data transmission?

It is interesting that the high data storage and transfer rates quoted above are so mind-boggling that NASA, in its briefings, speaks of two new units of data measurement which are both about 10^{13} bits: (1) data equivalent to the contents of the Library of Congress and (2) data equivalent to a day's transmission of TV pictures. (The derivation of the units is given in Tables 3.19 and 3.20.)

3.3.3 Prediction

All the preceding discussions in Sec. 3.3 have dealt with the storage requirements of the problem. Once these have been analyzed, it is the task of the designer to estimate how much memory the program (which solves this problem) will take. Since memory can be filled, overwritten several times in the execution of the program, and shared by various computations, the two analyses are not identical.

---

[1] Information briefing to NASA Research and Technical Advisory Committee, November 1976.

[2] Digital Equipment Corporation (1973) quotes the data densities of the RK8E disk as 1.6 million 12-bit words, and of the TA8E cassette as 93,000 bytes (8 bits). The newest Winchester disk technology can accommodate 5–25 million bytes per disk.

Table 3.19 Information content of a day of TV pictures

1. Sixty fields per second of interlaced pictures = 30 pictures per second.

2. Each picture contains 525 lines, and the horizontal sweep frequency is about 16 kHz (16,000) bits per line).

3. Bits per picture = $525 \times 16 \times 10^3 = 8.4 \times 10^6$.

4. Bits per second = $30 \times 8.4 \times 10^6 = 2.5 \times 10^8$.

5. Bits per day = $60 \times 60 \times 24 \times 2.5 \times 10^8 = 2.2 \times 10^{13}$.

Source: Arguimbau (1948), pp. 14, 128, 129.

Table 3.20 Information content of the Library of Congress

1. Assume there are 10×10^6 books in the library.

2. Assume 300 pages per book, or a total of 3×10^9 pages.

3. Assume 15 words per line and 40 lines per page, or 600 words per page.

4. Words in the library = $600 \times 3 \times 10^9 = 1.8 \times 10^{12}$.

5. Information content per word:
   a. Method 1: Assume 26 letters plus the space symbol are all equiprobable; then the H (letter) = $\log_2(27) = 4.76$ bits. Assuming an average of 5 independent letters per word, we obtain H(word) = 23.8 bits. However, not all the letters are equiprobable, nor are they all independent. Thus, let us say H(word) ≈ 10 bits.
   b. Method 2: Assume that the author has a vocabulary of 16,000 words $\approx 2^{14}$. If each word is equiprobable, H(word) = $\log_2 16,000 \approx 14$. However, we know not all words are equiprobable (cf. Zipf's law), so assume H(word) ≈ 10 bits.

6. Information content of library = $10 \times 1.8 \times 10^{12} = 1.8 \times 10^{13}$ bits.

This section addresses itself to the analysis during the design stage of the required memory size.

One approach to program memory sizing is to identify the algorithms which are responsible for the majority of the memory usage and analyze the required memory. Examination of the research literature on algorithms will be helpful in establishing whether the memory requirement for the particular algorithm in question has already been studied and documented.[1] Of course one must make allowances for overlay techniques, common subroutines, etc.

Another approach is to decompose the memory requirement into three parts:

$$\text{Memory requirement} = \text{Program length} + \text{variable and constant storage length} + \text{data-structure storage length} \quad (3.67)$$

[1] See Aho et al. (1974) and Lawler (1971).

Table 3.21 Number of tokens per machine instruction for several computers

Type of instruction	Examples	Tokens per instruction
Stack instructions	PDP-11, Burroughs 5500*	1 (1 operator)
Single-address computers	PDP-8	2 (1 operator + 1 operand)
Two-address computers	PDP-11, IBM-360	3 (1 operator + 2 operands)

*Bell and Newell (1971), p. 257.

The estimate of the data-structure storage length must come from an analysis of the structures and algorithms to be used in the design. The variable and constant storage length come from an analysis of the input parameters and constants, the temporary storage required, and the output parameters required. The estimate of the program length can be obtained by utilizing the Zipf length and estimating operator and operand types, as in Sec. 3.2.8. Of course, the token length n is not what we are after; we want the machine instruction length. We can obtain the machine instruction length by dividing the number of tokens by the average number of tokens per instruction in the machine language for the computer in question. An example of such computations for several computers is given in Table 3.21.

Of course, most computers have a mixture of different types of instructions, and one may wish to estimate or determine statistics based on past experience for the average number of tokens per instruction for any particular computer. This technique is explored in more detail in the problems at the end of this chapter.

3.3.4 Effect of Memory Limitations on Program Development

In discussing the cost of memory, until now we have implicitly, if not explicitly, considered the penalty of extra memory in terms of dollars. In the aerospace business and certain other applications, not dollars but cubic inches, pounds, or watts are the critical parameters. Most of us have had the experience of participating in or watching the installation of a large, ground-based digital computer. A room is chosen, and if necessary, walls are broken down to enlarge the floor space. Special air conditioning and wiring are installed, and the equipment is properly situated over load-bearing walls and columns. Of course, no such thing happens in a satellite or aircraft.

As was discussed in Chap. 1, the military and NASA have been pioneers in coming up with new and complex tasks for electronics and computers. This has resulted in drastic increases in the on-board storage requirements of Department of Defense software (see Fig. 1.1). In aircraft, electrical power is derived from generators connected to the jet engines, and although it is not limitless, the main constraints are generally volume and weight. In the case of satellites, volume and weight are obvious constraints; however, so is power. In the Nimbus weather satellite, horizon scanners were designed to provide position stabilization (attitude

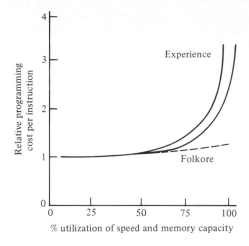

Figure 3.21 Cost of programming versus percent utilization of memory. *(From Boehm, 1981, p. 21)*

control) for small motions, and rate gyroscopes were designed into the system to provide stabilization and damping signals for larger motions. It was later discovered that the gyroscopes drew too much power and thus had to be dropped. The initial result was that the first redesign with only horizon scanners and electrical filter networks (to provide rate damping by differentiating position) proved unstable for many values of initial injection velocities (the large-angle nonlinearities of the horizon scanners for the tumbling satellite produced coupled instabilities). In the case of the LEM-Apollo guidance computer, a smaller memory than desired was used because the solar panels and batteries were able to support only a modest memory power drain. In fact, Barry Boehm has collected data to show (see Fig. 3.21) that when one approaches the 100 percent utilization of on-board memory, the programming effort and debugging effort rise enormously. (MIL-STD-1679 requires less than 80 percent memory utilization; see Table 6.19.)

One can almost envision the two hypothetical scenarios that follow:

Scenario 1: Inexperienced program manager During the first week of the program the manager announces that only 16K of core are available and the team will have to make do with that. After 3 months the programming team has a final design, part of the code, and estimates that the complete design will require 19K of core. The manager tells them that they should be smart enough to eliminate 3K and "squeeze it in." They walk away from the meeting mumbling about code overlays and other clever tricks, and then the woe begins.

Scenario 2: Experienced program manager During the preliminary stages the manager estimates that the job will require 14K to 18K of memory. He agrees with the others who are managing the design to try to do the job in 16K, but he may be back to them. He tells his design team that he has 12K of core and it is going to be awfully tight, but to see what they can do and to get back to him with the details of their preliminary design as soon as they have it ready. The manager puts the extra 4K in his back pocket. They return in a month with long faces and an estimate of 19K. After detailed review all agree that the best they can do is to trim the requirement to 18K; however if they left out or modified feature P, Q, or R they could trim it to about 15K. (They feel that all these features are noncrucial.) The program manager goes back to the management team and tells them (1) they can have all their functions if they will give him an extra 4K of core; (2) if they can do without or modify function P, Q, or R, he can do the job with 16K; and (3) if they don't believe him and the evidence he presents they should be prepared for sizable cost and time overruns or give the job to someone else to manage. One hopes that they will choose alternative 2, the manager and his crew will do the job in 13.5K with no tricks, and everyone will be pleased.

Maybe you don't believe these scenarios; however, you should, because every experienced aerospace software manager has heard of or lived through such events.

3.4 PROCESSING TIME

3.4.1 Introduction

The run time of a computer program or the processing time of a software system is a system performance parameter which varies in importance from crucial to minor depending on the application. In the satellite data-transmission application discussed in Sec. 3.3.2, the ground antenna must track the satellite as it moves at a rate of $0.4°/\text{min}$ overhead. If radar tracking is used, position data arrive and are fed to the computer, position calculations and predictions are made, and servo (or electronic scan) drive signals are sent to the antenna control system. Clearly, only a certain amount of time is available for calculations, and if this is exceeded, a tracking data point is lost. If too many tracking points are lost, the antenna no longer follows accurately. At the other extreme, the time required to evaluate a formula, once, on a hand-held calculator might vary from 1s to 1 min (depending on the power and speed of the calculator), yet the $60:1$ variation might be unimportant.

3.4.2 Algorithmic Complexity

In many projects the heart of the problem, or at least a major portion of it, involves a computation, search, manipulation or some other operation which is specified by a solution algorithm. The corresponding program, or software system with this algorithm embedded, is essentially a computer language transformation of the algorithm. Thus a study of the complexity of the algorithm establishes a basis for a subsequent study of the complexity of the problem.

We are now faced with the problem of extending the heuristic ideas of a complexity measure discussed in Sec. 3.2.2. Our heuristic concept of complexity really relates to how difficult or convoluted the problem is. The use of the term *algorithmic complexity*[1] or *computational complexity*[2] really deals with the amount of storage or running time required in the implementation of an algorithm. In fact in Aho et al. (1974) the authors use the terms *space complexity* and *time complexity*. In this text *algorithmic complexity* will not be used further, but the terms *algorithmic storage analysis* and *algorithmic processing-time analysis* will be substituted.

Although space and time problems can overwhelm even the largest known computers, they are especially troublesome in advanced real-time computer systems. The fundamental problem is that people frequently pose problems and attempt to solve them with a computer when they are beyond their intellectual span of control and beyond the speed and storage capacities of known computers. The special problems of storage in airborne and space-borne computers and processing time in real-time systems were discussed in Sec. 3.3.2.

3.4.3 Algorithmic Processing-Time Analysis

In general, the goals of algorithmic time analysis are to classify a broad spectrum of physical problems into homogeneous groupings, to discuss the various ways of approaching problems within the grouping, and to compute the related processing times. The work in this area usually requires some mathematical maturity, considerable emphasis on proofs, and rather complete descriptive models of automata and data structures. Although it is assumed that many of the readers of this book will possess such a background, many will not. Thus, the purpose of this section will be to present the types of problems which are involved and to summarize some of the known results. Readers who wish a deeper understanding of this subject are referred to Aho et al. (1974).

The immediate reaction of many to the problem of algorithmic time limitations is that this can easily be solved by a faster computer. If we let n stand for the size of the problem, then we can show that for problems where the processing time is *linearly* related to n, increasing the computer speed (say, measured in MIPS, millions of instructions per second) does help considerably. In the cases where the processing time increases as n^2 or n^3 or exponentially, the increase in MIPS is of no real help for large n. Note that if the processing time increases as 2^n it is called exponential, since $2^n = e^{0.69n} \approx e^n$. This is easily illustrated by Tables 3.22 and 3.23, which are from Aho. It is assumed that one repetition of the algorithm takes 1 ms. In the case of exponential time complexity, the 1-h problem size is a factor of 10^5 smaller than it would have been if the time complexity were linear. In the second table, we see the effects of a tenfold increase in MIPS. In the exponential case, the 1-h problem size increases only from 21 to 24.

Before we go further in this section we might ask, What are the consequences if an algorithm is shown to have exponential (or larger) time complexity? First of

[1]Aho et al. (1974).
[2]Lawler (1971).

Table 3.22 Limits on problem size as determined by growth rate

Algorithm	Time complexity	Maximum problem size		
		1 s	1 min	1 h
A_1	n	1000	6×10^4	3.6×10^6
A_2	$n \log n$	140	4893	2.0×10^5
A_3	n^2	31	244	1897
A_4	n^3	10	39	153
A_5	2^n	9	15	21

Source: Aho et al. (1974), Fig. 1.1, p. 3.

Table 3.23 Effect of tenfold speedup

Algorithm	Time complexity	Maximum problem size before speedup	Maximum problem size after speedup
A_1	n	s_1	$10s_1$
A_2	$n \log n$	s_2	Approximately $10s_2$ for large s_2
A_3	n^2	s_3	$3.16s_3$
A_4	n^3	s_4	$2.15s_4$
A_5	2^n	s_5	$s_5 + 3.3$

Source: Aho et al. (1974), Fig. 1.2, p. 3.

all it is possible that n is of modest size, and that by using good programming and a fast computer we can solve the problem. It is also possible that our initial analysis of the problem is faulty, and that we can find a different algorithm which solves the problem and is of a lower order of complexity. Last, we can attempt to find an approximate solution to the problem which is of lower order. An example follows which illustrates the reductions which can be achieved in processing time due to a change in algorithm.

Suppose we wish to write a computer program that helps us with switching-circuit design.[1] We can characterize a switching function with three inputs and a single output as a switching function of three variables. If we let x, y, and z be the inputs, then we can write the switching function as $f(x, y, z)$. Commonly we specify the switching function by the truth table shown in Table 3.24. If we let n be the number of variables in the problem ($x_1, x_2, \ldots, x_n$), then we can view the first n columns in the truth table as making up an n-bit binary number.

Each row in the truth table is one of r binary numbers, and since there are 2^n rows in the table, $r = 2^n$. If we consider the last column in the table, we observe

[1]See Kohavi (1970), p. 55, or any standard switching theory book.

Table 3.24 Truth table for the switching function

1. $f(x, y, z) = xy\bar{z} + xyz$

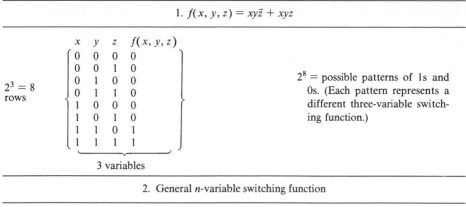

$2^3 = 8$ rows

x	y	z	$f(x, y, z)$
0	0	0	0
0	0	1	0
0	1	0	0
0	1	1	0
1	0	0	0
1	0	1	0
1	1	0	1
1	1	1	1

2^8 = possible patterns of 1s and 0s. (Each pattern represents a different three-variable switching function.)

3 variables

2. General n-variable switching function

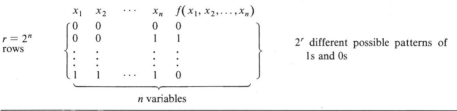

$r = 2^n$ rows

x_1	x_2	$\cdots$	x_n	$f(x_1, x_2, \ldots, x_n)$
0	0		0	0
0	0		1	1
:	:		:	:
1	1	$\cdots$	1	0

2^r different possible patterns of 1s and 0s

n variables

that a new switching function is created each time the bit pattern is changed in the last column. Since each of the r rows can have a 0 or a 1 in this column, there are 2^r possible switching functions. However, $r = 2^n$, and there are $2^{(2^n)}$ possible switching functions.

Suppose we wish to store in our computer the name of each of the switching functions, its minimum form, and a circuit realization which utilizes certain types of logic gates. Our intention is to input the $r = 2^n$ "function" bits and to have the computer locate and output the minimum form and logic circuit. We must store $2^{(2^n)}$ logic circuits in our memory. A discussion of ways to minimize this storage requirement is omitted here. We address ourselves here to the running-time problem. If we are to directly compare our function bit pattern with the $2^{(2^n)}$ patterns stored in memory, we have a case of a higher order than exponential time complexity. The solution is feasible for $n = 3$ (256 patterns), marginally for $n = 4$ (64K patterns), and impossible for $n = 5$ (about 4 billion patterns).

By now the reader will have probably realized that a direct comparison of patterns was a poor choice. If we consider the bit pattern under the function column to be an r-bit binary number, then we can perform a binary search which involves $\log_2 r = n$ comparisons. We are still in trouble with the storage, but the processing time is now only of order n.

In exploring the ways one can construct an algorithm to solve a problem, it is often instructive to consider various data structures such as lists, queues, and

Table 3.25 Algorithmic time complexity for a variety of computations

Type of Algorithm	Reference*	Order† (maximum)
Sorts		
1. Bubble sort	Aho et al. (1974), p. 77	$O(n^2)$
2. Radix (bucket) sort	Aho et al. (1974), p. 78	$O(n)$
3. Comparison sort	Aho et al. (1974), p. 87	$O(n \log_2 n)$
4. General	Wirth (1976), p. 56	Very comprehensive discussion
Search		
1. Linear	Donovan (1972), p. 81	$O(n)$
2. Binary	Aho et al. (1974), p. 114	$O(\log(n+1))$
3. Hash	Aho et al. (1974), p. 114	Possibly better than binary
Graphs		
1. Minimum cost spanning tree	Aho et al. (1974)	$O(n \log n)$
2. Minimum cost	Aho et al. (1974)	$O(n^3)$
3. Minimum cost all positive weights	Lawler (1974)	$O(n^2)$
4. Hamiltonian property	Lawler (1971)	$O(n^2)$
5. Planarity	Lawler (1971)	$O(n)$
6. Trees	Wirth (1976), p. 189	Comprehensive treatment
Matrices		
1. Multiplication	Aho et al. (1974)	$O(n^3)$
2. Multiplication (improved algorithm)	Borodin and Munro (1975), p. 4	$O(n^{2.81})$
3. Inversion	Aho et al. (1974)	$(3/2) \times O$ (multiplication)
Fast Fourier transform		
1. Calculation	Borodin and Munro (1975), p. 81	$O(n \log n)$
Polynomials (integer arithmetic)		
1. Multiplication	Aho et al. (1974)	$M(n)$ = time to multiply two integers of size n.
2. Division	Aho et al. (1974)	$D(n)$ = time to divide an integer of size $2n$ by an integer of size n.
3. Squaring	Aho et al. (1974)	$S(n)$ = time to square an integer of size n.
4. Reciprocals	Aho et al. (1974)	$R(n)$ = time to take reciprocal of an integer of size n.
5. Relationships	Aho et al. (1974)	$S(n) \leq C_1 R(n) \leq C_2 M(n)$ where C_1 and C_2 are constants. $D(n) \leq 4C_3 M(n) + C_4 n$ where C_3 and C_4 are constants.
6. $D(n)$	Aho et al. (1974)	$O(n \log n \log \log n)$
7. $M(n)$	Borodin and Munro (1975), p. 88	$O(n \log n \log \log n)$

Table 3.25 (*continued*)

Type of Algorithm	Reference*	Order† (maximum)
Polynomials (interpolation and evaluation)		
1. Through k points (interpolation)	Aho et al. (1974)	$O(k \log^2 k)$
2. Of degree n evaluated at $n^{1/2}$ points	Borodin and Munro (1975), pp. 48, 70	$O(n^{(\log_2 7)/2})$
Statistics and probability		
1. Median of n numbers	Lawler (1971) Wirth (1976), p. 82	$O(n)$
2. Probability of a union of n independent events	(See Eq. (A-11), App. A)	$O(2^n)$

*See also Trakhtenbrot (1963).

†The notation $O(n^2)$ means that for large n the computation depends upon n^2. Thus, computation times of the form $K_1 + K_2 n^2$ or $K_3 n + K_4 n^2$ would both be $O(n^2)$.

stacks as the basis for an efficient technique. Similarly set, graph, and recursive models of the problem should be explored.

This entire subject is too vast and complex for treatment here. In order to suggest to the reader the types of algorithms and time complexities which have been computed, a summary is given for several selected problem areas in Table 3.25.

Clearly, many algorithms have been studied in detail, and the designer is well advised to examine the theoretical results and discussions in the literature before undertaking the design of such an algorithm.

3.4.4 Analysis and Prediction

Introduction Most of the work on analysis or simulation of processing time has focused on the computer system. The hardware-software complex is divided into major subsystems, and a processing time is assigned to each entity. Then a Monte Carlo (simulation) or Markov (analytical) probabilistic model is made and the system is studied. Also one can focus on specific portions of a large system such as the operating system or the virtual memory organization. These detailed studies are beyond the scope of this book and the reader is referred to the literature.[1]

In the following sections of this chapter we treat the important but less well-studied problem of how to analyze the running time of a segment of code or a program module.

[1]Ferrari (1978); Freiberger (1972).

Monte Carlo models In a large software system, the program can generally be characterized by a number of functional paths through the program, each consisting of many modules. If the processing times of each module are deterministic, we can calculate the processing time along each path as the sum of the individual processing times:

$$T_i = \sum_{\substack{\text{all} \\ j}} t_{mji} \tag{3.68}$$

where
$$T_i = \text{processing time for path } i$$
$$t_{mji} = \text{processing time for module } j \text{ on path } i$$

If each of the i paths is executed with a frequency f_i, then the mean processing time $\bar{T}$ (see Eq. (A.34)) is given by the equation:

$$\bar{T} = \sum_{\substack{\text{all} \\ \text{paths}}} T_i f_i \tag{3.69}$$

The path frequencies can be calculated from a knowledge of the physical problem, or they can be measured, assuming that their number is not so large as to make the problem intractable.

In many cases, the module processing times are probabilistic rather than deterministic because (1) the module contains a DO WHILE or DO UNTIL loop which varies over a range of execution times; (2) the module contains an "idle" loop which waits for an interrupt signal or for an I/O device for a variable amount of time before it can proceed; or (3) the module operation is very complex and we simply model this behavior with an "average" processing time. In all of these cases, we can represent the program as having a number of states with particular processing times and probabilities of transition from one state to the other. Such a stochastic problem can be represented by a Monte Carlo model. Each module represents a state of the process. The parameters in the model are the processing times for each module (which can be deterministic or probabilistic) and the probabilities that each module is called from the control program. The problem is modeled by a simulation program (possibly using GPSS language, for example). The model is run many times and the results are collected and statistically analyzed. The engineering of such a system is discussed in the article by McCammon (1975), and the concept of simulation in the chapter by Graham (1973). The reader is referred to the literature for further details on Monte Carlo models.[1]

Timing experiments In certain cases we can directly calculate or measure the running time of a program. If the entire program is small enough, or if it is easily broken into small modules, then calculation or experimental measurement is feasible.

---

[1]Shooman (1968); Hammersley and Handscomb (1975).

One obvious case in which a running-time calculation can be made is a small (say, 100-line) assembly language program (module). Unless the assembly language contains higher-level macros or other such constructions, one assembly instruction produces one machine language instruction, and the execution times of the machine language instructions are well known. Sometimes the execution times for the two legs of a branch instruction are a little different, but in this case we could estimate the mean time or just take the average (assuming a 50-50 division). The total processing time is just the sum of the constituent instruction-processing times.

This is not the full story, since loops in the program radically change the definition of token length with respect to programming effort or with respect to running time. A DO I $= 1$ TO N loop adds only a few operators and operands for the DO and END statements, which constitute the beginning and end of the loop. However, in computing run time, we must unwrap the loop N times and account for the cumulative effect on the operator and operand count due to the looping. This means we must be able to analyze the structure of the algorithm to define the looping.

Of course, if there is an I/O device with an "idle" loop in the code, the time is no longer deterministic.

Another case in which timing measurements are easily made is a small or modest-sized program on an embedded (dedicated) computer which does not do multiprocessing. If a higher-level language is being used, we can time the execution times of various segments of the code and use Eqs. (3.68) and (3.69). In many cases we can predict the operating times of higher-level-language instructions by constructing an experimental formula. Suppose we wish to calculate the processing time of a higher-level-language statement such as W $=$ X $*$ Y $*$ $*2$ $+$ $\sin(Z)$. We could set up a DO I $= 1$ TO N loop and run and time the execution of the empty loop (no instructions in it) for various values of N. The experiment could be repeated for V $=$ X, V $=$ X $*$ Y, V $=$ Y $*$ $*2$, V $= A + B$, and $V = \sin(Z)$, and a predictive formula could be obtained. A similar approach was taken with respect to 14 short programs used to check the speed of six different versions of Basic.[1]

Benchmark tests and formulas The testing of run time of computer programs is often really a test of the basic speed of the computer system with respect to a standard package of programs (a benchmark). Generally the question is posed, How fast is computer A with respect to computer B? Such tests are useful in selecting a computer for a particular application.[2] These techniques are also useful in estimating how long it will take to run a program already working on computer A, on computer B.[3] Run-time formulas have been devised to supplement or replace the timing experiments. Knight[4] has devised a formula which

[1] Burton (1978).
[2] Bell and Newell (1971), p. 49; Burton (1978).
[3] Shooman et al. (1970).
[4] See Bell and Newell (1971), p. 51, and Turn (1974), p. 73, 74.

utilizes 29 factors plus five weighting numbers[1] in a formula to compute the processing time for 1 million operations of a computer. The weighting numbers are relative instruction frequencies.

Graph analysis In Chap. 2 we discussed the importance of drawing higher-level flowgraphs or pseudo-code to detail and represent the program design. Such a representation can easily be studied to produce a looping analysis. Most of the examples in the literature of looping analysis have started with a program flowgraph;[2] however, one could equally well have used pseudo-code as the point of departure. More research is needed on these approached to produce practical analyses.

Number of operators processed Since processing time is primarily the execution time needed for operator processing, we can focus on operator-processing speed. One can apply the Zipf length to operators alone and estimate the operator length of the program. Again we need a looping analysis, since a module with an operator length of 100 which is inside a DO I = 1 TO 15 loop must be counted as an effective operator length of 1500. The effective length is then multiplied by the average operator time determined by either an arithmetic average of the operator-processing times or a weighted average if available.

One encounters difficulty if the program has a DO WHILE $Z > 0$ loop. Unless one can determine the number of loop repetitions encountered before Z becomes nonpositive, the loop length is unknown. In fact, it may vary with input parameters and thus be probabilistic. The best approach is to estimate the minimum and maximum number of repetitions and continue the analysis using both values. If after the processing-time analysis is completed this loop turns out to be critical, then additional analysis must be performed. We may have to adopt a bottom-up approach to the design of this module and write the code as soon as possible. Once the code is available, it may be easier to estimate the minimum, average, and maximum number of repetitions of this loop. Of course, one can also write a simple driver program for this module and exercise it on the computer for a representative distribution of input parameters. If we keep careful track of the time for each run, we will have an estimate of the run-time probability density.

Much of the material presented in this section is still in the research stages, and much more work is needed in these areas.

3.5 SUMMARY

The basic premise of this chapter was that we could develop a complexity metric that could be used to analyze a problem and develop a complexity index that

---

[1]Zelkowitz (1976), p. 160. Also see Bell and Newell (1971), p. 50.

[2]Beiser (1971), vol. 1, Chap. 7; White and Booth (1976), p. 220; Sholl and Booth (1975), p. 414; Booth (1979).

correlates well with the number of development man-hours and program bugs. In addition, we desired storage and run-time analysis techniques. The area of complexity theory is still evolving; however, much substantial theory exists. Storage analysis and run-time analysis are more heuristic at this point in time.

We now summarize in the following list some of the major areas presented in this chapter:

1. An attractive theory, that of software science, has been introduced and developed.
2. Much of the work in the literature has been devoted to validating the length equations. Much still needs to be done to reduce the theory to a practical and popular means of analysis.
3. The topological measures of complexity analysis, cyclomatic and knot complexity, still need additional theoretical and practical development.
4. Not much theory was presented in the area of storage analysis; however, heuristic methods are widely used in practice.
5. In the area of timing analysis, simulation methods are universally used in practice; however, little theory exists except in the early research stages.

Although complexity analysis still has far to go, the most striking need in this area is for practitioners to begin applying on a wide scale the theories which presently exist.

PROBLEMS

3.1 Choose 10 books with which you are familiar and classify their relative complexity using the classifications of Table 3.1.

3.2 Design a parserlike program to automatically count operators and operands in a programming language of your choice. Give a high-level design in terms of flowcharts, pseudo-code, or HIPO diagrams.

3.3 Select a sample of English text which is 250 words long and test it to see if Zipf's law holds. Graph the results as in Fig. 3.2 and check the slope. Check the validity of Eqs. (3.9) and (3.11).

3.4 Select a second sample of English text from a different source and repeat Prob. 3.3. Compare the results.

3.5 Derive Eqs. (3.21) through (3.21g).

3.6 Derive Eqs. (3.22) through (3.26).

3.7 Select a program in a language of your choice and check to see if the operators and operands alternate. Repeat for a program in a different language. Compare the results.

3.8 Generate a program by simulation composed of alternating operators and operands and test to see how well Eqs. (3.38) and (3.40) apply.

3.9 Repeat Prob. 3.8 without the requirement that operators and operands alternate, and test Eq. (3.41).

3.10 Choose a modest-sized computer program (in any language) which you have written or which is in any textbook or report.

    (*a*) Count the number of unique operators and operands η_1 and η_2. (Note: $t = \eta_1 + \eta_2$.)

    (*b*) Count the total number of operators and operands.

    (*c*) Use the data of parts *a* and *b* to test the validity of Eqs. (3.11) and (3.27).

(d) Plot on log-log paper the operator frequencies versus rank to see if they follow Zipf's law.

(e) Repeat part d for operands.

(f) Repeat part d for operators plus operands (tokens).

3.11 Using the program of Prob. 3.10, compute the following quantities:

(a) Information content H

(b) Halstead volume V

(c) Level l

(d) Effort E

3.12 On the basis of the quantities computed in Prob. 3.11 and the ratios developed in the chapter text, estimate the following:

(a) The number of man-hours necessary to code and test the program.

(b) The number of initial bugs expected in the code.

(c) The number of anticipated lines of code if the program were to be written in assembly language.

(d) Repeat part c assuming Fortran will be the language.

(e) Repeat part c assuming PL/1 will be the language.

3.13 Repeat Prob. 3.10 for a different program.

3.14 Repeat Prob. 3.11 for the program of Prob. 3.13.

3.15 Repeat Prob. 3.12 using the computations of Prob. 3.14.

3.16 Using Prob. 2.3 of Chap. 2 estimate:

(a) The number of operators required in the problem solution

(b) The number of input and output quantities required in the problem solution

(c) The number of intermediate variables which will be required

(d) The total number of tokens (operators plus operands) which will represent the length of the finished program

3.17 Using the estimated of Prob. 3.16, repeat Probs. 3.11 and 3.12.

3.18 Repeat Probs. 3.16 and 3.17 for Prob. 2.4 of Chap. 2.

3.19 Repeat Probs. 3.16 and 3.17 for Prob. 2.5 of Chap. 2.

3.20 Repeat Probs. 3.16 and 3.17 for Prob. 2.8 of Chap. 2.

3.21 Choose any problem of moderate size that you wish (from a text or otherwise) and draw the control flowgraph and compute the cyclomatic complexity by the formula involving the number of vertices and edges and by counting the number of graph faces (mesh loops).

3.22 Prove that H is maximized in Eq. (3.42) if all the p_j's are equal.

3.23 For the case where $i = 2$, plot H versus p_1 in Eq. (3.42).

3.24 Derive Eqs. (3.45) to (3.47).

3.25 Draw a flowchart that shows how to solve the maverick coin problem for all cases.

3.26 Show that all paths in the flowchart of Prob. 3.25 generate at least 3.59 bits of information and thus represent valid solutions.

3.27 Choose a weighing sequence which is not a solution to Prob. 3.25 and show that at least one path generates less than 3.59 bits of information.

3.28 Choose an example and show how to minimize N and H in Eqs. (3.59) and (3.60).

3.29 Study Halstead's work on modularization (1977) and compare this work with the results of Prob. 3.28.

3.30 Code a problem in three different languages and calculate the levels. Explain the results.

3.31 The instructor will assign the same problem to be coded in various languages by different class members. The composite results are then studied.

3.32 Choose a programming example and use Eq. (3.63) to estimate the number of man-months needed for the project.

3.33 Draw flowcharts of two structured and two nonstructured programs with a cyclomatic complexity of 5.

3.34 The following problem (from Ledgard, 1975, p. 67) involves a payroll computation. From the problem statement below:

  (*a*) Estimate the operator-operand length of the program.
  (*b*) Estimate the number of lines of assembly code required.
  (*c*) Estimate the number of lines of Fortran code required.
  (*d*) Estimate the number of man-hours required to write and test the program.

Payroll problem statement

1. The program is to accept card inputs with data for each employee, print the weekly paycheck (fill in amounts on a preprinted form), and compute and output certain weekly averages for the total payroll.
2. The input data on each card contains name of employee, social security number, rate of pay (hourly wage), and hours worked per week. The number of employees (and input cards) varies a bit from week to week.
3. The paycheck must contain name, social security number, and dollar amount of net pay.
4. The net pay is the gross pay minus taxes (assume a 4 percent rate) minus social security (assume a 1.75 percent rate).
5. The weekly average number of hours is to be printed at the end of the payroll computation; it is the total hours divided by the number of employees.

3.35 Compute the cyclomatic complexity for the three designs given in Prob. 2.13 using

  (*a*) The number of faces of the planar graph
  (*b*) The number of edges, vertices, and parts

3.36 Repeat Prob. 3.32 using the constants given in Tables 3.16 and 3.17.

3.37 Design an experiment such as those described in Sec. 3.2.10 under "Human Performance and Information Theory." Perform the experiment and analyze the results.

3.38 As a problem for classroom illustration, the instructor should collect the data from student homework and analyze in class:

  (*a*) Data collected in Prob. 3.10
  (*b*) Data collected in Prob. 3.16

3.39 Analyze the data of Table 3.13 by plotting and fitting the best straight line (least squares) and computing the correlation coefficient. (Use statistical computer program packages if available.)

  (*a*) Compare the actual number of tokens with estimate 1.
  (*b*) Compare the actual number of tokens with estimate 2.
  (*c*) Compare estimate 1 with estimate 2.

3.40 Check the results given in Table 3.12.

3.41 We wish to explore the validity of the alternating operator-operand assumption used in the derivation of the Halstead length formula. To do this take a copy of any program you select and mark operators with an *x* and operands with an *o*. The sum of the total number of *x* and *o* symbols is the number of tokens in the program. Count the number of paired symbols (*xx*, *oo*), the number of triplets (*xxx*, *ooo*), etc. Calculate the percentage of program tokens which are singles (*x*, *o*), pairs, triplets, etc. What is your conclusion about the alternating hypothesis?

3.42 Compute the knot complexities and cyclomatic complexities for three programs and compare.

3.43 What is the knot complexity of a structured program?

3.44 Can we apply Zipf's law to pseudo-code to predict program length? Explain why or why not.

3.45 Select programs in the following languages[1] and compute the number of lines of source code, the number of tokens, and the ratio of tokens per line.

  (*a*) PL/1
  (*b*) Fortran

[1] The instructor may modify the language list to suit the class's background.

    (*c*) Basic
    (*d*) Algol
    (*e*) Pascal
    (*f*) Assembler (of your choice)

3.46 As a problem for classroom illustration, the instructor should collect all the data produced by the students' homework solutions of Prob. 3.45 and analyze them in class.

3.47 Can we apply Zipf's law to an algorithm to predict the length of the program module which implements the algorithm? Explain why or why not.

3.48 How can we define, describe, and characterize complexity of problem, algorithm, language, and program?

3.49 A program is written to solve for and print out the roots (real and imaginary) of a cubic equation, $Ax^2 + Bx^2 + Cx + D = 0$. The approach to be used extracts the real root first, then uses the quadratic formula for the remaining roots.
    (*a*) Estimate the number of operator and operand types.
    (*b*) Calculate the program length using the Zipf formula.
    (*c*) Calculate the program volume, level, and effort.
    (*d*) Estimate the number of man-hours needed for the software.

3.50 Assume that we are to change the design of Prob. 3.49 so that the roots not only are to be computed but are to be classified as well: all negative real, all real but one or more positive, complex with all real parts negative, complex with at least one positive real part. How do the measures in Prob. 3.49 change? Explain.

3.51 A program is written to solve for and print out the roots (real and imaginary) of a cubic equation, $Ax^3 + Bx^2 + Cx + D = 0$. The approach to be used extracts the real root first, then uses the quadratic formula for the remaining roots.
    (*a*) Estimate the number of operator and operand types.
    (*b*) Calculate the program length using the Zipf formula.
    (*c*) Calculate the program volume, level, and effort.
    (*d*) Estimate the number of man-hours needed for the software.

3.52 Choose a problem which is basically a data storage task. Define the data structure and analyze the memory requirements.

3.53 Choose one of the examples given in Table 3.25, write a program to implement the algorithm, test the algorithm for several values of n, and compare the theoretical and experimental results.

3.54 Write one or more programs in a language which you can run on several computers. Use this as a benchmark to test and compare the performance of the computers. Comment on the results.

3.55 Based on your list of inputs and outputs (operands) and an estimate of the number of operators for problem A, estimate the token length of the program using the Zipf-law formula and again using Halstead's formula.

3.56 Five different versions of an IF THEN ELSE construct are given in Table 2.14, written in different languages.
    (*a*) Compute the information content V for each program.
    (*b*) Compute the Halstead level for each program.
    (*c*) Compute the Halstead effort E for each program.
    (*d*) Estimate the programming time for each of these programs and the number of bugs.
    (*e*) Comment on the results. Does sample size matter?

3.57 Repeat Prob. 3.56 for the DO WHILE constructs given in Table 2.15. How do the Halstead-level values compare for the two problems?

CHAPTER
FOUR

PROGRAM TESTING

4.1 INTRODUCTION

4.1.1 Importance of Testing

In Chap. 1 we treated the various phases of the life cycle of system software. This discussion was summarized again by Fig. 3.1, which delineated 17 different phases in the life cycle. If we wish to simplify our conceptual model of software development, we can categorize all phases as either design or testing. Consequently, initial formulation of requirements and specifications would be viewed as the early phases of design. The first test phase would be module testing; this would be followed by integration testing. An allied process is the localization and determination of the cause of error. Similarly, error correction is another phase of design (actually a redesign). Thus, we have alternating sequences of design and testing throughout the project.

If we examine the overall structure of software development (see Table 1.5), we see that testing accounts for approximately 30 to 50 percent of the total development effort. If we discuss life-cycle costs including maintenance, then the percentage of the total cost attributable to development testing is considerably reduced; however, the maintenance effort also involves much testing. The inescapable conclusion is that software testing is a vital and major part of any software development or maintenance effort.

It is important to remember that the purposes, the methods, and the tools of testing change throughout the various phases of the development cycle. For example, let us take the unit (module) testing that occurs subsequent to the initial coding of a particular module. The initial test is essentially that which is performed on the software by the syntax-checking program within the compiler (or assembler) that is used. Clearly, the code cannot be correct if the syntax is wrong. Subsequently, the programmer inputs a set of data and examines the output results to see if at least the gross features of operation are correct. The middle phase of such module testing would involve a comprehensive exploration of the way in which the software executes the various functions for which it was designed. The last phase of module testing would involve a concerted effort to test the various stress points, or extremes of the range of variables, and also other known, or suspected, test cases, which would root out unusual difficulties. A similar cycle is repeated during system integration testing.

During acceptance testing, two distinct viewpoints prevail. The developer of the software tries to demonstrate all the features and run various tests which work, so as to convince the purchaser that the software is sound and should be accepted. The purchaser, on the other hand, strives to think up stressful and unusual cases to assess how bug-free and trouble-free the software is at the present moment, and whether it is acceptable at this time without further testing, debugging, and development.

The range of techniques employed in testing is extremely broad. When we attempt to test specifications and requirements, the only truly viable technique is to hold a design review.[1] The design review is essentially a conference lasting from one day to as much as a week. The design review should include a group of those intimately involved with the project (buyer, seller, and user), as well as a few experts not closely involved who are willing to contribute their efforts to help the group explore the validity of the requirements and specifications. The group may be aided by flowcharts, specification tools, various design tables and tools, etc. However, the end criterion which is applied is that most human quality—judgment. On the other hand, toward the middle of a development cycle, we may employ the most inhuman technique of testing by machine. That means that we have software (a test-generator program) which tests other software (the program which we are developing) and compares the actual results with precomputed results.

Another important consideration is, Who does the testing? This point is generally overlooked, or poorly understood by the student programmer who has had experience mainly with writing small programs for personal use. Such a programmer writes, tests, and debugs the programs single-handedly and eventually gets them to work well enough for the purposes at hand. If other people have trouble using them, or discover errors, the designer has, by this time, often lost interest and is not about to continue further testing and debugging of the program. The experienced, and perhaps cynical, program manager immediately comments, "You don't think I'm going to let my programmers test their own programs, do you? That's like letting the wolf watch the sheep!" As a programmer

---

[1]Should the research presently under way on specification tools prove feasible (see Sec. 6.2.2), an important new technique will become available for general use.

gains testing experience, his or her viewpoint often undergoes the following evolution:

1. Who needs testing? I wrote the program myself and I know that it works perfectly.
2. Oops. My perfect program just blew up. I will not test my (own) programs.
3. In fact, I won't commit any new program to production. I'll test and retest.
4. There's a happy medium. Part of the art of testing is to know when to stop testing.

Actually, the most common situation lies somewhere in between.

The programmer who originally writes the code generally carries out the module testing, whereas a separate test group often performs the integration testing.[1] The responsibility for fixing bugs found during module testing obviously lies with the programmer who generated the code initially. The responsibility for fixing bugs found during integration testing may lie with the designer, or may be shared between the designer and the integration-test group. It is important to use formal methods to avoid incomplete error records. Once integration testing has begun, a program is placed under configuration control,[2] and formal procedures must be used to change the code in any way. Thus, it is unlikely that errors will not be properly documented after this milestone has been reached.

It is also important to recognize significant differences in the way we test various-sized programs. Yourdon has categorized program complexity and its relation to testing as shown in Table 4-1.

4.1.2 Range and Scope of Tests

Another factor which has become clearly understood and documented only in the last few years is the tremendous cost of errors found late in the program-development process. In Fig. 1.5 we saw the high relative cost of correcting errors which survive until later stages of the development cycle. The principle of early testing is simply and clearly stated by A. Scherr:

> The importance of early testing cannot be emphasized enough. Code should be exercised with as many test cases as possible as early as possible. Test cases should not be "saved" until an appropriate point in the cycle. The argument that a programmer's code is not ready for being subjected to test cases is valid only up to a point. Given that a certain function in the system is being tested, all test cases pertaining to that function should be attempted. If an avalanche of errors are detected, it is better to know sooner than later that the associated code is poor.

---

[1]Musa (1976) has found that the exchange of programs among design personnel for module testing produces beneficial results.

[2]A management process in which a master version of the system is maintained by a configuration manager to whom any changes must be submitted in writing for approval before being inserted in the master version. This person may also control the written record of each test.

Table 4.1 Project complexity related to test difficulty

Category	Defining features	Main concern
1. Simple	1. Is less than 1000 source statements in length. 2. Is generally written by one programmer in 6 months or less. 3. Usually has no interactions with other programs or systems.	Single programmer-tester. Noncritical. Quality of result depends on quality of individual.
2. Intermediate complexity	1. Is less than 10,000 source statements. 2. Is generally written by 1 to 5 programmers in less than 2 yr. 3. Has few, if any, interactions with other systems. 4. Generally consists of 10 to 100 modules.	Quality of result depends on individual quality and management thoroughness.
3. Complex	1. Has less than 100,000 source statements. 2. Is generally written by 5 to 20 programmers over a period of 2 to 3 yr. 3. Consists of several subsystems. 4. Often interacts with other systems. 5. Generally consists of 100 to 1000 modules.	Since there is a mix of programmer skills, the end result is largely dependent on the use of modern, formal techniques of design and management.
4. Very complex*	1. Contains less than 10^6 source statements. 2. Is written by a group of 100 to 1000 programmers over a period of several years. 3. Requires continuing development and maintenance by people other than the original development team. 4. Generally consists of 1000 to 10,000 modules. 5. Generally consists of several major subsystems, with complex interactions between the subsystems; there are also likely to be complex interactions with other, separately developed systems. 6. Often involves additional complexities, such as real-time processing, telecommunications, and multitasking.	Same as 3.
5. Super complex*	1. Has between 1 million and 10 million instructions. 2. Generally has more than 1000 programmers, working over a period of several years, often approaching a decade or more of development time. 3. Nearly always includes real-time processing, telecommunications, and other complexities.	Same as 3.

Table 4.1 (*continued*)

Category	Defining features	Main concern
	4. Is often involved in critical processes, e.g., air traffic control or air defense.	
	5. Normally has an extraordinarily high requirement for reliability (e.g., one such project in Australia specified a mean time between failures for its system of 47 *years*).	

Source: Yourdon (1975), Chap. 7.
*Yourdon uses the colorful terms *nearly impossible* and *utterly absurd* for these two categories.

Furthermore, errors can frequently be corrected more efficiently in a batch than one at a time. Taken to the extreme, it is more efficient to re-write a program all at once than a little at a time.[1]

In Sec. 4.1.1, the opposite goals of the producer and user (contractor and customer) of software were discussed. A similar conflict exists, at least at a subconscious level, between the goals of the program manager and those of the program designer-tester during the test phase of program development. The manager views testing as the means whereby the imperfections in a program are discovered. Then debugging will localize and identify the error, redesign will correct the error, and retest will verify the correction. Outwardly, the program designer-tester agrees with this approach; however, this person's ego may really be striving to show how good the program is, i.e., how many test cases work well. This is succinctly stated in the following truisms:[2]

1. If your goal is to show the absence of errors, you won't discover many.
2. If your goal is to show the presence of errors, you will discover a large percentage of them.

Techniques for ensuring that personnel adopt the right approach and attitude are discussed in Chap. 6.

The reader should keep in mind that we are viewing testing in a broad sense, as we include the following five types of tests and the many variations on these themes which exist in practice:[3]

1. Code reading (desk checking, "eyeballing," hand execution), by programmer or colleague

[1]Scherr (1973), p. 178.
[2]Myers (1976), p. 170
[3]Myers (1976), p. 170.

2. Machine testing: valid output for given input, complete output, no spurious output
3. Program proofs or alternate program representations
4. Simulation testing: simulation of hardware, input-output devices, and signals (i.e., radar inputs, operator inputs, input from other computers, CRT outputs, etc.)
5. Design reviews: team conference on all relevant aspects of the design utilizing all available information, test results, etc., compiled to date

Actually, the process of design reviews, which was discussed in Chap. 3, can be viewed as a generalization of code reading. The design review team utilizes all the inputs it can obtain (listings, flowcharts, data flowgraphs, specifications, HIPO charts, etc.) and reads, walks through, and assesses the design. Simulation testing is really just another form of machine testing in which the host machine may differ from the actual computer to be used and so the host simulates the actual. The host may also simulate interfaces and signals to real-time I/O equipment.

4.1.3 Interaction with Reliability, Design, and Management

The different views of testing by designers and managers were discussed above. Also, at various stages of this chapter we will discuss alternative philosophies and approaches used in testing. Thus, we will outline some of the management prerogatives and decisions which must be made during program development. Our previous discussion regarding the cost of errors found early in a program, compared with those found later in a program, would under naive interpretation lead to the decision to spend all the testing budget at the beginning of the program. Clearly this is not a valid approach, because some errors manifest themselves, and can be exhibited only after system integration. Therefore, we must have some test effort during the latter phases of program development. Techniques for the best distribution of dollars among the various phases of program development will be discussed in Chap. 6.

Clearly, design and testing interact strongly. In fact, there are a number of respected scholars in the software area who believe that a proper design can result in such a low error rate that only a minimal amount of testing is required. This author does not agree with that position. No matter how few errors the designer "builds" into a program, we will always need a substantial amount of testing to ferret them out. I have often used the following analogy in this regard: An error-free program is like perpetual motion—something to be sought which is, in reality, unattainable. This does not mean that design of extremely-low-friction mechanisms is not a fruitful endeavor, just as design theories to produce software with very small initial error content are a very fruitful endeavor. An example of the former is the use of exotic vibratory bearing, floated suspension, and electrostatic suspension systems for inertial navigation gyroscopes. (The friction torques are responsible for drift errors in this very precise navigational instrument.) In the case of software, structured programming and chief-programmer design teams (see Sec. 6.5.4) have shown evidence of being able to significantly lower the initial error content of software.

The interaction of reliability and testing comes about in a number of different ways. First of all, in Chap. 5, we will see that most of the software reliability models discussed are related to residual bugs in the program. Obviously, testing removes residual bugs and improves the reliability of the program. It is a technical decision that establishes the minimum amount of testing necessary to remove enough bugs to produce a system with an acceptable reliability. It is generally a management decision which sets the maximum amount of testing which should be done to produce a high-quality, reliable system. One should note that the engineering viewpoint is a conservative one which does not claim anything more than an acceptable system that meets its requirements. Thus, it sets a lower bound on the estimated amount of testing required. On the other hand, management should aim for a high-quality, reliable system that will well satisfy the customer. The management estimate should be an upper bound on the amount to be spent on testing. If the upper and lower bounds are not in reasonable agreement, major effort must be placed on resolving the differences before the project proceeds, since a serious mistake at this point can strongly affect the profit picture. If the upper bound is much larger than the lower bound, then one of the following must be true:

1. The engineer-designers are much too optimistic about the quality of the code they will produce and have left too little time (manpower) for testing and debugging.
2. The manager has adopted a cautious attitude and has made an estimate incorporating too large a safety factor.
3. There is a substantial difference in interpreting the specifications, or the differences between "acceptable" and "good."

In any event, the differences must be analyzed and the situation resolved. If the project is in the bidding stages, one is faced with a Hobson's choice: a low bid which stands a good chance of winning but allows the company to "lose its shirt," or a comfortable high bid which stands little chance of winning. Of course, it is possible that the lower bound will exceed the upper bound. Again the discrepancy must be resolved, because the stakes are high and the results of an error are serious. In fact, one could characterize the reasons for such a crossing of estimates by the same three possibilities just listed, except that the words *engineer-designer* and *manager* should be interchanged. In essence one must determine who is the optimist, who is the pessimist, and who is to be believed.

The reliability models proposed in Chap. 5 contain a few undetermined parameters. The method proposed for determining these parameters is to test the system using the ultimate system simulator with scenario tests, or to use as extensive a test as is available. The data collected from these tests should be the number of successes and failures, the time to failure, and the running time of any tests without failure. These data are treated in the same way as reliability test

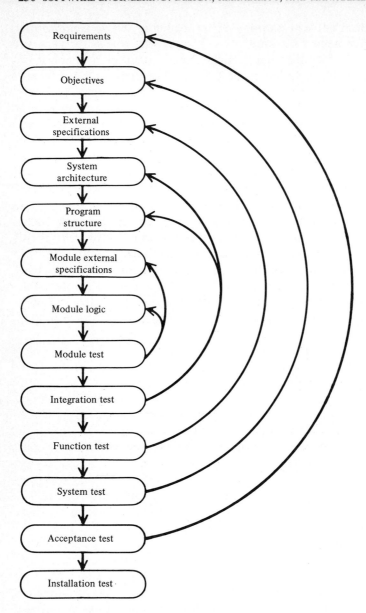

Figure 4.1 The testing processes and their relationships to the design processes. *(From Myers, 1976 Fig. 10.2, p. 174)*

data. Lastly, one of the reliability models in Chap. 5 relates the probabilities of failure along particular paths in a program to the number of tests that have exercised that path.

4.1.4 Diversity of Tests

As one proceeds through the development of any large product in general, and software in particular, one encounters a broad variety or diversity of different types of tests. This is illustrated by the diagram in Fig. 4.1, where the forward path represents the sequence of progression in time as the various stages of the project are accomplished. The feedback paths represent tests which are performed to detect errors that creep into the numerous stages of development.

Another way to classify tests is to focus upon the properties of a good program, and to test the quantitative or qualitative measures associated with program validity. One such list of factors to consider in devising tests is given in Table 4.2. The reader will notice that many of these factors are the so-called -ility factors associated with projects in general and are not really peculiar to software. Others, such as storage and recovery testing, are really unique to the software problem. Each project team will have to determine which of these factors are to

Table 4.2 Considerations in program design

 1. Modularity
 2. Consistency
 3. Efficiency
 4. Debuggability
 5. Risk factors
 6. Resources to implement (man-hours and computer hours)
 7. The sequence of decision
 8. Generality
 9. Readability
10. Portability
11. Maintainability
12. Reliability
13. Simplicity
14. Quality
15. Adaptability
16. Availability
17. Ease of recovery
18. Storage requirements
19. Running time
20. Installability

Table 4.3 Basic testing definitions

Testing, as we have previously discussed, is the process of executing a program (or a part of a program) with the intention or goal of finding errors.

A *proof* is an attempt to find errors in a program without regard to the program's environment. Most proof techniques involve stating assertions about the program's behavior and then deriving and proving mathematical theorems about the program's correctness. Proofs can be considered a form of testing although they do not involve a direct execution of the program. Many researchers consider proofs to be an alternative to testing, a view that is largely incorrect and explored further in Chapter 17 [in Myers].

Verification is an attempt to find errors by executing a program in a test or simulated environment.

Validation is an attempt to find errors by executing a program in a given real environment.

Certification is an authoritative endorsement of the correctness of a program, analogous to the certification of electrical equipment by the Underwriters Laboratories. Testing for certification must be done against some predefined standard. At the time of writing this book a few certification efforts had been established, such as the certification of COBOL compilers and mathematical subroutines by the United States National Bureau of Standards and Federal COBOL Compiler Testing Service and certification of mathematical software by the NATS project.

Debugging is not a form of testing. Although the words debugging and testing are often used interchangeably, they are distinct activities. Testing is the activity of finding errors; debugging is the activity of diagnosing the precise nature of a known error and then correcting the error. The two are related because the output of a testing activity (detected errors) is the input to a debugging activity.

These definitions represent one view of testing: the view of the testing environment. A second set of definitions listed below represents another view of testing: the types of errors that are expected to be found and the standard to which the program is being tested.

Module testing or *unit testing* is the verification of a single program module, usually in an isolated environment (i.e., isolated from all other modules). Module testing also occasionally includes mathematical proofs.

Integration testing is the verification of the interfaces among system parts (modules, components, and subsystems).

External function testing is the verification of the external system function as stated in the external specifications.

System testing is the verification and/or validation of the system to its initial objectives. System testing is a verification process when it is done in a simulated environment; it is a validation process when it is performed in a live environment.

Acceptance testing is the validation of the system or program to the user requirements.

Installation testing is the validation of each particular installation of the system with the intent of pointing out any errors made while installing the system.

Simulation testing* is the exercise of the software in conjunction with a simulation program and often some peripheral hardware which replicate the real operating environment as closely as possible. The computer used to run the software and the simulation program may be the computer to be used in the field or a development computer.

Field testing* is the initial operation of the actual hardware-software system in the field in a test mode (limited or full capabilities) to ferret out as many remaining errors as is feasible.

Source: Myers (1976), pp. 172–173.
*These definitions supplied by the author.

be included in the testing procedure in terms of the goals, requirements, and applications of the software. In addition, the relative weight, importance, and proportional expenditure of effort must be determined.

4.1.5 Definitions of Test Terms

All definitions are difficult, but definitions are especially important in this new field of software engineering. A selected set of definitions taken from Myers is given in Table 4.3. In some respects a few of these definitions focus on the means of accomplishing the task rather than the definition of the task itself. Also, other forms of testing, such as checking of flowcharts and code reading, are omitted. The reader may also wish to consult the IEEE definitions.[1] In all cases these definitions basically have the same flavor, and only minor nuances separate one from the other.

4.2 STATISTICS ON THE TESTING PROCESS

4.2.1 Introduction

A fundamental point of departure in the study of the test process is the examination and study of statistical data on testing. Unfortunately, this area suffers from a paucity of data. We will adopt the position of studying carefully whatever partial data are available to extract as much information as possible from the data, and to digest from its benefits and drawbacks guidelines for future data-collection efforts.

4.2.2 Test Hours

A good overall discussion of the role of testing in system development can be found in the article describing the system testing of Bell Laboratories TSPS telephone switching system.[2] A more quantitative overview of the magnitude and cost of system testing can be obtained by studying the data gathered by Weinwurm (reprinted in Sackman, 1967, p. 202), and shown in Figs. 4.2 and 4.3. For each log-log plot we fix by eye a simple straight-line approximation. For the man-months versus instructions plot of Fig. 4.2. we obtain

$$\log (\text{MM}) = \log I - 2 \tag{4.1}$$

$$\text{MM} = 0.01I \tag{4.2}$$

where
$$\text{MM} = \text{man-months of effort}$$
$$I = \text{number of new instructions}$$

---

[1] Center for Software (1979).
[2] Heller et al. (1970).

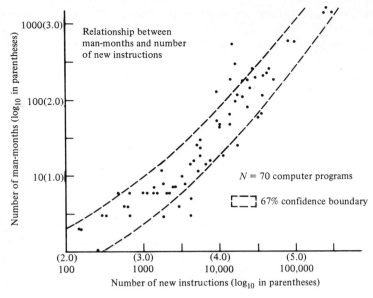

Figure 4.2 Relationship between man-months and number of instructions. *(From Weinwurm, 1965)*

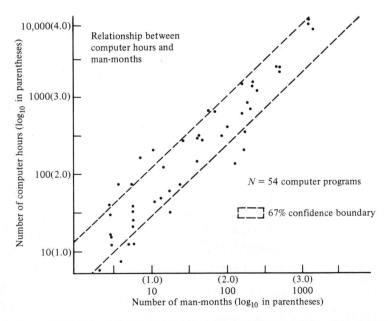

Figure 4.3 Relationship between computer hours and man-months. *(From Weinwurm, 1965)*

Similarly, from the computer hours versus program man-hours data, we can derive the relationship

$$\log(\text{CH}) = \log(\text{MM}) + 1 \tag{4.3}$$

$$\text{CH} = 10\text{MM} \tag{4.4}$$

where $\qquad\qquad\qquad$ CH = the number of computer hours

Combining Eqs. (4.2) and (4.4) yields

$$\text{CH} = 0.1I \tag{4.5}$$

Clearly, one must inquire further before such simple relationships can be applied. The data were taken from a 1965 report;[1] are they still valid? Were the instructions measured in machine instructions? (Probably, since the report must be based on data in the early 1960s, when almost all programming was in assembler.) Are the test hours module, integration, simulation, or total test hours? For further exploration of these data the reader is referred to Weinwurm's report.

4.2.3 Discovery and Correction Times

Another source of data on testing is the paper by Shooman and Bolsky (1975), which is also analyzed from a reliability viewpoint in Chap. 5. The purpose of the study was the collection of basic data on error types as well as diagnosis (of errors) and correction times. In Chap. 5, Fig. 5.3 the data-collection form for the 4000-machine-word program called STUDY is presented. The form, called a supplementary TR/CR (trouble report–correction report) form was completed for 63 TRs collected over a 9-month period during the test and integration phase. Effort expended in diagnosis was characterized by the number of runs to diagnose, the computer time expended, and the working time for each individual error. Similar data were recorded for the correction effort, in addition to the number of cards changed, added, or deleted in order to effect the correction. The frequency distributions of the data collected are given in Figs. 4.4, 4.5a, b, and c, and 4.6a, b, and c and are summarized in Table 4.4.

4.2.4 Difficulty versus Time

In addition to the data which are presented in the figures and Table 4.4, two hypotheses concerning testing were evaluated. Many people theorized that the bugs which were hard to detect were also hard to correct. None of the 63 bugs which were found seemed to possess this correlation, as confirmed by inspection of the data pairs and via a scatter plot. Another popular hypothesis is that the easy bugs are detected first and the hard bugs detected later. No such result was found for the experiment in question, leading to three possible conclusions: (1) intuition is wrong and there really is no difference in effort expended for early and late bugs; (2) the result is correct for the program in question, for some

[1]Weinwurm (1965).

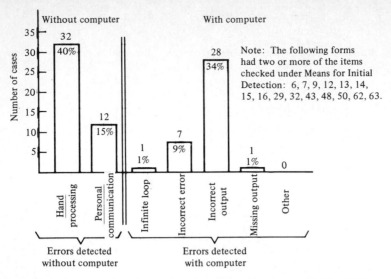

Figure 4.4 Means of initial error detection. *(From Shooman and Bolsky, 1975)*

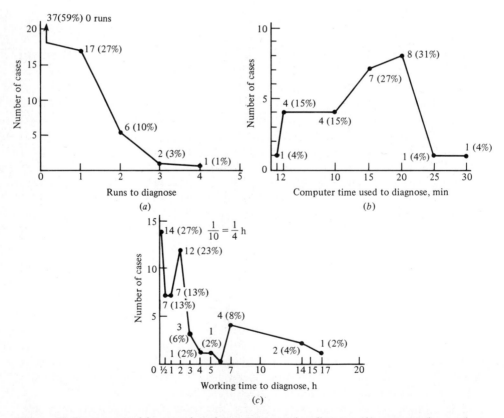

Figure 4.5 Resources used for error detection: (*a*) runs used to diagnose; (*b*) computer time used to diagnose; (*c*) working time to diagnose. Values shown alongside each data point represent number of cases and percentage of the 63 TRs exhibiting that time. *(From Shooman and Bolsky, 1975)*

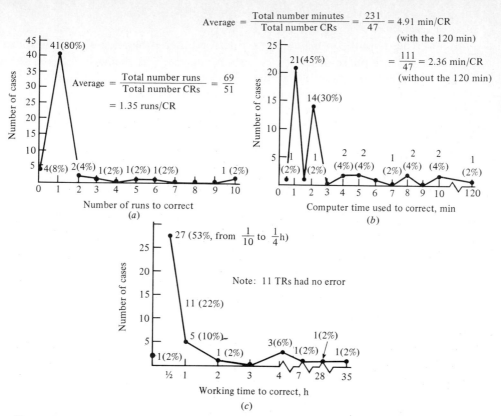

Figure 4.6 Resources used for error correction: (*a*) number of runs; (*b*) computer time used; (*c*) working time. Values shown alongside each data point represent number of cases and percentage of the 63 TRs exhibiting that time. *(From Shooman and Bolsky, 1975)*

Table 4.4 Summary of error diagnosis and correction data

1. The fraction of errors corrected without the computer (i.e., by hand processing or personal communication) was 55%, and the remaining 45% involved some form of computer testing or operation.

2. The number of runs to diagnose had an exponential-like distribution, with a mean of 0.61 runs.

3. The average computer time used to diagnose was 13.5 minutes, and no distributional pattern could be determined.

4. The study of working time in hours needed to diagnose yielded two reasonable interpretations: (1) a bimodal frequency distribution with "one day" bugs taking an average of 1.22 hours, and "two day" bugs taking an average of 10.43 hours or alternatively, (2) a unimodal distribution as the underlying pattern with a mean of 2.46 hours, where the multiple peaks are just due to the small sample size.

5. The number of runs to correct had an average of 1.35 run per error, and 80% required only 1 run.

6. The distribution of computer time used to correct had two large peaks, at one and two minutes, and an average of 4.9 (2.36 if the 120 point is neglected) minutes.

7. The working time to correct was amenable to two interpretations (as in item 4), with a spike almost at the origin for one of the modes. The average time was 1.98 hours.

Source: Shooman and Bolsky (1975).

reason, yet the hypothesis may still be true for other programs; (3) the result holds only for this phase of this (or another) program. The reader is referred to Shooman and Bolsky's paper for a fuller discussion.

Clearly, more experimentation is needed in this area to clarify some of the issues raised. Several experiments involving programs in different languages and of different types (control, data-management, mathematical, character-string-handling, etc.) would be most desirable.

4.3 TEST PHILOSOPHY AND TYPE

4.3.1 Introduction

In many ways testing is a very individualistic process, and the number of different types of tests varies as much as the different development approaches. For many years, our only real defense against programming errors was careful design and testing based on the native intelligence of the programmer. We are now in an era in which many modern design techniques are helping us to reduce the number of initial errors inherent in the code. Similarly, the different test methods are beginning to cluster themselves into several distinct approaches and philosophies. In this section we will discuss a number of different test techniques that are intimately related to the design process.[1]

In the latter sections of this chapter we will introduce test concepts that are somewhat independent of the design approach. Some aspects of testing are closely allied to the management decisions that must be made during system development and relate to costs, personnel selection and deployment, and management scheduling and control. These management-related issues are discussed in Chap. 6 and include topics such as acceptance tests and their relationship to contract warranty, guarantee, penalty, or incentive clauses; the effect of individual skills; design and code reviews and structured walk-throughs; and the role of independent organizations in the testing process.

4.3.2 Module Testing

If we are speaking about a small program, it is developed and tested essentially as a unit or entity by one person. Of course, when we begin to discuss large software systems developed by a group of individuals, each individual module will be tested, by itself and along with the other modules during system integration testing. In Chap. 2 we indicated that the design could be done top-down or bottom-up and the coding could also be accomplished via either approach. Similarly, the testing can be top-down or bottom-up. Thus, if we consider the design, coding, and development phases there are eight different combinations.

---

[1] Hetzel (1973); Myers (1976); Myers (1979); Yourdon (1975), Chap. 7.

Of course, these approaches are not equally probable. It is most likely that if the design proceeds top-down, so do the coding and testing.

4.3.3 Integration Testing

It is clear that certain errors which relate to the interaction of different program modules cannot be found by unit testing, but can be found only by an interactive test. The process by which individual modules are put together to realize major subsections and functions of a program is known as *system integration*.[1] When tests are performed which exercise interfaces among program modules, this is known as *integration testing*. The progress of integration testing is often measured by the number of instructions coded and tested (see Figs. 5.7 and 5.8), or the number of functions or modules implemented and tested.[2] Integration testing is followed by either simulation testing or initial field testing, which can be viewed as the ultimate integration test.

4.3.4 Top-Down versus Bottom-Up Testing

In Chap. 2 we introduced the concept of top-down design and discussed a number of intuitively appealing reasons favoring its use. One can make a similar list of the advantages (and disadvantages) of top-down testing. A weighting of the pros and cons of these test strategies as well as others will be done in the next section. In this section we will briefly discuss the salient features of the different test approaches.

In top-down testing, we begin with the control program and examine the way it receives data, how it passes control and data to the various program modules, how the modules pass data back to the control program, and how the control program (sometimes through an output module) passes data to the output device. Clearly, the control program must be coded before we can begin top-down testing. If the system were to be coded bottom-up, the control program would be written last, and if we insisted on top-down testing, the other modules of code would essentially sit around untested until the control program was finished. Thus, if we wish to use top-down testing, in all likelihood we will precede it by top-down coding. However, there is no reason why a top-down-coded and -tested program cannot be designed either top-down or bottom-up.

So far, for clarity, we have spoken only of either pure top-down or pure bottom-up test strategies. Obviously, mixed strategies are possible and in fact are often desirable; these will be discussed in Sec. 4.3.5. As long as we speak of "pure" strategies, we can compare the likelihood of the eight possible development combinations by use of the diagram given in Fig. 4.7.

---

[1]If a customized computer is being built, then there is hardware integration, software integration, and finally system integration, when both are melded.

[2]This measure of progress should be supplemented by the use of reliability models which estimate and project the mean time between software failures. See Chap. 5 and Musa (1978).

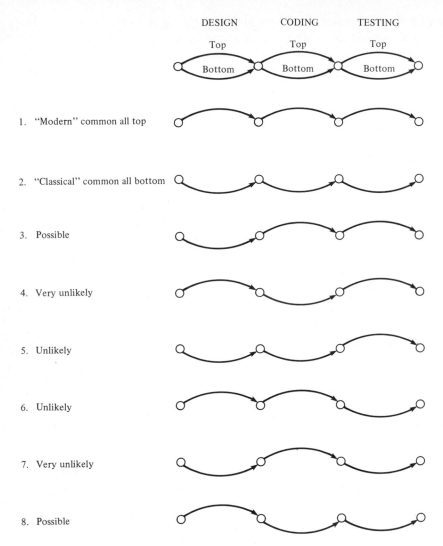

Figure 4.7 Sequences of pure development strategies for the design, coding, and test phases of software development.

In Fig. 4.7, we focus on the three stages of development—design, coding, and testing—and assume that each can be done top-down or bottom-up. In most of today's literature, *modern techniques* or a similar term is used to refer to a development which has proceeded top-down in all three phases. At the other extreme, the term *classical* refers to a development which has proceeded bottom-up all the way. We should be careful about labels, since through common usage *classical software development* has come to mean the old-fashioned techniques of the 1950s and 1960s and has taken on a pejorative tone. On the other hand, *top-down* and *modern software development* are terms which have become euphemisms for modern and good. A more sophisticated evaluation would conclude that we should consider modern techniques wherever possible, because of their many benefits. However, we should be alert for those special situations in which the classical technique is best. In other cases a mixed strategy will be best. In the next section we will discuss mixed strategies in which both top-down and bottom-up approaches are used during one or more development phases. In Fig. 4.7 we consider only pure strategies during each phase, but we allow switching of strategies from phase to phase. If we allow a single switch of strategies during the three phases, it is most likely that the coding and testing phases will match. If the design phase is to be iterated once or twice, it may not matter so much whether the design is pure top-down, pure bottom-up, or mixed. A switch between the coding and testing stage is unlikely, and two switches are very unlikely.

During the test phase one of the biggest differences between top-down and bottom-up testing is the need for test stubs and module drivers. In a top-down-coded program which is to be tested top-down, we need, at the minimum, an output statement for each module within the control structure to indicate that control has passed through the module during the tests of the control structure. These dummy lines of code are referred to as *test stubs*. The test stubs are removed or modified and augmented at the later stage when module coding has begun. Sometimes test stubs must contain facilities for passing of parameters to the module and back from the module. As an example, consider the word-processing system which was discussed in Chap. 2. Assume the control program is working and we wish to test whether it is properly interfaced with the editor module. A simple editor stub would merely print out a message to the effect that the editor module had been entered. A more elaborate stub would provide for the passing of some text to a simulated buffer area, simulated storage of the buffer, and a simulated text recall and print function. In special cases, the test stub may be almost a simple, limited simulation of the real program. It can contain an output section which prints the input parameters it has been sent from the control program, the time (from a real-time hardware clock) of entry, the processed output parameters, and the time of departure along with any appropriate messages. The elaborateness of the test stub is a function of (1) how easy it is to write, (2) the thoroughness with which we wish to test the control interfaces at this early stage, and (3) the length of time which will elapse before the editor module is available. Sometimes, in the case of a highly modular system which is undergoing evolutionary development, we will have an old version of an editor available which can be interfaced easily and serve as a full-scale test stub. Clearly, one of the advantages of bottom-up coding is that when we come to testing, no test stubs are needed.

As in most practical engineering situations, there is no advantage without a corresponding disadvantage. If we decide to do bottom-up coding followed by bottom-up testing in order to avoid the need for writing test stubs, then we find we must write test drivers. The test driver is a simulated program which passes data to the module under test and receives data which the module has processed.

In the case of our word-processing example, if we were doing bottom-up testing on the text editor, we would need a driver program to pass text to the editor and to accept and verify that the editor had passed text and control back to the control program. The complexity and cost of the driver program are related to the role of the module in the program. If the module being tested is a key one, such as the text editor in our word-processing example, then it may require a fair amount of work to code a driver program. Just as in our discussion of test stubs, if we have an old version of a program which performs many of the same functions as the new one being developed, we may be able to use or modify portions of the old program to serve as our driver. Once the bottom-up coding has reached the level of the control program, we can either discard the driver programs and write the control program or use the driver programs as the preliminary design for the control program. An example of a test stub and a *test driver* for the text editor module of our word-processing example is given in Table 4.5.

Table 4.5 An example illustrating test stubs and driver programs (written in pseudo-code)
Module 3.0 of Fig. 2.3.

---

1. ┌─TEST STUB FOR EDIT TEXT MODULE
   INITIALIZE
   OUTPUT MESSAGE "TEXT EDITOR ENTERED"
   OUTPUT "CONTROL INPUT WAS FUNCTION = ", "C FUNCT"
   OUTPUT BUFFER CHARACTER STRING
   ┌─IF C FUNCT = CHANGE
   │ THEN
   │ CHANGE SECOND WORD IN BUFFER TO * * * *
   │ ELSE
   │ ADD AT END OF BUFFER ???
   └─END IF
   OUTPUT NEW BUFFER CHARACTER STRING
   └─END TEST STUB

Notes: (1) We assume CFUNCT = CHANGE OR APPEND. No other functions are supported in the test stub, and even these are simulated. (2) A fixed buffer length is being passed.

2. ┌─TEST DRIVER FOR EDIT TEXT MODULE
   DECLARE BUFFER 2500 CHARACTERS LONG
   FORM A 500 CHARACTER TEST MESSAGE
   SET CFUNCT = DESIRED CONTROL TO BE TESTED
   INPUT NEW CHARACTER STRING
   TRANSMIT CONTROL AND NEW STRING TO EDIT TEXT MODULE
   RECEIVE CONTROL FROM EDIT TEXT MODULE AND
       STOP OR REINITIALIZE.
   └─END TEST DRIVER

4.3.5 Mixed Testing

As might be expected, in the big, cruel, realistic world, there is seldom anything such as pure top-down or bottom-up testing. In many cases a mixed or modified version of top-down or bottom-up testing is probably more efficient and desirable. The obvious approach is to try to choose some mixed approach which retains all the good features of the two techniques and eliminates or greatly reduces most of the bad features. Since ours is not the best of all possible worlds, the main focus of this section will be to discuss what can be done in practice to eliminate or mitigate some of the bad features of pure top-down or bottom-up testing without compromising the known good features.

In our subsequent discussion we will follow in part the terminology and methodology of Myers.[1]

The big bang approach If we convince ourselves that in a well-done, highly modular design the interaction among modules is minimal, then integration testing merely consists of verifying the interfaces. Furthermore, if we carefully specify the interfaces, interface errors will be kept to a minimum; thus integration testing is really just a final check on the interfaces. If this is true, we can save much of our testing time by performing bottom-up coding and unit testing on each module first. When all modules have been individually coded and unit-tested in isolation, we do our integration all at once.[2] Myers has chosen to call this the "big bang" method. Although we have not as yet tried to evaluate the relative merits and demerits of the approach, a pejorative tone has already been introduced via the choice of term. Obviously a proponent of the big bang technique would envision that the final integration phase would be shortened to a few days or weeks and the modules would all by and large "play" well together. If this is so, the cost savings due to a shortened integration-test period would be significant; however, in practice this method has serious problems, as discussed in Sec. 4.4.

Modified top-down testing As we pointed out in Chap. 2, one of the limitations of top-down design is that problems involving critical modules cannot be tested immediately but must wait until the control structure is completed. The obvious approach is to do a modified top-down design. In a similar fashion, we can do modified top-down testing. This means that while integration testing of the control structure is in progress the critical module is being exercised with a test driver program. Of course the critical module and all other modules have already undergone unit testing. Thus, it is difficult to make a distinction between unit

---

[1]Myers (1976), Chap. 10.

[2]Such an approach is also tempting from a management viewpoint in a project which is behind schedule. One shortens the module test phase and declares that integration testing has begun, thus reaching an important milestone.

testing and modified top-down testing with respect to one particular module. During unit testing, we concentrate on the internal functions of the module; however, in the integration-test phase we focus on communication of this module with the control program. Another way of describing modified top-down testing is to call it top-down testing augmented by intensive unit testing of critical modules.

Top-down–bottom-up testing If there is more than one critical module, or if the critical module is totally pervasive, we are virtually forced to consider working from both ends toward the middle. (This concept immediately conjures up in the author's mind the meeting of the two parts of the transcontinental railroad in Promontory, Utah, in 1869.) Clearly, the important thing is that the two efforts meet in the middle. Also of great importance is the choice of those modules that are to be designated for top-down and those for bottom-up integration. As was previously stated, critical modules are obvious choices for bottom-up; however, one should give ample weight to the additional costs of writing test drivers and test stubs. We must take care that in our attempt to enjoy the best of both worlds, we do not also have to endure the worst of both. Myers[1] calls this top-down–bottom-up approach to testing "sandwich testing." Further, he discusses the addition of intensive unit testing to the bottom-up–top-down method and calls it "modified sandwich testing."

4.3.6 Regression Testing

Regardless of which testing approach is used, when an error is discovered it is corrected, and thereby the software is changed. The question then arises, Do we have to go back and repeat all previous tests? Such repetition, in whole or in part, is known as *regression testing*. In fact, in Chap. 5 we will discuss error-generation models in which a certain proportion of all code changes will result in the creation of new errors. Cost usually prevents us from repeating all previous tests; however, it is feasible and prudent to repeat a portion of the tests. Also, in highly modular software with well-designed interfaces, regression testing can be limited to the module which has been changed and its interfaces. Some guidelines or rules for performing regression testing should be specified in the test plan.

4.4 A COMPARISON OF TEST METHODS

4.4.1 Introduction

Now that we have described several different types of tests, we will evaluate the merits and deficiencies of each test and comment on the time to use each approach. It is very important that there be a lot of testing. Testing will always be

[1](1976), pp. 186–187.

our last line of defense against residual errors. Also, until we prove the ability of modern design and coding techniques to greatly decrease initial error content, testing will remain the best technique for reducing the error content.

Because we are seldom able to predict what types of tests will be most effective in uncovering errors, there should be a mix of different types of tests throughout the development process. This means that there should be module and integration testing, code reading, design and code reviews, program proofs, simulation testing, and field testing. In fact, if we use a two-stage development approach, there is ample opportunity to introduce several types of testing. For example, one could quickly assemble a preliminary prototype using bottom-up design and testing and then follow it with a top-down design and test of the final product. Some of these topics will be covered in later sections of this chapter, as well as in Chap. 6. From the user's viewpoint, one of the most important tests is the demonstration and acceptance test run before the program is accepted. This subject will be treated in Chap. 6.

4.4.2 Features of the Various Approaches

We now focus on the good and bad features of the various approaches to integration testing developed in the preceding section. Many of these factors are subjective or relative; however, most experienced practitioners would agree with those listed in Table 4.6.

4.4.3 Comparison of the Approaches

Myers (1976) uses a matrix to evaluate and compare the various types of tests (Table 4.7). He rates the various attributes as positive (favorable), zero (neutral), and negative (unfavorable) and assigns scores of $+1$, 0, and -1 to each. In addition, he ranks each characteristic on a scale of 0 to 3 in terms of importance. This author finds that the matrix presentation is a valuable technique for comparing the test methods; however, the numerical weighting procedure does not seem useful, for several reasons. First of all, the individual ratings of good and bad attributes are somewhat subjective, and a few of them seem to be based more on each practitioner's viewpoint and experience than on fundamental principles. The relative weightings are even more subjective. This author suggests that such a matrix be constructed (augmented by other features of local or specific interest) during the early design phases. The designers can then fill in their own ratings and use this as an aid in formulating the integration-test procedures to be specified in the test plan.

Additional comments must be added to our discussion of the big bang method. This author has discussed the big bang method with several practitioners, and they all swear at it and not by it. It seems to be universally accepted that it causes chaos and results in many errors slipping through to the field deployment phase. In addition, it is difficult to localize the source of error. Unlike other techniques, the big bang method does not start from a basic system which works,

Table 4.6 A comparison of the features of different integration test philosophies

Technique	Major features	Advantages	Disadvantages	Comments
1. Top-down	*a.* Control program tested first. *b.* Modules integrated one at a time. *c.* Major emphasis on interface testing.	*a.* No test drivers needed. *b.* Control program plus a few modules forms a basic early prototype. *c.* Interface errors discovered early. *d.* Modular features aid debugging.	*a.* Test stubs needed. *b.* Early phase requires slow manpower buildup. *c.* Errors in critical modules which occur at a low level are found late.	*a.* An early working program raises morale. *b.* It is hard to maintain a pure top-down strategy in practice.
2. Bottom-up	*a.* Allows early testing aimed at proving feasibility and practicality of particular modules. *b.* Modules may be integrated in various clusters as desired. *c.* Major emphasis is on module functionality and performance.	*a.* No test stubs needed. *b.* It is easier to adjust manpower needs to number of available personnel. *c.* Errors in critical modules found early.	*a.* Test drivers needed. *b.* Many modules must be integrated before a working program emerges late in the development process. *c.* Interface errors discovered late.	*a.* At any given point in time more code has been written and tested than if top-down testing is used. *b.* Some people feel that bottom-up is a more intuitive test philosophy.
3. Modified top-down	Same as top-down except one or two major modules are tested bottom-up.	Same as top-down except errors in critical module(s) found early.	Same as top-down except a test driver is needed for the critical module(s).	Same as top-down.
4. Top-down –bottom-up	Combines all the major features, advantages, and disadvantages of top-down and bottom-up.			Not a pure philosophy.
5. Modified top-down –bottom-up	Same as top-down–bottom-up but more emphasis on critical module(s).			Not a pure philosophy.

Table 4.7 Qualitative comparison of various integration testing approaches

Characteristics	Bottom-up	Top-down	Modified top-down	Big bang	Sandwich	Modified sandwich
Integration	Early +	Early +	Early +	Late −	Early +	Early +
Time to a basic working program	Late −	Early +	Early +	Late −	Early +	Early +
Module driver (code or tool) needed	Yes −	No +	Yes −	Yes −	In part 0	Yes −
Stubs needed	No +	Yes −	Yes −	Yes −	In part 0	In part 0
Work parallelism at beginning	Medium 0	Low −	Medium 0	High +	Medium 0	High +
Ability to test particular paths	Easy +	Hard −	Easy +	Easy +	Medium 0	Easy +
Ability to plan and control the sequence	Easy +	Hard −	Hard −	Easy +	Hard −	Hard −
Machine inefficiencies	Judged as not significant					
Confusion*	Low +	Low +	Low +	High −	Low +	Low +
Cost*	Average 0	Average 0	Average 0	Low +	High −	High −
Time*	Average 0	Average 0	Average 0	Long −	Average 0	Average 0
Residual errors*	Average 0	Low +	Low +	High −	Low +	Low +

Source: Myers (1976).
*Rows added by this author.

Table 4.8 A comparison of the effectiveness of different types of tests in revealing different categories of errors

Error type	Module test	Integration test	Code reading	Design review
Logic	Good	Average	Average	Poor
Documentation error	Poor	Average	Good	Good
Overload or overflow of range	Good	Good	Average	Poor
Timing errors	Average	Good	Average	Average
Throughput	Poor	Good	Average	Average
Recovery errors	Poor	Good	Average	Average
Support Software errors	Average	Good	Average	Good
Hardware errors	Poor	Good	Poor	Average
Specifications and requirements	Poor	Average	Average	Good

to which is added a new module; thus, any troubles which occur cannot be attributed to the new module or its interfaces, as they can when other techniques are used.

Another way to compare various types of tests is to list the kinds of errors which occur and to rate each test category as to its efficiency in detecting the error types. Such a comparison appears in Table 4.8. Note that no single test technique is uniformly good over the spectrum of error types.

4.5 DEBUGGING

4.5.1 Introduction

Once an error has been discovered, we begin an investigation to localize the error, i.e., to find out which module or interface is causing it. Then, this section of code (or pseudo-code) is studied to determine the cause of the problem. This process is called *debugging*; it generally involves further specialized testing and code reading to pinpoint the source of the error. As discussed in Chap. 5, many people call the external manifestation of a problem an error (external error) and its internal cause a fault (internal error). Using this terminology, we can say that after testing has uncovered an error, debugging begins in order to determine the associated fault(s). Once a fault has been located, a redesign is devised to correct the fault, and the original test, some of the diagnostic tests, and some regression tests are performed to ensure that the fault has been removed and the error corrected. If the initial correction is not valid, the process is repeated until a valid solution is found. Sometime the redesign removes the detected fault(s) but creates new faults, which may be immediately detected or may remain hidden for some time until detected later. The effects of a "five steps forward and one step backward" type of process are discussed further in Chap. 5.

4.5.2 Debugging Techniques

Most programmers have learned through experience several techniques for debugging. Generally these are applied in a trial-and-error manner. In this section we will describe some of these techniques, while in the following section we will concentrate on overall debugging philosophies related to the individual techniques.

A number of popular debugging techniques[1] are described in Table 4.9. In general, none of these techniques should be used without a thorough prior analysis of the symptoms of the error resulting in a hypothesis concerning the cause of the error. Such analysis techniques are discussed in the next section.

[1]From Yourdon (1975), Myers (1979), and Bruce (1980).

4.5.3 Debugging Strategies

As previously stated, the heart of the debugging process is not the debugging tools discussed in Table 4.9, but the underlying strategy used to deduce the cause of the error.

One obvious technique is that of trial and error. The debugger looks at the error symptoms, reaches a snap judgment as to where in the code the underlying error might be, and jumps in to roam around in the program with one or more debugging techniques from the standard kit of tools. Obviously, this is a slow and wasteful approach.

Another technique, called *backtracking*, is to examine the error symptoms to see where they were first noticed. One then backtracks in the program flow of control to a point where the symptoms have disappeared. Generally, this process brackets the location of the error in the program. Subsequent careful study of the bounded segment of the code generally reveals the cause. Another obvious variation of backtracking is forward tracking, where we use print statements or other means to examine a succession of intermediate results to determine at what point the results first become wrong. *If we assume that we know the correct values of the variables* at several key points within a program, we can adopt a binary-search type of strategy. A set of inputs are injected near the middle of the program and the output is examined. If the output is correct, the error is in the first half of the program; if the output is wrong, the error is in the second half of the program. This process is repeated as many times as is feasible to bracket the erroneous portion of the code for final analysis.

Two more general approaches to debugging are those of induction and deduction (Myers 1976, pp. 133–140).

The inductive approach comes from the formulation of a single working hypothesis based on the data, on the analysis of existing data, and on specially collected data to prove or disprove the working hypothesis. A description of the steps follows;[1] a flowchart of their application sequence is shown in Fig. 4-8.

1. *Locate the pertinent data.* A major mistake made when debugging a program is failing to take account of all available data or symptoms about the problem. The first step is the enumeration of all that is known about what the program did correctly, and what it did incorrectly (i.e., the symptoms that led one to believe that an error exists). Additional valuable clues are provided by similar, but different, test cases that *do not* cause the symptoms to appear.
2. *Organize the data.* Remembering that induction implies that one is progressing from the specific to the general, the second step is the structuring of the pertinent data to allow one to observe patterns. Of particular importance is the search for *contradictions* (i.e., "the error occurs only when the customer has no outstanding balance in his margin account").
3. *Devise a hypothesis.* The next steps are to study the relationships among the clues and devise, using the patterns that might be visible in the structure of the clues, one or more hypotheses about the cause of the error. If one cannot devise a theory, more data are necessary, possibly obtained by devising and executing additional test cases. If multiple theories seem possible, the most probable one is selected first.

[1] Myers (1976), pp. 134–135.

Table 4.9 A comparison of various debugging techniques

Techniques	Features	Advantages	Disadvantages
1. Core dumps	A printout of all registers and relevant memory locations is obtained and studied. All dumps should be well documented and retained for possible use on subsequent problems.	1. The complete contents of memory at a crucial instant of time are obtained for study. 2. Can be cost-effective if used to explore validity of a well-formulated error hypothesis.	1. Require some CPU time, significant I/O time, and much analysis time. 2. Wasteful if used indiscriminately (i.e., at noncrucial instant or without an error theory or debugging plan). 3. Hexadecimal numbers are cumbersome to interpret and it is difficult to determine the address of source-language variables.
2. Traces	Essentially similar to core dumps, except the printout contains only certain memory and register contents and printing is conditional on some event occurring. Typical conditioning events are entry, exit, or occurrence of (1) a particular subroutine, statement, macro, or database; (2) communication with a terminal, printer, disk, or other peripheral; (3) the value of a variable or expressions; and (4) timed actuations (periodic or random) in certain real-time systems. A special problem with trace programs is that the conditions are entered in the source language and any changes require a recompilation. (See Yourdon, 1975, pp. 296–297.)		

3. Print statements	The standard print statement in the language being used is sprinkled throughout the program to output values of key variables.	1. This is a simple way to test whether a particular variable changes as it should after a particular event. 2. A sequence of print statements portrays the dynamics of variable changes.	1. They are cumbersome to use on large programs. 2. If used indiscriminately, they can produce copious data to be analyzed, much of which are superfluous.
4. Debugging programs*	A program which runs concurrently with the program under test and provides commands to (1) examine memory and registers; (2) stop execution of the program at a particular point; (3) search for references to particular constants, variables, registers. (For more details see Yourdon, 1975, pp. 298–321.)	1. Terminal-oriented real-time program. 2. Considerable flexibility to examine dynamics of operation.	1. Generally works on a machine language program. 2. Higher-level-language versions must work with interpreters. 3. More commonly used on microcomputers than large computers.

* One of the early successful debugging programs was written in the 1960s for the PDP-8 computer in the days before low-cost magnetic-tape and -disk peripheral devices and used punched paper tape. It was called DDT (dynamic debugging tape), and like the insecticide of the same name had a reputation as a good bug eliminator.

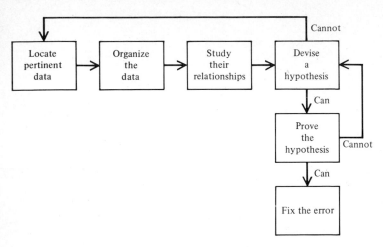

Figure 4.8 The inductive debugging process. *(Myers, 1979, p. 134)*

4. *Prove the hypothesis.* A major mistake at this point, given the pressures under which debugging is usually performed, is skipping this step by jumping to conclusions and attempting to fix the problem. However, it is vital to prove the reasonableness of the hypothesis before proceeding. A failure to do this often results in the fixing of only a symptom of the problem, or only a portion of the problem. The hypothesis is proved by comparing it to the original clues or data, making sure that this hypothesis *completely* explains the existence of the clues. If it does not, either the hypothesis is invalid, the hypothesis is incomplete, or multiple errors are present.

The process of deduction begins by enumerating all causes or hypotheses which seem possible. Then, one by one, particular causes are ruled out until a single one remains for validation. A description of the steps follows;[1] a flowchart of their sequence appears in Fig. 4-9.

1. *Enumerate the possible causes or hypotheses.* The first step is to develop a list of all conceivable causes of the error. They need not be complete explanations; they are merely theories through which one can structure and analyze the available data.
2. *Use the data to eliminate possible causes.* By a careful analysis of the data, particularly by looking for contradictions,... one attempts to eliminate all but one of the possible causes. If all are eliminated, additional data are needed (e.g., by devising additional test cases) to devise new theories. If more than one possible cause remains, the most probable cause, the prime hypothesis, is selected first.
3. *Refine the remaining hypothesis.* The possible cause at this point might be correct, but it is unlikely to be specific enough to pinpoint the error. Hence, the next step is to use the available clues to refine the theory (e.g., "error in handling the last transaction in the file") to something more specific (e.g., "the last transaction in the buffer is overlaid with the end-of-file indicator").
4. *Prove the remaining hypothesis.* This vital step is identical to step 4 in the induction method.

[1]Myers (1976), pp. 137–138.

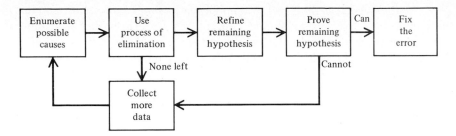

Figure 4.9 The deductive debugging process. *(Myers, 1979, p. 137)*

The reader is referred to Myers for further details of the method and to his interesting analogies between computer program debugging and the investigation of a crime.

4.5.4 Compiler Diagnostics

A long-standing test tool often overlooked is compiler checking and diagnostics. Of course, compiler checks work only on syntax errors and particular kinds of run-time errors.

A recent magazine article by Codling had an interesting discussion of compiler diagnostics and some of their failings.[1] One of the basic problems which he cites is that almost all compilers have been written by highly experienced assembly language programmers, who are used to the intricacies of assembly language coding and errors. Their conception of what constitutes a proper and acceptable error message may be quite different from that which the user would specify. For example, the diagnostic E20174 is certainly much less useful than the error message ILLEGAL EXPRESSION USED AS A SUBSCRIPT. Some of the reasons compiler writers give for not using English error test messages are (1) they take up too much space and time and (2) one should become experienced enough in seeing the error messages to memorize them. The first comment is no longer as valid as it was at one time, because of the lower cost of main memory, and because most systems have ample disk space on which they can store English text. The second comment is almost self-contradictory. A programmer who continually sees the same error message coming out should, rather than try to memorize its meaning, look into the reasons why he or she continually makes the same error over and over again in coding and doesn't catch it. Another problem is that sometimes when English text is printed in an error message, it contains very little information. Responses such as SYNTAX ERROR or ILLEGAL CHARACTER are not of very much help.

---

[1] Codling (1977).

Some compilers, such as the PL/1F compiler, give valuable information in an attributes table, which is printed along with the listing. This attributes table contains various levels of warnings which have been picked up by the compiler scan and which are noted. Other compilers[1] provide a symbol in the output when the scan fails or provide other error-detection features.[2] At this point in the evolution of programming, there is no excuse for compilers without meaningful error messages.

4.6 GRAPH MODELS OF TESTING

4.6.1 Introduction

In Chap. 2 we used a program graph model to discuss structured programs and the effects of structuring on the control flow in a program. In Chap. 3 we utilized the concept of graph cyclomatic complexity as a measure of program complexity. In this section we will use the program graph and its associated theoretical properties to help us classify various types of tests in terms of the graph structure, and to count or estimate how many tests are needed to traverse each program path. We will require some knowledge of graph properties for our discussion; these are briefly defined in this section and developed with a bit more care in App. C.

4.6.2 Graph Covers and Paths

We begin by introducing graph terminology that will help describe various types of tests. Since we are dealing with a graph model of the program, we wish to first define the concept in terms of the graph and then the analogous program concept. In the case of a graph cover, the concept is not clearly defined in abstract graph theory. It is mainly introduced in applications; thus, we begin our definition by first discussing the testing application.

One obvious test objective is to ensure at the close of testing that all parts of the program have been tested at least once. This may appear trivial in a short program, but is a major problem in a huge piece of software. In fact, the minimum number of tests necessary to accomplish this objective is an important measure of the test effort. Intuitively, the concept of a cover would mean a set of tests which cover (exercise) all instructions in a program. By a cover we might also mean a set of tests which exercise all control paths or flows in a program. As we shall see shortly, these two types of covers are similar but not identical. Last, we should mention that in testing a program we generally begin at the start point and finish at the end point.

---

[1] Ruston (1978). See "The Polytechnic Load and Go System Known as PLAGO," App. 3, and "The PL/C Compiler," App. 2.

[2] Freeman (1964).

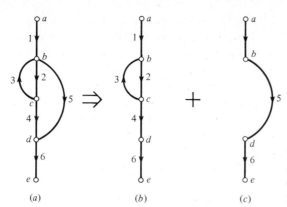

Figure 4.10 An example of path testing: (*a*) program graph; (*b*) test 1 (1, 2, 3, 2, 4, 6); (*c*) test 2 (1, 5, 6). Note that test 1 plus test 2 forms a path-test cover.

We now define a path as a sequence of edges which when traversed in the arrow direction form a connection from the start vertex to the stop vertex. We assume that the term *program path* means a graph path that includes only a single traversal of any loops which are encountered. We call the traversal of a path a *path test*.

We will now introduce the concept of a vertex cover and an edge cover of a graph. A subgraph G' is said to be a *vertex cover* of a connected graph G if G' is connected and contains all the nodes of G. A subgraph G'' is said to be an *edge cover* of a connected graph G if G'' is connected and contains all the edges of G.

If we consider the graph associated with the digraph shown in Fig. 4.10, there are two obvious vertex covers—1, 2, 4, 6 and 1, 2, 5, 6—and one obvious edge cover—1, 2, 3, 4, 5, 6.[1] Clearly, a single path test (either 1, 2, 4, 6 or 1, 2, 3, 5, 6) would traverse the vertex cover. Two path tests would be required to traverse the above-mentioned edge cover, e.g., test 1, 2, 3, 5, 6 and test 1, 2, 4, 6. Since we are dealing with connected graphs, all vertices are connected by an edge or set of edges; thus, an edge cover must also be a vertex cover. Since an edge cover is the more general concept, we will imply an edge cover in future discussions whenever we use the term *cover*, unless specified to the contrary. Note that the concept of a path-test cover, defined in the next section, is a stronger one than that of an edge cover.

4.6.3 Path Testing

Making use of the definitions of the previous section, and adapting a theorem from Knuth (1968), we can describe a path-test cover.

Any test path of the digraph can be constructed by a traversal of any path from the start node to the stop node plus a unique number of traversals of each of the independent loops (circuits in the circuit basis; see App. C). A set of path tests which includes an edge cover is called a *path-test cover*. A set of path tests will traverse a graph cover if the set of path tests includes all the independent

---

[1] Note that a cover need not contain any paths on the digraph.

loops. Since we have shown in Sec. 3.2.11 that the number of independent loops is equal to the cyclomatic number, the maximum number of path tests needed to traverse a cover is $v(G)$. Clearly, if we can find a way to make each path test traverse, say, two circuits, we will only need $v(G)/2$ tests.

It is important that we understand that so far we are treating upper bounds only on the number of path tests necessary to cover the program graph; we should also understand the definition of such a cover. At no time have we discussed an optimum or most efficient test; this will be covered later in this section.

We now consider four very similar program graphs and their associated tests to illustrate heuristic and systematic approaches to determining a path-test cover, and to further refine the concept of $v(G)$ as an upper bound on the number of path tests. In the program graph shown in Fig. 4.10a, we see it is not a connected digraph, since we have not added a phantom path as explained in Sec. 3.2.11. Heuristically, we are able to find a cover composed of the two tests 1, 2, 3, 4, 6 and 1, 5, 6. In fact, if we could test all the arcs in one path test it would be even easier. A graph which has a path containing all the edges only once each is said to be a Euler graph.[1] The graph in Fig. 4.10a is not a Euler graph; however, the graph in Fig. 4.10c is. Thus, the lower bound on the number of path tests needed to cover a graph is unity, which is reached only if the entire graph is a Euler graph. Of course, in practical cases, it is unlikely that we wish to do only a single path test even if it constitutes a cover. It is best, at least at the outset, to test smaller portions of the program which deal with only one or two functions (or features) of the program. Thus, if we have a choice of the number of tests between the maximum $v(G)$ and the minimum of 1 needed for a path-testing cover, we would probably opt closer to the maximum. Although Fig. 4.10 was not made into a strongly connected digraph, we were still able to choose heuristically a path-testing cover. The only reason for relating path testing to strongly connected digraphs, cyclomatic complexity, and independent loops is that it provides a general (not necessarily optimum) approach to finding a path-test cover, namely:

1. Locate all independent loops.
2. Choose path tests which include one or more new loops.
3. Continue choosing path tests until all loops and all edges have been used at least once.

The existence of a systematic method is of utmost importance in large problems, where heuristic methods become confusing.

4.6.4 Number of Paths

Introduction Assume that a programmer has decided to subject a program to a path test. To begin with we need a set of input data which will drive the program

---

[1] Marshall (1971), p. 31.

along all paths. This is a very difficult problem in the case of a large program, and is discussed in several of the following sections. A simpler problem which can greatly help the solution of the former one is the identification of all paths. By identification we mean a tracing of the path on the flowchart or program graphs, an enumeration of the edge sequence forming each path, or a matrix representation involving edge-vertex incidence matrices. Even this problem can prove difficult, and a starting point may be to first compute the maximum number of paths in the program.

One might ask, what need do we have to compute the number of paths when we can enumerate them and merely count their number?

1. It is useful to have a count so that it can serve as a cross-check on enumeration.
2. When we are formulating a test plan, knowledge of the number of path tests is useful in allocating test resources. Later, when the details of the test plan are needed, an enumeration can be performed.
3. If we consider the number of path tests to be a complexity measure, then we may wish to compute the number of path tests for several programs and study the correlation with other variables.
4. If exhaustive enumeration is difficult, we may be satisfied with enumeration of some fraction of the total number of tests. We need to know the number of tests first if we are to take this approach.

This section will focus on means of computing the number of paths and enumerating all paths. As we will see shortly, one must also define carefully the meaning of a path in a program with loops.

Graph bounds We begin our discussion by focusing on methods to count the number of loops. Obviously, in a program as simple as the one modeled in Fig. 4.10, inspection is all that is needed. However, in practical cases we need a general approach. A simple set of bounds can be obtained on the number of paths, N_p, in a graph without loops.[1] Consider a graph with n decisions (IF STATEMENTS). The structure shown in Fig. 4.11a represents the maximum number of paths which can be created with n deciders, that is, 2^n. Similarly, Fig. 4.11b represents the minimum number of paths which can result in a program with n deciders, namely, $n + 1$. Unfortunately, these bounds are often very wide. For example, if $n = 13$, then the minimum number of paths is 14 and the maximum is 8192. This technique can be improved if the graph is dissected at each merge point. Then bounds are computed for each subsection and the graph lower bound is computed as the product of the individual lower bounds. Similarly, the upper bound is computed as the product of the individual upper bounds. The process is illustrated in Fig. 4.12. For the entire graph $n = 6$ and $n + 1$ and 2^n yield a set of bounds $7 \leq N_p \leq 64$. For the decomposition we obtain $27 \leq N_p \leq 64$. Inspection

---

[1]Shooman (1974a); Popkin and Shooman (1978); Baggi and Shooman (1979).

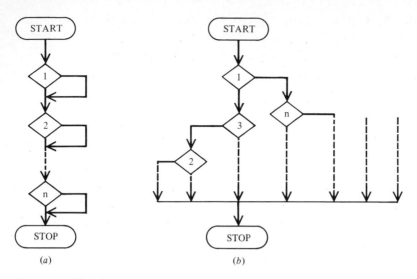

Figure 4.11 Flowchart bounds on the number of paths in a graph: (*a*) branch–merge, an upper bound; (*b*) branch–no merge, a lower bound.

shows that the actual number of paths is 27 in this case. Exact techniques are available for computing the number of paths.

Algebraic equations Again, if we consider programs without loops, the control structure is made up of the three fundamental substructures shown in both flowchart and control-graph form in Fig. 4.13. In Fig. 4.13*a*, N_A is the number of paths which pass through branch A, and by inspection, this is the sum of N_B and N_C. Similarly, in Fig. 4.13*b*, since there are two ways to get to B from A, $N_A = 2N_B$. Last, in Fig. 4.13*c*, the number of paths which pass through A is N_C, which is also the number passing through B. If we use these three relationships and work down in the program, we can write a simple set of algebraic equations which can be solved for N_p by either backward or forward substitution.

A simple example illustrates the method. Assume that the computer is to determine the winner of a card game in which player A is dealt two cards (A_1, A_2), as is player B (B_1, B_2). If either or both players have a pair, the highest pair wins. If there are no pairs, the highest card wins, and if both players have the same high card, then the highest second card determines the winner. Identical hands with or without pairs are ties.

A flowchart for this program is given in Fig. 4.14. The computation of the number of paths is given in Table 4.10. Clearly, one could also dissect the entire problem into three parts by dissecting the graph just above the C-D decider and at C and D. We could then compute $N_p = 4(N_C + N_D)$ and apply the method of Table 4.10 to compute N_C and N_D. We now consider extending this method to graphs with loops.

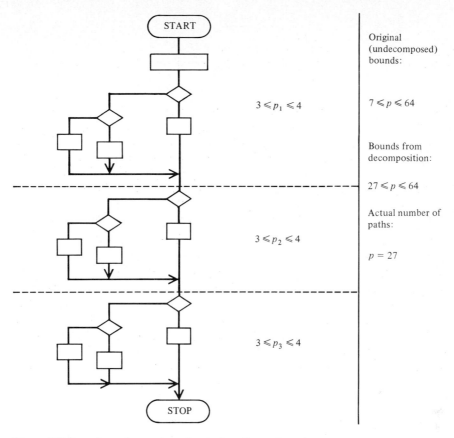

Original
(undecomposed)
bounds:

$3 \leqslant p_1 \leqslant 4$

$7 \leqslant p \leqslant 64$

Bounds from
decomposition:

$27 \leqslant p \leqslant 64$

Actual number of
paths:

$3 \leqslant p_2 \leqslant 4$

$p = 27$

$3 \leqslant p_3 \leqslant 4$

Figure 4.12 Bounds on the number of paths in a dissected graph.

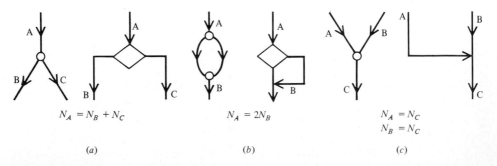

$$N_A = N_B + N_C$$

$$N_A = 2N_B$$

$$N_A = N_C$$
$$N_B = N_C$$

(a)   (b)   (c)

Figure 4.13 Elementary graph substructures.

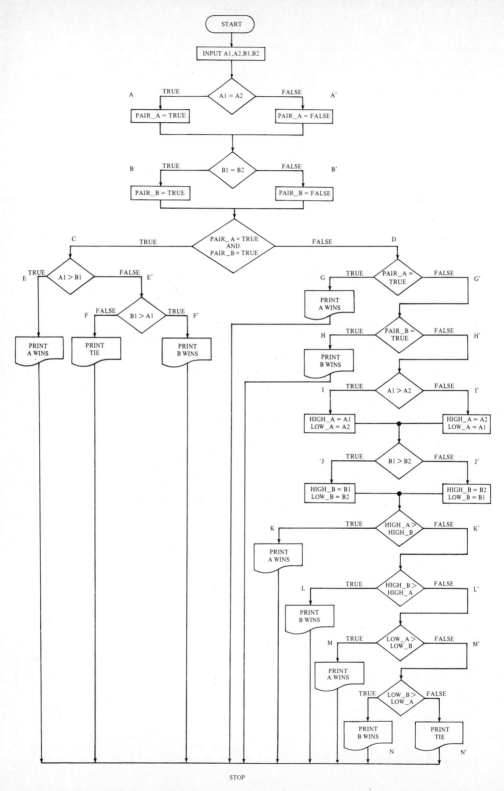

Figure 4.14 Flowchart for computer solution of a card game.

Table 4.10 Number of paths calculated in the flowchart of Fig. 4.14

Algebraic relationship	Number of paths
$N_P = N_A + N_{A'} = 2 \times N_{A'}$	$2 \times N_{A'}$
$N_{A'} = N_B + N_{B'} = 2 \times N_{B'}$	$4 \times N_{B'}$
$N_{B'} = N_C + N_D$	$4 \times (N_C + N_D)$
$N_C = N_E + N_{E'} = 1 + N_{E'}$	$4 \times ((1 + N_{E'}) + N_D)$
$N_{E'} = N_F + N_{F'} = 1 + 1 = 2$	$4 \times (3 + N_D)$
$N_D = N_G + N_{G'} = 1 + N_{G'}$	$4 \times (3 + 1 + N_{G'})$
$N_{G'} = N_H + N_{H'} = 1 + N_{H'}$	$4 \times (4 + 1 + N_{H'})$
$N_{H'} = N_I + N_{I'} = 2 \times N_{I'}$	$4 \times (5 + 2 \times N_{I'})$
$N_{I'} = N_J + N_{J'} = 2 \times N_{J'}$	$4 \times (5 + 4 \times N_{J'})$
$N_{J'} = N_K + N_{K'} = 1 + N_{K'}$	$4 \times (5 + 4 \times (1 + N_{K'}))$
$N_{K'} = N_L + N_{L'} = 1 + N_{L'}$	$4 \times (5 + 4 \times (1 + 1 + N_{L'}))$
$N_{L'} = N_M + N_{M'} = 1 + N_{M'}$	$4 \times (5 + 4 \times (2 + 1 + N_{M'}))$
$N_{M'} = N_N + N_{N'} = 1 + 1 = 2$	$4 \times (5 + 4 \times (3 + 2)) = 100$

Number of paths in a looping graph We now must define precisely what we mean by a path. In Fig. 4.10c there is no ambiguity, since 1, 5, 6 is the only possible path. In Fig. 4.10b we have paths (1, 2, 4, 6), (1, 2, 3, 2, 4, 6), (1, 2, 3, 2, 3, 2, 4, 6), (1, 2, 3, 2, 3, 2, 3, 2, 4, 6), etc. All these edge sequences satisfy the definition of a path; however, if we are looking for a path-test cover, only the first two are required. Thus, in order to remove this ambiguity, we will deal only with program paths which were previously defined so that any loops are traversed only once. This immediately suggests a method of converting a graph with loops into a loopless one. Once this is done, the previous methods may be employed. The approach, essentially, is to split any node X which is the terminus of a feedback path into nodes X and X'. The split portion of the node with feedback edge attached is then connected to the end node or another convenient node below so

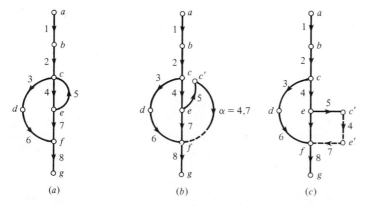

Figure 4.15 The use of node splitting to replace a graph having a loop with an equivalent loopless graph. (*a*) Original graph; (*b*) graph with node c split; (*c*) equivalent loopless graph.

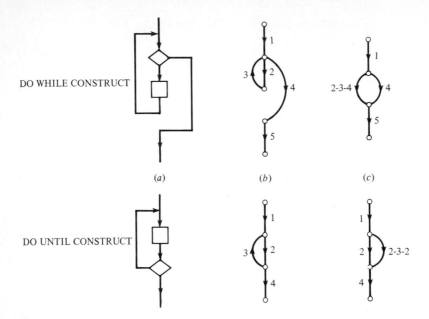

DO WHILE CONSTRUCT

(*a*)   (*b*)   (*c*)

DO UNTIL CONSTRUCT

Figure 4.16 Equivalent graphs of structured-program control structures: (*a*) flowchart; (*b*) graph; (*c*) equivalent graph.

as to remove the loop.[1] In order to preserve the program path structure (for subsequent enumeration methods, not for path counting), other nodes are replicated as needed. The procedure is illustrated by the example given in Fig. 4.15.

In the case of a structured program, counting the number of paths is easy, since the graph can be dissected at each entry and exit point to a control structure as required. IF THEN ELSE structures are treated as simple decisions. A DO CASE structure with k values of the index i represents k paths. DO UNTIL and DO WHILE structures are essentially replaced by two parallel paths (no-loop or once-around-the-loop), as shown in Fig. 4-16. Once the looping structures are replaced, either inspection or the method of Table 4.10 can be used.

Program-path enumeration Now that we know how to count the number of program paths, we can focus on methods for enumerating the actual paths. A simple method of enumeration is based on the "algebraic equation" method of path counting. We begin by considering a loopless graph with n edges. Each edge in the graph is labeled $X_1, X_2, \ldots, X_n$. Our object is to generate an algebraic expression consisting of sums and products of the X_n terms. When this expression is expanded, the terms represent the program paths. An example illustrates the procedure.

[1] Similar techniques are used to eliminate feedback loops in evaluating the transmission of signal flowgraphs, which are commonly used in the automatic control field. See Mason and Zimmerman (1960), Chap. 4.

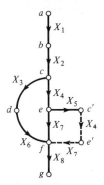

Figure 4.17 Version of Figure 4.15c with variables denoting each edge of the graph.

Consider the graph given in Fig. 4.17. Since it is clear that edges 1, 2, and 8 must be part of all paths, we can write:

$$PGF = X_1 X_2 \alpha X_8 \tag{4.6}$$

where   PGF = path-generating function

α = path-generating function for the subgraph from c to f

Now the path-generating function for α, PGF_α, is given as follows:

$$PGF_\alpha = (X_3 X_6 + X_4 \beta) \tag{4.7}$$

where β = the path-generating function for the subgraph from e to f. In a similar manner we can compute:

$$PGF_\beta = (X_7 + X_5 X_4 X_7) \tag{4.8}$$

Substitution of Eqs. (4.8) and (4.7) into Eq. (4.6) yields:

$$PGF = X_1 X_2 [X_3 X_6 + X_4 (X_7 + X_5 X_4 X_7)] X_8 \tag{4.9}$$

Expansion of Eq. (4.9) yields:

$$PGF = X_1 X_2 X_3 X_6 X_8 + X_1 X_2 X_4 X_7 X_8 \tag{4.10}$$
$$+ X_1 X_2 X_4 X_5 X_4 X_7 X_8$$

Comparison of Eq. (4.10) with Fig. 4.17 shows that all the paths have been enumerated. This methods works with loopless graphs, and we have already shown that one can transform a graph with loops into a loopless graph; thus the enumeration method is general and works for all graphs. Again we may comment that in the case of structured programs, the computation is conceptually simple and merely involves an algebraic expression with products, parentheses, and sums of terms. Of course, in a very large problem, the computation becomes lengthy and a computer solution is required.

Relationship of paths and cyclomatic complexity The number of path tests associated with a program is an important measure of program complexity. In fact, several authors have devised complexity measures related to this metric. Attempts

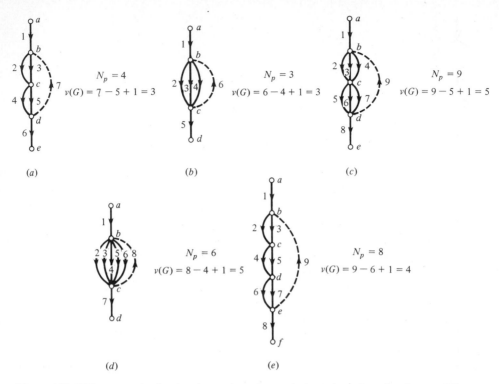

$$N_p = 4$$
$$v(G) = 7 - 5 + 1 = 3$$

$$N_p = 3$$
$$v(G) = 6 - 4 + 1 = 3$$

$$N_p = 9$$
$$v(G) = 9 - 5 + 1 = 5$$

(a)   (b)   (c)

$$N_p = 6$$
$$v(G) = 8 - 4 + 1 = 5$$

$$N_p = 8$$
$$v(G) = 9 - 6 + 1 = 4$$

(d)   (e)

Figure 4.18 Different graphs showing that cyclomatic complexity and number of paths may differ.

have been made to use the cyclomatic complexity number introduced in Chap. 3 as a measure of the number of test paths. However, the cyclomatic complexity number $v(G)$ and the number of path tests N_p differ, as shown in the five different examples given in Fig. 4.18. We can state that $v(G)$ is a lower bound on N_p. To prove this we consider the "tree method" of computing the cyclomatic complexity of a graph, which was stated in Chap. 3. Using this method $v(G)$ is defined as the number of edges which must be removed from the graph to break all loops yet still leave a tree. Thus, each of these removed branches is associated with a different loop, and any path test must cover all these loops as a minimum.

Polynomial complexity Ruston (1979) developed a complexity measure which is related to the topology of the program graph. Basically, for loopless program graphs, one develops a polynomial representation for each decider structure. An IF THEN ELSE is represented by a polynomial $p(x) = x$. When the IF THEN ELSE has additional decisions within the THEN and ELSE clauses, the polynomials for each clause are added to obtain the total graph polynomial, that is $p(x) = p_T(x) + p_E(x)$. For the loopless graph given in Fig. 4.11a, the polynomial $p(x) = x^n$, and for that of Fig. 4.11b, $p(x) = x + n - 1$. Combining these rules, we can readily see how the polynomial of a complex graph is calculated, as shown in Fig. 4.19.

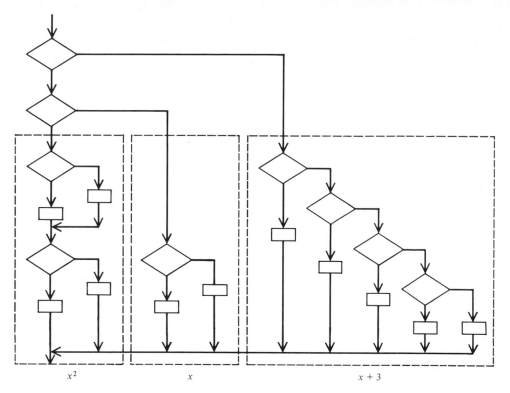

x^2 x $x + 3$

Figure 4.19 Example showing the use of the polynomial complexity measure: $x^2 + 2x + 3$ realized as a sum of $(x^2) + (x) + (x + 3)$.

4.6.5 Program Paths versus Graph Paths

So far our approach to testing has been to draw a program graph and orient our testing philosophy and categorization to the graph properties. It soon becomes apparent that the graph path approach has a number of important drawbacks. The material in this section and in Sec. 4.7 will be directed toward illuminating some of the problems caused by the fact that the program graph contains no information about the content of the program statements. Furthermore, we will modify and augment the program graph to remedy some of these defects and to achieve further realism in our abstract model.

It should be obvious at this point that the program flowchart is an abstract program model which is graphlike and yet provides information on the program statements.

These concepts are best illustrated by the analysis of an example. In Fig. 4.20 we find the problem statement, the flowchart, and the program graph for an illustrative problem. Note that in Fig. 4.20(c) we have added an arc from vertex k to vertex b to ensure that the digraph is strongly connected. In Fig. 4.21a we have chosen a heuristic cover consisting of two path tests, which traverse all branches. In Fig. 4.21b a path cover is presented which comprises four path tests.

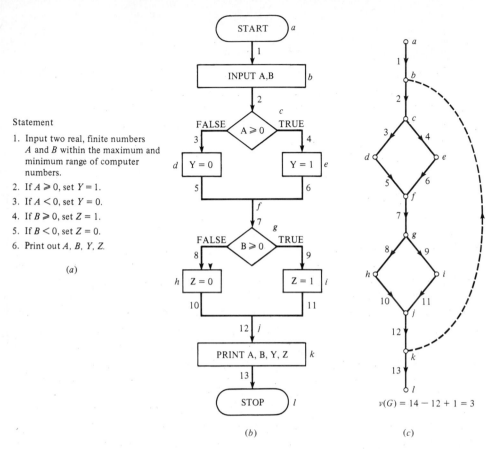

Statement

1. Input two real, finite numbers A and B within the maximum and minimum range of computer numbers.
2. If $A \geqslant 0$, set $Y = 1$.
3. If $A < 0$, set $Y = 0$.
4. If $B \geqslant 0$, set $Z = 1$.
5. If $B < 0$, set $Z = 0$.
6. Print out A, B, Y, Z.

(a)

$v(G) = 14 - 12 + 1 = 3$

(b)

(c)

Figure 4.20 Comparison of problem statement (a), flowchart (b), and graph (c).

An elementary analysis of the flowchart in Fig. 4.20b shows that there are basically four classes of input data, given in Table 4.11. Thus, if we wish to test each class of input data, we will need four path tests, i.e., those shown in Fig. 4.21. Furthermore, if we consult an experienced designer, we will most likely be cautioned to make sure we test the equal conditions in the predicates (expressions) of the two deciders (IF statements). This will result in nine tests, as shown in Table 4.12.

A further problem exists if not all the graph paths are program paths. For example, suppose we examine the flowcharts of Figs. 4.20b and 4.22; we find they are identical except for the predicate of the second decider. Clearly the graphs of the two flowcharts are the same. However, if we were to construct a test table equivalent to Table 4.12 for the flowchart of Fig. 4.22, we would find only seven test cases, since as long as $A = 0$, the predicate of the second decider is always false, regardless of the value of B. The situation would become even more complicated if the predicate of the second decider were $A + B \geq 0$. In such a case we would have to specify not only the sign of variables A and B, but their relative

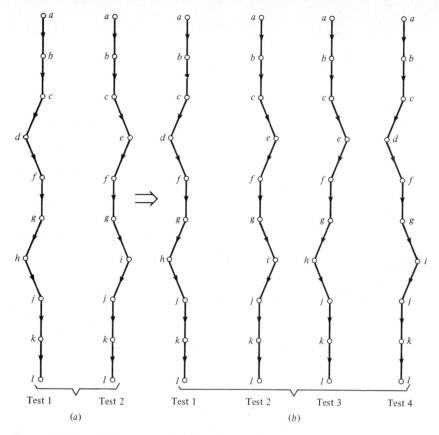

Figure 4.21 Two different covers for the example of Fig. 4.12: (*a*) two tests (edge cover); (*b*) four tests (path cover).

Table 4.11 Input data classes for the problem of Fig. 4.19

Test (path)	Input data
1	$A < 0, B < 0$
2	$A \geq 0, B \geq 0$
3	$A < 0, B \geq 0$
4	$A \geq 0, B < 0$

magnitudes as well. Thus the number of path tests is an upper bound on the number of program paths.

Much current research is devoted to the subject of graph models of programs as related to software testing.[1] Some additional issues which are discussed in the

[1]Deb (1977); Laemmel (1975*a*, 1975*b*, 1976); Laemmel (1966), App. A, "Path Enumerating Functions."

Table 4.12 Improved data classes

Test (path)	Input data
1	$A < 0, B < 0$
2	$A > 0, B > 0$
3	$A < 0, B > 0$
4	$A > 0, B < 0$
5	$A = 0, B = 0$
6	$A = 0, B < 0$
7	$A > 0, B = 0$
8	$A < 0, B = 0$
9	$A = 0, B > 0$

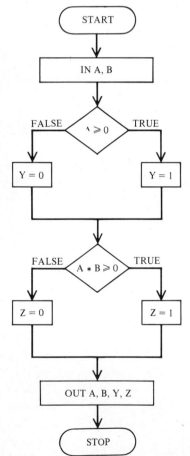

Figure 4.22 A modification of Fig. 4.20(b) in which only the predicate of the second decider is changed.

literature or are possibly being researched are as follows:

1. How can we represent a graph in terms of a branch-node incidence matrix, which can be used at the appropriate data structure for any computational program?
2. What is the significance of paths where we traverse a loop more than once?
3. If the value $v(G)$ is a lower bound and N_p an upper bound on the number of program tests, how close are these bounds in practice?
4. What is the relationship among $v(G)$, polynomial complexity, and the path-counting and enumerating procedures described above?

The reader is referred to the references and the problems at the end of the chapter for a further discussion of these issues.

4.7 CHOICE OF TEST DATA

4.7.1 Introduction

In the previous section we defined two types of tests which were based on a graph model of the program. The arc cover test guarantees only that each instruction is executed at least once. This is a very minimal type of test; a better type of test is to execute every path. In many large systems we may be unable to run a complete test of all paths. Of course, the ultimate test is an exhaustive one, which is essentially a test of each program path for all values of input data and all initial conditions (initial values stored in register and memory). In all except trivial cases, an exhaustive test is impossible. Thus, it is important to have approaches which guide one as to how to choose a subset of the paths if it is not feasible to test them all. Similarly, if we can test all paths at least once but still have additional test resources, we must decide how to distribute the additional tests along the paths.

Another problem arises in using the graph model of the previous section. The graph does not depict all features of program operation. For example, a subroutine call is not represented in a program graph. Also there is no way to represent the number of iterations performed by a DO I = 1 TO N loop. One method of representing such a DO group is to unwrap the loop as shown in Fig. 4.23. A list of the conditions which are difficult to depict in a graph model is given in Table 4.13. Note that many of these conditions are also difficult to show even in a flowchart model.

For all these reasons, we explore in the next section various heuristic methods of choosing test data.

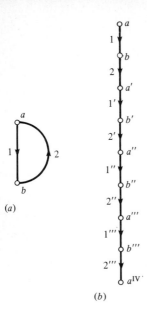

(a)

(b)

Figure 4.23 Modeling of a DO group: (*a*) simple model; (*b*) unwrapped model.

Table 4.13 Program properties that are difficult to represent in a graph model

Property	Graph	Flowchart
Decider predicate	Not represented	Represented
Assignment statements	Not represented	Represented
Input	Not represented	Statement
Output	Not represented	Statement
Iteration	Unwrapped loop	Statement or structure
Declaration	Not represented	Not represented
On condition	Not represented	Not represented
Interrupt	Not represented	Not represented
Segmentation	Not represented	Statement
Variable scope	Not represented	Not represented
Subroutine	Not represented	Statement
Macro call	Not represented	Statement

4.7.2 Practical Testing

As we have already suggested, practical testing in many cases reduces to the two questions: How many test cases should we choose, and how should we distribute these test cases? We now direct ourselves to the latter question.

As a vehicle for focusing this discussion and that of the next section on exhaustive testing, we introduce the following problem, which appeared on a recent doctoral examination in computer science at the Polytechnic Institute of New York.[1]

Problem statement

An assembly language program which solves for the roots of a quadratic equation $Ax^2 + Bx + C = 0$ has been written on a minicomputer with a 12-bit word length. The computation is done using integer arithmetic. Each time the program runs, values for A, B, and C within the range -10 to $+10$ are entered via a terminal. The syntactical bugs detected by the assembler have all been corrected and a few test cases yield the right answers. We are concerned with testing for any remaining logical bugs.

Questions

1. How would you choose a set of test values for A, B, and C to ensure that the program is exhaustively tested?
2. On the basis of the number of tests generated in part 1 and the typical CPU speed of such a computer, estimate how long the exhaustive test would take. (In order to estimate the running time of the program, assume that the memory cycle time is 1μ, the program is 200 instructions long, and the machine has hardware Multiply instructions.)
3. Based on your knowledge of the algorithm (the quadratic formula) and some intuition as to how bugs may occur, how would you construct a good comprehensive but nonexhaustive test?

In Sec. 4.8 we will deal with questions 1 and 2. In this section we will introduce different philosophies for selecting test cases based on an answer to question 3.

Input-space testing The most obvious approach is one based on the input data, and formally we will view the input parameters as variables which specify an *input space*. In fact, the three input parameters A, B, and C form a three-dimensional input space. Since the computer word length is 12 bits, there can be at most $2^{12} = 4096$ different number representations for A, B, and C. Thus, we can characterize our input space by a three-dimensional cube with 4096 points along each axis and 2^{36} combinations (points) inside the volume of the cube. Our

---

[1] From Shooman (1974c).

problem is to select a set of test values in the input space which is much smaller than 2^{36} yet gives adequate test coverage. In general we wish to choose our points "far enough apart" that they cover the space well; however, if there is an area with a high probability of error, we wish to concentrate our points there.[1] Although we cannot solve the problem analytically, and will have to rely on heuristic approaches, we can still formulate it. We will make the assumption that in the neighborhood of each test point there is a sphere of radius r. The probability p that any point within this sphere excites a latent bug is 0 when $r = 0$, and increases as r increases; that is, $p = g(r)$. If we wish to minimize the probability of an undetected bug, we choose more points or decrease the $g(r)$ function.

Solution-space testing Instead of concentrating on the input space we can concentrate on the output (solution) space. First of all, there exists a transformation T which maps the input space into the solution space, which we may loosely call the solution. In addition, the program may be considered to be another mapping T' which, if not identical to T, differs only in insignificant, small details. Assuming that mapping T is known, one can always establish corresponding points in the solution space for each value in the input space. The solution space has as many dimensions as there are outputs in the program, plus a possible additional dimension if the sequence of output values is of importance. There is no requirement that the input and output spaces have the same number of dimensions. Similarly, there is an inverse transformation T^{-1} which allows one to determine points in the input space which correspond to particular points in the output space. The inverse mapping from output space to input space need not be unique, since more than one set of input variables may generate the same output. The mapping T from input to output should be unique, since each set of input parameters can determine only one solution.

There is one apparent counterargument to this last statement. In certain cases one set of input data produces the correct output, whereas at other times the same set of test data produces an incorrect result. Such a transient error, if not due to a hardware transient condition, seems to contradict the uniqueness argument. If we have a multiprocessor system, a real-time input system, or a processor which does not uniquely initialize its internal state at the beginning of each problem, then an additional dimension in the input space representing the sequence or initial state accounts for these variations.

In some problems it is more sensible to plan our tests based on the solution space rather than the input space. In cases where the system has different classes of output solutions it may not be clear what range of input values generate each class. Thus, if we are to choose a certain number of test cases in each class we can

---

[1]Some authors have stated without proof that if we find one bug in a module, there are sure to be others nearby. This author feels the statement is correct if the module was particularly difficult, was written by an inexperienced or less skilled programmer, or is special in some other way. Without such supporting evidence, there seems no reason to accept this conjecture.

start with a nominal output solution in each case and scatter our test points about it. This is also an aid in computing the correct solution against which we will compare our results. Rather than go through the difficult problem of gathering an analytical or computer-calculated solution for each test point, we can expand the solution about the initial test point in a multidimensional Taylor series. The partial derivatives for these expansions may be obtained either analytically or by computing delta increments based on a pair of solutions. In the same manner in which we defined a set of spheres and a $g(r)$ function in the input space we may define a similar set of spheres and a $g'(r)$ function in the solution space.

In other cases, where the characteristics of the solution are dependent on input data, input-space-based tests are probably superior. For example, there are many cases of business data processing where the character of the input data generally determines the character of the output. Also, if we have some idea of the actual distribution of the input data, an input-space approach allows us to choose our test cases in proportion to observed input occurrence rates.

Program paths There is still a third position one can take in viewing program testing, i.e., based on the program topology. Each path in the flowchart represents either a single solution class or several solution classes. Thus, we should require that a comprehensive test traverse each path in the program at least once. If we add the further requirement that a number of representative solution cases be generated along each path then we approach the solution-space viewpoint. On the other hand, if we require that each path be traversed for several values of the input parameters, we begin to approach the input-space viewpoint.

In our search for unusual combinations of events which might constitute program bugs, we can center our attention on the predicates of the deciders which actuate the transfer of control, and their relationship to the input variables and other calculated variables whose values affect branching. This should yield an additional class of unusual test conditions.

Test-related reliability models If we view operation of our system as some randomly determined (uniformly distributed) path in the output (input) space, then the ratio of successful test points to total points in our output (input) space would represent an approximation to the probability of success on any one computational sequence. If the output points were not equally likely, then each test point could be weighted by its occurrence frequency. If we choose the most frequently occurring points as our test points, the approximation should be closer to the true value for a fixed test size. Carrying our model one step further, if we assume a functional form for $g(r)$ then we should include not discrete test points, but probability masses within each test sphere. One possible functional form for the $g(r)$ function is to make it inversely proportional to the gradient of the solution at the test point. Last, if we know the rate at which unique solutions are processed, we can compute the failure rate and the mean time between failures.

Laemmel (1980) has developed a model which relates the probability that an error occurs in the field, P_e, to the probability that the tester misses the error, P_m, and the probability that the user excites the error, P_u:

$$P_e = P_m P_u \tag{4.11}$$

The simplest assumption we can make is that the module has N possible equally likely input values and that W of these cause errors. This means that

$$P_u = \frac{W}{N} \tag{4.12}$$

If t independent tests are performed, the probability of missing an error t times is:

$$P_m = \left(1 - \frac{W}{N}\right)^t \tag{4.13}$$

Combining Eqs. (4.11) to (4.13) yields

$$P_e = \frac{W}{N}\left(1 - \frac{W}{N}\right)^t \leq \frac{W}{N}e^{-Wt/N} \tag{4.14}$$

A plot of P_e versus W/N is given in Fig. 4.24.

The conclusion is that for P_e to be a small number, t has to be much greater than N/W. Equation (4.14) gives us an approximate way to compute the required number of tests for a specified reliability.

Laemmel also treats the case of unequal probabilities of uncovering an error and dependencies among the errors, and discusses optimal test strategies. The reader is referred to the report for the complete results.

Another model relating the reliability to the testing process was developed by Girard and Rault (1973).

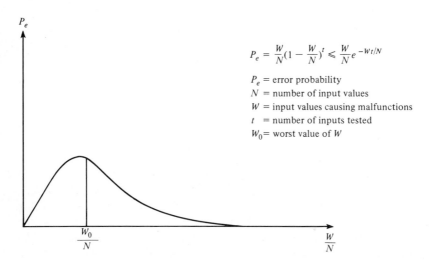

$$P_e = \frac{W}{N}(1 - \frac{W}{N})^t \leq \frac{W}{N}e^{-Wt/N}$$

P_e = error probability
N = number of input values
W = input values causing malfunctions
t = number of inputs tested
W_0 = worst value of W

Figure 4.24 Plot of P_e versus W/N from the model of Eq. (4.14).

Solving a system of equations One can formulate a direct approach to the choice of test data. Assume we have a loopless graph, in which the path structure is determined by the deciders. If we further assume that each decider has a predicate which can be represented by an inequality, then the two branches are (1) equality satisfied and (2) equality not satisfied. If we write a separate inequality for each decider, we have reduced the problem to the solution of a set of equations. Furthermore, if we use the node-splitting transformation shown in Fig. 4-15 we can extend this method to looping graphs.

The main problem with such an approach is that the solution of a set of inequalities is a difficult task. Some work has been done on applying this approach.[1] Also, some current research is attempting to apply the methods of linear programming to the solution of the set of inequalities one obtains.[2]

4.7.3 Guidelines for Test-Data Generation

In the above discussions of input space, output space, and program paths, we were able to properly formulate the problem; however, no techniques of analysis or synthesis emerged. In this section we will discuss a practical approach which is taken in almost all programming projects, i.e., a formulation of test cases based upon experience and engineering judgment. At least we have described the problem well enough that we should be able to define the various classes of test data we will use. We then choose a number of normal cases for each class. Once we have investigated the neighborhood of each of our test points, we should try to construct a number of unusual cases not represented in our previous testing which may cause trouble. Based on the test concepts previously discussed, four possible techniques for generating these unusual cases are suggested in Table. 4.14.

We can best illustrate the procedure for choosing test data by reference to a particular problem. The example to be used is the classical one of a program which receives three numbers representing the sides of a triangle and classifies the kind of triangle such sides form. The flowchart of the problem is given in Fig. 4.25. A set of test data for testing a completed program corresponding to Fig. 4.25 is given in Table 4.15. The sets of normal data were chosen to cover all the cases in the solution space. In a simple problem such as this we can have confidence that we have found all cases. However, in a complex problem, things are not so obvious. The analyst may wish to use HIPO diagrams and data flowgraphs to aid in this search. The range of data classification was devised to scatter a few tests along the program paths. The number of tests to be chosen and the method of choosing are not obvious. In a complex problem it may be useful to calculate the gradient of the solution so as to choose test cases which are "spread apart," rather than bunch them arbitrarily or spread them uniformly in input space. The test

---

[1] Mohanty (1976).
[2] Shooman and Ruston (1979).

Table 4.14 Suggested rules for generating test data

1. Generate one set of test data to exercise each major feature of the program.

2. Examine the solution to devise unusual cases not covered by any of the "standard" test cases (e.g., boundary lines between solution classes, extremes of solution, etc.).

3. Examine the input parameters and generate test cases which are representative of unusual or bad input data. Obvious values to include are combinations with zero, negative data, or endpoints of the range. Also, erroneous or so-called garbage inputs should be tried.

4. Compute the gradient of the solution, and choose some test cases which are generated by following the maximum gradient. This should produce a trajectory in the input space along which the solution is changing at a fairly rapid rate.

5. Using the techniques of Sec. 4.6, we can check to see if the tests selected by rules 1, 2, and 3 form an arc cover. If not, additional tests are added; furthermore, additional tests may be added to cover any unusual control sequences.

6. Choose additional cases along each test path by judicious selection or random generation until the test resource budget is used up.*

---

*It is good management practice to keep some of the testing resources in a reserve budget to cover contingencies or special problems which occur without asking higher management for increased resources.

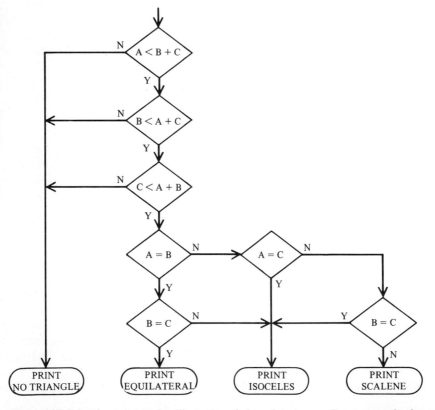

Figure 4.25 Triangle program for illustrating choice of test case. Program reads three integers representing the sides of a triangle and classifies whether the triangle is scalene, isosceles, equilateral, or invalid. *(From Myers, 1979, p. 197)*

Table 4.15 Types of tests for the triangle program

Data	Test case (*a*)	Sequences (*b*)	(*c*)
1. Equilateral	10, 10, 10	—, —, —	—, —, —
2. Isosceles	10, 10, 17	10, 17, 10	17, 10, 10
3. Scalene	8, 10, 12	8, 12, 10	10, 12, 8
4. Not a triangle	10, 10, 22	10, 22, 10	22, 10, 10
5. Degenerate case	10, 5, 5	5, 10, 5	5, 5, 10

Range of data

1. Run tests 1 to 4 over again for a range (say, 5 to 10 values), being sure to include the largest and smallest integer which the program will accept.

Abnormal data

1. Zero data	0, 0, 0	—, —, —	—, —, —
	0, 0, 17	0, 17, 0	17, 0, 0
	0, 10, 12	0, 12, 10	12, 0, 10
2. Negative data	−10, −10, −10	—, —, —	—, —, —
	−10, −10, +17	−10, +17, −10	+17, −10, −10
	−8, 10, 17	−8, 17, 10	17, −8, 10
3. Missing data	—, —, —	—, —, —	—, —, —
	10, —, —	—, 10, —	—, —, 10
	8, 10, —	8, —, 10	—, 8, 10
4. Garbage input	A, B, C	—, —, —	—, —, —
	= , +, −	—, —, —	—, —, —
	8, 10, A	8, A, 10	A, 10, 8
	7E3, 10.75, A	10.75, 7E3, A	A, 7E3, 10.75
5. Maximum-minimum data	Include maximum- and minimum-sized integers in the test set, and values above and below these values.		

cases given under the heading of abnormal data have been generated with reference to rule 3 of Table 4.14. Note that the emphasis of all these test cases is to look for weak spots and find errors, rather than to continue testing features or input regions which have already been tested.

We now use rule 5 of Table 4.14 to ensure that the tests already chosen constitute an arc cover. (In general they will do so; however, this is a good technique for checking.) In Fig. 4.26 we relabel the flowchart, draw the program graph, and compute $v(G) = 8$. In Table 4.16 we explore the coverage of the test paths and find that tests 1 through 4*c* provide an arc cover. We note that although $v(G) = 8$, we have chosen 10 tests in Table 4.16 and about 120 tests in Table 4.15. As an aside we note that since $v(G) = 8$, this problem is about the maximum size McCabe recommends for a single module.

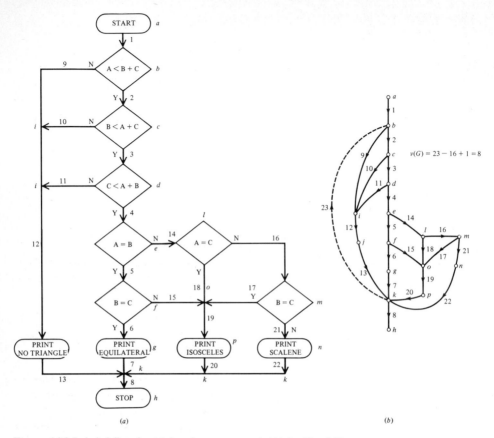

(a)   (b)

Figure 4.26 Labeled flowchart (a) and program graph (b) for Fig. 4.25

Table 4.16 Coverage check for tests given in Table 4.15

Test number	Data	Arcs covered
1.	10, 10, 10	1, 2, 3, 4, 5, 6, 7, 8
2a.	10, 10, 17	1, 2, 3, 4, 5, 15, 19, 20, 8
2b.	10, 17, 10	1, 2, 3, 4, 14, 18, 19, 20, 8
2c	17, 10, 10	1, 2, 3, 4, 14, 16, 17, 19, 20, 8
3a.	8, 10, 12	1, 2, 3, 4, 14, 16, 21, 22, 8
3b.	8, 12, 10	1, 2, 3, 4, 14, 16, 21, 22, 8
3c.	10, 12, 8	1, 2, 3, 4, 14, 16, 21, 22, 8
4a.	10, 10, 22	1, 2, 3, 11, 12, 13, 8
4b.	10, 22, 10	1, 2, 10, 12, 13, 8
4c.	22, 10, 10	1, 9, 12, 13, 8

4.8 EXHAUSTIVE TESTING

4.8.1 Introduction

Software designers often state that a program could be made free of errors if it were only exhaustively tested. If one questions the speaker further, one finds that while the spirit of the phrase *exhaustive testing* is well understood, the exact definition is not known. The purpose of this section is to try to quantify (by example) what an exhaustive test is and to show clearly why it is impossible. The example which will be used is the one given in Table 4.11.

4.8.2 Possible Sources of Error

In order to solve the stated problem, we must start with some physical under-standing of how errors might occur. We assume that the assembler is capable of detecting all syntactical errors and that these have been eliminated. Thus, the only remaining errors are either algorithmic or logical. In our case we are quite sure of our algorithm if we agree to use the quadratic formula:

$$r_1, r_2 = \frac{-B \pm \sqrt{B^2 - 4AC}}{2A} \tag{4.15}$$

This formula can be proved to be correct and only requires some care in the handling of the case of complex roots. An obvious approach is to test the discriminant at the beginning of the program and, if it is negative, to jump to a complex-roots subprogram which separately computes real and imaginary parts. Also, we must handle the case where $A = 0$ individually to avoid division by zero in Eq. (4.15). It seems that if these special cases are properly handled, then the algorithm in Eq. (4.15) is correct. (Have we neglected any other special cases?)

If we had chosen to use a numerical solution (perhaps the Newton-Ralphson method) to find the roots, we would have to carefully investigate the validity of the algorithm. Does it converge? What are the special cases? Do they converge? (Are we sure we have investigated all special cases?)

Now we must consider the possibilities of logical errors, assuming that we have satisfied ourselves on the issue of algorithmic errors. One logical error would be the writing of an incorrect transfer of control (IF [expression] THEN ELSE, DO WHILE [expression], etc.) in the program. In terms of graph terminology we say the *decider* (transfer of control) element is incorrect if its *predicate* (expression) is incorrect. In general the expression in the predicate of a decider takes the form

$$(\text{expression 1}) \text{ comparison operator } (\text{expression 2}) \tag{4.16}$$

For example, $x - y > 3$, $x^2 + 2z = x - 14$, etc.

Another possibility for logical error involves overflow of the finite word length, differences between positive and negative zero, etc. Since we are assuming the program is written in assembly language, all these problems must be considered as possible error sources in our testing.[1] This means we have the possibility that the program will work for certain sets of data but will give errors for others.

4.8.3 Exhaustive Test

As discussed above, the logical and arithmetic calculations involved in the program may fail for certain values of the program variables. The program variables are created by particular combinations of the input values (polynomial coefficients) A, B, and C given in Eq. (4.15). In a general way we may say the program maps A, B, and C into a set of program variables and then maps the program variables into two output roots r_1 and r_2. To exhaustively test the program we must exhaustively test the two mappings. Unless we explore further the nature of these two mappings our test must consist of trying all possible combinations of A, B, and C and obtaining computer solutions for r_1 and r_2. In addition we must check the solutions by some independent means: (1) using paper, pencil, Eq. (4.15), and a desk calculator; (2) using a different root-solving program with a different algorithm; (3) plotting the solutions on top of root locus plots; (4) testing to see if $(B/A) = -(r_1 + r_2)$ and $(C/A) = r_1, r_2$; (5) substitution of the roots in the equation to see if the result is nearly zero. The more different the checking technique, the better, since this will reduce the small but finite possibility that two independent solution schemes arrive at the same wrong result.[2]

Since we are assuming a 12-bit word length in our computer, one bit will be for the sign and the remaining 11 various number combinations. Thus, we could scale our problem so that the range from 0 to ± 10, at most, is represented by 11 bits, as is the range of 0 to -10. This way, there would be at most, $2^{12} = 4096$ bit representations for each of the coefficients A, B and C.

4.8.4 Intractability of an Exhaustive Test

The exhaustive test proposed is intractable for several reasons. First of all it is impossible to check the 64×10^9 combinations needed.[3] Second, the test time is prohibitive.

---

[1] Many people feel that higher-level-language programs have fewer bugs because the computer automatically takes care of number conversions and arithmetic. Thus, an entire class of errors is removed (cf. Table 2.25).

[2] Strictly speaking, the fact that the independent check may have the same error as the program it is checking challenges the basic philosophy of "perfect testing." As a practical matter we can argue as follows: The program under test has a small error probability ε_1, and the checking program has an error probability ε_2. The probability that any two errors are the same is δ_{12}. Thus, the probability that both methods yield the same wrong answer (assuming independence) is $\varepsilon_1 \times \varepsilon_2 \times \delta_{12}$, which can be made tiny enough to neglect.

[3] In this particular problem we could have a second computer check to see if $(B/A) = -(r_1 + r_2)$ and $(C/A) = r_1 r_2$. In general this is not possible.

Assuming that the average instruction takes 2.5 memory cycles (for example, some take 1, some 2, and multiply and divide might take 5), that a memory cycle is 1 μs, and that a typical run traverses 100 of the 200 instructions, we have a run time of 250 μs. The time to complete the entire test services is then

64×10^9 combinations $\times 250 \times 10^{-6}$ s per combination

$$= 16 \times 10^6 \text{ s} \approx 5000 \text{ h}$$

Even if we assume an electronic memory with 0.1 μs cycle time, the test time is still about 3 weeks.

Another problem is, How do we check the output? Assuming we don't have one computer check another, as was previously suggested, a human must separately compute and check a fantastic amount of output. If we assume 5 columns of printer output per line and 60 lines per page we obtain[1]

$$\frac{64 \times 10^9 \text{ output combinations}}{5 \text{ columns of output} \times 60 \text{ lines per page}} \approx 200 \times 10^6 \text{ pages of output}$$

$$\frac{200 \times 10^6 \text{ pages}}{400 \text{ pages per inch} \times 12 \text{ in/ft}} \approx 40,000 \text{ ft high.}$$

Clearly output checking can be even more of an impossibility than run time in many cases.

4.8.5 An Additional Test Dimension

If the input variables A, B, and C are read via analog-to-digital converters, the program will probably contain an "idle input loop" which accepts input values in the order in which they become available. Thus, we must add a fourth dimension to our input space, the sequence in which the input values occur. In terms of our example, this fourth sequence dimension contains the six points which correspond to the permutations of A, B, and C, (ABC, ACB, BCA, BAC, CAB, CBA). In a similar but more complex manner, if the computer system is a multiprocessor then some sort of processor sequence represents the added dimension.[2] This point is discussed further in Sec. 4.10.

4.9 SIMULATOR, SCENARIO, AND OPERATIONAL TESTS

4.9.1 Introduction

Because we assume that testing is the basic method of catching errors, and since simulator, scenario, and operational testing is the last stage of testing, we are now really speaking about the last line of defense against errors. The distinctions

---

[1]Printing time may exceed the computation time.
[2]Even in the case of a single processor, initial states of storage (registers, memory, mass storage) create the possibility of differing initial conditions.

between simulated, scenario, and operational testing are very fine and are being drawn here mainly to bring out three approaches to what might be termed the broader area of functional testing. By simulation, we mean some approximation to the "real thing." If we are strict about that definition, essentially all the tests in this section will be simulation. More specifically, we refer to a test phase in which the software development has progressed sufficiently so that system integration is fairly well advanced or complete, and we wish to test the system at a higher level which roughly approximates actual operation.[1] Thus, the purpose of these tests is to duplicate in as realistic a way as possible the actual operation of the software. Obviously the cost of such tests is fairly expensive; therefore, they should be well planned to develop the maximum amount of information and ferret out the maximum number of residual errors. Of course if we inspect Fig. 1.5 we see that the cost of finding errors and fixing them during functional testing is still less expensive than the cost of finding and fixing them during actual operation; therefore, its use is well justified. Also, there is a class of errors involving incompatibilities in timing and interfacing between major pieces of peripheral, input-output, or multiple-processor equipment which cannot be exercised prior to functional testing.

4.9.2 Simulation

When we consider simulation of the actual system, we must address ourselves to three main areas: the computer hardware, the computer software, and the mission. Often, we will not have the final hardware available to us, since that too may be under development and in the final stages of testing. Thus, we may have a software simulator for the actual hardware or an early prototype version of the actual hardware to work with. Second, there may be some sections of the software which have not been completed, and these must be replaced with either test stubs or earlier prototype modules which perform essentially the same functions. Last, we may find that the actual mission is such a complex one that we can only simulate the actual functions to be performed. For example, suppose we were designing a satellite tracking system which (1) controls the radar, (2) gathers the data base on located items, (3) decides which located items are satellites, and (4) records their orbital elements in the data base. Clearly, there would be difficulties in fully simulating the mission. First of all, the huge radar antenna which was to be controlled and which was to feed signals back to the computer concerning objects it located might not be available. In such a case we might have to use a total simulation (software) of the radar antenna, or use some other small antenna which was available and perhaps track the moon as a simulated mission.

---

[1]In Chap. 5, Sec. 5.9.12, we will discuss the concept of using functional tests early during development as a means of experimentally measuring the failure rate of the software, and from this measurement deriving the parameters of the reliability model which is introduced there. For this purpose, we would like the functional tests to be developed as early as possible and be available for use early in the system-integration phase of development.

4.9.3 Scenario Tests

By a scenario test, we mean the portion of our functional testing which deals with simulation of the mission. Obviously, in a large, complex example such as the satellite-tracking system discussed above, it would be quite a task to define a simulation of the mission. A true scenario of the system would involve locking-on (acquisition) of a radar target, continued tracking of the target, computer identification of the target, further tracking to determine its orbital elements, storage of the target identification number and orbital elements, and relinquishing of the target. Similarly, the scenario for the simulated moon-tracking mission would involve the same search, acquisition, tracking, identification, orbital-elements measurement, storage, and relinquishing phases. (If we wished our scenario to include tracking of more than one target, we might just recycle the moon, reacquire it, and retrack it several times.) Clearly, in some large and complex problems, we will develop a series of scenarios to use in the functional test.

4.9.4 Operational Testing

In constructing a scenario test for a computer system, we must carefully study the system requirements to choose appropriate scenarios. First of all, the scenarios should be representative of the major operational modes of the system. Returning to our example of the satellite-tracking system, it is clear from even our sketchy description of the problem that there will be many separate modes of operation. Suppose we attempt to discuss in more detail the scenario tracking mode. If we know that it is a harder task to track and identify small objects as opposed to larger ones, we might wish to repeat this scenario phase twice, once with a small object and once with a large object (perhaps a third time with nearby large and small objects to see if the system confuses them). If there are significantly different problems associated with tracking of satellites for low-altitude and high-altitude orbits, we will have two more cases for which we will want to construct scenarios. Thus, by just considering the tracking phase alone, we will have delineated four to six separate scenarios. In most cases, the selection of the group of scenarios to use in testing should be done in conjunction with the user.

Another major problem in formulating scenarios is the difficulty of calculating and specifying the correct answer. Unless we have a set of cases for which computation of the correct result is easy, it may be difficult to generate the correct solution via a different process. In the case of the satellite trajectory, we must specify the orbital elements of the satellite, compute its path, and simulate the radar signals. Then during testing, we compare the program calculations of orbital elements with the known values. In some cases, an auxiliary program might be needed to determine the correct response to a particular test.

We should include field testing under the operational testing category. Clearly, there are a few, if a limited number of, situations in which we can run a real operational test. In some cases the test system may be slightly different (in general configuration) from the system we are studying, or some pieces of the system may consist of prototype components (rather than the actual design to be installed). However, it may be the closest possible at this time (or within a reasonable cost) to "the real thing." Often in tests of this sort, the operational task is simplified. For example, the number of data entry and output points may be smaller than the number which we will see in full-scale operation.

In some cases field operation is planned as the last phase of development, involving installation of the computer hardware in the field and pilot operation for several months. Furthermore, if one plans on a warranty to cover maintenance of the software, one should prepare for the warranty period with a period of field testing. The subject of warranty contracts is discussed further in Chap. 6. All these caveats notwithstanding, operational testing is the closest one can possibly come to actual operation. If it can be arranged, at a reasonable cost, it should be included in every development contract.

4.9.5 Mixed Simulation and Operational Testing

In some cases, we are able to begin a simulation early in the development cycle and, as portions of the system are designed, substitute the actual components for their simulations. A clear historical example of this technique will now be discussed.

We can liken the kind of functional testing which we have just discussed to the ways in which control-system designers worked with an analog computer in the 1950s. Specifically, suppose that we were planning a flight control system for an aircraft. After we had an initial paper-and-pencil design of the system, we would simulate, on an analog computer, the control-system transfer function. Similarly, we would write a set of differential equations and derive the associated transfer function for the flight dynamics of the aircraft. These differential equations would then also be simulated on the analog computer. The complete simulated system would then be tested. As particular major control components (hydraulic actuators, gyroscopes, etc.) were designed and tested, they would be integrated into the system so as to replace the portions of the analog computer which simulated their operations. This would allow us to explore certain nonlinear effects such as saturation, dead zone, etc. The effect of all these nonlinearities could often be computed by nonlinear analysis; however, the computer would always serve as a check on the validity of the approximate analysis. Thus, as the development progressed, more physical pieces of the system design would be patched onto the analog computer and tested for validity.

Toward the end of such a test, most of the flight control system would be replaced with real equipment or at least engineering models except for the airframe; thus the computer simulation of the airframe would be retained. The result is that a simulation would grow in realism as the project progressed, and as actual hardware became available. Our goal in functional testing of a digital system should be the same. Limitations on the size, cost, and availability of the components of the system sometimes prevent us from achieving a functional test as close to real operation as we would like; however, even a modest success in approximating reality is of great help.

4.9.6 Related Tests

An operational test might also be designated a reliability or acceptance test. The construction of such tests based on Table 4.14 are discussed in Chap. 6.

The purpose of a reliability demonstration test is to verify that the system will meet contract reliability, availability, and maintainability specifications. Obviously, it must be a functional test, and most military contracts call for an operational test. This is to provide the user with a sample of how well the system works in practice and is a necessary preliminary to legal acceptance of the deliverable contract item.

It is important to remember that during early development a week's worth of testing with few or no errors found represents poor progress. However, the same week of testing with few or no errors may represent a major achievement if it occurs at the end of operational testing, or especially during acceptance testing.

4.10 CLASSIFICATION OF TESTS

4.10.1 Introduction

In the preceding sections of this chapter we have discussed a number of different types of tests. Some of the ideas encountered focused on the number of tests. Others were based on abstract program models (flowcharts or graphs), or on functional tests. In this section we will define a numerical classification scheme which will include the previous test types and some additional ones. The classes of tests which we will now discuss correspond to the tests which are used in the middle phases of testing.

4.10.2 Rationale for Classification

In devising a classification scheme, it is natural to desire that it correspond to an increasing (or decreasing) hierarchy of thoroughness and difficulty. Clearly, the upper range of our numerical scheme should correspond to an exhaustive test. At the lower end of the range, we will require only that each instruction be executed at least once.

We might liken the types of tests to the test procedures applied to a newly purchased car. The first and most rudimentary check would be to compare the list of accessories ordered with the delivered list on the car window, to see if they are all present and work. For example, the owner might check to see that the car was supplied with an AM/FM radio, and that it works on both AM and FM; that it contains a V-6 engine and not a straight six or a V-8, and that the engine starts; that the hood lamp, glove-box lamp, and trunk lamp were installed and work, etc. This checklist type of test would be the lowest-level test. At the other extreme would be functional testing, i.e., use of the auto for 3 months. However, between these extremes the owner would try many things during the first week of driving: drive the car up a hill with and without the air conditioner on, try the heater on a cool day and the air conditioner on a hot one (or alternate the two functions), accelerate from rest to 60 mi/h and execute a panic stop, etc.

Thus, the philosophy underlying the test classification which we will use applies to product testing in general. However, the specific details will apply to software in particular.

4.10.3 Completeness and Continuity Checking—Type 0

Our lowest level of program testing will be analogous to the checklist type of test described in our auto example. Intuition tells us that in testing a mechanism, one basic principle is to try to exercise the parts. In the case of a program, we must test each instruction at least once. We will call such a primitive test a type 0 test.[1] Such a test is very much expedited by a modern compiler which produces counts of the number of times each statement is executed. A type 0 test is a *necessary but not sufficient condition* for thorough testing of the program. In fact, when such a test is employed, one often finds design flaws. For example, it is sometimes impossible to reach a section of code; upon detailed investigation we find that an error was corrected by inserting a patch to bypass a block of code and the block was never removed.

Obviously, a type 0 test can be performed at the module level as well as at the system-integration level; however, it is more common to allow the individual coder (or tester) freedom at the module stage to proceed as he or she wishes and only enforce regimentation at the integration stage.

In terms of the graph theory concepts previously introduced, a type 0 test is an arc cover test.

A common way to carry out a type 0 test is to exercise each function at least once and to check the code, pseudo-code, flowchart, or graph to ensure that each instruction is executed at least once. For example, in a word-processing system we might check to see that the editor can be reached, that each editor function works, etc. At this stage of testing, it is unnecessary to check interactions of features. Thus, we don't have to enter the editor system, change a word, store it on disk, and then recall the new version. Even such a low-level test requires a great deal of effort and bookkeeping in a large system, unless a computerized tool is developed as an aid. Some practitioners have even suggested that a machine architectural feature be added which reserves a machine word bit for such checking. A special instruction would be added to zero all these bits initially, and whenever a machine instruction was executed, the respective check bit could be set to 1. Thus, a memory dump (or a search for nonset bits) could be used to reveal which sections had not been tested.

4.10.4 All Graph Paths Executed—Type 1

One of the problems in testing a program at a level higher than type 0 is the dependence between the data and the decider predicates in the program. Intuition

[1] Workshop on Reliable Software (1974).

tells us that once we have completed the type 0 test we should try to test all paths in the program. Our problem is that if we use a graph model as our program abstraction, we are unable to define program paths and must work with graph paths. Thus, testing all the paths in the graph is a lower-order test than testing all the program paths, and we call these tests type 1 and type 2, respectively.

In trying to solve the problem of constructing a program to test graph paths, it is convenient to call graph path testing and program path testing *forced execution* and *natural execution*, respectively. By natural execution, we mean the tester (human or machine) reads the decider predicates, computes whether they are true or false based on the current values of the program variables, and branches left or right accordingly.

The artificial concept of forced execution can be used to simplify the problem.[1] By forced execution we mean that the tester only recognizes the fact that a decider has been reached as the program is traversed. Once a decider is discovered, it forces further execution of the program for two cases, one where the decider is true and one where the decider is false. Clearly, forced execution will involve traversal of all the paths of the graph and will include some which can never be reached because of the decider predicate dependencies. For such a technique to be useful, the benefits of a simplified test tool must outweigh the disadvantages of extra, unreachable test cases. In most situations the number of forced execution tests is not terribly larger than the number of naturally executed tests. Furthermore, in our definition of forced execution we include a technique for shortening the running time of each test by forced execution of program loops.

Much of the execution time of a program is taken up by the repetitive execution of DO loops within the program, especially in the case of nested loops. Thus, we must invent a technique to ensure that each DO loop is traversed only once.

On second thought, we know from experience that many errors are committed when we exit from a loop. Thus, we define forced execution of a DO loop as testing the loop twice, once for the first execution and once for the final execution.

A technique for forced execution of all graph paths has been suggested by Professor Arthur Laemmel of the Polytechnic Institute of New York.[2] This technique was developed for loopless programs and has been extended by Dennis Baggi to include techniques for treating DO WHILE constructs.[3] Thus, it can be used for all basic structured programs. Baggi has implemented the test driver in PL/1 for testing PL/1 programs.[4] Clearly, the program could be broadened to test programs in other languages. The reader is referred to the literature and the problems at the end of the chapter for a further discussion of forced execution and automated testing.[5]

[1] Shooman (1974b).
[2] Shooman (1974b).
[3] Baggi and Shooman (1978), p. 278.
[4] Baggi and Shooman (1979).
[5] Deutsch (1982).

Laemmel's schemes for implementing a driver program to automatically test each path are as follows:

1. *Each* DO loop should be written in a special form *when the program is originally coded* so that inclusion of a test mode variable M allows one to execute the loop only for zero and one repetition of the loop. (This tests loop control structure primarily and not statements within the loop.)

$$DO\ I = 1\ TO\ 25$$

   would become

$$DO\ I = 1\ TO\ M * 25 + (1 - M) * T$$

   and we see M = 0 for test, and M = 1 for run. In the test mode we let T equal 0 for no repetitions and 1 for one repetition of the loop.[1] Similarly we would write our IF statements using mode and test variables as follows:

$$IF\ X + Y > 0 \quad THEN\ Z = X$$
$$ELSE\ Z = Y$$

   would become

$$IF\ M * (X + Y) + T > 0 \quad THEN\ Z = X$$
$$ELSE\ Z = Y$$

   For normal operation we let M = 1 and T = 0. During test we let M = 0 and T = +1 to test the THEN clause and M = 0 and T = −1 to test the ELSE clause.

2. Associate a boolean variable with each IF statement and DO loop. Generate (or store) a sequence of binary numbers such that the bit values perform essentially the same function as M and T above. One convenient way to generate the binary numbers is to use the outputs at each stage of a binary counter with a bit string as an input.

4.10.5 All Program Paths Executed—Type 2

We have only defined the concept of forced execution as a strategy to ease the problem of program path testing. Thus, the next highest level of program testing is to naturally test each program path at least once, which we define as a type 2 test. Note that a type 1 test includes an arc cover of the program graph and thus a type 0 test is a subset of a type 1 test. Since we have said nothing about minimality, there can be more than one type 1 test, and an implementation of this test category is not unique. A type 2 test executes all the paths of the program

---

[1] The exact operation of DO I = 1 to 0 and DO I = 0 to 1 depends on the language and the compiler; small modifications in this procedure may be required in some cases.

flowchart (including the information in the decider predicates), and similarly the type 2 test is not unique.

4.10.6 Exhaustive Testing—Types 3 and 4

In earlier sections of this chapter we discussed two different types of exhaustive tests, those for systems in which the input sequence or initial conditions can change (more complex) and those for fixed initial conditions and input sequences (simpler). Thus, we define a type 3 test as an exhaustive test for a system where input sequence and initial conditions are fixed. Similarly, a type 4 test is an exhaustive test for a system where either the initial conditions or the input sequence (or both) can change during program execution.

It is clear that in many smaller problems we can really test all the program paths; thus a practical test will include a type 2 test plus repetition of some of the test paths for several values of input data. Thus this might be called a type 2.3 test. Similarly, if we continued to execute testing so that we began to approach an exhaustive test, we might call this a type 2.8 test.

In Table 4.17, we summarize the test class definitions which we have evolved and discuss typical "in-between" classifications.

Table 4.17 Classification of tests

Test type	Basis	Features
0	Completeness and continuity checking	All instructions in code executed at least once (checklist).
0.5	....	Many graph paths executed at least once (partial type 1 test).
1	Graph path test	All graph paths executed at least once (100% graph path coverage).
1.5	....	Many program paths executed at least once (partial type 2 test).
2	Program path test	All program paths executed at least once (100% program path coverage).
2.5	....	All program paths executed for many values of input parameters (partial type 3 test).
3	Exhaustive test	All program paths executed for all values of input parameters (exhaustive test).
4	Exhaustive test	All program paths executed for all values of input parameters, all sequences of inputs, and all combinations of initial conditions (exhaustive test for multiprocessing, multiprogramming, and real-time systems with nonfixed input sequence).

4.11 SUMMARY

This chapter, like most of the chapters in this book, is a mixture of practical observations and techniques along with more quantitative analysis and models. The major features which emerged are:

1. Testing is at present the most important process for perfecting programs and is aimed at detecting errors.
2. Many and varied types of tests must be employed: code reading, module testing, integration testing, operational testing, and field testing.
3. The test philosophy depends somewhat on the design philosophy. A top-down design generally results in top-down testing, which requires test stubs. A bottom-up development most frequently leads to bottom-up testing, which requires test drivers.
4. Debugging follows the location of an error and is aided by focusing on a deductive or inductive model. Once a model is established, judicious use of dumps, traces, print statements, and debugging programs is helpful.
5. Various operational-type tests are discussed: simulation, functional tests, and field tests.

The quantitative concepts in this chapter try to focus on practical yet basic models which can be applied to the testing process:

1. Some basic data are presented regarding the effort required to find, localize, and correct errors.
2. A graph model of a program is established and the concept of an arc cover and graph paths is established.
3. The difference between graph paths and program paths is defined.
4. Several techniques are developed for computing the number of paths in a loopless graph.
5. The methods of item 4 are extended to looping graphs via node-splitting methods.
6. An enumeration procedure is developed.
7. The number of graph paths is compared with the cyclomatic complexity number and the polynomial complexity.
8. Test-oriented reliability models are discussed.
9. Techniques are developed for the choice of test data.
10. An example of exhaustive testing showing its impracticability is discussed.
11. A test classification is introduced which ranks tests from type 0 (all instructions executed at least once) up to types 3 and 4 (exhaustive testing).

The overall objective of this chapter is to raise the art of testing to a collection of engineering techniques and, in a few areas, to elevate it to the level of a scientific discipline.

PROBLEMS

4.1 A certain program is to be written in PL/1. The initial estimates are that it will entail 5000 lines of PL/1 (source) code, which is deemed equivalent to 25,000 lines of machine (object) code. Assume the average productivity of the programming group is 10 lines of PL/1 code per day and the development schedule is 2 years.

(*a*) Estimate the number of man-months needed to develop this program.

(*b*) How many man-months will be required to
    (i) Uncover and localize the errors?
    (ii) Correct and retest the code?

(*c*) How many computer hours will be required for parts *b*(i) and *b*(ii)?

(*d*) Assuming that the length of time for each phase is proportional to the cost, how long will the test phase take? How many tester-debuggers will be required for the test phase?

(*e*) Sketch the anticipated manpower deployment versus time for each of the three testing philosophies (top-down, bottom-up, big bang) given in Sec. 4.3.

4.2 Compute the number of paths through the control graph and compare it with the number of test cases and cyclomatic complexity (see Prob. 3.16) for the designs given in Prob. 2.13.

4.3 In Prob. 4.1 we used average values in the estimation process, based upon a single set of data. Perhaps we are on safer ground if we also estimate the minimum and maximum expected hours and costs. We therefore wish to repeat Prob. 4.1 using an appropriate worst-case analysis to compute upper and lower bounds on our estimates.

Assume that the worst-case (best-case) value for productivity is given by the mean value plus or minus one standard deviation (see Fig. 4.2). Compute worst-case upper and lower bounds on total man-months and computer hours.

4.4 The worst-case analysis of Prob. 4.3 is often a gross approximation. A better estimate can be obtained by using the simple statistical formula given below:

$$t_{TD} = N\left(\bar{t}_d + \bar{t}_l + \bar{t}_c + \bar{t}_v\right)$$

$$\sigma_{TD} = N\sqrt{\sigma_{t_d}^2 + \sigma_{t_l}^2 + \sigma_{t_c}^2 + \sigma_{t_v}^2}$$

where $\bar{x}$ = mean value of x
    σ_x = standard deviation of x
    t_{TD} = total number of man-hours to test and debug
    t_d = total number of man-hours to detect an error
    t_l = total number of man-hours to locate an error
    t_c = total number of man-hours to correct an error
    t_v = total number of man-hours to verify the correction
    N = total number of program errors discovered

(*a*) (*Optional*) State the assumptions involved and derive the above equations.
    Hint: What do we know about sums of random variables?

(*b*) By analogy to the equations above, write similar expressions for the total number of computer hours.

(*c*) Repeat Prob. 4.2 using the formulas of this problem.

(*d*) Why does this method produce tighter bounds than the worst-case technique of Prob. 4.3?

4.5 Suppose that the triangle problem described in Fig. 4.15 is to be programmed on a PDP-8 computer in assembly language. We wish to perform an exhaustive test. Design such a test following the example of Sec. 4.8.

(*a*) Compute the number of test cases.

(*b*) Estimate the length of the program using the method of Sec. 3.2.8.

(c) Estimate the time to run the exhaustive test.

(d) How much output do you expect?

(e) How will you check the results?

4.6 Define a software-development project of your own choosing, one described in this or another book or one you have worked on, or create one.

(a) Write a set of requirements sufficiently detailed to define the project.

(b) Write a test plan for the project including:

(i) A definition of the phases of testing and an estimate of their starting time and duration after project initiation.

(ii) A brief description of the module- and integration-test phases, who will perform the testing, and how.

(iii) Estimates of the number of man-hours and computer hours which will be needed for each phase of testing.

4.7 Check the data in Figs. 4.2 and 4.3 versus the results of the experiment summarized in Table 4.4. Do the two agree or disagree? Do you need to correct for the results of increased productivity, inflation, increased machine speed? If so how could you estimate these factors?

4.8 For an example of your choice, design, code, and test a simple control structure. Design a test stub (see Table 4.5) for one of the modules of this program and use it to test the interface.

4.9 For an example of your choice, design, code, and test a simple module. Design a module driver, code it, and use it to test the module interface.

4.10 Test a program of your own choosing, and uncover several program errors. Localize the cause of these errors, and explain how you found the causes. Did you use the techniques of Table 4.9? Explain why or why not.

4.11 Define a set of tests which form a test cover for each of the programs in Prob. 2.13.

4.12 Can the methods illustrated in Figs. 4.11 and 4.12 be applied to the examples given in Figs. 2.5, 2.8, and 4.14? Explain. If valid, use these methods to calculate the number of paths in the graphs.

4.13 Repeat Prob. 4.12 using the node-splitting method where appropriate.

4.14 Apply the methods of Fig. 4.13 to calculate the number of paths in the graphs of the examples given in Figs. 2.5, 2.8, and 4.22. Compare these results with those obtained in Probs. 4.12 and 4.13.

4.15 Make up a set of test data for the examples given in each of the following problems:

(a) Problem 2.1

(b) Problem 2.3

(c) Problem 2.4

(d) Problem 2.5

(e) Problem 2.8

(f) Problem 2.9

(g) Problem 2.36

(h) Problem 2.37

(i) Problem 2.46

4.16 Suppose that the example of Sec. 4.8 is to be programmed in Basic. Basic utilizes floating-point numbers and accepts numbers in the range from 9.99999E + 99 to 1.00000E − 9. How does Basic accomplish this on a 12-bit PDP-8 computer? Does this change the exhaustive-test analysis in Sec. 4.8? How?

4.17 Make up a set of test data following the methods of Table 4.15 for the quadratic equation problem of Sec. 4.8.

4.18 Discuss, define, or calculate the following:

(a) Define and contrast module and integration testing.

(b) How many errors would you anticipate would be found during integration testing of a 1000-instruction Fortran program which should compile into about 5000 machine words? Explain.

(*c*) For the following program define a type 0 and a type 3 test.

```
START
INPUT        (A, B, C)
     IF  A > 5
         THEN   X = 10
         ELSE   X = 1
     END
     IF B > 10
         THEN Y = 20
         ELSE Y = 2
     END
     IF C > 15
         THEN Z = 30
         ELSE Z = 3
     END
PRINT (X, Y, Z)
STOP
```

4.19 The Library of Congress has a CRT-terminal-based information-retrieval system which includes 81 million cross-referenced entries to the more than 20 million books and pamphlets. There are four basic commands which are typed into the system, followed by depressing the ENTER key.

Name	Syntax	Operation
BROWSE	b (keywords)	The computer searches for the keyword(s) and finds the closest match in its alphabetical listing of keywords. It then displays about 20 numbered lines of consecutive keywords with the matched word near the middle along with the number of references to that keyword.
SELECT	s (line number on screen)	The computer creates a file with all the references associated with the keyword in it. The first reference is numbered 1, the second 2, etc.
FIND	f (author's name)	The computer searches for the author's name and displays the number of references authored by him or her and places the references in a file.
DISPLAY	d (reference number)	The computer displays on the CRT the information normally found on a library catalog card for the given reference number. Used to display the file following BROWSE/SELECT or FIND commands.

(*a*) Devise a set of test data to be used to thoroughly test normal operations of the system.

(*b*) What test data should you use to test abnormal operations? Give specific test inputs and describe the classes of tests.

4.20 Locate a number of operational programs (or subroutines) which solve for the roots of quadratic equations (you may include also root-solving programs for higher-order polynomials and treat the quadratic as a special case) in different languages and on different computers. Use the test data prepared in Prob. 4.17, test the programs, and record the results.

4.21 The node-splitting method is to be applied to the examples given in Figs. 2.21 and 3.16. Calculate the number of paths for each example.

4.22 Repeat Prob. 4.20 for a root-solving program which solves polynomials up to the tenth order.

4.23 Some designers feel that software is intrinsically more complex than hardware; however, this really depends on the problem. If you own a digital watch, especially one with chronograph and alarm features, consider the following:

(*a*) Draw a diagram which explains the various states of the watch.

(*b*) Label each control button and each display element.

(*c*) Calculate the number or combinations of mode-state and control inputs (single and combined) which can occur.

(*d*) Suppose that we wished to perform an exhaustive test; one would have to repeat (*c*) for all alphanumeric display values.

Do you really believe that software is more complex than hardware?

4.24 Draw a flowgraph for the pseudo-code program given and calculate the cyclomatic complexity.

```
C       EXAMPLE
LOOP:  DO WHILE Z > 0
       A = B + 1
       IF A > 10
            THEN X = A
            ELSE Y = Z
       END IF
       IF < 5
            THEN PRINT X, Y
            ELSE IF Y = 2
                 THEN GO TO LOOP
                 ELSE C = 3
                 END IF
       END IF
       G = H + R
       END DO
       IF F > 0
            THEN PRINT G
            ELSE PRINT K
       END IF
       STOP
```

4.25 Airline A contracts with software house B to write a flight-routing program. You work for software house C, which is hired by the airline to write and perform an acceptance test. Based on the following facts, devise a set of acceptance-test inputs and explain the reasons for your choices. The pilot inputs departure and destination points and desired flight altitudes based on the weather and the aircraft. The program reads in the winds en route and constructs three flight plans[1] (altitudes,

---

[1] The pilot must file and obtain prior FAA approval for flight plans. In case of prior "choice" by another pilot or interference with another route, additional, alternative routes must be available.

speeds, directions, and five position-check points along the way) for minimum fuel consumption and flight time.

4.26 You are in the initial planning stages for a dental office computer system. The prototype system will be a bottom-up design and the final system a top-down (design, code, and test) office computer system. The program is to run on a DEC PDP-11 minicomputer. The system functions are to maintain the appointment schedule and do billing for a practice of 2000 patients, 3 dentists, 2 hygienists, 3 assistants, and a dental technician. The appointment and billing schedule is to be maintained for 3 months ahead of the current date. Bills which are more than 3 months overdue and appointments more than 3 months ahead will be maintained on a paper record. Your job is to:

(*a*) Explain how you will test the system: model, integration, simulation or field test, regression testing, etc.

(*b*) Discuss the use of test devices and program stubs in conjunction with this job.

(*c*) Estimate the program size and the number of man-hours which you will need for testing and how you believe it will break down by phase.

4.27 Write a set of inequalities which constrain the decision variables in Fig. 2.8 so that they can be solved for the set of values which will test each program path. Give a set of test values which satisfies this set of equations and will drive the program down each path. How would the problem change if we wished to test not only the greater-than and less-than but also the equal values of each decision? Code the program, place print statements in each branch, and use the test data to test the program.

4.28 Design and code the example of 4.8. Enumerate all the paths in the program. Show that if we traversed all the paths for all possible input values this would define the same exhaustive test which was developed in Sec. 4.8.

4.29 Choose an existing program and modify it for test-driver operation as was done according to Laemmel's technique in Sec. 4.10.4. Test the program and interpret the results.

4.30 How could you write a program which would automatically modify another program and test it as was done in Prob. 4.29? Design such a program and apply it to the example of Prob. 4.29. Do the results agree with the manual modifications?

FIVE

SOFTWARE RELIABILITY

5.1 INTRODUCTION

The term *reliability* has a dual meaning in modern technical usage. In the broad sense, it refers to a wide range of issues which pertain to the design of a product which will operate well for a substantial time period. Methods for designing reliable programs were discussed in Chap. 3 specifically, and threads of these ideas are woven into most of the chapters. In a narrower sense, reliability is a metric which is the probability of operational success of the software. Since this metric can be predicted, measured during program development, and demonstrated upon program completion, reliability analysis and testing serves as one of the most important means of measuring the quality of software and managing its development.

The chapter begins by exploring the basis of software reliability. An explanation is given as to how a probabilistic model can be used to describe a deterministic problem. The different modes of hardware, software, and human operator failure are discussed and the probabilistic sample space for software errors is introduced. The mathematical tools of reliability theory are then developed.

Definitions are given for the terms *reliability*, *availability*, *maintainability*, and *software errors*. Brief examples are given of how the metrics may be measured. Data from the literature on software error collection and classification are introduced.

The software reliability and availability models to be introduced in this chapter depend on error content; thus several techniques are given for estimating the number of residual software errors.

The older reliability models which have been shown to work in practice are macro models; i.e., they treat all errors as equal and suppress any information about program structure. Newer, so-called micro models include some details of path structure, but still have to be tested in practice.

The availability models in this chapter are based on Markov probability models. A basic discussion of the mathematics and the resulting models is included.

Several techniques for measuring the model parameters are given and illustrated with computations based on operational data.

The chapter concludes with a discussion of the problems involved in creating a software reliability data base.

5.2 THE CONCEPT OF SOFTWARE RELIABILITY

5.2.1 Probabilistic and Deterministic Models

Those who are unfamiliar with probabilistic models often question the validity and basis of the concept. For example, in the case of hardware reliability, failures of equipment are concrete events which occur as a result of particular, and generally well-defined, reasons. If the winding of a motor burns out, the copper wire has been heated to a temperature above its melting point and held there long enough for some particular spot to melt and interrupt the circuit. The cause of the high temperature would most likely be a local hot spot in the winding, or a large current transient with a long enough duration to cause significant temperature rise. These are certainly deterministic events; however, we are unable to predict when they will occur. Thus, the model of failures becomes a probabilistic one and the random element (the random variable) is the time to failure.[1]

In a similar manner, one can explore the meaning of a probabilistic software error model. The first mention of such an approach generally draws the comment,

---

[1] The reader must realize that probabilistic models are useful in the description of phenomena which are basically random in nature as well as those which are deterministic. A classical example of the debate as to whether a probabilistic model describes a random or deterministic process evolves from Albert Einstein's views on quantum theory. Although Einstein's work on the photoelectric effect was fundamental to the development of quantum theory, he never accepted the hypothesis that the behavior of matter was governed by random phenomena. Einstein viewed quantum mechanics as *a very useful and valuable probabilistic model describing a deterministic process.* Thus, once we learned enough about the underlying physics, we could replace the temporary, makeshift model by a more exact deterministic description. A famous Einstein quotation on this point was "I shall never believe that God plays dice with the world." Quantum theorists such as Bohr strongly disagreed, and maintained that the world was in truth probabilistic. (See *"Einstein, the Life and Times,"* Ronald W Clark, World Publishing Co., New York, 1971, p. 69 and p. 537.)

Table 5.1 Typical failure mechanisms

Failure mode	Examples of failure mechanisms		
	Hardware	Software	Human
Poor-quality fabrication	1. Bad solder joints. 2. Defective component installed. 3. Mechanical misalignment.	1. Typographical error in entering an instruction which eludes compiler checks. 2. Wrong version of a subroutine included by mistake. 3. Program has small incompatibility with operating system or hardware.	1. Reload control button pushed in error during operation. 2. Operator mounted wrong disk on drive. 3. Operator put radar control switch into track position rather than scan position.
Design error	1. Component with too low a rating specified. 2. Metal parts exposed to a corrosive atmosphere. 3. When we load an address from the front panel of a minicomputer, it erroneously clears the accumulator.	1. When we return from subroutine A to the main program we fail to clear all registers as we should. 2. The THEN ELSE branches are mistakenly interchanged in an IF statement. 3. The series expansion used for a special mathematical function does not converge for certain values.	1. The human is required to enter data in response to a system request. One of the requests is ambiguous and wrong data are entered. 2. Assume that following system crash the operator must reenter certain key data. If the key sequence is illogical many errors will occur. 3. The operator follows an incorrect explanation in the operator's manual and inadvertently clears all memory.

Overload of the component	1. A capacitor with a maximum rating of 50 V is used in a circuit where 100-V transients occasionally occur. 2. An unexpected heavy load on a gear train breaks off some gear teeth. 3. The hardware cannot keep up with an input of 300 band, even though specifications call for operation at this rate.	1. A timesharing system designed to handle 24 terminals performs poorly when over 20 terminals are connected and its crash rate rises. 2. The input module of a text-editing system cannot keep up with a very fast typist. 3. An air traffic control system has a capacity of 100 planes. When more than 100 planes are entered, targets on the screen disappear without warning.	1. An air traffic controller cannot handle more than 50 targets without overloading his or her vigilance capacity and making many errors. 2. The operator forgets the right sequence of commands on occasion because there are too many steps. 3. The human cannot react fast enough to enter control commands in an emergency situation.
Wear-out	1. A mechanical clutch begins to slip after 5000 hours of operation. 2. The insulation on certain wires cracks after 10 y, causing shorts. 3. High humidity eventually causes leakage failure of certain types of integrated-circuit packages.	1. No analogous effect.	1. Possibly errors due to cumulative fatigue.

"Software is deterministic because it doesn't wear out, but hardware is probabilistic because it does wear out." This oft-repeated statement is a mixture of truth, half-truth, and misunderstanding. First of all, the program execution is certainly deterministic; however, the development process is probabilistic and litters the program with many types of residual software errors, which are discussed in the following section.

5.2.2 Failure Modes

It is true that hardware wears out; however, only a small percentage of hardware failures are due to this cause. The general reason for a failure is called the mode of failure, e.g., poor quality of fabrication, design error, overload of the component, wear due to old age (wear-out). Out of the four failure modes just mentioned, all but wear-out apply equally well to hardware and to software. Failure in all cases is defined as system failure. Thus, the term *hardware failure* refers to a system failure traceable to some component malfunction, and the term *software failure* refers to a system failure traceable to some error in the software. The detailed cause of a failure is referred to as the *failure mechanism*.

Some typical failure mechanisms for each of the four failure modes given above are listed in Table 5.1. Note that examples of human operator errors (called by some "skinware" errors) are also given. In general, when a system is tested, failures occur, and they must be investigated. As the cause is determined, they are classified as hardware, software, or human. Those errors which remain have undetermined or unknown causes. Table 5.1 is meant to be not exhaustive but illustrative. In the case of firmware (programs in read-only memories) the same device can have both hardware and software failure modes.

5.2.3 Probabilistic Sample Space

In defining a probability model one should begin by defining the space of all possible occurrences (probability space) and the rules for selection of each outcome. In the case of a probability model for program errors, we begin by considering all the paths in a program. For each path there are many combinations of initial conditions and input values comprising mutually exclusive execution sequences. Once software is placed in use, a certain number of residual errors exist. Thus, some of the execution sequences result in system failures. The choice of inputs and initial conditions selects which of the execution sequences will be processed. A software failure occurs when an execution sequence containing an error is processed.

5.3 RELIABILITY THEORY

Reliability theory is essentially the application of probability theory to the modeling of failures and the prediction of success probability. This section assumes that the reader has an introductory knowledge of probability theory and builds on this to summarize some of the key points in reliability theory. The reader without such a background or one needing review is referred to App. A.

5.3.1 Reliability Mathematics

Modern probability theory bases many of its results on the concept of a random variable, the probability density function, and the cumulative probability distribution function. In the case of reliability, the random variable of interest is the time to failure, **t**. We can develop the basic relationships needed by focusing on the probability that the time to failure **t** is in some interval $(t_1, t_1 + \Delta t)$

$$\text{Probability that } t_1 \leq \mathbf{t} \leq t_1 + \Delta t \equiv P(t_1 \leq \mathbf{t} \leq t_1 + \Delta t) \qquad (5.1)$$

The above probability can be related to the density and distribution functions, and the results are

$$P(t_1 \leq \mathbf{t} \leq t_1 + \Delta t) = f(t_1)\Delta t = F(t_1 + \Delta t) - F(t_1) \qquad (5.2)$$

where

$f(t_1)$ = value of the probability density function at point t_1

$F(t_1)$ = value of the cumulative probability distribution function at point t_1

If we divide by Δt in Eq. (5.2) and let $\Delta t \to 0$, we obtain from the fundamental definition of the derivative the fact that the density function is the derivative of the distribution function:

$$f(t) = \frac{dF(t)}{dt} \qquad (5.3)$$

Clearly, then, the distribution function is the integral of the density function (note: x is just a dummy variable of integration):

$$F(t) = \int_0^t f(x)\,dx \qquad (5.4)$$

We can now define the probability of failure by time t_1, $P_f(t_1)$, as the probability that the time to failure occurs in the interval $0 \leq \mathbf{t} \leq t_1$, which, from Eq. (5.2), is given by

$$P_f(t_1) = P(0 \leq \mathbf{t} \leq t_1) = F(t_1) - F(0) \qquad (5.5)$$

The random variable **t** is only defined for the interval 0 to $+\infty$ (negative time has no meaning), and as a consequence $F(0)$ must be zero. Utilizing this result and Eq. (5.4), we can write Eq. (5.5) for any time as

$$P_f(t) = F(t) = \int_0^t f(x)\,dx \qquad (5.6)$$

One can also define the probability of success at time t_1, $P_s(t_1)$, as the probability that the time to failure is larger than t_1, that is, that $\mathbf{t} > t_1$. If we define an item as having two mutually exclusive states, success and failure, then from the fundamental laws of probability we can write for any time t

$$P_s(t) + P_f(t) = 1 \qquad (5.7)$$

The probability of success is the reliability which is generally denoted by $R(t)$, and Eqs. (5.6) and (5.7) yield

$$R(t) = P_s(t) = 1 - P_f(t) = 1 - F(t) = 1 - \int_0^t f(x)\, dx \qquad (5.8)$$

Mathematically, Eq. (5.8) summarizes most of what we need to know about reliability theory. However, when we start to study failure data for various items we find that the density function $f(t)$ is not very convenient. Intuition leads us to compute a new function, the failure rate function (hazard function), which is defined in the following section and related to Eq. (5.8).

5.3.2 Failure Rate

In order to study the reasons for failure, we classify system failures according to mode as electrical, mechanical, thermal, corrosion, design errors, procedural errors, software errors, damage in shipment or assembly, assembly errors, etc. Each part or component has its own unique list, yet many of the same modes occur in different types of hardware, software, firmware, and operator tasks. To further complicate the issue, many of these failure modes occur at different phases in the lifetime of an item. For example, design errors, assembly and part problems, and damage in shipment or assembly usually (but not always) evidence themselves early in the lifetime of an item. Similarly, corrosion generally takes some time to cause failures; thus, its effects are noticed later in the life span.

The best way to study these temporal effects is in terms of the failure rate function (hazard function) $z(t)$. This should not be confused with the density function $f(t)$ of classical probability, which was utilized in the preceding section. The difference in definition is developed completely in App. B and is summarized here.

The hazard function $z(t)$ is defined in terms of the probability $P_f(t)$ that a failure occurs in some interval t_1 to $t_1 + \Delta t$, given that the system has survived up to time $\mathbf{t}$:

$$P(t_1 \le \mathbf{t} \le t_1 + \Delta t \,|\, \mathbf{t} > t_1) = z(t_1)\,\Delta t \qquad (5.9)$$

The first term in Eq. (5.9) is a so-called conditional probability, which is shown in App. B to be given by

$$P(t_1 \le \mathbf{t} \le t_1 + \Delta t \,|\, \mathbf{t} > t_1) = \frac{f(t_1)\,\Delta t}{R(t_1)} = z(t_1)\,\Delta t \qquad (5.10)$$

Combining Eq. (5.3) with Eq. (5.10) for any time t yields

$$\frac{1}{R(t)} \frac{dF(t)}{dt} = z(t) \qquad (5.11)$$

From Eq. (5.8), we observe that $dF(t)/dt = -dR(t)/dt$ and substitution in Eq. (5.11) and rearrangement yields

$$\frac{dR(t)}{R(t)} = -z(t)\,dt \tag{5.12}$$

The differential equation given in Eq. (5.12) is simply solved by integrating both sides with respect to t:

$$\ln R(t) = -\int_0^t z(x)\,dx + c \tag{5.13}$$

Realizing that at $t = 0$ the system is initially good and $R(0) = 1$ provides us with the initial condition. Exponentiating both sides of Eq. (5.13) and substituting the initial condition simplifies to

$$R(t) = \exp\left[-\int_0^t z(x)\,dx\right] \tag{5.13a}$$

Equation (5.13) is the fundamental equation relating reliability to failure rate. If through study of data or by assumption we can model the failure rate by a constant, $z(t) = \lambda$, then Eq. (5.13a) becomes the familiar exponential function

$$R(t) = e^{-\lambda t} \tag{5.14}$$

Similarly, if the failure rate is linearly increasing, $z(t) = Kt$, and a Rayleigh function is obtained:

$$R(t) = e^{-Kt^2/2} \tag{5.15}$$

A more careful mathematical development of Eq. (5.13a) is provided in App. B.

The hazard function was first used by actuaries (they called it force of mortality), who recognized that this function was needed to set the premium for a healthy 30-year-old applicant for life insurance. Contrast this with the fixing of an insurance fee for newborns for a certain future period, say, the thirtieth year. For the latter premium we would use the density function $f(t)$. Figure 5.1 depicts one

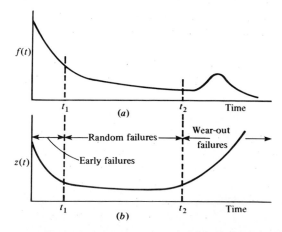

Figure 5.1 General form of failure curves: (a) failure density; (b) hazard rate.

commonly observed shape for failure rate and density function. The $z(t)$ curve shown is "affectionately" called the bathtub curve because of its shape and represents the behavior of many (but not all) systems and components.

The early failures are generally design defects, material defects, assembly errors, and transportation damage. Similarly, the wear-out failures are due to corrosion, mechanical wear, chemical changes, etc. In the case of high-quality electronic components which have been designed for long life, the wear-out period seldom occurs during the normal lifetime, and burn-in (a factory operating test) is used to weed out the initial defectives before shipment. Thus, many components will have a constant hazard due to a mixture of various failure modes. Note that the $z(t)$ function (but not $f(t)$) separates the behaviors well if we talk about decreasing, constant, and increasing hazard regions.

In the case of software, there is a different set of failure modes: incorrect specification, misunderstood specifications, algorithmic error, input data error, program logic error, etc. At the computer system level there are hardware and operator failures as well. True, there is no software wear-out failure mode; however, the complexity of the other software failure modes which do exist rivals or surpasses the difficulties in analyzing hardware failures.

In fact, in a general way, all the software errors are human design errors. Many of these would be analogous to design errors in a complex electronic system. Failure would not occur until the particular system mode and signal sequence occurred. Similarly, a logic error in some instruction may become evident only as a result of a particular combination of input data. The main difference between hardware and software reliability is that the design error failure mode should be infrequent in well-designed hardware but its analog, the program logic error, is the most frequently observed software failure mode.

5.3.3 Definition of Software Reliability

A formal definition of software reliability includes: (1) an appropriate definition of system success, (2) the operational conditions of the software, and (3) specification of the random variable in question. One definition which has been proposed in the literature and is accepted by many is as follows:[1]

> Software reliability is the *probability* that the program *performs successfully*, according to specifications, *for* a given *time period*.

The specifications must include precise statements of the host machine(s), the operating system and support software, the operating environment, the definition of success, details of any hardware interfaces with the host machine, complete details of the ranges and rates of input and output data, and the operational

---

[1]Dickson, Hesse, Kientz, and Shooman (1972) and Shooman (1973*d*). A slightly modified version of this definition is given in Sec. 5.5.3.

procedures. Although not a necessity, it would be helpful if the specification also included a definition of hardware failure and operator errors.

A careful definition of software errors will be needed for the measurement and demonstration phases of reliability. Theoretically, we can define software failures in the abstract; however, in practice our raw data are in terms of system failures. When a system failure occurs, we record all available data and subsequently analyze and divide our errors into hardware, software, operator, and unresolved errors. If our unresolved category is larger than 10 to 20 percent, the situation becomes too muddled and uncertain to proceed until the definitions and diagnostic techniques are improved.[1] Thus, the utility of our software reliability definition is improved not only by saying what software reliability is, but also by delineating what it isn't.

The random variable included in the definition is operating time, **t**. We must carefully define **t** since there are many time variables of interest during software development. There is operating time; calendar time during operation; calendar time during development; working time (man-hours) during coding, development testing, and debugging; and the computer test times throughout the various stages of the program. Operating time is the cumulative time the computer is up and working once the system has become operational. Clearly, there is also the downtime of the computer during operation. If the development phase is defined in terms of subphases, other time variables appear.

The choice of time as the random variable assumes that failures occur due to random traversing of paths in the program which contain bugs for some value(s) of the input parameters. These bugs are residual because they have been undetected during development, because the path has been tested for other parameter values and the program has worked well. The program size has not allowed exhaustive testing, and so these bugs have remained hidden. This means that as operating time increases, the probability of encountering at least one bug increases.

Other models of software failure may require a different random variable. For example, in a time-shared system it is well known that failures generally occur when the system is heavily loaded, i.e., is servicing many users. If such is the case, perhaps we should establish user hours. Thus, if n is the number of users and t is operating time in hours as previously defined, our random variable might be cumulative values of nt. Similarly, we could visualize a program which primarily operates in an idle condition waiting for input data to arrive either periodically or aperiodically. If failures occurred only when the data arrived and processing began and failed, then a different choice of random variable would be in order, i.e., the number of input cycles. If the input arrival rate were periodic, then operating time and cycles would be linearly related; however, in the aperiodic case they would not, and cycles would have to be used. Musa suggests that we use

---

[1]Musa found that the unresolved category represented less than 5 percent of all errors. See Musa (1975), p. 320.

total execution (CPU) time of the program as our time variable.[1] There are many analogous hardware examples. In the case of a transistor, time is the best choice; however, for a relay, cycles may be better, and in an automobile, miles traveled is generally used.

5.4 THE CONCEPT OF SOFTWARE REPAIR AND AVAILABILITY

5.4.1 Introduction

If one examines systems from the reliability standpoint, two major classifications appear—repairable and unrepairable systems. Examples of repairable and unrepairable hardware systems are a radar system and an unmanned satellite, respectively.

In the case of software we might classify a batch Fortran system and a computer-controlled air traffic control system as respectively repairable and unrepairable systems. By repair of software, we mean either debugging and error correction of the code or reinitialization of a program to clear an error which has occurred as a result of a particular input or a particular system state. If we define success of the batch Fortran system from the user's viewpoint as "I want two-hour turnaround time," then there is a repair capability. If on the first morning run (say, 9:00 a.m.) the system "bombs," then it can be reloaded, or reinitialized, or even have some minor debugging done to restore the system so that card decks submitted at 9:00 a.m. can be rerun at 10:00 a.m. and results can be ready by 11:00 a.m. In the case of the air traffic control system, any downtime for repair during a busy traffic period may interfere with the control of traffic necessary for the prevention of an accident. Thus, in such a system the only way in which operation can continue during a repair is if we have a duplicated system of both hardware and software.[2]

5.4.2 Downtime

The above discussion focuses on the concept of repair to prevent system failure (downtime). In the case of many systems a small amount of downtime can be tolerated. Therefore, even if a system is down for short periods it can be a "good system." Suppose that once per week our batch processing system were down so that the 9:00 a.m. run was available at 11:00 a.m. rather than 10:00 a.m. This would cause little trouble. Similarly, if an air traffic control system were down for 10 to 20 s, it might be tolerable if the mode of failure were relatively noncrucial. For example, suppose that the air traffic control system was composed of a central processor (CPU), a display processor (minicomputer), and a video display

[1] Hamilton and Musa (1978).
[2] Bernhard and Goldberg (1975).

(CRT). If the CPU failed but the minicomputer and CRT were still displaying the positions previous to the failure, no problems would occur for 10 to 20 s. This assumes that there was no imminent collision and the system updated the display as soon as the CPU was up again. A numerical measure of the system's uptime and downtime is discussed in Sec. 5.4.3.

5.4.3 Software Repair

The reliability and availability of repairable systems is based on the concept of error correction or software reinitialization. In the case of error correction, the repair rate is the average rate measured in corrections per hour for a complete repair. The complete repair time consists of recognition that there is a problem, diagnosis of the error, correction of the error, testing of the correction, and reinitialization of the system. The repair time is obviously a random variable, and the simplest models use the mean repair time or its reciprocal, the repair rate. Note that since we have removed another error from the program, the new failure rate is decreased (see Secs. 5.8 and 5.9).

Even the act of reloading or reinitializing a system to restore operation constitutes a repair if it is successful in returning the program to operation. Conceptually, the process is far different from debugging to remove an error, but the end result, restoring the system to operation, is functionally the same. The repair rate would again be represented in the simplest model as the reciprocal of the mean time to reinitialize the system. Since no bugs have been removed (they have only been bypassed), the failure rate remains the same.

The effect of repair on system reliability is best illustrated by a few simple examples. First, let us consider two computers with independent redundant programs as discussed in Sec. 2.7.2. Initially, let us assume no repair capability. If a software error occurred in one program, thereby crashing the system, the second computer would take over and operation would continue without interruption until the second computer program failed due to another error. By assumption, the two programs are independent. The probability of system failure is low, since it is the product of two small numbers, the probabilities of failure for each unit. If we now permit repair, we further reduce the probability of failure. Now as soon as one program fails, repair (either debugging or reinitialization procedures) begins, and if the repair is completed before the second program fails, operation is not interrupted. In this case, system failure requires the simultaneous occurrence of three events: (1) failure of program 1, (2) failure of program 2, and (3) inability to repair program 1 before program 2 fails. Thus, repair helps to decrease the system failure probability, thereby increasing system reliability.

If the system in question is a single program running on a single computer, then the system fails when the first error is discovered. The ability to repair the software does not help the reliability in this case, since the minute the system goes down a failure is recorded. However, the system is obviously better if we can repair and restore it quickly to operation. A new function, the system availability, is defined in the next section to measure such improvements.

5.4.4 Definition of Software Availability

Whenever a system can undergo repair, it is important to use availability as well as reliability to measure the system goodness. The definition of software availability parallels that of software reliability, but with important differences:

> Software availability is the *probability* that the program *is performing successfully*, according to specifications, *at* a given *point in time*.

Of course the same comment as in Sec. 5.3.3 regarding the use of random variables other than time also applies here. The important difference between reliability and availability is that reliability means no failures in the interval 0 to t, whereas availability means only that the system is up at time t. Thus it could be available at time t if it did not fail in the interval 0 to t (reliability), or if it failed once and was repaired once, or if it failed twice and was repaired twice, and so on. A good insight into the definition and usefulness of the availability concept is obtained if we consider measurement of the availability of an existing system.

Consider an idealized and simplified situation in which we have 100 identical computers all with the same operating system (same release, configuration, hardware and software corrections,[1] etc.), and similar or equivalent input streams (as regards variety, load, features used, etc.). Assume that at the same instant we inspect all the installations and find 97 are up and 3 are down; then the availability of the system is estimated to be $97/100$. If we repeated this calculation many times during some time period, then the average of the estimates should approach the true availability. Similarly, if all the systems are being operated in a normal manner (no new releases, personnel changes, major job stream changes, etc.), then they should all exhibit the same availability. If we obtain careful records for one system of the downtimes $(t_{d_1}, t_{d_2}, \ldots)$ and the uptimes $(t_{u_1}, t_{u_2}, \ldots)$ then the steady-state availability is given by

$$A_{ss} = \frac{T_{up}}{T_{up} + T_{down}} \tag{5.16}$$

where

$$T_{up} = \sum t_{u_i} \tag{5.16a}$$

$$T_{down} = \sum t_{d_i} \tag{5.16b}$$

(See App. B.) If we calculate A_{ss} for each of the 100 systems, then the average of the results should approach the true availability.

We have just defined availability in two ways: (1) the ratio of systems up at some instant to the size of the population studied, and (2) the ratio of observed

---

[1] Errors always surface subsequent to the initial distribution of a new operating system release. The organization supporting the operating system corrects the design, removing some of these errors, and circulates periodic changes. Some users incorporate such changes immediately, others later, and some wait for the next release. Similar comments apply to a new hardware design.

uptime to the sum of the uptime and downtime. The first definition is a convenient way to introduce the concept of availability. The second definition is a convenient way to measure availability of a deployed system. Such measurements are useful for several purposes:

1. To quantify the present level of availability and compare it with other systems or stated goals
2. To track the availability over a time period to see if it increases as errors are removed or possibly decreases as more and more complex input streams are applied and excite lurking residual errors
3. Planning for adequate repair personnel, facilities (mainly test time for software and replacement parts or units for hardware), and alternative service if necessary during downtimes

The reader must realize that we have oversimplified the concept of availability. Availability is actually a time function; it has the value of unity at time zero and decreases to some steady-state value after several failure-repair cycles. Thus, Eq. (5.16) will yield a value closer to unity if applied early in time rather than later after the steady state is reached. In practice, much of reliability theory deals with the steady-state region. The concepts of transient and steady-state availability are dealt with mathematically in App. B.

In many cases, we wish to estimate the system availability during design. In such cases neither one of the above two definitions of availability is convenient and a third formulation is more useful. We assume that we are in steady state and that the average value of uptime $\bar{t}_u$ is given by the mean time to failure (MTTF) and that the average value of downtime $\bar{t}_d$ is given by the mean time to repair (MTTR). Substitution of these average values in Eq. (5.16) yields

$$A_{ss} = \frac{\text{MTTF}}{\text{MTTF} + \text{MTTR}} \tag{5.17}$$

Various techniques can be employed to estimate MTTF and MTTR so that Eq. (5.17) can be utilized. This is discussed further in Sec. 5.10. A more fundamental derivation of Eq. (5.17) is given in App. B.

5.5 SOFTWARE ERRORS AND FAULTS

5.5.1 Introduction and Definition

We begin our discussion of software errors with a focus on the concept of system failures. Our underlying objective is to model the reliability of the system; thus any definition of errors should be tied to system failure. We may define a hardware error as a system failure due to a hardware cause. The hardware cause is called a hardware fault and may be a hardware failure, a noise or timing problem, or a design error. Sometimes a fault does not result in a system failure. For example, when one of two redundant elements experiences a fault and the second element continues successful operation, no error occurs. If a system failure is traceable to a human act of commission or omission, we call this a human error. The underlying cause may be inattention, wrong judgment, panic, task overload, or other factors, and to be consistent, such conditions should also be called faults. Not all human faults result in errors, and good human engineering will require simultaneous or successive human actions to provide protection against single faults in crucial situations. A software error occurs when a system failure is experienced which is traceable to an underlying software fault. Again, not all software faults will result in system failure if some of the design techniques discussed in Secs. 2.7.2 and 2.7.4 are employed. In imprecise colloquial speech we call either errors or faults "bugs."

Note that in defining errors and faults, we have in no way quantified the severity of an error. Obviously, there are catastrophic, major, minor, and cosmetic errors. For simplicity, the reliability models, which we will soon discuss, treat all errors as equal. Thus, initially, no differentiation will be made among errors as to severity or the amount of redesign effort (lines of code added, deleted, or changed) needed to eliminate the error.

5.5.2 Errors, Specification Changes, and Corrections

Code changes are made for many reasons; however, we are primarily interested in changes which are made to correct a fault causing an error. In addition, changes to correct or to add documentation, as well as changes to implement new or changed requirements (specifications), impact the work schedule and are also of interest. Since all changes are generally mixed together in recording data, it is necessary to indicate the reason for the change. Errors are then segregated into at least three categories: documentation, changes in specifications, and changes to correct errors. The former two categories of changes are discussed further in Chap. 6.

System performance specifications may be either explicit or implicit. For example, when Bell Laboratories develops a switching computer system for a telephone network, it specifies the number of lines to be served, call rates, types of phone equipment, etc., in an explicit, quantitative fashion. It does not specify that the caller will be an American who is accustomed to the use of our telephone system and not a European to whom our system is strange. The latter is an implicit specification.

Inherent in the above definitions and discussion is the assumption that system failures can be and are detected and recorded. Furthermore, it is assumed that each failure episode is sufficiently well investigated so that the underlying fault can be detected and classified as hardware, software, operator, or unresolved, and that the unresolved category is small, say, less than 20 percent. The detection of errors can be effected by monitoring the system (or simulated system) performance or by reading the code and finding a fault which will cause an error.

We must amplify on the previous definition of error in order to cover the cases of repetitious errors, multiple errors caused by one fault, and multiple faults which cause one error. We may think of faults as causes and errors as effects. Thus, if a single fault results in an associated single system failure, we call it a single error. If system failure exists and we are sure it is a software problem, then a software error exists regardless of whether or not we can find the corresponding fault. In practice intermittent or nonrepeatable software errors often fall into this subset of the unresolved category.

Some practitioners will consider that a software error exists only when a code change is introduced in the program, tests are made, and it is shown that the system failure no longer occurs. At this point we are essentially splitting hairs. We might liken this situation to that of a witness for the prosecution in a murder trial. Assume that the witness saw the defendant shoot the victim and notebooks were found in which the defendant planned the crime. At this point, the witness would say that the defendant is a murderer. However, a lawyer present as a spectator might refuse to call the defendant anything but a defendant in a murder trial until the jury verdict is in.

It is useful to comment that not all errors are fixed. This means that even if a code change is tested to verify the fault, this code change may not be incorporated into the official version of the program. Sometimes, in the case of a minor error, the fault is not fixed. As an example, one may cite the Lunar Excursion Module (LEM) guidance computer for the Apollo moon landing program.[1] The computer consisted of about 32K of read-only memory (ROM), which was constructed with the appropriate 1–0 patterns by weaving wires into a core memory (called a rope), plus about 2K of random-access memory (RAM). Once the final program was woven into the rope, changes could be made only by (1) reweaving the rope (very closely) or (2) locating a nearby Jump to Read-Write Memory instruction, devising an ingenious patch[2] which took up a block of scarce read-write memory, and then jumping back to the rope memory past the error point. In this case, once the rope was woven, the few subsequent errors were classified as anomalies or discrepancies. All discrepancies were serious enough to require a correction, while anomalies were not corrected. The astronauts and others in the program were advised of the anomalies and taught to ignore them or given a simple "work around" sequence. As an example, one anomaly concerned the round-off in the computer due to decimal-to-binary and binary-to-decimal conversion. The standard procedure when an astronaut entered data into the computer via the console data entry pad was to follow the entry by display to ensure correctness. When this

---

[1] Private communication, Steve Copps, Draper Laboratory, MIT, Cambridge, Mass., January 1972.

[2] The term *patch* refers to changes made to an existing program in machine language (to avoid recompilation of the source program or remanufacturing a ROM). Generally the change begins by a Jump to Subroutine instruction and ends with a Return from Subroutine instruction. Patches almost always lead to loss of program control, thus, an important reason for instituting configuration control techniques is to limit the use of patches to a few temporary, special cases.

was done, the displayed numbers often differed from the numbers entered by one digit in the last decimal place. The difference was numerically insignificant and the astronauts were told to ignore it.

One important class of external errors for which no fault can be found is transient errors. These exist for too short a time to be isolated. If a transient error occur *n* times, it is still only counted as a single error if the symptoms are the same. Conceptually, many faults can combine to cooperatively cause one error. We expect that this is an event with a low probability of occurrence. Since only a single failure occurs, this would be classified as one error.

A more common multiple error case is where one fault causes *m* different failures. Initially, if the *m* errors are known but no corresponding fault has been found, then we classify this result as *m* errors. At a later time when the common fault is found, the cumulative record is changed to a single error. Thus, one must be careful in the initial data taking, the detective work to analyse the error, and the bookkeeping.

5.5.3 New and Old Errors

In modeling the dynamics of the debugging process, it is useful to know whether an error is old or new. To be more precise, we might use the terminology *previously fixed errors* and *generated errors*. We define these terms as follows:

A *previously fixed error* is one which *recurs* in substantially the *same form* after the programmer has terminated work on a code change believing that the error has been corrected. A conclusive decision that an error is a previously fixed one can be made only on the basis of study of the corresponding fault.

A *generated error* is one which does not exist until it is *created* as a by-product of a *code change* made to correct another error. A generated error is usually best diagnosed by finding the corresponding fault. However, it is sometimes possible to base such a classification on the error, e.g., if a newly created variable appears in the wrong output form.

Thus, we have three additional error classifications: undetected, previously fixed, and generated.

Using the above definitions of error, we can improve somewhat on the previous definition of software reliability (see Sec. 5.5.1).

Software reliability is the *probability* that a given *software system operates* for some *time period* without software *error*, on the machine for which it was designed given that it is used within design limits.

The definition of the term *error* has been improved; however, we are still at the mercy of the specification. At least we have agreed that the specification must embody quantitative design limits on input data, performance, etc. We would expect that the above definition will work well where the hardware-software computer complex is performing a well-defined operational task with clearly stated, measurable goals.

5.5.4 Classification and Causes of Errors

In the previous section we have taken the first step and defined program errors and faults; we can now venture further and attempt to classify program errors and faults by type and cause.

Before we begin, it is useful to explore some of the hypotheses which people hold about program errors.[1] There are many logical reasons to support these hypotheses and some data; however, in most cases no controlled tests have been run to prove their validity.

Hypothesis: Bugs per line constant Code written in higher-level languages has a smaller initial error content. Three reasons are advanced for this: (1) In a higher-level language such as PL/1, for example, exceptional conditions such as zero divide, overflow, etc., are automatically handled; however, if one writes in machine language, one must handle these problems each time oneself, and errors of omission are bound to occur. (2) Second, some people propose that the number of faults created per line of code is the same whether one writes in higher-level language or machine language. Since each line of a language such as PL/1 expands into 5 to 10 lines of machine language, if this effect is true, there should be a corresponding reduction in error content by a factor of 5 to 10. (3) Finally, certain types of faults which exist in machine language don't occur in higher-level languages (see Table 2.24).[2]

Hypothesis: Memory shortage encourages bugs The inherent error content of some programs is claimed to be related to the lack of available memory capacity. The theory is that if the memory is very cramped, the software writers will have to resort to overlays and other coding "tricks" to squeeze the desired function into the allocated memory space. It is assumed that these tricks introduce great complexity and are the source of many faults. This effect is often cited by designers of airborne computers, where the allocation of another block of 4K of memory is a major design decision.[3] (See Fig. 3.21.)

Hypothesis: Heavy load causes errors to occur Many people have commented that a whole class of software errors occur only when the system is operating with a heavy load. This effect is very hard to document, since it is difficult to define the concept of computer load. Certainly, it is related to the number of users in a timesharing system or the number of processes being multi-processed in a batch system; however, this is probably not the entire story. Certainly, the complexity of the jobs being processed and how diverse a mix of facilities they require during their execution is significant. Also, a large reduction in performance is equivalent to a failure.

---

[1] Shooman (1974*b*); Amster and Shooman (1974); Schwartz (1971).
[2] For a good discussion of this point, see Brooks (1975), p. 235.
[3] Boehm (1973); Brooks (1975), pp. 98–103.

Hypothesis: Tuning reduces error occurrence rate Many people have noticed that a hardware-software complex can be tuned so that the system runs well. This is not the well-known optimization of system parameters, but has to do with the removal of known errors for a class of input data. Thus, if the same software is subjected to a significantly different set of inputs, an entire new crop of errors will occur. Of course we could retune the program by eliminating the new errors so that the program would run well with the new inputs.

Each of the above arguments is supported partially by data and mostly by common sense; however, a definitive study and development of these points is lacking at present in the research literature.

Anyone who has done extensive debugging knows that there are types of faults which repeat themselves over and over again. Also some classes of faults occur only in assembly language programming, some only in higher-level-language programming, and some in both. The following list represents some bug types:

1. Array overwrite
2. Off by 1 in indexing or shifting
3. Wrong flag bit
4. Complement arithmetic problems
5. Initialization
6. Pointer problems
7. Wrong transfer of control
8. Indirect addressing problems

No doubt, in reading the above incomplete list, the reader is tempted to take a pencil and add many which have been omitted. Each programmer uses different terminology; however, there obviously is a common set of underlying fault types.

Another point to be considered is that different programming styles and levels may give rise to different error types. For example, there have to be some fault types which occur in top-down but hardly ever in bottom-up programming and vice versa. Similarly, the faults which occur in higher-level language, assembly language, and microprogramming will differ. Also, the type of programming done on a large IBM 4341 computer, a DEC VAX computer, and an Intel 8086 microprocessor will differ.

Unfortunately, no definitive list of fault types has yet emerged from the literature, but a good start has been made by TRW.[1]

---

[1]Thayer, et al. (1978), pp. 27–32.

5.5.5 A Data-Collection Experiment

Most of the approaches to data collection in the literature have used different techniques for classification of program bugs.[1] The approach discussed below focused on program changes and the reasons which necessitated the changes.

One study described in detail below, was carried out at Bell Laboratories in Madison, N.J., and had several initial objectives:[2]

1. To characterize errors

The first objective was to design a form which could be used to develop detailed information on the frequency and types of errors which occurred, and the effort in programmer hours and computer hours expended to detect and correct these bugs. However, if you ask five programmers to compose a list of the types of errors they encounter in their programs, there would be a great diversity of terminology. In addition to the use of different names for the same error, there would be much overlap and confusion of terms. Thus, establishing a working set of error types which would appear on the data collection form, and from which we would force the programmer to choose in reporting the results, was our initial area of study.

Our mode of approach was to discuss a list of possible error types with a fairly large number of programmers and program managers experienced in the field and sympathetic to, but critical of, our intended objectives. The authors formulated, on their own, a draft form based upon these discussions and present it to a subset of this group at an initial conference. This form was subsequently distributed to all the attendees of this conference, and after private feedback was received from them, the final copy of version 1 of the form was produced. This was then circulated to another group[3] of program managers, and a meeting was held to evaluate version 1. From this meeting emerged version 2 in draft form, which was commented on and corrected to obtain the final copy of version 2.

This process was repeated perhaps four or five times until it seemed to be settling down and the final form emerged. This is not to say that each time the process was repeated new changes were not suggested; however, toward the end of the process these seemed to become second-order effects rather than primary changes. Of course, the real test of such a form must be made on the basis of whether programmers can accurately complete it in a reasonable amount of time, and whether the data obtained are of subsequent benefit.

2. To determine if data could be collected

Another objective of this study was to satisfy the questions which were often raised in the initial planning of this investigation regarding the amount of time

---

[1] Boehm et al. (1975); Rubey (1975); Enders (1975); Shooman and Bolsky (1975); Itoh and Izutani (1973); Presson (1980).
[2] Shooman and Bolsky (1975).
[3] There was some overlap between the groups.

used in filling out forms of the type described above. The program managers felt, by and large, that their personnel were heavily burdened with meeting the milestones for the project. Therefore, even if the managers agreed, in spirit, with the purposes of the study, they were loath to agree to it, unless a data collection scheme could be devised which would both be effective and consume little of the programmer's time.

3. To study error density and compare with previous data

A third objective was to compare the overall error count obtained for this program with previous data which have appeared in the literature.

4. To develop data on resource expenditure during integration testing

The fourth objective of this study was to obtain information on the expenditure of resources during the integration phase. Thus, we included information on the form concerning the cost of locating and correcting each bug in terms of programmer hours and computer hours.

Only the first and second objectives will be discussed in this section; however, the results associated with objective 3 were discussed in Sec. 4.2.4 and the results related to objective 4 are treated in Sec. 6.2.

During the planning of this experiment one manager suggested that we utilize historical information, i.e., debugging forms which were already on file. Thus, we would select an appropriate project, read forms on file, and fill out our own data collection form for each error. This suggestion was implemented on a batch of approximately 50 regular trouble report–correction report (TR/CR) error-reporting forms used on the project studied (see Fig. 5.2).

The trouble report (TR) portion is filled out by the person who discovers the bug in the program, and a verbal description of trouble encountered is written in the appropriate section on the form. The second half of the form is the correction made to remedy the difficulty described in the TR portion. Sometimes, both the TR and CR are completed by the same individual, and at other times by two different individuals.

The 50 TR/CR forms used in this initial study were a few months old. Two persons—one an experienced programmer (who had not originally initiated any of the forms), and one a technical clerk—read the TR/CR forms. Each one first tried to understand the causes of the errors, and the results were checked with the originator(s) of the TR and CR forms. It was assumed that the information supplied by the originators was correct, and thus the programmer and the clerk were rated on their ability to understand and replicate the conclusions reached by the TR and CR originators. Both the programmer and the clerk scored about 25 percent correct when their responses were compared with the assumed correct forms.

The conclusion drawn from this study was that the verbal information contained in the TR/CR form is suitable if one programmer is trying to record

System Software
Trouble Report/Correction Report

TR

ORIGINATED BY		EXT.	ROOM	DATE	TR NUMBER

PIDENT (Program identification)		LEVEL	PRIORITY E U R	REASON FOR CHANGE ☐ ERROR ☐ IMPROVEMENT

COMPUTER RUN	TYPE OF ACT.	TEST ID	DUMP TAPE NO.	LOG TAPE NO.

ORGINATION APPROVAL (Supervisor)	DATE	RESPONSIBLE PA/FA (Manager)	DEPT

DESCRIPTION

SCM LOG-IN (Coordinator)	DATE	APPR. FOR ACTION	DATE	REFERRED TO	DEPT

CR

ORGINATED BY		EXT.	ROOM	DATE	CR NUMBER

PIDENT		LEVEL	LIBRARY ID	VOLUME SER. NO.

DESIGN APPROVAL	DATE	BELLFLOW COMMENTS UPDATED (Flowchart) ☐ YES ☐ NO ☐ NA

DESCRIPTION

CHANGE RECEIVED	DATE	CHANGE INTEGRATED	DATE

RELEASED IN	PIDENT	LEVEL

Page 1

Figure 5.2 System software trouble report–correction report.

and document errors for personal use or for another programmer,[1] but that the descriptions were not clear enough for the purposes of our study. Thus, we decided that the only way in which such data could be obtained was to have programmers fill out our more complete, supplementary form along with the regular TR/CR form.

[1]Obviously the programmer assigned to the CR has prompt and ample access (person-to-person, telephone, or written inquiries) to the TR programmer while the information is still fresh.

It is possible that if the programmer were to keep all copies of program runs, encircle and number the bugs on the listing with colored pencil, and insert marginal notes describing what was wrong, then a complete history of the debugging process could be obtained. It was felt that this would be a much more difficult procedure than simply filling out a supplementary TR/CR form attached to the regular TR/CR form. (See Fig. 5.3.)

Many criteria were considered in choosing the program (called the STUDY program) which served as the vehicle for this investigation.[1] The STUDY program was about to enter the test and integration phase, was 4000 machine words long, and was a control-type program designed to interface with many other programs in a large program system. There were no major changes in functional specifications during the period of data collection; therefore, we may assume that most of the changes which were made were to correct errors rather than to satisfy new or changed functional requirements.

In designing the supplementary form, we chose to separate the reason for and the nature of the change since errors occurring due to different causes might be fixed in the same way and vice versa. The error-classification results of the study are given in Figs. 5.4, 5.5, and 5.6. Figure 5.4 shows the reason for changes, Fig. 5.5 shows the nature of the change, and Fig. 5.6 gives the reason why, if a change is not needed.

The predominant feature in Fig. 5.4 is that most of the changes (96 percent) were due to a correction of an error rather than to a new requirement verifying our assumption. Second, within the correction category, over 65 percent of the reasons for a correction were checked as due to a programming bug. Therefore, it would seem prudent, in repeat studies of this type, to be certain to divide the category of "programming bug" into several more detailed subcategories. We would have been much aided in this study by the preexistence of a set of standard bug categories such as those discussed in Sec. 5.5.4. On the other hand, some of the categories with very low percentile responses which have similar titles could very well be combined. However, the STUDY program was a control program, and the distribution of reason for change and nature of change might be different for an input-output or computation program.

For nature of change about 90 percent of the responses fell into the two categories "fix instruction" and "structural." Again, it would be desirable to break down these categories to achieve a better description of the nature of the change. For example, it might be appropriate to categorize these as syntax error, program error, structural error, and instruction fix.

Approximately 20 percent of the TRs which were issued did not require a change, and as shown in Fig. 5.6 no change needed generally means there was no error. Thus, a TR form had been generated, but upon complete investigation, it was found that there was no error, and no correction was required. In other cases no change was required because the problem was in the support software itself, or

---

[1]Shooman and Bolsky (1975).

**To Be
Filled
Out by
Originator
of**

**TR
FORM**

**CR
FORM**

Supplementary TR/CR Corm

Directions: 1. Fill out this form in conjunction with each TR/CR form.
2. Attach this form to the regular TR/CR form. When both
the TR and CR originators have completed their respective portions of
this form, detach it and send it, along with a photo copy of the TR/CR form,
to M. I. Bolsky.

T1. TR No. _____ Date This Form Completed _____
Program Coded in (Language) _____
T2. Means of Initial Detection — √ only for corrections (not new reqs.)
— More than one category may be √ 'ed

☐ a. Hand processing   ☐ d. Interrupt error (code _____)
☐ b. Personal communication   ☐ e. Incorrect output or result
☐ c. Infinite loop   ☐ f. Missing output
  ☐ g. Other — explain

T3. Effort in diagnosing the error — Do not include effort spent in
initial detection.

a. No. of runs to diagnose _____ Elapsed computer time (minutes) _____
b. Working time to diagnose: Days _____ Hours _____

C1. CR No. _____ Date This Form Completed _____
C2. Category — More than one category may be √ 'ed.

<table>
<tr><td colspan="2">Software Change Required</td><td>Software Change Not Required</td></tr>
<tr><td>Reason for Change</td><td>Nature of Change</td><td>☐ Problem is in hardware</td></tr>
<tr><td>New Requirement</td><td>☐ Documentation</td><td>☐ Problem is in support</td></tr>
<tr><td>☐ Mission</td><td>(preface or</td><td>software</td></tr>
<tr><td>☐ Engineering model</td><td>comments)</td><td>☐ Error was in test itself</td></tr>
<tr><td>☐ Software implemen-</td><td>☐ Fix instruction</td><td>☐ Error is not repeatable</td></tr>
<tr><td>tation</td><td>☐ Change constants</td><td>☐ There was no error</td></tr>
<tr><td>☐ Hardware</td><td>☐ Structural</td><td>☐ Other — explain</td></tr>
<tr><td>☐ Other — explain</td><td>☐ Algorithmic</td><td></td></tr>
<tr><td>Correction</td><td>☐ Other — explain</td><td></td></tr>
<tr><td>☐ Misinterpretation</td><td></td><td></td></tr>
<tr><td>of spec</td><td></td><td></td></tr>
<tr><td>☐ Wrong spec</td><td></td><td></td></tr>
<tr><td>☐ Incomplete spec</td><td></td><td></td></tr>
<tr><td>☐ Program bug</td><td></td><td></td></tr>
<tr><td>☐ I/O software</td><td></td><td></td></tr>
<tr><td>☐ Operating system</td><td>Correction (continued)</td><td></td></tr>
<tr><td>☐ Support software</td><td>☐ Software interface (e.g., interface with another task)</td><td></td></tr>
<tr><td>☐ Card handling</td><td>☐ Hardware interface (e.g., timing error)</td><td></td></tr>
<tr><td>☐ Other — explain</td><td></td><td></td></tr>
</table>

C3. Difficulty of Correction
a. No. of runs to correct _____ Elapsed computer time (minutes) _____
b. Working time to debug: Days _____ Hours _____
c. No. of cards: Changed _____ Added _____ Deleted _____

C4. Other Relevant Information
a. Type of program: Control ☐ Arithmetic ☐ Hybrid ☐ Dataset ☐
b. Complexity of program: Simple ☐ Medium ☐ Complex ☐
c. Other information?

Comments — Use reverse side of sheet.

Figure 5.3 Supplementary TR/CR form.

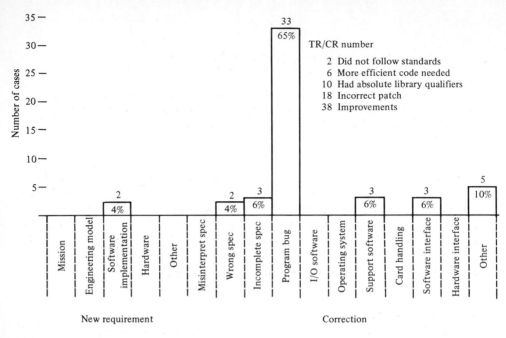

Figure 5.4 Reason for change.

was an interface incompatibility *in another* program which called STUDY or was called by STUDY.

This section has shown the reader some of the practical difficulties in conducting even a modest programming experiment. Any readers who are contemplating a data collection experiment are advised to first consult experimental studies in the literature, and to plan with care.

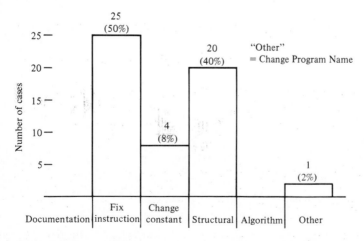

Figure 5.5 Nature of change.

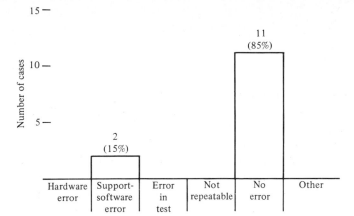

Figure 5.6 Software change not required.

5.6 ESTIMATING THE NUMBER OF BUGS IN A COMPUTER PROGRAM

5.6.1 Introduction

One of the major problems in software development is that there are few quantities which one can use as a measure of project progress. Thus, it is very difficult to estimate the state of a project and how much more time is needed to finish the software. Traditionally, software managers record the number of lines of code written and the estimated total number of lines of code in the final program (see Fig. 5.7). Most managers use the number of lines of code debugged (see Fig. 5.8) and the total number of errors removed from a program for

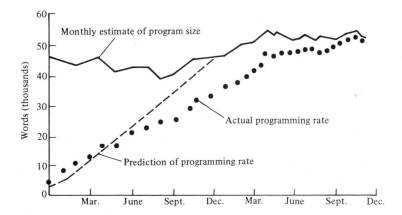

Figure 5.7 Curves of the number of lines of code written (actual and estimated) and estimates of program size. (For similar curves, see Giloty et al., 1970.) *(From Brooks, 1975, p. 92)*

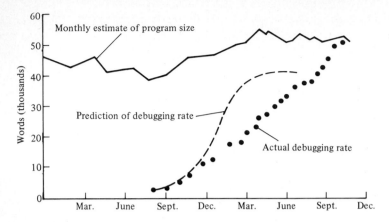

Figure 5.8 Cumulative number of instructions debugged, actual and predicted. *(From Brooks, 1975, p. 92)*

measuring project progress (see Fig. 5.9). The obvious inference is that once the cumulative-number-of-errors-removed curve begins to approach a horizontal asymptote, the debugging is nearing completion.

The author, an engineer and a student of probability, does not believe in perfection, and feels that the achievement of such an asymptote does not represent the removal of all bugs. It represents the removal of most bugs, or, more

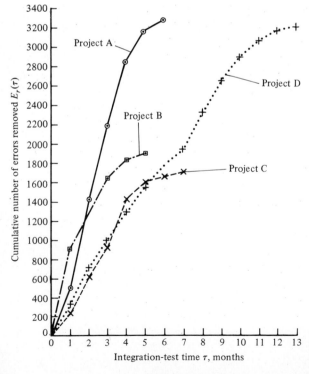

Figure 5.9 Cumulative curves of the number of errors removed versus test time for four projects involving applications programs. (See Table 5.2 for source of data.)

specifically, those which one could ferret out using the test methods and test data employed in the project. A few managers and software analysts feel these estimates are useless, since it is too difficult to define and count bugs. As a rebuttal, I cite the hypothetical case in which the manager of a computer-controlled chemical plant schedules the installation of a new release of an operating system over a weekend. During mid-morning there is computer trouble and the process is shut down for 2 hours. Since a hardware error is suspected, all the hardware diagnostics are run and they check perfectly. To avoid further interruptions of production, the old version of the operating system is reloaded and the plant resumes operation and production. It is certain that the manager of the chemical plant believes in software errors and knows how to define them.

In the remainder of this section we discuss various models and methods for estimating and measuring the number of errors in a program.

5.6.2 Error-Removal Data

Introduction The first thought which comes to mind when we are investigating how to judge the number of bugs left in a program is to compare this program with previous ones. Inherent in such a suggestion is the assumption that the total number of bugs in similar programs is approximately constant. We now have to define what is meant by *similar programs* and *approximately constant*.

We begin with a discussion of the term *approximately constant*. First of all, we are discussing a macroscopic model of a complex stochastic process, the debugging of a large piece of software by a team of programmers. Thus, the quantity to be estimated (number of errors) is not a fundamental physical constant such as the speed of light, but merely a parameter in a probabilistic model. Second, we need this constant for initial planning purposes and rough initial prediction. Thus, even if our constant can only be initially estimated with an accuracy of 50 to 100 percent, this accuracy is still satisfactory for the intended purposes. Later estimation will be more accurate.

The definition of similarity is more complex. First of all, we must assume an equivalent skill mix in each of the programming teams. Second, we must assume that similar techniques were used to test the software. We might expect the same constant for all bottom-up unstructured programs; however, a different constant might be valid for the class of top-down structured programs. Also, we must define *similar* in terms of the phase of the development. If we focus on a conventional bottom-up development process, there are three phases: module coding and test, system integration and test, and, last, field operation. Definitions of these phases may differ somewhat in practice. For convenience in very large systems, the task is divided into several processes; thus system integration is a two-phase task divided into a process-integration phase followed by system integration of the processes. Also, in many large systems it is recognized that the best test is actual operation. Thus, often the first several months of field test are actually the last part of final integration and test. In such cases the release date (when ownership of the software is transferred from developer to user) occurs several months after, rather than at the beginning of, field deployment.

Table 5.2 Number of errors removed per month for seven different large programs

	Errors			
Month	Application A: 240,000 instructions	Application B: 240,000 instructions	Application C: 240,000 instructions	Application D: 240,000 instructions
1	514	905	235	331
2	926	376	398	397
3	754	362	297	269
4	662	192	506	296
5	308	70	174	314
6	108	.....	55	183
7	.....	.....	60	158
8	.....	.....	.....	368
9	.....	.....	.....	337
10	.....	.....	.....	249
11	.....	.....	.....	166
12	.....	.....	.....	108
13	.....	.....	.....	31
Total errors	3272	1905	1725	3207
Average per month	545	381	246	247

	Errors		
Month	Supervisory A: 210,000 instructions	Supervisory B: 240,000 instructions	Supervisory C: 230,000 instructions
1	110	250	225
2	238	520	287
3	185	430	497
4	425	300	400
5	325	170	180
6	37	120	50
7	5	60	.....
8	.....	40	.....
Total errors	1325	1890	1639
Average per month	189	236	273

Source: Dickson, Hesse, Kientz, and Shooman (1972) and Shooman (1972c). Hesse's raw data were in terms of program changes, and the data in this table and the Hesse paper were adjusted by dividing by an estimated 17 changes per error.

Error data—some examples Some of the first data which were published in the open literature[1] for the number of errors removed per month were collected from three manufacturers on their operating systems and from a government agency on four versions of an applications program (see Table 5.2). The size (measured in machine language instructions) for these programs was between 210K and 240K.[2]

[1] Dickson, Hesse, Kientz, and Shooman (1972).
[2] The abbreviation K as used here is not in the engineering sense, where K = 1000, but in the computer science sense, where $K = 2^{10} = 1024$.

All those in the supervisory category were similar types, as were all those in the applications program category.

From Table 5.2 we see that among the application programs the total number of errors (we assume each change is an error and denote the total by E_T)[1] varies between 3270 and 1725, a range of 1.9:1. In the case of the supervisory programs, $1325 \le E_T \le 1890$, and the range is about 1.4:1. Lumping all the programs together, the range for E_T from smallest to largest is about 2.5:1.

Similarly we can examine the rate at which errors are removed as a function of debugging time τ. Denoting this error rate, $r(\tau)$, we can compute the average value of $r(\tau)$ over the interval 0 to τ, which is also given in Table 5.2. Note that the average rates vary by about 2.9:1 among the seven examples. Thus, we may formulate a new hypothesis that the error removal rate per month for similar programs is approximately the same. We must add two conditions to our definition of similarity: (1) that the manpower levels are similar and (2) that the amount of testing per month is similar.

In the case of the seven programs previously discussed, all were about 0.25 million words long. If we are to compare the number of errors for large and small programs, it seems reasonable to normalize in some way and deal with an "error density." The initial attempt at normalization was to divide E_T and $r(\tau)$ by the total number of machine language instructions, I_T.[2]

Hypothesis: Constant normalized number of errors The normalized number of errors in similar programs is approximately constant. (The normalization is performed by dividing the total number of errors by the number of machine language instructions.)

Hypothesis: Constant normalized error-removal rate The normalized removal rate for errors in similar programs is approximately constant. (The normalization is performed by dividing the rate of error removal per month by the number of machine language instructions.)

We now examine how well typical data fit these hypotheses.

Error density—large programs The normalized data for the total number of instructions and average removal rate ρ_A [$E_T/(I_T \times$ development time)] for several systems is compared in Table 5.3. The variation in E_T/I_T and ρ_A can be stated in standard statistical terms. The mean values are 10.2×10^{-3} and 0.43×10^{-3}, respectively, and assuming a normal distribution and a 75 percent

---

[1] In some of the author's research papers E_T has also been called E_0.

[2] The normalization of E_T through division by I_T was conceived prior to the research on token length as a measure of complexity, which is developed in Chap. 3. It now appears that it might be better to normalize with respect to token length. If this is true, then future software data-gathering efforts should record not only I_T but token length as well.

Table 5.3 Computation of normalized total errors and error rates

Program	Size	$E_T/I_T (\times 10^{-3})$	$\rho_A (\times 10^{-3})$
Supervisory A	210K	6.14	0.875
Supervisory B	240K	7.97	0.096
Supervisory C	230K	7.48	1.25
Application A	240K	13.20	2.20
Application B	240K	7.70	1.54
Application C	240K	7.00	1.00
Application D	240K	12.90	0.995
TSPS no. 1	100K	20.00	1.67
Mean		10.2	1.32
Standard deviation		4.4	0.43

Source: Supervisory programs A–C and application programs A–D: Dickson, Hesse, Kientz, and Shooman (1972) and Shooman (1972c). TSPS no. 1 from Heller et al. (1970), p. 2712.

confidence interval,[1] we obtain $5 \times 10^{-3} \le E_T/I_T \le 15 \times 10^{-3}$ and $0.83 \times 10^{-3} \le \rho_A \le 1.82 \times 10^{-3}$.

Two of the greatest difficulties in analyzing data of the type given in Table 5.3 are (1) differences and often lack of precision in reporting the development phase of the project (module test, integrating test, field test, etc.) and (2) the fact that source rather than object code size is given and we are unsure if comments and nonexecutable statements are included. For example, Walston and Felix (1977) report on 60 IBM projects in a data base with size ranging from 4K to 467K and written in 28 different high-level languages. (They do not specify how many, if any, assembly languages are represented.) They report a median value of 3.1 errors per 1000 source lines and a quartile range (25 to 75 percent) of 0.8 to 8.0. If we wish to compare these values with the E_T/I_T values given in Table 5.3, we must calculate a source-to-object code expansion factor. Assuming that of the 60 programs, 30 are assembly language (1:1 expansion factor), 15 are medium high-level (1:4 expansion factor), and 15 are quite high-level (1:6 expansion factor), one obtains a weighted expansion factor equal to 3:1. Use of this factor produces a computation yielding $E_T/I_T = 3.1/3 \times 1000 = 1.03 \times 10^{-3}$, which is less by a factor of 10 than the values quoted in Table 5.3. This gives rise to a number of conjectures (explanations):

1. The IBM data are circa 1973 to 1977 and the data in Table 5.3 are circa 1965 to 1970. Perhaps programming has improved and fewer errors are committed now.
2. The IBM data may contain field testing data for many projects, which are sometimes substantially lower.

[1]A 75 percent confidence interval for a random variable **x** which is normally distributed with mean μ and standard deviation σ is $(\mu - 1.15\sigma) \le x \le (\mu + 1.15\sigma)$. See App. A.

3. Perhaps the error expansion factor of 3:1 is in error.
4. The definitions of error may be much different.
5. The data in Table 5.3 are for assembly language programs. Perhaps the high-level-language programs in the IBM data base contain fewer errors.
6. We all know that IBM employs good personnel, but are they that good?

Again, it is important to know the full history of a programming project before we can make an accurate comparison.

We now study the error density for small programs.

Error density—small programs One small program we have already discussed is the STUDY program (Sec. 5.5.5), which contained approximately 4000 machine words and had 63 bugs removed. The ratio $E_T/I_T = 15.8 \times 10^{-3}$, and it compares well with the data in Table 5.3. In the paper by Itoh and Izutani (1973), two similar programs were debugged with and without a test tool. The results were $E_{T_1} = 335$, $I_{T_1} = 14{,}302$, and $E_{T_1}/I_{T_1} = 23.4 \times 10^{-3}$ and $E_{T_2} = 345$, $I_{T_2} = 16{,}037$, and $E_{T_2}/I_{T_2} = 21.5 \times 10^{-3}$; again good agreement is obtained. Another set of data for small programs appears in Table 5.4.

Thus, using a 50 percent confidence interval as previously, we obtain $11.9 \times 10^{-3} \leq E_T/I_T \leq 26.7 \times 10^{-3}$ and $1.15 \times 10^{-3} \leq \rho_A \leq 2.71 \times 10^{-3}$. Note that the values given in Table 5.4 (and by Itoh) are somewhat higher than those in Table 5.3. One explanation for this is that Akiyama's and Itoh's data cover three phases of program development: module debugging M, integration testing I, and field deployment F.

Error density versus development phase When we analyze the data in Table 5.4 plus Itoh's data by phase, we obtain the results of Table 5.5. After dissecting

Table 5.4 Computation of normalized total errors and debugging rates

Program	Size	$E_T/I_T(\times 10^{-3})$	$\rho_A(\times 10^{-3})$
MA	4.03K	25.4	2.54
MB	1.32K	13.7	1.37
MC	5.45K	17.1	1.71
MD	1.67K	15.6	1.56
ME	2.05K	34.6	3.46
MF	2.51K	14.7	1.47
MT	2.10K	12.4	1.24
MG	0.70K	22.9	2.29
MH	3.79K	13.2	1.32
MX	3.41K	23.4	2.34
Mean		19.3	1.93
Standard deviation		6.4	0.68

Data from Akiyama (1971).

Table 5.5 Computation of normalized debugging by phase (see Akiyama, 1971 and Itoh, 1973)

Program	Size	Module debug errors, E_M	$E_M/I_T (\times 10^{-3})$	Integration debug errors, E_I	$E_I/I_T (\times 10^{-3})$	Field debug errors	E_F/I_T $(\times 10^{-3})$
Akiyama:							
MA	4.03K	58	14.4	40	9.9	4	0.99
MB	1.32K	9	6.8	8	6.1	1	0.76
MC	5.45K	79	14.3	14	2.5	1	0.18
MD	1.67K	21	12.6	5	3.0	0	0
ME	2.05K	54	26.3	14	6.8	3	1.5
MF	2.51K	21	8.4	15	5.9	0	0
Total	17.03K	242	.....	96	....	9	.....
Mean	2.83	40.3	13.8	16	5.7	1.5	0.57
Standard deviation	1.45K	24.9	6.3	11.3	2.5	1.5	0.56
Itoh:							
With FADEBUG-1 Code	14.3K	261	18.3	74	5.2	...	.....
Without FADEBUG-1 Code	16.0K	245	15.3	100	6.2	...	.....

Akiyama's and Itoh's data, we find that E_I/I_T for integration errors was about 6×10^{-3}, which is a little smaller than the average of 10×10^{-3} in Table 5.3. Note that very few errors were found in the field (Itoh gave no field data). On the basis of the total number of errors found by Akiyama and Itoh's two data sets in Table 5.5, we find that module debugging discovered 69 percent, 78 percent, and 71 percent; integration found 28 percent, 22 percent, and 29 percent; and field deployment uncovered 3 percent of the known errors. Hyman has studied errors found after release compared with errors found during system integration for three large operating systems. (He did not have module data.) He found that 56 percent of the errors were found during integration and 44 percent in the field. Additional data on failures found in the field[1] are referenced in the paper by Amster and Shooman (1975). One of the problems in analyzing such data is clearly defining the differences between terms such as *integration test, functional test, field trials*, and *operational testing*. Similarly, Itoh (in Itoh and Izutani, 1973) speaks of *module, component,* and *system test* and reports 34 percent, 37 percent, and 29 percent of the total errors, respectively.

Although additional data would be welcome to further explore the supposition that the number of bugs per line is constant, there is sufficient evidence to

[1]Hyman (1973); Amster and Shooman (1975).

accept the hypothesis at this point.[1] Unfortunately the data in Table 5.5 along with Hyman's results are too sketchy to be definitive on how error finding is distributed between the phases of development.

Summary—Error-removal data A considerable amount of space has been spent in this chapter on error data because a good understanding of the error-removal process is so fundamental to software reliability. The conclusions can be summarized as follows:

1. Collection of error data is difficult and costly because of imprecise terminology, because the users of such data are not the collectors, and because of company proprietary policies; however, several useful studies have been published.
2. The data for both large and small programs seemed reasonably consistent within each group and between groups for E_T/I_T.
3. A value of E_T/I_T between 0.5×10^{-2} and 2×10^{-2} seems to be a reasonable guideline.
4. For the small programs studied, about 70 percent of the errors were found during module testing, 25 percent during integration testing, and less than 5 percent after release.
5. For the operating systems studied, 55 percent of the errors were found during integration and 45 percent after release. The additional number found during module testing was unknown.
6. More definitive research must be done with the existing data sets and new data sets before we can establish a reliable data base of software error data.[2]

We now turn to an investigation of how the error-removal rates vary over the development phases.

5.6.3 Models of Cumulative Errors and Error Rate

Errors and error rate We now look in more detail into the rate of removal of bugs from computer programs. We are looking for error behavior during debugging which will possess some generality for both large and small programs. Thus, in addition to plotting the error-removal rate $r(\tau)$, we will plot a normalized error-removal rate. If we let $E_r(\tau)$ represent the number of errors removed in the

---

[1] The one piece of negative data which does not validate the hypotheses is the paper by Raymond J. Rubey (1975), in which he cites data on 12 programs, *not described*, which vary from 3K to 17K and have E_T/I_T ratios from 10 to 500×10^{-3}. The author feels the pro evidence far outweighs the con evidence.

[2] This is one of the stated goals of the Data and Analysis Center for Software (DACS) sponsored by the Rome Air Development Center, Griffiss Air Force Base, Rome, NY, 13441.

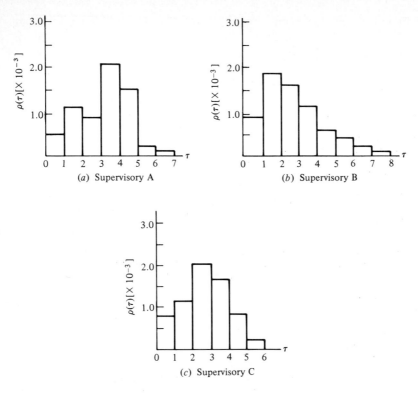

Figure 5.10 Normalized error rate versus debugging time for three supervisory programs.

interval 0 to τ, we obtain

$$r(\tau) = \frac{dE_r(\tau)}{d\tau}$$

$$\rho(\tau) = \frac{r(\tau)}{I_T} = \frac{\text{errors/total number of instructions per month}}{\text{of debugging time}} \tag{5.18}$$

where $\qquad I_T \equiv$ total number of machine language instructions

$\qquad \tau \equiv$ months of debugging time

In Table 5.2 we see that the average number of bugs removed per month $\bar{r}$ varies between 545 and 189 for the seven systems. In Table 5.3 we see that the normalized average rate ρ_A varies between 2.20×10^{-3} and 0.875×10^{-3}. If we calculate $\rho(\tau)$ for the data of Table 5.2, we obtain the graphs shown in Figs. 5.10 and 5.11. Although several curve shapes might be fitted to these data,[1] one characteristic is common for all curves: the normalized error rate decreases over the entire curve, or at least over the latter two-thirds or half of the curve. Initial behavior of $\rho(\tau)$ differs from example to example in Figs. 5.10 and 5.11. If we

---

[1] Dickson, Hesse, Kientz, and Shooman (1972); Shooman (1972c).

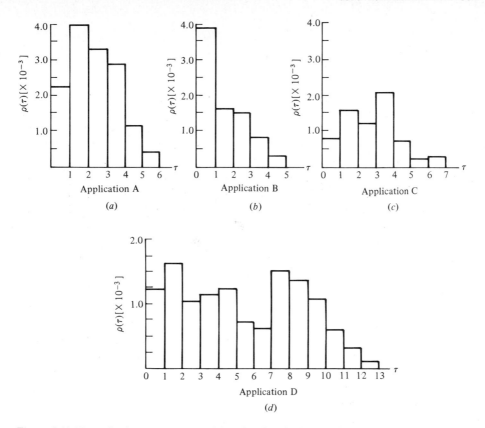

Figure 5.11 Normalized error rate versus debugging time for four applications programs.

compare Fig. 5.9 with Fig. 5.11, we see that it is easier to observe variations over the time interval by studying the $\rho(\tau)$ (rate) curves rather than the $E_r(\tau)$ (cumulative) curves. Obviously the amount of extra effort needed to plot and study both rather than a single curve is well warranted.

Since we are interested in the normalized total number of errors removed rather than the actual number $E(\tau)$, we will define a cumulative normalized error curve $\varepsilon(\tau)$, which is the area under the $\rho(\tau)$ curve:

$$\frac{E(\tau)}{I_T} = \varepsilon(\tau) = \int_0^\tau \rho(x)\,dx = \text{cumulative errors/total number of instructions}$$

(5.19)

$\rho(\tau)$ is of course the slope of the $\varepsilon(\tau)$ curve:

$$\rho(\tau) = \frac{d\varepsilon(\tau)}{d\tau}$$

(5.20)

A curve of the cumulative error data for supervisory system A of Fig. 5.10 is shown in Fig. 5.12. Except for the normalization factor, Fig. 5.12 shows the same

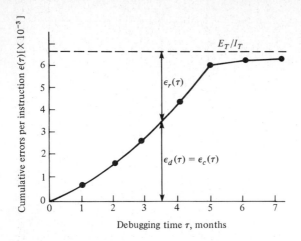

Figure 5.12 Cumulative error curve for supervisory system A given in Fig. 5.10.

behavior as the curves of Fig. 5.9; all build up initially with a constant or increasing slope, followed by a decreasing slope, and finally the curves appear to become asymptotic.

Exponential error-removal model One very tempting hypothesis is to assume that the rate of error detection $dE_d(\tau)/d\tau$ in any time period is proportional to the number remaining in the program, $E_r(\tau)$. If we also assume that all detected errors are immediately and accurately corrected, then $E_c(\tau) = E_d(\tau)$. If the number of generated errors during the debugging process, $E_g(\tau)$, is *zero*, then we have a simple error-balance equation; i.e., what remains is what we started with, E_T, minus what was removed:

$$E_r(\tau) = E_T - E_c(\tau) \tag{5.21}$$

If we rewrite Eq. (5.21) in terms of normalized quantities, i.e., divide all terms by the total number of object instructions, we obtain

$$\frac{E_r(\tau)}{I_T} = \frac{E_T}{I_T} - \frac{E_c(\tau)}{I_T} \tag{5.22}$$

$$\varepsilon_r(\tau) = \frac{E_T}{I_T} - \varepsilon_c(\tau) \tag{5.23}$$

$$\varepsilon_d(\tau) = \varepsilon_c(\tau) \tag{5.24}$$

The interpretation of Eq. (5.23) is shown in Fig. 5.12.

In any sizable program, it is impossible to remove all errors; thus even as τ becomes large,

$$\varepsilon_c(\tau) < E_T/I_T \tag{5.25}$$

$$\varepsilon_r(\tau) > 0 \tag{5.26}$$

If we set the rate of error detection proportional to the number of residual errors $\varepsilon_r(\tau)$ (see Eqs. (5.23) and (5.24)), we obtain

$$\frac{d\varepsilon_d(\tau)}{d\tau} = \frac{d\varepsilon_c(\tau)}{d\tau} = k_1 \left[\frac{E_T}{I_T} - \varepsilon_c(\tau) \right] \tag{5.27}$$

where k_1 is the constant of proportionality. As a result of rearranging terms, the differential equation becomes

$$\frac{d\varepsilon_c(\tau)}{d\tau} + k_1 \varepsilon_c(\tau) = \frac{k_1 E_T}{I_T} \tag{5.28}$$

Summing the homogeneous and particular solutions to this first-order differential equation, we obtain

$$\varepsilon_c(\tau) = \frac{E_T}{I_T} + A \exp(-k_1\tau)$$

Substituting the initial condition that at $\tau = 0$, $\varepsilon_c(0) = 0$, we obtain $A = -E_T/I_T$. Thus, the cumulative error function becomes the familiar exponential rise to the asymptote E_T/I_T:

$$\varepsilon_c(\tau) = \frac{E_T}{I_T} \left[1 - \exp(-k_1\tau) \right] \tag{5.29}$$

Differentiating Eq. (5.29), we obtain an exponential error rate:

$$\frac{d\varepsilon_d(\tau)}{d\tau} = \frac{d\varepsilon_c(\tau)}{d\tau} = \frac{k_1 E_T}{I_T} \exp(-k_1\tau) \tag{5.30}$$

Observation of Figs. 5.10 and 5.11 shows that although the exponential model of Eq. (5.30) approximately fits the overall behavior, there are significant deviations. First of all, many of the debug-rate curves show an initial increase during the first few months. Also in some cases there seems to be somewhat of a plateau in the middle of the debugging period. Musa also has analyzed error data which support the exponential assumption.[1]

Error-removal rate versus effort In the statistics presented in Figs. 5.10 and 5.11, one essential ingredient is missing, i.e., the number of people involved in testing and the extent of their efforts. Ideally, we might wish to measure this in terms of the skill of the programmers and the efficiency of their techniques. An easier and possibly satisfactory expedient would be to merely record the number of man-hours or man-months of work expended on testing and correction[2] and normalize both ρ and ε with respect to this factor. (Musa uses test time.) Thus we may

---

[1] Musa (1979*a*).

[2] The author is aware that personnel and months cannot be arbitrarily traded over a large range (see Sec. 6.3.6). The old joke that "one woman can produce a baby in nine months, but nine women can't produce a baby in one month" conveys the concept precisely. What we are referring to is a debugging effort which is sensibly staffed but in which the manpower varies by a factor of, say, 2 or 3 over the duration of debugging.

define

$$\rho = \text{errors/instruction/month} \tag{5.31}$$
$$\rho' = \text{errors/instruction/man-month}$$

which yields

$$\rho = M\rho' \tag{5.32}$$

where $M \equiv$ average number of programmers working on testing and correction during a month.

If we postulate that ρ' should be roughly constant for similar sizes and classes of programs, then we can postulate that the shape of $\rho(\tau)$ in Figs. 5.10 and 5.11 is dependent on the assigned manpower. Thus, we could explain a curve which initially increased and then decreased in several ways:

1. The underlying behavior of $\rho'(\tau)$ is constant, but initially only limited manpower was assigned and was gradually increased. Later in the testing, after significant progress was achieved, the manpower was reduced and assigned to other projects.
2. The underlying behavior of $\rho'(\tau)$ is exponential, but initially only limited manpower was assigned. Once the manpower built up to its peak, it was held constant.
3. A variant of explanation 2 is to postulate that initially it is reasonably easy to formulate tests which reveal a large number of errors, but it requires a large amount of time to *correct* these errors. Thus, with limited manpower and a few scheduled batch runs per day, the programmer may still *detect* a large number of errors initially but only correct a portion of these. Since in all probability only the corrected errors rather than the detected errors are scored, this explanation would yield a constant saturation error-correction rate for a period of time followed by an exponentially declining tail. The exponential tail in the error-correction rate would begin when the initial testing group (alone or augmented by reinforcements) reduced the total of the backlog queue plus the newly arrived errors below their saturation level. The above explanation implies that the time behavior of the number of detected and corrected errors could differ appreciably.

One may quantitatively introduce the concept of varying manpower into the exponential error-rate model of the previous section in a simple manner. If in Eq. (5.27) we include the fact that the detected errors should also be proportional to the manpower, we may write

$$k_1 = k_2 M \tag{5.33}$$

where k_2 is a new constant of proportionality. Thus Eqs. (5.29) and (5.30) become

$$\varepsilon_c(\tau) = \frac{E_T}{I_T}[1 - \exp(-k_2 M_\tau)] \tag{5.34}$$

$$\frac{d\varepsilon_c(\tau)}{d\tau} = \frac{k_2 M E_T}{I_T}\exp(-k_2 M_\tau) \tag{5.35}$$

From Eq. (5.34) we see that the $\varepsilon(\tau)$ curve has the same basic behavior and asymptote but the time constant is now a product of two constants. The $\rho(\tau)$ curve experiences both amplitude and decay rate changes when M is changed.

Further investigation of the validity of the models proposed in this section requires a detailed set of error statistics which include the difference (if any) between error-detection and -correction rate and the manpower assigned as a function of time. Unfortunately, few such data have appeared in the open literature. Itoh (in Itoh and Izutani, 1973) cites values of 1.24, 2.85, and 11.87 man-hours per error for the module, component, and system test phases.

Collection of man-hour data should not be too difficult if advance planning is done. In most cases each programming project is assigned a work number, and the personnel fill out weekly time cards indicating how they have spent their time during the month.[1] Such data should be readily available in business records. In fact, if one were planning to collect data on a programming project, it would be valuable to assign different work numbers to the design, coding, testing, debugging, etc., phases so that there would be semiautomatic data analysis of man-hours.

5.6.4 Estimating the Number of Residual Errors E_T

In the preceding sections we have developed several models to explain how the number of remaining errors in a program decreases as debugging progresses. All these models contain the constant E_T; thus in this section we explore methods for estimating the value of this constant while debugging is in progress. Obviously, the utility of the methods depends on how early in the integration-test phase a reliable estimate of E_T can be obtained.

Seeding models The so-called bug seeding method is an outgrowth of a technique used to estimate the number of animals in a wildlife population or fish in a pond.[2] The technique is best illustrated by discussing the estimation of the number of a specific species of fish, say, bass, N, in a small pond which contains no other type of fish. We begin by procuring a suitable number of bass, N_t, from a fish hatchery and tag each one with a means of identification which will remain reliably attached for the length of the measurement period. The N_t tagged fish are then added to the N original fish and allowed to mix and disperse. After an appropriate number of days a sample is fished from the lake (by hook or net) and separated into n_t tagged bass and n untagged bass. If we assume that there was no difference in the dispersion or ease of catching of the tagged and untagged fish,

---

[1]Of course, one would occasionally have to correct the data for "loading effects," i.e., the week when all programmers in the shop who are temporarily without project numbers charge to project Z—the big program with money.
[2]Bailey (1951); Feller (1957).

then we can set up the following equation, which equates the proportions of tagged fish in the fished sample to the original fraction seeded.[1]

$$\frac{N_t}{N + N_t} = \frac{n_t}{n + n_t} \qquad (5.36)$$

We may solve the above equation for N in terms of the known quantities N_t, n, and n_t, yielding the following:[2]

$$\hat{N} = \frac{n}{n_t} N_t \qquad (5.37)$$

By direct analogy we may consider N to be the unknown number of bugs in the program at the start of debugging and $N_s = N_t$ to be the number of seeded bugs (unknown to the debugger). After τ months of debugging, the bugs which have been removed are examined by someone (other than the debugger) who has a list of the seeded bugs. This tester classifies them as n_s which come from the seeded group and n which were not seeded. Direct substitution in Eq. (5.37) yields

$$\hat{N} = \frac{n}{n_s} N_s \qquad (5.38)$$

The possibility of seeding bugs in a program and of using this technique to measure the initial bug content was first suggested by Mills.[3] The results of the early experiments in this area were inconclusive for two reasons. First of all, it was difficult to make up realistic bugs. Consider the analogous fish problem of matching ages of the bass, not to mention the realistic situation where one has, say, three types of fish—bass, perch, and pickerel. Now one must also match the unknown ratios in seeding the tagged fish unless all types of fish are equally easy to catch. Also, are hatchery-bred fish as easy to catch as pond-bred fish? The second problem with the early seeding experiments was that the measuring technique of bug seeding was used to evaluate the effectiveness of code reading (as opposed to machine testing) as a means of debugging programs. Thus, the results of the two experiments somewhat clouded a crisp evaluation of either.

A different approach was suggested by Hyman (1973) which circumvented the problem of seeding bugs. He proposed that one employ two (or more) independent debuggers to work on the same program initially. Suppose that it is estimated that debugging will take 4 months and that debugger number 1 is assigned to the program for 4 months (or the duration of the job). Debugger number 2 is assigned to the job for only one or two months at the beginning of the project. The two debuggers work independently, and after a few weeks the results of their efforts are evaluated by a third analyst, who estimates the number of program bugs N by a formula similar to Eq. (5.38) (to be derived below).[4] The

---

[1] See derivation in App. A, Sec. A.9.4, "Maximum-Likelihood Estimators."

[2] The circumflex above N is the standard statistical symbol meaning an estimate of the quantity.

[3] Ditto, Hurley, Kessler, and Mills (1970).

[4] For pedagogical clarity we speak of a third analyst, who could in fact be debugger number 1 or number 2 or both working together if only a single estimate is planned. For multiple estimates over a time period, a third person is needed to avoid destruction of independence.

estimates are repeated every few weeks, and when the third analyst is satisfied that the value N is sufficiently well estimated, the results of debugger number 2's work are given to debugger number 1 and debugger number 2 is reassigned. Now, after one-quarter to one-half of the project has been debugged, we have a reasonable estimate of the total number of bugs in the program, and knowing the number of bugs already removed, by subtraction we obtain the number of remaining bugs. In addition, only a portion of debugger number 2's findings duplicate debugger number 1's. Thus, debugger number 1 is able to rapidly incorporate much of debugger number 2's work, thereby producing almost a step change in the number of bugs found. In most cases the benefits should far outweigh the costs—one or two extra man-months of debugging time (the cost may be minor, zero, or negative if debugger number 2 really finds many independent errors which shorten debugger number 1's efforts). We now discuss a detailed development of the estimation formulas.[1]

In order to develop our two-debugger estimation procedure, we begin with the following notation:

τ = development time in months; interval 0 to τ_1 is the measurement period

B_0 = number of bugs in program at $\tau = 0$

B_1 = number of bugs found in program by debugger number 1 up to time τ_1

b_c = number of bugs which debugger number 2 finds up to time τ_1 which are common, i.e., in set B_1

b_I = number of bugs which programmer number 2 finds up to time τ_1 which are independent, i.e., not in set B_1

$B_2 = b_c + b_I$ = number of bugs found in program by debugger number 2 up to time τ_1

If we really believe that the bugs we would seed in a bug seeding experiment are identical to the indigenous bugs, then instead of seeding, we could merely locate a certain number of bugs and tag them (identify them). Of course the problem here is that much work must transpire in order to identify a group of bugs. Since it should not matter which set of bugs we choose as the tagged set (as long as they are representative), we should be able to treat the identified set as if they were a tagged set of bugs. In order to proceed, we must make some fundamental assumptions, which we will state as hypotheses:

Bug characteristics unchanged as debugging proceeds When a large program is debugged, the bugs found during the first several weeks (months) are representative of the total bug population.

Independent debugging results in similar programs When two independent debuggers work on a large program, the evolution of the program is such that the differences between their two versions are small enough that they can be neglected.

---

[1]Shooman (1973c); Rudner (1976).

Common bugs versus representative When two independent debuggers work on a large program, the bugs which they find in common are representative of the total population.

Assuming that the above hypotheses are valid, we can treat the quantity B_1 as if it were the seeded group N_s in Eq. (5.38). Similarly, b_c becomes n_s and B_2 becomes n. Substituting these quantities in Eq. (5.38) and solving for the original number of bugs $B_0 = N$ yields

$$\hat{B}_0 = \frac{B_2}{b_c} B_1 \tag{5.39}$$

We can even derive an approximate expression for the variance of B_0. Suppose that the values of B_1 and B_2 are fixed; i.e., we agree to continue the work of both of our debuggers until the values B_1 and B_2 are obtained. Then any variation in B_0 will be due to variations in b_c. We may guess the variance to be of the form[1]

$$\text{var } B_0 = \frac{\hat{B}_0^2}{b_c} \tag{5.40}$$

Substitution of Eq. (5.39) in Eq. (5.40) yields

$$\text{var } B_0 = \frac{B_1^2 B_2^2}{b_c^3} \tag{5.41}$$

This problem has been studied in more depth, and using the tools of modern statistical estimation theory, and an improved set of estimation formulas is as follows:[2]

$$\hat{B}_0 = \frac{B_2(B_1 + 1)}{b_c} - 1 \tag{5.42}$$

$$\text{var } B_0 = \frac{(B_1 - b_c + 1)(B_0 + 1)(B_0 - B_1)}{b_c(B_1 + 2)} \tag{5.43}$$

Since $B_1 \gg 1$ and $B_2 B_1/b_c \gg 1$, Eq. (5.42) reduces to Eq. (5.39). Similarly, in Eq. (5.43), since $B_0 \gg 1$ and $B_1 \gg 2$, the expression becomes

$$\text{var } B_0 \approx \left(\frac{B_1}{b_c} - 1 \right) \frac{B_0^2}{B_1} \left(1 - \frac{B_1}{B_0} \right) \tag{5.44}$$

If we further substitute Eq. (5.39) into Eq. (5.44) and let $B_1 > b_c$ and $B_2 > b_c$, we obtain

$$\text{var } B_0 \approx B_1^2 B_2^2 / b_c^3 \tag{5.45}$$

Thus Eqs. (5.41) and (5.43) agree if B_1 and $B_2 > 1$ and b_c is small. The reader is

---

[1] See the discussion in App. A, Sec. A.8.
[2] Bailey (1951); Rudner (1976).

Table 5.6 Means and variances—values for a hypothetical debugging experiment (where $B_1 = 55$ and $B_2 = 25$)

Common bugs b_c	$\hat{B}_0$	var $\hat{B}_0$	$\sigma_{\hat{B}_0}$	Accuracy of estimate: $(\hat{B}_0 - 100)/100 \times 100\%$
10	139	949	30.81	+39%
15	92.3	171.5	13.1	−8%
20	69	30.95	5.56	+31%

referred to the literature[1] for a further discussion of the estimation formulas; however, some numerical examples follow.

As an example suppose that there are 100 bugs in a program and debugger 1 finds 55 bugs and debugger 2 finds 25 bugs. If 10 of the bugs are common ones, substitution in Eqs. (5.42) and (5.43) yields the values given in row 1 of Table 5.6. Similarly, appropriate values are given in rows 2 and 3, respectively, for common bug counts of 15 and 20. A better picture of the meaning of these results is shown in Fig. 5.13, where the estimated values along with a ± 20 percent confidence band is plotted. Note how the value of $\hat{B}_0$ changes from an overestimate to an underestimate of the true value as b_c changes. Thus, we must be very careful in identifying b_c accurately since the result is very sensitive to b_c. As would be expected, the confidence bands close in as b_c/B_2 increases.

The hypothetical example implies that for the modest extra cost of a second debugger for a month or so, a fairly accurate estimate can be obtained for B_0. Clearly this depends on a large enough fraction of common bugs. The ability of this method seems promising, but it still must stand the test of practice.

The concept of bug seeding has also been suggested in a somewhat different context, as a means of evaluating the "detecting power" of a test program.[2] Two identical versions of a program at some stage of debugging would be prepared. The first would be seeded with errors and the second used without modification. The test program (really the collection of test data cases) is evaluated by testing both programs, comparing results, and evaluating the utility of the test based on the percentage of seeded errors found.

Regression models A common technique for predicting the future behavior of any time function is to plot the previous data, fit a curve to the data, and extrapolate the curve into the future. Often it is appropriate to model the data by a simple curve and use the method of least squares to determine the parameters yielding the best fit. This entire process has been formalized in statistics under the

[1] Rudner (1976).
[2] Girard and Rault (1973).

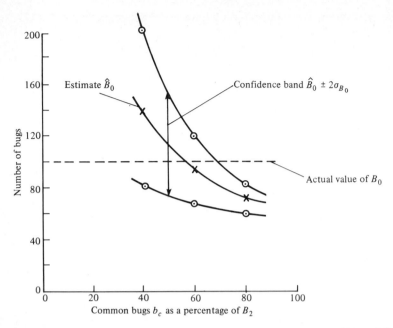

Figure 5.13 Illustration of the sensitivity of the estimation formulas, of Eqs. (5.42) and (5.43) to the ratio b_c/B_2, for the data given in Table 5.6.

name *regression analysis*. If a straight line is used as the model, one uses linear regression to find values for the slope and intercept parameters which best fit the data. If a polynomial model is hypothesized, then polynomial regression is employed to find the polynomial coefficients.

If one takes a set of data on changes in a program and plots the cumulative number versus time, one will obtain curves which are similar to Fig. 5.9. Ellingson (1967) has used regression analysis on the cumulative number of bugs to predict the number of bugs which will be removed at development milestones in the future. Coutinho (1973) has also attempted to investigate the predictive properties of cumulative error plots by plotting them on log-log paper. Nathan (1979) has used the concept of growth curves to model the improvement of software as errors are removed. More work on this approach is presently in progress.

It would seem that until a comprehensive model is developed of how bugs are removed, the above techniques may be of less use than the modeling techniques discussed in Sec. 5.7.

5.6.5 Error Generation during Debugging

The error models developed in Sec. 5.6.3 all were based upon the fundamental assumption that errors were corrected in the debugging process but no new ones were introduced. Thus, the number of errors must start at some initial value, which we called E_T, and be monotonically nonincreasing (i.e., decreasing or constant). The concept was that after sufficient debugging, the number of errors removed would approach the total number of errors originally present; thus the notation E_T was adopted. In practice, the debugging process is an imperfect one. Thus, a certain amount of generation of errors is associated with any debugging procedure. Therefore, the total number of errors does not remain a constant. Some of the ways in which errors may be generated are:

1. A typographical error may arise, invalidating the result of an error correction.
2. The correction may be based upon faulty analysis; thus complete error removal is not accomplished.
3. The correction is accomplished; however, it is accompanied by the creation of a new error.

Model for generated errors Depending upon the efficiency of debugging, the error-generation rate could be greater than, equal to, or less than the error-correction rate. The resulting error behavior in the three cases is shown qualitatively in Fig. 5.14. Note that Fig. 5.14*a* is the case where there is no error generation

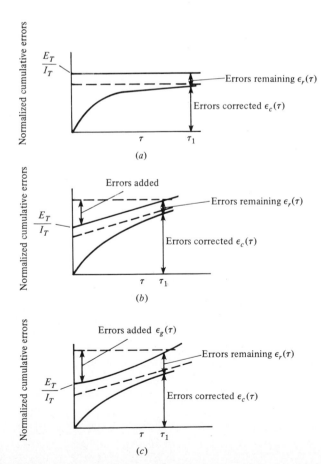

Figure 5.14 Cumulative errors debugged versus months of debugging: (*a*) approaching equilibrium, horizontal asymptote, no generation of new errors; (*b*) approaching equilibrium, generation rate of new errors equal to error-removal rate; (*c*) diverging process, generation rate of new errors exceeding error-removal rate.

(compare Fig. 5.12). The time τ_1 is when debugging stops. Note that the number of errors remaining is greater than zero in each case.

Error-balance equation We wish to develop a set of equations which will describe the three cases given in Fig. 5.14. We begin by writing a difference equation for the number of errors in the program,[1] which is a generalization of Eq. (5.21):

Errors present at time τ_i = errors present at time τ_{i-1}

$$+ \text{errors generated in the interval } (\tau_i - \tau_{i-1})$$

$$- \text{errors removed in the interval } (\tau_i - \tau_{i-1})$$

If we let

$$E_g(\tau_i, \tau_{i-1}) = \text{number of errors generated in the interval } (\tau_i - \tau_{i-1})$$

$$E_d(\tau_i, \tau_{i-1}) = \text{number of errors detected in the interval } (\tau_i - \tau_{i-1})$$

$$E_c(\tau_i, \tau_{i-1}) = \text{number of errors corrected in the interval } (\tau_i - \tau_{i-1})$$

then the number of errors remaining in a program at time τ_i, $E_r(\tau_i)$, is given by the following difference equation:

$$E_r(\tau_i) = E_r(\tau_{i-1}) + E_g(\tau_i, \tau_{i-1}) - E_c(\tau_i, \tau_{i-1}) \tag{5.46}$$

Conversion of the above difference equation to a differential equation is performed by grouping terms, dividing both sides by $(\tau_i - \tau_{i-1}) \equiv \Delta\tau$, and taking limits:

$$\lim_{\Delta\tau \to 0} \frac{E_r(\tau_i) - E_r(\tau_{i-1})}{\Delta\tau} = \lim_{\Delta\tau \to 0} \frac{E_g(\tau_i, \tau_{i-1})}{\Delta\tau} - \lim_{\Delta\tau \to 0} \frac{E_c(\tau_i, \tau_{i-1})}{\Delta\tau} \tag{5.47}$$

The left-hand side of Eq. (5.47) is recognized as the rate of change of errors remaining, i.e., the derivative of E_r with respect to τ. The right-hand side is composed of two terms which, as the limit is approached, become the rates of error generation and correction, respectively. The notation for error rates is given below.

$$r_g(\tau_i) \equiv \text{generation rate of new errors at time } \tau_i$$

$$r_c(\tau_i) \equiv \text{correction rate of errors at time } \tau_i$$

$$r_d(\tau_i) \equiv \text{detection rate of errors at time } \tau_i$$

Using the above definitions, Eq. (5.47) becomes

$$\frac{dE_r(\tau)}{d\tau} = r_g(\tau) - r_c(\tau) \tag{5.48}$$

(See Eq. (5.18).) In Eq. (5.48) the term accounting for error generation includes all the cases discussed previously which are created by debugging changes.

[1]Shooman and Natarajan (1976a).

As in the previous models, we normalize the number of errors and error rates by dividing by the program size, I_T. We will proceed in a similar manner to normalize Eq. (5.33):

$$\frac{E_r(\tau)}{I_T} \equiv \varepsilon_r(\tau) \qquad \frac{r_g(\tau)}{I_T} \equiv \rho_g(\tau) \qquad \frac{r_c(\tau)}{I_T} \equiv \rho_c(\tau)$$

$$\frac{d\varepsilon_r(\tau)}{d\tau} = \rho_g(\tau) - \rho_c(\tau) \tag{5.49}$$

Error correction- and generation-rate models The best way to formulate models for the generation and correction rates in Eq. (5.49) is to base them on a study of experimental data. Unfortunately, there are few data on this subject. Two fragmentary pieces of data are quoted by Miyamoto and Musa.

I. Miyamoto (1975) comments that he studied the types of changes made on a system during the system integration and testing stages. The 1245 errors were divided into four categories, one of which was "corrections for preceding erroneous debugging." The erroneous debugging category represented 8.5 percent of all the errors. He commented that experience within his company indicated that a 5 to 8 percent rate for erroneous debugging was observed on other projects. Also he postulated that erroneous errors are more commonly generated early in the debugging process, and that as the effect of the change control board began to be felt and as the programmers became more experienced (with the particular software?), the erroneous error rate decreased.

Musa (1975) observed that for the four systems he studied, the number of generated errors averaged 4 percent of the total.

Since no detailed data are available on the time behavior and dependence of $\rho_g(\tau)$ and $\rho_c(\tau)$, we will make a number of assumptions based on intuition and mathematical convenience. In general if $\rho_g(\tau) = 0$, we have the result shown in Fig. 5.14a. If $\rho_g(\tau)$ is modest in size and less than $\rho_c(\tau)$, we obtain the case depicted in Fig. 5.14b. The hopefully rare but disastrous case where $\rho_g(\tau) > \rho_c(\tau)$ is that depicted in Fig. 5.14c.[1]

A number of assumptions regarding the nature of the generation and correction terms were made on the basis of intuition regarding the dynamics of the debugging process and so that the resulting differential equation was mathematically tractable. The mathematical development appears in the references[2] and the assumptions and the resulting error equations are given in Table 5.7. A few selected cases are discussed in the remainder of this section.

---

[1] The author has spoken with a few experienced program managers who believe that some of their scrapped projects followed the behavior in Fig. 5.14c. Unfortunately, when the projects were scrapped, the error data were lost, and generally a new team of "super programmers" was brought in to start all over.

[2] Shooman (1973a); Shooman and Natarajan (1976a, 1976b).

Table 5.7 Error Generation Models

The basic equation is Eq. (5.49):

$$\dot{\varepsilon}_r(\tau) = \frac{d\varepsilon_r(\tau)}{d\tau} = \rho_g(\tau) - \rho_c(\tau)$$

$$\varepsilon_r(\tau = 0) = \frac{E_T}{I_T} = \varepsilon_T$$

Case	Equation	Solution
1. Generation and correction proportional to detection: $\rho_g(\tau) = \alpha\beta\rho_d(\tau)$ $\rho_c(\tau) = \beta\rho_d(\tau)$	$\dot{\varepsilon}_r(\tau) = \beta(\alpha - 1)\rho_d(\tau)$	If $\alpha < 1$, $\varepsilon_r(\tau)$ is a decreasing function. If $\alpha > 1$, $\varepsilon_r(\tau)$ is an increasing function.
2. No generation, correction proportional to detection, and detection is constant: $\rho_g(\tau) = 0$ $\rho_c(\tau) = \beta\rho_d(\tau)$ $\rho_d(\tau) = \text{constant} = \rho_0$	$\dot{\varepsilon}_r(\tau) = -\beta\rho_0$	$\varepsilon_r(\tau) = \varepsilon_T - (\beta\rho_0)\tau$ 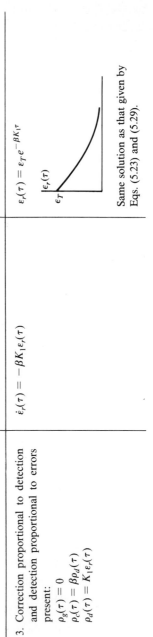
3. Correction proportional to detection and detection proportional to errors present: $\rho_g(\tau) = 0$ $\rho_c(\tau) = \beta\rho_d(\tau)$ $\rho_d(\tau) = K_1\varepsilon_r(\tau)$	$\dot{\varepsilon}_r(\tau) = -\beta K_1\varepsilon_r(\tau)$	$\varepsilon_r(\tau) = \varepsilon_T e^{-\beta K_1\tau}$ Same solution as that given by Eqs. (5.23) and (5.29).

4. Generation proportional to product of errors present and detection; correction proportional to detection:
$$\rho_g(\tau) = a p_d(\tau)\varepsilon_r(\tau)$$
$$\rho_c(\tau) = b p_d(\tau)$$

$$\dot\varepsilon_r(\tau) = [a\varepsilon_r(\tau) - b]\rho_d(\tau)$$
For $\rho_d(\tau) = $ constant $= \rho_0$:
$$\dot\varepsilon_r(\tau) = [a\varepsilon_r(\tau) - b]\rho_0$$

$$\varepsilon_r(\tau) = (\varepsilon_T - b/a)e^{a\rho_0\tau} + b/a$$
If $\varepsilon_T < b/a$, then $\varepsilon_r(\tau)$ is an inverted exponential.

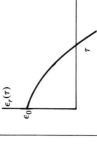

If $\varepsilon_T > b/a$ then $\varepsilon_r(\tau)$ is a growing exponential.

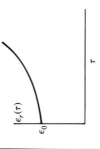

a. Let $\rho_g(\tau)$ be the sum rather than the product of terms:
$$\rho_g(\tau) = a_1\rho_d(\tau) + a_2\varepsilon_r(\tau)$$
$$\rho_c(\tau) = b p_d(\tau)$$

$$\dot\varepsilon_r(\tau) = a_1\rho_d(\tau) + a_2\varepsilon_2(\tau) - b\rho_d(\tau)$$
$$= (a_1 - b)\rho_d(\tau) + a_2\varepsilon_r(\tau)$$
Let $\rho_d(\tau) = \rho_0$
$$\dot\varepsilon_r(\tau) = (a_1 - b)\rho_0 + a_2\varepsilon_r(\tau)$$

Compare this with case 4. Note that the form is the same except that a_1 decreases the effect of b.
$$\varepsilon_r(\tau) = \left[\varepsilon_T - \frac{(a_1 - b)}{a_2}\right] \times e^{a_2\rho_0\tau} + \frac{a_1 - b}{a_2}$$

Table 5.7 (*continued*)

The basic equation is Eq. (5.49):
$$\dot{\varepsilon}_r(\tau) = \frac{d\varepsilon_r(\tau)}{d\tau} = \rho_g(\tau) - \rho_c(\tau)$$
$$\varepsilon_r(\tau = 0) = \frac{E_T}{I_T} = \varepsilon_T$$

Case	Equation	Solution
5. Generation proportional to number of errors present; correction either manpower- or detection-limited: $$\rho_g(\tau) = a_1\varepsilon_r(\tau)$$ $$\rho_c(\tau) = \begin{cases} b_1 \text{ for } \varepsilon_r(\tau) > \varepsilon_1 \\ b_2\varepsilon_r(\tau) \text{ for } \varepsilon_r(\tau) \le \varepsilon_1 \end{cases}$$	$$\dot{\varepsilon}_r(\tau) = -b_1 + a_1\varepsilon_r(\tau)$$ for $\varepsilon_r(\tau) > \varepsilon_1$ $$\dot{\varepsilon}_r(\tau) = -b_2\varepsilon_r(\tau) + a_1\varepsilon_r(\tau)$$ for $\varepsilon_r(\tau) \le \varepsilon_1$	If $\varepsilon_r(\tau) > \varepsilon_1$, $$\varepsilon_r(\tau) = (\varepsilon_T - b_1/a_1)e^{a_1\tau} + \frac{b_1}{a_1}$$ (Same solution form as case 4) If $\varepsilon_r(\tau) \le \varepsilon_1$, $$\varepsilon_r(\tau) = \varepsilon_1\exp[(a_1 - b_2)(\tau - \tau_1)]$$ (i) If $1 < b_2/a_1$, then $\varepsilon_r(\tau)$ decays exponentially. (ii) If $1 > b_2/a_1$, then $\varepsilon_r(\tau)$ oscillates as shown in Fig. 5.16c.
a. Let $$\rho_g(\tau) = c_1\rho_c(\tau)$$ $$\rho_c(\tau) = \begin{cases} b_1 \text{ for } \varepsilon_r(\tau) > \varepsilon_1 \\ b_2\varepsilon_r(\tau) \text{ for } \varepsilon_r(\tau) \le \varepsilon_1 \end{cases}$$	$$\dot{\varepsilon}_r(\tau) = c_1\rho_c(\tau) - \rho_c(\tau)$$ For $\varepsilon_r(\tau) > \varepsilon_1$. $$= (c_1 - 1)\rho_c(\tau) = (c_1 - 1)b_1$$ Normally $0 \le c_1 \le 1$. Therefore we rewrite $$\dot{\varepsilon}_r(\tau) = -(1 - c_1)b_1$$ for $\varepsilon_r(\tau) \le \varepsilon_1$. $$\rho_c(\tau) = b_2\varepsilon_r(\tau)$$ $$\dot{\varepsilon}_r(\tau) = (c_1 - 1)\rho_c(\tau)$$ $$= (c_1 - 1)b_2\varepsilon_r(\tau)$$ $$= -(1 - c_1)b_2\varepsilon_r(\tau)$$	$$\varepsilon_r(\tau) > \varepsilon_1$$ $$\varepsilon_r(\tau) = \varepsilon_1 - (c_1 - 1)b_1\tau$$ $$\varepsilon_r(\tau) \le \varepsilon_1$$ $$\varepsilon_r(\tau) = \varepsilon_1\exp[-(1 - c_1)b_2(\tau - \tau_1)]$$ (Same form as case 5)

Generation proportional to errors present and detection rate The hypothesis of case 4 of Table 5.7 assumes that generation of new errors is a function of not only the detection rate, but also the number of remaining errors. Clearly, the larger the number of detected errors, the greater the number of changes required, and in this case the probability of creating an error increases. Also, each time we make a change there is a chance that this will interact with existing errors, thus creating new errors. Assuming generation is a simple product of these two functions and correction is proportional to detection,

$$\rho_g(\tau) = a\varepsilon_r(\tau)\rho_d(\tau) \tag{5.50}$$

$$\rho_c(\tau) = b\rho_d(\tau) \tag{5.51}$$

where a and b are proportionality constants.

Substituting Eqs. (5.50) and (5.51) into Eq. (5.49), we obtain

$$\frac{d\varepsilon_r(\tau)}{d\tau} = \dot{\varepsilon}_r(\tau) = a\varepsilon_r(\tau)\rho_d(\tau) - b\rho_d(\tau) \tag{5.52}$$

If we make the further assumption that the detection rate is a constant, ρ_0, Eq. (5.52) becomes

$$\dot{\varepsilon}_r(\tau) = a\varepsilon_r(\tau)\rho_0 - b\rho_0 \tag{5.53}$$

Equation (5.53) can be readily solved by taking Laplace transforms or by classical differential equation theory, yielding

$$\varepsilon_r(\tau) = (\varepsilon_T - b/a)e^{a\rho_0\tau} + b/a \tag{5.54}$$

where $\qquad \varepsilon_r(\tau = 0) \equiv \varepsilon_T$

The behavior of Eq. (5.54) depends upon the relative values of ε_T and b/a. Since the probability that ε_T is exactly equal to b/a is very low, we are left essentially with two possibilities. If $\varepsilon_T > b/a$, then $\varepsilon_r(\tau)$ builds up exponentially. If $\varepsilon_T < b/a$, the number of errors decreases and becomes negative for large τ. The two cases are shown in Fig. 5.15.

The fact that the number of errors can become negative has no physical meaning. Thus, this model leads to a contradiction. Either the initial assumption and the model are valid only for a short time period, or our initial assumptions were wrong.

A different form for the correction term in Eq. (5.51) can be developed if we assume that the correction rate is proportional to the detection rate, which in turn is dependent on the debugging manpower. A particular form for the manpower dependency is discussed in the next section.

Manpower-limited model Discussions with program managers have led to the conclusion that the correction rate is sometimes manpower-limited. Thus, we postulate a new model where the correction rate remains constant during the early stage of debugging (manpower-limited). We assume that later in the program another stage is reached where the correction rate is proportional to the number of remaining errors. During both these correction stages we assume the error

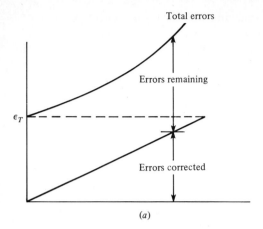

(a)

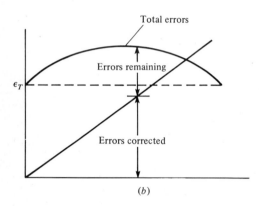

(b)

Figure 5.15 The model developed under the assumptions of case 4, Table 5.7. (a) $\varepsilon_0 > b/a$. (b) $\varepsilon_0 < b/a$.

generation rate is proportional to the product of the number of remaining errors and the number of detected errors, as in Eq. (5.50). The transition from the early-stage model of error correction to the later-stage model may be considered to occur at a critical value of the remaining number of bugs which we call ε_1.

These assumptions lead to

$$\rho_g = k_1 \varepsilon_r(\tau)\rho_d(\tau) \qquad \text{for all} \quad \varepsilon_r(\tau) \tag{5.55}$$

$$\rho_c = k_2 \rho_d(\tau) \qquad \text{for} \quad \varepsilon_r(\tau) > 1 \quad [\text{region 1}] \tag{5.56a}$$

$$= k_3 \varepsilon_r(\tau)\rho_d(\tau) \qquad \text{for} \quad \varepsilon_r(\tau) \le 1 \quad [\text{region 2}] \tag{5.56b}$$

If we make the further assumption that $\rho_d(\tau)$ is a constant, we obtain

$$\rho_g = a_1 \varepsilon_r(\tau) \tag{5.57}$$

$$\rho_c = b_1 \qquad \text{for} \quad \varepsilon_r(\tau) > \varepsilon_1 \tag{5.58a}$$

$$= b_2 \varepsilon_r(\tau) \qquad \text{for} \quad \varepsilon_r(\tau) \le \varepsilon_1 \tag{5.58b}$$

where

$$a_1 = k_1 \rho_d(\tau)$$
$$b_1 = k_2 \rho_d(\tau)$$
$$b_2 = k_3 \rho_d(\tau)$$

Substituting Eqs. (5.57) and (5.58a) into Eq. (5.49) we get for the early phase where $\varepsilon_r(\tau) > \varepsilon_1$ (called region 1):

$$\frac{d\varepsilon_r(\tau)}{d\tau} = a_1 \varepsilon_r(\tau) - b_1 \tag{5.59}$$

A solution of Eq. (5.59) is of the same form as Eq. (5.53):

$$\varepsilon_r(\tau) = (\varepsilon_T - b_1/a_1)e^{a_1\tau} + b_1/a_1 \tag{5.60}$$

If $\varepsilon_T > b_1/a_1$, the debugging is out of control and Eq. (5.60) indicates that the errors build up exponentially with time. On the other hand, if $\varepsilon_T < b_1/a_1$, the correction process is efficient and the errors reduce with time. Once the errors fall to the critical value ε_1, a transition takes place in the error-correction rate and substitution of Eqs. (5.57) and (5.58b) into Eq. (5.49) yields

$$\frac{d\varepsilon_r(\tau)}{d\tau} = a_1 \varepsilon_r(\tau) - b_2 \varepsilon_r(\tau) \tag{5.61}$$

Letting the time elapsed in reducing the number of errors to ε_1 be τ_1, a solution of Eq. (5.60) yields

$$\varepsilon_r(\tau) = \varepsilon_1 \exp\left[(a_1 - b_2)(\tau - \tau_1)\right] \tag{5.62}$$

Equation (5.62) gives rise to two cases, depending upon whether $1 > b_2/a_1$ or $1 < b_2/a_1$. If $1 < b_2/a_1$, then $\varepsilon_r(\tau)$ decays exponentially to zero as τ goes to infinity. On the other hand, if $1 > b_2/a_1$, then $\varepsilon_r(\tau)$ increases exponentially, thereby reentering region 1. A physical explanation for why the switch in regions may occur is that if the manager removes some of the personnel on the project prematurely, b_2 is thereby decreased. If it is later noticed that the errors are increasing, some personnel are brought back and a transition to region 2 will soon occur.[1] We thus can have an oscillating model.

It is convenient to categorize the models as

Case 1   The unstable model
Case 2   The controlled model
Case 3   The oscillatory model

The three cases are shown in Fig. 5.16 and summarized in case 5, Table 5.7. For a detailed analysis of these cases and a discussion of the results, the reader is referred to the references.[2]

---

[1]Brooks (1974).
[2]Shooman and Natarajan (1976a, 1976b).

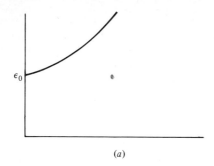

(a)

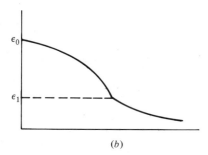

(b)

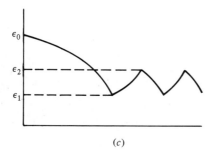

(c)

Figure 5.16 Remaining errors plotted as function of months of debugging. (*a*) Unstable model. Errors build up indiscriminately. (*b*) Controlled model. Debugging is efficient. (*c*) Oscillatory model.

5.7 RELIABILITY MODELS

5.7.1 Introduction

Reliability has for many years meant two related but distinct things. In general terms reliability related to the concept of dependable and error-free operation. The second meaning was the mathematical definitions given in Secs. 5.3.3 and 5.5.3. In this section we deal with models based upon the definitions of Sec. 5.5.3 and the error models of the preceding section. Some critics of mathematical software reliability models carp, "I don't have to be able to measure the reliability of a program to know how to improve it." This author would answer, "I agree, and perhaps for small problems that's good enough; however, I wouldn't want to tackle a big problem with one hand tied behind my back." Furthermore, although the achievements in the computer software field are very impressive, they have not in general been achieved in a cost-effective manner, and useful analytical tools are most welcome. Even though some of these models are less precise than we would like, they are of considerable use at present, and will continue to grow in accuracy, applicability, and usefulness.

System, hardware, and operator reliability The three major uses of software reliability models may be broadly categorized as (1) prediction, (2) comparative analysis, and (3) development control. In the case of prediction, let us assume that a good-sized hardware-software computer system is to be built for government or industry use. The user demands a certain system reliability and states it *quantitatively* in the contract by specifying the probability of error-free operation for a given time period, or the mean time between failures. The system contractor's job in the proposal phase is to predict (estimate on the basis of the preliminary configuration and specifications) the reliability for the hardware, the software, and the operator. Assuming independence, the reliability of the system is the product of the hardware, the software, and the operator reliabilities. Thus, the system reliability is as follows:[1]

$$R_{SY} = P(S \cdot H \cdot O) = P(S)P(H|S)P(O|S \cdot H) \tag{5.63}$$

Assuming independence of hardware, software, and operator failures,

$$P(H|S) = P(H)$$

$$P(O|S \cdot H) = P(O) \tag{5.64}$$

$$R_{SY} = P(S)P(H)P(O) = R_S R_H R_O$$

where

$$R_{SY} \equiv \text{reliability of the system}$$

$$R_S = P(S) \equiv \text{reliability of the software}$$

$$R_H = P(H) \equiv \text{reliability of the hardware}$$

$$R_O = P(O) \equiv \text{reliability of the operator}$$

A similar analysis of the system mean time to failure (MTTF) in terms of the hardware, software, and operator MTTF is given shortly.[2]

Clearly, to meet a system specification for the reliability, the hardware, software, and operator reliability must each exceed the system reliability by

[1] Where S, H, and O stand for the events in which the software, the hardware, and the operator perform without error, respectively, and the center point means intersection. For a discussion of the significance of independence and conditional probabilities, see App. A, Sec. A.3.

[2] With the advent of read-only memory (ROM), much software now resides in such devices and is called *firmware*. It is interesting that ROMs can exhibit two sets of failure modes. If the basic program a ROM contains has an error, it fails like software; and if the integrated-circuit chip fails, the firmware fails like hardware. The "science" of jargon took a big step forward when at a recent meeting people began to describe human operator procedures and actions as *skinware*.

enough that their product equals or exceeds the system reliability. Whether the contractor is to write the software personally or subcontract it, it is necessary to estimate the software reliability to see if the proposed approach can meet the specifications. Although prediction techniques are not precise, they can ensure that the proposed design is at least feasible in the reliability sense. Any shortfall in reliability encountered later should be corrected using standard improvement techniques. Failure to estimate the software reliability is a gamble. It may turn out well, in which case the software manager has performed as expected, and intuition and hard work have been substituted for engineering analysis. But if the intuitive estimates are mistaken and delays involving many extra man-months ensue, then the software manager will be held responsible for poor judgment.

Often the system reliability is specified along with the hardware reliability, with no mention of software or operator reliability. The reader should realize that this still represents an implied constraint on the $R_S R_M$ product. The following example is taken from a case history for a new product which was a process controller performing measurements in real time on a batch of samples and producing reports as output.[1] It also illustrates the problem of apportioning[2] the system reliability among the three failure modes.

The reliability goal set for the entire system was 500 h MTBF, although the rationale behind this choice was never fully investigated. The failure rates of the hardware, software, and operator must all be included in a prediction of system reliability. Unfortunately, the initial thinking excluded the software and the operator. An estimate was made of the computer hardware reliability, and after a few iterations with the minicomputer manufacturer's reliability group, an MTBF estimate of 630 h for the computer hardware emerged. Since this seemed to predict a modest safety factor, the matter was closed until much later, when questions about the software failure rate were raised.

How should the system reliability goals have been set initially? The author suggests that because of the lack of any other relevant information on the system, it is reasonable to require that the MTBF of the software be equal to the MTBF of the hardware. In addition, we might require that the operator MTBF[3] be 5 times greater than that of the hardware and software, in this case 2500 h. If hardware, software, and failures have a constant failure rate (exponential density function), and if all failures are system failures, then we can write (see Eqs. (5.14), (5.16), and (5.64)):

$$R(t) = \exp\left[-(\lambda_S + \lambda_H + \lambda_O)t\right] \tag{5.65}$$

$$\text{MTBF} = \frac{1}{\lambda_S + \lambda_H + \lambda_O} = \frac{1}{\dfrac{1}{\text{MTBF}_S} + \dfrac{1}{\text{MTBF}_H} + \dfrac{1}{\text{MTBF}_O}} \tag{5.66}$$

[1] Shooman (1979a).
[2] Lloyd and Lipow (1977), App. 9A, pp. 267–270.
[3] Since the operator manually loads the batch of samples and chooses the mode of system operation, there is ample opportunity for an occasional human error.

where λ_S, λ_H, λ_O = the failure rates of software, hardware, and operator, respectively, and MTBF_S, MTBF_H, MTBF_O = the mean time between failures of software, hardware, and operator, respectively. Substitution of MTBF values of 500, 500, and 2500 into Eq. (5.66) yields a system MTBF of 227 h. Based on the previously described hardware prediction, the 500-h goal for the hardware seems to be realistic and reachable. To be on the safe side, if we really hope to meet the 500-h and 2500-h goals for the software and operator, we should design toward slightly higher goals to leave a little safety margin to cushion us against estimation errors, unknown contingencies, bad luck, etc. One should then investigate whether the software and reliability goals are realistic by making predictions or obtaining data on predecessor systems or similar systems.

To illustrate the use of reliability models in comparative analysis, we assume that during the proposal or initial design phases, two or three alternative approaches are being considered. The choice will be made among these alternatives. In order to make an intelligent choice, as much engineering information must be gathered as possible about the different designs. One of the quantities to be used in the overall evaluation is the reliability; thus, estimates of the software, hardware, operator, and systems reliability of all the design alternatives must be made.

Last, reliability can be used as one of the tools for development control during the development cycle. If operational tests are made on the system and combined with a software reliability model, the reliability of the system under development will be an accurate and useful measure to judge the present state of development and to estimate how much more debugging is needed to reach an acceptable level of reliability.

After some thought about how to construct a software reliability model, two viewpoints emerge—the macro approach and the micro approach. In the macro approach we ignore the differences between types of statements, details of the control structure, etc. We step back and examine the number of instructions, the number of errors removed, and the overall details of the control structure and base our model on these features. Constants for the model can be evaluated from data on past systems as well as analysis of test data on the software being developed. In the case of the micro approach, a detailed analysis of the statements and the control structure is performed, leading to a detailed model structure. Most of the models developed to date[1] have been macro models, and the remainder of this section is devoted to a discussion of such models. The development will focus on how to use tests performed on the program to produce failure data and how to use such data to estimate the parameters of the reliability models.

---

[1]Twenty-four reliability–error analysis models are listed in the survey report "Quantitative Software Models," Data Analysis Center for Software, Rome Air Development Center, March 1979. See also Littlewood (1980) and Adams (1980).

5.7.2 Stochastic Model

The accepted approach to building a stochastic model is to first define the random variable of interest. In the preceding section the random variable of interest was the number of errors in a program. In this section our random variable is the time to failure of the software. More exactly, we are assuming that the software is first placed into operational use at $t = 0$. We only count operational time and exclude downtime for hardware maintenance and diagnosis, evening or weekend downtime, etc. When a system failure occurs, operational time stops and the failure must be diagnosed. If the failure is due to an operator error, the system is reinitialized, tested, and placed into operation again and the "operational time clock" is restarted. If the failure is due to hardware, the hardware is repaired or replaced, the system is reinitialized, tested, and placed in operation, and counting of operational time is continued. If the failure is due to a software error, we record the operational time as the time to software failure t_f. We can describe our probability model by defining a sample space and drawing theoretical conclusions; however, in some ways a clearer conceptual representation is obtained if we use the frequency approach to probability and talk about the outcome of hypothetical (or real) experiments.

Suppose we place 1000 identical systems into operation and carefully monitor their operational times as described above. If we wait long enough, we will record at least one software failure of every system. If we consider the sequence of times to first failure of the 1000 systems, we have $t_{f1}, t_{f2} \dots t_{f1000}$. We can then plot a histogram (frequency distribution) of these failure times. If we let the number of systems monitored approach infinity, the normalized version (the vertical axis representing the fraction of systems in the interval) approaches the probability density function.

Another way of hypothetically gathering the sequence of failure times is to consider a single system which is put in operation at $t = 0$ and allowed to run until the first software failure. This time is recorded as t_{f1}, *no software corrections are made*, the system is reinitialized, and operation continues.[1] Once the second software failure occurs, we record the time between failures as t_{f2} and continue until t_{f1000} is obtained. We can now treat the data as was done above. Of course in a real system whenever we find a software bug, we record it, and most of these are fixed in the field, or fixes are accumulated for the next release. Thus as bugs are fixed, the time between failures should steadily increase. Data accrued over $2\frac{1}{2}$ years on 478 times between failures for two IBM 370/165 systems at Hughes Aircraft Company were analyzed.[2] The times between failure were recorded and average values reported over 6-month intervals (see Table 5.8). The MTBSF[3] over

---

[1] We are assuming in this hypothetical system that the set of events which excited the software failure have disappeared and upon reinitialization, the system resumes operation. Further discussions of reliability data collection and analysis appear in Sec. 5.7.11 and Sec. 5.9.

[2] Reynolds and Van Kinsbergen (1975).

[3] Although we can draw some fine theoretical differences, for practical purposes, the terms *mean time to failure* (MTTF) and *mean time between failures* (MTBF) are the same. For a definition of the mean time to failure (MTTF), see App. B.

Table 5.8 Variation in mean time between software failures (MTBSF) for two IBM 370/165 systems

	Second half 1972	First half 1973	Second half 1973	First half 1974	Second half 1974	Total 2 1/2 yr
MTBSF, h	7.69	7.98	8.97	11.51	9.04	8.86

Source: Reynolds and Van Kinsbergen (1975).

the first 6 months was 7.84 h, while over the last 18 months it was 9.84 h, or an increase of about 26 percent. Thus, even though the system MTBSF slowly improved, the number of software corrections made in the field was probably small. Additional data on MTTF for software can be found in several of Musa's papers.[1]

5.7.3 A Bug-Proportional (Macro) Model

Introduction In the following sections we will discuss micro reliability models. A simple semimicro model will be presented which involves measurement or estimation of a number of system parameters, as well as the necessity for decomposition of the program. Often we are at the early estimation stages in program design, and have too vague a knowledge of the final software to structure such a model. There are also times when in even a later stage of program development we may be unwilling or unable to formulate a micro model. Thus, macro models of the type discussed in this section are of great practical importance.

The basic philosophy behind this macro model is that software errors are caused by the uncovering of residual bugs in a program. Furthermore, if we consider all bugs to be alike, the program to be large and essentially nonrepetitive in nature, then the failure rate should be proportional to the number of remaining bugs. We use the models of Sec. 5.6 to describe the number of remaining errors and relate this to the failure rate, and then use classical reliability theory to complete the model. In order to compute the constants of the resulting models we use historical data, tagging techniques, or the results of simulated operation.

Basic assumptions We assume that operational software errors occur because of the occasional traversing of a portion of the program in which a hidden software bug is lurking. We begin by writing an expression for the probability that a bug is encountered in the time interval Δt after t successful hours of operation: $z(t)\,\Delta t$ (see Eq. (5.6)). We make the assumption that this probability is proportional to the fractional number of remaining bugs $\varepsilon_r(\tau)$. (See Eq. (5.23).)[2]

---

[1] Musa (1975), Fig. 4; Hamilton and Musa (1978); Musa (1979).
[2] Musa (1979) presents data which substantiate this assumption.

Thus, we obtain

$$P(t < \mathbf{t}_f \le t + \Delta t \,|\, \mathbf{t}_f > t) = z(t)\,\Delta t = K\varepsilon_r(\tau)\,\Delta t \tag{5.67}$$

$$z(t) = K\varepsilon_r(\tau) = K[(E_T/I_T - \varepsilon_c(\tau)] \tag{5.68}$$

where $\mathbf{t}_f \equiv$ operating time to failure (occurrence of a software error)

$P(t < \mathbf{t}_f \le t + \Delta t \,|\, \mathbf{t}_f > t) \equiv$ probability of failure in interval Δt, given no previous failure.

$K =$ an arbitrary constant[1]

Note that in Eq. (5.68) two time variables appear: first there is t, the operating time in hours of the system, and second there is τ the debugging time in months (or more generally, the debugging resource variable). Once the assumptions in Eq. (5.68) have been made, the reliability and mean time to failure functions follow directly from classical reliability theory.

Reliability model By combining Eqs. (5.68) and (5.13) and assuming that K and $\varepsilon_r(\tau)$ are independent of operating time t, we obtain for the reliability function

$$R(t) = e^{-[K\varepsilon_r(\tau)]t} = e^{-K[(E_T/I_T) - \varepsilon_c(\tau)]t} \tag{5.69}$$

For a fixed value of τ, $K\varepsilon_r(\tau)$ is a constant which we call γ for convenience.

$$R(t) = e^{-\gamma t} \tag{5.70}$$

Basically the above equation states that the probability of successful operation without software errors is an exponential function of operating time. When the system is first turned on, $t = 0$ and $R(0) = 1$. As operating time increases, the reliability monotonically decreases as shown in Fig. 5.17. We depict typical reliability functions for three values of debugging time, $\tau_0 < \tau_1 < \tau_2$. From this curve we may make various predictions about the system reliability. For example, looking along the vertical line $t = 1/\gamma$, we may state:

1. If we spend τ_0 hours of debugging, then $R(1/\gamma) = 0.35$.
2. If we spend τ_1 hours of debugging, then $R(1/\gamma) = 0.50$.
3. If we spend τ_2 hours of debugging, then $R(1/\gamma) = 0.75$.

The constants of the model must be determined as discussed in Sec. 5.7.6 to complete the model.

---

[1] In earlier work (see Dickson, Hesse, Kientz, and Shooman, 1972) an attempt was made to achieve a semimicro model by splitting K into two factors: K, an arbitrary constant, and r_p, the instruction-processing rate. This elaboration is not included here, since, to date, no data have been obtained to define or calculate r_p. (In some previous papers the proportionality constants were called C or K'.)

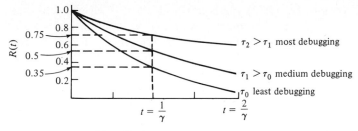

Figure 5.17 Variation of reliability function $R(t)$ with debugging time τ.

MTTF model A simple way to summarize the results of the reliability model is to compute the mean time to (software) failure MTTF by substituting Eq. (5.69) into Eq. (5.16), yielding

$$\text{MTTF} = \frac{1}{K\varepsilon_r(\tau)} = \frac{1}{K[E_T/I_T - \varepsilon_c(\tau)]} \tag{5.71}$$

In order to interpret Eq. (5.71), one must assume a model for $\varepsilon_c(\tau)$. For simplicity, let $\rho(\tau)$ be modeled by a constant rate of error correction ρ_0 (see Dickson, Hesse, Kientz, and Shooman, 1972, and Prob. 5.21 for other models); then $\varepsilon_c(\tau) = \rho_0\tau$ and solution of Eq. (5.71) yields

$$\text{MTTF} = \frac{1}{K(E_T/I_T - \rho_0\tau)} = \frac{1}{\beta(1 - \alpha\tau)} \tag{5.72}$$

For convenience we define normalized parameters

$$\beta = \frac{E_T}{I_T}K \quad \text{and} \quad \alpha = \frac{\rho_0 I_T}{E_T}$$

In Fig. 5.18, $\beta \times \text{MTTF}$ is plotted versus $\alpha\tau$. We see that the most improvement in MTTF occurs during the last quarter of the debugging. This is an extremely important point. If we have no model to guide us, we may expend our resources, patience, and credibility during the debugging process short of achieving our goals. Suppose that our budget allows $\tau = 0.8/\alpha$ months of debugging,

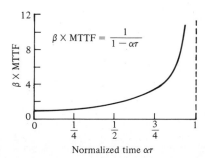

Figure 5.18 Comparison of MTTF with debug time for the constant-error debug-rate model.

which upon substitution into Eq. (5.72) yields a MTTF of $5/\beta$. If we could only continue debugging till $\tau = 0.9/\alpha$ ($12\frac{1}{2}$ more resources), we would achieve a 100 percent improvement, obtaining a MTTF of $10/\beta$. Of course if $\rho(\tau)$ is not constant, then other shapes of the MTTF versus τ curve are obtained, but all evidence the steep rise in MTTF with increasing τ.

One can qualitatively explain the shape of the MTTF curve given in Fig. 5.18. Suppose $E_T = 1000$ and during the first quarter of the debugging period we remove 250 errors. The difference in the MTTF displayed by the program with 750 residual errors is only 33 percent greater than that at the start (1000 errors), since MTTF is proportional to the reciprocal of the number of remaining errors (see Eq. (5.71)). Once we reach the last phase of debugging with 100 errors left, the MTTF has increased tenfold. Removal of another 50 errors provides another factor of 2 gain for a total increase of 20. Thus, removal of the same number of errors early in the integration process has much less effect on MTTF than when the removal takes place near the end.

Further examination of Eqs. (5.71) and (5.72) reveals that when $\tau = 1/\alpha$, the MTTF $\rightarrow \infty$. This is mathematically correct but not very satisfying, since we have postulated that zero errors is unreachable. If we assume that $\varepsilon_r(\tau)$ cannot be reduced below $\varepsilon_{min}(\tau)$, then at some point τ_1, $\varepsilon_r(\tau \geq \tau_1) = \varepsilon_{min}(\tau)$ and MTTF is fixed at $1/K\varepsilon_{min}(\tau)$. In fact, if we assume one remaining error, we might consider $1/K$ to be a sort of upper bound on the MTTF. This and other, similar assumptions are explored in the problems at the end of the chapter.

Experiment verification—Miyamoto's data The macro model developed above has been verified by two investigators in the literature. Isao Miyamoto (1975) analyzed the software errors accumulated on a 500-line real-time message-switching system developed between 1968 and 1970. He categorized the errors into five categories and observed 96 errors of the severest level during the integration and test stages. The final system exhibited a software MTBF of 396.5 h and a hardware MTBF of 480 h.[1] The growth curve of mean time between software errors which he calculated is given in Fig. 5.19 and compares very well with the shape predicted by the model in Fig. 5.18.

We can further analyze Miyamoto's data. He estimates that at the end of debugging, when the MTBF has risen to 396.5 h, there are 6 remaining errors and 371 have been removed (see Miyamoto, 1975, Fig. 7). The program size is not explicitly stated; however, we are told by the author that his system is a dual-processor one, with 512K of memory in each machine; thus we assume a program size of 500,000 instructions. At the end of testing, we conclude that Eq. (5.22) becomes

$$6/500,000 = (377/500,000) - (371/500,000)$$

From Eq. (5.71) we obtain

$$396.5 = \frac{1}{K \times 6/500,000}$$

---

[1]The system operated 13 hours a day; thus 30.5 (days between failures) $\times$ 13 = 396.5 (CPU hours).

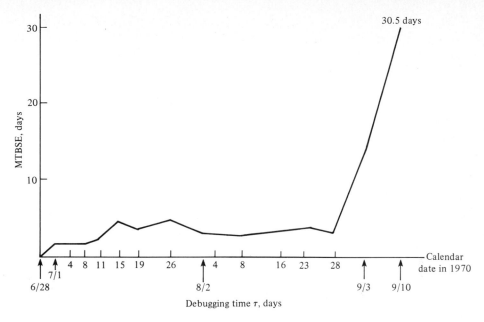

Figure 5.19 Growth curve of software reliability (mean time between software errors). *(From Miyamoto, 1975, Fig. 6)*

Solving for K yields a value of 210. If we compute the ratio 371/500,000 we obtain 7.4×10^{-4}. Note that this value is smaller than the ratios E_T/I_T quoted in Tables 5.3 and 5.4. However, we must remember that Miyamoto's data are for the *last few months* of integration testing. If we examine the literature[1] we find other low values of E_T/I_T for *certain situations*. In the case of early *field testing* of the No. 1 ESS ADF electronic telephone switching system, 135 corrections per month for 4 months occurred for the 250,000-word program, yielding a ratio of 0.0022. Also, the often quoted *New York Times* Information Bank program recorded 21 errors out of 83,324 lines of code for a ratio of 2.5×10^{-4} during *acceptance testing*.

The message of the above data analysis is clear: one obtains different parameter values in different phases and for different applications. Thus, analysts who are seeking historical data for estimation of reliability should search for examples which closely match their intended application (either in the literature or, better yet, within their own companies).

Experimental verification—Musa's data J. D. Musa (1975) develops a model very similar to the macro model just described and has applied it to four programming projects. Musa used the models to predict the progress of the projects at the outset and to manage the software as it was developed; then he compared the operational performance with the predictions. A plot of the mean time to failure

---

[1]Amster and Shooman (1974).

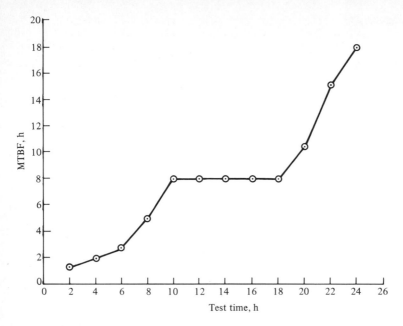

Figure 5.20 MTBF versus test time for project 1. *(Replotted from the data of Fig. 3., Musa, 1975)*

versus test time is given in Fig. 5.20 for Musa's Project 1. Again the overall behavior of Fig. 5.18 is verified; however, if we look more closely at Fig. 5.20, a plateau between 10 and 18 test hours is apparent. Note that Musa's ordinate is test hours rather than development days.

In many cases, we can readily appreciate that test time and development days will be roughly proportional to each other. The plateau in the figure is open to two interpretations. One might observe that the plateau might have represented a period during which essentially the same tests which were performed during the interval 0–10 h are rerun (as is done in regression testing). Note that if we eliminate the 10–18-h time segment, the curve increases monotonically. The alternative interpretation is that there are two types of tests which were run: the first type was successful in eliminating errors over the 0–10-h period and was continued for another 8 h without improvement until it was clear that no further progress could be made, and then at 18 h a new type of test was begun. However, neither of these two interpretations conflicts with the macro mode developed. Since the derivation of Eq. (5.72) depended on the assumption of a constant rate of error correction, so did the particular shape of Fig. 5.10. Clearly, in the case of an actual development, the error-correction rate would vary. The main features which all three curves (Figs. 5.18 to 5.20) have in common are a monotonically nondecreasing behavior (except for minor ripples) and a sharp rise near the end of the test or development time.

Musa's results strongly support the utility of such models, and the final predictions of the software MTBF correspond closely to the observed times. (See

Table 5.9 Comparison of measured and predicted MTBF, h

	Project 1	Project 2	Project 3	Project 4
Measured (during use period	14.6	31.4	30.3	9.2
Predicted (at end of test period) using maximum likelihood point estimate	19.1	35.2	24.4	12.3
50% confidence range	13.5–28.8	> 19.8	> 12.9	6.4–23.6
New or modified instructions*	19,500	6600	11,600	9000
Total program size	21,700	27,700	23,400	33,500
Number of programmers	9	5	6	7
Project length, months	12	11	12	10

Source: Musa (1975).
*Size given is the number of assembly or machine language instructions.

Table 5.9.) The errors between measurement and prediction were $+30.8$ percent, $+12.1$ percent, -19.5 percent, and $+33.7$ percent, with an average deviation of 24 percent. The reader is referred to Musa's paper for further details of his model and how he computed the results.

5.7.4 Other Macro Models

As previously discussed, there are perhaps a few dozen software reliability models which have been reported in the literature. In this section we will discuss a few of the more popular models and their relationship to the macro model introduced in Sec. 5.7.3.

History of software reliability models Most of the models associated with software reliability have appeared between 1970 and 1980. A few efforts predated these models. In 1967, G. R. Hudson described an error-removal model similar to that described in Sec. 5.6.[1] Also, Barlow and Scheuer developed a model for hardware system debugging which could also have been applied to software debugging.[2]

[1] Hudson (1967).
[2] Barlow and Scheuer (1966).

The first software reliability models were developed by this author and by Jelinski and Moranda in early 1971. In the fall of 1970 at a Northern New Jersey ASQC Conference, George Levenbach of Bell Labs alerted this author to the need for a software reliability model, which led to a proposal to the Polytechnic for a sabbatical leave to study this problem. Soon thereafter, the author began consulting for the U.S. Army on hardware and software reliability models for project SAFEGUARD. This work led to the paper authored by the author and his coworkers on the SAFEGUARD reliability model which was submitted in June 1971.[1] The author also began a 3-year consulting relationship at Bell Laboratories in early 1971 under Levenbach's direction working on software reliability models for SAFEGUARD and other Bell System projects. During a consulting visit to Bell Labs in Whippany the author heard Jelinsky and Moranda present a short overview of their model. The first open presentation of this author's model[2] and the Jelinski-Moranda model[3] was at a conference held at Brown University, November 22 to 23, 1971. To the best of this author's knowledge, the two models were concurrently and independently developed.

Failure-rate-based models As was previously stated, many software reliability models have been developed (see Data and Analysis Center for Software, 1979). Rather than attempt to be exhaustive, we discuss a few of the other models published in the literature, specifically those with features akin to the model described in Sec. 5.7.3. The author feels that this group of models is the most practical and should find wide usage in the field during the 1980s. For a comparison of several of these models, the reader is referred to the literature.[4] Specifically, we will discuss the Jelinski-Moranda model, the Schick-Wolverton model, and the Musa model.

Jelinski-Moranda model Jelinski and Moranda (1972) proposed a hazard function of the form

$$z(t) = \phi[N - (i - 1)] \tag{5.73}$$

where ϕ = constant of proportionality

N = total number of errors present

i = number of errors found by debugging time τ_i

Comparison of Eq. (5.73) with Eqs. (5.68) and (5.22) shows them to be equivalent

---

[1] Dickson, Hesse, Kientz, and Shooman (1972).
[2] Shooman (1972c).
[3] Jelinski and Moranda (1972).
[4] Schick and Wolverton (1978); Sukert (1977).

for

$$E_T = N \tag{5.74}$$

$$\frac{K}{I_T} = \phi \tag{5.75}$$

$$\varepsilon_c(\tau) = \frac{i-1}{I_T} \tag{5.76}$$

Equations (5.74) and (5.75) are merely notational differences and Eq. (5.76) is nearly the same and would be identical if

$$\varepsilon_c(\tau) = i/I_T \tag{5.76a}$$

Schick-Wolverton model In another paper Schick and Wolverton (1972) modify Jelinski and Moranda's model and assume that the failure rate is proportional to the number of remaining errors and increases with operating time t:

$$z(t) = \phi[N - (i - 1)]t \tag{5.77}$$

One rationale for postulating an increase in $z(t)$ would be if operation were viewed as a succession of different trials which gradually closes in on the remaining errors (sampling without replacement). This author disagrees with this assumption. On the contrary, he feels that $z(t)$ should decrease with t during development testing since latter errors are the subtle ones which take a long while to encounter in operation. Similarly, in most cases of large, intricate, well-tested real-time systems the hazard will remain constant once the initial field debugging of a new release is finished. The small number of subsequent "patches" generated between releases should not be significant. Failure will be caused by rare combinations of input data and path traversals, with the time between failures governed by an exponential distribution, yielding a constant hazard. Additional experimental data are necessary to choose among these hypotheses.[1]

Musa model Musa (1975) has developed a model similar to those previously described, has investigated the assumptions (1979a), and has collected extensive data on the application of his model and how it compares with subsequent field experience.[2]

He defines τ to be the execution time or central processor time used in testing the program (rather than months of calendar development time; see Fig. 5.20), and τ' to be the execution time of the program after release. The reliability model which he obtains is

$$R(\tau') = \exp(-\tau'/T) \tag{5.78}$$

---

[1] Musa (1979).
[2] Musa has submitted data on 16 projects to the DACS data repository. See also Table 5.9.

where T is the mean time to failure, which is defined by the expression

$$T = T_0 \exp\left(\frac{C\tau}{M_0 T_0}\right) \tag{5.79}$$

The parameters in the Eq. (5.79) are

$T_0 = $ MTTF at start of test ($\tau = 0$)

$C = $ ratio of equivalent operating time to test time

$M_0 = $ number of failures which must occur to reveal all errors ($M_0 = E_T$)

$\tau' = C\tau$

Note that the exponentially increasing MTTF given in Eq. (5.79) roughly matches the shape of Fig. 5.18. The MTTF given in Eq. (5.79) is equivalent to an exponentially decreasing removal rate; see Eqs. (5.30), (5.68), and (5.71).

If we wish to compare Musa's model with the one developed in Sec. 5.7.3, we must account for the differences in the various time definitions. We begin by setting t equal to τ'; thus Eq. (5.69) becomes

$$R(\tau') = \exp[K\varepsilon_r(\tau')]\tau' \tag{5.80}$$

Similarly, the MTTF associated with Eq. (5.80) becomes

$$\begin{aligned}
\text{MTTF} &= \frac{1}{K\varepsilon_r(\tau')} = \frac{1}{K[E_T/I_T + \varepsilon_c(\tau')]} \\
&= \frac{1}{\dfrac{KE_T}{I_T}[1 - (I_T/E_T)\varepsilon_c(\tau')]}
\end{aligned} \tag{5.81}$$

Further, if $\varepsilon_c(\tau')$ is assumed to increase linearly as in Eq. (5.72), $\varepsilon_c(\tau) = \rho_0 \tau'$ and Eq. (5.81) becomes

$$\text{MTTF} = \frac{1}{\dfrac{KE_T}{I_T}[1 - (I_T/E_T)\rho_0 \tau']} \tag{5.82}$$

If we let $\tau = 0$, τ' also is zero, and from Eqs. (5.79) and (5.82) we obtain the initial values of MTTF. (Note $M_0 = E_T$.)

$$T_0 = \frac{I_T}{KM_0}$$

Thus, Eq. (5.82) becomes

$$\text{MTTF} = \frac{T_0}{1 - (I_T/M_0)\rho_0 \tau'} \tag{5.83}$$

If we compare the series expressions of e^x and $(1 - x)^{-1}$ we see that

$$e^x = 1 + x + \frac{x^2}{2!} + \cdots$$

$$\frac{1}{1 - y} = 1 + y + y^2 + \cdots$$

The first two terms are identical and the third term differs only by a factor of 2. Thus, Eqs. (5.79) and (5.83) will behave similarly over the range where

$$\frac{1}{T_0} \approx I_T \rho_0 \qquad (5.84)$$

One advantage of the Musa model is that it allows us to use actual test data rather than simulator data. The disadvantage is that the input stream is less representative of operation and in fact the constant C in Musa's model is introduced to compensate for this fact. Of course the introduction of C results in an additional parameter which must be estimated from past experience and historical data.

A micro model of a somewhat different nature based on bayesian statistics is developed by Littlewood (1980). He compares his model for goodness of fit with Musa's model and the Jelinsky-Moranda model (equivalent to the micro model of Eqs. (5.68) and (5.69)).

Other related reliability models based on other assumptions are discussed in the literature.[1]

We now turn in the next two sections to a discussion of how we can experimentally measure reliability and use these measurements to determine the unknown parameters K and E_T of the micro model given in Eq. (5.69).

5.7.5 Experimental Reliability Data

If we had just deployed a large hardware-software system for field use, we could monitor its reliability by carefully recording the operating time and documenting each failure in detail. Thus, we could obtain the times between failure. Investigation of each failure should allow one to classify all failures as hardware, software, operator, or unclassified. If we segregate the software times between failure and plot their average week by week, we will have a quantitative measure of operational software reliability. We would expect the operational MTTF to increase for the first month (year, in some cases) or so as software errors detected in service are removed, then gradually to level off to a relatively constant value. This is, of course, an after-the-fact evaluation of the software design and does not allow one to measure progress and/or need for improvement of the software design while it is under development.

---

[1]Lloyd and Lipow ((1977), Chap. 17); Littlewood and Verrall (1974); Goel and Okumoto (1978).

The earliest stage at which an entire system can be functionally tested is during system integration using the system simulator (functional test) program. If this test is performed at the beginning of system integration, the result will be a succession of very short runs and immediate crashes. Most software test personnel would instinctively comment that this is as expected since the system is still in "poor shape," and such a test should be delayed until the end when the system is in "good shape." A bit of reflection leads one to the conclusion that it is just this frequent crashing which leads to a quantitative measurement of the poor initial reliability.

We now focus on the test data and how they should be analyzed. The necessary information which must be recorded for each run of the system test program is how long the test ran, whether an error occurred, if the error is a software error, and the time of failure. Sufficient dumps and other documentation must be recorded for subsequent analysis in order to segregate errors into hardware, software, or operator errors.

There are n total runs, r of these represent failure, and $n - r$ represent success. The $n - r$ successful runs represent $T_1, T_2, \ldots, T_{n-r}$ hours of success,[1] and the r unsuccessful runs represent $t_1, t_2, \ldots, t_r$ successful run hours before failure.[2] The total number of successful run hours H is given by

$$H = \sum_{i=1}^{n-r} T_i + \sum_{i=1}^{r} t_i \tag{5.85}$$

Assuming that the failure rate is constant, we denote it by λ and compute it as the number of failures per hour:[3]

$$\text{Failure rate} = \lambda = \frac{r}{H} \tag{5.86}$$

The MTTF for a constant failure rate is the reciprocal (see App. B) of the failure rate:

$$\text{MTTF} = \frac{1}{\lambda} = \frac{H}{r} \tag{5.87}$$

Equations (5.86) and (5.87) represent the total system failure rate and MTTF.

Since we are interested in software failures, we assume that the outputs as well as dumps are carefully investigated for the r failures. Based on the above analysis, the failures are divided into r_H hardware failures, r_S software failures, r_O operator failures, and r_U unclassified failures. Hopefully, the unknown ratio r_U/r will be 25 percent or smaller so that most of the data are classifiable.

---

[1] In many programs the running time will not vary, and all T_i will equal T.

[2] We are of course assuming that the times t_i at which the program fails are carefully recorded or estimated in all cases.

[3] Shooman (1968), p. 476.

The software failure rate and MTTF are defined by

$$\lambda_S = \frac{r_S}{H} \tag{5.88}$$

$$\text{MTTF}_S = \frac{H}{r_S} \tag{5.89}$$

Based on the results of this occasional test we can plot λ_S and MTTF_S versus τ, the debugging time. Such charts should allow a quantitative measure of the progress in improving software quality. After τ_a hours of debugging we would have a measure of MTTF and $R(t)$, and by *extrapolation* of the curves, we could *predict* MTTF and $R(t)$ after $\tau_b > \tau_a$ months of debugging. Unless we knew the functional form of the variations in $R(t)$ and MTTF with τ and could determine an appropriate extrapolation scheme, accurate predictions would be limited to small excursions into the future.

5.7.6 Estimation of Macro Model Constants

The primary purpose of the software reliability models developed in the previous section is to allow early prediction of the operational software reliability which will be experienced after release. In order to use these models, we must be able to estimate the model parameters. If we are in the early design phases of a program (say, during the proposal phase), the only way to estimate the model parameters is to rely on past data. If we assume that a handbook has been prepared containing 25 to 30 different projects and their respective values of K and E_T, then parameter estimation during the design phase is possible.[1] We assume that each project in the handbook has a concise description of the project type, size, development philosophy, language, duration, reliability goals, etc. The analyst would then select two to four different systems which fit most closely and use these values to obtain an average estimate, a worst-case estimate, and a best-case estimate. A tabulation of some of the values obtained in the past for K and E_T is given in Table 5.10. The accuracy of such an estimation procedure depends on how closely we can match our new project to past experience (this depends on the number of examples in the data base and how well they are described), and some experience with such a handbook.

Until such a handbook or equivalent data base exists, we must forgo any but the most approximate estimates during the design phase and focus on parameter estimates made during development. For most projects the earliest stage at which appropriate error data exist is once configuration control is in effect. Since configuration control generally starts at system integration, this becomes the earliest point at which we can collect data and estimate the software reliability model parameters.

---

[1]Development of a software reliability handbook was planned in 1981 at the Rome Air Development Center but delays have occurred.

Table 5.10 Typical values of K and E_T for the reliability model in Eq. (5.69)

System description	K'	$K = K'I_T$	E_T	E_T/I_T	Comments
Collective experience during integration testing	—	—	—	10^{-2}	See Tables 5.2, 5.3
Real time message switching system, end-of-integration testing	4×10^{-4}	210		7.4×10^{-4}	Miyamoto (1975); see Sec. 5.7.3
No. 1 ESS telephone switching system, field testing	—	—	—	2.2×10^{-3}	See Sec. 5.7.3
New York Times Infor-mation Bank, acceptance testing	—	—	—	2.5×10^{-4}	See Sec. 5.7.3
Real time command and control, integration testing					
Software Package 1	6×10^{-5}	1.4	140	6.5×10^{-3}	Musa's data;
Software Package 2	4×10^{-5}	1.1	62	2.2×10^{-3}	see Table 5.8 and
Software Package 3	12×10^{-5}	2.8	40	1.7×10^{-3}	Shooman and Schmidt
Software Package 4	20×10^{-5}	6.7	55	11.6×10^{-3}	(1982)
Shuttle data proces-sing software, simu-lation testing	5×10^{-4}	1400	417	1.5×10^{-4}	Richeson (1981)
Real time process control system, early field testing					
Assumption 1	2×10^{-2}	1000	82	1.6×10^{-3}	See Fig. 5.21
Assumption 2	2.6×10^{-2}	1300	92	1.8×10^{-3}	
Assumption 3	1.3×10^{-2}	650	182	3.6×10^{-3}	

We assume that a simulator program has been run and that data of the type described in the preceding section have been collected. Since it is early in the integration phase, only a small amount of simulator data are available and use of an underlying model will improve the accuracy of the estimation process. As the project progresses, more data are available, and the variance of the parameter estimates should decrease and the resulting estimate become more accurate. If the hypothesized model is correct, then predictions using this technique should be superior to the extrapolation technique of the previous section.

Three different procedures have been developed for estimating the parameters K and E_T: a moment estimation procedure, a maximum-likelihood estimation (both discussed in Shooman, 1973b), and, last, the familiar least-squares method (Shooman, 1979b).

Moment estimates We restate the software reliability model defined in Eqs. (5.69) and (5.71) and assume the data collection and analysis of Sec. 5.7.5 has taken place.

$$R(t) = \exp\left[-K\left(\frac{E_T}{I_T} - \varepsilon_c(\tau)\right)t\right] \tag{5.90}$$

$$\text{MTTF} = \frac{1}{K[E_T/I_T - \varepsilon_c(\tau)]} \tag{5.91}$$

Note that if we assume a known program size and careful collection of error data, then I_T and $\varepsilon_c(\tau)$ are known values and only the constants K and E_T remain to be determined. These two unknowns, K and E_T, can be evaluated by running a functional test after two different debugging times $\tau_1 < \tau_2$ chosen so that $\varepsilon_c(\tau_1) < \varepsilon_c(\tau_2)$. We then equate the MTTF expressions given by Eqs. (5.89) and (5.91) at times τ_1 and τ_2:[1]

$$\frac{H_1}{r_{S_1}} = \frac{1}{K[E_T/I_T - \varepsilon_c(\tau_1)]} \tag{5.92}$$

$$\frac{H_2}{r_{S_2}} = \frac{1}{K[E_T/I_T - \varepsilon_c(\tau_2)]} \tag{5.93}$$

The above two equations allow us to solve for our constants. Taking the ratio of Eq. (5.92) to (5.93) and using Eq. (5.89) and removing our normalization,

$$\hat{E}_T = -\frac{\left[(\lambda_{S_2}/\lambda_{S_1})E_c(\tau_1) - E_c(\tau_2)\right]}{(\lambda_{S_2}/\lambda_{S_1}) - 1} \tag{5.94}$$

Once $\hat{E}_T$ has been computed from Eq. (5.94), we obtain $\hat{K}$ by substituting Eq. (5.94) into Eq. (5.92), and removing normalization.

$$\hat{K} = \lambda_{S_1}I_T/[\hat{E}_T - E_c(\tau_1)] \tag{5.95}$$

The "hats" above E_T and K in Eqs. (5.94) and (5.95) denote estimates of the parameter. Note that if there is no additional error removal between τ_1 and τ_2 so that $E_c(\tau_1) = E_c(\tau_2)$ and $\lambda_{S_1} = \lambda_{S_2}$, the numerator and denominator of Eq. (5.94) become zero; i.e., Eqs. (5.92) and (5.93) are no longer independent and the estimate fails.

If the operational tests are run k times during development, one can compute values of E_T and K for adjacent values of τ_i and τ_{i+1}. Thus one could plot a curve of E_T versus τ and K versus τ. If the assumptions inherent in the model are true, these curves should appear as statistical fluctuations about a horizontal line. Any apparent growth or decay with τ would indicate that a different hypothesis might be required and may suggest the appropriate functional form. Other appropriate statistical tests could be used to study the constancy of these parameters. Also the

[1]In Shooman (1973b), r was used to denote successes; thus the terms r and $(n - r)$ are interchanged.

k sets of data can be pooled using a best linear unbiased estimate (or other technique).[1]

In statistical terms, the evaluation of model parameters is called parameter estimation. Specifically, equating expressions as was done in Eqs. (5.92) and (5.93) is a form of the moment method of parameter estimation. Another estimation technique, maximum-likelihood estimation (MLE), can be used to develop a difference estimate.[2]

Maximum likelihood estimation One of the most powerful techniques of parameter estimation is the maximum-likelihood estimation (MLE) method, which is developed in App. A. The method begins by constructing a density function called the likelihood function $L(t_1, t_2, \ldots, t_n, T_i, T_2, \ldots, T_{n-r}; E_T, K)$. This function represents the probability of obtaining the observed results (time to failure $t_1, t_2, \ldots, t_r$ and times without failure $T_1, T_2, \ldots, T_{n-r}$). The best choices (optimum value) of E_T and K are those which maximize L. The details of how L is constructed and how it is maximized (by setting $\partial L/\partial E_T$ and $\partial L/\partial K = 0$) is given in App. A. The result is a pair of equations for $\hat{K}$ and $\hat{E}_T$. Given two tests, with r_1 and r_2 failures and H_1 and H_2 total hours, we obtain (see App. A, Eqs. (A.74) and (A.75)):

$$\hat{K} = \frac{r_1 + r_2}{\left[\hat{E}_T/I_T - \varepsilon_c(\tau_1)\right]H_1 + \left[\hat{E}_T/I_T - \varepsilon_c(\tau_2)\right]H_2} \tag{5.96}$$

$$\hat{K} = \left(\frac{1}{H_1 + H_2}\right)\left[\frac{r_1}{\hat{E}_T/I_T - \varepsilon_c(\tau_1)} + \frac{r_2}{\hat{E}_T/I_T - \varepsilon_c(\tau_2)}\right] \tag{5.97}$$

Although Eqs. (5.96) and (5.97) require numerical solution, as is often the case with MLE, most statisticians believe that MLE estimates are superior to moment estimates.[3] Furthermore, it is not too difficult to implement an iterative computer solution of Eqs. (5.96) and (5.97). In most cases a simple graphical technique will suffice, using a calculator for the computations. The first step is to solve Eqs. (5.96) and (5.97) to obtain starting values for E_T and K. Values of E_T above and below the starting value are substituted into Eqs. (5.96) and (5.97). The curves of K versus E_T given by both of the equations are plotted on the same axes and their intersection determines $\hat{E}_T$ and $\hat{K}$.

The MLE method also allows us to compute the variance of $\hat{K}$ and $\hat{E}$. Although it is difficult to obtain the exact variance of MLE estimators, the theory does allow us to approximate the variance. The approximations approach the exact values and assume a normal distribution as the number of failures r_2

---

[1] Freeman (1963), pp. 265–268.
[2] Shooman (1972a).
[3] Shooman (1968), Sec. 2.10; Freund (1962), Chap. 9.

becomes large (see App. A). For two tests we obtain

$$\text{var } \hat{K} \underset{\text{large } r}{\rightarrow} \frac{\hat{K}^2}{r_1 + r_2} \tag{5.98}$$

$$\text{var } \hat{E}_T \underset{\text{large } r}{\rightarrow} \frac{I_T^2 \varepsilon_r(\tau_1)^2 \varepsilon_r(\tau_2)^2}{r_1 \varepsilon_r(\tau_2)^2 + r_2 \varepsilon_r(\tau_1)^2} \tag{5.99}$$

If we have m sets of test data, we can treat the collection in several ways, as described in App. A. In most cases, the best approach will be to generalize the MLE equations for $m \geq 3$. This is done in the appendix, yielding

$$\hat{K} = \frac{\displaystyle\sum_{j=1}^{m} r_j}{\displaystyle\sum_{j=1}^{m} \left[\hat{E}_T/I_T - \varepsilon_c(\tau_j) \right] H_j} \tag{5.100}$$

$$\hat{K} = \frac{\displaystyle\sum_{j=1}^{m} \frac{r_j}{E_T/I_T - \varepsilon_c(\tau_j)}}{\displaystyle\sum_{j=1}^{m} H_j} \tag{5.101}$$

$$\text{var } \hat{K} \underset{\text{large } r}{\rightarrow} \frac{\hat{K}^2}{\displaystyle\sum_{j=1}^{m} r_j} \tag{5.102}$$

$$\text{var } \hat{E}_T \underset{\text{large } r}{\rightarrow} \frac{I_T^2}{\displaystyle\sum_{j=1}^{m} \frac{r_j}{\varepsilon_r(\tau_j)^2}} \tag{5.103}$$

Accuracy of the MLE estimates Of course the accuracy of the entire model is related to the correctness of the hypotheses that the number of errors remains constant and that the original failure rate is proportional to the remaining errors.

The next assumption is that the functional test program used is a reasonable replica of actual operation. Most probably the deviations from reality will be due more to omissions of possible events than to inclusion of extraneous or poorly modeled events, in which case the procedure discussed in this paper should yield optimistic values for R and MTTF. In addition, it is necessary to compute the correct result for each case used in simulation; thus cost limits the number of cases which can be utilized. Ideally, we would like to initialize each test run with randomly chosen values of the parameters and initial system state.

Another complication is that the functional test programs are generally a collection of tests with increasing severity, rather than a single program. In order to strike a balance between cost of testing and accuracy of the simulation, an intermediate test should probably be chosen. If we assume that diagnosed results and test times are available for all tests, then the problem arises of how to mix the easy and difficult test results with our "standard" test results. One suggestion is that this be done by deriving a heuristic weighting factor for test severity.

Another area for error is in the diagnosis of errors. If we are concerned over the unresolved failures r_U, as well as the accuracy with which r_S is determined, we might assign some uncertainty to r_S (for example 10 percent and bound λ_S by worst-case values (see Eq. (5.88)):

$$\frac{0.9\, r_S}{H} < \lambda_S < \frac{1.1 r_S + r_U}{H} \tag{5.104}$$

Last, we observe that the estimates of K and E_T obtained from Eqs. (5.96) and (5.97) depend upon the difference between $\varepsilon_c(\tau_1)$ and $\varepsilon_c(\tau_2)$. Those experienced in the analysis of software errors realize that because of looseness of the error-reporting process, inseparably mixed in with valid software errors are specification changes, minor documentation changes, no errors, etc. Thus, it is desirable that $E_c(\tau_1) - E_c(\tau_2)$ should be 10 or more to minimize the above effects.

Least-squares parameter estimates We continue with our discussion of methods of parameter estimation because the measurement of model parameters is central to the use of a reliability model in practice. The last parameter estimation method we will discuss is that of least squares. Although the MLE method can be shown to have more advantages in terms of speed of convergence to the correct answer, the least-squares method is the simplest to understand. In addition, the variance of the parameter estimates can be easily judged by visual inspection of how close the experimental points lie on the least-squares straight line.

We begin our estimation procedure by rewriting the failure-rate equation, Eq. (5.68). The failure rate is assumed to be a constant once we stop debugging; however, it decreases from one test interval τ_i to the next. We write $z(t) = \lambda_i$, and rearranging Eq. (5.68) we obtain

$$\frac{E_c(\tau_i)}{I_T} = \frac{E_T}{I_T} - \frac{1}{K}\lambda_i \tag{5.105}$$

Thus, a plot of $E_c(\tau_i)/I_T$ versus λ_i yields a straight line with an intercept of E_T/I_T and a slope of $-1/K$. Thus, one can plot the experimental values of $E_c(\tau_i)/I_T$ obtained from recorded error data versus the λ_i values obtained from Eq. (5.98). One can then choose the best straight line by eye or use least-squares estimation.[1] Most computer program libraries as well as advanced programmable calculators have programs for least-squares fitting.

An example[2] of the use of the least-squares fitting is given in Fig. 5.21. The data on error removals in the example were not carefully recorded, and three

---

[1] Shooman (1968), pp. 464–470.
[2] From Shooman (1979b).

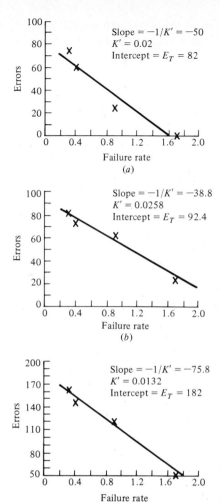

Figure 5.21 Least-squares fits of data to Eq. (5.106): (*a*) assumption 1; (*b*) assumption 2; (*c*) assumption 3. *(Using TRS-80 computer and Radio Shack Statistics Package No. 26-1703)*

different assumptions were made regarding the errors. Also, since I_T was not accurately known, Eq. (5.105) was used in the unnormalized form

$$E_c(\tau) = E_T - \frac{1}{K'}\lambda_i \qquad (5.106)$$

where

$$K' = \frac{K}{I_T}$$

The least-squares estimation was done using the statistics package for the Radio Shack TRS-80 computer.

Choice among estimation techniques Several techniques of parameter estimation have been presented. Thus, a question naturally arises as to which one to use. In the author's opinion the answer is all three. In most cases one will wait for weeks before enough data are collected. Thus, it is not unreasonable to spend half a day to a full day on the analysis of these data. Specifically, it is suggested:

1. The analyst should perform an estimate of I_T during the proposal or early design phase and estimate E_T as $0.005 \le I_T \le 0.02 I_T$. Estimate the token length n at the same time using the methods of Sec. 3.2.8. The value of E_T is estimated as $10^{-2}n$ using the constant of Table 3.16.[1] (If better historical data are available to compute the number of errors per token, then they should be used instead of Table 3.16). Also examine the values of E_T in Table 5.10. Use judgment to arrive at a value to use for E_T. (If the seeding-tagging model discussed in Sec. 5.6.4 is shown to be effective through future work, then this will be a preferred method to estimate E_T.)
2. Estimate K during the proposal or early design stages from Table 5.10 or your own historical data base by matching your project characteristics as closely as possible to the data base.
3. On the basis of the results of steps 1 and 2 compute a reliability and MTTF model. Assuming a value of ρ_0, the error removal rate, predict how long τ, the integration-test time, must be to reach the desired $R(t)$ or MTTF.
4. Consider revisions of design and development plan if the reliability estimate is below your goal.
5. During the course of the project repeat steps 1, 2, 3, and 4 if additional information becomes available.
6. When configuration control begins (generally at the start of integration testing) begin collecting accurate error data $E_c(\tau)$ and test data as per Sec. 5.7.5.
7. Use least-squares estimation first because it is easy and provides an overall feel for the accuracy of the estimate.
8. Compute moment estimates using Eqs. (5.93) and (5.94).
9. Compute MLE estimates and variances using Eqs. (5.100) to (5.103).
10. Compute a confidence interval or band for $R(t)$ and MTTF using the method given on pp. 484–486 in Shooman (1968).

It must be stated again that reliability estimates such as the ones described above are practical and have been employed in a number of cases with good success. Their accuracy will improve as more data such as those of Table 5.10 are collected, analyzed, published, and circulated in the open literature.

5.7.7 Binomial-Type Error Models

The models to be discussed in this section and the next are micro models; i.e., they look within the program and attempt to model the interaction of errors and

---

[1] We note that I_T is the number of equivalent machine code lines and each line of machine code represents two tokens, one operator, and one operand. Thus $10^{-2}n$ is equivalent to $0.005 I_T$.

program structure. The difficulties encountered in formulating a micro model and the need to define a probabilistic sample space also shed light on the basis and utility of the macro models we developed in the preceding sections.

Error categories We begin our discussion by classifying errors into four categories:

1. Syntax and typographical errors
2. Bad input data or data base errors
3. Bad instruction (logical)
4. Bad sequence of instructions and data

The majority of errors are of types 3 and 4; however, it is difficult to provide a theoretical structure (sample space) for these more complex cases. We begin therefore by considering errors in category 1 which is easier to treat theoretically. Assuming that we are writing our program in a higher-level language, the syntax checker will find almost every syntactical error, and it is only a very rare case which will not be detected. Similarly, many of the typographical errors will be found either by the syntax checker or by a careful reading of a program listing. For example, if we make a typographical (spelling) error in a keyword or a label name (which is the target of a GO TO or a subroutine call), an "illegal statement" or "undefined label" error message should occur.

An example is given in Table 5.11 of a typographical error which the syntax checker will not find. The program calculates distance in terms of acceleration and velocity, where nonlinear effects occur at high velocities. In statement d VELOC is spelled VELOX by mistake, and a logical error occurs which the compiler cannot find. (Of course a careful reading of the program listing should find it.) For VELOC > 10, statement d will be executed; however, a new variable VELOX is created rather than a new value being assigned to VELOC as was intended. Thus, at statement e the wrong (old) value of VELOC will be used. Thus, the majority of syntactical errors (human misunderstandings or mental lapses of the coder) and typographical errors (keypunch or terminal typing errors) can be found by the compiler or program reading. However, some will survive into later stages of debugging, and we will formulate a sample space (probabilistic model) for such errors.

Table 5.11 Example of an undetected typographical error

$a.$ ACCEL = 10
$b.$ VELOC = 10*T
$c.$ IF VELOC > 10
$d.$ THEN VELOX = 10*T − 0.1*T**2
$e.$ DIST = 5 + VELOC*T/2

Sample space for typographical errors We begin by recalling the model used in binomial sampling.[1] Suppose there are N balls in an urn, n of which are black and $N - n$ of which are white. If we pick a ball from the urn (blindfolded, and assuming a homogeneous distribution), the probability of drawing a white ball is $(N - n)/N$ and that of drawing a black ball is n/N. If we replace the ball drawn, mix, and draw again, the probabilities on the second draw do not change. The probability of drawing a white ball (or black ball) in j independent draws (with replacement) is given by the binomial distribution (see Eq. (A.21)). If the balls are drawn without replacement, the probabilities change. If on the first trial we draw a white ball, the probabilities on the second trial are $(N - n - 1)/(N - 1)$ and $n/(N - 1)$. On the other hand, if the first draw is a black ball, the probabilities on the second trial are $(N - n)/(N - 1)$ and $(n - 1)/(N - 1)$. The probabilities of k white (black) draws without replacement in j trials are given by the hypergeometric distribution.[2]

We now consider surviving syntax or typographic errors which involve only a single statement and will show up if that statement is executed in the program. There is a clear analogy between this problem and the binomial and hypergeometric models discussed above. Suppose there are N statements in the program and in the past we have found that the probability of an error on any one statement is q. We let the black balls be analogous to an error; then the probability of an error is $q = n/N$. Now if each test involves only a single statement, we can use the binomial distribution to *estimate* the probability of finding k errors in j independent trials (if $N > n \gg j$) as

$$P(k \text{ errors in } j \text{ trials}) = \binom{j}{k}\left(\frac{n}{N}\right)^k\left(1 - \frac{n}{N}\right)^{1-k} \tag{5.107}$$

where

$$\binom{j}{k} = C_k^j \equiv \begin{array}{c} \text{the number of} \\ \text{combinations of } j \\ \text{things taken } k \text{ at a time} \end{array} = \frac{j!}{k!(j-k)!}$$

This approach assumes that we know n from measurements such as those previously described or know q from historical data (see Amster and Shooman, 1974, for data on typographical errors).

In general we will correct the errors as we find them, so a better model is to use the hypergeometric distribution:

$$P(k \text{ errors in } j \text{ trials}) = \frac{\binom{n}{k}\binom{N-n}{j-k}}{\binom{N}{j}} \tag{5.108}$$

[1] See App. A, Sec. A.4.
[2] For a full discussion of the hypergeometric distribution see Wadsworth and Bryan (1960), pp. 59–63.

For large samples with few errors and few trials ($N > n \gg 2$) one can show that Eq. (5.108) approaches Eq. (5.107) (see Wadsworth and Bryan, 1960).

A sample space for logic errors in general If we consider the normal way in which a program is executed, more than a single statement is tested in each run. If during the first test s_1 statements are executed, we can still use Eq. (5.108) but must consider the number of trials j to be equal to s_1. On the second trial we execute s_2 statements, consisting of s_a statements which are the same and $s_2 - s_a$ statements which are different. Assuming we have corrected all the errors found on the first trial, we now have only n' left. We now use Eq. (5.108) again with $j = s_2 - s_a$ and $n = n'$. Thus we optimize our tests if we minimize the value s_2 by proper choice of a second test.

The model described above can be extended to type 2 data and data base errors, if we assume that the data are stored in the program at the beginning of operation and that each data value is stored in a separate location in memory. Then if those data errors are independent of the program errors, we can use Eq. (5.108) separately for data errors. If the two phenomena are mutually exclusive, we can add the probabilities.

The case of errors of type 3 or 4 is much more difficult to describe. In such cases the errors involve the interaction of several statements or data values, and the interactions are hard to describe and model. Research is currently in progress directed at formulating combinatorial error models such as those described above.[1]

5.7.8 Structural (Micro) Models

The universal approach for dealing with complex problems is to divide the whole into several subproblems in such a way that each subproblem is now of a size which can be comprehended and dealt with. Such a subdivision process is called *decomposition* and is difficult in the case of a computer program, for the following reasons.

Program analysis and decomposition One of the basic prerequisites in decomposing a program into logical or functional elements is the existence of techniques which can be used to analyze the program parts and how they fit together. The particular form of such an analysis is not of great importance as long as it decomposes the system into smaller functional entities which are easier to model (in a reliability sense) and as long as it clearly describes the logical interrelationships among the parts. The utility of such decomposition techniques is one of the fundamental reasons for the successes achieved in the hardware and reliability areas.

---

[1] For analysis of a related topic—dumping of data bases into storage to recover from catastrophic errors—see Vold and Sjogren (1973).

Three different decomposition techniques widely used in reliability analysis are (1) failure mode, effect, and criticality analysis (FMECA), (2) the reliability block diagram (RBD), and (3) fault-tree analysis (FTA). These three techniques are illustrated by the safety analysis of an automobile braking system given in App. B.5. The FMECA technique is essentially a table listing the possible modes of failure, mechanisms of failure, and consequences (related to system operation) of the failure. The FMECA can be used by itself to write a probabilistic expression for the system reliability (or suggest design improvements to increase reliability). More commonly, an FMECA is used as a prelude to constructing an RBD or performing an FTA. The RBD is much like a PERT graph or control-system block diagram.[1] However, in an RBD the cause-and-effect nature of the inputs and outputs is chosen to depict the logical topology of the diagram (i.e., if the system contains two elements both of which must work for the system to work, they are in series; and if the system works if either element works, they are in parallel). The success of the system depends on success of all elements along at least one path (from input to output) in the final RBD. An FTA focuses on the logical combination of events which can cause system failure. The diagram looks like an inverted tree with the top event (stump and trunk) representing system failure and the branches the causes of the failure. If system failure is caused by *either* of two hazards, the hazards (branches) are connected to the top event via an OR logic gate. If two hazards must *simultaneously* occur, then the connecting event is an AND logic gate. (The symbols are borrowed from digital switching circuit theory). The analysis is concluded by writing a probabilistic expression for system failure in terms of unions and intersections of the element hazards.

Unfortunately, no equivalent decomposition process exists in the software field in general. This is precisely the major design problem which software engineering faces and is one of the prime reasons why top-down modular or structured design seems to have so bright a future, as will be discussed in the next section.

Effects of structured and modular programming   One of the effects of structured or modular programming is to provide a framework within which to decompose the software. If we think in terms of a top-down control structure and a group of 25 to 100 statement modules, one already has the start of a decomposition analysis. The control structure itself provides the logical relations between modules, program paths, and system success. Similarly, in the case of a modular design implemented by callable subroutines and a calling program, the structure is well delineated. In fact, even if one module is callable from several points in the program, the effect of such shared use can be modeled easily.

The design representation which is used in the project will provide the detailed description of each element in the decomposition. As was pointed out in Chap. 2, detailed flowcharts are too large and complex to be of much use. With

---

[1] PERT is the acronym for Program Evaluation Review Techniques; it is discussed briefly in Sec. 6.3.2.

the advent of top-down structured design, the use of high-level flowcharts to indicate how the control structure interacts with the modules has become popular. Some analysts, however, prefer to use pseudo-code indicating only the main programming features of the section to be written. Once pseudo-code or a flowchart is developed, it is used as the basis of decomposition and analysis.

Path decomposition model The decomposition model which will be proposed in this section is based upon several assumptions. We first assume that the program has been designed using a structured or modular philosophy. As a result, there emerges a natural structure of the program which can be described as consisting of a number of paths, cases, parts, modules, or subprograms. The decomposition focuses upon this natural structure. In general we will use the term *paths* from now on as a generic term to designate the paths, cases, parts, modules, subprograms, or any other natural substructures. We also assume that the majority of the paths are independent of each other. (One could probably tolerate some type of limited dependence in the model if it could be easily modeled or shown to have a negligible effect on the numerical results.)

The decomposition model[1] will be developed from the probabilistic viewpoint of relative frequency. We will hypothesize a sequence of tests which either uncover a bug (failure) or run to completion without uncovering a bug (success). We begin our development of the model by defining the following variables and parameters:

N = number of tests

i = number of software paths (cases, parts, modules, etc.)

t_i = time to run case i $\left(\text{if time is not deterministic we can substitute the mean value of } t_i, \bar{t_i}\right)$

q_i = probability of error on each run of case i (probability of no error $p_i = 1 - q_i$)

f_i = frequency with which case i is run

n_f = total number of failures in N tests

H = total cumulative test time, h $\left(\text{see Eq. } (5.85)\right)$

Note that in the above set of definitions we have defined N as the number of tests. Thus, we are modeling actual or simulated operation by a succession of N tests—path traversals—of the system. We also assume that the input data vary on each traversal. This is the reason why we have assigned a nonconstant quantity, q_i, for the probability of encountering a bug on a particular run.

Suppose there were no variation in input parameters and three successive tests each traversed path j. Then the probability of encountering an error on the first trial would be q_j. Since we have "perfect" dependence, the conditional probability of encountering an error, on the second traversal of the same path

---

[1]Shooman (1976).

with the same parameters given that an error was found on the first traversal, is unity. Similarly, the probability of encountering an error on the traversal of the same path with the same parameters the third time is also unity. Thus, the probability of an error on three traversals of path j is $q_j \times 1 \times 1 = q_j$.

Since we have assumed a variation in parameters on each run in our model, each test is independent, and the probability of encountering one bug on three successive traversals of path j is given by the binomial distribution (Eq. (5.107)), where $j = 3$, $k = 1$, and $n/N = q_j$:

$$P(1 \text{ error in 3 trials}) = \binom{3}{1} q_i^1 (1 - q_i)^3 = 3q_i(1 - q_i)^3 \qquad (5.109)$$

Similarly, the expected number of errors in N tests of path j is as follows:

$$\text{Number of failures} = Nq_j \qquad (5.110)$$

where N is the number of runs and q_j the probability of error along path j.

In general, the N total tests are distributed along each path so that Nf_1 tests traverse path 1, Nf_2 tests traverse path 2, etc. Thus, successive application of Eq. (5.110) to each of the i paths yields the number of failures in N tests:

$$n_f = Nf_1 q_1 + Nf_2 q_2 + \cdots + Nf_i q_i = N \sum_{j=1}^{i} f_j q_j \qquad (5.111)$$

We can now compute the system probability of failure on any one test run q_0 as

$$q_0 \equiv \frac{n_f}{N} = \sum_{j=1}^{i} f_j q_j \qquad (5.112)$$

Similarly we can compute the system failure rate z_0 by first computing the total number of test hours for the successful and unsuccessful runs. We compute the total number of traversals of path i as Nf_i as was previously done. Out of these Nf_i traversals a fraction p_i will be successful and will accumulate a total of $Nf_i p_i t_i$ hours of successful operation. If we assume that the time-to-failure distribution for the $Nf_i q_i$ traversals which result in failure is rectangular, then each trial which results in failure runs $t_i/2$ hours on the average before failure. Thus, the total test time accumulated in N runs is given by

$$H = Nf_1 p_1 t_1 + Nf_1 q_1 \frac{t_1}{2} + Nf_2 p_2 t_2 + Nf_2 q_2 \frac{t_2}{2}$$

$$+ \cdots + Nf_i p_i t_i + Nf_i q_i \frac{t_i}{2}$$

$$= N \sum_{j=1}^{i} f_j t_j \left(p_j + \frac{q_j}{2} \right) \qquad (5.113)$$

Substitution for $p_j = 1 - q_j$ in Eq. (5.113) and simplification yield

$$H = N \sum_{j=1}^{i} f_j t_j \left(1 - \frac{q_i}{2} \right) \qquad (5.114)$$

We now compute the system failure rate z_0 as

$$z_0 = \lim_{N \to \infty} \frac{n_f}{H} \tag{5.115}$$

and substitution from Eq. (5.11) and (5.114) into Eq. (5.115) yields in the limit

$$z_0 = \frac{\displaystyle\sum_{j=1}^{i} f_j q_j}{\displaystyle\sum_{j=1}^{i} f_j \left(1 - \frac{q_j}{2}\right) t_j} \tag{5.116}$$

We now wish to examine and interpret Eqs. (5.112) and (5.116) under the special conditions listed in Table 5.12. Note that the units of z_0 are failures per hour. Assuming that we can determine the set of values (f_j, q_j, t_j) for all the i paths, then Eq. (5.116) can be evaluated at the particular stage in the development process and used instead of Eq. (5.68) as the failure-rate expression in Eqs. (5.69) and (5.71). Furthermore, if we equate Eqs. (5.68) and (5.116) for case 1 of Table 5.12 we find that K can be computed from

$$K = \frac{I_T z_0}{E_r(\tau)} \tag{5.117}$$

We can now comment on the sample space for the macro model of Sec. 5.7.3. In the macro model all errors are considered equal and are lumped together regardless of their path association. Thus, the macro model depends on an input which randomly selects the path of program traversal. Suppose we select a particular test group composed of, say, five programs and run the batch several times until we are satisfied that all errors have been corrected. We can now rerun the same program with the same parameters and have an apparent error-free program.[1] Thus, in any true simulation test we must be careful to randomly change inputs each time so as to randomize the input.

Measurement of micro model parameters In order to implement the model developed in the previous sections, we must develop numerical values for the sets of parameters f_j, q_j, and t_j. Of course, in keeping with the concept of structured programming and levels of structures within levels, one could merely state that we continue decomposition to lower levels until we end up with a new set of f_j', q_j', and t_j' parameters at a lower level. This is just begging the question, and answers as to how we could measure or estimate our parameters at a higher level are also, by and large, answers as to how we would do the measurement at a lower level.

The parameter sets f_j and t_j are related to the design, size, and complexity of the control structure and program modules. The determination of the f_j can be made by a study of the physical meaning of the paths and the distributions of input parameters which drive one along the program paths. If the program is complex, or there is really no information on input statistics, we can take one of

---

[1] This is called *tuning* the program.

Table 5.12 System probability of failure and failure rate for special cases

Constraint	Probability of failure	Failure rate
General; see Eqs. (5.112) and (5.116)	$q_0 \equiv \sum_{j=1}^{i} f_j q_j$	$z_0 \equiv \dfrac{q_0}{\sum_{j=1}^{i} f_j \left(1 - \dfrac{q_j}{2}\right) t_j}$
Case 1: $q_j \ll 1$ Small failure probability	$q_0 = \sum_{j=1}^{i} f_j q_j$	$z_0 = \dfrac{q_0}{\sum_{j=1}^{i} f_j t_j}$
Case 2: $q_j \ll 1$ $f_1 = f_2 = \cdots = f_i = f = \dfrac{1}{i}$ Small failure probability; uniform path frequencies	$q_0 = \dfrac{1}{i} \sum_{j=1}^{i} q_j$	$z_0 = \dfrac{\sum_{j=1}^{i} q_j}{\sum_{j=1}^{i} t_j}$
Case 3: $q_j \ll 1$ $f_1 = f_2 = \cdots = f_i = f = \dfrac{1}{i}$ Small failure probability; uniform path frequencies; equal failure probabilities	$q_0 = q$	$z_0 = \dfrac{i_q}{\sum_{j=1}^{i} t_j}$
Case 4: $q_j \ll 1$ $f_1 = f_2 = \cdots = f_i = f = \dfrac{1}{i}$ $q_1 = q_2 = \cdots = q$ $t_1 = t_2 = \cdots = t$ Small failure probability; uniform path frequencies; equal failure probabilities; equal test times	$q_0 = q$	$z_0 = \dfrac{q}{t}$

two approaches. Assume f_j has a uniform distribution (see case 2 of Table 5.12) or insert counters in the various paths, and experimentally determine the f_j. The experimental approach requires that the program be in reasonably good shape so that a simulated test program can be run. Clearly, if a counter c_j is placed in each path so that it registers one count for each path traversal, and if we run N tests, then $f_j = c_j/N$. For a more detailed discussion of a simulation program see Sec. 5.7.3 and Shooman (1973). In fact, both micro and macro models require experimental measurement of parameters via simulation, and there is no reason why both models cannot be used and compared.

The set of t_j parameters can also be either calculated or measured. If the program is written in assembly, machine, or microprogramming code, one can estimate quite closely the run time of a sequence of code by summing the operating times of each instruction. In the case of a higher-level language (Fortran, PL/1, Cobol, etc.), the analysis is more complex, because each statement may expand into, say, 10 machine language statements. Several approaches are possible and have been discussed in Sec. 3.4.4. Of course, if the program and a simulation are available, one can merely run several test runs for each path, record the times, and use average values for each path.

The estimation of the q_j parameters is somewhat more difficult. During the early stages of design or development, one can try to estimate q_j using historical data. One way to derive the q_j parameter is to obtain values for failure rate from historical data or measurement and use Eq. (5.86) to calculate z_0. Then if we know t_j or t we can use case 3 or 4 of Table 5.12 and solve for q. This process can be repeated as the program is written and better values for q_j determined.

There is a possibility that one could calculate q_j from a more basic procedure. Knuth (1970) has shown that most Fortran statements are relatively simple and fall into one of several cases. If each of these classes also has a characteristic error rate, then by analysis of the q_j values for several examples, we should be able to derive characteristic values for the q_j parameters.

Another approach to the problem of computing, measuring, or estimating q_j is to treat each of the j cases as a separate module of code and to use the macro model techniques previously discussed in Sec. 5.7.3.

One should be cautious in applying such a two-state technique. The macro model already introduced depends to a certain extent on the fact that several programmers and styles are mixed in a big program so that average bug-removal rates and other similar parameters can be used. If we now apply this theory to a module, there is a good chance that only a single programmer has worked on the module. If we individually measure a q_j for each module, there is no problem; however, if we use historical data to establish "average values" of the parameters, then some of the q_j's will be overestimated and some will be underestimated. Even in this case there is a good chance that these errors will in part cancel so that the overall failure rate will still be a good estimate. (Just such a phenomenon has been observed to occur very frequently in hardware reliability analysis.)[1]

[1]Shooman (1968), Chap. 5.

An example of how we can define paths and begin a decomposition of a program is illustrated by using a quadratic root solving program in Shooman (1976).

5.8 AVAILABILITY MODELS

5.8.1 Introduction

As was previously discussed in Sec. 5.4.4, in addition to reliability, availability is an important measure of performance of any system. Many computer systems do not have the rigid requirements that a real-time system has for continuous operation. Time-shared systems and batch systems can, and often do, go down without causing severe problems to the user. The real item of importance here is how frequently the system goes down and for how long it stays down. The analytical expression given in Eq. (5.16) clearly measures this property.

The mathematical technique generally used to model system availability is a Markov model. A brief summary of the theory and application of Markov models is given in App. A, Sec. A.8, and App. B, Sec. B.6. In fact, Eq. (5.16) can be simply derived by evaluating Eq. B.93 for $t \to \infty$. The student who is unfamiliar with Markov models should study the appropriate sections in App. A and App. B before proceeding with this section.

5.8.2 The Basic Many-State Markov Model[1]

In this section, we will describe the assumptions and the configuration of the basic Markov model, so as to reveal the essential details. Useful generalizations of the basic model will be discussed later.

We assume that the software system under consideration is fairly large, of the order of 10^4 words (or more) of code, so that statistical deductions become meaningful. Software systems for which performance evaluations are relevant will usually be large. We assume that the system contains initially (at $t = 0$) an unknown number of bugs n. The variable t is taken to be the operating time of the system measured from initial activation.

The time origin could be chosen as the beginning of the phase known as process integration and test. In such a case, the model would be useful for an evaluation of the quality of the software during final simulation or field testing. It would also provide a measure of the software availability which would be useful in managing this crucial state in software development, and would provide a quantitative index of its field performance.

In most large systems the first 6 months to 1 year of deployment is essentially a "shakedown cruise," during which errors are discovered and fixed in the field by the users or through a software group which supports field operation from the development site. In such a case, the time origin $t = 0$ might be the time at which field deployment starts.

[1] Much of this section is based on Trivedi and Shooman (1975).

The basic Markov model assumptions are that at most one error is discovered or fixed (debugged, tested, and a code change inserted) in any instant of time, and that the transitions between states in the model depend only on the state we are in and the state we are going to and not on the past history of states.

Let the sequence of system up states be $\{n, n - 1, n - 2,...\}$. This is the set of states in which the system exists if no error has occurred, or if an error has just been repaired. Similarly, let the set of down states of the system be $\{m, m - 1, m - 2,...\}$. In general, the system will be in state $n - k$ if the $(k - 1)$th error has been corrected and the kth error has not yet occurred, while the system will be in state $m - k$ after the kth error has been discovered but not yet corrected $(k = 0, 1, 2,...)$. The configuration of the states of the model, together with the transition probabilities between states, is shown in Fig. 5.22.

Figure 5.22 depicts a Markov process of the discrete-state continuous-time type. The Markov model is therefore defined by the set of transition probabilities $\{p_{ij}\}$, where p_{ij} denotes the probability of a transition from state i to state j and depends only on the states i and j, and not on any of the previous or later states. The probability of transition from state $n - k$ to state $m - k$ is $\lambda_{n-k} \Delta t$, for $k = 0, 1, 2,...$. Similarly, the transition probability from state $m - k$ to state $n - k - 1$ is $\mu_{m-k} \Delta t$, for $k = 0, 1, 2,...$. The transition rates λ_j and μ_j depend, in general, upon the present state of the system. In the context of our software system, we note that λ_j represents the error occurrence rate, while μ_j represents the error-repair rate. The transition probability matrix of our system is then given in Table 5.13 where $(i, j) = (n, m), (n - 1, m - 1), (m - 2, m - 2)....$.

5.8.3 Expressions for Availability of the System

We will now derive expressions for the availability $A(t)$ and the reliability $R(t)$ in terms of the state-occupancy probabilities defined by:

$$P_{n-k}(t) \equiv P\{\underline{S}(t) = n - k\}; k = 0, 1, 2,... \tag{5.118}$$

$$P_{m-k}(t) \equiv P\{\underline{S}(t) = m - k\}; k = 0, 1, 2,... \tag{5.119}$$

Note: The notation $\underline{S}(t) = k$ means the system is in state k.

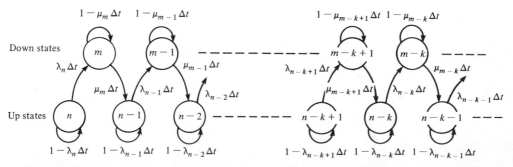

Figure 5.22 A many-state Markov model for software performance evaluation.

Table 5.13 The Markov transition probability matrix for the model defined in Fig. 5.28.

$$
\begin{bmatrix}
1 - \lambda_n \Delta t & \lambda_n \Delta t & 0 & 0 & 0 & \cdots & \cdots & \cdots & \cdots & \cdots \\
0 & 1 - \mu_m \Delta t & \mu_m \Delta t & 0 & 0 & \cdots & \cdots & \cdots & \cdots & \cdots \\
0 & 0 & 1 - \lambda_{n-1} \Delta t & \lambda_{n-1} \Delta t & 0 & \cdots & \cdots & \cdots & \cdots & \cdots \\
0 & 0 & 0 & 1 - \mu_{m-1} \Delta t & \mu_{m-1} \Delta t & \cdots & \cdots & \cdots & \cdots & \cdots \\
\cdots & \cdots & \cdots & \cdots & \cdots & \cdots & \cdots & \cdots & \cdots & \cdots \\
0 & 0 & 0 & 0 & 0 & \cdots & 1 - \lambda_{n-k} \Delta t & \lambda_{n-k} \Delta t & 0 & \cdots \\
0 & 0 & 0 & 0 & 0 & \cdots & 0 & 1 - \mu_{m-k} \Delta t & \mu_{m-k} \Delta t & \cdots \\
\cdots & \cdots & \cdots & \cdots & \cdots & \cdots & \cdots & \cdots & \cdots & \cdots
\end{bmatrix}
$$

The expression for system availability at time t ($t \geq 0$) is obtained easily from the definition given in Sec. 5.5:

$$A(t) \equiv P\{\text{system up at time } t\}$$
$$= P_n(t) + P_{n-1}(t) + P_{n-2}(t) + \cdots$$
$$= \sum_{k=0}^{\infty} P_{n-k}(t) \qquad (5.120)$$

Thus, the availability of the system at time t is obtained by simply summing all the up-state occupancy probabilities.

We would now like to briefly discuss a variation of the basic Markov model (model I) just introduced. We will refer to this variation as model II. The structure of this model and the background assumptions involved are essentially identical to those discussed earlier for model I. The basic Markov assumptions are also in effect, and we will not repeat these here.

The essential difference between the two Markov models, models I and II, is in the input modeling of the error-occurrence rate λ and the error-repair rate μ. In general, then, as input to model I, the following two functions must be supplied (modeled):

$$\lambda \equiv \lambda_{n-k} = \lambda(k) \qquad (5.121)$$
$$\mu \equiv \mu_{m-k} = \mu(k) \qquad (5.122)$$

The configuration of states for the basic Markov model (model I) is represented in Fig. 5.22. It is seen that the probability of any transition in the time interval $(t, t + \Delta t)$ is given by $\lambda_i \, \Delta t$ or $\mu_i \, \Delta t$, where the quantities λ_i and μ_i are functions of k, the number of bugs removed for the case of model I.

In model II, it is assumed that the error-occurrence rate λ and the error-repair rate μ are both explicit functions of time t. That is,

$$\lambda \equiv \lambda(t) \qquad (5.123)$$
$$\mu \equiv \mu(t) \qquad (5.124)$$

The idea involved here is that as the system is debugged, λ and μ will change, and in fact, λ and μ may be directly modeled as functions of t from the error data of the past history of the software system. Figure 5.22 still represents the basic model, but for model II, the quantities λ_i and μ_i are taken to be functions of t, as indicated in Eqs. (5.123) and (5.124). Figure (5.122) represents the configuration of states for model II.

In the following section the solutions of the basic many-state Markov models (models I and II) are discussed.

5.8.4 Solutions of the Many-State Markov Models

Besides the fact that the solutions of the basic many-state Markov models (models I and II of Sec. 5.8.3) and the actual implementations of these solutions are nontrivial problems, a number of illustrative and important points are manifested

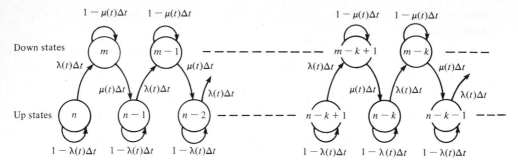

Figure 5.23 Variation of the basic many-state Markov model: model II.

while undertaking the solution of the models. In this section, we will discuss various aspects of the solutions of models I and II. For the special case of constant λ and μ, both models reduce to the same Poisson type of process. An analytical solution is developed for this case. The general cases of arbitrary λ and μ are of course the more important and interesting ones to study, especially from an applications point of view. We will discuss the solution of both models I and II in this general case. This section is concluded with a discussion of the computer implementations of the solutions and various computational aspects thereof.

Solution of model I Let us assume, for the purposes of this subsection, that the model parameters λ and μ are functions of the state of debugging achieved in the software system, i.e., the λ and μ variations are described in general by:

$$\lambda_{n-l} \equiv \lambda(k) \cdot \quad k = 0, 1, 2, \ldots \tag{5.125}$$

$$\mu_{m-k} \equiv \mu(k) \quad k = 0, 1, 2, \ldots \tag{5.126}$$

where k represents the number of bugs that have been removed from the system.

In order to verify initially the validity of the model, it is assumed that the error-occurrence rate λ_j and the error-repair rate μ_j are both constant and do not depend upon the stage at which the system exists in the debugging process.

Since λ and μ are constants, the set of differential equations corresponding to Fig. 5.22 can be written as shown below. The dependent variables in these differential equations are the state-occupancy probabilities $P_n(t)$ and $P_m(t)$.

By inspection of Fig. 5.22,[1] we obtain the following set of ordinary first-order differential equations, where we have used the notation that $\dot{f}(t) \equiv df(t)/dt$.

$$\dot{P}_n(t) = -\lambda P_n(t)$$

$$\dot{P}_m(t) + \mu P_m(t) = \lambda P_n(t)$$

$$\dot{P}_{n-1}(t) + \lambda P_{n-1}(t) = \mu P_m(t)$$

$$\dot{P}_{m-1}(t) + \mu P_{m-1}(t) = \lambda P_{n-1}(t) \tag{5.127}$$

$$\vdots$$

[1]Shooman (1968).

Since we assume that state n is the initial state of the system, the following initial conditions hold:

$$P_n(0) = 1 \tag{5.128}$$

$$P_{n-k}(0) = 0 \qquad k = 1, 2, 3, \ldots \tag{5.129}$$

$$P_{m-k}(0) = 0 \qquad k = 0, 1, 2, \ldots \tag{5.130}$$

The solution of the governing state equations for model I is formidable; however, we have three approaches: (1) apply classical differential equation theory for the solution of a set of n linear first-order equations; (2) use Laplace transform theory; and (3) use numerical analysis techniques to reduce the differential equation to difference equations and solve the latter on a computer. It turns out that careful application of method 1 or 2 leads to a closed-form result for the state probabilities;[1] however, the formula is complex and a computer evaluation is still needed. Thus, the third method is the preferred approach.

Solution of model II The configuration of states for model II is shown in Fig. 5.22. At present, we do not consider how $\lambda(t)$ and $\mu(t)$ are obtained or modeled. The system differential equations can be obtained from Fig. 5.22 and may be shown to be:

$$\dot{P}_n(t) = -\lambda(t)P_n(t) \tag{5.131}$$

$$\dot{P}_{n-k}(t) + \lambda(t)P_{n-k}(t) = \mu(t)P_{m-k+1}(t) \qquad k = 1, 2, 3, \ldots \tag{5.132}$$

$$\dot{P}_{m-k}(t) + \mu(t)P_{m-k}(t) = \lambda(t)P_{n-k}(t) \qquad k = 0, 1, 2, \ldots \tag{5.133}$$

The initial conditions are once again assumed to be:

$$P_n(0) = 1 \tag{5.134}$$

$$P_{n-k}(0) = 0 \qquad k = 1, 2, 3, \ldots \tag{5.135}$$

$$P_{m-k}(0) = 0 \qquad k = 0, 1, 2, \ldots \tag{5.136}$$

Numerical solutions of the above equations were implemented by using the Euler and the Runga-Kutta methods. Great care had to be exercised in grouping terms to overcome the effects of round-off errors. Details of the solutions are presented in Trivedi and Shooman (1975) and are summarized in the following section.

5.8.5 Results of Solutions for Many-State Markov Models I and II

We have described the solutions of the basic many-state Markov models (models I and II) in some detail in the preceding section. We will now present some typical results obtained using the methods and procedures that have been discussed. Results obtained for the case of constant parameters by both the analytic solution and the numerical solution are presented for comparison.

[1] Trivedi and Shooman (1975).

Because of the numerical difficulties in the solutions which were just mentioned, it was necessary to define and compute a check function along with our solution. Fortunately, from the theory of probability we know that the sum of all possible outcomes of a stochastic process must sum to unity, and thus the sum of all the Markov state probabilities must sum to unity.

We define the following notation,

$$A(t) = \sum_{k=0}^{k_{max}} P_{n-k}(t) \qquad \text{(up states)} \qquad (5.137)$$

$$B(t) = \sum_{k=0}^{k_{max}} P_{m-k}(t) \qquad \text{(down states)} \qquad (5.138)$$

so that if k_{max} is chosen sufficiently large, then we should have

$$\Sigma(t) = A(t) + B(t) \approx 1 \text{ for all } t \qquad (5.139)$$

and we will accept as correct only those values of $A(t)$ which correspond to t values satisfying the inequality

$$|\Sigma(t) - 1.0| \leq \varepsilon \qquad (5.140)$$

We somewhat arbitrarily choose $\varepsilon = 0.005$ in the solution that follows as the limit of validity.

Our first solution is for a model I case where $\lambda = 1.0$ and $\mu = 2.0$. The up-state probabilities are given in Fig. 5.24. Note that the $k = 0$ function is the reliability function, starting at 1 at $t = 0$ and decreasing exponentially. The other

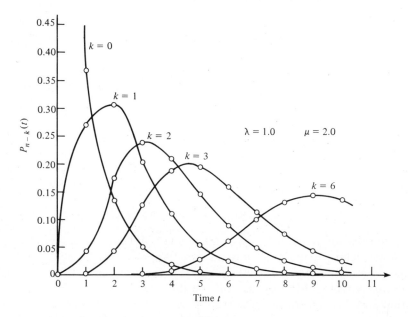

Figure 5.24 Up-state occupancy probabilities $P_{n-k}(t)$.

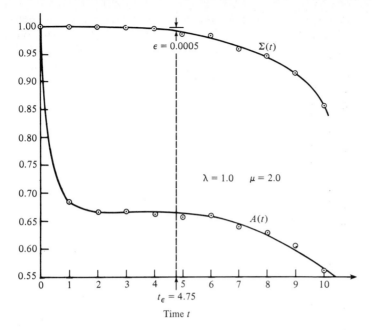

Figure 5.25 Availability and sigma function (constant parameter case, from exact solution).

functions form a regular family and were obtained via computer evaluation of a closed-form solution of Eq. (5.127). The sum of the up-state probabilities is the availability (see Eq. (5.137)) and is given in Fig. 5.25. This same case is solved a second time using numerical analysis techniques.[1] The results of the two solutions are identical, as they should be, for small t; however, the numerical solution is valid for times larger than the exact solution because of the peculiar way in which the round-off errors build up in each case.

We now consider a case in which the failure rate λ decreases with the state number k, as shown in Fig. 5.26, and the availability function is given in Fig. 5.27. Note that because the failure rate in this example goes to zero, the availability changes slope and rather than becoming asymptotically constant, as in Fig. B.20, it increases toward unity. This is of course more representative of a real software system, which improves as the testing or "shakedown" progresses.

We conclude our examples with a model II example for the case of the error-occurrence and correction rates shown in Fig. 5.28. The availability function is given in Fig. 5.29. Note that in this case the function changes slope and rises asymptotically to the steady-state value 0.8. This steady-state value can also be obtained by substituting λ and μ steady-state values into Eq. B.93 and letting $t \to \infty$. In fact this is the basis of the approximate solution technique of the next section.

[1] Trivedi and Shooman (1975).

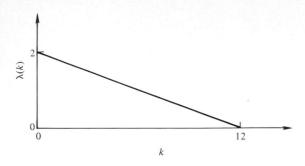

Figure 5.26 Model selected for error-occurrence rate for model I example.

5.8.6 Approximate Solutions

Because of the computational difficulties which are encountered even with a computer in solving for the state probabilities and system availability for the models developed in the previous sections, a simplified computational procedure is much to be desired. Also, much of the detailed techniques of solution were not included here since they are presented in Trivedi and Shooman (1975). The technique hinted at at the close of the preceding section can be generalized to allow an easy approximate solution, which yields insight and will suffice in many cases.

The technique for solving for the steady-state availability in terms of the values of λ and μ is discussed following Eq. (B.93). For a two-state model,

$$\lim_{t \to \infty} A(t) = \frac{\mu}{\lambda + \mu} \tag{5.141}$$

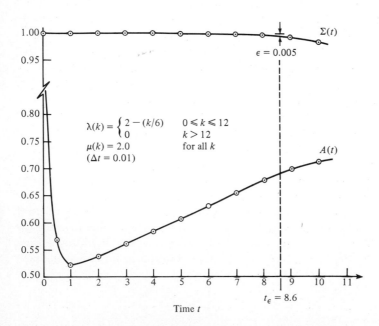

Figure 5.27 Availability and sigma function (model I example).

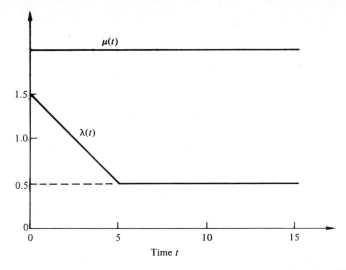

Figure 5.28 Error-occurrence and error-correction rate models selected for model II example.

For the case when $\lambda = 1.0$ and $\mu = 2.0$, Eq. (5.141) gives

$$\lim_{t \to \infty} A(t) = \tfrac{2}{3}$$

Note that this result agrees with the computed value in Fig. 5.25, where we see from the figure that for $t > 2.5$, $A(t)$ maintains a constant value of $\tfrac{2}{3}$. Thus, in the steady state (t sufficiently large), our many-state Markov model gives the same

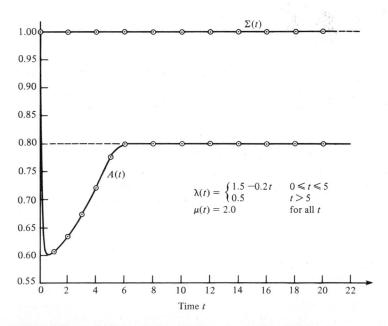

$$\lambda(t) = \begin{cases} 1.5 - 0.2t & 0 \leqslant t \leqslant 5 \\ 0.5 & t > 5 \end{cases}$$
$$\mu(t) = 2.0 \qquad \text{for all } t$$

Figure 5.29 Availability and sigma function (model II example).

result for availability as the two-state model considered above, as would be expected in the case of the basic many-state Markov models in which there are only two sets of states, the system up and the system down states.

Even in the cases where λ and μ are not constant, i.e., in the general cases of models I and II, we may use the two-state Markov model analogy as follows. For example, consider the example depicted in Fig. 5.27. Let us denote by $\hat{A}(t)$ the estimate of $A(t)$ obtained by assuming a piecewise-constant variation of λ and μ in time t. That is, at time t, the values of $\lambda(k)$ and $\mu(k)$ may be estimated by using the estimate $\hat{k}(t)$ for k introduced previously. Let us denote these estimates of λ and μ by $\hat{\lambda}$ and $\hat{\mu}$, respectively. Then

$$\hat{A}_\infty \equiv \lim_{t \to \infty} \hat{A}(t) \tag{5.142}$$

$$= \lim_{t \to \infty} \frac{\mu(\hat{k}(t))}{\mu(k(t)) + \lambda(\hat{k}(t))} \tag{5.143}$$

$$= \frac{\hat{\mu}}{\hat{\mu} + \hat{\lambda}} \tag{5.144}$$

By hypothesis, we will define $\hat{A}_\infty$ to be 1 at $t = 0$. Note that the above definition for $\hat{A}_\infty$ will be used in piecewise-constant manner; i.e., although λ and μ are not really constant, we assume them to be slowly varying in suitable intervals of time so that we may compute values of $\hat{A}_\infty$ for all t values of interest. The results obtained are given in Fig. 5.30, which shows these points superimposed on the

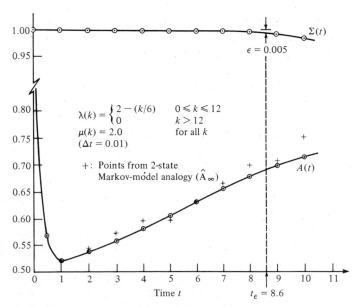

Figure 5.30 Availability and sigma function (model I example) compared with two-state Markov model estimates.

actual curve of $A(t)$ versus t (from Fig. 5.27). It is observed, in Fig. 5.30, that fairly good approximate agreement between $\hat{A}_\infty$ and A is obtained, as may be reasonably expected.

5.8.7 Extensions of the Model

The Markov availability model has been extended beyond the detail described above in two ways. First, some manufacturer's data for repair times were obtained and analyzed and combined with failure-rate data from the literature to provide values for λ, and numerical values for $A(t)$ were calculated. Second, one can introduce terms which model bug growth in the model by adding "backward" transition paths. Both these extensions are discussed in Trivedi and Shooman (1975).

5.9 DATA COLLECTION, STORAGE, AND RETRIEVAL

5.9.1 Introduction

A basic stumbling block in improving the estimation process and the reliability of software is the lack of adequate data. Because of the great need and high cost of collecting such data, we explore in some detail in this section why the data are needed, how they should be collected, and how they are to be stored and retrieved.

Historically, progress in science, and even more so in engineering, has occurred when theoretical hypotheses are verified by experiment or emerge from an analysis and study of data. As various models become available and are verified, data will be needed to estimate the constants in the models. In such cases we need a large enough statistical sample that we can determine the constants with sufficient accuracy. Remember that the standard deviation goes as $\sim 1/\sqrt{n}$ where n is the number of independent experimental data items. Since costs of experimentation generally increase linearly with n, there is a substantial economic problem accumulating sufficient data. The standard solution to this problem is for some unifying organization (the military, a professional society, a trade organization, etc.) to establish a data repository and thus share the cost among the users.[1]

5.9.2 Problems in Software Data Collection

Now that we have stated the great need for large quantities of data, we should review briefly the difficulties and problems in collection, storage, and use. One obvious problem indigenous to all operational data collection systems is that the

---

[1]In 1975, the Rome Air Development Center funded two organizations to study and plan an Air Force software data repository. In 1978 the DACS organization was formed to serve this need.

collection must be done at the operational level; however, it is difficult to obtain the cooperation of operational personnel over the long term to accurately and conscientiously record the necessary data. A prime reason for this is that the data collection organization generally does not employ the collectors but only instructs, guides, and cajoles them with the sometimes hesitant approval of their immediate superiors. This problem is indigenous to many data collection efforts; however, there are some additional special hurdles which are somewhat unique to software:

1. The creation of software is a human activity and thus the relevant variable list is swelled by a number of difficult to define and measure human traits.
2. Once a project has reached a certain state, it is almost impossible to recover data from past phases on a variable newly defined as important.
3. Programmers are historically less disciplined than engineers and scientists, and the boring aspects of data collection are increased to an even higher degree than normal.
4. Definitions, which are always a problem, are especially difficult in the software area.

One immediate answer to the above problems is to write a piece of software merely to collect software data. This is generally not feasible because of the expense. Suppose we wished to use six programmers for 6 months of an experiment. These 3 man-years could cost between $100,000 and $200,000, depending on salary and overhead rates. The alternative is to locate an ongoing development job and collect the data as a by-product. The problem here is that the development manager views the data collection as a nuisance in most cases, and the quality of the data is suspect. Of course, as a middle ground you may offer the manager manpower help in debugging as repayment for cooperation. By pooling resources, one can provide a large enough data base to investigate questions such as, Are PL/1 programs more reliable than Fortran programs?

5.9.3 Two Examples of Distortion of Terms

In order that the reader fully appreciate the importance of adherence to definitions, two examples are given to illustrate the chaos caused by conflicting groups with different goals who defined terms to meet their own desires rather than objectively.

The first example involves a large military computer system in which the hardware was to be subjected to a reliability demonstration test in excess of 1000 h in which seven or fewer failures were permitted for acceptance. After about 100 h, 50 "incidents" had been recorded and the military wished to cancel the test and give the contractor more time to improve the system before rescheduling the test. To the military's surprise, the contractor was anxious to continue the test. Upon careful investigation, it was found that no firm definition of a failure existed, and the contract called for a failure board (approximately half military and half contractor) to define what was a failure. The contractor apparently felt he could define most of the incidences as pattern failures (multiple repetitions of the same failure), which count only once. The result was a postponement of the demonstration test, an investigation by an independent panel, renegotiation of the contract, delay of a few years, and an eventual waiver permitting the contractor to deliver the system with one-third the mean time between failures that the contract initially called for. Clearly, the failure data which the contractor would have reported to a data base in this project would differ greatly from those the customer would submit. The difference would be in the definition of terms (arising out of disparate goals).[1]

The second example not only involves a large military computer system; it also deals with estimates of the software reliability. A prototype hardware system, once removed from the actual system, was being used as a test vehicle for an early release of the software. A diagnostic test was devised in order to ensure that hardware was error-free before new features to be added to the software were tested. A typical operating scenario was defined and the appropriate input signals were recorded on tape to serve as the diagnostic. This test tape was then to be used as a powerful diagnostic test to check out the hardware. The diagnostic was run many times during each test week, generally during slack periods in the test schedule. Not only were any anomalies extensively documented with core dumps, *but the time at which the anomaly occurred in the test cycle was recorded*. It was assumed (by many) that since the basic software had been well debugged, there would be only hardware failures and any failures of the software would be due to new features. All anomalies were thoroughly investigated so that the expected hardware defect could be located and fixed. As the reader may have anticipated, about one-half of the anomalies turned out to be software bugs. Upon more careful study, the *n* anomalies were divided into hardware, software, operator, and unknown groups, as discussed in Sec. 5.7.5. The software and hardware failure rates and MTBF were computed and plotted over the many weeks which the data encompassed. A disagreement then occurred between groups of analysts. Group 1, the probabilistic analysis group, was primarily trying to evaluate the data as typical software failure data and secondarily as a measure of the system software and hardware reliability. Group I felt that:

1. The data prototype system was close enough to the real system to be of some validity (say, in obtaining an estimate of software MTBF accurate to an order of magnitude).
2. The data were repeatable and sensible and could be "trusted."
3. The scenario test was a useful tool in measuring the software reliability.

---

[1] The difficulty in classifying errors is illustrated by the following story. A follow-up news item (*New York Times*, Oct. 5, 1980) described the death of or damage to 3000 old mice that were part of a research study of the aging process. A computer-controlled valve failed in the temperature control system, the mice were exposed to great heat, and the computer-monitored temperature warning signal operated but was overlooked by the laboratory personnel. Is this a hardware failure, a software failure, or some combination of failures? The consequences of this failure were also high—years of delay for the results, costs to replace the aged mice, and lost man-years for the experimenters.

The second group, composed of members of the design team developing the software, took a much different position. First of all, it pointed out that the prototype and final software contained considerable error-recovery capability and, because of the nature of the scenario test, error recovery was "turned off" when the scenario tests were run. Group 1 agreed that this weakened the utility of the data as a predictive tool; however, the data still could be used as a *worst-case estimate* (if the still-to-be-tested error-recovery features didn't work well). Group 2 insisted that this one fact alone made the data *totally useless* for estimation. In addition, group 2 insisted that the tape rewind time, which was about equal to the exercise run time of the tape, be counted as operating time. This more than doubled the operating time, and consequently the MTBF. Group 1 disagreed and considered this incorrect. Finally, group 2 reanalyzed the anomaly data and found that a number of software failures should be shifted to the hardware or unknown category. Since group 2 consisted of the software designers, group 1 was unable to intelligently comment on those changes. Finally, group 2 decided to remove most of the remaining software errors, because it claimed that it had diagnosed their cause and that fixing them and verifying the fixes was so routine and well understood that it could be considered accomplished. The estimate of MTBF by group 2 now increased by about an order of magnitude or more. Group 1 was willing to call this figure (except for the tape rewind time) an estimate of the potential reliability given further software debugging and test. At this point both groups recognized the disagreement, documented their own separate positions, and went on to other tasks.

Now if these data were to be added to data base, whose data should be accepted? Group 1? group 2? both sets?[1] neither set? Clearly, a precise definition of terms at the onset may have helped narrow the differences; however, there was essentially a management decision to be made here at a level higher than either group 1 or group 2. (Group 2 ranked one organizational level higher than group 1.)

5.9.4 History of Hardware-Reliability Data Collection—Parallels and Differences in the Software Area

For 25 to 30 years people have been collecting hardware reliability data, and it is useful to review what they have learned in the process before planning the collection of software reliability data. One basic problem is that field engineers and technicians often view data collection as a "pain in the neck" that requires time and bothersome paperwork. Also, if many unexpected failures occur in one month, there is a tendency to minimize their number so as not to make things "look bad" for maintenance personnel. In addition, there are many honest mistakes which occur.

---

[1] One as a set of data for the present software and the other as an estimate of the data expected from the improved software?

One method for minimizing these problems is to have a member of the reliability group that is collecting the data permanently attached (or a frequent and extended visitor) to the field site. In addition, any training, motivation, etc., which can be offered is useful. Finally, professionals skilled in human engineering should be asked to advise the group responsible for devising data collection forms, or other data acquisition methods. In the case of software we can envision that some data will be collected automatically by the operating system; however, these are generally just syntactical errors as opposed to logical errors.

One of the biggest problems with hardware data is that the failure rates reported are a strong function of the environment: temperature, humidity, voltage level, vibration, etc. Thus, for the data to be meaningful, one must understand and take these factors into account. Similar factors in software include firmness of configuration control, quality of documentation, skill of programmers, programming tools and facilities available, choice between top-down and bottom-up design techniques, language and operating system used, computer hardware, etc.

Three techniques used in the hardware area to deal with this problem are:

1. To try to plot or derive an equation for failure rate as a function of each of the variables.[1]
2. To describe the environment in story form on one or two pages and to store (or print) this description with the data (see GIDEP/FARADA[2]). This works fairly well as long as the data base is large enough that the analyst can pick and choose in order to try to match a data base project to his or her own project fairly closely.
3. To try to make up a set of environmental factors (in hardware these are called K factors) by which to multiply. This is the most widely used system; however, its success is completely dependent on the quality of the data and the analysis used in determining the K factors. A software analogy would be to decide that the average initial number of errors E_T can be adjusted for the mix of programmers' skills.

As previously stated, most data collection efforts suffer from inadequate theoretical support and documentation. This is one area which has been inadequately treated in almost all the hardware data bases with which the author is familiar. One problem is that data collection, although vital, is a tedious and often boring task. Furthermore, the data base manuals often resemble cookbooks with no explanation of how the data or formulas have been arrived at. On occasion it is vitally important that a senior analyst understand all the ramifications of the data base, because in general no adequate documentation exists. One simple

---

[1] Not very feasible, since this requires extensive and complete knowledge about how the variables affect reliability.

[2] One of the several standard military data base systems used to collect hardware reliability data. The abbreviation stands for Government Industry Data Exchange Program/Failure Rate Data.

solution is to write an appendix or companion volume which discusses the background of the data, their limitations, etc.

One way of remedying this situation is to appoint an advisory body to "govern" a software reliability data base. The board should be composed in a broad fashion of both theoretical and practical people. One should choose *very good* people for this board and should make the chairman an outside person and the executive secretary the data base manager.

5.9.5 Use of the Data Base as a Research Tool

The data recorded in the data base should be suitable for general research use. For example, if should contain information on operating hours, uptime, downtime, failures, and other such variables for operational software. One use could be in the verification of prediction models. One could use a model to predict $R(t)$ and $A(t)$, and then the predicted values could be compared with $R(t)$ and $A(t)$ values in the data base for similar systems. Similarly, data on cost or schedule or any predictions used which might be necessary to test other models should be recorded.

If we are to develop any measure of program quality, we will need data to test our models. Basic information on design technique, language, test techniques employed, program skill, number of bugs removed at each stage, etc., will be needed. Many of the items discussed in this section are data which are needed only infrequently and thus can be stored on microfilm or microfiche.

5.9.6 Specific Types of Data to Be Stored

One important class of software data to be collected and stored is time-to-failure data. In the case of such data, it is important to store the raw data. One of the most troublesome parts of many of the present data banks is that for convenience the raw data are processed and stored. In many cases this seriously hampers the analyst who wishes to explore the data in detail.

When you talk of raw reliability data, many people erroneously think that a vast amount of data must be stored. In fact, all that is needed is:

1. Identification number
2. Number on test
3. Length of test
4. Individual failure times

In most cases of highly reliable items (or software) item 4 will not be so large, 5 or 10 or 20, say. In addition, item 4 can always be placed in secondary storage if necessary. In fact, if we decide to store failure type, mode, etc., we already have to store each failure. Thus, we are only storing one more characteristic about the failure, i.e., its time of occurrence.

It is important that all data be traceable to this source. On occasion when one takes failure data, it is necessary to trace the data to the source. Thus, the data should be coded so that they can be traced back via identifying levels. This becomes especially critical when someone has a special need, i.e., has to do a programming project with all rank amateur programmers and needs data on this group.

Another important area in which one wishes to collect software data is the type of errors. This deserves special consideration. Just as the first step in entomology is to classify insects, we should do the same in studying computer bugs. If we ever hope to eliminate or minimize the number of errors in one category by a novel design technique, it is necessary to know how many of such errors occur and to test out the technique to see if it helps. Also some prediction models might make use of error types and their frequency of occurrence. After we classify, we can then begin to do the equivalent of comparative anatomy. We can then formulate some cause-and-effect hypotheses on how to create poisons to kill particular bugs. The analogy is clear; however, the big problem is that no one has yet agreed on a scheme or schemes of classification which are generally applicable to model coding, integration testing, field-release bugs, etc. Also, when we talk about timesharing, real time, batch, etc., we get different classes of bugs. We may have to change categories over the first year or two of operation in order to settle on one or more classification of bugs.

Thus, we must have recorded the various types of man-hours and computer hours. Another important study area is the computation of optimum points to switch from one development phase to another, minimizing cost and number of residual bugs. If we have sufficient data, we can make economic models for such switches. Thus, we must ensure that the data contains appropriate data on man-hours, test hours, etc.—by phase of development for both bottom-up and top-down development philosophies.

Many important data exist which are associated with operational measurements and demonstration tests. In general all large software systems are subjected to simulated operation by driving programs and simulations, generally near the end of the test. In most cases the running time of the runs which did not complete is not recorded, and thus these vital data are lost for reliability purposes. It is important that the participants in data collection not throw away these vital data as well as other test data which occur during development.

5.9.7 Multiple Levels of Storage

One tool which can help in many ways in a data base is the concept of multiple levels of storage. Before we propose a set of multiple levels of storage, let us attempt to calculate the amount of data that must be added to a hypothetical software reliability data base per year. As a model we focus on a data base such as the one the Air Force is planning which was mentioned previously. We start with an estimate of $3 billion spent per year by the Air Force for software (see

Table 1.2). Assuming that 20 percent is for coding of instructions, this represents yearly $600 times 10^6. If we assume a programmer's time is worth $50,000 per year including supervision and overhead loading, we have $(6 \times 10^8)/(5 \times 10^4)$ = 12,000 man-years per year of coding effort.

Let us assume that each programmer can code between 1000 and 10,000 higher-level-language instructions per year. If we assume that a higher-level-language instruction expands into about 5 machine language instructions, we are talking about 5000 to 50,000 lines of machine code per programmer per year or for 12,000 programmers the "equivalent force" of from 60×10^6 to 600×10^6 lines of machine code for the entire Air Force per year. We use the previous estimate that there are 1 percent bugs per line of code. Also we assume that this percentage is the same for the module-coding phase, the system-integration phase, and the operational deployment phase, and adding, we have 0.03 bugs per line. Using our previous estimate of lines, this yields 1.8×10^6 to 18×10^6 bugs per year. Assuming that there are 10 data descriptors (words) per bug which must be stored, we have 18×10^6 to 180×10^6 words per year of storage. If the data are coded into various binary bit patterns, all these data can be stored on a few reels of magnetic tape, as well as held online in a large disk system for immediate access.

As a permanent backup record, either microfilm or microfiche of each report can be used. If we assume that each bug will be reported on an $8\frac{1}{2}$- by 11-in form and that we can store 100 frames per microfiche card, we have 1.8×10^4 to 18×10^4 microfiche cards per year.

5.10 SUMMARY

In many ways this chapter on software reliability is the most satisfying and in other ways the least satisfying portion of this book. The error reliability and availability models developed provide a quantitative measure of the goodness of software. This measure can be used as a management guide for gauging the progress of the project, as discussed in this chapter and the following one. The frustration is that as we begin to make progress on analytical models, the depth of our ignorance about how we can analyze software and the extent of the lack of experimental failure data surface. This summary lists the major accomplishments of this chapter along with the thorny unanswered questions begging for future research and study.

The major accomplishments of this chapter are:

1. The concept of software reliability is introduced by describing the probabilistic process whereby residual software errors cause system failures when excited during operation.
2. The basic mathematics of reliability and failure-rate theory is introduced and the natures of system failures due to hardware and software causes are compared.
3. Definitions of reliability and availability are given and the concepts are discussed.

4. A residual software error model is developed on the basis of the initial number of errors in the program and records of the number of errors removed. Some data and error-removal models are explored.
5. Seeding and tagging techniques are developed for measuring the initial number of errors in the program.
6. A macro software reliability model is introduced which assumes that the failure rate is proportional to the number of remaining errors, and it is compared with other models in the literature.
7. The macro model is extended to include error generation as well as removal.
8. Methods of measuring the two model constants, initial number of errors and proportionality constant, are based upon simulation tests performed on the program during development.
9. Three statistical estimation techniques, least squares, moment estimates, and maximum-likelihood estimates, are used to compute values for the model constants from the data.
10. An operational software availability model is introduced based on Markov assumptions for error discovery and removal.
11. The final section discusses the kind and quantity of data which should be collected in a national software reliability data repository. Such a repository should be designed to provide raw data for estimating software reliability model parameters and for testing of newly proposed theories.

The still unanswered questions are:

1. How many past examples do we need in a data base to provide adequate estimate accuracy?
2. How much difference is there between the estimates obtained from the three estimation techniques and how does this affect the reliability and MTTF computations?
3. A number of case histories based upon applying the various models to additional practical situations are necessary to (a) improve our ability to employ these models with assurance and (b) establish their limitations and suggest avenues for improvement.

PROBLEMS

5.1 Formulate a table similar to Table 5.1 with examples drawn from objects familiar to you. Typical objects might include home appliances, home entertainment equipment, instruction manuals, an automobile, banking, etc. Use specific examples wherever possible.

5.2 Failure data for 10 hypothetical electronic components are given in the accompanying table. Compute and sketch the following quantities:
  (a) The hazard function $z(t)$
  (b) The density function $f(t)$
  (c) The distribution function $F(t)$
  (d) The reliability function $R(t)$

Failure data for 10 hypothetical electronic components

Failure number	Operating time, h
1	8
2	20
3	34
4	46
5	63
6	86
7	111
8	141
9	186
10	266

5.3 Repeat Prob. 5.2 for the failure data grouped in the intervals given in the accompanying table.

Failure data for 172 hypothetical components

Time interval, h	Failures in the interval
0–1000	59
1001–2000	24
2001–3000	29
3001–4000	30
4001–5000	17
5001–6000	13
	Total 172

5.4 A system is to be designed to have a reliability greater than or equal to 0.9 over 1000 h and a minimum availability of 0.99 over that period. Using steady-state availability theory, compute the required values of the failure rate λ and the repair rate μ.

5.5 Make a list of program errors you have encountered in your experience.

5.6 Use a set of forms similar to those given in Figs. 5.2 and 5.3 to record and document errors in a program you are developing. Analyze the data when the project is completed.

5.7 Use the data collected in Prob. 5.6 to prepare a set of curves like those shown in Figs. 5.7 and 5.8.

5.8 The error-removal data given in Table 5.1 are to be fitted with the exponential model given in Eq. (5.30). The model parameters k_1 and E_T are to be determined in the following manner:

  (*a*) Plot the data on logarithmic paper and fit a best straight line by eye.

  (*b*) Repeat, using a least-squares program (see Prob. 1.3). Sketch the model on top of the data and comment on the accuracy of the fit.

5.9 The data of Prob. 5.8 are to be analyzed using the model of Eqs. (5.34) and (5.35) and assuming the manpower-deployment profiles shown in the accompanying figure.

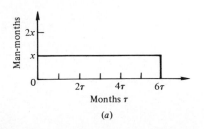

(a)

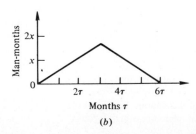

(b)

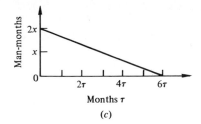

Months τ

(c)

5.10 Verify the derivations and solutions of the differential equations given in Table 5.7.

5.11 Using average values derived from the data discussed in Sec. 5.6.2, estimate the following for a program which has been estimated to be 10,000 words of object code.

(a) The total number of program errors which you anticipate will be found during development.

(b) The distribution of the estimated program errors among module-testing, integration-testing, and early field-release phases of development.

(c) Using the data from Sec. 4.2 estimate the number of personnel needed for testing and debugging if 6 months are available for all three phases.

(d) Repeat part c for computer hours.

5.12 If we assume that Prob. 5.11 is to be a bottom-up development, would you expect any of the answers to change if we switched to a top-down design? Explain.

5.13 Assume that the following four time histories are observed for four different programming projects.

(a) When would you release these projects: at 6 months, before 6 months, after 6 months? Explain.

(b) Comment on the various features and shapes of the curves.

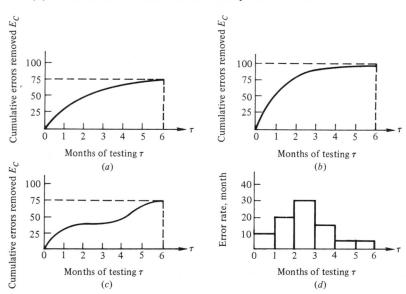

5.14 After 1 month of integration testing a 10,000-machine-word-long program, the MTBF = 10 h and 15 errors have been removed. After 2 months the MTBF = 15 h and 25 errors have been removed.

(a) Fit a model to this set of data and sketch the predicted MTBF function versus development time.

(*b*) How long must integration testing be in order to achieve a 100-h MTBF? How many errors will have been removed and how many will remain at this point?

5.15 Assume that the programs of Prob. 5.13 are 10,000 lines (of object code) long. Use the model of Sec. 5.7.3 to compute:

(*a*) The reliability function for the software if it is released after 4, 5, or 6 months. Sketch.

(*b*) The MTBF for the software if it is released after 4, 5, or 6 months. Sketch.

5.16 The following data have been obtained by the recording of errors removed and by simulation testing during the integration-test phase on a 100,000-instruction program.

1. July 1, 1976: Integration testing started, 0 errors found.
2. August 2, 1976: One hundred total errors removed, MTBF = 0.4 h.
3. September 1, 1976: Three hundred total errors removed, MTBF = 2 h.

Using the above data,

(*a*) Estimate the total numbers of errors in the program.

(*b*) Estimate how much longer you must test and debug in order to achieve an MTBF of 10 h.

(*c*) For the test time chosen in part *b*, sketch the reliability function versus operational time.

(*d*) Sketch the MTBF function versus development time.

5.17 A program which is 24,000 machine instructions in length is undergoing integration testing. After 1 month of testing 20 errors have been removed and the MTBF of the software is measured on a simulator to be 10 h. After 2 months of testing, 50 errors have been removed and the MTBF is similarly measured to be 20 h.

(*a*) Using the error-reliability model discussed in the notes compute the model parameters E_T and K.

(*b*) How many *errors* must be found and corrected before the MTBF of the software has risen to 60 h?

(*c*) Estimate how much integration testing *time* will be required to raise the MTBF to 60 h.

(*d*) Sketch the MTBF versus the integration-test time.

(*e*) If we release the software after the MTBF has been improved to 60 h, sketch the reliability function versus operating time.

(*f*) How long can the software operate (if released as in part *e*) before the reliability has dropped below 0.90?

5.18 Assume the debugging example associated with Table 5.6 took 2 months for the two debuggers to find 10 common bugs. Assume that from the third month forward only one debugger will work on the software. Using the model of Eqs. (5.34) and (5.35) sketch the anticipated error-removal rate using the mean value, the upper confidence estimate, and the lower confidence estimate for B_0.

5.19 Choose reasonable values for the constants in case 5 of Table 5.7, and study the behavior of the model. What parameter changes would be needed for unstable, controlled, and oscillatory behavior?

5.20 Assume that the design costs for achieving reliable human behavior are x, those for achieving reliable hardware are $2x$, and those for achieving reliable software are $4x$. If the system MTBF is to be 1000 h, use Eqs. (5.65) and (5.66) to "apportion" the MTBF values for the human, the hardware, and the software.

5.21 Assume that the error-removal rate is proportional to the assigned testing and debugging manpower, and assume that the three manpower deployment profiles given in Prob. 5.9 are representative of the integration-test process which extends from 0 to τ months. The model given in Eqs. (5.71) and (5.72) corresponds to a constant profile, and we may assume that $\rho_0 = cx$, where c is the number of errors found and corrected per man-month. Reformulate the reliability model for the two triangular manpower profiles, sketch the three reliability functions and the three MTBF curves, and interpret the results.

5.22 Discuss and explain the differences among the Shooman, Musa, Moranda, and Schick-Wolverton software-reliability models.

5.23 Compute and evaluate the sensitivities of R and MTBF to inaccuracies in estimating K and E_T in the Shooman model. Assume an error of 20 percent in K and E_T. What are the equivalent errors in R and MTBF?

5.24 Select a program of your choice and make up a representative set of test data. Insert a set of counters in the program, run the test data, and estimate the f_i frequencies needed for the structural model of Sec. 5.7.8.

5.25 Check the approximate points in Fig. 5.30 which were obtained by using the two-state approximate model (see Eqs. (5.142) to (5.144). Do your computations agree?

5.26 The data shown below were taken from early field trials of a software system. Since there was confusion as to how many errors were found (accurate records were not kept), three assumptions were made. Construct a reliability model for each of the three assumptions and compute and sketch $R(t)$ and MTTF.

Reliability computations

Time period 1979	Test hours	Software failures	Failure rate z, h^{-1}	MTBF, h	Cumulative number of errors removed at beginning of period		
					Assumption 1	Assumption 2	Assumption 3
March 19–30	24	41	1.71	0.59	0	25	50
April 1–30	64	58	0.91	1.10	25	60	120
May 1–31	56	23	0.41	2.43	60	74	148
June 1–13	32	10	0.31	3.20	74	81	162

MANAGEMENT TECHNIQUES

6.1 INTRODUCTION

The reader with experience on large complex projects of any nature realizes that it is a struggle to complete such a project, meet specifications, and stay within budgeted costs. In general, this can only be accomplished if strong and effective management techniques are used. The purpose of this section is to instruct the dubious or uninitiated reader of the necessity for discipline and organization for a software project.[1] Following this introduction, the body of the chapter introduces and places in perspective the tools and techniques at our command.

6.1.1 The Need for a Development Methodology

Anyone who has been associated with a large project involving many people and advanced technology soon realizes that there must be a coherent management philosophy and methodology to control and guide the project to successful completion. In many cases success is as much a function of quality management as of quality engineering and design. Why should we treat software management specially when technical management is a well-developed field? One reason is that a large percentage of experienced software engineers do not possess management skills. Similarly, many of the individuals possessing the necessary management skills do not understand software or the software development process. In addition, during its rapid growth, the programming profession has developed

---

[1]"Engineering Management" (1978); Reifer (1979).

many bad habits which have led to low-quality software and are hard to break. Last, there are unique aspects of software development without direct hardware analogs; thus not all the lessons learned about past hardware development are applicable to software.

Readers experienced in the software field find ample proof of the above statements from their own experiences. However, for the new reader a few brief examples will be given to reinforce these points.

In the early 1970s the author was asked to join an impartial, external review team for a large, computer-controlled military weapons system which was experiencing hardware reliability problems. Since a major portion of the project was software, it was agreed that I should also question the developer about the reliability and progress of the software. The hardware manager presented a rather complete block-diagram model of the system hardware and each of the major subsystems. He then presented a PERT[1] chart of the hardware development indicating major milestones[2] and the appropriate calendar dates. When asked questions about schedule and progress he invariably referred back to these diagrams. A complete discussion ensued as to how the reliability of the hardware was predicted and how well the first two prototype systems were meeting the required MTBF. (The estimated MTBF was 275 h, the contract called for 150 h, and a prototype system used for operator training was exhibiting 80 h.)

The software manager focused his presentation on a table listing the names of the major modules in the system and their estimated size. (His presentation would have been vastly improved if he had had a few high-level HIPO diagrams to detail the design.) He then presented a PERT chart containing some difficult to understand milestones and one key segment: the time allotted for the final integration of the software modules on the final hardware. When questioned about software reliability he asked what the term meant. After an explanation, the software manager replied that they hadn't given software reliability any thought and they didn't know how to estimate it, but they had good programmers who made very few errors and thus it was really unimportant. The software manager was then questioned why only 3 weeks were allotted for integration of the software when other, similar projects took 6 to 12 months for such a task. He again explained that they had very superior programmers and could do the job in 3 weeks! After participating in the committee's final report to the military, this author lost contact with the problem until about 4 years later. I then learned that the project was delivered about 2 years late and the company obtained a contract waiver reducing the system MTBF to about 50 h. In addition there were many software problems and delays during integration far beyond the allocated 3 weeks. It is difficult to say exactly how the software management affected the system development; however, it was clearly weak and played a strong role in the delays and poor final quality.

[1] Hiller and Lieberman (1974), Chap. 5, "Network Analysis Including PERT-CPM."

[2] A milestone is a significant event in the system life cycle, represented by a node in the PERT graph. The branches connecting the nodes are labeled with time or other resources required to move from one milestone to the next.

As a second example of the need for a formal software development methodology, we consider Landes' comments on an Air Force specification for software development, designed for use along with existing hardware development specifications in the system acquisition process:[1]

> A software document of this kind presents a new way of doing business for the government. Traditionally, the government would specify all requirements of the hardware in the system and leave the software to the discretion of the contractor. One or two sentences describing the functions of the software were considered sufficient to deal with the software aspect of a system.
>
> The imposition of a specification of this nature changes everything radically. We feel confident that we know enough about software development to mandate that a set of tools and procedures be applied to an ongoing effort. We know that telling the contractor how he should design his programs in general, how he should restrain [mandate structured or modular design, etc.] code and the selection of the language used, how he should keep track of the software development status, etc., will result in more reliable timely software. . . .
>
> It often happens that smaller projects, which combine hardware and software are sometimes managed by an engineer who is fully competent in hardware, e.g., radar technology, but is totally innocent of the correct way to buy software. Having a Standard from which he can select appropriate procedures and tools for use in his effort will be a great help.

Most readers will agree that the only way contractors can be monitored by buyers (or project managers by their superiors) is if a formal development methodology is in use. In the following section we point out that formal procedures are also necessary for internal software development.

6.1.2 External versus Internal Software Development

Many different relationships exist between the user and the developer of a software system. In the simplest such relationship, the user and the developer are the same person. For example, suppose that the software manager of a company is asked by the manufacturing manager to write a parts inventory program. No formal agreement would be written in general, just a brief memo describing the nature of the project.

Some managers feel that it is unnecessary to treat an in-house development in a formal fashion. However, it is important that formal documents be used for the control and management of such a project. An experienced reader can cite many examples of internal development which failed for the lack of such formal documentation. A request for proposal from the manufacturing group to the software group might seem silly; however, a memorandum stating what they wanted developed, what use they would put it to, and when they wanted it would be the minimum acceptable paperwork. The response of the software group should be a memorandum proposing (1) what it will develop, (2) some idea of the approach to be taken, (3) a preliminary design, (4) the cost, and (5) the development schedule. Also it is important to determine how the manufacturing

[1]Landes (1978).

group will verify that the design is proceeding satisfactorily (perhaps via their representative at design reviews). Such documents contain the same information as a request for a proposal and a proposal, except that they are written in memorandum form and do not contain the so-called boiler plate (equal opportunity employment clause, limitation of travel to American airline companies, etc.) typical of U.S. government proposals. The important point is that even if Joe, the leader of the software group is very friendly with Pete, the leader of the manufacturing group, formal documents are needed. The form of the documents is not of great importance: they can be short business letters formalizing oral agreements. But their content and effect on the technical and managerial aspects of the project are of major importance.

At the other extreme we discuss a large external contract, the development of a new air traffic control system for the New York area. All would agree that such a huge, complex external project requires formal methods. Undoubtedly, the FAA would handle the contracting of the system, and numerous companies would bid in response to the request for proposal. The winning bidder would develop the system as prime contractor using several subcontractors for parts of the system hardware and software. Possibly another party would be responsible for the acceptance testing, installation, and field trials of the software and hardware. Last, the operational group, the air traffic controllers, would use the system. Obviously such a large and intricate project requires formal contracting documents, design reviews, lists of deliverable items, a development plan, a test plan, milestones, delivery schedules, etc., to control the project.

Except for legal formalities, the management of an internal and an external project should be similar. The size and scope of the project will ordinarily have a greater effect on the level of detail required than whether it is an external or internal project. In all cases, it is important to focus on the entire life cycle (see Table 1.4 and Fig. 3.1) and especially the boundaries between phases. Each of the boundaries between development phases should be clearly defined by the issuance of a document. Such a document should state what has been accomplished during the preceding phase and present or reference all the relevant documents. Generally the issuance of such a document will be preceded by a design review which aims at evaluating and validating the draft of the document. As a minimum, at least the three boundaries between the requirements, the specifications, the design, and the program should be validated. The best procedure is to have the validation done as each phase is completed, as shown in Fig. 6.1. Note that each group is required to attest to the fact that the boundary is valid from complementary viewpoints. As discussed before, the results of such validation studies should be reported via a written document. If errors are found at the interface they are fixed before proceeding to the next phase. Unfortunately, the validation is too often left until the end of the program, as shown in Fig. 6.2. In this case, any serious errors which are found are more costly to fix (compare Fig. 1.5), since the implications of the changes often reverberate up and down the development chain.

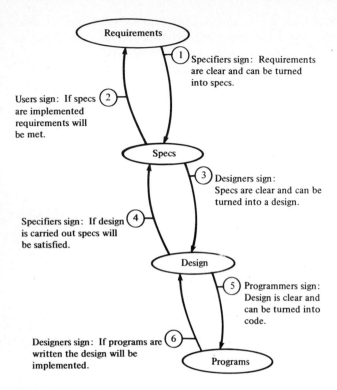

Figure 1. Requirements — Specs — Design — Programs

1 Specifiers sign: Requirements are clear and can be turned into specs.

2 Users sign: If specs are implemented requirements will be met.

3 Designers sign: Specs are clear and can be turned into a design.

4 Specifiers sign: If design is carried out specs will be satisfied.

5 Programmers sign: Design is clear and can be turned into code.

6 Designers sign: If programs are written the design will be implemented.

Figure 6.1 Phase-by-phase validation of the development process. *(From McCabe, 1975)*

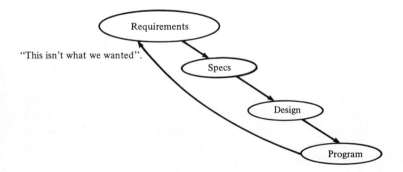

"This isn't what we wanted".

Requirements — Specs — Design — Program

Figure 6.2 Validation by comparing the program with the requirements. *(From McCabe, 1975)*

6.1.3 Quality Assurance

The role of quality assurance is well established in the hardware manufacturing area. It covers the inspection and test of incoming materials, maintenance of standards for workmanship, calibration of equipment, and acceptance testing. Many related functions are generally considered phases of engineering design: (1) reliability prediction, (2) demonstration testing, (3) functional testing of system or subsystem, and (4) environmental testing. However, in some organizations these tasks may be assigned to the quality control organization. Engineering design, prototyping, engineering testing, manufacturing engineering, and document control are always treated as engineering functions. It is not important exactly which organization is responsible for which function as long as *all* functions *are* performed and the groups work together harmoniously. Over the years experience has taught us that it is important for the reliability and quality control function to have an independent reporting channel which reaches a level one step higher than the project director. This is needed because all too often a project director is faced with too short a schedule, too few development dollars, and very difficult performance specifications. Thus, the task is impossible and some constraints must be broken to satisfy others. Traditionally, the first constraints which are ignored are reliability and quality. To put it another way, one military staff manager said of his project line-managers, "I've heard them holler at contractors because the schedule was late, because the cost was too high, because it was too big or heavy, because the performance was too low, but never because the quality or reliability were poor—even though they often are." In a typical case a system may be delivered where all 10 of the required functions work more or less but the quality is poor.

The role of quality assurance in software development is less clear-cut. There is no prototyping (except as the first phase of a two-phase design[1]), no incoming parts are to be inspected, and software quality measures are still unstandardized. Again the important theme is that all functions be covered. The decision whether they are done by the design group, a software quality group, or a software engineering group is of lesser importance. In smaller organizations, these functions will generally be performed by the design group. In large organizations, the responsibility is often shared between the software design group and a software engineering (or quality) group. If there is more than one group involved, they both must have access to the same high-level manager, or conflicts will be resolved by the project manager, whose built-in biases have already been described.

In the case of software, to ensure independence and objectivity the testing function is often divorced from design and given to another group. The test function could be delegated to quality assurance; however, it is probably best to entrust it to another programming group which specializes in testing. In some

[1]Brooks (1975), Chap. 22, "Plan to Throw One Away."

contracting situations, the test group is actually a third-party subcontractor different from the design contractor or the user.

6.1.4 Life-Cycle Management

The age-old cliché penny-wise and pound-foolish applies to large system developments as well as it does to common life situations. In a medium- to-large scale project, the software development takes 2 to 5 years and the project manager may change during the course of development. In addition, within user organizations, system development funds may come from one organization and operational funds from another. Because of the diverse nature of funding, it is difficult to negotiate design trade-offs which require higher acquisition costs but yield extra reliability and quality features which pay for themselves in lower field maintenance costs. A study of military reliability showed that the Air Force Systems Command allocated funds and managed the development of new weapons systems while the Air Force Logistics Command paid for maintenance of the systems in the field.[1] At that time the Systems Command did not apportion development funds for design improvements which minimized subsequent maintenance. In addition the Logistics Command had no funds for correction of design weaknesses, which contributed substantially to low operational reliability and availability and high repair costs.

The lesson we must learn from the above problems is that a software system must be designed initially with a view toward life-cycle costs. This is especially important since present estimates are that from 50 to 90 percent of the cost of software is spent in the maintenance phase. This is discussed in detail in Sec. 6.6, where we find that maintenance covers not only fixing of errors in the field, but also design of new features and enhancements.

6.1.5 Outline of the Chapter

As in previous chapters we will attempt to focus on quantitative techniques for managing software development. Unfortunately, the state of the art of software management is largely a collection of qualitative techniques. Thus, much of the story in this chapter will be told via checklists of what to do and not to do, case histories, and examples.

Quantitative methods exist in several areas, such as performance, quality and reliability, and cost. In these cases a thorough review of the quantitative methods in use and their limitations will be presented.

The chapter concludes with an examination of some selected success and failure stories.

---

[1]Gault, Horner, McMillan, Naka, Shooman, and Ware (1975).

6.2 REQUIREMENTS, SPECIFICATIONS, AND INITIAL DESIGN

6.2.1 Contracting for Software

Contract law is not an area of major concern for programmers or software engineers; however, they should have some awareness of the problems involved.[1] Any large company will have a legal department with experience, legal expertise, and responsibility for software contracts. Nevertheless, the technical manager or lead programmer can often help the legal department on certain key issues. This is even more important in a smaller company, and a software manager or designer should be sensitive to some of the issues involved in software contracting. Furthermore, if the argument that management thinking is rooted in computer hardware holds (see Sec. 1.1.5), we should expect that top-level legal thinking and experience are also hardware-oriented.

Lest the reader feel that technical matters are peripheral to legal ones, we relate the following story. A major consumer of software contracted with a small developer for a software system. The specifications clearly called for the software to support the full ASCII character set (7-bit code) of 128 symbols.[2] The terminal devices specified for initial use with the system were designed to use the more common 64-character subset (6-bit code). For some unknown reason, the contractor decided that because the terminal required only 64 characters, the entire design would be based on the 64-character subset, and the 128-symbol specification was ignored. Well into the design, the contractor's technical manager called his counterpart at the customer's laboratory and inquired whether the 128-character-set specification was an error. When he received the immediate reply that the full 128-character set was vital for future applications an unhappy set of circumstances ensued. The contractor found that to implement the full 128-character set would mean a scrapping of the present design, a complete redesign, and a tremendous additional cost. The issue was eventually settled in the courts. The contractor delivered to the customer those portions of the design which were still valid, received partial payment, and suffered a severe financial loss. The user had to find a new contractor, and only a portion of the work already accomplished was reusable. Understandably, the total cost of the partial payment and the new contract far exceeded the amount budgeted for the system, and much time was lost. In this situation there were only losers and no winners. Was there sufficient technical review of the legality and clarity of the contract? It is hard to tell, but obviously something went wrong.

As a partner in the contracting process, the software manager should try to avoid known pitfalls. Wooldridge (1973, Chap. 9) cites seven basic rules to follow in software negotiations (see Table 6.1). Even where the legal staff is in charge, it is still useful to know the major concerns, some of which are discussed below.

[1] Reddien (1979).
[2] Tanenbaum (1976, pp. 34–35) offers a description of ASCII code.

Table 6.1 Rules to follow in software contracting

1. Get legal advice from the beginning.

2. Negotiate with a senior person.

3. Negotiate with only one person.

4. Document all verbal agreements.

5. Make sure the contract specifies everything you will get: the prices, the terms, the conditions.

6. Do not announce the final decision until the contract is signed.

7. Remember that no matter what the contract says, success with software depends first of all on a good business relationship between buyer and seller.

Source: Wooldridge (1973), p. 134.

Field maintenance is a high-cost item, and it is vital to ensure that the contract is crystal-clear regarding who has the responsibility for field maintenance. Similarly, a clear policy should be stated for dealing with requests by customers for improvements, or changes during the course of the contract. A firm legal policy tempered with good judgment is required. For example, if a long-time customer asks for a $1000 change on a $1 million contract, one simply agrees. However, it is wise to inform both the legal staff and the customer in writing that there is a cost involved and the contractor is absorbing it in the interests of good will. This is especially important if the customer's next request for a change would cost $50,000. Some hardware-oriented managers erroneously feel software changes are inexpensive. They must be educated to understand that the retesting of the system after such a change takes time and someone has to pay the cost.

As is often the case, much of a legal document deals with worst cases, and ample consideration is given to (1) penalties for late delivery, (2) performance below specifications, and (3) premature termination of the contract. In a more typical case, the important contract provisions are those pertaining to (4) what constitutes good software and (5) how soon one is paid for one's work.

The book by Brandon and Segelstein (1976) provides actual sample contracts as well as practical guidance. It is useful to study the nine key objectives of a data processing contract given in Table 6.2 and a sample contract.[1]

6.2.2 Software Requirements

Introduction One of the key problems in any software (or hardware) design is to formulate a complete and correct set of requirements for the system. Then one

---

[1]Brandon and Segelstein recommend that one obtain a copy of the standard U.S. Government General Services Administration (GSA) contract document for the acquisition of computer hardware and software.

Table 6.2 Key objectives of a data processing contract

1. As protection against potential disaster, unanticipated at the time the relationship was initiated. These disasters can include business termination of the vendor, or potentially of the user; the reassignment of personnel whose relationships were vital to the implementation of the contract; or a natural disaster, act of God, strike, or other event which might disrupt the implementation of the computer installation activity.

2. A clear documentation of the agreement between the parties, and the commitments made by each party to the other. Time has a way of erasing memory of individuals involved in a contractual relationship. Thus, it is useful to commit to paper in one document the totality of commitment on both sides of an agreement.

3. To delineate clearly the responsibility for the performance of specific tasks which may affect the proper performance by the other party.

4. To provide clear technical and legal descriptions so that future participants in the process will be able to decipher the terms of the relationship.

5. To provide a point of reference in the event the relationship breaks down, without affecting the progress of the joint implementation activity.

6. To establish quantitative, mechanistic measures of performance where it is feasible to do so.

7. To alert management to the problems associated with computer implementation, and to increase their sophistication by providing a comprehensive document describing the relationship.

8. To overcome arrogance on the part of certain vendors in the industry, in part emanating from certain monopolistic practices which have become traditional in the computer industry.

9. To provide some means of recourse and some definition of remedies, if all else fails.

Source: Brandon and Segelstein (1976), p. 2.

must produce a set of specifications which when properly implemented yield a system meeting the requirements. We began a discussion of the management of this process in Sec. 6.1.3. In this section, we explore in more depth the content and form of computer program requirements (*what* must be accomplished) and the specification (*how* it is to be accomplished).

Often there is confusion and it is difficult to determine where requirements leave off and specifications begin. In order to clarify the situation, we define the initial stages of a software development in terms of an example and the block diagrams given in Fig. 6.3*a* and *b*. In Fig. 6.3 we have depicted the initiation of the project as a definition and expression of need. The formalization of these needs leads to a requirements document, which will generally be the *statement of work* in a *request for proposal* (RFP) if the user is to contract the work to a second party. In fact, a user who does not have sufficient in-house expertise may hire a third party to prepare the requirements document. Once the potential developers receive the request for proposal and decide to bid, they prepare a proposal. The proposals prepared by the bidders contain preliminary specifications, a preliminary design, a cost estimate, a preliminary test plan, and a management plan. Once a choice has been made and the contract is awarded, a detailed design and specification are evolved by the contractor, with the cooperation and participation of the user.

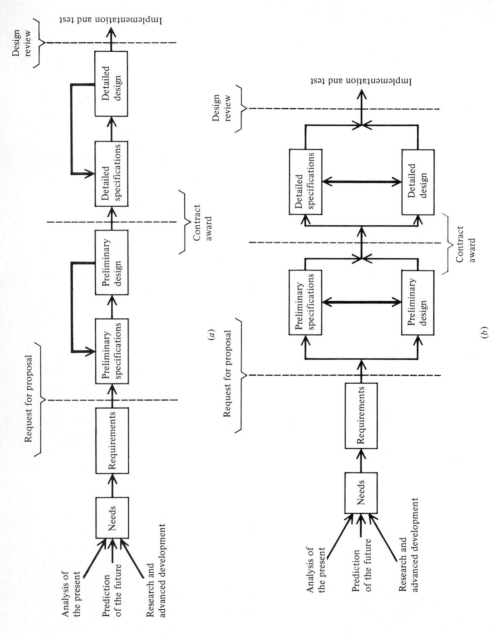

Figure 6.3 The preliminary portion of the development cycle for a contracted project: (*a*) series (with feedback) specifications and design phases; (*b*) semiparallel specifications with design phases.

In Fig. 6.3*a* we have shown the specification process to precede the design process. However, as design proceeds we often find that the specifications are less than ideal and additions or corrections are needed. Thus, we have shown feedback from the design phase to the specification phase. Sometimes managers try to shorten the length of the development cycle by working on the specifications and design in parallel with regular communication between the two groups as shown in Figure 6.3*b*. We can illustrate the differences between the development times of Fig. 6.3*a* and *b* if we assume that preliminary specification and design take 3 man-months each. Then in Fig. 6.3*a* we could have a three-member team prepare the preliminary specifications in 1 month and the same group take one more month for the preliminary design. Thus, the proposal would cost 6 man-months (plus other, fixed costs) and take 2 months to complete. In the case of Fig. 6.3*b*, we would have one three-member team work on preliminary specifications for 1 month and constantly check with a second three-member team working on the design in parallel. The cost would still be 6 man-months (plus other, fixed costs), but the proposal would take only 1 month to complete. In general, the series process is less prone to confusion and error and should be used during the detailed phase. In many cases, the pressures of the contracting process may force us to abandon the series approach for the semiparallel one. If this is the case, the manager should be aware of the dangers of such a choice and try in every way to minimize confusion and assure good communication. This may require scheduled hour-long conferences (mini design reviews) every few days between the specification and design groups.

Requirements We now discuss some of the specific material which should be included in a set of requirements. Consider the table of contents for a typical requirements document (see Table 6.3). Chapter 0 serves as an overview and introduction. The next two chapters deal with the host computer and the peripheral hardware (displays, terminals, communications equipment, memories, etc.) which are to be used in the system. In some cases, these items will be prechosen and included in the requirements, while in other cases the choice or design of such equipment will be part of the development. If hardware development is required the function and performance requirements of the equipment must be sufficiently detailed that designs have a sufficient foundation to prepare preliminary specifications and a preliminary design. One must not include the details of implementation (unless they are already prescribed), but must mainly focus on external behavior. Most of the other items in Table 6.3 are self-explanatory; however, Chap. 6 should be carefully done. Designers often tend to think that operation will always do things correctly and build in little or no defensive programming. Similarly, Chap. 9 is important. The design of a system which will be used for 3 years and discarded may be fundamentally different from one which will have a 10-year life span and be improved (enhanced) three or four times over this span.

Unless most design decisions have been made, one must not tell the designer how to implement the requirements, for in doing so we preclude any design

Table 6.3 A table of contents for a typical requirements document

Chapter	Contents
0 Introduction	Organization principles; abstracts for other sections, notation guide.
1 Computer characteristics	If the computer is predetermined, a general description with particular attention to its idiosyncrasies; otherwise a summary of its required characteristics.
2 Hardware interfaces	Concise description of information received or transmitted by the computer.
3 Software functions	What the software must do to meet its requirements, in various situations and in response to various events.
4 Timing constraints	How often and how fast each function must be performed: This section is separate from section 3 since "what" and "when" can change independently.
5 Accuracy constraints	How close output values must be to ideal values to be acceptable.
6 Response to undesired events	What the software must do if sensors go down, the pilot keys in invalid data, etc.
7 Subsets	What the program should do if it cannot do everything.
8 Fundamental assumptions	The characteristics of the program that will stay the same, no matter what changes are made.
9 Changes	The types of changes that have been made or are expected.
10 Glossary	Most documentation is fraught with acronyms and technical terms. At first we prepared this guide for ourselves; as we learned the language, we retained it for newcomers.
11 Sources	Annotated list of documentation and personnel, indicating the types of questions each can answer.

Source: Heninger (1979, p. 3). Three additional sections are suggested for this outline: 1(a), "Software Characteristics"; 2(a), "Software Interfaces"; and 6(a), "Defensive Programming Techniques." See the subsection "Requirements" in Sec. 6.2.2 of this book.

initiative or creativity on his or her part. In such a case one really ends up writing a combined requirements-specifications document. There are times when such an approach is good; however, it should be the result of a considered management decision rather than due to an inexperienced or overzealous individual who writes the requirements.

This author would add two additional sections to the outline: 1A, Software Characteristics, and 2A, Software Interfaces. The software characteristics section should include any prior decisions about (1) design philosophy, (2) language, (3) algorithms, or (4) data structures which are to be used. Similarly, the software interfaces section should discuss any explicit or implicit decisions concerning (1) existing operating systems, (2) compilers, (3) interpreters, (4) assemblers, (5) existing software development tools, and (6) any existing code modules, sub-routines, or data bases which are to be used.

An additional section which will be valuable in many cases would be Chap. 6A, Defensive Programming Techniques. This section should include the expected ranges of any input variables, key intermediate variables, and any output vari-ables. It should also discuss whether defensive programming techniques such as range checking, parallel (redundant) computation and checking, rollback, or error-recovery techniques are to be utilized. In a broad sense these techniques are all responses to undesired events; however, that title seems to imply passive response, whereas the term *defensive programming* seems to also include active procedures to control such errors.

Heninger (1979) rightly stresses ease of use in her article, since the document will be constantly referred to by many users with different backgrounds. Clear, simple, and unambiguous English is essential, along with a glossary, a table of contents, an index, and an effective top-down and modular organization.

Heninger counsels against inclusion of tutorial material, assuming that the document is to be used by experienced programmers. This author counsels just the opposite. Too often problems arise because the implementer has not under-stood something that the user felt was obvious or implied. The user *must* generate a tutorial narrative describing the intended application and defining the different modes of operation.

A mode of system operation which is often overlooked is that of error correction. If a credit card billing system with 100,000 accounts generates errors involving 0.1 percent of the users each month, there will be about 100 errors per month to correct. Unless the system is specifically designed to handle such corrections with special editing and checking features, error correction in the system will be a disaster. This is an almost universally neglected feature of software system design, and the after-the-fact fixes used to patch things up are generally intolerable.

In any event, a narrative tutorial document should be included as an appendix to the requirements document or clearly referenced as necessary prior reading. There are often many versions of the requirements documents due to (1) periodic corrections and additions, (2) multitiered requirements, if subcontractors are involved, or (3) evolution in a really large system as conflicts or omissions are found. Thus, a flexible and clear numbering and dating system is required.

6.2.3 Software Specifications

The specifications are essentially a description of how each item in the require-ments is to be realized based on a specific implementation. The computer, language, and operating system are chosen prior to the writing of the specifica-tions. Often some of the preliminary design is in progress or completed. Thus, the specifications contain details of what must be done and how it is to be accom-plished. Major algorithms, equations, and approaches to design are included and named. Further details of these items will be given in the preliminary design, which is documented using HIPO diagrams or an equivalent representation. Clearly, in a smaller project, the requirements and specifications documents might be combined, or the specifications and preliminary design combined. Specifications will experience even more changes over the life cycle than requirements, as the design evolves. For the same reasons stated under Requirements in Sec. 6.2.2 a good numbering and dating system is mandatory for specification documents.

Requirements—specification tools There are many techniques which can be used to aid in the writing of precise requirements and specifications. Standard mathematical notation should be used to document equations or algorithms whenever appropriate.

Another useful technique is to construct tables of all the input and output variables and group them in some logical fashion. In fact since mnemonic names will be chosen for these variables at some stage in the design, why not have users choose the abbreviations most meaningful to them and place them in the requirements rather than leave the choice to the designer or programmer?

Many researchers have tried to go beyond the above tools and produce a formal language which could be used to transform formal requirements into precise specifications.[1] They have also attempted to verify the resulting programs with respect to the precise specification. This author feels that some of the developments are still in the research stages; however, some are now used in practice. The most advanced one (in terms of practicality) is that associated with the ISDOS project at the University of Michigan.[2] The system utilizes a problem-statement language called PSL. Once the problem has been entered into the computer in PSL, various features of the problem description can be listed and explored interactively using the problem-statement analyzer (PSA) program. Details of these tools are described in the references; however, the reader may visualize the tool as providing roughly the same information as a set of manually generated HIPO diagrams.

6.2.4 An Example

The following example is introduced to clarify the differences among requirements, specifications, and preliminary design. The author needs a simple means to record and retrieve information on his books, reports, and technical papers. The size of the collection and dispersion between his home, Brooklyn Campus, and Long Island Campus offices make it difficult for the author to continue relying on memory and browsing the bookshelves to perform these functions.

A simple statement of requirements is given in Table 6.4, which follows the outline in Table 6.3. A set of preliminary specifications is given in Table 6.5. In the interests of simplicity and low cost of development it was decided to use existing editor–word-processing programs to implement the requirements. A

---

[1] *Proc. Specifications of Reliable Software Conf.* (1979).
[2] Teichroew, (1976; 1977).

Table 6.4 Requirements for a catalog and information-retrieval system for technical books, reports, and papers

Introduction	A simple, cost-effective system which shows information similar to that contained on a library catalog card shall be developed. Automatic search of data base by author or topic from the home or from Brooklyn or Farmingdale office shall be possible.
Chapter 1	Computer and operating system characteristics—The computers available at the various locations are a Radio Shack TRS-80 with dual floppy disks at home; DEC PDP-11/40 and 11/60 computers and terminal access to a PDP-11/70 at Farmingdale; and terminal access to a PDP-11/70 and an IBM 4341 at Brooklyn. The PDP-11 computers use the Bell Labs UNIX operating system (see Sec. 6.7.6), and the TRS-80 uses the DOS and the NEWDOS operating systems with a wide variety of additional software.
Chapter 2	Hardware and software interfaces—The PDP-11/70 computer is a single machine, physically in Brooklyn, and accessible from either Brooklyn or Farmingdale via modems and telephone tie lines. The TRS-80 has an RS-232 interface and a telephone modem. A communications package is presently under development to tie the TRS-80 to the PDP-11/70 (it is anticipated that this communications program will be completed in 6 months). At present about two-thirds of the material in the Farmingdale office (which represents about 60% of the total) is on 3×5 index cards, cross-referenced by author, title and subject.
Chapter 3	Software functions—The prime functions of the software are: 3.1 Create in appropriate format a data base which contains the same information as a library card catalog. 3.2 Allow easy addition and deletion and correction of the data base. 3.3 Allow searching of the data base by author, subject, keywords, or title. 3.4 Provide hard copy of items found in the various searches. 3.5 Data base shall provide a means via access number (like library call number), author, title, etc., which is compatible with the way the items are stored on the library shelves so that the copy may be easily found once identified.
Chapter 4	Running time—Since the data base will not be that large it is anticipated that search time will not be critical. A maximum search time of 15 s per search will be used as a working goal, subject to future study and experimentation. A more critical time requirement is the telephone connect time for a session from the home location. If the home location is to access a computer at the Brooklyn or Farmingdale location, connect times may cost $10 to $30 per hour depending on location and time of day.
Chapter 5	Accuracy—Since the basic operations to be performed are string searches rather than numerical computation, accuracy requirements are not relevant to this problem.

Table 6.4 (*continued*)

Chapter 6	Response to undesired events, and defensive programming—The effect of an unrecognizable command or a search which fails shall be an error message to that effect. A prime objective of the system is to protect the data base; thus hard copy and magnetic copy of the data base must be maintained in a safe location. Also, one should guard against operator errors which destroy part or all of the data base.
Chapter 7	Basic functions—Since simplicity and low cost (in terms of development time) are important goals, the use of complex searches using compound keywords may be deleted if necessary. All other functions are required.
Chapter 8	Fundamental assumptions—There is no need that the objectives be expanded into a multiuser (merging of other libraries) system. It is possible that the system will be attractive to others, yet this is not a requirement. The operability from all three locations is a fundamental assumption.
Chapter 9	Changes—The system must initially manage the present collection of 1000 to 2000 books and 1000 to 2000 papers and reports. The size of the collection may double over the next 5 to 10 years. The addition of items to the data base as well as its initial creation should be as easy as possible.
Chapter 10	Definition of terms—A glossary of terms, a summary of operating instructions, and a sample session must be included in the specifications. Online instructions will also be provided.
Chapter 11	Related documents—The preliminary specifications and/or design will contain references to existing library information systems.

Table 6.5 Preliminary specifications for a catalog and information-retrieval system for technical books, reports, and papers

Introduction	As a simple low-cost solution to the requirements given in Table 6.4, a system is proposed based on existing text editors and a separate system at home to save on telephone charges.
Chapter 1	Computers and operating systems—The PDP-11/70 computer will be used to store the master data base in Brooklyn. Access to the system from Brooklyn and Farmingdale will be via terminal using the facilities of the UNIX operating system. Access from the home location will be via a duplicate data base maintained on TRS-80 floppy disks and accessed via the DOS or NEWDOS operating systems. For occasionally more complex searches, the TRS-80 will access the PDP-11/70 using the RS-232 interface and the telephone modem.
Chapter 2	Hardware and software interfaces—The present editor programs (UNIX Editor on the PDP-11/70 and Electric Pencil and Scripsit on the TRS-80) are available and adequate to provide

Table 6.5 (*continued*)

	the required searching functions. The present communications program available for the TRS-80 allows it to be used with RS-232, modem, and telephone as a terminal into the PDP-11/70. The ability to provide disk transfer capabilities in two directions for updating and creating a duplicate data base depends on completion of the new communications package under development.
Chapter 3	Software functions—All functions required in Secs. 3.1 to 3.4 can be provided via the string search commands of either the UNIX Editor or Pencil/Scripsit. UNIX is more powerful and provides facilities for compound keyword searches. The biggest portion of the job will be initial entry into the data base. Thus, a two-step design is proposed. The existing card file will be maintained at present and a number of nonindexed items will be entered into the system on a trial basis to provide an experimental data base. The experimental data base will contain records in the same format as (1) The existing data base or (2) the Polytechnic Library card, or (3) a subset of 1 or 2. In addition, alphabetized lists of authors, keywords, and titles will be prepared. Experiments will be conducted on the data base and the various lists to determine the optimum approach for the detailed specifications. Access-numbering techniques will be fixed in the detailed specifications.
Chapter 4	Running time—The experimental data base can be replicated (concatenated with itself) n times to provide a long enough file to determine experimentally the anticipated search times. The TRS-80 system will be used at home for all functions except complex searches, which will require direct access to the PDP-11/70 via terminal mode.
Chapter 5	Accuracy—The string length and file length limits of some of the file manipulation and string search commands may cause some problems. These should be investigated before the detailed specifications are written.
Chapter 6	Response to undesired events—A detailed list of error messages which are built into the editor programs will be prepared for the detailed specifications. Defensive operator procedures will also be provided in the detailed specifications.
Chapter 7	Methods for complex searches in UNIX will be given in the detailed specifications.
Chapter 8	Fundamental assumptions—Any changes from those in the requirements will be given in the detailed specifications.
Chapter 9	Changes—The detailed specifications will contain a plan and procedures for adding the existing documents to the data base.
Chapter 10	Definition of terms—The glossary of terms and online instructions will be provided in the detailed specifications.
Chapter 11	Related documents—References to UNIX, Pencil, Scripsit, and several library information systems available to the Polytechnic Library will be referenced.

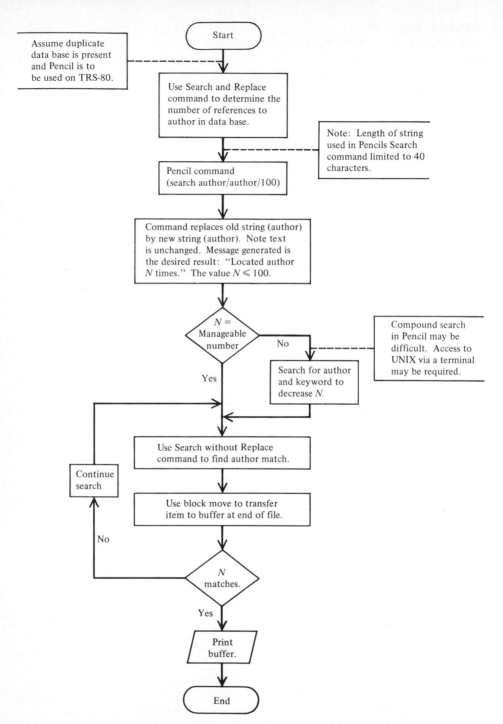

Figure 6.4 Preliminary design of an author search (see Sec. 3.3 of Table 6.4).

portion of the preliminary design of an author search is given in Fig. 6.4. The reader should note how the detail expands as we move from requirements to specifications to design.

6.3 PERFORMANCE, RELIABILITY, AND QUALITY MEASURES

The subject of project management deals largely with motivating, coordinating, and guiding the professionals who are performing various tasks on the project. Much of project management depends on personnel interaction, subjective evaluations, and judgment. It is of the utmost importance to utilize quantitative measures wherever they exist to support qualitative judgments.

This section discussed performance measures (memory sizes and running time), reliability, and quality metrics. These first two topics have already been discussed in Chaps. 3 and 5, and only a brief recapitulation is given. In fact, it is assumed that because of advances in memory technology and reduced cost, memory size is a crucial design issue only in special cases and we need not add to the discussion which appeared in Chap. 3.

The new material to be introduced in this section is that on quality metrics.

6.3.1 Performance Measures

When one speaks of the performance of a complex system, in general more than one index is used. An automobile might be rated in terms of top speed, the number of miles per gallon, and the time to accelerate from 40 to 60 mi/h in a passing maneuver. When we apply the term *performance* to a computer system, often we imply a single measure, the time to process a particular program. In many applications this is too simplistic a measure and the scope must be broadened.

In the case of a batch system designed to process a wide variety of program sizes and types, one generally defines performance with respect to a group of typical computer programs representative of the expected job stream and calls this package a benchmark.[1] The computer system is then tested for average processing speed $\bar{T}$ by timing the length of time t_b it takes to process the benchmark package of N programs. The average processing time is given by

$$\bar{T} = t_b/N \tag{6.1}$$

One use of such benchmark programs is to compare various compilers which operate on the same machine or to compare the hardware and software of competitive vendors before buying a system.[2] This is somewhat harder to do in a

---

[1] The term *benchmark* has also been used to denote a check program. For example, the Nuclear Regulatory Commission needed to check the accuracy and validity of a program which performed civil engineering design computations on nuclear reactor structures. They used as a "benchmark" a set of problems which had already been checked theoretically and run on another, similar and well-trusted computer program.

[2] Ferrari (1978), p. 33.

multiprocessor or time-shared system because one also has to specify what all the others (users) are doing to fully specify the load on the system. Clearly such a performance measure is a combination of the operating system and the computer. Of course if we wish to compare the speed of two competitive program designs, assuming a fixed operating system and computer, one can use the same experimental technique.

If we have two different designs and wish to compare their processing times, one approach is to code each one and then test them both on the computer, using the appropriate operating system and language translator. Unfortunately this approach requires duplicate design and coding work and presupposes that the target computer and system software are available. This approach cannot be used for estimates early in the system design process; thus software and hardware simulators of the target machine and system software are often used for such comparisons. An analytical method one can use in such circumstances is to deal with the total number of instructions, the processing time of each instruction (or class of instruction), and the expected instruction mix (see Table 6.6). One can then compute the processing time T in terms of the processing times t_i for the k instructions and the occurrence frequencies f_i and the number of instructions I_T (see Sec. 3.4.4):

$$T = I_T \left(\sum_{i=1}^{k} f_i t_i \right) \tag{6.2}$$

If k represents the number of instruction classes, then we must use $\bar{t}_i$, the average processing time in Eq. (6.2). Of course such computations are done at the assembly language level. Equation (6.2) holds for sequential control flow. When

Table 6.6 Typical instruction mixes

Instruction category	Commercial scientific weights*	Commercial nonscientific weights*	Command control†	This forecast‡
Fixed add	0.10	0.25	0.16	0.70
Floating add	0.10	0.00	......	0.00
Multiply (fixed or floating)	0.06	0.01	0.152	0.30
Divide	0.02	0.00	0.008	0.00
Fetch, store, logic	0.72	0.74	0.68	0.00

Source: Turn (1974), p. 73. See also Bell et al. (1978), pp. 356–360 and 541–552.
  *Formulated by K. E. Knight (see Bell and Newell, 1971).
  †See G. N. Nomicos, "Advanced Data Processing Systems Study, Part IV: Advanced Processor Concepts," IBM, Aug. 25, 1969.
  ‡The fixed-add instruction represents all "short instructions."

we encounter branches and loops, we must use the techniques given in Eqs. (3.68) and (3.69).

More elaborate formulas involving the expression of computing power in terms of instruction mix have been devised by Knight.[1] Interesting comparisons of the relative computing power of the IBM 360 series of computers appear in Bell and Newell (1971, p. 584). The author and his colleagues used Eq. (6.2) to roughly show that except for floating-point calculations, the PDP-11/20 computer had the same processing speed for a language translator as the IBM 360/50.[2]

The measurement of system performance and the isolation of the factors which affect performance in a complex time-shared or multiprocessing or multiprocessor computer system is a difficult problem. A good reference describing the application of statistical estimation and correlation-regression techniques to such measurements is the proceedings of a 1971 Office of Naval Research conference.[3]

A somewhat different problem arises when a piece of software has already been built and its processing time is too slow. This is a common problem in real-time systems. A good line of attack is to run the software through a program which provides frequency counts of the number of times an instruction is executed.[4] The designer then focuses on the program areas with large execution counts (see the discussion of the work of Holthouse and Cohen in Sec. 2.8.2). Another approach is to look for a faster algorithm (see Sec. 3.4.2).

6.3.2 Reliability

We have already discussed reliability extensively in Chap. 5. Thus, our approach here is merely a brief recapitulation of its utility and an exhortation that it indeed be used. Reliability estimates should first appear during the initial stages of design. Then during integration testing they can be used to determine how much more testing is required.

If we use the model of Eq. (5.69) we need to estimate the total number of errors and the proportionality constant, E_T and K, by using the methods of Sec. 5.7.6. Rough estimates for these parameters can be obtained from previous data (see Tables 5.4, 5.5, and 5.10). An example is given below which illustrates how reliability estimation can be done during preliminary design.

Let us suppose that we are about to bid on a computer system for a particular task and that our initial estimates are that the program will consist of about 30,000 PL/1 statements. Assuming that each PL/1 statement expands into 5 lines of machine language, the program will result in 150,000 lines of object code. The specifications are such that the MTTF must be 100 h.

[1] Bell and Newell (1971), pp. 49–52; Ferrari (1978), p. 294.
[2] Shooman et al. (1970).
[3] Freiberger (1972).
[4] Knuth (1970); Knuth and Stevenson (1973).

If we use the 1 percent figure developed in Tables 5.4 and 5.5, we obtain: $E_T = 0.01 \times 150,000 = 1500$ errors. Using Miyamoto's value of K (approximately 200) computed in Sec. 5.7.3, and Eq. (5.71), we can obtain a value for E_c, the number of errors which must be found and corrected, to yield the specified 100-h MTTF:

$$100 = \frac{1}{200(1500/150,000 - E_c/150,000)} \tag{6.3}$$

Solving for E_c yields 1492; thus about eight errors would be left undiscovered. Now other estimates of test time, development cost, and total cost can be made based on the above model and the computed values.

Since our estimates are based on the assumed values for E_T and K, it is instructive to perform a simple sensitivity analysis by varying both parameters by a factor of 10. Varying K affects our estimate of the number of removed errors E_c and thus the number of remaining errors. For $K = 2000$, there are 0.8 remaining errors and 1499.2 corrected errors; while for $K = 2$, there are 80 remaining errors and 1420 corrected errors. Notice that neither of these changes appreciably affects the initial estimate of E_c needed to obtain a 100-h MTTF. If we similarly perturb E_T by a factor of 10 while holding K constant at 200, we find that for $E_T = 15,000$ we must remove 14,992 errors, leaving 8, whereas if $E_T = 150$, we remove 142 errors, leaving 8. Our initial estimates of testing time will be proportional to the number of error removals anticipated.

Clearly, the best results will be obtained if one has good estimates for K and E_T based upon historical data. One should try to find data for a similar program size, a similar application, a similar mix of programming skills, and a project performed within one's own company. The important parameter for initial estimation is E_T, which can be obtained by studying the historical records of previous programs completed in the near past. Also it is easy to gather such data for ongoing programs if a decision to do so is made early in the project. In fact, the compilation of such historical data both within a company and from the literature should be the first priority of a software quality and reliability group.

Later in the project, when integration testing is about to begin, we can apply the methods of Sec. 5.7.5 to obtain better estimates of K and E_T. Of course the estimates made during early design can be updated as a final design begins to emerge. Toward the end of integration testing, the prime question is how much more testing must be done to ensure a good system. If reliability of the end product is a strong factor in this decision (as it is in many cases), then we can begin focusing on the estimates of the number of remaining errors and the MTTF, which should be fairly accurate at this point. Thus, MTTF versus development time graphs such as those shown in Figs. 5.18 to 5.20 become a significant measure of progress. In this case the value of K is the sensitive parameter, since by now we should have an accurate value for E_T. Again we observe that the macro model holds only for a case where there are still remaining errors. Thus, as $E_r(\tau) \rightarrow 1$ the model assumptions become invalid. This implies that an MTTF $= I_T/K$ should serve as an upper bound on the range of valid predictions for the model. For our hypothetical example, MTTF $\rightarrow 150{,}000/200 = 750$.

In one case the author did a study on a system under development with a software MTTF goal of 500 h. The exhibited MTTF was a few hours, and the "bound" I_T/K yielded 100 to 150 h, depending on the values estimated for K. This analysis contributed to the scrapping of the software and concentration on the development of backup software as the primary system.[1]

The analyst may wish to use a formal statistical procedure for "averaging" together the initial estimates of K and E_T along with those determined later via testing.

6.3.3 Quality Metrics

Qualitative approaches Reliability is the most important single measure of quality. However, there are other attributes which are also of considerable importance. Some of these attributes describe the technical qualities of a good design, while others relate to the ease of producing the design. A list of many of these important good qualities (sometimes called the "ilities" list) appears in Table 6.7 along with a brief definition.

Clearly there is much overlap among the quantities, precise definitions have yet to be formulated, and quantitative measurement is difficult. For example, how would we define a metric for visibility (see Table 6.7)? Should one use the number of hours it takes an average manager unfamiliar with the program to understand the design?

The definition of portability is based upon one given by Gilb:

> The application shall be constructed so that total system portability is not less than 95 percent in total.
> This implies a guarantee that the consultant software house will undertake to convert to any standard Cobol environment of major manufacturer for a maximum price of 5% $(100 - 95)$ of the original programming/debugging cost [exclusive system analysis and design].
> This includes all programs, machine language subroutines, control cards, necessary software, job operational specifications, physical file conversion and logical file data conversion.
> The operational cost and reliability are to remain at the same level as for 100% portable programs and files.[2]

This definition was used in two contracts which Gilb helped negotiate. The purchaser wished the program to run on a computer which had not as yet been selected. In order to be sure that such a contract clause could be enforced, it

[1]Shooman (1979*b*).
[2]Gilb (1977), p. 66.

Table 6.7 Quality metrics and their definition*

Technical measure

Maintainability	Basically a measure of how difficult and costly it will be to correct errors found in the field. A mathematical definition is given in Chap. 5.
Adaptability (changeability)	How difficult and costly it is to introduce new features into the program after release. Also how difficult it is to extract certain functions from the program and incorporate them in other programs. Clearly a well-structured, modular program will be highly adaptable.
Utility (usability)	How well the program satisfies its intended function. Perhaps we could measure this by asking all the users of the program to grade each program feature on a scale A, B, C, D, F (after defining our meaning of each grade) and averaging the results.
System security (privacy)	How difficult it is for unauthorized persons to gain access to information in or control of a computer system. This covers the gamut of (1) the "hacker" at the university computer center who wishes to demonstrate prowess, (2) the busybody who seeks access to your private records, (3) the government or industrial spy, and (4) the computer criminal.†
Installability	Most large systems which are designed for general-purpose use go through a system-generation phase, to customize the software to the specific computer system. Perhaps we might measure this by the number of hours spent installing the software divided by the development man-hours for software plus hardware.
Simplicity	Is the design straightforward and direct or is it sophisticated and complex? In all systems the greatest enemy of reliability is complexity; thus the measures developed in Chap. 3 can be used.
Portability	This most important quality is the ease of transferring a software system to a different computer and/or operating system. One measure is the cost to develop divided by the cost to modify (see text).
Understandability	How easy it is to understand and use the software. To measure this we could ask an impartial panel of users to grade the system as suggested in the case of utility.

Managerial measures

Testability	How easy is it to test the software? Perhaps a program with a lot of bugs which are easy to find and correct is better than one with fewer initial bugs which are hard to find and remove; perhaps not. A metric might be the test cost divided by development cost.
Viability (explainability, justifiability)	Is the design one which can be easily explained to management, and can we easily trace and control the progress of the development with easily definable and measurable milestones?
Risk	What is the probability that (1) the system will be delivered on time, (2) there will be no cost overruns, and (3) the user will be satisfied?

*See Jensen and Tonies (1979), pp. 82–86; Gilb (1977); and Boehm et al. (1978).
†See Hoffman (1973) and Parker (1976).

432

would be prudent to use a set of benchmark programs as a standard in judging whether the clause has been satisfied.

Unfortunately, the state of software quality metrics is far from satisfactory. The author has observed much research activity in this area during the last few years, but little supported research and still fewer results. It is to be hoped that the future will bring a better understanding of these issues and practical quantitative measures.

The reader should not infer that nothing can be done presently. In most cases the good qualities listed in Table 6.7 can be qualitatively evaluated and used in a metric fashion (see Table 4.7) in comparing competitive designs. If each quality can be ranked in terms of numerical values from 0 to 10, a semiquantitative analysis can be made (see Gilb, 1977, for a discussion of the MECCA method).

Analytical approaches This section summarizes three analytical approaches which have been proposed in the area of software quality. One important study in this area was done by S. Amster et al. at Bell Labs.[1] The group set out to investigate whether one could set up an objective measure of software quality. Their research had an immediate goal. They wished to determine whether the quality of two software systems consisting of 1000 programs could be readily improved by rewriting selected programs.

The approach was to assemble a board of expert programmers who would rate a randomly selected sample of the programs by reading and analyzing them on the basis of five different (called dependent) variables Y_1 to Y_5. The variables Y_1 to Y_4 were estimates of the percentage reduction in (1) object code achievable by easy transformation, (2) object code achievable by complete restructuring, (3) source statements via easy transformations, and (4) source statements via complete restructuring. The last dependent variable, Y_5, was a quantitative estimate of program clarity based on a 14-point scale from 1 (best) to 14 (worst). The eight attributes given in Table 6.8 were used to guide the experts in the ranking.

The experiment also utilized 29 different independent variables X_1 to X_{29}, listed in Table 6.9, which could be counted with an analysis program (called a *data extractor*). These variables were chosen by studying the programs, by using ideas from the literature, by intuition and judgment, etc. Extensive statistical correlation and regression analysis was performed. Each one of the dependent Y's could be predicted quite well (correlation coefficients were 0.90, 0.91, 0.93, 0.77, 0.86) by using from 5 to 7 different X variables. Variables X_6, X_{10}, and X_{21} were the most common, occurring in 3 out of the 5 equations for the Y's.

Some of the conclusions of the study were:

1. It appears feasible to objectively identify program quality if an experiment is performed to correlate subjective measures with the relevant variables.
2. Labels are useful even in structured programs, and do not degrade quality.

---

[1]Amster et al. (1976).

Table 6.8 Attributes used to guide experts in their clarity ranking

1. Concise (lack of verbosity in number of source statements)

2. Straightforward (lack of tricky, obscure code)

3. Understandable (good comments, formatting, use of mnemonics)

4. Clear control structure (good use of structured programming, lack of undue complexity, modularization)

5. Uniform style (changes well integrated; few, if any, "historical reasons" for the present state of the program)

6. Self-contained with respect to documentation

7. Appropriate use of macros

8. Appropriate use of change levels, i.e., adherence to change control procedures

Source: Amster et al. (1976).

Table 6.9 List of independent variables used

X_1 := (DO loops-IJNOs)/machine operations
X_2 := (.As + A0s + ughs)/source statements
X_3 := longest run of labels/labels
X_4 := longest run of labels/source statements
X_5 := longest run of labels
X_6 := identifiers referenced/identifiers
X_7 := flags/source statements
X_8 := (DECLAREs + ACTs)/source statements
X_9 := labels
X_{10} := machine operations/source statements
X_{11} := machine operation fetches/machine operations
X_{12} := machine operation moves/machine operations
X_{13} := (fetches + moves + stores)/machine operations
X_{14} := source statements
X_{15} := ACTs/source statements
X_{16} := DECLAREs/source statements
X_{17} := A0s/source statements
X_{18} := ughs/source statements
X_{19} := source level comments/source statements
X_{20} := simple assignment statements/source statements
X_{21} := DOs/source statements
X_{22} := (BREAKs + CALLs + DOs + ELSEs + IFs + RETURNs + ITERATEs + WHENs + DO loops + GOTOs)/source statements
X_{23} := SRJs/machine operations
X_{24} := UCJs/machine operations
X_{25} := BASEs
X_{26} := DATAs
X_{27} := macro definitions
X_{28} := (IFs + WHENs + DO loops + CALLs)
X_{29} := X_{28}/source statements

Source: Amster et al. (1976).

3. Programs get more complex as their size increases.
4. Complete restructuring of programs is more likely to reduce object code size than mechanical transformations.
5. The clearer a program, the more difficult it is to make reductions in source code by complete restructuring.
6. Program clarity did not correlate with the number of GOTOs for programs with less than 40 GOTOs. However, clarity decreased with the number of GOTOs for programs with more than 40 GOTOs.

The reader is referred to the paper for further details.

Halstead has also studied programming quality from a different viewpoint. He studied the potential volume V^* and related it to clarity and simplicity of algorithmic expressions, which he calls purity. An example which he uses for illustration is the result R of squaring the sum of two operands P and Q. If we have a language with a matching built-in primitive, the algorithm is

$$SQDSUM(PQR)$$

Other possible algorithms are:

$$(P + Q) \times (P + Q) \to R$$

$$P + Q \to R \times R \to R$$

$$P + Q \to T, T \times T \to R$$

Halstead studied 18 different versions of this algorithm and considers six different classes of impurities to exist, including unfactored expressions, common subexpressions, etc. The reader is referred to Halstead's book for a full discussion of his approach.[1]

Another study attempting to quantify program quality was conducted by TRW[2] and dealt with 12 low-level metrics: structuredness, device independence, completeness, accuracy, consistency, device efficiency, accessibility, communicativeness, self-descriptiveness, conciseness, legibility, and augmentability. The lower-level metrics are assumed to be related to seven higher-order metrics: portability, reliability, efficiency, human engineering, testability, understandability, and modifiability. The structuredness of the programs was related to the nine different metrics given in Table 6.10. Those metrics which rated high in the evaluation areas are marked by an asterisk, and the one which rated very high is

---

[1] Halstead (1977), Chap. 7.
[2] Boehm et al. (1977), pp. 97–105.

Table 6.10 Evaluation of nine different metrics for measuring structuredness

Metric number	Original metric number	Definition of metrics to measure structuredness	Correlation with quality	Potential benefit	Quantifiability	Ease of developing automated evaluation	Completeness of automated evaluation
1	10.13*	Have the rules for transfer of control between modules been established and followed?	A	5	AL	E	P
2	10.12*	Are the modules limited in size?	AA	4	AL	E	P
3	1.14*	Has the ordering: commentary header block, specification statements, then executable code been followed?	A	3	CC	E	C
4	7.11*	Do all subprograms contain at most, one point of exit?	AA	4	AL	E	C
5	10.9*	Do all subprograms and functions have only one entry point?	A	4	AL	E	C
6	10.8(*)	Is program flow always forward, with commented exceptions?	AA	4	AL	M	P
7	10.11	Is the overlay structure consistent with the subprogram's sequencing?	A	5	ER		
8	6.8	Is the program subdivided into modules in accordance with readily recognized functions?	A	5	TR		
9	4.7*	Is the program written in a standard set of constructs available in the particular programming language used (preferably a national standard such as ANSI)?	AA	4	CC	E	P

Correlation with software quality

A = Always a nonnegative correlation between high score for the metric and possession of the associated primitive characteristic.
AA = Almost Always the above correlation.
U = Usually the above correlation.
S = Sometimes the above correlation.

Potential benefit

5 = Extremely important for metric to be satisfied; major potential troubles if not.
4 = Important for metric to be satisfied.
3 = Fairly Important for metric to be satisfied.
2 = Some incremental value for metric to be satisfied.
1 = Slight value, no real loss if not.

Quantifiability

AL = Can be done cost effectively via an automated ALgorithm.
CC = Can be done cost-effectively via an automated Compliance Checker if given a checklist.
UR = Requires an Untrained human Reader.
TR = Requires a Trained human Reader.
ER = Requires an Expert human Reader.
EX = Requires the program to be EXecuted.

Ease of developing automated evaluation

E = Easy, M = Medium difficulty, D = Difficult

Completeness of automated evaluation

C = Total, P = Partial, I = Inconclusive results

Source: Boehm et al. (1973).

437

marked by an asterisk in parentheses. A discussion of the other metrics appears in the report.

The reader who wishes to study this subject further is referred to other related studies: (1) the relationship between the quality of an information system and how satisfied users are with that system;[1] (2) the use of utility theory to study user attitudes in a time-shared system;[2] (3) how a user can input data and how errors occur in the input phase;[3] and (4) the use of expert opinion to quantify certain concepts (consensus estimation, Delphi method).[4]

6.4 COST ESTIMATION

6.4.1 Introduction

The computer age began about 40 years ago when experimental digital computers first appeared. Extensive use of computers dates back only 25 years, and higher-level language only 20 years. Cost estimation probably began when the first sizable programming projects were designed in the 1950s. In the 1960s estimates were much too optimistic, and large cost overruns often occurred; however, in the 1970s considerable progress has been made in cost estimating. To quote Putnam and Wolverton (1977, p. i):

> The typical 200–300 percent cost overrun and similar schedule slippage is no longer tolerable when the cost is measured in millions of dollars and the most optimistic schedule expectation is three years or more until an operating product is available to run on the machine. Manpower cost and schedule have to be predictable within reasonable engineering limits *before* investment decisions are made. Heretofore this has not been possible. Today we can handle a wide variety of software projects adequately.

An important feature of cost modeling is that estimates are made for every project. In addition, actual costs are kept throughout the project, and projected and actual costs are compared at key milestones. This is probably the reason why cost models are much more developed at present than other software engineering models.

In the next section we investigate how development costs have varied over the past two decades and how we expect them to change in the future.

6.4.2 Development Costs per Instruction

In many ways cost estimation and control is the heart of the management task in software development. Only in recent years has a reasonable body of cost data

---

[1] Lucas (1975).
[2] Grochow (1972).
[3] Gilb and Weinberg (1977); Sontz (1973), p. 136.
[4] Shooman and Sinkar (1977).

appeared in the open literature. Thus, it is easier to document present software costs than to compare them with past history or to forecast the future. In Chap. 1 we projected the exponential growth in software size during the decade of the 1960s (see Fig. 1.1). If we are to prevent software development costs from growing at a rate proportional to size, we must effect order of magnitude reductions in the cost per instruction. Generally we measure the unit cost of software in terms of dollars per instruction or instructions developed per man-day (productivity). We can roughly gauge the progress in software construction by exploring three sets of data.

Weinwurm versus Shooman-Bolsky data As a hypothetical example we assume a program which is 150,000 object words in length and use Weinwurm data, circa 1965, to predict productivity at that time. From Eq. (4.2) we estimate 1500 man-months of development time for the entire project (and from Eq. (4.5) we obtain 15,000 total computer test hours). Dividing the 150,000 words by 1500 man-months yields 100 words per month, or, for a 20-working-day month, 5 words per day. We can compare these values with those obtained by Shooman and Bolsky for the integration-test phase in Table 4.4, where the average number of man-hours for diagnosis and correction per error was $2.46 + 1.98 = 4.4$ h. Assuming that the number of errors is about 1 percent of the code size (see Table 5.3), we would anticipate 1500 errors and a total of 6660 h. Dividing this by 8 h per day yields 832.5 man-days. However, the test phase is about 40 percent of the total task (see Table 1.5), and the Shooman-Bolsky data represent perhaps one-half of the test phase; thus we divide by 0.2 and obtain 4162.5 man-days. Dividing 150,000 words by 4162.5 man-days yields a productivity of 36 words per day, which indicates an improvement of over 7:1 from 1964 to 1975.

Similarly, from Table 4.4 the testing time including diagnosis and correction is $13.5 + 4.9 = 18.4$ min or 0.307 hours per error, and multiplying by 1500 errors yields 461 h. This is approximately a 30:1 improvement from 1965 to 1975. (No doubt some of this is due to improved design and test methods; however, faster computing time must also play a large role.)

SDC data The System Development Corporation published a report in 1966 containing an analysis of a group of 169 SDC programs. The sample of programs included large, small, assembly, and higher-level software for a variety of applications and machines. The results are shown in Fig. 6.5. *Only product effort* (coding) was included and the time for design, management, and integration testing *were excluded*. If we assume that production time is a stable fraction of the total effort (from Table 1.5, we might estimate it at 20 percent), then the mean value is 200 instructions per man-month in 1960 and 1000 instructions per man-month in 1970. This predicts a 5:1 improvement. Assuming a 20-day month and that production is 20 percent of the entire task, the improvement is from 2 instructions per day to 10 instructions per day.

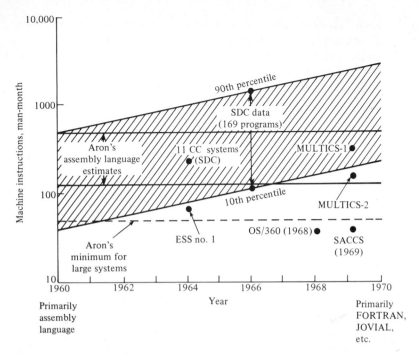

Figure 6.5 Estimated software productivity, 1960–1970. *(From Fleishman, 1966)*

Wolverton data A third study, reported by Wolverton, shows a band of productivity data for current experience and another band for new technology (see Fig. 6.6). If we assume for discussion a program size of 100K object instructions, we see that current experience is about 5 man-hours per instruction and new technology should yield about 1.3 man-hours per instruction. Assuming an 8-h working day, these values convert to 1.6 and 6.2 instructions per day, predicting an improvement for new technology of about 4:1.

Based on the above crude extrapolations, it appears that it will be a difficult task to obtain a 10:1 improvement in software productivity during the 1980s; however, this is certainly not beyond our grasp. Much of this depends on how large an improvement modern programming techniques will yield and how quickly existing programmers will adopt these methods.

6.4.3 Cost-Estimation Models[1]

Introduction Some of the earliest cost-estimation models[2] were formulated in the 1960s. In almost all cases, cost estimation is based either directly or indirectly on

[1] See Shooman (1979).
[2] Frielink (1965); Sackman (1967), p. 202 (a discussion of Weinwurm's 1965 SDC report); LaBolle (1972).

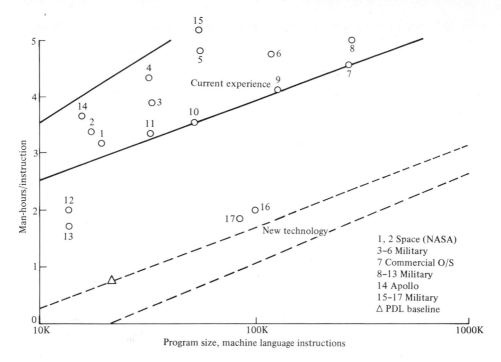

Figure 6.6 Estimated productivity improvement due to new technology. *(From Putnam and Wolverton, 1977)*

past historical data. Sometimes the collected data are translated into tables or graphs indicating the productivity (instructions per man-day, man-month, or man-year). Another approach is to formulate a parametric model, a mathematical function of several variables, suggested by previous experimentation and engineering judgment. Statistical techniques are then applied to the data in order to reduce the number of model variables (analysis of variance and correlation) and to compute the constants in the equation (parameter estimation).

Before we discuss the various cost-estimation models, we will discuss the definition of the term *productivity*. Care must be taken, since the definition in the literature may change from one model or data base to the next. First of all, what constitutes a line of code? a line of higher-level language? a line of assembly code? a line of machine language? a machine instruction? or the number of bytes? Furthermore, in counting lines does one count comments, job control language, declarations, test code (test drivers and test stubs)? In computing productivity, does one divide the total number of instructions written by the total number of man-days for the project? What about the variance in human ability?

In general, the productivity measures discussed in this book assume that only the number of executable object code (machine code) instructions are counted, and that the total of man-days for the entire project is a sum for several workers of mixed ability resulting in an "average level" of talent. In all cases the reader should check all these questions before proceeding with any model or data base. Jones (1978) gives an excellent discussion of these issues.

Classification of cost models A number of authors have attempted to classify cost-modeling procedures. One classification scheme proposed by LaBolle focuses on the mathematical technique used to produce the cost estimate (see Table 6.11). Clearly, techniques 3 and 4 in the table involve more structure than techniques 1 and 2, and all other things being equal, they should yield better estimates.

Wolverton classifies the different techniques of cost estimation in a slightly different way in Table 6.12. His categories relate more nearly to which group does the estimation and the type of data base used. In the top-down method, the overall cost is estimated and then apportioned among the identified work packages and modules. The bottom-up method starts by separately estimating each work package and module and combining the individual estimates to obtain an overall estimate. Wolverton suggests that top-down and bottom-up estimating be done together with each method serving as a check on the other.

There appear to be a few arguments why method 4 of Table 11 and method 5 of Table 12 should be superior to the other techniques. Both techniques involve estimating at a lower level, i.e., breaking the software into many low-level work packages. In such a case, the individuals who do the estimates for the packages probably have more experience with previous software of the same type and can thus give more accurate estimates. Second, there are statistical reasons, discussed in Sec. 6.6.4, why independent estimates of low-level portions of the system which are summed should be more accurate than an overall estimate.

The following sections discuss a number of different techniques which are popular in the open literature. The examples selected for discussion are not

Table 6.11 Classification of general cost estimating techniques

To make cost estimates, one or more of four general approaches are used: (Note these approaches apply to widgets, Apollo, shoe laces, income tax, and computer programming.)

1. *Unit cost or price* e.g., cost per instruction, cost per subprogram, routine or module or cost per program system, cost per activity.
2. *Percentage of total cost* e.g., computer programs are X% of the cost of a library retrieval information system.
3. *Specific analogy* e.g., the design requirements for this computer program system are similar to the one done last year except for X, Y, and Z, so the cost will be $A (the cost of last year's job) modified by factors X, Y, and Z.
4. *Parametric equations* e.g., this program system requires X displays, Y modules, Z types of data so:

$$\text{COST}, C = K_1 X + K_2 Y + K_3 Z$$

where K_i are predetermined parameters

Note: "Seat-of-the-pants," "top-of-the-head" (pulling numbers out of the air) estimating may use one or more of the approaches without articulating the parameters or the approach used.

Source: LaBolle (1972).

Table 6.12 Classification of approaches to cost estimation*

1. *Top-down estimating*: The estimator relies on the total cost of large portions of previous projects that have been completed to estimate the cost of all or large portions of the project to be estimated. History coupled with informed opinion (or intuition) is used to allocate costs between packages. Among its many pitfalls is the substantial risk of overlooking special or difficult technical problems that may be buried in the project tasks, and the lack of details needed for cost justification.

2. *Similarities and differences estimating*: The estimator breaks down the jobs to be accomplished to a level of detail where the similarities to and differences from previous projects are most evident. Work units that cannot be compared are estimated separately by some other method.

3. *Ratio estimating*: The estimator relies on sensitivity coefficients or exchange ratios that are invariant (within limits) to the details of design. The software analyst estimates the size of a module by its number of object instructions, classifies it by type, and evaluates its relative complexity. An appropriate cost matrix is constructed from a cost data base in terms of cost per instruction, for that type of software, at that relative complexity level. Other ratios, empirically derived, can be used in the total estimation process, for instance, computer usage rate based on central processing unit (CPU) time per instruction, peripheral usage to CPU usage, engineers per secretary, and so forth. The method is simple, fast, convenient, and useful in the proposal environment and beyond. It suffers, as do all methods, from the need for a valid cost data base for many estimating situations (business versus scientific, real-time versus nonreal-time, operational versus nonoperational).

4. *Standards estimating*: The estimator relies on standards of performance that have been systematically developed. These standards then become stable reference points from which new tasks can be calibrated. Many mature industries, such as manufacturing and construction, use this method routinely. The method is accurate only when the same operations have been performed repeatedly and good records are available. The pitfall is that custom software development is not "performed repeatedly."

5. *Bottom-up estimating*: This is the technique most commonly used in estimating government research and development contracts. The total job is broken down into relatively small work packages and work units. The work breakdown is continued until it is reasonably clear what steps and talents are involved in doing each task. Each task is then estimated and the costs are pyramided to form the total project cost. An advantage of this technique is that the job of estimating can be distributed to the people who will do the work. A difficulty is the lack of immediate perspective of the most important parameter of all: the total cost of the project. In doing detailed estimates, the estimator is not sensitive to the reasonableness of the total cost of the software package. Therefore, top-down estimation is used as a check on the bottom-up method.

The estimation process is nearly always a combination of two or more of the basic classifications given above.

* Wolverton (1974).

exhaustive, but only illustrate current usage. In most cases, only a brief discussion of the technique and the data base is given. The reader is referred to the references for a complete description.

SDC study Cost data on 74 computer programs written between 1962 and 1966 were gathered by System Development Corporation (SDC) and analyzed under a U.S. Air Force contract.[1] The end result is the graph given in Fig. 6.7, which

[1]Sackman (1967); LaBolle (1972).

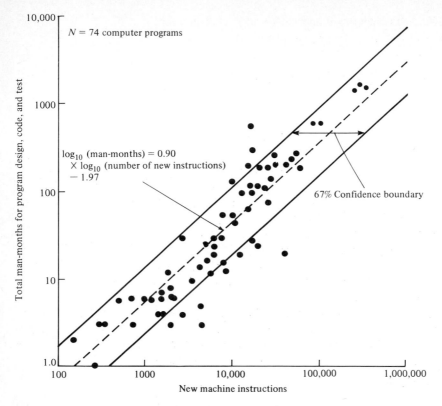

Figure 6.7 Cost data collected by Program Management Project at System Development Corporation (SDC) under U.S. Air Force Contract (1962–1966). Note that this graph is almost identical with the data given in Fig. 4.2.

depicts cumulative effort versus program size. The dotted line in the figure represents the most likely value, and the two solid lines are a 67 percent confidence boundary.

Aron study Aron published a set of data in 1969 in which he categorized productivity in terms of project duration and difficulty.[2] The data are presented in matrix form in Table 6.13, where the duration of the project is broken into three categories, as is the difficulty. Thus, nine different cells appear in the table, and the productivity varies from a low of 5 instructions per man-day to a high of 40 instructions per man-day.

Wolverton's studies In a prizewinning paper, Wolverton (1974) describes a wealth of data on cost estimation. We have selected one of his graphs, which is shown in

[2]Aron (1969).

Table 6.13 Aron's productivity table*
(Assuming 20 working days a month and 250 working days a year)

| Difficulty | Duration, months | | | Comments |
	6–12	12–24	More than 24	
Easy	20	500 (25/day)	10,000 (40/day)	Very few interactions
Medium	10	250 (12.5/day)	5,000 (20/day)	Some interactions
Difficult	5	125 (6.25/day)	1,500 (6/day)	Many interactions
Units	Instructions per man-day	Instructions per man-month	Instructions per man-year	

*From Aron (1969).

Fig. 6.8. In this figure the project difficulty is plotted along the x axis and the dollar cost per instruction along the y axis. A family of 10 curves is presented for new instructions and old (modified) ones. The range of cost given varies from a low of $15 per instruction for easy algorithms and old code to $75 per instruction for all kinds of time-critical processors.

Walston and Felix studies Walston and Felix (1977) began gathering data in 1973, and by 1977 there were 60 programs in their data base. For purposes of comparison, we have assumed that the average age of their programs can be dated from 1975. The programs ranged from 4000 to 467,000 lines of code, 12 to 11,758 man-months. Twenty-eight different higher-level languages were used, and 66 computers were represented. The data are presented in the same manner as in Fig. 6.7, and the least-squares fit to the data results in the equation

$$E = 5.2L^{0.91} \tag{6.4}$$

where

$$E = \text{total effort in man-months}$$
$$L = \text{thousands of lines of delivered source code}$$

A host of other data are presented in the paper on how various variables affect the productivity. In addition, a parametric equation is developed involving 29 different variables; however, the numerical values of the coefficients are not given in the paper. Additional data on the effects of reused code, multiple development locations, terminal input and documentation, machine, and schedule times appear in Walston and Felix (1977).

Doty study Doty Associates conducted a cost study for the U.S. Air Force which was published in 1977 (Doty, 1977). The results are a set of formulas similar to

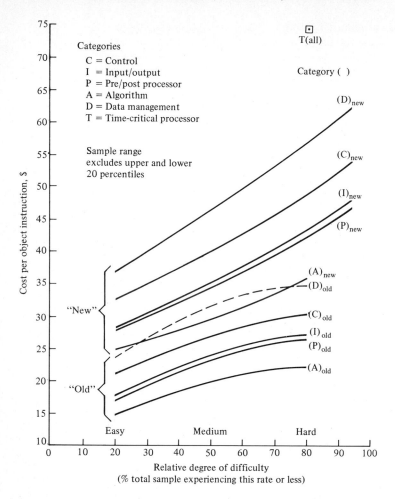

Figure 6.8 Cost per object instruction versus relative degree of difficulty. *(From Wolverton, 1974)*

Eq. (6.4) which are given in Table 6.14. The program applications are divided into four categories, and separate formulas are given for object code (assembly language) and source code (higher-level language). For purposes of comparison, the data were considered to be from an average (representative) year, 1976. It is important to note that these data largely sustain the often repeated hypothesis that it takes the same length of time to write x lines of code in a higher-level language as in assembly language. For example, suppose we say $x = 1000$ lines for convenience; then $I = 1$ and Table 6.14 predicts (average of all) 4.8 man-months for writing 1000 lines of assembly code and 5.3 man-months for writing 1000 lines of higher-level-language code. The corollary to the above hypothesis is that the increased productivity of writing in a higher-level language is due to the reduced size (by a factor of 3 to 7, typically) of a higher-level-language program.

Table 6.14 Software development manpower estimating algorithms

| Application | Object code | | Source code | |
	Estimator	Standard error	Estimator	Standard error
All	$MM = 4.790I^{0.991}$	62.2	$MM = 5.258I^{1.057}$	50.7
Command and control	$MM = 4,573I^{1.228}$	41.1	$MM = 4.089I^{1.263}$	41.1
Scientific	$MM = 4.495I^{1.068}$	72.1	$MM = 7.054I^{1.019}$	72.1
Business	$MM = 2.895I^{0.784}$	12.4	$MM = 4.495I^{0.781}$	10.7
Utility	$MM = 12.039I^{0.719}$	58.1	$MM = 10.078I^{0.811}$	51.7

MM = Man-Months required for analysis, design, code, debug, test, and checkout.
I = Number of delivered instructions expressed in either Object or Source Code in thousands.
Source: Doty (1977).

(Additional cost advantages of higher-level-language programs due to their superior clarity become evident when we consider program enhancement and maintenance. These phases of the software life cycle were not covered in the Doty study.)

The RCA PRICE S system During the late 1960s and early 1970s, RCA developed a cost model for pricing its own military hardware projects. The success of this model[1] led to the leasing of the program at a yearly fee. Other cost-estimation programs have been added to the product line, including most recently PRICE S, which performs software pricing.[2] Because this is a proprietary product, fewer details of the system are available in the open literature than of other techniques. The authors claim that in addition to parametric equations, the product contains simulation and feedback models for certain aspects of programming behavior. A typical output from the PRICE S system is shown in Table 6.15. A brief description of some of the terms used as input to the model is given in Table 6.16. The reader is referred to the references and to Sec. 6.4.5 of this book for a further description of this example.

Other models Many other studies and data exist in the open literature, and the author senses that even more are available within company private reports. A few additional sources should be cited to guide the reader who wishes to probe further. A draft report of a study conducted by Nelson (1978) contains a large amount of data on productivity. One of the results of his study is shown in Fig.

[1]"RCA's Uncanny System" (1976).
[2]Freiman and Park (1979).

Table 6.15 A typical Basic PRICE S output* (With costs in thousands of dollars)

```
                        --- PRICE SOFTWARE MODEL ---

                     DATE 06/26/78  TIME 16:43:13

SAMPLE CASE                                        MOBILE RADAR

                          INPUT DATA
FILENAME: SAMPLE                                   DATED: 07/22/77

DESCRIPTORS
  INSTRUCTIONS  36000     APPLICATION  0.0     RESOURCE     3.500
  FUNCTIONS         0     STRUCTURE    0.0     LEVEL        2.600
                                              INTEGRATION  0.500

APPLICATION CATEGORIES    NEW DEVELOPMENT      SYSTEM CONFIGURATION
                  MIX     DESIGN    CODE       TYPES      QUANTITY
  DATA S/R        0.0     1.00      1.00         0           0
  ONLINE COMM     0.08    1.00      1.00         1           1
  REALTIME C&C    0.08    1.00      1.00         2           2
  INTERACTIVE     0.23    1.00      1.00         1           2
  MATHEMATICAL    0.28    0.50      0.70        ***         ***
  STRING MANIP    0.26    1.00      1.00        ***         ***
  OPR SYSTEMS     0.07    1.00      1.00        ***         ***

SCHEDULE
  COMPLEXITY      1.250
  DESIGN START    SEP 77   IMPL START  DEC 77   T&I START   MAR 78
  DESIGN END      MAY 78   IMPL END    JUL 78   T&I END     FEB 79

SUPPLEMENTAL INFORMATION
  YEAR            1977     ESCALATION  0.0      TECH IMP    1.00
  MULTIPLIER      1.000    PLATFORM    1.4      UTILIZATION 0.80


                          PROGRAM COSTS

COST ELEMENTS             DESIGN     IMPL    T & I     TOTAL
  SYSTEMS ENGINEERING      323.       18.     277.      618.
  PROGRAMMING               42.       83.     113.      239.
  CONFIGURATION CONTROL     74.       25.     171.      271.
  DOCUMENTATION             54.        8.      68.      130.
  PROGRAM MANAGEMENT        30.        8.      34.       72.
       TOTAL               525.      141.     664.     1330.

                          ADDITIONAL DATA

DESCRIPTORS
  INSTRUCTIONS  36000     APPLICATION  5.299    RESOURCE   3.500
  FUNCTIONS       400     STRUCTURE    4.961    LEVEL      2.600

SCHEDULE
  COMPLEXITY      1.250
  DESIGN START    SEP 77   IMPL START  DEC 77   T&I START   MAR 78
  DESIGN END      MAY 78   IMPL END    JUL 78   T&I END     FEB 79

                          SCHEDULE GRAPH
SEP 77                                                  FEB 79
************** DESIGN ***************
       ********* IMPLEMENT **********
               *************** TEST & INTEGRATE ***************
```

* From Freiman and Park (1979).

Table 6.16 A brief explanation of some of the categories of input data used in the PRICE S model*

Mobile radar system

Instructions	Number of machine language executable inst. (36,000)
Functions	Number of blocks in HIPO chart
Application	Index running from math. to real-time control
Structure	Crosscheck of function and level inputs
Resource	Skill, experience, productivity
Level	Average level of work breakdown (from HIPO)
Integration	Measure of amount of integration necessary
Complexity	Factors which effect development time
Escalation	Inflation factor
Platform	Environment
Tech. imp.	Technology improvement
Utilization	Fraction of maximum speed and memory utilized

* From Freiman and Park (1979).

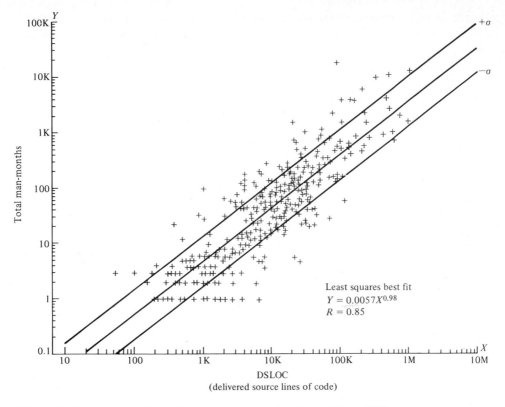

Figure 6.9 Total man-months of effort versus program size. *(From Nelson, 1978)*

6.9, which is of the same form as Fig. 6.7. The details of the data which Nelson used were not described.

Additional information on how project management and cost relate to productivity is given by Daly (1977).

A good reference for various cost data related to computer hardware and software is Phister (1979).

6.4.4 Practical Difficulties versus Theoretical Advantages

There are many practical problems which occur in cost estimation. As an example we discuss some of the difficulties in applying Wolverton's top-down method. Some of the obvious problems with the method are (1) that no historical data may be available for certain packages and (2) that special problems may be overlooked which appear only in more detailed, lower-level analysis. If we decide to use this technique and adopt a fixed-price attitude, we can use the ratios of the historical package cost to total cost estimate to apportion the fixed price among the packages. However, there is an obvious problem with such a fixed-price allocation policy. Suppose the marketing, management, and software engineering groups agree that the software price bid must be $1 million in order to win the contract. However, based on historical data for all the identified packages, the estimated total cost is $1,300,000. This conflict leads to a number of interpretations:

1. The $1,300,000 estimate is based upon older data, and in more recent times productivity has improved and we should be able to do the job for $1 million.
2. There were errors in the cost estimates for some of the packages and a lesser cost can be anticipated. In actuality, if our data base is rich enough, we should not estimate just one value for each package, but three values: the maximum, minimum, and average. This would yield an expected cost estimate along with a worst-case and a best-case cost estimate.
3. The cost will really be $1,300,000. The company had better bid $1,300,000 or not bid at all. Of course it is possible that the project is vitally important to the company since much additional business is virtually assured to the successful bidder. In such a case, upper management may carefully consider the facts and decide to "buy in" (underbid and supplement the budget with company funds).

The bottom-up technique in bottom-up estimating has a statistical advantage over the other methods if the individual estimates are independent and unbiased. The design is detailed to the module level and several programmers give independent cost estimates for each module. These estimates are then pyramided to form the total cost estimate. There are several advantages of this method. Line programmers are better able to anticipate particular difficulties or possibilities of adapting previous code than a higher-level manager. Another important benefit is based on statistical averaging.

If m different programmers *independently* estimate each module cost c_i, and if each estimate has a variance σ_i^2, then we can make the following statistical statements about the total project cost c_p:

$$c_p = c_1 + c_2 + \cdots + c_m \qquad (6.5)$$

The standard deviation of the project cost σ_p is given by

$$\sigma_p^2 = \sigma_1^2 + \sigma_2^2 + \cdots + \sigma_m^2 \qquad (6.6)$$

If all the modules are of equal size and have the same standard deviation, then Eqs. (6.5) and (6.6) become

$$c_p = mc \qquad (c_1 = c_2 = \cdots = c_m = c) \qquad (6.7)$$

$$\sigma_p = \sqrt{m}\,\sigma \qquad (\sigma_1 = \sigma_2 = \cdots = \sigma_m = \sigma) \qquad (6.8)$$

If we compute the ratio of project variance to project cost (Eq. (6.8) divided by Eq. (6.7)), we obtain

$$\frac{\sigma_p}{c_p} = \frac{\sqrt{m}\,\sigma}{mc} = \frac{1}{\sqrt{m}}\frac{\sigma}{c} \qquad (6.9)$$

The result is that the project ratio is *smaller* than the module ratio by a factor of $1/\sqrt{m}$. Thus, for a fixed c, the accuracy of the estimated cost increases as m increases.

A heuristic explanation is that some programmers estimate too high and some too low, and since total cost is the sum of individual costs, there will be some algebraic canceling of the errors. If this cancellation is to hold, the assumption is that all module estimates are independent. Suppose one programmer makes an estimate for three modules; if these three estimates are not independent, then the error reduction will go something like $1/\sqrt{m-2}$, rather than $1/\sqrt{m}$.

Obvious signs of *dependence* among programmers would be conversations such as the following between two programmers: "How did your module estimate come out?" "Mine was five man-months." "Gee. I only came up with three and I think my module is a harder one. I had better increase my estimate."

Another problem which would invalidate the predicted decrease in variance is statistical bias. One can be sure that bias will exist if any of the following comments is heard at lunch: (1) "We sure got raked over the coals for our low-cost estimate of the job we just finished. I don't think anyone is going to make that mistake again on this new job we are now bidding." (2) "This company always underbids the job. The lawyers and managers always seem to be able to renegotiate a higher price later, based on the claim that the customer has asked for a new requirement or an enhancement. Since the requirements and specifications are so loosely drawn on most jobs, a skilled negotiator can make up the low costs that way." Thus, it is important that the manager obtain valid, unbiased estimates of cost.

It would seem that bottom-up estimating is a superior procedure; however, it suffers from one major fault: there is no perspective on what the total cost will be or the reasonableness of the estimate until the estimate is completed. Thus, a combination of top-down and bottom-up cost estimating would be preferable.

6.4.5 A Comparison of Cost-Estimating Models

A detailed comparison of the models discussed above as well as others in the literature is beyond the scope of this book. We shall content ourselves with a discussion of the models presented in Sec. 6.4.3 and of how they can be used to estimate the cost of one particular example. The results will then be compared and discussed.

Since the only data available to the author on the PRICE S system are in the example given in Table 6.15, this example will be the one chosen for comparison. The system in question is the software to support a mobile radar. It is estimated that 36,000 instructions will be needed; the breakdown within the total program by application category is given for the seven application categories. Only the mathematical category involves any reuse of previously developed code. The resulting estimate of total programming costs is $1,330,000, which is entered as method 1 in Table 6.17. (Note that the examples are ordered by age and that Nelson's data appear last because the age of the data base was unknown.)

Table 6.17 Summary of results for comparative study

Method	Estimate (thousands)	Base year	Inflation correction	Estimate corrected to 1978	Difference
1. Price system	$1330	1978	......	$1330	......
2. Doty formulas	832	1976?	1.06^2	935	-30%
3. Walston and Felix formula	525	1975	1.06^3	625	-53%
4. Wolverton family of graphs by type	$925 < 1139 < 1360$	1973	1.06^5	$1238 < 1524 < 1820$	$+15\%$
5. Aron table	531	1969	1.06^9	897	-33%
6. SDC graph	$251 < 628 < 1465$	1966	1.06^{12}	$505 < 1264 < 2948$	-5%
7. Nelson graph	$209 < 754 < 1675$	?	?		

Assumptions:
1. One man-year with overhead costs $50,000
2. One man-month with overhead costs $50,000/12 = $4187
3. One man-day with overhead costs $4187/20 = $209
4. One man-hour with overhead costs $4187/20 \times 8 = $26

In the case of the SDC study, Fig. 6.7, and Nelson's study, Fig. 6.9, the estimate is made by entering the x axis of the graph at 36,000 instructions and reading off the most likely and the confidence-interval values from the y axis. The results for both data bases are given in Table 6.17. The estimate for the Walston and Felix study was obtained by substitution in Eq. (6.4), which also appears in the table.

In the cases of the Doty, Aron, and Wolverton modes, more detailed computations are required, and these are given in Table 6.18. The most difficult phase of these computations was deciding on how to map the seven application categories used with the PRICE model into the six categories given in the Doty model, and into the easy, medium, and hard categories of Aron's model. The only categories which seemed to be identified by the same names or similar names were the real-time C and C (also called *control* or *command and control*) and the mathematical (also called *algorithm* or *scientific*). In these two cases, even though the terms were similar, it is likely that each author interpreted the terms differently. In the other cases, this author had to make judicious engineering estimates as to which categories corresponded. The details appear in Table 6.18, and the results are summarized in Table 6.17.

In order to compare the results, any model which estimated dollar costs was listed in the second column of Table 6.17. In cases where the estimates resulted in man-hours, man-days, man-months, or man-years, the conversion factors given at the bottom of Table 6.17 were used.

In preparing Table 6.17, a correction for inflation is required, since the largest costs in programming are salary-related and the span of years for the

Table 6.18 Detailed calculations—for models with instruction classes

A. Wolverton family of graphs

Category	Fraction, %	New	Number of lines	$/Instruction Easy	Medium	Hard	Cost, $ Easy	Medium	Hard
Online communication	0.08	100%	2,880 I-new	27	35	42	77,760	100,800	120,960
Real-time C and C	0.08	100%	2,880 C-new	33	38	48	95,040	109,440	138,240
Interactive	0.23	100%	8,280 I-new	27	35	42	223,560	289,800	347,760
Mathematical	0.28	40% old	4,032 A-old	15	20	23	60,480	80,640	92,736
		60% new	6,048 A-new	25	30	35	151,200	181,440	211,680
String manipulation	0.26	100%	9,360 A-new	25	30	35	234,000	280,800	327,600
Operating system	0.07	100%	2,520 C-new	33	38	48	83,160	95,760	120,960
Totals							925,200	1,138,680	1,359,936

B. Aron Model

Category	Size	MM/instruction	18 months MM	$ = MM × 4187
Easy—Mathematical	10,080	1/500	20.16	84,410
Easy—string manipulation	9,360	1/500	18.72	78,381
Medium—communication	2,880	1/250	11.52	48,234
Medium—interaction	8,280	1/250	33.12	138,673
Hard—real time	2,880	1/125	23.04	96,468
Hard—operating system	2,520	1/125	20.16	84,410
Total				$530,576

C. Doty model

Category	Formula	MM	$ = MM × 4,187
Online communication	$MM = 4,495(2.88)^{1.068}$	13.91	58,246
Real-time C and C	$MM = 4,503(2.88)^{1.228}$	16.51	69,110
Interactive	$MM = 4,495(8.28)^{1.068}$	42.97	179,924
Mathematical	$MM = 4,495(10.08)^{1.068}$	53.02	221,987
String manipulation	$MM = 4,495(9.36)^{1.068}$	48.98	205,095
Operating system	$MM = 12,039(2.52)^{0.719}$	23.40	97,972
Total			832,334

various data bases is large. The assumption was made that 1978 was the base year, and inflation was modeled as 6 percent compounded interest. (The assumption was later checked with data in Phister, 1979, as well as gross national product deflator data in several world almanacs, and the 6 percent model seemed to agree at the points checked to within 5 percent.) For a more accurate price deflator, one should consult government statistics for the price deflator which applies to just wages.[1] (One could also use the results of the periodic surveys of data processing salaries conducted by *Datamation* magazine.) Since the base year of Nelson's study was in doubt, no corrected estimate was made for method 7.

It is interesting to observe that five out of the six corrected estimates agreed within about 30 percent. Several workers in the cost-modeling field have commented to the author that they believe a variation of 15 to 20 percent between methods is to be expected once sufficient experience reveals the nuances of a particular method.

6.4.6 Penalty-Incentive and Warranty Cost Models

Because of the uncertainties in contract cost and schedule, it would seem natural that a customer would explore the concept of penalty-incentive contracts. Such a contract puts the burden of checking proposed costs for reasonableness on the contractor. In a fixed-price contract, there is always a nagging doubt that the low bidder made some mistakes and estimated too low. On the surface it would seem that such an outcome is desirable from the customer's viewpoint since it will result in a bargain; however, this may not be the case. The result may be that as the project progresses, the contractor finds ways to recoup the looming losses and this may compromise the quality of the software, or significantly delay delivery.

In the case of a penalty-incentive contract, the bidder must carefully cost the project and manage it to meet the incentive milestones. In such a case, the focus of the customer's vigilance must be broadened from cost and schedule to include performance and quality. Thus, the penalty-incentive contract should result in a higher level of management awareness, tracking, and control of cost, delivery schedule, and quality on the part of the contractor.

Wolverton presents an interesting example of a penalty-incentive contract, which is described in Figs. 6.10 and 6.11. In Fig. 6.10 we see that incentive packages are based on time of acceptable completion for each of the key milestones in the development process. In addition, any incentive fee which was missed at a previous milestone can be earned back if a subsequent milestone is met. The total incentive is 15 percent if the final milestone is met.

In Fig. 6.11 the penalty assessment structure is detailed. The penalties are assessed linearly over a 60-day period, as shown in the figure. In addition to delay penalties, there are cost-overrun penalties, shown in Fig. 6.12. The contractor shares 20 percent of any cost overruns up to 22.5 percent, and 30 percent of any overruns between 22.5 percent and 37.5 percent up to a maximum of 9 percent.

---

[1] More detailed models of inflation appear in the problems at the end of the chapter.

•Determination of fee

Milestone 2	Functional specification and test plan	1.8% of total target cost
Milestone 4	Detailed design specification	7.2%, or difference between fee paid for MS 2 (above) and 9% of total target cost
Milestone 5	Updated detailed design specification	4.5%, or difference between fee paid through MS 4 (above) and 13.5% of total target cost
Milestone O/D	Operational demonstration and customer acceptance	1.5%, or difference between fee paid through MS 5 (above) and 15% of total target cost

•Fee profile (max)

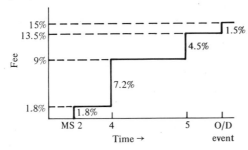

Figure 6.10 Incentive fee structure. *(From Wolverton, 1974)*

● Schedule-performance incentive
Incentive-fee schedule (based on total target cost of $5 million)*

MS 2	$ 1,500 per day, not to exceed $ 90,000
MS 4	$ 7,500 per day, not to exceed $450,000
MS 5	$11,250 per day, not to exceed $675,000
O/D	$12,500 per day, not to exceed $750,000

● Fee penalty profile

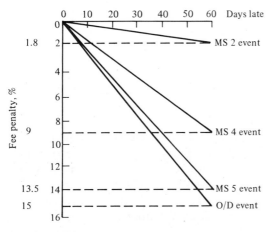

*For illustrative purposes only

Figure 6.11 Penalty assessment structure. *(From Wolverton, 1974)*

● Cost incentive

Condition	Result
If allowable cost exceeds target cost by not more than 22.5%	Fee shall be reduced by 20% of such excess

● Fee Penalty profile

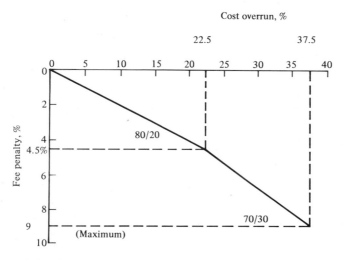

Figure 6.12 Penalty assessment structure (continued). *(From Wolverton, 1974)*

Wolverton's example illustrates the structure of a typical penalty-incentive contract. Before entering into such contracting arrangements, both the contractor and the customer should be fully aware of the risks involved. A fundamental study of such issues appears in Marshall's work (1969; 1974).

In recent years customers have shown an interest in warranty contracts. Such contracts are especially interesting to customers who have experienced high maintenance cost during the first year after a new software system is acquired. They are also attractive to those customers who do not have adequate programming staffs and must contract for software maintenance. A 1-year warranty period during which the contractor fixes all errors sounds very appealing. Again a careful study of the underlying risks is in order. Balaban (1979) discusses the use of warranties in hardware procurements.

Another means of structuring a penalty-incentive contract is to use a quantitative acceptance test. The customer (or a third party) writes N test cases which are unknown to the contractor. If the contractor's software passes more than x percent of the cases, the contractor earns an incentive. If fewer than x percent are passed, the contractor pays a penalty equal to the cost of writing N new test cases and is also penalized for the size of the time delay T before the retest.

6.5 MANAGING THE DEVELOPMENT PROCESS

6.5.1 Philosophy and Approach

Modern engineering projects often involve tasks so large and complex that they overwhelm the intellectual and work capacity of one or a few individuals. Thus, we are forced to pursue them as group projects, and the task of the manager is to guide and coordinate the project personnel. If this is done skillfully, the task complexity is conquered by the organizational coherence and directed progress. Poor management only exacerbates the situation in that organizational complexity and incoherence adds to the task complexity.

Management style is difficult to quantify, and many approaches will work.[1] It is imperative for the manager to keep in mind that the main objective is to fight complexity with organization (not to pile complexity upon complexity). Thus, rather than postulating one approach, this section focuses upon some of the tools which have evolved in recent years.

6.5.2 Milestones and Time Lines

In Sec. 6.4 we discussed methods for estimating the total manpower and resources needed for a programming project. In this section, we study the categorization of these resources and how to control and meter their expenditure. The discussion is continued in Secs. 6.5.6 and 6.5.7.

Several tools have been developed to aid in the management of large hardware projects: work breakdown structure, Gantt charts, PERT-CPM techniques. All these techniques can be applied to a computer project.

The term *work breakdown structure* (WBS) is a term popularized by the military[2] to describe the decomposition and naming of the various subtasks which form the tree or hierarchy structure of a large project. The important events in project development, the so-called milestones[3] (or, as Brooks says, perhaps they are millstones), are the initiation and termination of the subtasks.

A Gantt chart[4] is a bar-graph-like diagram in which the left margin is a column of the activities for the project. The top margin is a time line of calendar weeks or months starting with project initiation and ending with the projected completion date. The horizontal bars on the chart extend between the anticipated beginning and end points. A typical example is given in Fig. 6.13. Often local conventions, additional symbology, and lower-level charts are used, including names of the individuals or groups assigned to individual tasks.

---

[1]Brooks (1975), pp. 78–83.
[2]MIL-STD 881 defines a WBS for aircraft, electronics, missiles, ordnance, ships, space, and surface vehicles. See Coutinho (1977), p. 280.
[3]Tausworthe (1977), pp. 8–11.
[4]Coutinho, (1977), p. 286.

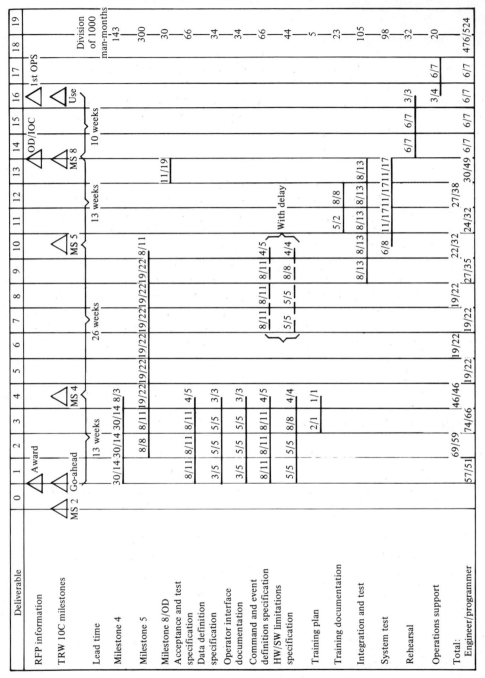

Figure 6.13 A Gantt chart for a computer project: manpower estimate with single-release milestone approach (single milestone). *(From Putnam and Wolverton, 1977)*

The program evaluation and review technique (PERT) represents project progress by a graph. Each node in the PERT graph represents a significant event in the project (milestone), and each branch is an activity which must be completed to move from milestone to milestone. The graph is a directed one since we assume that the activities are irreversible. A PERT diagram for the construction of a house is shown in Fig. 6.14. The dummy branches (dashed lines) do not indicate actual activities, but are needed to denote the sequence of events. For example, one should not complete the exterior siding (milestone 8) before the rough exterior plumbing (milestone 5) is completed. The numbers appearing in boldface represent project completion times, and the numbers in parentheses are the earliest and latest cumulative milestone completion times since project initiation. The method continues by evaluating the paths through the network and

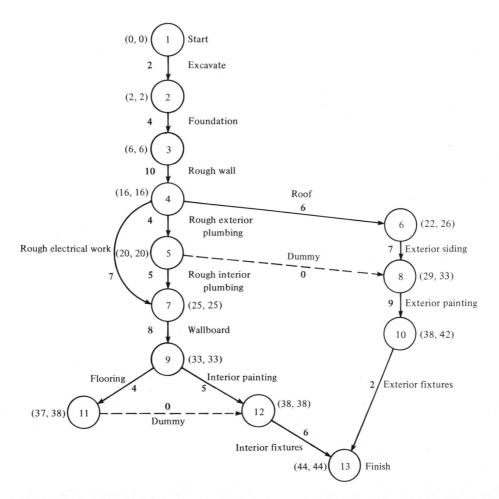

Figure 6.14 Initial PERT diagram for construction of a house. *(From Hiller and Lieberman, 1974)*

searching for the critical minimum path time. For a further discussion of PERT and CPM (critical path method), the reader is referred to Hiller and Lieberman (1974, pp. 229–241) and an example of PERT applied to a BASIC program.[1]

We should remind the reader that we have already discussed two other techniques for measuring project progress. The code-completed-and-debugged graphs of Figs. 5.7, 5.8, and 5.9 and the reliability models of Chap. 5 (see the discussion in Sec. 5.7.6) can be used to quantify progress.[2]

It is important that higher management realize that, in a top-down design, progress may have to be measured by the percentage of modules which have been pseudo-coded at some level of depth of the HIPO diagrams rather than by the number of lines of code written and tested.

6.5.3 Design, Quality, and Management Standards

All large organizations and projects generate much paperwork. This seems inevitable (see Sec. 6.6.1); thus rather than commenting on quantity, we will focus on the relevance, completeness, and quality of the paperwork. Standard techniques can be used to aid communication and allow the economy of reuse from one project to another. Toward this end, standards organizations produce, disseminate, and maintain standards documents and manuals.[3]

The largest standards efforts are those associated with U.S. government agencies, especially the Department of Defense. Many of the present military standards which apply to the development of software are listed in Table 6.19. A detailed discussion of the contents of these standards is beyond the scope of this text; however, the reader is urged to obtain copies of the pertinent documents. Even if the reader's task is not government-related, there is much valuable information in this collection of documents.

Suppose one decides to utilize an entire set of military standards. Additional work must be done to (1) fill in gaps in the collection, (2) choose among alternatives, and (3) detail the methods of implementation. Company practices must be decided and codified, and this takes the form of one or more company standards manuals which reference other standards documents. One typical organization of a standards manual for a large company is given in Table 6.20. The level of detail in each section of such a manual may differ significantly. In some sections the content will be a few sentences defining the item but leaving the implementation up to the reader. At the other extreme there are sections which spell out exactly how the task is to be executed. Some professionals argue that a standard should be essentially a glorified checklist of the necessary activities and that any more detail will constrain and stifle design initiatives, preventing creative solutions. Others feel that unless the tasks are spelled out in detail, they will be

---

[1]Sabean et al. (1978).

[2]Matejka and Sandler (1978).

[3]Wooldridge (1977); also, private correspondence with Mr. M. G. Mesecher of Sperry Systems Management, Great Neck, N.Y., September 1977.

Table 6.19 Military (and commercial) software-development standards

1. Military Standard, Weapon System Software Development, MIL-STD-1679 (Navy), December 1, 1978

2. Preliminary version of "Software Quality Testing Criteria for Tactical Digital Systems," TADSTAND 9, Chief of Naval Material, August 18, 1978

3. RADC Software Development Specification, CP 0787796100D, discussed on pp. 88–91 of Landes (1978)

4. DOD Directives 5000.29 and 5000.31 on software development

5. Language Evaluation and Coordinating Committee, DOD Common High Order Language, Phase 1 Reports and Analyses, AD-B950 587, June 1978

6. Military Specifications Software Quality Assurance Program Requirements, MIL-S-52779(AD), April 5, 1974

7. Military Standard Configuration Management Practices for Systems, Equipment, Munitions, and Computer Programs, MIL-STD-483 (USAF), June 1, 1971

8. Military Standard Technical Reviews and Audits for Systems, Equipment, and Computer Programs, MIL-STD-1521S(USAF), June 1, 1976

9. Standard for Software Quality Assurance Plans, P730/D4-R, August 25, 1978, Software Engineering Technical Committee of the IEEE Computer Society

---

done in a minimal and perfunctory fashion, and there is enough flexibility to substitute different but equally effective or superior procedures. Because of the present lax use of standards in the field, the author sides with the groups urging a detailed standard. Note that in matters such as the type of design representations to be used (see Sec. 5.4 of Table 6.20), one can specify a list of approved techniques and leave the choice up to the project manager. However, in all probability it will be necessary to enforce uniformity among the designers on any one project.

It is clear that a standards manual as extensive as that outlined in Table 6.20 will be produced only by the largest of companies for large projects. However, it behooves the software manager, even on more modest projects, to examine each function in Table 6.20. If there is no intention of performing that function, then why not, or who will, or what will be done instead?[1]

6.5.4 Humans as System Elements, Programmers, and Managers

Introduction The human is the heart of the design and coding process. Thus, the subject of this section is of prime importance. Furthermore, in most large systems several humans interface with the computer hardware and software (e.g., air traffic controller, word processing, business data entry, military command and control, etc.). Last, programming managers possess all the human frailties which

---

[1]Rosengard (1979).

Table 6.20 An outline of a comprehensive software-development standards manual for a large company

---

1. Management techniques
   1.1 Writing of requirements and specifications
   1.2 Management of proposal, development, and deployment phases of the life cycle
   1.3 Estimation of cost, memory, time, schedule, personnel
   1.4 Configuration control
   1.5 Design reviews
   1.6 Data collection and assessment
   1.7 Software quality control
   1.8 Organization of the development team
   1.9 Maintenance phase management
2. System engineering methods
   2.1 Feasibility study
   2.2 Performance analysis
   2.3 Reliability analysis and tests
3. Language manual(s)
   3.1 Language standards
   3.2 Coding style
4. Programming design and style guide
   4.1 Naming conventions
   4.2 Good procedures
   4.3 Calling conventions
   4.4 Choice of top-down, bottom-up, mixed, or modular programming styles
   4.5 Recommended data structures
   4.6 Recommended algorithms
   4.7 Recommended approaches to generic problems which are unique in the design of systems in the specific applications area
5. Program-development standard
   5.1 Implementation of requirements (plans, schedules, scope of development)
   5.2 Initial design (system specifications, problem definition)
   5.3 Structural design (top-level functional specifications, high-level information flow diagram)
   5.4 Detailed design (low-level design representations such as pseudo-code, flowcharts, HIPOs)
   5.5 Programming (detailed coding and documentation, module testing)
   5.6 Testing (integration and system testing)
   5.7 Validation (field and acceptance)

---

shape the development process. As important as all these topics are, our state of knowledge is poor in most of these areas. Thus, the purpose of this section is to raise the pertinent issues, place them in perspective, summarize some of the known facts, and refer the reader to the literature. Three references which cover many of these topics are Weinberg (1971), Shneiderman (1980), and Mehlmann (1981).

The human as a system element Modern computer complexes continue to rely heavily on human beings for data input, output interpretation, and high-level command and control. At one extreme the computer performs the main task and the human only enters data and distributes results. An example of such a system would be a payroll computation. Errors are not too frequent in such systems except when the system is initially installed or changes are made. However, we all know the high visibility and great annoyance associated with such errors. One way of further reducing the error rate of such systems is to use defensive programming (see Sec. 2.7.4). Another approach is to improve a major source of errors, the data entry phase. This subject is discussed in detail in Gilb and Weinberg (1977) and in Shneiderman (1980). At a higher level we concern ourselves with a language for input and output. For example in the Apollo space project, the astronauts could operate the on-board navigation and guidance computer via a verb-noun language.[1] Typical verbs and nouns were *display*, *load*, *restart*, *angles*, *time*, *velocity*.

At a still higher level, we concern ourselves with the human as a command, communications, and control element. Important issues are:

1. How much information should the human store and the computer store?
2. In what form should the computer present information to the human for decision making?
3. How can we best harness the great human abilities of error checking, insight, and overall assessment of a situation?
4. How can we provide status information, optimization of normal operation, special procedures for emergency control, operator restoration of a damaged system?

Again, we are at the beginning in these areas and the reader is referred to the literature.[2]

Programmer expertise We all know how important individual differences are in the quality and speed associated with any technical task. Individual differences among programmers are especially large.

Early experimental evidence of the large variations in programmer expertise became available in 1967. The goal of Grant and Sackman's study (1967) was to compare timesharing (online) systems versus batch (offline) systems with respect to development time (debugging time), program size, and running time. The results of the experiment are discussed in detail in two books by Sackman (1967, Chap. 9, and 1970). The experiment (which was a Latin-square statistical design) involved 12 different programmers and two different programs, an algebraic program and a maze program (Sackman, 1967, pp. 379, 387).

The following conclusions were drawn from the experiment:

1. The online cases took 50 to 300 percent less time to debug the programs than the offline cases.

---

[1] General Motors (n.d.).
[2] General Motors (n.d.); Swain and Goffman (1980); Mackie (1977); Sheridan and Ferrell (1976); Schmall (1979).

2. The offline cases required about 30 percent less CPU time than the online cases, but this difference was not statistically significant.
3. The algebra task was a longer and harder problem than the maze.
4. More experienced programmers tended to write shorter programs.
5. The individual performance differences were huge, up to 18:1 for debug hours, 15:1 for code hours, 6:1 for program size, and 13:1 for run time.

The fifth conclusion is the most important result of the entire experiment. If such large individual differences exist it is almost immaterial how you design your programs as long as you get the best people. The real problem is that there are too few exceptional individuals available. Thus, we are still concerned with methods of promoting a poor programmer to an average one, and an average performer to a good performer.

Project organization We now turn very briefly to the topic of project organization and personnel interaction. Large programming projects involve many people, much stress, much interaction, and all the dynamics of interpersonnel relationships. We are interested in any insight into these human relationships and any management philosophies which aid development.

One basic myth we should debunk is that the manager of a programming project and the chief technical person must be one and the same person. Brooks (1975, pp. 78–83) calls them the producer and the technical director or architect. He very rightly points out that all the permutations are possible, i.e., (1) the producer and technical director may be the same person, (2) the producer may be boss and the director the second in command, and (3) the director may be boss and the producer the second in command.

Mills[1] has conceived of a programming organization called the "chief programmer team" in which a "superprogrammer" (perhaps 10 times as productive as an ordinary programmer) is the leader. The superprogrammer is surrounded by a team of associates who support him or her in much the same way that a renowned surgeon is supported by associates and assistants. Brooks (1975, pp. 33–37) gives an excellent summary of this approach, via his description of the roles of each team member, paraphrased as follows:

1. The surgeon (chief programmer). He personally defines the functional and performance specifications, designs the program, codes it, tests it, and writes its documentation. It is assumed that he will work in a high-level structured language (perhaps in pseudo-code for certain portions), and he is fully supported by the other members of the team and by extensive software tools.
2. The copilot (second in command). He has the skills of a surgeon, but less experience. He serves as a sounding board for the surgeon and may write some code or represent the group at meetings. In an emergency, he can assume the duties of the chief programmer.

[1]Mills (1971); Baker (1972).

3. The administrator. The surgeon is boss, and must make all important decisions. However, the administrator serves a key function in removing administrative burdens from the surgeon and in carrying out the directives. On more modest projects, one administrator can serve two different teams.
4. The editor. Although the surgeon writes the documentation (at least in draft form), he should not be burdened with polishing the language, proofreading the typing, detailing the references, etc. This is the editor's job.
5. The secretaries. Both the administrator and the editor will need secretaries. (Possibly, the editor and one secretary may be assigned part- or full-time to the project from a technical reports section.)
6. The program clerk (program librarian). He is charged with the job of submitting the programs, retrieving and delivering the output listing to the surgeon, and keeping records of all the runs and the status of each program. He is responsible for configuration control of the software, and distribution of official versions and listings to other team members.
7. The toolsmith. He writes any special tools which the surgeon desires and maintains any other available tools.
8. The tester. He provides test cases for the surgeon to use, writes any needed test stubs or drivers, and is responsible for obtaining the correct answers to the test cases.
9. The language lawyer. He is an expert on the particular language being used and is responsible for special studies on how to do difficult things and utilize special features of the language, and serves as a consultant to the surgeon and the other team members.

The first major trial of the chief programmer team was on the programming of the often cited *New York Times* information bank system. The productivity for this project was 65 lines per day (for design, programming, debugging, and testing). The mixtures of high-level and low-level code and difficulty ratings are shown in Table 6.21.

We can use the percentage data of Table 6.21 along with the center-column data in Table 6.13 to obtain a comparative productivity figure from Aron's data:

$$0.06 \times 6.25 + 0.59 \times 12.5 + 0.35 \times 25 = 16.5 \text{ lines/day} \qquad (6.10)$$

Table 6.21 Lines of source coding by difficulty and level*

Difficulty	Level High	Low	Total	%
Hard	5,034	.....	5,034	6
Standard	44,247	4,513	48,760	59
Easy	27,897	1,633	29,530	35
Total	77,178	6,146	83,324	100

*From Baker (1972).

Table 6.22 Analysis of project staffing by time and type of work*

Work type	Chief	Backup	Analyst	Staff time (man-months) Programmer 1	2	3	4	5	Technician	Manager	Sec'y	Total	% Total
Requirements Analysis	2.5	1.0	8.0	0.5	...	...	...	...	...	...	...	12.0	9
System design	4.0	4.0	4.5	1.0	...	...	...	...	...	...	...	13.5	10
Unit design, programming, debugging, and testing	12.0	14.0	10.0	13.0	4.5	2.8	3.7	4.5	...	...	...	64.5	49
Documentation	2.0	2.0	4.5	1.5	0.2	0.2	0.3	0.3	...	...	...	11.0	8
Secretarial	...	...	...	...	...	...	...	...	...	...	7.0	7.0	5
Librarian	...	...	...	...	...	...	...	...	5.5	...	2.0	7.5	6
Manager	3.5	2.0	...	...	...	...	...	...	...	11.0	...	16.5	13
Total	24.0	23.0	27.0	16.0	4.7	3.0	4.0	4.8	5.5	11.0	9.0	132.0	100

*From Baker (1972), p. 113.

Thus, the productivity data on the *New York Times* job indicate a 4:1 improvement over Aron's data. This is a major achievement. However, the reason for the improvement could be one or more of the factors given below:

1. The programmers involved were so superior that any method they used would have shown a similar improvement.
2. The improvement was due to the superiority of the chief programmer team structure.
3. The improvement was due to the fact that 93 percent of the code was written in a higher-level language. (Aron's data are for low-level languages.)
4. If we look at the breakdown of total staff time shown in Table 6.22 we find that the 83,324 instructions required a total effort of 132 man-months, or 631 instructions per man-month. Dividing by 20 working days per month we obtain an overall productivity of 32 instructions per day. Thus, some of the ancillary tasks required in the project have reduced the productivity by a factor of 2. Were these items included in Aron's data?

The *New York Times* job also resulted in a low error rate. We obtained error ratios of $E_T/I_T = 0.00892$ during integration testing, and assuming that there are 80 percent as many errors after release, we have 0.0071. The *New York Times* job found 21 errors during acceptance testing for an error ratio of 0.00025. During the first year of field use the error ratio was 0.00030. Other projects have also demonstrated low error ratios. Early field use of the Bell Labs telephone switching system ESS No. 1 ADF demonstrated about 0.0034 changes per instruction per year, and after 7 years of operation, this value had dropped to 0.00016.[1]

Since productivity is related to group dynamics, it is important to stress that the program is a group effort and not just a collection of individual efforts. It is difficult for some programmers to admit that "his" program had 15 errors, yet if the entire software were spoken of as having 100 errors, any one programmer might be more comfortable in saying the portion of the software he or she wrote contained 15 errors. Weinberg (1971) has called the treatment of a programming job as a group project "egoless programming." This point is well illustrated by Brooks' comment (1975, p. 33) about chief programmer teams. "Absolutely vital to Mills' concept is the transformation of programming *from private art to public practice* by making *all* the computer runs visible to all team members and identifying all programs and data as team property, not private property." Clearly, the program librarian can be of great help here by recognizing that all team members have equal library privileges and all program information is included within the library, be it on paper, magnetic tape, disk, or cards.

6.5.5 Change Control

It is imperative that at some point in a programming project a single person be placed in charge of maintaining the official version of the program. The hardware

---

[1]Amster and Shooman (1975), pp. 678–679.

analogy is clear. Assume we were building a hardware system costing several million dollars. We would not allow each engineer to keep a personal master copy of the mechanical and electrical drawings for the system, nor allow changes without *review and approval* each time someone thought of an improvement or designed a correction.

It is an interesting commentary on the state of the software management art that two books dealing with software management which the author consulted had no discussions of configuration control, change control, or related concepts. Two other books, which focus on systems management in general, did discuss these topics and mention that the same problem exists in both hardware and software systems.[1] An excellent discussion of software change control is given by Ellingson (1973).

The term *configuration management* refers to the control and change management of all documents related to a program: requirements, specifications, design documents, etc. The term *baseline* is often used to refer to some official version of a document which is then updated via changes. In the case of hardware, configuration management primarily refers to paper documents. In the case of software, it applies to information stored on magnetic tape or magnetic disk, paper reports and listings, and any other form of permanent, stored information about the system. In the case of either hardware or software systems, requirements and specifications will exist as paper documents (however, they might also be stored on microfilm, tape, or disk as the master copy). If one plans to use program librarians, regardless of whether a chief programmer team is or is not planned, one of the librarians could be put in charge of change control and configuration management. In large problems two or more personnel will be needed for these tasks. If no program librarians are planned, one of the programmers can be assigned the task. The subject of document control, i.e., documentation, is discussed further in Sec. 6.6.2.

In the case of software, the configuration manager is generally called the *code control* or *change manager*, and instead of the term *baseline*, we will speak of the release, build, assembly, or version number. The change manager will not make any official changes in the present code release unless the change is submitted in writing, on a standard form, which is then approved by either a committee, the designer of the code, or the change manager. All new code releases emanate from the change manager.[2]

Most of the modern program development systems provide easy ways to keep each release of the code, facilities to compare the releases and print out the differences, and powerful text editors which help to prepare and update all documents (see the discussion of the PWB Source Code Control System, Sec. 6.7.6).

---

[1] Coutinho (1977); Hajek (1977).

[2] If the change manager is a younger or junior employee he or she probably needs the support of a committee. A more senior programmer can make the majority of the decisions alone.

6.5.6 Manpower and Computer Deployment Models

Introduction In Sec. 6.4, we dealt with the estimation of total costs for software development. Once overall costs have been projected, it is important to estimate the expected rate of resource expenditure and to determine a matching schedule of personnel availability. Too many times personnel are assigned to a new project as they become available (when other projects terminate) with no real thought to the project's ability to absorb their services in its *present* state. We already discussed work parallelism during the test phases of a project in Table 4.7. Similarly, in Sec. 5.6.5, we discussed the possibilities that if the debugging activity was error-detection (test-time) limited, addition of debuggers probably would do little good. However, reduction of manpower later in the project can cause problems if the reduction is premature.

The Putnam-Norden model The most promising analytic work in this area is Putnam's resource deployment model.[1] We shall shortly describe the theoretical development of the Putnam model, which follows the Rayleigh curve shown in Fig. 6.19(*b*). Note that for small values of t, the exponential term is nearly unity, and a virtually linear buildup is obtained. For large values of time, the exponential decay overpowers the linear buildup and the function decreases. As shown in the figure, a peak occurs between these two extremes.

Unfortunately, most computer programs are planned on the basis of a linear deployment as shown in Fig. 6.15, but actual experience indicates that the shape of Fig. 6.16 is generally true. The result is depicted in Fig. 6.17, where (1) an excess at the beginning results in waste, (2) insufficient help is available to satisfy the peak needs, and (3) additional effort is wasted later in the development cycle because it is too late to be effective. The shaded rectangle in the figure represents extra effort which must be applied to compensate for the losses.

Model development Putnam based his model development on earlier work by Norden (1963). Norden reasoned that each of the several phases in the development cycle of an engineering project would have a typical "humped" shape such as that shown in Fig. 6.18. The sum of these curves would be another hump-shaped curve. The cumulative curve was modeled by the Rayleigh curve shown in Fig. 6.19(*b*). Other curves (e.g., gamma, beta) could be used; however, the Rayleigh curve has some interesting properties: (1) the curve is determined by one scale parameter K and one shape parameter a; (2) it has the value zero at $t = 0$; and (3) it reaches a peak and has an exponential decay. Norden lists some of the important features of the curves given in Fig. 6.19(*a*) and (*b*):

1. The manpower-utilization rate reaches a maximum at $t = (1/2a)^{1/2} \equiv t_d$("development time").

---

[1]Putnam and Wolverton (1977), pp. 1–112.

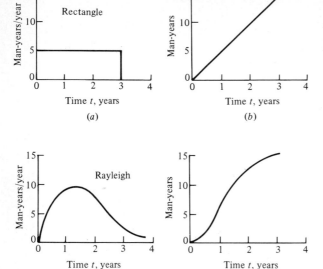

Figure 6.15 A naive view of how manpower should be applied on software-development projects: (*a*) man-years per year versus development time *t*; (*b*) cumulative effort in man-years versus development time *t*. (*From Putnam and Wolverton, 1977*)

Figure 6.16 A realistic view of the way manpower should be applied to software projects to avoid wasted effort: (*a*) man-years per year versus development time *t*; (*b*) cumulative effort in man-years versus development time *t*. (*From Putnam and Wolverton, 1977*)

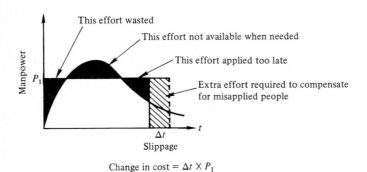

Change in cost = $\Delta t \times P_1$

Figure 6.17 An illustration of how effort is wasted when constant manpower is applied to a software-development project. (*From Putnam and Wolverton, 1977*)

2. The slope of the rate of manpower utilization (Y'') is initially $2Ka$ and decreases to zero at the peak.
3. The slope of Y' (Y'') becomes increasingly negative after the peak is passed, reaches a negative maximum (inflection point) at $t = (3/2a)^{1/2}$, and then increases asymptotically toward zero.

Inspection of Fig. 6.19(*a*) shows the parameter K to be the total manpower expended. If we have a reasonable estimate of K, we can quickly determine the parameter a by estimating the initial slope of Y'. In general, we use regression analysis to determine values for K and a from data (see Putnam and Wolverton,

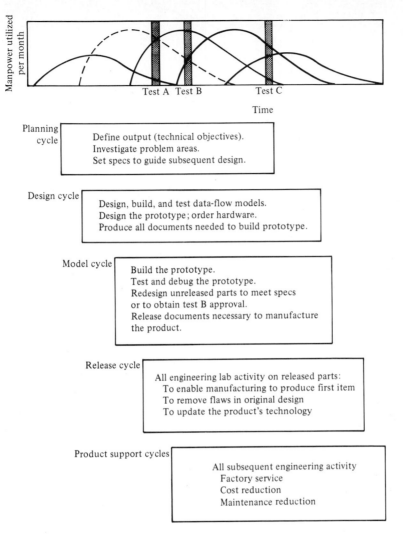

Test A Test B   Test C

Time

Planning
  cycle
Define output (technical objectives).
Investigate problem areas.
Set specs to guide subsequent design.

Design cycle
Design, build, and test data-flow models.
Design the prototype; order hardware.
Produce all documents needed to build prototype.

Model cycle
Build the prototype.
Test and debug the prototype.
Redesign unreleased parts to meet specs
or to obtain test B approval.
Release documents necessary to manufacture
the product.

Release cycle
All engineering lab activity on released parts:
  To enable manufacturing to produce first item
  To remove flaws in original design
  To update the product's technology

Product support cycles
All subsequent engineering activity
  Factory service
  Cost reduction
  Maintenance reduction

Figure 6.18 Typical manpower pattern of an engineering project. *(From Norden, 1963, Fig. 3)*

1977). Two examples showing the use of this model to fit actual data are given in Fig. 6.20. We now consider a third set of manpower data and utilize simplified parameter estimation procedures to determine K and t_d.

The Putnam model applied to SAFEGUARD data As an example, we will fit a Putnam model to the manpower data for project SAFEGUARD, which is studied in some detail in Sec. 6.7.3. The manpower-utilization rates for the 7 years from 1979 to 1975 are 188, 699, 1175, 1261, 1113, 780, and 191 man-years.[1] Since this

---
[1]Stephenson (1977).

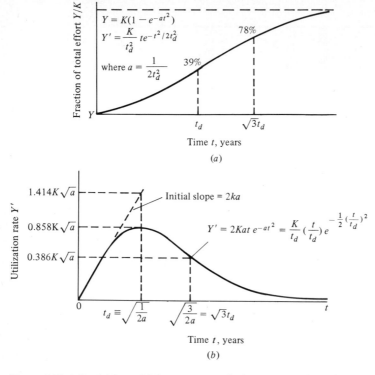

$$Y = K(1 - e^{-at^2})$$
$$Y' = \frac{K}{t_d^2} te^{-t^2/2t_d^2}$$
where $a = \dfrac{1}{2t_d^2}$

Time t, years

(a)

Initial slope = $2ka$

$$Y' = 2Kat\, e^{-at^2} = \frac{K}{t_d}\left(\frac{t}{t_d}\right) e^{-\frac{1}{2}\left(\frac{t}{t_d}\right)^2}$$

$$t_d \equiv \sqrt{\frac{1}{2a}} \qquad \sqrt{\frac{3}{2a}} = \sqrt{3}\,t_d$$

Time t, years

(b)

Figure 6.19 A Rayleigh model for manpower deployment. (a) Cumulative manpower utilization in percent of total resources. Intervals 0 to t_d and 0 to $\sqrt{3}\,t_d$ represent 39 percent and 78 percent. (b) Manpower utilization rate $Y'(t)$.

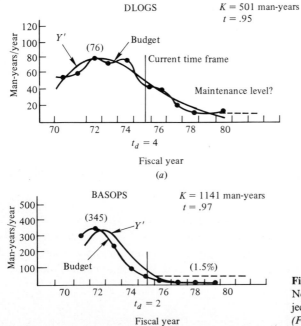

DLOGS $K = 501$ man-years $t = .95$

$t_d = 4$

Fiscal year

(a)

BASOPS $K = 1141$ man-years $t = .97$

$t_d = 2$

Fiscal year

(b)

Figure 6.20 The use of the Putnam-Norden model for two military projects. *Note: r =* correlation coefficient. *(From Putnam and Wolverton, 1977, p. 13)*

is retrospective data, we know that the cumulative manpower expended, K, equals 5407 man-years. We will assume K is unknown and judge the validity of the model by how well the curve shape fits the actual data and the accuracy with which K is estimated.

A plot of the SAFEGUARD data appears in the "stepwise" curve of Fig. 6.21. One approach to determining the two parameters K and a is to fit the peak, another is to use regression, and the simplest is to transform the basic equation so

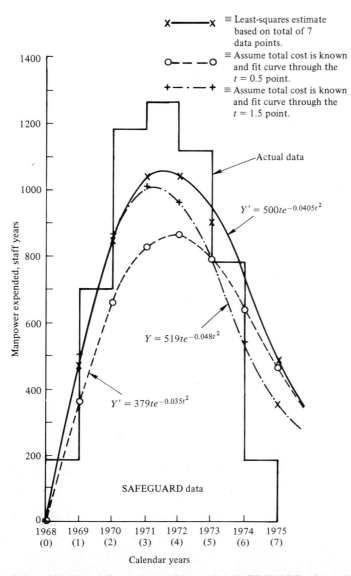

Figure 6.21 Plot of the manpower from project SAFEGUARD, along with three model estimates.

that we can use linear least-squares techniques.[1] The transformation is derived below.

We begin with Rayleigh model (see Fig. 6.19)

$$Y' = \frac{Kt}{t_d^2} e^{-(t^2/2t_d^2)}$$

where

$$a = 1/\left(2t_d^2\right) \qquad (6.11)$$

Dividing both sides of Eq. (6.11) by t, taking logarithms to the base 10, and redefining terms yields

$$\log\left(\frac{Y'}{t}\right) = \log K/t_d^2 - \frac{\log e}{2t_d^2} t^2 \qquad (6.12)$$

where $\log e = 0.4343$

Letting

$$w = \log\left(Y'/t\right) \qquad (6.13)$$

$$A = \log\left(K/t_d^2\right) \qquad (6.14)$$

$$B = -\log\left(e\right)/2t_d^2 \qquad (6.15)$$

and substituting into Eq. (6.12) yields

$$w = A + Bt^2 \qquad (6.16)$$

Thus, using the transformations, we can plot w versus t^2 on log-log paper and fit a straight line. The parameter A will be determined from the intercept with the line $t = 0$, and B will be obtained from the slope. Knowing A and B, we can determine a and K by substituting in Eqs. (6.14) and (6.15).

The data for SAFEGUARD are plotted as a stepwise curve in Fig. 6.21. Note that it is important that we consider the data to represent the half-interval points and not the end points; e.g., the value of 188 for the year 1969 should not be considered the value after 1 year of development, but the average value for the year and most representative of the value reached after $\frac{1}{2}$ year of development. The data were plotted on semilog paper after transforming according to Eqs. (6.12) to (6.16). One set of points was computed assuming that the data values were at $t = 1, 2, 3, 4, 5, 6,$ and 7 years; whereas the other set assumed that $t = 0.5, 1.5, 2.5, 3.5, 4.5, 5.5,$ and 6.5 years. The half-year data points yielded a better fit, especially at the initial point. The points for 1975 fell well below the experimental curve. The most likely explanation is that this project was not normally terminated, since work was abruptly stopped once the U.S.-Soviet treaty banning antiballistic missile systems was signed.

The model parameters were determined from the data in the following manner:

1. The intercept with the $t = 0$ axis in the figure is at $\log\left(Y'/t\right) = \log 500 = 2.7$ $= A$.

[1]Box and Pallesen (1977).

2. The slope of the line is $-(\log 500 - \log 100)/40 = 0.0175 = B$.
3. Substitution into Eqs. (6.11) to (6.16) yields the values $a = 0.0403$ and $K = 6219$.

The value of K estimated by the model, 6219, is about 15 percent higher than the actual value of 5407. (Remember our comment about the abrupt termination of the project.)

Of course the real use of such a model is not to study past projects (which is really only done to validate and gain experience with the model), but to use it to predict the future. We now show how the model could have been used after year 1 and year 2 to predict the manpower expenditures for the remaining years of the project. A good procedure is to use the best current estimates of total manpower expenditures K. Thus, our task reduces to finding the value of a, given the value of K. Many procedures could be used; however, a simple one is to pass the model through the data point, i.e., at $t = \frac{1}{2}$ (the first-year point); substitute in Eq. (6.10) $Y'(\frac{1}{2}) = 188$, $K = 5407$ (we assume the true value is known), $t = \frac{1}{2}$; and solve numerically the resulting equation

$$ae^{-0.25a} = 0.03477 \tag{6.17}$$

yielding $a = 0.035$. Using the same procedure at $t = 1.5$ we obtain the value $a = 0.048$. These two results are shown in Fig. 6.21.

Another point which Putnam studied should be emphasized at this point. He postulated that the ratio K/t_d^2 is a measure of complexity and consequently programming rate. In Fig. 6.22 we show a comparison of programming rate versus K/t_0^2 for a number of different projects. Note that the value for SAFEGUARD for $K/t_d^2 = 5407/3.5^2 = 441$ corresponds with the SAFEGUARD point in the figure.

Another observation is that the initial slope of the model fixes the manpower buildup rate. In Fig. 6.19(b) we see that the initial slope is equal to $2Ka$. If we set this equal to a manpower buildup rate proportional to K ($B\% \times K$), then $a = B\%/2$. Since $t_d = \sqrt{\frac{1}{2}a}$ we obtain:

$$t_d = (1/B\%)^{1/2} \tag{6.18}$$

Brooks (1975) cites Vyssotsky's observation that a project cannot sustain more then a 30 percent manpower buildup per year. Substitution in Eq. (6.18) yield for $B = 30$ percent, 20 percent, and 10 percent values of $t_d = 1.825$, 2.23, and 3.16, respectively.

For further discussion of these points, additional examples, and extensions of this work the reader is referred to Putnam and Wolverton (1977) and the problems at the end of this chapter.

As previously stated, the major resource expended is manpower. However, significant amounts of computer time and librarian, technical editing, and typing time are also expended in software development. We have already discussed computer resources in a number of places in the book. A discussion of technical editing resource requirements will be given in Sec. 6.6.1.

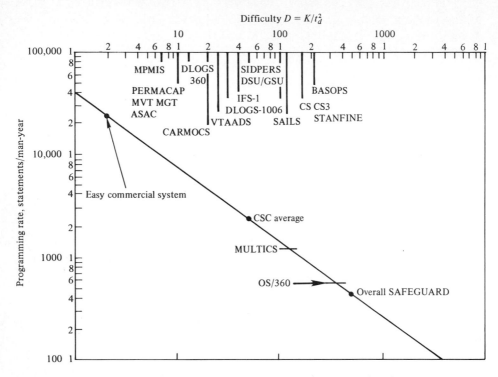

Figure 6.22 Difficulty measure versus programming rate. *(From Putnam and Wolverton, 1977, p. 21, Fig. 15)*

6.5.7 Productivity versus Program Size

Introduction Many people have observed that as the number of people on a project increases, the productivity (measured in instructions per day) decreases. Another way to observe this phenomenon is to plot the total number of man-months needed to complete the project versus the size of the project. If the productivity is constant, such a curve should be a straight line. The dotted line in Fig. 6.23 represents a constant productivity, whereas the data which Brooks presents are nonlinear and indicate that productivity decreases with program size.

If we assume that an individual programmer always handles the same-size portion of a large project, then the number of programmers is proportional to project size. If we hypothesize that a portion of each programmer's time is spent in communicating with other programmers, then the total hours the programmer expends on the job are reduced by the communication time to yield "productive hours." (Actually the communication time is highly important, and although we call it nonproductive time, this is not meant in a pejorative sense.) Thus we can write

$$T = T_p + T_c \tag{6.19}$$

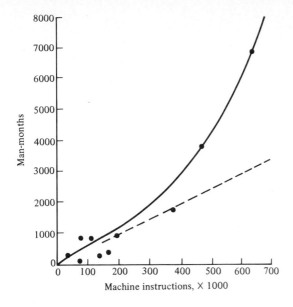

Figure 6.23 Programming effort as a function of program size. *(From Brooks, 1975, Fig. 18)*

where T = total work time of a programmer
T_p = productive working time
T_c = communication time

Communication time proportional to number of programmers and total time We can assume that the communication time is proportional to the number of people each programmer must communicate with. This in turn depends on the management and design structure of the computer project. In order to show the effect of communication time, we make a worst-case assumption, i.e., that each of the N_p programmers must communicate with all the other programmers. Thus, based upon this assumption, the number of interfaces is the number of combinations of N_p things taken 2 at a time:

$$\binom{N_p}{2} = \frac{N_p!}{2!\,(N_p - 2)!} = \frac{N_p(N_p - 1)}{2} \tag{6.20}$$

If there are L total lines of code to be developed and T_p is measured in months, then the productivity in lines per month is given by

$$P = \frac{L}{N_p T_p} \tag{6.21}$$

If we assume that a certain fraction K of the total work time T is spent communicating with *each* interface, then the communication time T_c is given by

$$T_c = KTN_p(N_p - 1)/2 \tag{6.22}$$

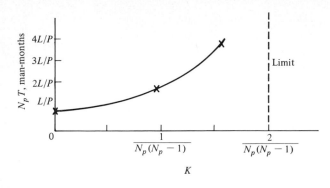

Figure 6.24 Predicted variation in man-months as a function of communication time parameter K (See Eq. (6.24)).

Substitution of Eq. (6.22) in Eq. (6.19) and solution for T yields

$$T = \frac{T_p}{1 - KN_p(N_p - 1)/2} \tag{6.23}$$

Multiplying both sides of Eq. (6.23) by N_p and substituting from Eq. (6.21) yields

$$N_p T = \frac{L/P}{1 - KN_p(N_p - 1)/2} \tag{6.24}$$

The numerator factor in Eq. (6.24) predicts a linear variation in man-hours with program length; however, the denominator factor produces a curve similar to Fig. 6.23, because of the increase in N_p for large programs.

We can study the man-hours for the project increase as a function of the communication time parameter K. If $K = 0$, then the number of man-months is given by S/P. As K increases, this factor grows and approaches infinity when the communication time consumes the total work time. See Fig. 6.24.

Communication time proportional to number of programmers In Eq. (6.22) we assumed a *fraction of the total* time was spent in communicating. If we assume that fixed amount of time K' is spent in coordinating each human interface over the length of the project, then

$$T_c = K'N_p(N_p - 1)/2 \tag{6.25}$$

If we substitute Eq. (6.25) into Eq. (6.19) and multiply by N_p, we obtain

$$N_p T = N_p T_p + K'N_p^2(N_p - 1)/2 \tag{6.26}$$

Substitution from Eq. (6.21) yields

$$N_p T = \frac{L}{P} + K'N_p^2(N_p - 1)/2 \tag{6.27}$$

The increase in man-hours with communication constant K' is shown in Fig. 6.25.

Note that the increase in programming time for large projects with increased numbers of programmers is predicted by both of the above models. Tausworthe (1977, pp. 322–327) models the communication time as proportional to N_p and

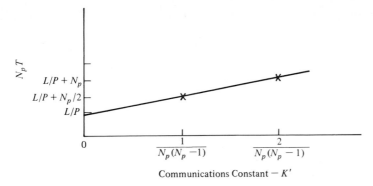

Figure 6.25 Predicted variation in man-months as a function of communication time parameter K' (See Eq. (6.27)).

obtains similar results. The above models and Tausworthe's are further explored in the problems at the end of the chapter.

This new and important line of research[1] should be pursued with some caution, since there are contradictory data. Nelson has shown that total man-months vary linearly with program size for the data which he studied (see Fig. 6.9).

6.5.8 Design Reviews

We have already discussed the usefulness of design reviews in the specification and design phases of program development (see Chap. 2). Another, equally important use is as a management tool. During the design phase, a design review is often less formal and may consist of a code walk-through, or a meeting to discuss the progress of the design. In the case of a design review held for management purposes, a wider and larger group of attendees is invited, and the entire procedure is more formal in nature.

As an example for discussion we assume that the company is organized in "matrix" fashion with a system, a software, and a hardware engineering staff, and a pool of technical managers. Personnel are drawn from each one of these staffs to cover particular projects. Assume (1) that the project in question began as a proposal several months ago, (2) that a proposal manager was assigned, (3) that a senior system engineer studied and interpreted the proposal requirements and specifications and formulated an overall approach, and (4) an experienced hardware engineer and an experienced software engineer (lead programmer or program analyst) were assigned to provide further details. Clearly, these four principles form a closely knit proposal team with additional support from engineering and programming if it is a large project, and help from the business and publications staff.

[1] Cormier (1980).

We assume that the company won the bid and that now the project is under way, led by the same team of four principals.

The project manager will schedule the formal design reviews to coincide with specific milestones in the management plan. The senior software engineer may schedule code walk-throughs and informal design reviews, and some will serve as "dress rehearsals" preceding a formal design review. Typical times (milestones) for the scheduling of formal design reviews for software development are given in Table 6.23. If hardware is to be built or interfaced, additional milestones will be required.

A typical list of attendees at a design review is given in Table 6.24. Not all these attendees will be present at all reviews, and others may be added; however, this is a typical list.

It is especially important that someone (preferably an independent software quality group) perform the quality assurance role outlined in Sec. 6.1.3. This role includes:

1. Checking that all necessary documentation is available, complete, and readable and has been approved
2. Witnessing some of the key integration-test results
3. Computing and interpreting reliability estimates
4. Running any demonstration or acceptance tests
5. Serving as a surrogate of the customer where appropriate

It is important that the manager of quality control (or that manager's superior) be separate and distinct from the program manager's supervisor. Often when the going gets tough and the project manager (and perhaps the manager's boss) are hard-pressed to get *something working* somewhere near the scheduled

Table 6.23 Typical milestones at which a design review should be scheduled for a software development

1. Before the last draft of the proposal for a very large project.

2. A few months after receipt of the contract once the technical aspects of the proposal and contract have been rechecked, the preliminary design is developed, and the preliminary specifications are written.

3. After the detailed specifications and the high-level (top-down) design are completed. In the case of a bottom-up design this would be after the design is complete for the one or two critical modules.

4. Once the (top-down) control structure has been tested and one or more modules are ready for investigation. In the case of a bottom-up development, the equivalent event would be when two or more modules have been written and tested and are ready for integration.

5. About halfway through the integration-test phase, when some reliable estimates should be available concerning the present reliability, the number of residual bugs, and the additional amount of testing required before the system is ready for release.

6. Just before the product is delivered to the customer for field or acceptance testing.

Table 6.24 A typical list of attendees at a design review

1. The project manager (who serves as chairman of the review and appoints a secretary)

2. The project manager's superior (especially when there is trouble or on very large projects)

3. The senior system engineer, the senior hardware engineer, and the senior software engineer plus some of their associates

4. A representative of each major software or hardware component

5. A program librarian (who may serve as secretary of the review)

6. A customer representative (at selected reviews)

7. A bright, experienced, and perceptive engineer not directly working on the project, who should be experienced in both software and hardware, be good in spotting implicit assumptions, and be adroit at recommending alternative designs and approaches

8. A representative from the software quality control group, who, *if he or she can avoid an adversary role and work well with the chairman*, may serve as secretary of the review.

time, quality is sacrificed for functionality. A separate and independent quality control organization can sympathize with the difficulties the project manager faces, but still must insist that quality be maintained.

The design review should have a certain amount of formality. An announcement should be distributed several weeks in advance, with a written agenda and list of invited attendees attached. Draft copies of the presentations and summaries should be distributed by the program manager at least 1 week in advance. If the drafts are unavailable, the review may have to be postponed. At the close of the design review, which may take between half a day and several days (depending on the size of the project and the stage of development), the project manager should write a summary memo. This will be addressed to his or her own management with copies to all of the attendees and other interested parties concerning the findings of the design review. The memo should contain an overall statement of whether progress is satisfactory, marginal, or unsatisfactory, and a list of any action items generated by the review. The final version of this memo should be signed by the project manager, some of the other principals, the customer's representative, the quality control group, and higher management as appropriate; it then becomes part of the permanent project documentation. The purpose of these signatures is to indicate acceptance and concurrence with the outcome of the design review, and the requirement of a written endorsement helps to focus on rather than bypass any important issues which have been raised.

Two important issues which should be on the agenda of every design review are the measurement of program debugging progress and the completeness of program documentation to date. The mere fact that key individuals must make a presentation to their peers is a strong incentive to see that adequate documentation is available. In fact, *copies of the complete file of documentation* for the project including specifications, high-level flowcharts, pseudo-code, HIPO diagrams, or other design representations should be circulated among the members of the design review team at the beginning of the review. If key issues arise which require detailed study of the documentation, the program manager should call a recess or send a subgroup into an adjacent room to caucus and report back to the review group.

6.5.9 Demonstration and Acceptance Tests

Demonstration or acceptance testing has become a standard feature of most hardware projects in recent years. Similar tests are gradually being adopted in the software development field. The terms *demonstration test* and *acceptance test* have particular meaning when written into a contract; however, their purpose is to prove to the customer that the software that is being handed over does the job for which it was intended.

Generally, in a demonstration test the contractor substantiates for the customer (at either's facilities) that each of the software functions works as intended. For example, if there are 15 different features or modes of software operation, this may require 15 separate sets of test data.

Normally, the term *acceptance test* is used to describe a more rigorous type of test in which each of the functions is exercised for a number of different test cases, including extreme and difficult conditions.

A three-phase acceptance test which the author has proposed is given in Table 6.25 (see also Sec. 4.7.3). Note that all programs should pass phase I of the test easily unless:

1. The wrong version or a bad reel of tape or a bad disk was inadvertently taken from the contractor's test site and will now not work properly at the customer's site.
2. There are incompatibilities between the development computer and the computer at the test site which prevent proper operation.
3. The contractor is way behind the schedule, and a business decision was made to proceed with the test even though there are known test cases which do not run properly. We assume that for the contractor's own good reasons it is better to accept the high probability that the system may fail part I (and surely part II) than to ask for a time extension.[1]

Once phase I is completed, phase II is initiated. If phase II is successfully passed, then phase III is started.[2] If phase II is failed, then the contract might specify that the contractor be given k months in which to prepare for a rerun of the acceptance test. In most cases the contract will also specify the penalty incurred by a failure of phase II. It is reasonable to set the penalty equal to the cost to the customer of making up a *new set of n test cases and the associated*

---

[1] An incentive contract (see Sec. 6.4.6) generally discourages such behavior.

[2] If neither project requirements nor specifications detail how the system should perform under a particular input, the contractor is not responsible for changing the design without compensation. This highlights why Chap. 6 in Table 6.3 and the abnormal-data category in Table 4.15 are items of prime importance.

Table 6.25 A proposed software acceptance test

Part I: Feature Check

The contractor is required to demonstrate that each of the m features (modes) of the system works properly by running one test case for each feature. These test cases have been previously determined and appear in the original contract or in subsequent documents *available to both contractor and customer*. Failure of part I requires a successful repeat of part I before the test can continue.

Part II: Comprehensive check

The customer supplies a set of n test cases *which are unknown to the contractor*, and the customers and the contractor's test teams work together to run these cases and check the results. Assuming that r of these tests are successful, then part II is passed if $r/n \times 100\%$ equals or exceeds the prespecified acceptance level, AL. The set n will include the boundaries of each feature, and any known stressful points as well as a distribution of values over the range of inputs. The contract document must specify the consequences of failing part II of the test.

Part III: Extraordinary-input check

The customer supplies a set of j test cases which probe to see how the system responds to input values outside the normal range, to garbage input, to input data in the wrong form or sequence, etc. Any anomaly from the behavior *specified in the contract* is deemed a failure. The contract document must specify the consequences of failing part III of the test.

---

answers. The contractor is given the first set of test cases and answers for help in preparing for the rerun. The contract should also specify a maximum number of times that the acceptance test can be taken (perhaps three) before the contractor is declared to be in default of contract and a contract renegotiation is instituted. If phase II is passed, phase III is begun. Any errors uncovered in phase III, plus all the remaining m-r errors from phase II, are segregated into two classes: those covered by the specifications and those not covered by the specifications. All those covered by the specifications must be promptly fixed and retested to complete successful performance of the acceptance test. Those errors not covered by the specifications are the customer's responsibility, and a separate negotiation (which may involve extra payment) is needed to decide if they are to be fixed or left in the system with appropriate warnings in the user's manual.

It is tempting to view part II of the test as if it were a statistical sampling test and to try to deduce a reliability value from the results. To date, the author has been unsuccessful in this regard because of the difficulty in enumerating the sample space of actual inputs and the relative frequency of these inputs.

6.6 SOFTWARE MAINTENANCE

6.6.1 Introduction

In recent years, studies of the maintenance phase of software development have revealed enormous costs, generally exceeding the development cost. Perhaps the most startling statement in this regard is that due to Gansler (1976): "One recent DOD study showed that Air Force avionics software costs something like $75 per instruction to develop, but the maintenance of the software has shown costs in the range of $4,000 per instruction." Some of these high costs are due to the difficulty of fixing software once it is deployed in the field (see Fig. 1.5). Also, in most cases the maintenance data include the cost of rewriting, testing, debugging, and integrating *new* features (often called enhancements) into the software. Such costs should be called modification or enhancement costs and treated as separate and distinct from maintenance; however, in practice they are lumped together. In both cases, the maintenance or modification costs will be strongly related to the quality of the documentation. Thus, we have chosen to include a discussion of documentation in this section.

Table 6.26 Problem areas in software maintenance reported by respondents

Rank	Problem area
1.	User demands for enhancements, extensions
2.	Quality of system documentation
3.	Competing demands on maintenance personnel time
4.	Quality of original programs
5.	Meeting scheduled commitments
6.	Lack of user understanding of system
7.	Availability of maintenance program personnel
8.	Adequacy of system design specifications
9.	Turnover of maintenance personnel
10.	Unrealistic user expectations
11.	Processing time of system
12.	Forecasting personnel requirements
13.	Skills of maintenance personnel
14.	Changes to hardware and software
15.	Budgetary pressures
16.	Adherence to programming standards in maintenance
17.	Data integrity
18.	Motivation of maintenance personnel
19.	Application failures
20.	Maintenance programming productivity
21.	Hardware and software reliability
22.	Storage requirements
23.	Management support of system
24.	Lack of user interest in system

Source: Lients et al. (1976), Table V.

A study of the reasons for the high costs of software in 1976 reported on 24 problem areas of software maintenance (see Table 6.26); demand for enhancements and poor documentation lead the list.

6.6.2 Documentation

Documentation is an all-encompassing term which includes many things in a computer program. The first item which most people think of is a listing of the program along with the program comments. This is of course only one of many items in a complete set of documentation. Contract documents, design documents, test documents, and design review documents are all included. A reasonably complete list of the documents which comprise a complete set of software documentation is given in Table 6.27.

If at all possible, one should designate a program librarian who is responsible for the system documentation. Programmers are still responsible for the technical writing; however, the librarian can do much in the way of editing, proofreading, and polishing to relieve the programmers of this chore. Clearly other aids such as a good online text-editing system, support from technical typing and editing, and a comprehensive software development tool (such as the *Source Code Control*

Table 6.27 A typical list of documentation for a programming project

1. Request for proposal*
2. Proposal document*
3. Any studies, papers, reports which support items 1 and 2**
4. Preliminary specifications
5. Preliminary design document (memo plus flowcharts, pseudo-code, HIPOS, etc.)
6. Detailed specifications
7. Detailed design document (formal report plus flowcharts, pseudo-code, HIPOS, etc.)
8. Documents supporting unit testing (test plans, lists of test cases and expected results, lists of errors, programmers' notebooks)
9. Documents specifying how configuration control is to be performed
10. Documents supporting integration test (test plans, lists of test cases and expected results, lists of errors, programmers' notebooks, computer records such as those produced by SCCS,*** or similar development tools)
11. Forms describing each error by number and how it was discovered, the diagnosed cause of the error, and how it was corrected (see Fig. 5.2)
12. Acceptance test plans and results
13. Field test plans, operational notebooks, and results
14. Documents resulting from design reviews or management decisions
15. Any related specifications and design guides.

*In the case of an in-house project, memos of direction and intent may serve the same role as these documents.
**Copies of the contract; any quality assurance plans and documents; engineering studies of reliability, memory requirements, processing time, or prior engineering or feasibility studies; etc.
***See Sec. 6.7.5, and Glasser (1978).

*S*ystem[1]), are of great help in performing the documentation task. In fact, some companies have even experimented with a scheme whereby each programmer is given a tape recorder and asked to dictate a record of any tests or changes made during that day. Once a week the tape is transcribed and a typed copy is produced. A more common procedure is to give each programmer a notebook with bound, numbered pages. All tests, changes, and events of note are to be entered daily along with the date and time (if significant). If tests are being run in an operational or simulated environment, then *it is crucial to carefully log in all operating times, times at which failures occur, and information on successful test runs. If an error reoccurs it is to be recorded as any other error with a notation that it is a reoccurrence of a specified previous error.* Failure to comply with the above simple documentation rules may invalidate the use of any of the test data for reliability estimates (see Chap. 5).

It is clear that editing, proofreading, reproduction, filing, distribution, updating, and control of the documentation for a sizable software development are a significant task. If the task organization is to include a program librarian it is generally that person's task to perform these services. If not, the task must be spread among the individuals on the project. Of course the danger here is that no one takes responsibility for this chore and it is badly neglected.

In fact, the assignment of responsibility for documentation is a key assignment in any software development project. The main problem is that it is a hard, unglamorous task, compared with testing and programming. We might liken designing to planning, shopping for, and preparing a fine meal and coding and testing to the cooking and serving tasks. This leaves documentation in the category of washing the dishes and taking out the garbage—hardly the most fun but still very necessary. One way to recruit someone to be in charge of documentation is look for a young programmer with little experience, who can be given the main task of documentation along with a small coding task. The job of documentation rapidly gives newcomers an overview of program development and builds their practical knowledge and insight.

The standard reply many programmers give when asked about documentation is that they will deliver relatively error-free code and so who needs the documentation? If the program is going to be used for only 1 or 2 years *without any changes*, then if the code is relatively error-free the code is sufficient. If the program is to be changed several times over a 10-year period, the documentation is more important than the code. We can always recode, and retest, especially if we have the complete test plan. Obviously, in any sensible project we want both code and documentation.

Some interesting data have been collected on the amount of documentation generated during a programming project.[2] The measure used in the cited study is the number of standard pages ($8\frac{1}{2}$- by 11-in) of documentation per K lines (1024

---

[1] Glasser (1978).
[2] Jones (1979).

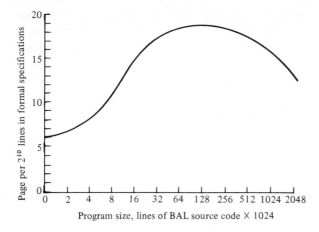

Figure 6.26 Number of pages of specifications versus program size.

lines) of code written in BAL (IBM System 360 assembly language). For programs written in assembler this metric was found to vary from a low of 2 pages per K lines to 68 pages per K lines. It was found that the most lines of documentation were written for medium-sized projects (see Fig. 6.26) and completeness declined with increased size (see Fig. 6.27). Additional data on size, cost, and completeness of program documentation are given in the reference.

6.6.3 Maintenance-Cost Models

Since cost is the most outstanding feature of the maintenance phase we will focus on maintenance cost models in this section. Fig. 6.17 shows how maintenance costs can show up as too high a tail on the right flank of the manpower curve. Similar results are depicted in Fig. 6.20 for actual data. Unfortunately, the

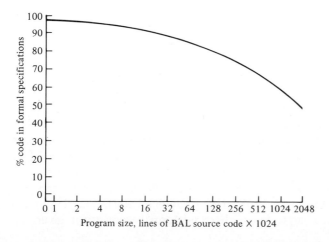

Figure 6.27 Completeness of specifications versus program size.

Putnam-Norden model does not predict the height of the sustaining maintenance tail, but only the way in which a "normal" development should taper off.

A simple model which illustrates how maintenance cost can build up frighteningly fast is due to Mills (1976). This model assumes that the programming work force F is constant and is normalized to be unity. After a project is completed, a (normalized) maintenance force M is left behind to deal with the maintenance, leaving a (normalized) development force D to handle new projects; thus

$$F = M(t) + D(t) \tag{6.28}$$

At $t = 0$, $M = 0$ and $D = F = 1$. If we let X be the fraction of development force left behind for maintenance at the end of a project, then

$$X = M/F \tag{6.29}$$

and at $t = 0$, X is not defined. Assume that we start our first project at 0. At the release of the first project, $t = t_1$ and we have

$$M(t_1) = XD(t_1) = X \times 1 = X \tag{6.30}$$

and
$$D = 1 - M = 1 - X \tag{6.31}$$

After the release of project 2,

M = assignment to first project + assignment to second project.

$$M = X + XD = X + X(1 - X) \tag{6.32}$$

and

$$D = F - M = 1 - M = 1 - [X + X(1 - X)] = (1 - X)^2 \tag{6.33}$$

Generalizing Eqs. (6.30) to (6.33) yields for the kth project release

$$M = 1 - (1 - X)^k \tag{6.34}$$

$$D = (1 - X)^k \tag{6.35}$$

If we assume that $X = 0.2$ (20 percent of the force is left behind for maintenance each time) and we have 6 projects of 2 years each, then substitution in Eqs. (6.34) and (6.34) yields

$$X = 0.2$$

$$M = 1 - (1 - 0.2)^6 = 1 - 0.8^8 = 0.74$$

$$D = (1 - 0.2)^6 = 0.8^6 = 0.26$$

Thus the 6 projects have gobbled up 75 percent of the total work force in maintenance of previous projects.

We can derive a different maintenance cost model which trades off warranty and integration-test costs. Assume we are in the integration phase and we wish to decide when to discontinue integration testing. If we stop too soon, we will save on test cost but will have more field errors to correct. We assume that there is a warranty period stated in the contract, T_w, during which all errors found are fixed by the contractor without charge. Even where no formal warranty is given, an implied one exists, especially where the customer has no staff or facilities capable of making the corrections. In such a case it is better to specify a warranty and add it to the cost of the contract, so as to be compensated for the services which will probably have to be provided anyway. The object of the following model is to choose the release time for minimum total cost.

We assume that our decision has no impact on the previous costs of design, unit test, etc., and that the cost for the minimum amount of integration testing which must be done is C_I. The cost of additional integration tests is C_I'. The cost of fixing errors caught in the field is C_F. Thus, the total cost which we are attempting to minimize is

$$C_T = C_I + C_I' + C_F \qquad (6.36)$$

We assume that additional test costs are proportional to the increased integration time τ:

$$C_I' = \alpha\tau \qquad (6.37)$$

Similarly, we assume that the maintenance cost is given by the product of the cost per error found in the field, β, the frequency of error discovery, z, and the length of the warranty period, T_w; thus

$$C_F = \beta z T_w \qquad (6.38)$$

Substituting in Eq. (6.38) for z as given in Eq. (5.64), we obtain

$$C_F = \beta K[(E_T/I_T) - \varepsilon_c(\tau)] T_w \qquad (6.39)$$

The minimum value is obtained by substitution of Eqs. (6.37) and (6.39) into Eq. (6.36), differentiating with respect to τ, and setting the result equal to 0. This yields

$$\frac{d\varepsilon_c(\tau)}{d\tau} = \frac{\alpha}{\beta K T_w} \qquad (6.40)$$

Thus we must plot or model the $\varepsilon_c(\tau)$ versus τ curve and determine when Eq. (6.40) is satisfied to obtain an optimum. This model is explored further in Prob. 6.27.

6.6.4 Growth Dynamics Models

Another study of maintenance growth[1] focuses on how the total resources of a program such as an operating system grow from the first release to the ith. The conclusion is that at some point it is too expensive to continue correcting errors and adding enhancements to a system and a better approach is to discontinue the system and write a new version. Some of the data Belady and Lehman present in support of their theory is given in Fig. 6.28, which shows the growth in changes introduced into a software system with increased release number.

---

[1] Belady and Lehman (1972).

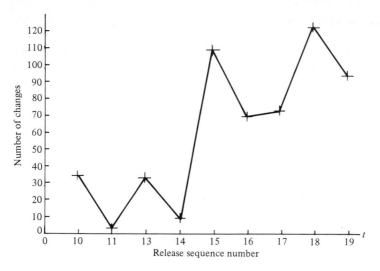

Figure 6.28 Growth in the number of residual errors with release number (see Fig. 2.8, Belady and Lehman, 1975).

A similar explanation of this phenomenon is given in Fig. 6.29. We assume that the first release contains N errors and as problems show up in the field they are corrected. When we are ready for release 2, the number of residual errors in release 1 is reduced to about $0.1N$ to $0.15N$. The enhancements added to release 2 create another crop of errors, which are added to the residual errors in release 1, so that the number of residual errors now equals about $1.1N$. The debugging on

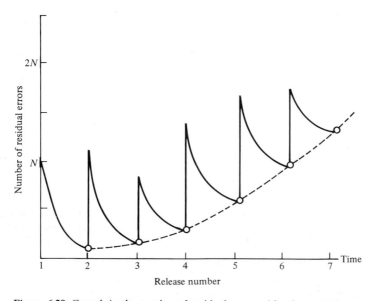

Figure 6.29 Growth in the number of residual errors with release numbers.

release 2 is less successful than that on release 1, because the documentation of release 1 is imperfect. The result is a residual error count equal to about $0.25N$. As can be seen from the figure, the inability to reduce the residual error level to that of release 1 or below results in a growing error level as shown by the dotted line.

Suppose that our strategy is to accept release 1 and hold onto it until release 3 is ready, at which time we install the now debugged version of release 2. If we continue this philosophy, we follow the solid curve between release 1 and release 2 and then the dotted line thereafter. The resulting curve should be compared with the hazard curve given in Fig. 5.1. The similarity of these shapes has led some to say that software does have a wear-out failure mode. A much better explanation is to say that the software exhibits an increasing failure rate due to the inability to control the growth of residual errors as enhancements are added.

For a further explanation of this phenomenon, the reader is referred to the literature.[1]

6.7 PAST SUCCESSES

6.7.1 Introduction

Before we close this volume, it is important that we dispel any sense of discouragement about our ability to design, predict, and develop high-quality software. In Chap. 1, we painted in broad strokes the magnitude of the problems. In Chaps. 2 to 6, we dwelt upon techniques for dealing with these problems. In many areas existing techniques are well developed and the practitioner should have ample tools to work with. (Of course, it may require considerable effort at the outset to learn how to apply some of the new and unfamiliar tools.) In other areas the author has presented the ideas prevalent in the literature and has indicated that good judgment and ad hoc solutions are required in many cases. We will study shortly a number of examples from the 1960s and 1970s in which designers were able to develop large, complex, and successful software systems, utilizing the meager set of tools then available. Unfortunately, the author was unable to assemble any failure studies to complement these success stories; however, case histories of the problems of software management have been described in the literature.[2]

One class of generally successful software is the system software written by computer manufacturers, namely, compilers, interpreters and assemblers, operating systems, diagnostic programs, utility programs, etc.

---

[1] Belady and Lehman (1971; 1975; 1977).

[2] One can cite the book by George Penney (1975), which deals mainly with the drafting of requirements, or Ben Schneider (1974), which wittily details the difficulties which an English teacher has in constructing a computerized theater information bank.

In the remainder of this chapter, we will focus on five large software projects, three of them commercial and two military. The main reasons for choosing this set of examples is their success, their glamor, and the fact that ample information is available in the literature describing the projects. We will focus on the SAGE air defense system, the SAFEGUARD antiballistic missile system, the SABRE airlines reservation system, the MULTICS timesharing system, and the UNIX timesharing system. In each case we will extract the lessons which can be learned from the project.

6.7.2 The SAGE Air Defense System

Introduction SAGE (Semi-Automatic Ground Environment) was probably the first real-time computer system.[1] The system was designed to provide air defense for the North American continent, based on military air power and ballistic missiles and the discovery and rapid development of radar and the atomic bomb during World War II. The military-political impetus was provided by Russia's first atomic bomb test in 1949 and the start of the Korean War in 1950.

In 1953 the U.S. Air Force decided on the concept of central processing of air defense data by a ground-based computer. By 1958 the New York Air Defense Sector became the first operational site. By 1963 the system consisted of 14 direction centers and 5 combat centers.

The total system capital cost (radar, data processing, communications, interceptors, and missiles) ran in excess of $10 billion, and in 1965 the operating costs were estimated at $1.8 billion (interceptor weapons, direction and combat centers). The large list of military, governmental, and commercial organizations involved in the development of the SAGE system is given in Table 6.28.

Hardware and software The prototype computer, the AN/FSQ-7 (Q-7 for short), was ordered from IBM in 1955 for the prototype system. The cost of the duplexed (one online and one backup) Q-7 and its auxiliary equipment is estimated at $20 million. It contained 58,000 vacuum tubes, consumed 1500 kilowatts of power, weighed 113 tons, and occupied an entire floor in the direction center. (The first electronic computer, ENIAC, circa 1946, contained 20,000 vacuum tubes, consumed 150 kilowatts, weighed 30 tons, and filled 40 equipment racks.) The SAGE computer had a 32-bit word length, single-address architecture, 69,000 words of magnetic core memory and 12 magnetic drums, and a total capacity of 150,000 words. Average instruction operating times were 10 μs, and transfer time from core to drum was 325 μs. The real-time program contained 100,000 instructions, partitioned into about 40 functions (subprograms) which could be classified

---

[1] Sackman (1967), Chaps. 3 and 4. The system was supplemented and replaced by a succession of air defense systems: the DEW (Distant Early Warning) line, the Mid-Canada Line, the Pine Tree Line, the BMEWS (Ballistic Missile Early Warning System), and the GIUK (Greenland–Iceland–United Kingdom) line.

Table 6.28 Main agencies involved in SAGE development

Military and government	Civilian organizations

Air Defense Command Headquarters
  Division commands
  Sector commands
  4620th Air Defense Wing/
    Air Defense Command
    Computer Programming
    and System Training Office
  Air Defense Systems Integration Division
    (superseded later by the Air Force Systems
    Command's Electronics Systems Division)
  Air Materiel Command
  Army Air Defense Command
  Canadian Defense Procurement Board
  Federal Airways Administration
  North American Air Defense Command
  Rome Air Development Center
  Royal Canadian Air Force
  Strategic Air Command
	American Telephone and Tele-
	  graph Company
	Bell Telephone Laboratories
	Bendix Corporation
	Boeing Company
	Burroughs Corporation
	General Dynamics/Convair
	General Electric
	Hughes Aircraft Company
	International Business Machines
	Lincoln Laboratory
	Lockheed Aircraft Corporation
	Martin Orlando Company
	McDonnell Aircraft Corporation
	MITRE Corporation
	Philco Corporation
	Radio Corporation of America
	System Development Corporation
	Western Electric Air Defense
	  Engineering Services

roughly into four equal-sized groups: input-output operations, human-to-computer communications, tracking and weapons control, and miscellaneous. The Q-7 support programs involved about 1 million instructions. One support program, the SPARS program, generated simulated inputs for training and testing and contained 120,000 words of machine code generated from 19,000 words of higher-level Jovial language.[1] Other instructions were coded in assembler.

In order to manage software changes in the system, about once a year a change-control committee met to decide what should be included in each new release. Between releases, some isolated changes were permitted via a different formal mechanism.

Program Development The development process for SAGE entailed (1) statement of the problem, (2) system requirements, (3) system configuration, (4) operational system description, (5) operational specifications, (6) program specifications, (7) transfer functions, (8) flow diagrams, (9) coded programs, (10) parameter testing (module testing), (11) assembly testing, and (12) system testing. The division of programming time among the various tasks is shown in Fig. 6.30. We can infer

---

[1] A version of Algol written by System Development Corporation for the IBM Military Computer AN/FSQ-32. Jovial is the acronym for *J*ules Schwartz's *O*wn *V*ersion of the *I*nternational *A*lgebraic *L*anguage. See Shaw (1963).

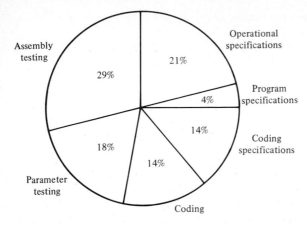

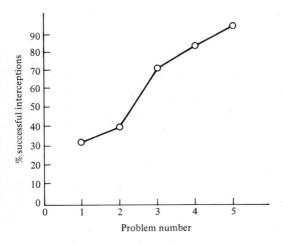

Figure 6.30 SAGE system: division of programming time. *(From Sackman, 1967, p. 201)*

Figure 6.31 Success of SAGE system as measured by results of simulated intercepts. *(From Sackman, 1967, p. 340)*

the basic success of the system by examining the results of simulated intercepts collected in a test to show the effects of operator training (see Fig. 6.31).

Because of the mingling of hardware, software, and interceptor expenditures in the system cost data, it is difficult to accurately estimate the software productivity for SAGE; however, it has been estimated that SAGE took 1800 man-years to write the *original* programs.[1] Dividing 600,000 instructions by 1800 man-years and 250 working days per year yields 1.33 instructions per day.

Thus, some of the principles of "modern" program design and management are not so new. As the famous philosopher George Santayana once said, "Those who do not study history are forced to repeat it."

[1] Burck (1964).

Lessons to be learned The important features of the SAGE system were:

1. It was the first large-scale real-time system.
2. It was developed over a 10-year period, 1953–1963, in an evolutionary fashion.
3. Development of the first operational site took 5 years; of the total system, 10 years.
4. It used primitive (by today's standards) hardware and software.
5. Many organizations were involved.
6. Several stages of requirements and specifications preceded development.
7. It used mostly assembly language with a productivity of 1.33 instructions per day.
8. The programs were divided into 40 functional modules averaging about 2500 instructions each.
9. It exhibited strong and modern management philosophy (much time spent on specifications, change control, much simulation testing).

Although the hardware was slow, bulky, and cumbersome and programming had just begun to evolve, the management seemed sound by current-day standards.

6.7.3 The SAFEGUARD Antiballistic Missile System

Introduction The SAFEGUARD system was developed while a controversy, in part technical and in part political, raged over whether the software for the project would ever work.[1]

For its time SAFEGUARD was the largest and most complex real-time system ever undertaken.[2] The purpose of the system was to provide a defense against an attack by intercontinental ballistic missiles. The system consisted of four major components: the long-range radar to detect incoming attack missiles, a short-range radar to aim the defensive missiles so as to intercept the attacking missiles, the defensive missiles, and a very large multiprocessor computer for data processing and control. The system entailed the development of approximately 2 million instructions and required 5000 man-years of effort.

Major features of the development Some of the interesting features of the system which had major impacts on the system development are listed below:

1. A large percentage of the total number of software instructions were real-time programs which had to be executed in milliseconds. This made for programming difficulties and low productivity (as is usually the case in real-time software).

---

[1] Alan Kaplan, the editor of *Modern Data* magazine, posed the question, "Is the ABM system capable of being practically implemented or is it beyond our current state-of-the-art?" The replies to this question were printed in the January and April 1970 issues of the magazine. John S. Foster, director of the Office of Defense Research and Engineering, led the proponents, and Daniel D. McCracken, chairman of Computer Professionals against ABM, led the opposition.

[2] "SAFEGUARD" (1975).

2. Because at the time no existing hardware architecture had sufficient processing power (measured in millions of instructions per second, or MIPS) to handle the task, a custom-designed multiprocessor system was undertaken.[1] The resulting computer had a processing power of over 10 MIPS.
3. The builders of the system felt that extra effort, above and beyond that normally required, was called for because such a large and complex real-time system had never been built before.
4. During the early stages of system development there was a continuing evolution and change of system specifications, and it took 2 to 3 years into the development cycle before a stable set of specifications was obtained.
5. Approximately 20 percent of the effort expended on the system engineering phase was for long-range system development. Since the plans were to produce an evolving group of ABM systems, this type of effort might not be justified for other applications.
6. The development cycle took approximately 7 years, and as late as 15 months before the end there were major changes in some of the system algorithms.
7. Since the hardware was being developed concurrently with the software, as is often the case, there were changes in the hardware which impacted the software development, causing new changes and delays.

Software development The system was developed in a high-level, specially written language similar to PL/1. During the course of development about five or six major releases of the software occurred. The deployment of manpower over the project life cycle has already been given in Fig. 6.21.

A breakdown of programming instructions by type is given in Table 6.29. For the overall project, 2,261,000 instructions were written and 5407 man-years of effort were required. Based upon 250 working days per year, this represents an overall productivity of 1.7 instructions per man-day. The variation in productivity varied from a low of 0.98 to a high of 6.40, depending on the type of program being written, as shown in the table.

The division of effort for the overall project among the various phases is given in Table 6.30. If we assume that the 5407 man-years were expended according to these ratios, then the overall productivity per phase was as shown in Table 6.31. It is interesting to note that the system engineering, the design, and the code and unit test phases all had roughly the same productivity, about 9 instructions per man-day. Suppose the integration phase (see Table 6.30) were divided into two subphases, the first test planning and execution and the second debugging and redesign; then the five resulting phases of system development would all have absorbed roughly the same amount (one-fifth) of the total effort. The developers noted that toward the end of the project, when more structured methods of programming were used, productivity rose.

---

[1] If present large, high-speed architectures had been available at that time, the computer and the operating system could have been simplified.

Table 6.29 Productivity of SAFEGUARD software by program type*

Software type	Size (instructions)	Instructions/ staff year	Instructions/ man-day
Real-time (total)	789,000	285	1.14
Real-time process (logical)	81,000	485	1.94
Real-time function (logical)	67,300	974	3.90
Real-time process (algorithmic/logical)	317,000	244	0.98
Real-time function (algorithmic/logical)	23,000	438	1.75
Hardware installation	350,000	1097	4.39
Hardware M & D	490,000	1601	6.40

*See Stephenson (1977).

Table 6.30 Distribution of total effort on SAFEGUARD by phase*

Phase	Percentage
Systems engineering	20
Design	20
Code and unit test	17
Integration testing	43
Total project	100

*See Stephenson (1977).

Table 6.31 Productivity per phase

Phase	Productivity, instructions/man-day
Systems engineering	8.5
Design	8.5
Code and unit test	10.0
Integration testing	3.9
Total project*	1.7

*Total project productivity $= 1/(\text{man-days/instruction})$

$$= 1 / \left(\frac{1}{8.5} + \frac{1}{8.5} + \frac{1}{10} + \frac{1}{3.9} \right)$$

System success The success of the system cannot be completely judged, because, obviously, no live war occurred, nor were any field trials ordered for the final system. However, actual intercepts of test targets did occur at the Meck Island test site, which proved feasibility of the system.

Stephenson (1977) measures the success of the system with respect to a set of five comprehensive and difficult government demonstration and acceptance tests. During this set of 57 different tests, which were conducted at the development site, only one software error affecting the primary objectives of the system was found. During the prior development period, about 5000 such errors were found and removed from the system.

Lessons to be learned The important features of SAFEGUARD were:

1. The question whether a software system as large as 2 million words could ever work was settled in the affirmative.
2. Technical and political considerations were finally separated, and diplomatic success caused an abrupt termination of the project.
3. The multiprocessor concept, although very complex, solved the MIPS problem.
4. Development took 7 years, and much effort was devoted to specification and requirements.
5. The productivity of 1.7 instructions per day represented an improvement of only 28 percent over SAGE, even though SAFEGUARD had the benefit of a higher-level language and 10 to 12 years' additional history.
6. If the instruction count for SAFEGUARD of 2.26×10^6 instructions includes simulation and training software, then SAGE was about one-half the size of SAFEGUARD.
7. The SAFEGUARD management process appeared to be of high caliber when measured against contemporary standards and was well documented.[1]
8. Code control and extensive simulation testing were emphasized.

Again, because of its abrupt termination, a study of the field-deployment phase of SAGEGUARD is unavailable.

6.7.4 The SABRE Airlines Reservation System

Introduction The knowledge learned on the SAGE project was transferred in many ways to the first large commercial real-time computer system, the SABRE Airlines Reservation System. This program was preceded by a long study period

---

[1] The data cited are from unpublished papers describing the system circa 1971 (significant changes have been made since then), which were furnished in a private communication by R. J. McGrath, then director of data processing for SABRE.

An interesting and thorough discussion of the design of a typical airline reservations system appears in Zelkowitz et al. (1979), pp. 157–178.

Table 6.32 Chronology of the SABRE system development

Preliminary study	1954–1958
Precontractual analysis	1958–1959
Contract	1959
Functional requirements	1960–1962
Program specifications	1960–1962
Coding	1961–1964
Single-path testing	1961
Equipment arrival	1962
Package testing	1961–1962
Final checkout	1963
Test city parallel operation[1]	1962–1963
First firm cutover[2]	1963
Several more cities cutover[2]	1963
Further cutover delayed pending addition of memory to 7090	1963
Remainder of American cities added to system	1963–1964

[1] Manual and semiautomatic system.
[2] Semiautomatic system alone.
Source: Parker (1965).

(1954–1959) involving representatives from the customer, American Airlines, and the contractor, IBM. In 1957 the study team was named Semi-Automatic Business Environmental Research, giving rise to the acronym for the system. Coding began in 1961 and all cities were connected to the initial system configuration by 1964. A list of the important milestones for the project is given in Table 6.32.

System configuration The initial system utilized two 7090 computers, one as online and one as backup, to provide highly reliable service to the 34 cities comprising 66 sites and 1012 terminals. The communication facilities which connected the terminals to the central computer complex totaled 31,000 miles of leased telephone lines. The system was initially designed to handle over 3 million passenger records and provide a 3-s response time to at least 90 percent of the requests and a 0.5-s response time to 75 percent of them. Extensive simulation and queuing analysis was done during the preliminary phases.[1] Raw data based upon telephone records of the previously existing manual system were utilized to determine the model parameters.

Difficulties occurred in managing the parallel operation system cutover phases. As new cities were added to the system the daily error rate grew to levels which threatened the viability of the operational system. The consulting firm of Arthur D. Little studied this problem[2] and came up with a simple and effective

[1] Rothstein (1965).
[2] Private communication, fall 1971.

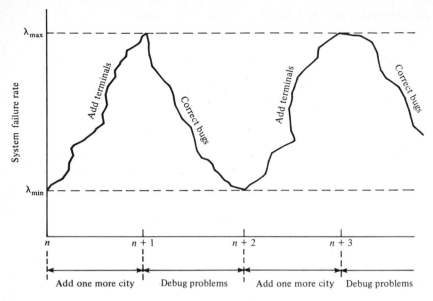

Figure 6.32 Cycles of network expansion: a solution to the problem of controlled network expansion.

solution. A maximum failure rate λ_{max} was determined beyond which system operation was considered unacceptable. At the other extreme a minimum failure rate λ_{min} was chosen at which operation was considered normal. In Fig. 6.32 we show the system initially at level λ_{min} with n cities operational. Terminals are added in one or more new cities until λ_{max} is reached. Then the configuration is frozen and debugging takes place until the failure rate drops to λ_{min}. Then the cycle is repeated.

Multilevel storage Because of the huge volumes of data, multitiered levels of storage facilities were utilized. The dual 7090 computers had 65,536 words of magnetic core memory (about the same as SAGE) and six high-speed drum memories containing 1,228,000 words with an access time of 11.25 ms (larger and faster than SAGE). The drums were used to store frequently used portions of the system such as programs, the next 10 days of "inventory," and the availability of other airline flights.

The next level of storage involved 16 disk files containing 118,400,000 words with an average access time of 115 ms. These disk files contained over 3.5 million passenger records, each one consisting of 220 characters of data. The last level of storage was magnetic tapes, which were run each night to back up the system and which were kept in storage at least 60 days in order to satisfy a Civil Aeronautics Board requirement. In the event of a computer CPU failure, the standby 7090 computer would cut onto line and operation would continue. In the event of a system crash involving both computers, or one of such a nature that the backup system could not take over so as to avoid system downtime, a variety of different

Table 6.33 Actions the system takes when an interrupt occurs (In order of priority)

1. If a transient or intermittent error occurred, it is possible that the instruction which led to the error can be re-executed and the program operation can be resumed.

2. Restart the program as a certain restart address.

3. If a core clobbered—reload the program.

4. If a faulty component; operate in a F/B (fallback) mode.

5. If the program cannot be reloaded; switch computers.

6. If the trouble is "solid," or permanent, the system goes off the air.

Source: McGrath (1971).

techniques could be utilized to continue system operation (see Table 6.33). In the case of a permanent failure, the previous night's backup tapes could be loaded into the system along with the journal tapes (record of the present day's transactions) to reestablish the system data base once the fault had been corrected.

Errors The types of errors encountered in the system are delineated in Tables 6.34 and 6.35. Details of the various program sizes and where they were stored appear in Tables 6.36 and 6.37.

Table 6.34 Most frequent causes of system interruptions

1. A hardware component failure
2. Noise pulses on a transmission or data channel line
3. Programming problems or bugs
4. Transient parity errors in computer circuitry
5. System overload, or a buildup of message or action queues
   in core

Table 6.35 Analysis by cause of 394 interruptions during a 3-month period

Number	Cause	%
181	Programming errors	46
116	Depletions or system overload	29
63	Hardware component failures	16
19	Procedural errors	5
15	Intentional to load system changes	4
Total 394		100

Table 6.36 Breakdown of program instructions by functional areas

Functional area	Size, instructions	%
Control program	25,000	3
Operational and functional programs	155,000	16
Schedule change and management reports	400,000	42
Special diagnostics	175,000	18
Drivers and simulators	200,000	21
Total	955,000	100

Table 6.37 Storage locations of the 120 separate program segments

Number	Location	%
273	Programs reside in the main, high-speed core storage cells.	23
726	Programs are stored on drums.	60
202	Programs are located on the disk files.	17
Total 1201		100

Reliability problems Some interesting features of this system and its operation might be noted. During the early stages of its operation some of the most troublesome problems involved the power supply to the dual computer system. This consisted of a primary system (commercial power), backed up by batteries and two 400-horsepower diesel generators. Voltage dips on the primary system as short as 2 ms had an adverse effect on system operation and sometimes caused loss of data bits. This was to a large extent alleviated by floating the backup battery supply across the line with an electronic switch cutting in the batteries whenever such a dip occurred. During the Northeast power blackout of November 9, 1965, the system was operating under diesel power within 35 min after the outage, and service to agents' terminals was restored within 3 hours and 2 minutes. (With the new electronic switching of the batteries, and a faster autostart diesel capacity, it is possible that no service would have been lost.)

Another interesting feature of the system is the ability to search for passenger names which have been entered with certain kinds of misspellings.

Development Certain features relating to management of the development are of interest. The development time was estimated at 47 months but actually took 56 months (giving an overrun of about 20 percent).

The total effort has been estimated as 400 man-years, and about 1 million lines of code were written (see Table 6.36). Assuming 250 working days per year, this yields a productivity figure of 5 instructions per man-day, quite a bit higher than SAGE or SAFEGUARD. However, SAGE was a real-time system, while SABRE was an operational data base system.

Operation American Airlines gauged the success of the system in the following terms. In 1962 the load factor for the airline was 57 percent, and by 1967 it had risen to 59.9 percent; much of this improvement was attributed to the SABRE system. For comparison purposes, the average load factor for the airline industry in 1967 was 54 percent. The system was still in daily use at the writing of this book.

Lessons to be learned The important features of SABRE were:

1. The precontract study period took 5 years.
2. The 1012 terminals represented the largest timesharing system ever attempted at that time.
3. Extensive engineering studies (simulation) were conducted during the study period.
4. The program was organized into 120 segments of about 8000 instructions.
5. The data base was one of the largest attempted at the time.
6. During the operational period cited in Table 6.35 the MTTF was about 55 h.
7. The SABRE management process appeared to be of high caliber when measured against contemporary standards.

6.7.5 The MULTICS Timesharing System

Introduction The *Mult*iplexed *I*nformation and *C*omputing *S*ervice[1] was a research project designed to serve as a second-generation timesharing system more advanced than its first-generation predecessors, the Dartmouth BASIC system and the MIT CTSS system (see Corbató and Vyssotsky, 1967, p. 715, for a brief history of prior timesharing systems). The project was begun in the mid 1960s by Bell Laboratories, MIT, and GE. In 1970 Bell Labs dropped out of the project, and when GE sold its computer line, its successor Honeywell teamed with MIT to complete the system. The project began on a modified and augmented GE 635 computer called the GE 645. (New models developed by Honeywell have replaced the GE 645.)

The system was initially conceived as a computer utility which would be available 24 hours a day and 7 days a week, as are the telephone and power systems, with the flexibility to evolve and continue to satisfy future needs. The primary language for the system was PL/1, both as a user language and for almost all the system software. It was envisioned that there would be a very large program library created by the systems programmers and the users which would

---

[1] Corbató and Vyssotsky (1967), Rosen (1972).

be available to all. In addition to PL/1, many other language processors would be supported.

Advanced features Some of the important technical features of the system are summarized by Corbató.

> ...a virtual memory system for each user involving two-dimensional addressing with segmentation and paging; the dynamic linking of program segment cross-references at execution time to minimize system overhead; the routine use of sharable, recursive, pure procedure programming within the system as the normal mode of operation; the pooled use of multiple processors, memory modules, and input-output controllers; and multiprogramming of all resources and of multiple users. Automatic management of the complex of secondary storage media along with backup, retrieval, and maintenance procedures for the stored information will be provided by a file system. (Corbató and Vyssotsky, 1967, p. 714.)

In order to achieve high-speed transfer of files, drum as well as disk storage units were used. A typical system configuration is shown in Fig. 6.33.

The virtual-memory features were implemented so that they appear invisible to the user. Batch processing is supported as a subset of the operating system, and users who wish to run under GECOS (the operating system for the GE 635–45 computers) can do so within the MULTICS system. The most current version of the user manual for the system is maintained online for speedy user access to the latest features.

System performance The author obtained some firsthand data on the early performance of MULTICS. The mean time between system crashes (MTBF) varied from about 3 to 9 h per month during 1970–1971.[1] During this period the system was under constant change.[2] Contrary to the common industry scheme of phased software releases, MULTICS development went on continually, and a feature completed or corrected by a systems programmer in the morning was added to the system and available for use immediately, or later that day.

The programmers and managers used the following as a rule of thumb: if more than one system crash occurred in a day, they would suspend system development for a few days. This would allow the users to enjoy some "undisturbed" computing time before system development was continued. Another version of MULTICS was being maintained by Honeywell at a Massachusetts facility. The latest version of the system was transferred from MIT to Honeywell every few months. The Honeywell facility using essentially a phased release philosophy had perhaps a 50-h MTBF.

The success of MULTICS should be measured not only by the commercial success realized by Honeywell, but by the influence that the ideas and experience have had on subsequent timesharing system design.

---

[1] Monthly reports, MIT computation center.
[2] Discussion during fall 1971 with Professors Corbató and Saltzer of MIT.

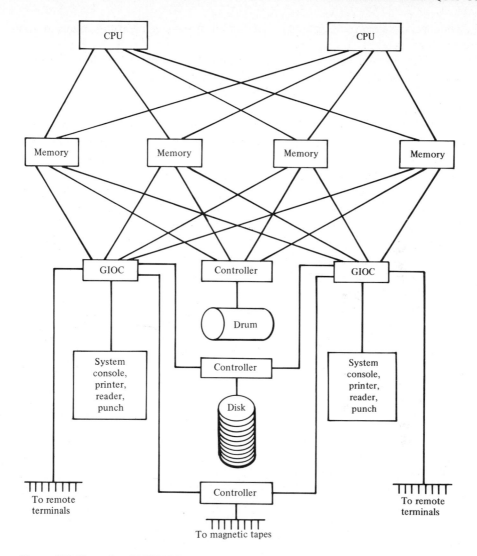

Figure 6.33 Examples of MULTICS system configuration. *(From Corbató and Vyssotsky, 1967, p. 720)*

In some ways the UNIX timesharing system, to be discussed in the next section, can be considered the "son of MULTICS."

Lessons to be learned Some of the lessons to be learned from the MULTICS project are listed below:

1. MULTICS was one of the first projects which demonstrated that large-scale system software could be efficiently written in PL/1.

2. The level of talent used on this project by all of the organizations involved was far above average.
3. The lack of phased release of software and conventional methods of supervising programmers did not prevent project completion.
4. The MTBF was a function of the development rate, and high activity meant poor reliability.
5. The experimental nature, lack of delivery schedules, the long evolution period, and the skill levels make it difficult to compare this project with a commercial development.

6.7.6 The UNIX Operating System

Introduction The term UNIX is a trademark for a family of powerful operating systems which have been written for several minicomputer systems. The first UNIX system was first developed at Bell Laboratories in the late 1960s and early 1970s, and by 1980 there were over 300 installations using the system within Bell Labs, various universities, government departments, and commercial facilities.[1] The system was developed and is maintained by Bell Laboratories, and is marketed by Western Electric under various licensing agreements. Universities are generally able to obtain a license, a complete set of documentation and manuals, and a copy of the software on disk for a nominal cost of a few hundred dollars. The cost to commercial users for the same set of materials and a license is several tens of thousands of dollars. Within the laboratories, the system is used for (1) support of telephone operations, (2) program development, (3) text processing, and (4) general-purpose computing.

System Development This example is unique among those we are discussing because there were no formal system specifications. The system concept grew out of the ideas of a single researcher (Ken Thompson), who was soon joined by a collaborator (Dennis Ritchie), and the two drew others into the fold as the project evolved. In 1969, Thompson, was able to obtain the use of an in-house cast-off PDP-7 minicomputer, for his sole use in programming research at Bell Labs. He set out to write a good, small operating system which would be useful to him and his colleagues in programming research. Thompson and Ritchie wrote the first version of UNIX in PDP-7 assembly language, and it became available in 1969–1970. Although no official release designations are in common use, the various versions of the system may be characterized in two different ways (see Table 6.38).

Hardware requirements The system hardware requirements are a minicomputer CPU with an architecture like that of a PDP-11, 24K to 48K words of main memory, a disk system with a capacity of 0.5 million to several million words, a

---

[1] Many new small- and medium-sized computer systems which have recently been released or are under development offer UNIX-like operating systems.

Table 6.38 Classification schemes for the various versions of the UNIX system

Machine classification

Version 1: On the PDP-7 and -9 computers
Version 2: On the PDP 11-20 computer
Version 3: (Incorporating multiprogramming, and the currently most widely used version), on the PDP-11/34, /40, /45, /60, and /70 computers
Version 4: On the PDP-11/70 and the Interdata 8/32 computers
Version 5: For the PDP-VAX system

Major features classification

(i) The standard system maintained by the UNIX Support Group at Bell Laboratories for Bell System projects.
(ii) The "Programmer's Workbench" version, also in wide use within Bell Laboratories, especially in areas in which text-processing and job-entry to other machines are important. Recently, PWB/UNIX has become available to outside organizations as well.
(iii) The "Sixth Edition" system (so called from the manual that describes it), which is the most widely used under Western Electric licenses by organizations outside the Bell System.
(iv) The version currently used in the Computing Science Research Center, where the UNIX system was developed, and at a few other locations at Bell Laboratories.

Source: Thompson and Ritchie (1978), pp. 1949, 1965. Newer versions have recently appeared.

terminal and/or printer, and some kind of storage device for loading and backup storage. The smallest configuration[1] available in 1980 was a DEC PDP 11-23 computer with 128K bytes of memory, a 10-megabyte Winchester disk, and an 8-in floppy disk. The experimental version of UNIX adapted by the Polytechnic Institute of New York for such a system supports four users, and the hardware as of 1982 cost about $12,000, including the four terminals.

Software facilities The present language facilities supported under UNIX are listed in Table 6.39. The first version of the system supported only one user; however, modern versions of the system on a machine the size of the PDP-11/70 or the VAX with ample disk space can support 40 to 60 users. Also, network facilities are provided for interconnection of several machines.

The developers were well aware of previous timesharing system research, and specifically, Ritchie worked on the MULTICS system when Bell Laboratories was still a member of the original triumvirate.[2] Many of the ideas for UNIX were adapted from MIT's successful CTSS timesharing system (circa 1960) (Lycklama, 1978). Furthermore, the text editor was an evolution of a previous text-editing system called QED.[3]

---

[1] Lycklama (1978).
[2] The influences of MULTICS and CTSS on UNIX are discussed by Thompson and Ritchie (1978).
[3] Thompson and Ritchie (1978), p. 1906.

Table 6.39 Major language facilities available under the UNIX operating system

1. The C language compiler
2. The text editor and spelling check programs
3. An assembler, linking loader, and symbolic debugger
4. Phototypesetting, equations, and statistical tables programs
5. Dozens of languages including Fortran 77, Ratfor, Basic, Snobol, APL, Algol 68, M6, TMG, Pascal
6. A compiler, compiler
7. Network communications with other PDP-11's and IBM 360 and 370 systems

The size of the present operating system is about 90,000 bytes or 45,000 two-byte words. No formal accounting of the resources expended in the development of UNIX is available in the literature. However, the authors estimate that the first version of the main system software took less than 2 man-years. Dividing 45,000 machine language words by 500 man-days yields the truly prodigious productivity rate of 90 words per day. Even though operating system software is perhaps an easier job than some of the embedded real-time computer system projects we have just discussed—Thompson and Ritchie are super programmers—it was still a significant feat.

Some of the most important features of the UNIX system are centered about the major programs listed in Table 6.39. The C programming language, developed by Ritchie, is a high-level, semi-PL/1-like language suitable for applications programming. It contains certain features such as register manipulation which also make it a useful systems programming language. In fact, the UNIX system was rewritten predominantly in the C language in 1973. This development resulted in essentially a self-maintaining system, a clearer expression and documentation of the design, and a more portable design. The rewriting increased memory size and run time by about one-third; however, the C language version also included many enhancements and improvements of the original design.

Clearly, the designers felt that any disadvantages in abandoning assembly language were far outweighed by the advantages which were realized. As an illustration of how useful the C language is in systems programming we cite its use in the so-called kernel of the operating system, which represents 5 to 10 percent of the total code. This kernel contained 10,000 lines of C language and 1000 lines of assembler code. About 200 of the lines of assembly code were written for efficiency reasons, and 800 were written to provide functions which were available in assembler but not in the C language.

Text processing Another important feature of the system is the powerful and comprehensive facilities for text processing of prose, mathematical equations, and statistical tables. The powerful text editor is supplemented by two different programs to check spelling and two powerful formatting programs. These facilities are useful in program creation and correction as well as in the creation, correction, and editing of written documents. The facilities for composition of

Table 6.40 Some of the important features of PWB/UNIX

(i) Many of its facilities were built in close cooperation between developers and users.

(ii) It has proven itself to be sufficiently reliable so that its users, who develop production software, have abandoned punched cards, private backup tapes, etc.

(iii) It offers a large number of simple, understandable program-development tools that can be combined in a variety of ways; users "package" these tools to create their own specialized environments.

(iv) Most important, the above were achieved without compromising the basic elegance, simplicity, generality, and ease of use of the UNIX system.

Source: Thompson and Ritchie (1978), p. 2177.

Table 6.41 Some reasons for the success of UNIX

(i) It is simple enough to be comprehended, yet powerful enough to do most of the things its users want.

(ii) The user interface is clean and relatively surprise-free. It is also terse to the point of being cryptic.

(iii) It runs on a machine that has become very popular in its own right.

(iv) Besides the operating system and its basic utilities, a good deal of interesting software is available, including a sophisticated text-processing system that handles complicated mathematical material and produces output on a typesetter or a typewriter terminal, and a LALR parser-generator.

Source: Thompson and Ritchie (1978), p. 1948.

equations and tables, and their linking to a phototypesetter,[1] provide high-quality master documents for reproduction which surpass those of all but a few existing systems.[2]

PWB UNIX A very interesting variant of the UNIX family is the Programmers Workbench, or PWB UNIX (see Table 6.40). The regular (research) version of UNIX was designed to provide an optimum set of facilities for programming research, and PWB UNIX was optimized for program development support. In addition to all the regular UNIX facilities, PWB UNIX possesses the ability to use UNIX as a remote job entry (RJE) vehicle into another computer, and various source code control SCCS features are provided. Also, networking is facilitated in PWB UNIX. For example, the Bell Labs BIS Division utilizes a UNIX system of five PDP-11/70 and two PDP-11/45 computers with a total of 275 user terminals.

Success of the system Among the reasons for the success of the system is its efficient and elegant design, which occurred not in spite of but (quoting the developers) because of the limitations on machine size; other reasons are given in Table 6.41. The UNIX software is judged to be very reliable, and the mean time

[1] Barnett (1965).
[2] Knuth (1979).

between software crashes is typically a few weeks. Reasons for such crashes are often that the system runs out of swap space or a nonrecoverable I/O error occurs during swapping. Typically, hardware failures occur more frequently than software failures, and the system software is not particularly tolerant of such hardware failures (this was not a design objective) or of power supply dips.

The SCCS system The purpose of the SCCS system is to capture all changes to a program which are under development. The initial version of the system is stored and identified, and each change entered is stored as a separate record. The system provides easy facilities to construct a listing or to execute any previous version of the software at any point in the development cycle. Commands are provided which automatically gather, calculate, and print out various statistics which are essential to the tracking and control of a software development. These facilities are extremely useful in supporting modern techniques of software management and control.

Lessons to be learned Some of the lessons learned from UNIX as stated by the developers of the system are as follows:

1. There is really no excuse for not providing a hierarchically arranged file system. It is very useful for maintaining directories containing related files, it is efficient because the amount of searching for files is bounded, and it is easy to implement.
2. The notion of "record" seems to be an obsolete remnant of the days of the 80-column card. A file should consist of a sequence of bytes.
3. The greatest care should be taken to ensure that there is only one format for files. This is essential for making programs work smoothly together.
4. Systems should be written in a high-level language that encourages portability. Manufacturers who build more than one line of machines and also build more than one operating system and set of utilities are wasting money.

6.8 SUMMARY AND CONCLUSION

The goal of this book is to encourage practitioners to try the existing software engineering techniques and evaluate their usefulness. They may reject some which are found lacking and accept others in a limited way, hoping for improved methods in the future. We hope that by now we have refuted the nihilist attitude: *There is little you can do to manage or measure software; the techniques don't work; so why waste your time?* The author rejects this pessimistic approach as well as that of the eternal optimist in Voltaire's satire, *Candide*, who says: "All is for the best in this best of all possible worlds."

Perhaps we might take as the moral of this book: *Sometimes life deals you a lousy hand of cards. Your job is to do the best with what you have and work hard to improve things as the game progresses.*

This work is dedicated to using what we have, which is very substantial, while we continue to improve our tools and techniques.

PROBLEMS

6.1 Discuss the differences among the following documents:
  (*a*) A needs document (system)
  (*b*) A requirements document (software)
  (*c*) A specification document (software)
  (*d*) A preliminary design document (software)

6.2 Write an *outline* for each of the documents discussed in Prob. 6.1 for the following examples:
  (*a*) An air traffic control system
  (*b*) A home computer/word-processing system which fits into half an attaché case
  (*c*) A personal financial records system for a homeowner
  (*d*) A robot welder for an auto assembly plant
  (*e*) Prob. 2.3
  (*f*) Prob. 2.4
  (*g*) Prob. 2.5
  (*h*) Prob. 2.6
  (*i*) Prob. 2.7
  (*j*) Prob. 2.8
  (*k*) A problem of your choice

6.3 What features of the contract do you feel will be most important for the examples of Prob. 6.2?

6.4 An existing program (or a newly developed one) is to be analyzed and tested to see how well Eqs. (6.1) and (6.2) predict running time. Obtain numerical values for the necessary terms in the equations through analysis or test. Test the program with a specified set of inputs to see if Eqs. (6.1) and (6.2) accurately predict running time.

6.5 Check the distribution of instruction types given in Table 6.6 with those which occur in two assembly language programs of your choosing.

6.6 Make up a set of instruction types that are similar to those in Table 6.6 but apply to a higher-level language.

6.7 Repeat Prob. 6.5 for two higher-level-language programs using the categories developed in Prob. 6.6.

6.8 Consider the quality measures listed in Table 6.7. Determine which of these are most important in the development of the problems given in Prob. 6.2. How would you define and measure these quantities in each case?

6.9 Consider the two designs discussed in Prob. 2.4. Compare these with respect to:
  (*a*) Operator-operand count
  (*b*) Predicted and actual run time
  (*c*) Estimated cost
  (*d*) Memory size
  (*e*) Relevant quality factors from Table 6.7.
Based on the above considerations, which design would you choose?

6.10 Repeat the comparison of Prob. 6.9 by assigning a maximum number of points X_i to each of the i factors such that a perfect score (sum of the X_i terms) is 100. Score each factor and see if your comparison changes.

6.11 Check the computations of Tables 6.17 and 6.18.

6.12 For a problem of your own choice, estimate the development costs for the software by the various methods as was done in Table 6.17.

6.13 From a reference source find the government inflation index for the last two decades and compare it with the model used in Table 6.17. Do you have a better model? Repeat Prob. 6.11 with this new model and discuss whether the results are significantly different.

6.14 Consult various salary surveys which have appeared in magazines and compare the results with Prob. 6.13.

6.15 Assume that in the later stages of a program most of the costs of software development are due to error removal. Use the results of Figs. 1.5, 4.5, and 4.6 to estimate the cost of error removal per stage. Using these results and the penalty fee profile of Fig. 6.11 (with events defined in Fig. 6.13) equate the penalty fees with the number of errors which must be removed.

6.16 Construct a Gantt chart for the examples of Prob. 6.2.

6.17 Construct a PERT diagram for the examples of Prob. 6.2.

6.18 For the examples given in Prob. 6.2:

(*a*) Estimate the number of man-months and the average number of people.

(*b*) Using the Rayleigh model and assuming a maximum manpower buildup rate (cf. Eq. (6.18)), plot the manpower profile for each project.

6.19 Repeat Prob. 6.18 assuming that the manpower buildup rate is actually one-half the maximum rate.

6.20 Verify the slopes, peaks, and inflection points of Fig. 6.19.

6.21 Check the calculations of Fig. 6.21.

6.22 Plot the cumulative curves related to Fig. 6.21 and calculate the maximum and average errors for each estimate.

6.23 Compare the results given in Figs. 6.23, 6.24, and 6.25 and comment.

6.24 For the problems given in Prob. 6.2, how many reviews are needed, and when should they be scheduled? Write an outline for each review.

6.25 Can you explain why the curves given in Figs. 6.26 and 6.27 have the shapes shown?

6.26 Sketch the cost of maintenance by a design group for the projects they produce using the model of Eqs. (6.28) to (6.35).

6.27 Use the model given in Eqs. (6.36) to (6.40) to estimate the typical warranty period T_W.

6.28 How does the behavior given in Fig. 2.7 affect software reliability?

6.29 Compare and contrast the software developments of: (*a*) SAGE, (*b*) SAFEGUARD, (*c*) SABRE, (*d*) MULTICS, and (*e*) UNIX.

6.30 Write a summary of your own programming project as was done in Sec. 6.7.

SUMMARY OF PROBABILITY THEORY*

A.1 INTRODUCTION

Several of the analytical techniques discussed in this text are based on probability theory. Many readers have an adequate background in probability and need only refer to this appendix for notation and brief review. However, some readers may not have studied probability, and this appendix should serve as a brief and concise introduction for them. If additional explanation is required, an introductory probability text should be consulted.[1]

A.2 PROBABILITY THEORY

"Probability had its beginnings in the 17th century when the Chevalier de Méré, supposedly an ardent gambler, became puzzled over how to divide the winnings in a game of chance. He consulted the French mathematician Blaise Pascal (1623–1662), who in turn wrote about this matter to Pierre Fermat (1601–1665); it is this correspondence which is generally considered the origin of modern probability theory."[2] In the eighteenth century Karl Gauss (1777–1855) and Pierre Laplace (1749–1827) further developed probability theory and applied it to fields other than games of chance.

---

*This appendix is largely extracted from Chap. 2 of *Probabilistic Reliability: An Engineering Approach*, by Martin L. Shooman, McGraw-Hill, New York, 1968.

[1]Wadsworth and Bryan (1960); Freund (1962); Drake (1967); Meyer (1970); Spiegel (1975).

[2]Freund (1962).

Today probability theory is viewed in three different ways:[1] the a priori (equally-likely-events) approach, the relative-frequency approach, and the axiomatic definition. Intuitively we state that the probability of obtaining the number 2 on a single roll of a die is $\frac{1}{6}$. Assuming each of the six faces is equally likely and that there is one favorable outcome, we merely take the ratio. This is a convenient approach; however, it fails in the case of a loaded die, where all events are not equally likely, and also in the case of compound events, where the definition of "equally likely" is not at all obvious. The relative-frequency approach begins with a discussion of an experiment such as the rolling of a die. The experiment is repeated n times (or n *identical* dice are all rolled at the same time in *identical* fashion). If n_2 represents the number of times that two dots face up, then the ratio n_2/n is said to approach the probability of rolling a 2 as n approaches infinity. The requirement that the experiment be repeated an infinite number of times and that the probability be defined as the limit of the frequency ratio can cause theoretical problems in some situations unless stated with care. The newest and most generally accepted approach is to base probability theory on three fundamental axioms. The entire theory is built in a deductive manner on these axioms in much the same way plane geometry is developed in an axiomatic manner. This approach has the advantage that if it is followed carefully, there are no loopholes, and all properties are well defined. As with any other theory or abstract model, the engineering usefulness of the technique is measured by how well it describes problems in the physical world. In order to evaluate the parameters in the axiomatic model one may perform an experiment and utilize the relative-frequency interpretation or evoke a hypothesis on the basis of equally likely events. In fact a good portion of mathematical statistics is devoted to sophisticated techniques for determining probability values from an experiment.

The axiomatic approach begins with a statement of the three fundamental axioms of probability:

1. The probability that an event A occurs is a number between zero and unity:

$$0 \le P(A) \le 1 \qquad\qquad \text{(A.1)}$$

2. The probability of a certain event (also called the *entire sample space* or the *universal set*) is unity:

$$P(S) = 1 \qquad\qquad \text{(A.2)}$$

3. The probability of the *union* (also called sum) of *two disjoint* (also called *mutually exclusive*) events is the sum of the probabilities:

$$P(A_1 + A_2) = P(A_1) + P(A_2) \qquad\qquad \text{(A.3)}$$

[1] Papoulis (1965).

A.3 SET THEORY

A.3.1 Definitions

Since axiomatic probability is based on set theory, we shall discuss briefly a few concepts of sets. The same concept often appears in set theory and in probability theory, with different notation and nomenclature being used for the same ideas. A *set* is simply a collection or enumeration of objects. The order in which the objects of the set are enumerated is not significant. Typical sets are the numbers 1, 2, 3, all 100 cars in a parking lot, and the 52 cards in a deck. Each item in the collection is an *element* of the set. Thus, in the examples given there are 3, 100, and 52 elements, respectively. Each set (except the trivial one composed of only one element) contains a number of *subsets*. The subsets are defined by a smaller number of elements selected from the original set. To be more specific one first defines the largest set of any interest in the problem and calls this the *universal set* U. The universal set contains all possible elements in the problem. Thus, a universal set of n elements has a maximum of 2^n distinct subsets. The universal set might be all cars in the United States, all red convertibles in New York, or all cars in the parking lot. This is a chosen collection which is fixed throughout a problem. In probability theory, the type of sets one is interested in consists of those which can, at least in theory, be viewed as outcomes of an experiment. These sets are generally called *events*. When the concept of universal set is used in probability theory, the term *sample space* S is generally applied. It is often convenient to associate a geometric picture, called a *Venn diagram*, with these ideas of sample space and event (or set and subset), and the sample space is represented by a rectangle (see Fig. A.1).

A.3.2 Axiomatic Probability

With the above background one can discuss intelligently the meaning of probability axioms 1 and 2 given in Eqs. (A.1) and (A.2). Equation (A.1) implies that the probability of an event A is a *positive number* between zero and one. From the relative-frequency interpretation we know that the probability of a certain event

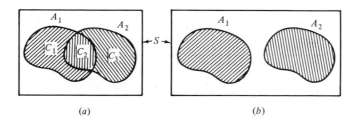

(a)   (b)

Figure A.1 Venn diagram illustrating the union of sets A_1 and A_2. (*a*) Ordinary sets. (*b*) Disjoint sets.

is unity and the probability of an impossible event is zero. All other events have probabilities between zero and unity. In Eq. (A.2) we let the event A be the entire sample space S, and not too surprisingly we find that this is a certain event. This is true because we say that S occurs if at least one element of S occurs.

A.3.3 Union and Intersection

The union of sets A_1 and A_2 is a third set B. Set B contains all the elements which are in set A_1 or in set A_2 or in both sets A_1 and A_2. Symbolically,

$$B = A_1 \cup A_2 \quad \text{or} \quad B = A_1 + A_2 \tag{A.4}$$

The $\cup$ notation is more common in mathematical work, whereas the $+$ notation is commonly used in applied work. The union operation is most easily explained in terms of the Venn diagram of Fig. A.1a. Set A_1 is composed of disjoint subsets C_1 and C_2 and set A_2 of disjoint subsets C_2 and C_3. Subset C_2 represents points common to A_1 and A_2, whereas C_1 represents points in A_1 but not in A_2, and C_3 represents points that are in A_2 but not A_1. When the two sets have no common elements, the areas do not overlap (Fig. A.1b), and they are said to be *disjoint* or *mutually exclusive*.

The intersection of events A_1 and A_2 is defined as a third set D which is composed of all elements which are contained in both A_1 and A_2. The notation is:

$$D = A_1 \cap A_2 \quad \text{or} \quad D = A_1 A_2 \quad \text{or} \quad D = A_1 \cdot A_2 \tag{A.5}$$

As before, the former is more common in mathematical literature and the latter more common in applied work. In Fig. A.1a, $A_1 A_2 = C_2$, and in Fig. A.1b, $A_1 A_2 = 0$. If two sets are disjoint, they contain no common elements, and their intersection is zero. (A set with no elements is called a *null set*.)

A.3.4 Probability of a Disjoint Union

We can now interpret the third probability axiom given in Eq. (A.3) in terms of a card-deck example. The events in the sample space are disjoint and (using the notation $S_3 \equiv$ three of spades, etc.)

$$P(\text{spades}) = P(S_1 + S_2 + \cdots + S_Q + S_K)$$

Since all events are disjoint,

$$P(\text{spades}) = P(S_1) + P(S_2) + \cdots + P(S_Q) + P(S_K) \tag{A.6}$$

From the equally-likely-events hypothesis one would expect that for a fair deck (without nicks, spots, bumps, torn corners, or other marking) the probability of drawing a spade is given by:

$$P(\text{spades}) = \tfrac{1}{52} + \tfrac{1}{52} + \cdots + \tfrac{1}{52} + \tfrac{1}{52} = \tfrac{13}{52} = \tfrac{1}{4}$$

A.4 COMBINATORIAL PROPERTIES

A.4.1 Complement

The complement of set A, written as $\bar{A}$, is another set B. Set $B = \bar{A}$ is composed of all the elements of the universal set which are not in set A. (The term A *not* is often used in engineering circles instead of A *complement*.) By definition the union of A and $\bar{A}$ is the universal set.

$$A + \bar{A} = U \tag{A.7}$$

Applying axioms 2 and 3 from Eqs. (A.3) and (A.2) to Eq. (A.7) yields

$$P(A + \bar{A}) = P(A) + P(\bar{A}) = P(S) = 1$$

This is valid since A and $\bar{A}$ are obviously disjoint events (we have substituted the notation S for U, since the former is more common in probability work). Because probabilities are merely numbers, the above algebraic equation can be written in three ways:

$$P(A) + P(\bar{A}) = 1$$
$$P(A) = 1 - P(A)$$
$$P(\bar{A}) = 1 - P(A) \tag{A.8}$$

A.4.2 Probability of a Union

Perhaps the first basic relationship to be deduced is the probability of a union of two events which are not mutually exclusive. We begin by extending the axiom of Eq. (A.3) to three or more events. Assuming that event A_2 is the union of two other disjoint events $B_1 + B_2$, we obtain

$$A_2 = B_1 + B_2$$
$$P(A_2 + A_2) = P(A_1) + P(B_1 + B_2) = P(A_1) + P(B_1) + P(B_2)$$

By successive application of this stratagem of splitting events into unions of other mutually exclusive events, we obtain the general result by induction

$$P(A_1 + A_2 + \cdots + A_n) = P(A_1) + P(A_2) + \cdots + P(A_n)$$
$$\text{for disjoint } A\text{'s} \quad \text{(A.9)}$$

If we consider the case of two events A_1 and A_2 which are not disjoint, we can divide each event into the union of two subevents. This is most easily discussed with reference to the Venn diagram shown in Fig. A.1a. The event (set) A_1 is divided into those elements (1) which are contained in A_1 and not in A_2, C_1 and (2) which are common to A_1 and A_2, C_2. Then $A_1 = C_1 + C_2$. Similarly we define $A_2 = C_3 + C_2$. We have now broken A_1 and A_2 into disjoint events and can apply Eq. (A.9):

$$P(A_1 + A_2) = P(C_1 + C_2 + C_2 + C_3) = P[C_1 + C_3 + (C_2 + C_2)]$$

By definition, the union of C_2 with itself is C_2; therefore

$$P(A_1 + A_2) = P(C_1 + C_2 + C_3) = P(C_1) + P(C_2) + P(C_3)$$

We can manipulate this result into a more useful form if we add and subtract the number $P(C_2)$ and apply Eq. (A.3) in reverse

$$P(A_1 + A_2) = [P(C_1) + P(C_2)] + [P(C_2) + P(C_3)] - P(C_2)$$
$$= P(A_1) + P(A_2) - P(A_1 A_2) \qquad (A.10)$$

Thus, when events A_1 and A_2 are not disjoint, we must subtract the probability of the union of A_1 and A_2 from the sum of the probabilities. Note that Eq. (A.10) reduces to Eq. (A.3) if events A_1 and A_2 are disjoint since $P(A_1 A_2) = 0$ for disjoint events.

Equation (A.10) can be extended to apply to three or more events

$$P(A_1 + A_2 + \cdots + A_n)$$

$$= [P(A_1) + P(A_2) + \cdots + P(A_n)] \qquad \leftarrow \binom{n}{1} = n \text{ terms}$$

$$- \left[P(A_1 A_2) + P(A_1 A_3) + \cdots + P\left(\underset{i \neq j}{A_i A_j}\right) \right] \qquad \leftarrow \binom{n}{2} \text{ terms}$$

$$\qquad\qquad (A.11)$$

$$+ \left[P(A_1 A_2 A_3) + P(A_1 A_2 A_4) + \cdots + P\left(\underset{i \neq j \neq k}{A_i A_j A_k}\right) \right] \leftarrow \binom{n}{3} \text{ terms}$$

$$\cdots\cdots\cdots\cdots\cdots\cdots\cdots\cdots\cdots\cdots\cdots\cdots\cdots\cdots$$

$$(-1)^{n-1} [P(A_1 A_2 \cdots A_n)] \qquad \leftarrow \binom{n}{n} = 1 \text{ term}$$

The complete expansion of Eq. (A.11) involves $(2^n - 1)$ terms.

A.4.3 Conditional Probabilities and Independence

It is important to study in more detail the probability of an intersection of two events, that is, $P(A_1 A_2)$. We are especially interested in how $P(A_1 A_2)$ is related to $P(A_1)$ and $P(A_2)$.

Before proceeding further we must define conditional probability and introduce a new notation. Suppose we want the probability of obtaining the four of clubs on one draw from a deck of cards. The answer is of course $1/52$, which can be written: $P(C_4) = 1/52$. Let us change the problem so it reads: What is the probability of drawing the four of clubs *given that a club is drawn*? The answer is $1/13$.

In such a situation we call the probability statement a *conditional probability*. The notation $P(C_4 \mid C) = 1/13$ is used to represent the conditional probability of drawing a four of clubs given that a club is drawn. We read $P(A_2 \mid A_1)$ as the probability of A_2 occurring conditioned on the previous occurrence of A_1, or more simply as the probability of A_2 given A_1.

$$P(A_1 A_2) = P(A_1)P(A_2|A_1) \tag{A.12a}$$

$$P(A_1 A_2) = P(A_2)P(A_1|A_2) \tag{A.12b}$$

Intuition tells us that there must be many cases in which

$$P(A_2|A_1) = P(A_2)$$

In other words, the probability of occurrence of event A_2 is independent of the occurrence of event A_1. From Eq. (A.12a) we see that this implies $P(A_1 A_2) = P(A_1)P(A_2)$, and this latter result in turn implies

$$P(A_1|A_2) = P(A_1)$$

Thus we define independence by any one of the three equivalent relations

$$P(A_1 A_2) = P(A_1)P(A_2) \tag{A.13a}$$

or

$$P(A_1|A_2) = P(A_1) \tag{A.13b}$$

or

$$P(A_2|A_1) = P(A_2) \tag{A.13c}$$

Conditional probabilities are sometimes called *dependent probabilities*.

One can define conditional probabilities for three events by splitting event B into the intersection of events A_2 and A_3. Then letting $A = A_1$ and $B = A_2 A_3$, we have

$$P(AB) = P(A)P(B|A) = P(A_1)P(A_2 A_3|A_1)$$
$$= P(A_1)P(A_2|A_1)P(A_3|A_1 A_2)$$

Successive application of this technique leads to the general result

$$P(A_1 A_2 \cdots A_n) = P(A_1)P(A_2|A_1)P(A_3|A_1 A_2) \cdots$$
$$P(A_n|A_1 A_2 \cdots A_{n-1}) \tag{A.14}$$

Thus, the probability of the union of n terms is expressed as the joint product of one independent probability and $n - 1$ dependent probabilities.

A.5 DISCRETE RANDOM VARIABLES

A.5.1 Density Function

We can define x as a random variable if we associate each value of x with an element in event A defined on sample space S. If the random variable x assumes a finite number of values, then x is called a *discrete random variable*. In the case of a discrete random variable, we associate with each value of x a number x_i and a probability of occurrence $P(x_i)$. We could describe the probabilities associated with the random variable by a table of values, but it is easier to write a formula that permits calculation of $P(x_i)$ by substitution of the appropriate value of x_i. Such a formula is called a *probability function* for the random variable **x**. More exactly, we use the notation $f(x)$ to mean a discrete probability density function associated with the discrete random variable **x**. (The reason for the inclusion of the word "density" will be clear once the parallel development for continuous random variables is completed.) Thus,

$$P(\mathbf{x} = x_i) = P(x_i) = f(x_i) \tag{A.15}$$

In general we use the sequence of positive integers $0, 1, 2, \ldots, n$ to represent the subscripts of the $n + 1$ discrete values of **x**. Thus, the random variable is denoted by **x** and particular values of the random variable by $x_1, x_2, \ldots, x_n$. If the random variable under consideration is a nonnumerical quantity, e.g., the colors of the spectrum (red, orange, yellow, green, blue, indigo, violet), then the colors (or other quantity) would first be coded by associating a number 1 to 7 with each. If the random variable **x** is defined over the entire sample space S, $P(A)$ is given by

$$P(A) = \underset{\substack{\text{for all } x_i \\ \text{values which} \\ \text{are elements of } A}}{\Sigma P(x_i)} = \underset{\substack{\text{for all } x_i \\ \text{in } A}}{\Sigma f(x_i)} \tag{A.16}$$

The probability of the sample space is

$$P(S) = \underset{\substack{\text{over all} \\ i}}{\Sigma f(x_i)} = 1 \tag{A.17}$$

As an example of the above concepts we shall consider the throw of one die. The random variable **x** is the number of spots which face up on any throw. The domain of the random variable is $x = 1, 2, 3, 4, 5, 6$. Using the equally-likely-events hypothesis, we conclude that

$$P(x = 1) = P(x = 1) = \cdots = \tfrac{1}{6}$$

Thus, $f(x) = 1/6$, a constant density function. This can also be depicted graphically as in Fig. A.2a. The probability of an even roll is

$$P(\text{even}) = \underset{i=2,4,6}{\Sigma} f(x_i) = \tfrac{1}{6} + \tfrac{1}{6} + \tfrac{1}{6} = \tfrac{1}{2}$$

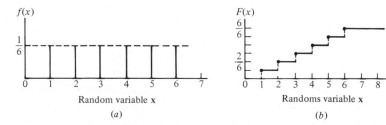

Random variable x

(a)

Randoms variable x

(b)

Figure A.2 (a) Line diagram depicting the discrete density function for the throw of one die. (b) Step diagram depicting the discrete distribution functions for the density function given in (a).

A.5.2 Distribution Function

It is often convenient to deal with another, related function rather than the density function itself. The *distribution function* is defined in terms of the probability that $\mathbf{x} \leq x$:

$$P(\mathbf{x} \leq x) \equiv F(x) = \sum_{\mathbf{x} \leq x} f(x) \qquad (A.18)$$

The distribution function is a cumulative probability and is often called the *cumulative distribution function*. The analytical form of $F(x)$ for the example in Fig. A.2 is

$$F(x) = \frac{x}{6} \qquad \text{for } 1 \leq x \leq 6 \qquad (A.19)$$

Equation (A.19) related $F(x)$ to $f(x)$ by a process of summation. One can write an inverse relation[1] defining $f(x)$ in terms of the difference between two values of $F(x)$

$$f(x) = F(x^+) - F(x^-) \qquad (A.20)$$

In other words, $f(x)$ is equal to the value of the discontinuity at x in the step diagram of $F(x)$. There are a few basic properties of density and distribution functions which are of importance: (1) since $f(x)$ is a probability, $0 \leq f(x) \leq 1$; (2) because $P(S) = 1$,

$$\sum_{\substack{\text{all} \\ x}} f(x) = 1$$

A.5.3 Binomial Distribution

Many discrete probability models are used in applications, the foremost being the binomial distribution and the Poisson distribution. The *binomial distribution* (sometimes called the *Bernoulli distribution*) applies to a situation in which an event can either occur or not occur (the more common terms are *success* or *failure*, a legacy from the days when probability theory centered around games of chance). The terms success and failure, of course, are ideally suited to reliability applications. The probability of success on any one trial is p, and that of failure is $1 - p$. The number of independent trials is denoted by n, and the number of successes by r. Thus, the probability of r successes in n trials with the probability of one success being p is

$$B(r; n, p) = \binom{n}{r} p^r (1 - p)^{n-r} \qquad \text{for } r = 0, 1, 2, \ldots, n \qquad (A.21)$$

where $\quad \binom{n}{r} = n!/r!(n-r)! \equiv \dfrac{\text{number of combinations of } n \text{ things}}{\text{taken } r \text{ at a time}}$

---

[1] The notations $F(x^+)$ and $F(x^-)$ mean the limits approached from the right and left, respectively.

$B_n(r; 9, p)$

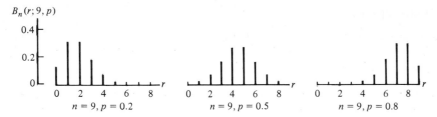

Figure A.3 Binomial density function for fixed n. *(Adapted from Wadsworth and Bryan, 1960. Used by permission.)*

A number of line diagrams for the binomial density function[1] are given in Fig. A.3. In Fig. A.3 the number of trials is fixed at nine, and the probability of success on each trial is changed from 0.2 to 0.5 to 0.8. Intuition tells us that the most probable number of successes is np, which is 1.8, 4.5, and 7.2, respectively. (It is shown in Sec. A.7 that intuition has predicted the mean value.)

Example 1 Clearly, we could use the binomial distribution to predict the probability of twice obtaining a 3, in six throws of a die:

$$r = 2 \qquad n = 6 \qquad p = \tfrac{1}{6}$$

$$B(2; 6, \tfrac{1}{6}) = \binom{6}{2}(\tfrac{1}{6})^2(1 - \tfrac{1}{6})^{6-2} = 15 \times 0.0131 = 0.196$$

Example 2 We can also use the binomial distribution to evaluate the probability of picking three aces on ten draws with replacement from a deck; however, if we do not replace the drawn cards after each pick, the binomial model will no longer hold, since the parameter p will change with each draw. The binomial distribution does not hold when draws are made without replacement, because the trials are no longer independent. The proper distribution to use in such a case is the hypergeometric distribution.[2]

$$H(k; j, n, N) = \frac{\binom{n}{k}\binom{N-n}{j-k}}{\binom{N}{j}} \qquad (\text{A.21}a)$$

where k = number of successes
j = number of trials
n = finite number of possible successes
N = finite number of possible trials

---

[1] We use the notation $B(r; n, p)$ rather than the conventional and less descriptive notation $f(x)$.
[2] Wadsworth and Bryan (1960), p. 59, or Freeman (1963), pp. 113–120.

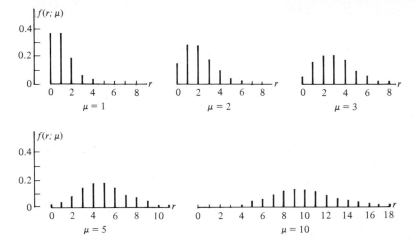

Figure A.4 Poisson density function for several values of μ.

A.5.4 Poisson Distribution

Another discrete distribution of great importance is the *Poisson distribution*, which can be derived in a number of ways. One derivation will be outlined in this section[1] and a second derivation in Sec. A.8. If p is very small and n is very large, the binomial density, Eq. (A.21), takes on a special limiting form, which is the Poisson law of probability. Starting with Eq. (A.21), we let np, the most probable number of occurrences, be some number μ

$$\mu = np \qquad \therefore p = \frac{\mu}{n}$$

$$B\left(r; n, \frac{\mu}{n}\right) = \frac{n!}{r!\,(n-r)!}\left(\frac{\mu}{n}\right)^r\left(1 - \frac{\mu}{n}\right)^{n-r}$$

The limiting form called the Poisson distribution is

$$f(r; \mu) = \frac{\mu^r e^{-\mu}}{r!} \tag{A.22}$$

The Poisson distribution can be written in a second form, which is very useful for our purposes. If we are interested in events which occur in time, we can define the rate of occurrence as the constant λ = occurrences per unit time; thus $\mu = \lambda t$. Substitution yields the alternative form of the Poisson distribution:

$$f(r; \lambda, t) = \frac{(\lambda t)^r e^{-\lambda t}}{r!} \tag{A.23}$$

Line diagrams for the Poisson density function given in Eq. (A.22) are shown in Fig. A.4 for various values of μ. Note that the peak of the distribution is near μ and that symmetry about the peak begins to develop for larger values of μ.

[1] See Shooman (1968), pp. 37–42.

A.6 CONTINUOUS RANDOM VARIABLES

A.6.1 Density and Distribution Functions

The preceding section introduced the concept of a discrete random variable and its associated density and distribution functions. A similar development will be pursued in this section for continuous variables. Examples of some continuous random variables are the length of a manufactured part, the failure time of a system, and the value of a circuit resistance. In each of these examples there is no reason to believe that the random variable takes on discrete values. On the contrary, the variable is continuous over some range of definition. In a manner analogous to the development of the discrete variable, we define a continuous density function and a continuous distribution function. We shall start with the cumulative distribution function.

The cumulative distribution function for the discrete case was defined in Eq. (A.18) as a summation. If the spacings between the discrete values of the random variable $\mathbf{x}$ are Δx and we let $\Delta x \to 0$, then the discrete variable becomes a continuous variable, and the summation becomes an integration. Thus, the cumulative distribution function of a continuous random variable is given by

$$F(x) = \int_{\substack{\text{over the}\\\text{domain of } \mathbf{x}}} f(x)\, dx \tag{A.24}$$

If we let $\mathbf{x}$ take on all values between points a and b

$$P(\mathbf{x} \le x) = F(x) = \int_a^x f(x)\, dx \quad \text{for} \quad a < \mathbf{x} \le b \tag{A.25}$$

The density function $f(x)$ is given by the derivative of the distribution function. This is easily seen from Eq. (A.25) and the fact that the derivative of the integral of a function is the function itself.

$$\frac{dF(x)}{dx} = f(x) \tag{A.26}$$

The probability that $\mathbf{x}$ lies in an interval $x < \mathbf{x} < x + dx$ is given by

$$P(x < \mathbf{x} < x + dx) = P(\mathbf{x} \le x + dx) - P(x \le \mathbf{x})$$
$$= \int_a^{x+dx} f(x)\, dx - \int_a^x f(x)\, dx = \int_x^{x+dx} f(x)\, dx$$
$$= F(x + dx) - F(x) \tag{A.27}$$

It is easy to see from Eq. (A.27) that if $F(x)$ is continuous and we let $dx \to 0$, $P(\mathbf{x} = x)$ is zero. Thus, when we deal with continuous probability, it makes sense to talk of the probability that $\mathbf{x}$ is within an interval rather than at one point. In fact since the $P(\mathbf{x} = x)$ is zero, we need not be very careful in the continuous case in specifying whether the interval is open or closed since

$$P(a \le \mathbf{x} \le b) = P(a < \mathbf{x} < b) = P(a \le \mathbf{x} < b) = P(a < \mathbf{x} \le b)$$

Thus, the density function $f(x)$ is truly a density, and like any other density function it has a value only when integrated over some finite interval. The basic properties of density and distribution functions previously discussed in the discrete case hold in the continuous case. At the lower limit of $\mathbf{x}$ we have $F(a) = 0$, and at the upper limit $F(b) = 1$. These two statements, coupled with Eq. (A.27), lead to $\int_a^b f(x)\,dx = 1$. Since $f(x)$ is a probability, $f(x)$ is nonnegative, and $F(x)$, its integral, is a nondecreasing function.

A.6.2 Rectangular Distribution

The simplest continuous variable distribution is the uniform or rectangular distribution shown in Fig. A.5a. The two parameters of this distribution are the limits a and b. This model predicts a uniform probability of occurrence in any interval

$$P(x < \mathbf{x} \leq x + \Delta x) = \Delta x (b - a)^{-1}$$

between a and b.

A.6.3 Exponential Distribution

Another simple continuous variable distribution is the exponential distribution. The exponential density function is

$$f(x) = \lambda e^{-\lambda x} \qquad 0 < \mathbf{x} \leq +\infty \tag{A.28}$$

which is sketched in Fig. A.5b. This distribution recurs time and time again in reliability work. The exponential is the distribution of the time to failure t for a great number of electronic-system parts. The parameter λ is constant and is called the *conditional failure rate* with the units fractional failures per hour. The distribution function yields the failure probability and $1 - F(t)$ the success probability. Specifically, the probability of no failure (success) in the interval $0 - t$ is given by

$$P_s(t_1) = 1 - F(t_1) = e^{-\lambda t_1}$$

A.6.4 Rayleigh Distribution

Another single-parameter density function of considerable importance is the *Rayleigh distribution*, which is given as

$$f(x) = Kx e^{-Kx^2/2} \qquad 0 < \mathbf{x} \leq +\infty \tag{A.29}$$

and for the distribution function

$$F(x) = 1 - e^{-Kx^2/2} \tag{A.30}$$

The density function is sketched in Fig. A.5c. The Rayleigh distribution finds application in noise problems in communication systems and in reliability work.

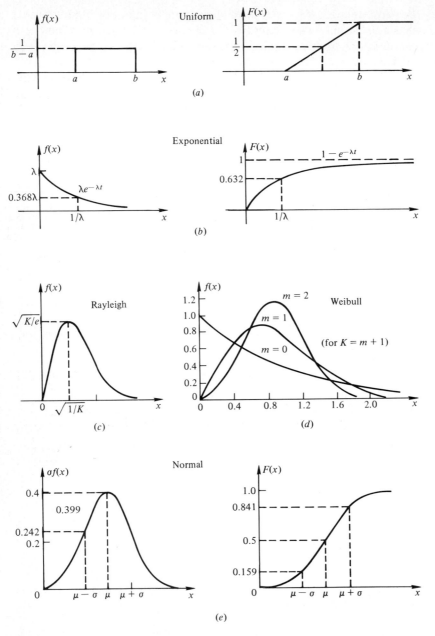

Figure A.5 Various continuous variable probability distributions: (*a*) uniform distribution; (*b*) exponential distribution; (*c*) Rayleigh distribution; (*d*) Weibull distribution; (*e*) normal distribution.

Whereas the exponential distribution holds for time to failure of a component with a constant conditional failure rate λ, the Rayleigh distribution holds for a component with a linearly increasing conditional failure rate Kt. The probability of success of such a unit is

$$P_s(t) = 1 - F(t) = e^{-Kt^2/2}$$

A.6.5 Weibull Distribution

Both the exponential and the Rayleigh distributions are single-parameter distributions which can be represented as special cases of a more general two-parameter distribution called the *Weibull distribution*. The density and distribution functions for the Weibull are

$$f(x) = Kx^m e^{-Kx^{m+1}/(m+1)} \qquad F(x) = 1 - e^{-Kx^{m+1}/(m+1)} \qquad (A.31)$$

This family of functions is sketched for several values of m in Fig. A.5d. When $m = 0$, the distribution becomes exponential, and when $m = 1$, a Rayleigh distribution is obtained. The parameter m determines the shape of the distribution, and parameter $K = m + 1$ is a scale-change parameter.

A.6.6 Normal Distribution

The best-known two-parameter distribution is the *normal*, or *gaussian*, distribution. This distribution is very often a good fit for the size of manufactured parts, the size of a living organism, or the magnitude of certain electric signals. It can be shown that when a random variable is the sum of many other random variables, the variable will have a normal distribution in most all cases.

The density function for the normal distribution is written as

$$f(x) = \frac{1}{\sigma\sqrt{2\pi}} e^{-x^2/2\sigma^2} \qquad -\infty < x < +\infty$$

This function has a peak of $1/\sigma\sqrt{2\pi}$ at $x = 0$ and falls off symmetrically on either side of zero. The rate of falloff and the height of the peak at $x = 0$ are determined by the parameter σ, which is called the *standard deviation*. In general one deals with a random variable x which is spread about some value such that the peak of the distribution is not at zero. In this case one shifts the horizontal scale of the normal distribution so that the peak occurs at $x = \mu$

$$f(x) = \frac{1}{\sigma\sqrt{2\pi}} e^{-(x-\mu)^2/2\sigma^2} \qquad (A.32)$$

The effect of changing σ is as follows: a large value of σ means a low, broad curve and a small value of σ a thin, high curve. A change in μ merely slides the curve along the x axis.

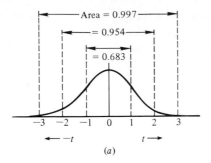

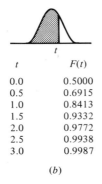

t	$F(t)$
0.0	0.5000
0.5	0.6915
1.0	0.8413
1.5	0.9332
2.0	0.9772
2.5	0.9938
3.0	0.9987

(b)

Figure A.6 Area under the normal curve: (a) for $-1 < t \le 1$, $-2 < t \le 2$, and $-3 < t \le 3$; (b) between $-\infty$ and various values of t.

The distribution function is given by

$$F(x) = \frac{1}{\sigma\sqrt{2\pi}} \int_{-\infty}^{x} e^{-(\xi-\mu)^2/2\sigma^2} \, d\xi \qquad (A.32a)$$

where ξ is a dummy variable of integration. The shapes of the normal density and distribution functions are shown in Fig. A.5e. The distribution function given in Eq. (A.32) is left in integral form since the result cannot be expressed in closed form. This causes no particular difficulty, since $f(x)$ and $F(x)$ have been extensively tabulated and approximate expansion formulas are readily available.[1] In tabulating the integral of Eq. (A.32) it is generally convenient to introduce the change of variables $t = (x - \mu)/\sigma$, which shifts the distribution back to the origin and normalizes the x axis in terms of σ units.

The area under the $f(x)$ curve between a and b is of interest since it represents the probability that x is within the interval $a < x \le b$. The areas for $-1 < t \le +1$, $-2 < t \le +2$, and $-3 < t \le +3$ are shown in Fig. A.6 along with a short table of areas between $-\infty$ and t.

The normal distribution can also be used as a limiting form for many other distributions. The binomial distribution approaches the normal distribution for large n.

---

[1]Abramovitz and Stegun (1972), pp. 931–936, Sec. 26.2.

A.7 MOMENTS

The density or distribution function of a random variable contains all the information about the variable, i.e., the entire story. Sometimes the entire story of the random variable is not necessary, and an excerpt which sufficiently characterizes the distribution is sufficient. In such a case one computes a few moments (generally two) for the distribution and uses them to delineate the salient features. The moments are weighted integrals of the density function which describe various geometrical properties of the density function.

A.7.1 Expected Value

It is easy to express the various moments of a probability distribution in terms of an operator called the *expected value*. The expected value of the continuous random variable $\mathbf{x}$ defined over the range $a < \mathbf{x} \leq b$ with density function $f(x)$ is

$$E(\mathbf{x}) = \int_a^b xf(x)\, dx \qquad (A.33)$$

For a discrete random variable $\mathbf{x}$ taking on values $x = x_1, x_2, \ldots, x_n$ the expected value is defined in terms of a summation

$$E(\mathbf{x}) = \sum_{i=1}^{n} x_i f(x_i) \qquad (A.34)$$

A.7.2 Moments

To be more general one defines an entire set of moments. The nth moment of the random variable $\mathbf{x}$ computed about the origin and defined over the range $a < \mathbf{x} \leq b$ is given by

$$m_r = \int_{-\infty}^{+\infty} x^r f(x)\, dx \qquad (A.35)$$

The zero-order moment m_0 is the area under the density function, which is, of course, unity. The first-order moment is simply the expected value, which is called the *mean* and is given the symbol μ

$$m_1 = E(\mathbf{x}) = \mu \qquad (A.36)$$

The origin moments for a discrete random variable which takes on the values $x_1, x_2, \ldots, x_n$ are given by

$$m_r = \sum_{i=1}^{n} x_i^r f(x_i) \qquad (A.37)$$

Is is often of importance to compute moments about the mean rather than the origin. The set of moments about the mean are defined as:

For continuous random variables:

$$m_r' = E\big[(\mathbf{x} - \mu)^r\big] = \int_{-\infty}^{+\infty} (x - \mu)^r f(x)\, dx \qquad (A.38)$$

Table A.1 Mean and variance for several distributions

Distribution	$E(\mathbf{x})$	var $\mathbf{x}$
Binomial	np	$np(1-p)$
Poisson	μ	μ
Exponential	$\dfrac{1}{\lambda}$	$\dfrac{1}{\lambda^2}$
Rayleigh	$\sqrt{\dfrac{\pi}{2K}}$	$\dfrac{3.43}{K}\left(1-\dfrac{\pi^2}{4}\right)$
Weibull	$\left(\dfrac{K}{m+1}\right)^{1-\varepsilon}\Gamma(\varepsilon)$ $\varepsilon \equiv \dfrac{m+2}{m+1}$ $\Gamma \equiv$ the gamma function	$\left(\dfrac{K}{m+1}\right)^{1-\delta}\Gamma(\delta) - [E(\mathbf{x})]^2$ $\delta \equiv \dfrac{m+3}{m+1}$
Normal	μ	σ^2

For discrete random variables:

$$m'_r = E\big[(\mathbf{x}-\mu)^r\big] = \sum_{i=1}^{n}(x_i - \mu)^r f(x_i) \qquad (\text{A.39})$$

The second moment about the mean, $m'_2 = \int_{-\infty}^{+\infty}(x-\mu)^2 f(x)\,dx$, is called the *variance* of $\mathbf{x}$, var $\mathbf{x}$, and is a measure of the sum of the squares of the deviations from μ. Generally this is expressed in terms of the standard deviation $\sigma = \sqrt{\text{var}\,\mathbf{x}}$. One can easily express var $\mathbf{x}$ and σ in terms of the expected-value operator:

$$\sigma^2 = \text{var}\,\mathbf{x} = E(\mathbf{x}^2) - \mu^2$$

The means and variances of the distributions discussed in Sec. A.5 are given in Table A.1.

A.8 MARKOV MODELS

A.8.1 Properties

There are basically four kinds of Markov probability models, one of which plays a central role in reliability. Markov models are functions of two random variables: the state of the system $\mathbf{x}$ and the time of observation $\mathbf{t}$. The four kinds of models arise because both $\mathbf{x}$ and $\mathbf{t}$ may be either discrete or continuous random variables, resulting in four combinations. As a simple example of the concepts of state and time of observation, we visualize a shoe box with two interior partitions which divide the box into three interior compartments labeled 1, 2, and 3. A Ping-Pong ball is placed into one of these compartments, and the box is periodically tapped on the bottom causing the Ping-Pong ball to jump up and fall back into one of the three compartments. (For the moment we neglect the possibility that it falls out onto the floor.) The states of the system are the three compartments in the box. The time of observation is immediately after each rap, when the ball has fallen back into one of the compartments. Since we specified that the raps occur periodically, the model is discrete in both state and time. This sort of model is generally called a *Markov chain model* or a *discrete-state discrete-time model*. When the raps at the bottom of the box occur continuously, the model becomes a discrete-state continuous-time model, called a *Markov process*. If we remove the partitions and call the long axis of the box the x axis, we can visualize a continuum of states from $x = -l/2$ to $x = +l/2$. If the ball is coated with rubber cement, it will stick wherever it hits when it falls back into the box. In this manner we can visualize the other two types of models, which involve a continuous-state variable. We shall be concerned only with the discrete-state continuous-time model, the Markov process.

Any Markov model is defined by a set of probabilities p_{ij} which define the probability of transition from any state i to any state j. If in the discrete-state case we make our box compartments and the partitions equal in size, all the transition probabilities should be equal. (In the general case, where each compartment is of different size, the transition probabilities are unequal.) One of the most important features of any Markov model is that the transition probability p_{ij} depends only on states i and j and is completely independent of all past states except the last one, state i. This seems reasonable in terms of our shoe-box model since transitions are really dependent only on the height of the wall between adjacent compartments i and j and the area of the compartments and not on the sequence of states the ball has occupied before arriving in state i. Before delving further into the properties of Markov processes, an example of great importance, the Poisson process, will be discussed.

A.8.2 Poisson Process

In Sec. A.4 the Poisson distribution was introduced as a limiting form of the binomial distribution. In this section we shall derive the Poisson distribution as the governing probability law for a Poisson process, a particular kind of Markov process. In a Poisson process we are interested in the number of occurrences in time, the probability of each occurrence in a small time Δt being a constant which is the parameter of the process. Examples of Poisson processes are the number of atoms transmuting as a function of time in the radioactive decay of a substance, the number of noise pulses as a function of time in certain types of electric systems, and the number of failures for a group of components operating in a standby mode or in an instantaneous-replacement situation. The occurrences are discrete, and time is continuous; therefore this is a discrete-state continuous-time model. The basic assumptions which are necessary in deriving a Poisson process model are as follows:

1. The probability that a transition occurs from the state of n occurrences to the state of $n + 1$ occurrences in time Δt as $\lambda \Delta t$. The parameter λ is a constant and has the dimensions of occurrences per unit time. The occurrences are

irreversible, which means that the number of occurrences can never decrease with time.

2. Each occurrence is independent of all other occurrences.
3. The transition probability of two or more occurrences in interval Δt is negligible. Another way of saying this is to make use of the independence-of-occurrence property and write the probability of two occurrences in interval Δt as the product of the probability of each occurrence, that is, $(\lambda \Delta t)(\lambda \Delta t)$. This is obviously an infinitesimal of second order for Δt small and can be neglected.

We wish to solve for the probability of n occurrences in time t, and to that end we set up a system of difference equations representing the state probabilities and transition probabilities. The probability of n occurrences having taken place by time t is denoted by

$$P(x = n, t) \equiv P_n(t)$$

For the case of zero occurrences at time $t + \Delta t$ we write the following difference equation

$$P_0(t + \Delta t) = (1 - \lambda \Delta t)P_0(t) \tag{A.40}$$

which says that the probability of zero occurrences at time $t + \Delta t$ is $P_0(t + \Delta t)$. This probability is given by the probability of zero occurrences at time t, $P_0(t)$, multiplied by the probability of no occurrences in interval Δt, $1 - \lambda \Delta t$. For the case of one occurrence at time $t + \Delta t$ we write

$$P_1(t + \Delta t) = (\lambda \Delta t)P_0(t) + (1 - \lambda \Delta t)P_1(t) \tag{A.41}$$

The probability of one occurrence at $t + \Delta t$, $P_1(t + \Delta t)$, can arise in two ways: (1) either there was no occurrence at time t, $P_0(t)$, and one happened in the interval Δt, (with probability $\lambda \Delta t$), or (2) there had already been one occurrence at time t, $P_1(t)$, and no additional ones came along in the time interval Δt, (probability $1 - \lambda \Delta t$). It is clear that Eq. (A.41) can be generalized, yielding

$$P_n(t + \Delta t) = (\lambda \Delta t)P_{n-1}(t) + (1 - \lambda \Delta t)P_n(t)$$

$$\text{for } n = 1, 2, \ldots \tag{A.42}$$

The difference equations (A.40) and (A.41) really describe a discrete-time system, since time is divided into intervals Δt, but by taking limits as $\Delta t \to 0$ we obtain a set of differential equations which truly describe the continuous-time Poisson process. Rearranging Eq. (A.40) and taking the limit of both sides of the equation at $\Delta t \to 0$ leads to

$$\lim_{\Delta t \to 0} \frac{P_0(t + \Delta t) - P_0(t)}{\Delta t} = \lim_{\Delta t \to 0} -\lambda P_0(t)$$

By definition the left-hand side of the equation is the time derivative of $P_0(t)$ and the right-hand side is independent of Δt; therefore

$$\frac{dP_0(t)}{dt} = \dot{P}_0(t) = -\lambda P_0(t) \tag{A.43}$$

Similarly for Eq. (A.41)

$$\lim_{\Delta t \to 0} \frac{P_n(t + \Delta t) - P_n(t)}{\Delta t} = \lim_{\Delta t \to 0} \lambda P_{n-1}(t) - \lim_{\Delta t \to 0} \lambda P_n(t)$$

$$\frac{dP_n(t)}{dt} = \dot{P}_n(t) = \lambda P_{n-1}(t) - \lambda P_n(t)$$

$$\text{for } n = 1, 2, \ldots, n \quad \text{(A.44)}$$

Equations (A.43) and (A.44) are a complete set of differential equations which, together with a set of initial conditions, describe the process. If there are no occurrences at the start of the problem, $t = 0$, $n = 0$, and

$$P_0(0) = 1, P_1(0) = P_2(0) = \cdots = P_n(0) = 0.$$

Solution of this set of equations can be performed in several ways: classical differential-equation techniques, Laplace transforms, matrix methods, etc. In this section we shall solve them using the classical technique of undetermined coefficients. Substituting a solution of the form Ae^{st} gives $s = -\lambda$, and substituting the initial condition $P_0(0) = 1$ gives

$$P_0(t) = e^{-\lambda t} \quad \text{(A.45)}$$

For $n = 1$, Eq. (A.42) becomes

$$\dot{P}_1(t) = \lambda P_0(t) - \lambda P_1(t)$$

Substitution from Eq. (A.45) and rearrangement yields

$$\dot{P}_1(t) + \lambda P_1(t) = \lambda e^{-\lambda t}$$

The homogeneous portion of this equation is the same as that for $P_0(t)$. The particular solution is of the form $Bte^{-\lambda t}$. Substituting yields $B = \lambda$, and using the initial condition $P_1(0) = 0 = A$ gives

$$P_1(t) = \lambda te^{-\lambda t} \quad \text{(A.46)}$$

It should be clear that solving for $P_n(t)$ for $n = 2, 3, \ldots$ will generate the Poisson probability law given in Eq. (A.23). (Note: $m \equiv r$.)

Thus, the Poisson process has been shown to be a special type of Markov process which can be derived from the three basic postulates with no mention of the binomial distribution. We can give another important interpretation to $P_0(t)$. If we let t_0 be the time of the first occurrence, then $P_0(t)$ is the probability of no occurrences:

$$P_0(t) \equiv P(t < t_0) = 1 - P(t_0 < t)$$

Thus, $1 - P_0(t)$ is a cumulative distribution function for the random variable **t**, the time of occurrence. The density function for time of first occurrence is obtained by differentiation:

$$f(t) = \frac{d}{dt}(1 - e^{-\lambda t}) = \lambda e^{-\lambda t} \quad \text{(A.47)}$$

This means that the time of first occurrence is exponentially distributed. Since each occurrence is independent of all others, it also means that the time between any two occurrences is exponentially distributed.

A.8.3 Transition Matrix

Returning to some of the basic properties of Markov processes, we find that we can specify the process by a set of differential equations and their associated initial conditions. Because of the basic Markov assumption that only the last state is involved in determining the probabilities, we always obtain a set of first-order differential equations. The constants in these equations can be specified by constructing a transition-probability matrix.[1] The rows represent the probability of being in any state A at time t and the columns the probability of being in state B at time $t + \Delta t$. The former are called *initial states* and the latter *final states*. An example is given in Table A.2 for a process with $n + 1$ discrete states. The transition probability p_{ij} is the probability that in time Δt the system will undergo a transition from initial state i to final state j. Of course p_{ii}, a term on the main diagonal, is the probability that the system will remain in the same state during one transition. The sum of the p_{ij} terms in any row must be unity, since this is the sum of all possible transition probabilities. In the case of a Poisson process, there are an infinite number of states. The transition matrix for the first five terms of a Poisson process is given in Table A.3. Inspection of the Poisson example reveals that the difference equations[2] for the system can be obtained simply. The procedure is to equate the probability of any final state at the top of each column to the product of the transition probabilities in that column and the initial probabilities in the row. Specifically, for the transition matrix given in Table A.2,

$$P_{s_0}(t + \Delta t) = p_{00} P_{s_0}(t) + p_{10} P_{s_1}(t) + \cdots + p_{n0} P_{s_n}(t)$$

If the p_{ij} terms are all independent of time and depend only on constants and Δt, the process is called *homogeneous*. For a homogeneous process, the resulting differential equations have constant coefficients, and the solutions are of the form e^{-rt} or $t^n e^{-rt}$. If for a homogeneous process the final value of the probability of being in any state is independent of the initial conditions, the process is called *ergodic*. A finite-state homogeneous process is ergodic if every state can be reached from any other state with positive probability. Whenever it is not possible to reach any other state from some particular state, the latter state is called an *absorbing state*. Returning to the partitioned shoe box example of Sec. A.8.1, if we allow the ball to hop completely out of the box onto the floor, the floor forms a fourth state, which is absorbing. In a transition matrix any column j having only a single entry p_{ij} along the main diagonal is an absorbing state.

---

[1] In App. B a flowgraph model for a Markov process will be developed which parallels the use of the transition matrix.

[2] The differential equations are obtained by taking the limit of the difference equations as $\Delta t \to 0$.

Table A.2 A transition matrix

Initial states		Final states				
		$s_0(t + \Delta t)$	$s_1(t + \Delta t)$	$s_2(t + \Delta t)$	$\cdots$	$s_n(t + \Delta t)$
$s_0(t)$	$n = 0$	p_{00}	p_{01}	p_{02}	$\cdots$	p_{0n}
$s_1(t)$	$n = 1$	p_{10}	p_{11}	p_{12}	$\cdots$	p_{1n}
$s_2(t)$	$n = 2$	p_{20}	p_{21}	p_{22}	$\cdots$	p_{2n}
. . . .						
$s_n(t)$	$n = n$	p_{n0}	p_{n1}	p_{n2}	$\cdots$	p_{nn}

Table A.3 The first five rows and columns of the transition matrix for a Poisson process

	$s_1(t + \Delta t)$	$s_1(t + \Delta t)$	$s_2(t + \Delta t)$	$s_3(t + \Delta t)$	$s_4(t + \Delta t)$
$s_0(t)$	$1 - \lambda \Delta t$	$\lambda \Delta t$	0	0	0
$s_1(t)$	0	$1 - \lambda \Delta t$	$\lambda \Delta t$	0	0
$s_2(t)$	0	0	$1 - \lambda \Delta t$	$\lambda \Delta t$	0
$s_3(t)$	0	0	0	$1 - \lambda \Delta t$	$\lambda \Delta t$
$s_4(t)$	0	0	0	0	$1 - \lambda \Delta t$

A.9 ESTIMATION THEORY

A.9.1 Introduction

Estimation theory[1] has to do with how one determines the parameters in a probabilistic model from statistical data taken on the items governed by the model. Specifically, in reliability work we place a group of components on life test and observe the sequence of failure times $t_1, t_2, \ldots, t_n$. On the basis of these data we compute time-to-failure models and hazard models, which it is hoped govern the behavior of other, similar items. The model parameters are computed from certain calculations made with the data. Estimation theory provides guidelines for efficient and accurate computations.

If only a few data are available, say, $n \leq 5$, the result must be questioned no matter how sophisticated the formula. If many data are available, $n \geq 100$, the results should be good as long as the formula used is sensible. (Many of the different computational schemes used converge as the number of data $n \to \infty$.) Estimation theory is probably of most help in the intermediate range $10 \leq n \leq 50$.

[1]Shooman (1968), pp. 80–96.

A *point estimation* formula computes one value which represents the parameter in question. For example, if we had data representing failure times of 10, 20, 25, 35, and 40 h, intuition would tell us to estimate the MTTF[1] as

$$(10 + 20 + 25 + 35 + 40)/5 = 26 \text{ h}$$

Thus, 26 h is a point estimate of the MTTF. Our discussion of the properties of point estimators will shed some light on how good such an estimate is. Of course, we could very properly argue that with only five data we cannot be very sure the MTTF is exactly 26 h, and it makes more sense to quote a range of values. If we say that we are fairly sure the MTTF is between 20 and 30 h, we are giving an *interval estimate*. Interval estimation will be discussed following point estimation.

A.9.2 Estimator Properties

In devising a point-estimator formula there are no hard and fast rules. The techniques to be discussed—moment methods, maximum likelihood, and least squares—all have a number of good features. We start out by postulating from intuition what seems to be a good property of an estimator, and if it can be computed in a reasonable mathematical fashion, we adopt it as one of our criteria of goodness. Any estimator which satisfies many of the goodness criteria is probably a useful estimator. In order to systematize the notation we shall let $\mathbf{x}$ be the random variable in question, and the mean and variance of $\mathbf{x}$ will be defined by

$$\mu_x = E(\mathbf{x})$$
$$\text{var } \mathbf{x} = \sigma^2 = E(x^2) - E^2(x)$$

The estimator of $\mathbf{x}$ is $\mathbf{w}$, which is a new random variable. The actual data values will be denoted by $x_1, x_2, \ldots, x_n$.

A.9.3 Moment Estimator

The moment method of point estimation is the simplest method in common use. If the numbers $x_1, x_2, \ldots, x_n$ represent a set of data, then a moment estimator for the kth origin moment is defined as

$$\check{m}_k = \frac{1}{n} \sum_{i=1}^{n} x_i^k \tag{A.48}$$

where $\check{m}_k$ stands for the moment estimate of m_k. Thus, using Eq. (A.48), we can generate a series of r values for the first r origin moments of the data. Similarly we can compute the first r origin moments from the density function in question. This latter set of equations will contain several unknown parameters $\theta_1, \theta_2, \ldots, \theta_j$, which we wish to estimate. We equate the first j data moments to the first j theoretical moments, and solve the resulting j simultaneous equations for the estimates $\check{\theta}_1, \check{\theta}_2, \ldots, \check{\theta}_j$. As an example consider the estimation of the parameter λ

---

[1]Mean time to failure, which is sometimes called by the equivalent term MTBF, mean time between failures.

of the exponential distribution:

$$m_1 = E(\mathbf{x}) = \int_0^{+\infty} x\lambda e^{-\lambda x}\, dx = \frac{1}{\lambda}$$

$$\check{m}_1 = \frac{1}{n} \sum_{i=1}^{n} x_i = m_1$$

$$\frac{1}{n} \sum_{i=1}^{n} x_i = \frac{1}{\lambda}$$

$$\check{\lambda} = \frac{n}{\displaystyle\sum_{i=1}^{n} x_i} \tag{A.49}$$

To illustrate the procedure for a two-parameter distribution we shall estimate μ and σ^2 for a normal distribution:

$$m_1 = \mu = \check{m}_1 = \frac{1}{n} \sum_{i=1}^{n} x_i$$

$$m_2 = \sigma^2 + \mu^2 = \check{m}_2 = \frac{1}{n} \sum_{i=1}^{n} x_i^2$$

Solving these two equations simultaneously,

$$\check{\mu} = \frac{1}{n} \sum_{i=1}^{n} x_i \tag{A.50}$$

$$\check{\sigma}^2 = \frac{1}{n} \sum_{i=1}^{n} x_i^2 - \left(\frac{1}{n} \sum_{i=1}^{n} x_i\right)^2 = \frac{1}{n} \sum_{i=1}^{n} x_i^2 - \check{\mu}^2 \tag{A.51}$$

A.9.4 Maximum-Likelihood Estimators

A different system of estimation, which is newer and is generally accepted as superior to moment estimation, is *maximum-likelihood estimation* (MLE). The computation is a little more difficult than that of moment estimates, and the philosophy behind it is somewhat more subtle and powerful. If we let each sample value be a random variable $\mathbf{x}_1, \mathbf{x}_2, \ldots, \mathbf{x}_n$ and the particular data values obtained be $x_1, x_2, \ldots, x_n$, we can write n marginal density functions[1] which represent the probability that $\mathbf{x}_i = x_i$

$$f(x_i; \theta)\, dx_i = P(\mathbf{x}_i = x_i)$$

Since the $\mathbf{x}_i$'s are independent, the joint density function can be written as the product of the marginal density functions:

$$\phi(x_1, x_2, \ldots, x_n; \theta) = L(x_1, x_2, \ldots, x_n; \theta)$$
$$= f(x_1; \theta)f(x_2; \theta) \cdots f(x_n; \theta) \tag{A.52}$$

---

[1] The theory of many random variables (see Shooman, 1968, p. 67) is analogous to a single random variable. In the simplest case, that of independence, the density function of all the variables (joint) is simply the product of the density functions of each variable (marginals), that is, $f_1 f_2 f_3 \cdots f_n$.

In Eq. (A.52) we have written each probability density as a function of θ, the parameter to be estimated. The joint density function ϕ is generally called the likelihood function L, as given in Eq. (A.52). We would expect that if we really knew the true value, called θ_{true}, and substituted it into the density for x_1, yielding $f(x_1; \theta_{true})$, then this density function would have a large value. Similar reasoning holds for $f(x_2; \theta_{true})$, etc. This of course implies that $\phi(x_1, x_2, \ldots, x_n; \theta_{true})$ will be large. In fact for any $\theta_1 \neq \theta_{true}$ we would expect that

$$\phi(x_1, x_2, \ldots, x_n; \theta_1) < \phi(x_1, x_2, \ldots, x_n; \theta_{true})$$

Since the integration of ϕ over all n variables must yield unity regardless of how ϕ is distributed, if ϕ is very high at one point, it is also concentrated about that point (assuming smooth variation and no large discontinuities). This means that the relative magnitude of the likelihood function will serve as a measure of how close to θ_{true} any estimate is. The obvious conclusion is that we shall obtain a good estimate for θ if we maximize L as a function of θ, that is, set $\partial L / \partial \theta = 0$. In other words, we are trying to maximize the probability that the set of data $x_1, x_2, \ldots, x_n$ represents a sample governed by the density function $f(x, \theta)$. To do this we choose the most likely value of θ.

As an example we shall derive the MLE for the parameter λ of the exponential distribution

$$f(x, \lambda) = \lambda e^{-\lambda x}$$
$$f(x_i, \lambda) = \lambda e^{-\lambda x_i}$$

$$L(x_1, x_2, \ldots; \lambda) = f(x_1, \lambda) f(x_2, \lambda) \cdots f(x_n, \lambda) = \prod_{i=1}^{n} f(x_i; \lambda)$$

$$= \lambda^n \prod_{i=1}^{n} e^{-\lambda x_i} = \lambda^n \exp\left(-\lambda \sum_{i=1}^{n} x_i\right)$$

Now to maximize we compute $\partial L / \partial \lambda$ and set it equal to zero. At this point the computation looks a bit messy since the derivative of a product of n functions leads to n differentiations. A simple modification of the procedure eliminates this extra labor. Because of the one-to-one nature of the mapping, the functions max z and max $(\log z)$ both coincide. Thus, we can deal with

$$\ln L(x_1, x_2, \ldots; \lambda) \equiv \mathcal{L}(x_1, x_2, \ldots; \lambda)$$

where $\mathcal{L}$ represents the log of the likelihood function.

$$\mathcal{L}(x_1, x_2, \ldots; \lambda) = \ln\left[\prod_{i=1}^{n} f(x_i; \lambda)\right] = \sum_{i=1}^{n} \ln f(x_i; \lambda)$$

$$\frac{\partial \mathcal{L}}{\partial \lambda} = \frac{\partial}{\partial \lambda}\left[\sum_{i=1}^{n} \ln f(x_i; \lambda)\right] = \sum_{i=1}^{n} \left[\frac{\partial}{\partial \lambda} \ln f(x_i; \lambda)\right]$$

where we have assumed that we can interchange the order of summation and differentiation. Substituting the exponential density,

$$\frac{\partial \mathcal{L}}{\partial \lambda} = \sum_{i=1}^{n} \frac{\partial}{\partial \lambda} \ln \lambda e^{-\lambda x_i} = \sum_{i=1}^{n} \frac{\partial}{\partial \lambda} (\ln \lambda - \lambda x_i)$$

$$= \sum_{i=1}^{n} \left(\frac{1}{\lambda} - x_i \right) = \frac{n}{\lambda} - \sum_{i=1}^{n} x_i$$

Equating $\partial \mathcal{L}/\partial \lambda$ to zero,

$$\frac{n}{\lambda} - \sum_{i=1}^{n} x_i = 0$$

$$\hat{\lambda} = \frac{n}{\displaystyle\sum_{i=1}^{n} x_i} \tag{A.53}$$

where $\hat{\lambda}$ means the MLE of λ. Equations (A.49) and (A.53) are identical and the moment estimate and MLE for the parameter λ of the exponential distribution agree. This is just a coincidence, and the moment and MLE of most functions will differ.

As an example of how the method applies to a two-parameter distribution we consider the normal distribution

$$f(x) = \frac{1}{\sigma \sqrt{2\pi}} e^{-(x-\mu^2)/2\sigma^2}$$

$$L(x_1, x_2, \ldots; \mu, \sigma) = \left(\frac{1}{\sigma \sqrt{2\pi}} \right)^n \prod_{i=1}^{n} e^{-(x_i - \mu)^2/2\sigma^2}$$

$$\mathcal{L}(x_1, x_2, \ldots; \mu, \sigma) = n \ln \frac{1}{\sigma \sqrt{2\pi}} - \sum_{i=1}^{n} \frac{(x_i - \mu)^2}{2\sigma^2}$$

Setting $\partial \mathcal{L}/\partial \mu = 0$ yields

$$\hat{\mu} = \frac{1}{n} \sum_{i=1}^{n} x_i \tag{A.54}$$

Similarly, for σ, setting $\partial \mathcal{L}/\partial \sigma = 0$ yields

$$\sigma^2 = \frac{1}{n} \sum_{i=1}^{n} (x_i - \mu)^2$$

Of course for μ we use $\hat{\mu}$ from Eq. (A.54):

$$\hat{\sigma}^2 = \frac{1}{n} \sum_{i=1}^{n} (x_i - \hat{\mu})^2 \tag{A.55}$$

The MLE has many good properties, one of which pertains to the variance of the MLE, which can be shown[1] to approach

$$\text{var } \hat{\theta} = -\frac{1}{nE\left[\dfrac{\partial^2 \ln f(x; \hat{\theta})}{\partial \hat{\theta}^2}\right]} \tag{A.56}$$

as n becomes large. Furthermore, the distribution of $\hat{\theta}$ approaches a normal distribution for large n with parameters $\mu = \hat{\theta}$ and $\sigma^2 = \text{var } \hat{\theta}$. Equation (A.56) can also be written in an equivalent form[2] which is a little simpler computationally:

$$\text{var } \hat{\theta} = -\frac{1}{\partial^2 \mathcal{L} / \partial \hat{\theta}^2} \tag{A.57}$$

As an example, the $\text{var } \hat{\mu}$ and $\text{var } \hat{\sigma}^2$ are computed for the normal distribution. For μ

$$\mathcal{L} = n \ln \frac{1}{\sqrt{2\pi}} - n \ln \sigma - \sum_{i=1}^{n} \frac{(x_i - \mu)^2}{2\sigma^2}$$

$$\frac{\partial^2 \mathcal{L}}{\partial \mu^2} = -\sum_{i=1}^{n} \frac{1}{\sigma^2} = -\frac{n}{\sigma^2}$$

$$\text{var } \hat{\mu} = \frac{\sigma^2}{n} = \frac{\hat{\sigma}^2}{n} \tag{A.58}$$

For $\sigma^2 \equiv v$,

$$\mathcal{L} = n \ln \frac{1}{\sqrt{2\pi}} - \frac{n}{2} \ln v - \sum_{i=1}^{n} \frac{(x_i - \mu)^2}{2v}$$

$$\frac{\partial^2 \mathcal{L}}{\partial v^2} = \frac{n}{2} \frac{1}{v^2} - \sum_{i=1}^{n} \frac{(x_i - \mu)^2}{v^3} = \frac{n}{2} \frac{1}{v^2} - \frac{n}{v^2} = -\frac{n}{2v^2}$$

$$\text{var } \hat{\sigma}^2 = \frac{2\hat{\sigma}^4}{n} \tag{A.59}$$

MLEs are now considered superior to moment estimates by most people.

Example—MLE estimates for bug seeding We can derive Eq. (5.36) in Sec. 5.6.4 by using MLE theory. We begin with the binomial density function $f(x) = B(r; n, p)$ given in Eq. (A.21) and substitute into Eq. A.52:

$$L(r, n; p) = \binom{n}{p} p^r (1 - p)^{n-r}$$

Proceeding with MLE theory to compute an estimator for p assuming we have r

---

[1] Freeman (1963), p. 259.
[2] Lloyd and Lipow (1962), p. 168.

successes in n trials, we obtain

$$\mathcal{L} = \ln\binom{n}{r} + r\ln p + (n-r)\ln(1-p)$$

$$\frac{d\mathcal{L}}{dp} = \frac{r}{p} + \frac{n-r}{1-p}(-1) = 0$$

Solving, we obtain the MLE estimator for p:

$$\hat{p} = \frac{r}{n} \tag{A.60}$$

Now suppose we have two samples from two populations; then

$$\hat{p}_1 = \frac{r_1}{n_1}$$

$$\hat{p}_2 = \frac{r_2}{n_2}$$

If we assume the populations have the same success probability, then we equate

$$\frac{r_1}{n_1} = \frac{r_2}{n_2} \tag{A.61}$$

If $r_1 = N_t$, $n_1 = N + N_t$, $r_2 = n_t$, and $n_2 = n + n_t$, we obtain the result given in Eq. (5.36).

The computation of the variance of N is much more difficult. However, we can obtain an approximate formula if we recognize that b_c will be the main source of variation and we observe that in both Eqs. (A.58) and (A.59) the var $\hat{\theta} \approx \hat{\theta}^2/n$. We can therefore guess the formula given in Eq. (5.40). It turns out we are on safe ground in our approximation since it checks well with Eq. (5.43) for a restricted range.

A.9.5 Least-Squares Estimates

The least-squares estimation technique is commonly applied in engineering and mathematics problems. We assume that a linear law relates two variables, the independent variable x and the dependent variable y:

$$y = ax + b$$

The experimental data relating y and x are a set of n pairs of points: $x_1, y_1; x_2, y_2; \ldots; x_n, y_n$. The error between the true value of the independent value and the first data point is

$$\text{error}_i = y - y_i = ax_i + b - y_i$$

The error measure for the accuracy of fit is given by the sum of the squared errors:

$$\text{SSE} = \sum_{i=1}^{n} (\text{error}_i)^2 = \sum_{i=1}^{n} (ax_i + b - y_i)^2$$

The best estimates of a and b are the values of a and b which minimize the sum of the *squared errors* (SSE). Thus, we compute $\partial SSE/\partial a$ and $\partial SSE/\partial b$, set each equal to zero, and solve for the resulting values of a and b, yielding

$$\tilde{a} = \frac{\sum\limits_{i=1}^{n} y_i(x_i - \bar{x})}{\sum\limits_{i=1}^{n} (x_i - \bar{x})^2} \qquad \bar{x} = \frac{1}{n} \sum\limits_{i=1}^{n} x_i$$

$$\tilde{b} = \bar{y} - \tilde{a}\bar{x} \qquad \bar{y} = \frac{1}{n} \sum\limits_{i=1}^{n} y_i$$

(A.62)

The symbol $\tilde{x}$ stands for the least-squares estimate of $\mathbf{x}$. A more detailed discussion and derivation appear in the references.[1]

We can of course perform least-squares estimation in a similar manner with a functional relationship between y and x other than the linear one considered above. As an example the reader is referenced to the discussion in Prob. 1.3 at the end of Chap. 1.

A.9.6 Interval Estimates

Rather than giving a point estimate of our unknown parameter θ it is often sensible to give an interval estimate for θ. Let us suppose we have an MLE for θ computed from physical data and its variance, which are given by $\hat{\theta}$ and $(\hat{\sigma}^2)_\theta$. If many data are available, n is large, and the distribution of $\boldsymbol{\theta}$ is approximately normal. We can thus discuss the probability that an interval about $\hat{\theta}$ really does contain the true value of θ. It is sensible to construct a symmetric interval $\hat{\theta} - k\hat{\sigma}_\theta \leq \theta \leq \hat{\theta} + k\hat{\sigma}_\theta$. This interval brackets the true value θ (some number) by an upper and lower limit. The limits are random variables, which are in turn functions of the random variables $\boldsymbol{\theta}$ and $\boldsymbol{\sigma}_\theta$. If $k = 1$, the normality assumption means we can write $P(\hat{\theta} - \sigma_\theta \leq \theta \leq \hat{\theta} + \sigma_\theta) = 0.683$. Thus, we are 68 percent sure that the interval constructed from the estimates brackets the true value θ. If we let $k = 2$ or 3, the interval grows, and the probability increases; i.e., our confidence that we have bracketed our parameter becomes greater. If we had used something other than the MLE, the estimate distribution might have been other than normal, and although the same procedure could be used, the numerical answer would have differed.

In fact suppose we had an MLE for a small sample size and were very wary about assuming a normal distribution for such a small sample. In this case we would want to know whether we could construct an interval estimate knowing μ and σ but not knowing the distribution of $\hat{\theta}$. The inequality given below, which was first developed by the Russian mathematician Chebyshev, gives us bounds on a probability interval which are independent of the distribution.

---

[1]Shooman (1968), pp. 91–94.

Table A.4 Comparison of Gauss and Chebyshev bounds

Interval	Chebyshev	Gauss	Rectangular	Normal
$\|\mathbf{x} - \mu\| \geq \sigma$	1.00	0.44	0.58	0.32
$\|\mathbf{x} - \mu\| \geq 2\sigma$	0.25	0.11	0.00	0.05
$\|\mathbf{x} - \mu\| \geq 3\sigma$	0.11	0.05	0.00	0.003

Given that $\mathbf{x}$ is a random variable with $E(\mathbf{x}) = \mu$ and var $\mathbf{x} = \sigma^2$, then for any positive number k the following inequality holds:

$$P(|\mathbf{x} - \mu| \geq k\sigma) \leq \frac{1}{k^2} \tag{A.63}$$

For a proof of this theorem see Meyer (1965, p. 128). A slightly tighter bound which improves on Chebyshev's inequality is due to Gauss.[1] If $f(x)$ is continuous and has one maximum (mode) at x_{max}, and if $x_{max} = E(\mathbf{x})$, then

$$P(|\mathbf{x} - \mu| \geq k\sigma) \leq \frac{4}{9k^2} \tag{A.64}$$

This bound is roughly one-half of Chebyshev's bound; however, more information on $f(x)$ is needed. For comparison purposes, the bounds calculated from Eqs. (A.63) and (A.64) are compared with the actual values for a normal and rectangular distribution in Table A.4. The Chebyshev bound of course holds for both the normal and rectangular case. The Gauss bound does not apply in the rectangular case because a rectangular distribution does not have a unique mode. The bounds are somewhat crude, but they are still good for first estimates in many problems. More advanced bounds of this type can be found in the literature.[2]

A.10 DERIVATION OF MLE ESTIMATES FOR MACRO MODEL PARAMETERS

In Sec. 5.7.6, MLE estimates for the two model parameters, K and E_T, were given in Eqs. (5.96) to (5.103). This section states the basic assumptions and derives these estimator equations.

A.10.1 Input Data

The input data available for estimation fall into classes: (1) periodic debugging data on error-removal rate $\rho_c(\tau)$ and cumulative number of errors removed $\varepsilon_c(\tau)$,

---

[1] Lloyd and Lipow (1977), p. 94.
[2] Savage (1961); Goodwin (1955).

and (2) occasional functional tests run on the software during integration. These functional tests are run after the software has had $\tau_1, \tau_2, \ldots$, and τ_k hours of integration testing. During *each* run of a functional test, several failures occur, and the sequence of i confirmed software failure times is $t_{1k}, t_{2k}, \ldots, t_{ik}$ for the kth functional test. The program size I_T is known.

A.10.2 Density Function

As in Chap. 5, we assume a direct proportionality between hazard and residual errors, and we obtain

$$R(t) = e^{-K\varepsilon_r(\tau)t} \tag{5.69}$$

Since $R(t) = 1 - F(t)$, the associated density function is given by $-dR(t)/dt$:

$$f(t) = K\varepsilon_r(\tau)e^{-K\varepsilon_r(\tau)t} \tag{A.65}$$

where

$$\varepsilon_r(\tau) = \frac{E_T}{I_T} - \varepsilon_c(\tau) \tag{5.23}$$

A.10.3 Estimator Formulas

The parameters to be estimated are the two unknowns in Eq. (A.65), K and E_T. Since there are two unknowns we will need two different sources of test data to determine the two parameters. We begin by deriving the MLE at a single test time τ and show that there is insufficient information to solve for K and E_T in general. Then we assume two sets of data at development times τ_1 and τ_2, and show that a set of two equations are obtained, which are solved to obtain the estimate. The estimator equations are finally generalized for m sets of test data at times $\tau_1, \tau_2, \ldots, \tau_m$.

Single test Assume we are dealing with a single test composed of a set of n runs, where r of these result in failure times $t_1, t_2, \ldots, t_r$ and $n - r$ complete $T_1, T_2, \ldots, T_{n-r}$ hours of operation without failure. When any test is terminated before all items have failed (as is true here), it is called a *truncated* test. A different likelihood function applies for truncated tests:[1]

$$L(t_1, t_2, \ldots, t_r; T_1, T_2, \ldots, T_{n-r}; K, E_T) = \frac{n!}{(n-r)!} \prod_{i=1}^{r} f(t_i)R(T_i) \tag{A.66}$$

Substitution of Eqs. (5.69) and (A.65) into Eq. (A.66) yields

$$L(t_1, t_2, \ldots, t_r; T_1, T_2, \ldots, T_{n-r}; K, E_T)$$

$$= \frac{n!}{(n-r)!} \prod_{i=1}^{r} K\varepsilon_r(\tau)e^{-K\varepsilon_r(\tau)t_i} \prod_{i=1}^{n-r} e^{-K\varepsilon_r(\tau)T_i} \tag{A.67}$$

[1] Shooman (1968), p. 476.

Taking the natural logarithm of L in Eq. (A.67) yields

$$\mathcal{L} = \ln L = \ln\frac{n!}{(n-r)!} + \sum_{i=1}^{r} \ln K\varepsilon_r(\tau)e^{-K\varepsilon_r(\tau)t_i} - \sum_{i=1}^{n-r} \ln e^{-K\varepsilon_r(\tau)T_i}$$

(A.67a)

$$= A + \sum_{i=1}^{r} \ln K\varepsilon_r(\tau) - \sum_{i=1}^{r} K\varepsilon_r(\tau)t_i - \sum_{i=1}^{n-r} K\varepsilon_r(\tau)T_i$$

where

$$A = \ln\frac{n!}{(n-r)!}$$

We derive one of the MLE equations by computing $\partial\mathcal{L}/\partial K$ and equating the result to zero:

$$\frac{\partial\mathcal{L}}{\partial K} = \sum_{i=1}^{r}\frac{1}{K} - \sum_{i=1}^{r}\varepsilon_r(\tau)t_i - \sum_{i=1}^{n-r}\varepsilon_r(\tau)T_i$$

$$= \sum_{i=1}^{r}\frac{1}{K} - \varepsilon_r(\tau)\left(\sum_{i=1}^{r}t_i + \sum_{i=1}^{n-r}T_i\right)$$

(A.68)

$$= \frac{r}{K} - H\varepsilon_r(\tau) = 0$$

where H is defined as in Eq. (5.85). From Eqs. (A.68) and (5.23) we obtain

$$\hat{K} = \frac{r}{H[E_T/I_t - \varepsilon_c(\tau)]}$$

(A.69)

We can now compute $\partial\mathcal{L}/\partial E_T$ and set it equal to zero.

$$\frac{\partial\mathcal{L}}{\partial E_T} = \sum_{i=1}^{r}\frac{1}{K\varepsilon_r(\tau)}\frac{\partial K\varepsilon_r(\tau)}{\partial E_T} - \sum_{i=1}^{r}t_i\frac{\partial K\varepsilon_r(\tau)}{\partial E_T} - \sum_{i=1}^{n-r}T_i\frac{\partial K\varepsilon_r(\tau)}{\partial E_T}$$

From Eq. (5.23) we see that

$$\frac{\partial K\varepsilon_r(\tau)}{\partial E_T} = \frac{K}{I_T}$$

Thus,

$$\frac{\partial\mathcal{L}}{\partial E_T} = \frac{r}{I_T\varepsilon_r(\tau)} - \frac{K}{I_T}\left(\sum_{i=1}^{r}t_i + \sum_{i=1}^{n-r}T_i\right) = 0$$

(A.70)

If we multiply Eq. (A.70) by I_T, we see that the result is the same equation as (A.68). Thus, we do not have a second independent equation, and the only way we can solve for both E_T and K is to use a historical value from a data base to evaluate either K or E_T and use Eq. (A.69) for the remaining parameter. Thus, in general we need another equation to compute both parameters.

Two tests Inspection of Eqs. (A.66) and A.67) shows that if we have two sets of data, we can write

$$L = L_1 \times L_2 \tag{A.71a}$$

$$\mathcal{L} = \mathcal{L}_1 + \mathcal{L}_2 \tag{A.71b}$$

$$\frac{\partial \mathcal{L}}{\partial \theta} = \frac{\partial \mathcal{L}_1}{\partial \theta} + \frac{\partial \mathcal{L}_2}{\partial \theta} \tag{A.72}$$

Thus, Eq. (A.68) becomes

$$\frac{\partial \mathcal{L}}{\partial K} = \frac{r_1}{K} + \frac{r_2}{K} - H_1 \varepsilon_r(\tau_1) - H_2 \varepsilon_r(\tau_2) = 0 \tag{A.73}$$

which leads to

$$\hat{K} = \frac{r_1 + r_2}{H_1 [E_T/I_T - \varepsilon_c(\tau_1)] + H_2 [E_T/I_T - \varepsilon_c(\tau_2)]} \tag{A.74}$$

Similarly for two sets of data Eq. (A.70) becomes

$$\frac{\partial \mathcal{L}}{\partial E_T} = \frac{r_1}{I_T \varepsilon_r(\tau_1)} + \frac{r_2}{I_T \varepsilon_r(\tau_2)} - \frac{KH_1}{I_T} - \frac{KH_2}{I_T} = 0$$

Simplifying, we obtain

$$\hat{K} = \left(\frac{1}{H_1 + H_2} \right) \left[\frac{r_1}{E_T/I_T - \varepsilon_c(\tau_1)} + \frac{r_2}{E_T/I_T - \varepsilon_c(\tau_2)} \right] \tag{A.75}$$

It is interesting to note the result of taking our test times τ_1 and τ_2 close together so that $\varepsilon_c(\tau_2) \approx \varepsilon_c(\tau_1)$: very few additional errors have been found between τ_1 and τ_2. In such a case Eqs. (A.74) and (A.75) become identical as in the single-test case, and the estimate fails.

Three or more tests If we have test data from m tests where $m \geq 3$, we can use several approaches to obtain our parameter estimates. Suppose for purposes of discussion that $m = 5$ and the tests occur at development times $\tau_1, \tau_2, \ldots, \tau_5$. We could proceed as follows:

1. Pair the data into four groups—$(\tau_1, \tau_2), (\tau_2, \tau_3), (\tau_3, \tau_4)$, and (τ_4, τ_5)—and use MLE equations (A.74) and (A.75) to obtain four sets of parameter estimates. Then we could study the variability of these estimates and average them.
2. Lump the data into two groups a and b by computing $r_a = r_1 + r_2 + r_3$, $H_a = H_1 + H_2 + H_3$, $r_b = r_4 + r_5$, and $H_b = H_4 + H_5$ and then apply Eqs. (A.74) and (A.75).
3. Generalize the MLE formulas for $m \geq 3$.

Since we have embarked on using MLE methods because of their superior properties (see Shooman, 1968), we should expect the third method to yield superior results.[1] It is easy to extend Eq. (A.71) to the case of m tests:

$$\mathcal{L} = \sum_{i=1}^{m} \mathcal{L}_i \tag{A.76}$$

Repetition of the preceding derivation using Eq. (A.76) shows that Eqs. (A.74) and (A.75) generalize to yield

$$\hat{K} = \frac{\displaystyle\sum_{j=1}^{m} r_i}{\displaystyle\sum_{j=1}^{m} H_j \left[E_T/I_T - \varepsilon_c(\tau_j) \right]} \tag{A.77}$$

$$\hat{K} = \frac{\displaystyle\sum_{j=1}^{m} \frac{r_j}{E_T/I_T - \varepsilon_c(\tau_j)}}{\displaystyle\sum_{j=1}^{m} H_j} \tag{A.78}$$

A.10.4 Solution of MLE Estimation Equations

The simultaneous solution of two nonlinear equations generally implies a computer program incorporating algorithms to obtain an initial starting point and effect an iterative solution. Clearly, if frequent estimation is to be done, such a program is desirable; however, in most cases Eqs. (A.77) and (A.78) can be easily solved with a good calculator and a piece of graph paper.[2] The sequence of steps is as follows:

1. Starting values are obtained from the moment estimator equations, Eqs. (5.94) and (5.95).
2. A graph of K (y axis) versus E_T (x axis) is prepared.
3. The moment estimate for E_T is used as a starting value.
4. The starting value of E_T is substituted in Eqs. (A.77) and (A.78) and both values (K and K') are plotted on the graph.
5. If K and K' are sufficiently close, we have reached a solution. If not, we continue.
6. If two or more values of K (and K') have been plotted, we extrapolate through the points to predict the intersection and use the predicted value of E_T as the next trial. If only one value of K (and K') has been determined, a new trial value for E_T is chosen, as, say, 10 percent above the initial moment estimate.
7. Return to step 4.

---

[1] See Shooman and Schmidt (1982). This paper shows that similar results were obtained for moment, MLE, and least-squares estimates.
[2] Shooman (1968), p. 468.

Variance of K and E_T An additional advantage of an MLE estimate over a moment estimate is that one can obtain values for the variance of $\hat{K}$ and $\hat{E}_T$ using MLE theory. Although an exact computation of var $\hat{K}$ and var $\hat{E}_T$ is difficult, for large r Eqs. (A.56) and (A.57) can be used to obtain an approximate result.

Differentiating Eq. (A.73) a second time we obtain

$$\frac{\partial^2 \mathcal{L}}{\partial K^2} = -\frac{r_1}{K^2} - \frac{r_2}{K^2} = -\frac{r_1 + r_2}{K^2} \tag{A.79}$$

In general we can see that for m tests

$$\frac{\partial^2 \mathcal{L}}{\partial K^2} = -\frac{r}{K^2} \tag{A.80}$$

where

$$r = \sum_{i=1}^{m} r_j$$

and substitution into Eq. (A.57) yields

$$\text{var } \hat{K} \underset{\text{large } r}{\rightarrow} \frac{\hat{K}^2}{r}$$

Similarly for E_T we compute the second derivative as

$$\frac{\partial^2 \mathcal{L}}{\partial E_T^2} = -\frac{r_1}{I_T \varepsilon_r(\tau_1)^2} \frac{\partial \varepsilon_r(\tau_1)}{\partial E_T} - \frac{r_2}{I_T \varepsilon_r(\tau_2)^2} \frac{\partial \varepsilon_r(\tau_2)}{\partial E_T}$$

and

$$\frac{\partial \varepsilon_r(\tau_1)}{\partial E_T} = \frac{\partial \varepsilon_r(\tau_2)}{\partial E_T} = \frac{1}{I_T}$$

Thus

$$\frac{\partial^2 \mathcal{L}}{\partial E_T^2} = -\frac{1}{I_T^2}\left[\frac{r_1}{\varepsilon_r(\tau_1)^2} + \frac{r_2}{\varepsilon_r(\tau_2)^2} \right] \tag{A.81}$$

and in general for m tests

$$\frac{\partial^2 \mathcal{L}}{\partial E_T^2} = -\frac{1}{I_T^2} \sum_{j=1}^{m} \frac{r_j}{\varepsilon_r(\tau_j)^2} \tag{A.82}$$

Thus, substitution of Eq. (A.82) into Eq. (A.57) yields

$$\text{var } \hat{E}_T \underset{\text{large } r}{\rightarrow} \frac{I_T^2}{\displaystyle\sum_{j=1}^{m} \frac{r_j}{\varepsilon_r(\tau_j)^2}} \tag{A.83}$$

One can state that in the limit as r becomes large $\hat{K}$ and $\hat{E}_T$ approach a normal distribution. Thus, one can establish a 95 percent confidence interval for K between $\hat{K} - 2\sqrt{\text{var } \hat{K}}$ and $\hat{K} + 2\sqrt{\text{var } \hat{K}}$ and similarly for E_T.

PROBLEMS

A.1 The following two theorems are known as De Morgan's theorems:[1]

$$\overline{A + B + C} = \overline{A}\,\overline{B}\,\overline{C}$$

$$\overline{ABC} = \overline{A} + \overline{B} + \overline{C}$$

Prove these two theorems using a Venn diagram. Do these theorems hold for more than three events? Explain.

A.2 We wish to compute the probability of winning on the first roll of a pair of dice by throwing a seven or an eleven.

   (*a*) Define a sample space for the sum of the two dice.
   (*b*) Delineate the favorable and unfavorable outcomes.
   (*c*) Compute the probability of winning and losing.
   (*d*) List any assumptions you made in this problem.

A.3 Suppose a resistor has a resistance R with mean of 100 Ω and a tolerance of 5%, i.e., variation of 5 Ω.

   (*a*) If the resistance values are normally distributed with $\mu = 100$ Ω and $\sigma = 5$ Ω, sketch $f(R)$.
   (*b*) Assume that the resistance values have a Rayleigh distribution. If the peak is to occur at 100 Ω, what is the value of K? Plot the Rayleigh distribution on the same graph as the normal distribution of part *a*.

A.4 A certain resistor has a nominal value (mean) of 100 Ω.

   (*a*) Assume a normal distribution and compute the value of σ if we wish $P(95 < \mathbf{R} < 105) = 0.95$.
   (*b*) Repeat part *a* assuming a Weibull distribution and specify the values of K and m.
   (*c*) Plot the density function for parts *a* and *b* on the same graph paper.

A.5 Let a component have a good, a fair, and a bad state. Assume the transition probabilities of failure are: from good to fair, $\lambda_{gf}\Delta t$, from good to bad, $\lambda_{gb}\Delta t$, and from fair to bad, $\lambda_{fb}\Delta t$.

   (*a*) Formulate a Markov model.
   (*b*) Compute the probabilities of being in any state.

A.6 Failure data at 10 points are recorded in the table associated with Prob. 5.2. Assume that the data can be fitted with a constant-hazard model. Estimate the failure rate using the following estimation techniques:

   (*a*) Moment estimation
   (*b*) Maximum-likelihood estimation
   (*c*) Least-squares estimation

[1]Problems A.1 through A.5 are taken from Shooman (1968).

SUMMARY OF RELIABILITY THEORY*

B.1 INTRODUCTION

B.1.1 History

Since its beginnings following World War II, reliability theory has grown into an engineering science in its own right. (The early beginnings are discussed in Chap. 1 of Shooman, 1968.) Much of the initial theory, engineering, and management techniques centered about hardware; however, human and procedural elements of a system were often included. Since the late 1960s the term *software reliability* has become popular, and now reliability theory refers to both *software* and *hardware reliability*.

B.1.2 Summary of the Approach

The conventional approach to reliability is to decompose the system into smaller subsystems and units. Then by the use of combinatorial reliability, the system probability of success is expressed in terms of the probabilities of success of the elements. Then by the use of failure rate models, the element probabilities of success are computed. These two concepts are combined to calculate the system reliability.

---

*This appendix has been abstracted from various sections of Chaps. 3, 4, 5, and 6 of *Probabilistic Reliability: An Engineering Approach*, by Martin L. Shooman, McGraw-Hill, New York, 1968.

When reliability or availability of repairable systems is the appropriate figure of merit, Markov models are generally used to compute the associated probabilities.

Often a proposed system does not meet its reliability specifications, and various techniques of reliability improvement are utilized to improve the predicted reliability of the design.

Readers desiring more detail are referred to Shooman (1968) and the references cited in that text.

B.1.3 Purpose of this Appendix

This appendix was written to serve several purposes. The prime reason is to provide additional background for those techniques and principles of reliability theory which are used in the software reliability models developed in Chap. 5. A second purpose is to expose software engineers who are not familiar with reliability theory to some of the main methods and techniques. This is especially important since many discussions of software reliability end up discussing how much of "hardware reliability theory" is applicable to software. This author feels the correct answer is "some"; however, the only way to really appreciate this answer is to learn something about reliability.

The third purpose is to allow readers who are software engineers to talk with and understand hardware reliability engineers. If a reliability and quality control (R & QC) engineer handles the software reliability estimates and the software engineer generates software reliability estimates, they must meet at the interface. Even if the R & QC engineer computes reliability estimates for both the hardware and the software, it is still necessary for the software engineer to work with him or her and provide information as well as roughly evaluate the thoroughness and quality of the software effort.

B.2 COMBINATORIAL RELIABILITY

B.2.1 Introduction

In performing the reliability analysis of a complex system, it is almost impossible to treat the system in its entirety. The logical approach is to decompose the system into functional entities composed of units, subsystems, or components. Each entity is assumed to have two states, one good and one bad. The subdivision generates a block-diagram or fault-tree description of system operation. Models are then formulated to fit this logical structure, and the calculus of probability is used to compute the system reliability in terms of the subdivision reliabilities. Series and parallel structures often occur, and their reliability can be described very simply. In many cases the structure is of a more complicated nature, and more general techniques are needed.

The formulation of a structural-reliability model can be difficult in a large, sophisticated system and requires much approximation and judgment. This is best done by a system engineer or someone closely associated with one who knows the system operation thoroughly.

B.2.2 Series Configuration

The simplest and perhaps most common structure in reliability analysis is the *series configuration*. In the series case the *functional* operation of the system depends on the proper operation of all system components. A series string of Christmas tree lights is an obvious example. The word *functional* must be stressed, since the electric or mechanical configuration of the circuit may differ from the logical structure.

A series reliability configuration will be portrayed by the block-diagram representation shown in Fig. B.1a, or the reliability graph shown in Fig. B.1b. In either case, a single path from cause to effect is created. Failure of any component is represented by removal of the component, which interrupts the path and thereby causes the system to fail.

The system shown in Fig. B.1 is divided into n series-connected units. This system can represent n parts in an electronic amplifier, the n subsystems in an aircraft autopilot, or the n operations necessary to place a satellite in orbit. The event signifying the success of the nth unit will be x_n, and $\bar{x}_n$ will represent the failure of the nth unit. The probability that unit n is successful will be $P(x_n)$, and the probability that unit n fails will be $P(\bar{x}_n)$. The probability of system success is denoted by P_s. In keeping with the definition of reliability, $P_s \equiv R$, where R stands for the system reliability. The probability of system failure is

$$P_f = 1 - P_s$$

Since the series configuration requires that all units operate successfully for system success, the event representing system success is the intersection of $x_1, x_2, \cdots, x_n$. The probability of this event is given by

$$R = P_s = P(x_1 x_2 x_3 \cdots x_n) \tag{B.1}$$

Expansion of Eq. (B.1) yields

$$P_s = P(x_1)P(x_2 \mid x_1)P(x_3 \mid x_1 x_2) \cdots P(x_n \mid x_1 x_2 \cdots x_{n-1}) \tag{B.2}$$

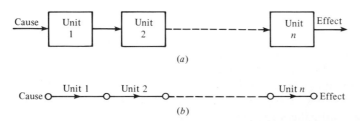

(a)

(b)

Figure B.1 Series reliability configuration: (*a*) reliability block diagram (RBD); (*b*) reliability graph.

The expression appearing in Eq. (B.2) contains conditional probabilities, which must be evaluated with care. For example, $P(x_3 \mid x_1 x_2)$ is the probability of success of unit 3 evaluated under the condition that units 1 and 2 are operating. In the case where the power dissipation from units 1 and 2 affects the temperature of unit 3 and thereby its failure rate, a conditional probability is involved. If the units do not interact, the failures are independent, and Eq. (B.2) simplifies to

$$P_s = P(x_1)P(x_2)P(x_3) \cdots P(x_n) \tag{B.3}$$

An alternative approach is to compute the probability of failure. The system fails if *any* of the units fail, and therefore we have a union of events

$$P_f = P(\bar{x}_1 + \bar{x}_2 + \bar{x}_3 + \cdots + \bar{x}_n) \tag{B.4}$$

Expansion of Eq. (B.4) yields

$$P_f = [P(\bar{x}_1) + P(\bar{x}_2) + P(\bar{x}_3) + \cdots + P(\bar{x}_n)]$$
$$- [P(\bar{x}_1 \bar{x}_2) + P(\bar{x}_1 \bar{x}_3)$$
$$+ \cdots + P(\bar{x}_i \bar{x}_j)] + \cdots + (-1)^{n-1}[P(\bar{x}_1 \bar{x}_2 \cdots \bar{x}_n)] \tag{B.5}$$
$$\underset{i \neq j}{}$$

Since

$$P_s = 1 - P_f \tag{B.6}$$

the probability of system success becomes

$$P_s = 1 - P(\bar{x}_1) - P(\bar{x}_2) - P(\bar{x}_3) - \cdots - P(\bar{x}_n)$$
$$+ P(\bar{x}_1)P(\bar{x}_2 \mid \bar{x}_1) + P(\bar{x}_1)P(\bar{x}_3 \mid \bar{x}_1) + \cdots + P(\bar{x}_i)P(\bar{x}_i \mid \bar{x}_j)$$
$$\underset{i \neq j}{}$$
$$- \cdots + (-1)^n P(\bar{x}_1)P(\bar{x}_2 \mid \bar{x}_1) \cdots P(\bar{x}_n \mid \bar{x}_1 \cdots \bar{x}_{n-1}) \tag{B.7}$$

The reliability expression in Eq. (B.7) is equivalent to that in Eq. (B.2) but is much more difficult to evaluate because of the many terms involved. Equation (B.7) also involves conditional probabilities; for example, $P(\bar{x}_3 \mid \bar{x}_1 \bar{x}_2)$ is the probability that unit 3 will fail given the fact that units 1 and 2 have failed. In the case of independence $P(\bar{x}_3 \mid \bar{x}_1 \bar{x}_2)$ becomes $P(\bar{x}_3)$, and the other conditional probability terms in Eq. (B.7) simplify, yielding

$$P_s = 1 - P(\bar{x}_1) - P(\bar{x}_2) - P(\bar{x}_3) - \cdots - P(\bar{x}_n)$$
$$+ P(\bar{x}_1)P(\bar{x}_2) + P(\bar{x}_1)P(\bar{x}_3) + \cdots + P(\bar{x}_i)P(\bar{x}_j)$$
$$\underset{i \neq j}{}$$
$$- \cdots + (-1)^n P(\bar{x}_1)P(\bar{x}_2) \cdots P(\bar{x}_n) \tag{B.8}$$

Equation (B.8) is still more complex than Eq. (B.3). It is interesting to note that the reliability of any particular configuration may be computed by considering either the probability of success or the probability of failure. In a very complex structure both approaches may be used at different stages of the computation.

The reliability of a series system is always worse than the poorest component and is generally a disappointment from a reliability standpoint. As an example let us consider a magnetic-core computer memory. The size of the memory is 100×100, or a total of 10^4 cores. The reliability of each memory cell is p. Assuming that all cells are used in a particular computation and that any cell error is a computational error, the computation reliability is given by p^{10^4}. If we wish an error rate of 1 in 10^3 computations, we can solve for the required value of p. Letting $q = 1 - p$,

$$p^{10^4} = (1 - q)^{10^4} = 0.999$$

Since $q \ll 1$,

$$(1 - q)^{10^4} \approx 1 - 10^4 q = 0.999$$

$$q = 10^{-7}$$

Thus, the failure probability must be four orders of magnitude smaller than the computational error probability.

B.2.3 Parallel Configuration

In many systems several signal paths perform the same operation. If the system configuration is such that failure of one or more paths still allows the remaining path or paths to perform properly, the system can be represented by a parallel model.

A block diagram and reliability graph for a parallel system are shown in Fig. B.2. There are n paths connecting input to output, and all units must fail in order to interrupt all the paths. This is sometimes called a redundant configuration.

In a parallel configuration the system is successful if any one of the parallel channels is successful. The probability of success is given by the probability of the union of the n successful events

$$P_s = P(x_1 + x_2 + x_3 + \cdots + x_n) \tag{B.9}$$

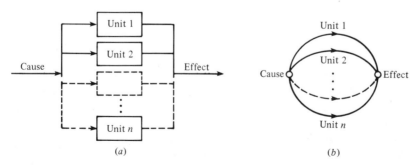

(a) (b)

Figure B.2 Parallel reliability configuration: (a) reliability block diagram; (b) reliability graph.

Expansion of Eq. (B.9) yields

$$P_s = [P(x_1) + P(x_2) + P(x_3) + \cdots + P(x_n)]$$

$$-[P(x_1 x_2) + P(x_1 x_3) + \cdots + P(x_i x_j)]$$
$${\scriptstyle i \neq j}$$
$$+ \cdots + (-1)^{n-1} P(x_1 x_2 \cdots x_n) \tag{B.10}$$

The conditional probabilities which occur in Eq. (B.10) when the *intersection terms* are expanded must be interpreted properly, as in the previous section (see Eq. (B.7)). A simpler formula can be developed in the parallel case if one deals with the probability of system failure. System failure occurs if *all* the system units fail, yielding the probability of their intersection

$$P_f = P(\bar{x}_1 \bar{x}_2 \bar{x}_3 \cdots \bar{x}_n) \tag{B.11}$$

where

$$P_s = 1 - P_f \tag{B.12}$$

Substitution of Eq. (B.11) into Eq. (B.12) and expansion yields

$$P_s = 1 - P(\bar{x}_1) P(\bar{x}_2 | \bar{x}_1) P(\bar{x}_3 | \bar{x}_1 \bar{x}_2) \cdots P(\bar{x}_n | \bar{x}_1 \bar{x}_2 \cdots \bar{x}_{n-1}) \tag{B.13}$$

If the unit failures are independent, Eq. (B.13) simplifies to

$$P_s = 1 - P(\bar{x}_1) P(\bar{x}_2) \cdots P(\bar{x}_n) \tag{B.14}$$

B.2.4 An *r*-out-of-*n* Configuration

In many problems the system operates if *r* out of *n* units function, e.g., a bridge supported by *n* cables, *r* of which are necessary to support the maximum load. If each of the *n* units is identical, the probability of exactly *r* successes out of *n* units is given by Eq. (A.21)

$$B(r; n, p) = \binom{n}{r} p^r (1 - p)^{n-r} \quad \text{for } r = 0, 1, 2 \ldots n \tag{B.15}$$

where *p* is the probability of success of any unit. The system will succeed if $r, r + 1 \ldots n - 1$, or *n* units succeed. The probability of system success is given by

$$P_s = \sum_{k=r}^{n} \binom{n}{k} p^k (1 - p)^{n-k} \tag{B.16}$$

If the units all differ, Eqs. (B.15) and (B.16) no longer hold, and one is faced with the explicit enumeration of all possible successful combinations. One can draw a reliability graph as an aid. The graph will have $\binom{n}{r}$ parallel paths. Each parallel path will contain *r* different elements, corresponding to one of the combinations of *n* things *r* at a time. Such a graph for a four-out-of-five system is given in Fig. B.3. The system succeeds if *any* path succeeds. Each path success depends on the

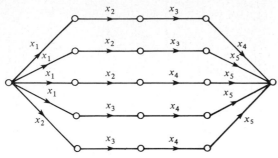

Figure B.3 Reliability graph for a 4-out-of-5 system.

success of four elements:

$$P_s = P(x_1x_2x_3x_4 + x_1x_2x_3x_5 + x_1x_2x_4x_5 + x_1x_3x_4x_5 + x_2x_3x_4x_5) \tag{B.17}$$

Expanding Eq. (B.17) involves simplification of redundant terms. For example, the term $P[(x_1x_2x_3x_4)(x_1x_2x_3x_5)]$ becomes by definition $P(x_1x_2x_3x_4x_5)$. Thus, the equation simplifies to

$$P_s = P(x_1x_2x_3x_4) + P(x_1x_2x_3x_5) + P(x_1x_2x_4x_5) + P(x_1x_3x_4x_5)$$
$$+ P(x_2x_3x_4x_5) - 4P(x_1x_2x_3x_4x_5) \tag{B.18}$$

It is easy to check Eq. (B.18). For independent, identical elements Eq. (B.18) gives $P_s = 5p^4 - 4p^5$. From Eq. (B.16) we obtain

$$P_s = \sum_{k=4}^{5} \binom{5}{k} p^k (1-p)^{5-k} = \binom{5}{4} p^4 (1-p)^1 + \binom{5}{5} p^5 (1-p)^0$$
$$= 5p^4 - 4p^5$$

B.2.5 Fault-Tree Analysis

Fault-tree analysis (FTA) is an application of deductive logic to produce a failure- or fault-oriented pictorial diagram, which allows one to analyze system safety and reliability. Various failure modes that can contribute to a specified undesirable event are organized deductively and represented pictorially.

First the top undesired event is defined and drawn. Below this, secondary undesired events are drawn. These secondary undesired events include the potential hazards and failures that are immediate causes of the top event. Below each of these subevents are drawn second-level events, which are the immediate causes of the subevents. The process is continued until basic events are reached (often called *elementary faults*). Since the diagram branches out and there are more events at each lower level, it resembles an inverted tree. The treelike structure of the diagram illustrates the various critical paths of subevents leading to the occurrence of the top undesired event. A fault tree for an auto braking system example is given in Sec. B.5, Fig. B.14.

Both FTAs and RBDs are useful for both qualitative and quantitative analyses:

1. They force the analyst to actively seek out failure events (success events) in a deductive manner.
2. They provide a visual display of how a system can fail, and thus aid understanding of the system by persons other than the designer.
3. They point out critical aspects of systems failure (system success).
4. They provide a systematic basis for quantitative analysis of reliability.

Often in a difficult practical problem one utilizes other techniques to decompose the system prior to effecting either an RBD or an FTA.

B.2.6 Failure Mode and Effect Analysis

Failure mode and effect analysis (FMEA) is a systematic procedure for identifying the modes of failures and for evaluating their consequences. It is a tabular procedure which considers hazards in terms of single-event chains and their consequences. The FMEA is generally performed on the basis of limited design information during the early stages of design and is periodically updated to reflect changes in design and improved knowledge of the system. The basic questions which must be answered by the analyst in performing an FMEA are:

1. How can each component or subsystem fail? (What is the failure mode?)
2. What cause might produce this failure? (What is the failure mechanism?)
3. What are the effects of each failure if it does occur?

Once the FMEA is completed, it assists the analyst in:

1. Selecting, during initial stages, various design alternatives with high reliability and high safety potential
2. Ensuring that all possible failure modes, and their effects on operational success of the system, have been taken into account
3. Identifying potential failures and the magnitude of their efforts on the system
4. Developing testing and checkout methods
5. Providing a basis for qualitative reliability, availability, and safety analysis
6. Providing input data for construction of RBD and FTA models
7. Providing a basis for establishing corrective measures
8. Performing an objective evaluation of design requirements related to redundancy, failure detection systems, and fail-safe character

An FMEA for the auto braking example is given in Sec. B.5, Table B.3.

B.2.7 Cut-Set and Tie-Set Methods

A very efficient general method for computing the reliability of any system not containing dependent failures can be developed from the properties of the reliability graph. The reliability graph consists of a set of branches which represent the n elements. There must be at least n branches in the graph, but there can be more if the same branch must be repeated in more than one path (see Fig. B.3). The probability of element success is written above each branch. The nodes of the graph tie the branches together and form the structure. A path has already been defined, but a better definition can be given in terms of graph theory. The term *tie set*, rather than path, is common in graph nomenclature. A tie set is a group of branches which forms a connection between input and output when traversed in the arrow direction. We shall primarily be concerned with *minimal* tie sets, which are those containing a minimum number of elements. If no node is traversed more than once in tracing out a tie set, the tie set is minimal. If a system has i minimal tie sets denoted by $T_1, T_2, \ldots, T_i$, then the system has a connection between input and output if at least one tie set is intact. The system reliability is thus given by

$$R = P(T_1 + T_2 + \cdots + T_i) \tag{B.19}$$

One can define a *cut set* of a graph as a set of branches which interrupts all connections between input and output when removed from the graph. The minimal cut sets are a group of distinct cut sets containing a minimum number of terms. All system failures can be represented by the removal of at least one minimal cut set from the graph. The probability of system failure is, therefore, given by the probability that at least one minimal cut set fails. If we let $C_1, C_2, \cdots, C_j$ represent the j minimal cut sets and $\overline{C_j}$ the failure of the jth cut set, the system reliability is given by

$$P_f = P(\overline{C}_1 + \overline{C}_2 + \cdots + \overline{C}_j)$$
$$R = 1 - P_f = 1 - P(\overline{C}_1 + \overline{C}_2 + \cdots + \overline{C}_j) \tag{B.20}$$

As an example of the application of cut-set and tie-set analysis we consider the graph given in Fig. B.4. The following combinations of branches are *some* of the several tie sets of the system:

$$T_1 = x_1 x_2 \quad T_2 = x_3 x_4 \quad T_3 = x_1 x_6 x_4 \quad T_4 = x_3 x_5 x_2 \quad T_5 = x_1 x_6 x_5 x_2$$

Tie sets $T_1, T_2, T_3,$ and T_4 are minimal tie sets. Tie set T_5 is nonminimal since the

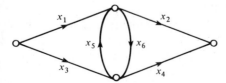

Figure B.4 Reliability graph for a six-element system.

top node is encountered twice in traversing the graph. From Eq. (B.19)

$$R = P(T_1 + T_2 + T_3 + T_4) = P(x_1 x_2 + x_3 x_4 + x_1 x_6 x_4 + x_3 x_5 x_2) \quad \text{(B.21)}$$

Similarly we may list *some* of the several cut sets of the structure

$$C_1 = x_1 x_3 \quad C_2 = x_2 x_4 \quad C_3 = x_1 x_5 x_3 \quad C_4 = x_1 x_5 x_4$$
$$C_5 = x_3 x_6 x_1 \quad C_6 = x_3 x_6 x_2$$

Cut sets C_1, C_2, C_4, and C_6 are minimal. Cut sets C_3 and C_5 are nonminimal since they are both contained in cut set C_1. Using Eq. (B.20),

$$R = 1 - P(\bar{C}_1 + \bar{C}_2 + \bar{C}_4 + \bar{C}_6) = 1 - P(\bar{x}_1 \bar{x}_3 + \bar{x}_2 \bar{x}_4 + \bar{x}_1 \bar{x}_5 \bar{x}_4 + \bar{x}_3 \bar{x}_6 \bar{x}_2)$$
$$\text{(B.22)}$$

In a large problem there will be many cut sets and tie sets, and although Eqs. (B.19) and (B.20) are easily formulated, the expansion of either equation is a formidable task. (If there are n events in a union, the expansion of the probability of the union involves $2^n - 1$ terms.) Several approximations which are useful in simplifying the computations are discussed in Messinger and Shooman (1967) and in Shooman (1968), p. 138.

B.3 FAILURE-RATE MODELS

B.3.1 Introduction

The previous section has shown how one constructs various combinatorial relia-bility models which express system reliability in terms of element reliability. This section introduces several different failure models for the system elements. These element failure models are related to life-test results and failure-rate data via probability theory.

The first step in constructing a failure model is to locate test data or plan a test on parts substantially the same as those to be used. From these data the part failure rate is computed and graphed. On the basis of the graph, any physical failure information, engineering judgment, and sometimes statistical tests, a failure-rate model is chosen. The parameters of the model are estimated from the graph or computed using the statistical principles of estimation, which are developed in Sec. A.9. This section discusses the treatment of the data and the choice of a model.

The emphasis is on simple models, which are easy to work with and contain one or two parameters. This simplifies the problems of interpretation and parameter determination. Also in most cases the data are not abundant enough and the test conditions are not sufficiently descriptive of the proposed usage to warrant more complex models.

B.3.2 Treatment of Failure Data

Part failure data are generally obtained from either of two sources: the failure times of various items in a population placed on a life test, or repair reports listing operating hours of replaced parts in equipment already in field use. Experience has shown that a very good way to present these data is to compute and plot either the failure density function or the hazard rate as a function of time.

The data we are dealing with are a sequence of times to failure, but the failure density function and the hazard rate are continuous variables. We first compute a piecewise-continuous failure density function and hazard rate from the data.

We begin by *defining* piecewise-continuous failure density and hazard-rate functions in terms of the data. It can be shown that these discrete functions approach the continuous functions in the limit as the number of data becomes large and the interval between failure times approaches zero. Assume that our data describe a set of N items placed in operation at time $t = 0$. As time progresses, items fail, and at any time t the number of survivors is $n(t)$. The data density function (also called empirical density function) defined over the time interval $t_i < \mathbf{t} \le t_i + \Delta t_i$ is given by the ratio of the number of failures occurring in the interval to the *size of the original population*, divided by the length of the time interval[1]

$$f_d(t) = \frac{[n(t_i) - n(t_i + \Delta t_i)]/N}{\Delta t_i} \quad \text{for } t_i < t \le t_i + \Delta t_i \qquad (B.23)$$

Similarly, the data hazard rate[2] over the interval $t_i < t \le t_i + \Delta t_i$ is defined as the ratio of the number of failures occurring in the time interval to the *number of survivors at the beginning of the time interval*, divided by the length of the time interval.

$$z_d(t) = \frac{[n(t_i) - n(t_i + \Delta t_i)]/n(t_i)}{\Delta t_i} \quad \text{for } t_i < t \le t_i + \Delta t_i \qquad (B.24)$$

The failure density function $f_d(t)$ is a measure of the *overall speed* at which failures are occurring, whereas the hazard rate $z_d(t)$ is a measure of the *instantaneous speed* of failure. Since the numerators of both Eqs. (B.23) and (B.24) are dimensionless, both $f_d(t)$ and $z_d(t)$ have the dimensions of inverse time (generally the time unit is hours).

The failure data for a life test run on a group of 10 hypothetical electronic components are given in Table B.1. The computation of $f_d(t)$ and $z_d(t)$ from the data appear in Table B.2.

The time intervals Δt_i were chosen as the times between failure, and the first time interval t_0 started at the origin; that is, $t_0 = 0$. The remaining time intervals

---

[1] In general a sequence of time intervals $t_0 < t \le t_0 + \Delta t_0$, $t_1 < t \le t_1 + \Delta t_1$, etc., is defined, where $t_1 = t_0 + \Delta t_0$, $t_2 = t_1 + \Delta t_1$, etc.

[2] Hazard rate is sometimes called hazard or failure rate.

Table B.1 Failure data for 10 hypothetical electronic components

Failure number	Operating time, h
1	8
2	20
3	34
4	46
5	63
6	86
7	111
8	141
9	186
10	266

Table B.2 Computation of data failure density and data hazard rate

Time interval, h	Failure density per hour $f_d(t)(\times 10^{-2})$	Hazard rate per hour $z_d(t)(\times 10^{-2})$
0–8	$\dfrac{1}{10 \times 8} = 1.25$	$\dfrac{1}{10 \times 8} = 1.25$
8–20	$\dfrac{1}{10 \times 12} = 0.84$	$\dfrac{1}{9 \times 12} = 0.93$
20–34	$\dfrac{1}{10 \times 14} = 0.72$	$\dfrac{1}{8 \times 14} = 0.96$
34–46	$\dfrac{1}{10 \times 12} = 0.84$	$\dfrac{1}{7 \times 12} = 1.19$
46–63	$\dfrac{1}{10 \times 17} = 0.59$	$\dfrac{1}{6 \times 17} = 0.98$
63–86	$\dfrac{1}{10 \times 23} = 0.44$	$\dfrac{1}{5 \times 23} = 0.87$
86–111	$\dfrac{1}{10 \times 25} = 0.40$	$\dfrac{1}{4 \times 25} = 1.00$
111–141	$\dfrac{1}{10 \times 30} = 0.33$	$\dfrac{1}{3 \times 30} = 1.11$
141–186	$\dfrac{1}{10 \times 45} = 0.22$	$\dfrac{1}{2 \times 45} = 1.11$
186–266	$\dfrac{1}{10 \times 80} = 0.13$	$\dfrac{1}{1 \times 80} = 1.25$

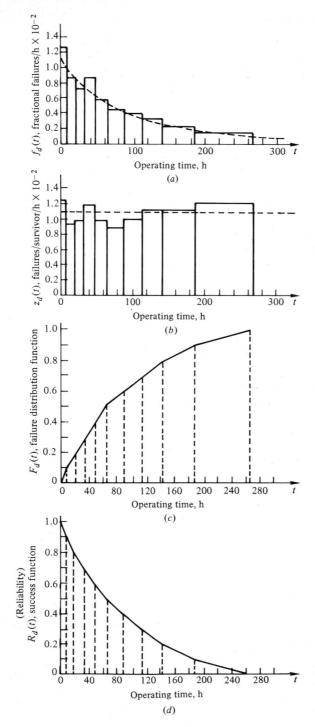

Figure B.5 Density and hazard functions for the data of Table B.1. (*a*) Data failure density functions; (*b*) data hazard rate; (*c*) data failure distribution function; (*d*) data success function.

t_i coincided with the failure times. In each case the failure was assumed to have occurred just before the end of the interval. Two alternate procedures are possible. The failure could have been assumed to occur just after the time interval closed, or the beginning of each interval t_i could have been defined as the midpoint between failures. In this book we shall consistently use the first method, which is illustrated in Table B.2.

Since $f_d(t)$ is a density function, we can *define* a data failure distribution function and a data success distribution function by

$$F_d(t) = \int_0^t f_d(\xi)\, d\xi \tag{B.25}$$

$$R_d(t) = 1 - F_d(t) = 1 - \int_0^t f_d(\xi)\, d\xi \tag{B.26}$$

where ξ is just a dummy variable of integration. Since the $f_d(t)$ curve is a piecewise-continuous function consisting of a sum of step functions, its integral is a piecewise-continuous function made up of a sum of ramp functions.

The functions $F_d(t)$ and $R_d(t)$ are computed for the preceding example by the appropriate integration of Fig. B.5a and are given in Fig. B.5c and d. By inspection of Eqs. (B.23) and (B.26) or Fig. B.5a and b we see that

$$R_d(t_i) = \frac{n(t_i)}{N} \tag{B.27}$$

In the example given in Table B.1, only 10 items were on test, and the computations were easily made. If many items are tested, the computation intervals Δt_i cannot be chosen as the times between failures since the computations become too lengthy. The solution is to divide the same scale into several equally spaced intervals. Statisticians call these *class intervals*, and the midpoint of the interval is called a *class mark*.

B.3.3 Failure Modes and Handbook Failure Data

After plotting and examining failure data for several years, people began to recognize several modes of failure. Early in the lifetime of equipment or a part, there are a large number of failures due to initial weakness or defects; poor insulation, weak parts, bad assembly, poor fits, etc. During the middle period of equipment operation fewer failures take place, and it is difficult to determine their cause. In general they seem to occur when the environmental stresses exceed the design strengths of the part or equipment. It is difficult to predict the environmental-stress amplitudes or the part strengths as deterministic functions of time; thus the middle-life failures are often called *random failures*.[1] As the item reaches old age, things begin to deteriorate, and many failures occur. This failure region is quite naturally called the *wear-out region*. Typical $f(t)$ and $z(t)$ curves[2] illustrating

[1]Actually all the failures are random; thus a term such as *unclassifiable as to cause* would be more correct.
[2]We are now referring to continuous hazard and failure density functions, which represent the limiting forms of $f_d(t)$ and $z_d(t)$ as discussed.

these three modes of behavior were shown in Chap. 5, Fig. 5.1. The early failures, also called *initial failures* or *infant mortality*,[1] appear as decreasing $z(t)$ and $f(t)$ functions. The random-failure, or constant-hazard-rate, mode is characterized by an approximately constant $z(t)$ and a companion $f(t)$ which is approximately exponential. In the wear-out or rising-failure-rate, region, the $z(t)$ function increases whereas $f(t)$ has a humped appearance.

It is clear that it is easier to distinguish the various failure modes by inspection of the $z(t)$ curve than it is from the appearance of the $f(t)$ function. This is one of the major reasons why hazard rate is introduced. Because of the monotonic nature of $F(t)$ and $R(t)$ these functions are even less useful in distinguishing failure modes.

The curve of Fig. 5.1(b) has been discussed by many of the early writers on the subject of reliability[2] and is often called the *bathtub curve* because of its shape. The fact that such a hazard curve occurs for many types of equipment has been verified by experience. Also when failed components have been dismantled to determine the reasons for failure, the conclusions have again justified the hypothesis of three failure modes. In fact most manufacturers of high-reliability components now subject their products to an initial burn-in period of t_1 hours to eliminate the initial failure region shown in Fig. 5.1. At the onset of wearout at time t_2, the hazard rate begins to increase rapidly, and it is wise to replace the item after t_2 hours of operation. Thus, if the bathtub curve were really a universal model, one would pretest components for t_1 hours, place the survivors in use for an additional $t_2 - t_1$ hours, and then replace them with fresh pretested components. This would reduce the effective hazard rate and improve the probability of survival. Unfortunately, many types of equipment have a continuously decreasing or continuously increasing hazard and therefore behave differently. It often happens that electronic components have a constant hazard and mechanical components a wear-out characteristic. Unfortunately, even though reliability theory is 3 to 4 decades old, not enough comparative analysis has been performed on different types of hazard models and failure data to make a definitive statement as to which models are best for which components.

Many failure data on parts and components have been recorded since the beginning of formal interest in reliability in the early 1950s. Large industrial organizations such as Radio Corporation of America, General Electric Company, Motorola, etc., publish handbooks of part failure-rate data compiled from life-test and field-failure data. These data and other information were compiled into an evolving series of part-failure-rate handbooks: MIL-HDBK-217, Government Printing Office, Washington, D.C., 1962; MIL-HDBK-217A, 1965; MIL-HDBK-217B, 1974; and MIL-HDBK-217C, 1980. Another voluminous failure data handbook is "Failure Rate Data Handbook" (FARADA), published by the GIDEP program.[3] The FARADA handbook includes such vital information as

---

[1] Some of the terms, as well as the concept of hazard, have been borrowed from those used by actuaries, who deal with life insurance statistics.

[2] Carhart (1953).

[3] Government Industrial Data Exchange Program, Naval Fleet Missile Systems, Corona, Calif.

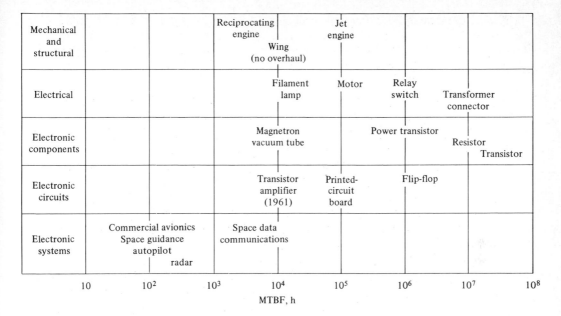

Mechanical and structural			Reciprocating engine Wing (no overhaul)	Jet engine			
Electrical			Filament lamp	Motor	Relay switch	Transformer connector	
Electronic components			Magnetron vacuum tube		Power transistor	Resistor	Transistor
Electronic circuits			Transistor amplifier (1961)	Printed-circuit board	Flip-flop		
Electronic systems	Commercial avionics Space guidance autopilot radar		Space data communications				
	10	10^2	10^3	10^4	10^5	10^6	10^7	10^8

MTBF, h

Figure B.6 Reliability of selected components. *(Nolos and Schultz, 1965)*

the *number on test*, the *number of failures*, and some details on the *source* of the data and the *environment*. This information allows one to use engineering judgment in selecting failure rates from this reference.

A comparison of typical equipment reliabilities in terms of mean time between failures, MTBF (to be defined shortly), is given in Fig. B.6.

B.3.4 Reliability in Terms of Hazard Rate and Failure Density

In the previous section, various functions associated with failure data were defined and computed for the data given in the examples. These functions were $z_d(t)$, $f_d(t)$, $F_d(t)$, and $R_d(t)$. In this section we begin by defining two random variables and deriving in a careful manner the basic definitions and relations between the theoretical hazard, failure density function, failure distribution function, and reliability function.

The random variable **t** is defined as the failure time of the item in question.[1] Thus, the probability of failure as a function of time is given as

$$P(\mathbf{t} \le t) = F(t) \tag{B.28}$$

which is simply the definition of the failure distribution function. We can define the reliability, which is a probability of success in terms of $F(t)$, as

$$R(t) = P_s(t) = 1 - F(t) = P(\mathbf{t} \ge t) \tag{B.29}$$

---

[1]In some problems, a more appropriate random variable is the number of miles, cycles, etc. The results are analogous.

The failure density function is of course given by

$$\frac{dF(t)}{dt} = f(t) \qquad \text{(B.30)}$$

We now consider a population of N items with the same failure-time distribution. The items fail independently with probability of failure given by $F(t) = 1 - R(t)$ and probability of success given by $R(t)$. If the random variable $N(t)$ represents the number of units surviving at time t, then $N(t)$ has a binomial distribution with $p = R(t)$. Therefore,

$$P[N(t) = n] = B[n; N, R(t)] = \frac{N!}{n!(N-n)!}[R(t)]^n[1 - R(t)]^{N-n}$$

$$n = 0, 1, \ldots, N \qquad \text{(B.31)}$$

The number of units operating at any time t is a random variable and is not fixed; however, we can compute the expected value $N(t)$. From Table A.1 we see that the expected value of a random variable with a binomial distribution is given by $NR(t)$ and leads to

$$n(t) \equiv E[N(t)] = NR(t) \qquad \text{(B.32)}$$

Solving for the reliability yields

$$R(t) = \frac{n(t)}{N} \qquad \text{(B.33)}$$

Thus, the reliability at time t is the average fraction of surviving units at time t. This verifies Eq. (B.27), which was obtained as a consequence of the definition of $f_d(t)$. From Eq. (B.29) we obtain

$$F(t) = 1 - \frac{n(t)}{N} = \frac{N - n(t)}{N} \qquad \text{(B.34)}$$

and from Eq. (B.30)

$$f(t) = \frac{dF(t)}{dt} = -\frac{1}{N}\frac{dn(t)}{dt}$$

$$f(t) \equiv \lim_{\Delta t \to 0} \frac{n(t) - n(t + \Delta t)}{N\Delta t} \qquad \text{(B.35)}$$

Thus, we see that Eq. (B.23) is valid, and as N becomes large and Δt_i becomes small, Eq. (B.23) approaches Eq. (B.35) in the limit. From Eq. (B.34) we see that $F(t)$ is the average fraction of units having failed between 0 and time t, and Eq. (B.35) states that $f(t)$ is the rate of change of $F(t)$, or its slope. From Eq. (B.35) we see that the failure density function $f(t)$ is *normalized* in terms of the size of the original population N. In many cases it is more informative to normalize with respect to $n(t)$, the number of survivors. Thus, we define the hazard rate as

$$z(t) \equiv -\lim_{\Delta t \to 0} \frac{n(t) - n(t + \Delta t)}{n(t)\Delta t} \qquad \text{(B.36)}$$

The definition of $z(t)$ in Eq. (B.36) of course agrees with the definition of $z_d(t)$ in

Eq. (B.24). We can relate $z(t)$ and $f(t)$ using Eqs. (B.35) and (B.36):

$$z(t) = - \lim_{\Delta t \to 0} \frac{n(t) - n(t + \Delta t)}{\Delta t} \frac{1}{n(t)} = Nf(t) \frac{1}{n(t)}$$

Substitution of Eq. (B.33) yields

$$z(t) = \frac{f(t)}{R(t)} \tag{B.37}$$

We now wish to relate $R(t)$ to $f(t)$ and to $z(t)$. From Eqs. (B.29) and (B.30) we see that

$$R(t) = 1 - F(t)$$

$$= 1 - \int_0^t f(\xi) \, d\xi \tag{B.38}$$

where ξ is merely a dummy variable. Substituting into Eq. (B.37) from Eqs. (B.35) and (B.33), we obtain

$$z(t) = - \frac{1}{N} \frac{dn(t)}{dt} \frac{N}{n(t)} = - \frac{d}{dt} \ln n(t)$$

Solving the differential equation yields:

$$\ln n(t) = - \int_0^t z(\xi) \, d\xi + c$$

where ξ is a dummy variable and c is the constant of integration. Taking the antilog of both sides of the equation gives:

$$n(t) = e^c \exp\left[- \int_0^t z(\xi) \, d\xi \right]$$

Inserting initial conditions

$$n(0) = N = e^c$$

gives

$$n(t) = N \exp\left[- \int_0^t z(\xi) \, d\xi \right]$$

Substitution of Eq. (B.33) completes the derivation

$$R(t) = \exp\left[- \int_0^t z(\xi) \, d\xi \right] \tag{B.39}$$

Equations (B.35) and (B.36) serve to define the failure density function and the hazard rate, and Eqs. (B.37) to (B.39) relate $R(t)$ to $f(t)$ and $z(t)$.[1]

B.3.5 Hazard Models

On first consideration it might appear that if failure data and graphs such as Fig. B.5a to d are available, there is no need for a mathematical model. However, in

---

[1] An alternative derivation of these expressions is given in Shooman (1968), p. 183.

drawing conclusions from test data on the behavior of other, similar components it is necessary to fit the failure data with a mathematical model. The discussion will start with several simple models and gradually progress to the more involved problem of how to choose a general model which fits all cases through adjustment of constants.

Constant hazard For a good many years, reliability analysis was almost wholly concerned with constant hazard rates. Indeed many data have been accumulated, like those in Fig. B.5*b*, which indicate that a constant-hazard model is appropriate in many cases.

If a constant-hazard rate $z(t) = \lambda$ is assumed, the time integral is given by $\int_0^t \lambda \, d\xi = \lambda t$. Substitution in Eqs. (B.37) to (B.39) yields

$$z(t) = \lambda \tag{B.40}$$

$$f(t) = \lambda e^{-\lambda t} \tag{B.41}$$

$$R(t) = e^{-\lambda t} = 1 - F(t) \tag{B.42}$$

The four functions $z(t)$, $f(t)$, $F(t)$, and $R(t)$ are sketched in Fig. B.7. A constant-hazard rate implies an exponential density function and an exponential reliability function.

The constant-hazard model forbids any deterioration in time of strength or soundness of the items in the population. Thus if $\lambda = 0.1$ per hour, we can expect 10 failures in a population of 100 items during the first hour of operation and the same number of failures between the thousandth and thousand and first hours of operation in a population of 100 items that have already survived 1000 h. A simple hazard model that admits deterioration in time, i.e., wear, is one in which the failure rate increases with time.

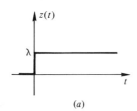

(a)

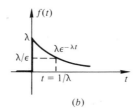

(b)

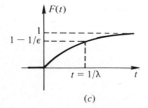

(c)

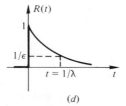

(d)

Figure B.7 Constant-hazard model: (*a*) constant hazard; (*b*) decaying exponential density function; (*c*) rising exponential distribution function; (*d*) decaying exponential reliability function.

Linearly increasing hazard When wear or deterioration is present, the hazard will increase as time passes. The simplest increasing-hazard model that can be postulated is one in which the hazard increases linearly with time. Assuming that $z(t) = Kt$ for $t \geq 0$ yields

$$z(t) = Kt \tag{B.43}$$

$$f(t) = Kte^{-Kt^2/2} \tag{B.44}$$

$$R(t) = e^{-Kt^2/2} \tag{B.45}$$

These functions are sketched in Fig. B.8. The density function of Eq. (B.44) is a Rayleigh density function.

The Weibull model In many cases, the $z(t)$ curve cannot be approximated by a straight line, and the previously discussed models fail. In order to fit various $z(t)$ curvatures, it is useful to investigate a hazard model of the form

$$z(t) = Kt^m \quad \text{for } m > -1 \tag{B.46}$$

This form of model was discussed in detail in a paper by Weibull (1951) and is generally called a *Weibull model*. The associated density and reliability functions are

$$f(t) = Kt^m e^{-Kt^{m+1}/(m+1)} \tag{B.47}$$

$$R(t) = e^{-Kt^{m+1}/(m+1)} \tag{B.48}$$

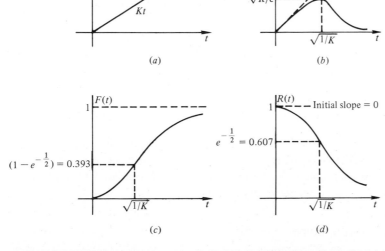

Figure B.8 Linearly increasing hazard: (*a*) linearly increasing hazard; (*b*) Rayleigh density function; (*c*) Rayleigh distribution function; (*d*) Rayleigh reliability function.

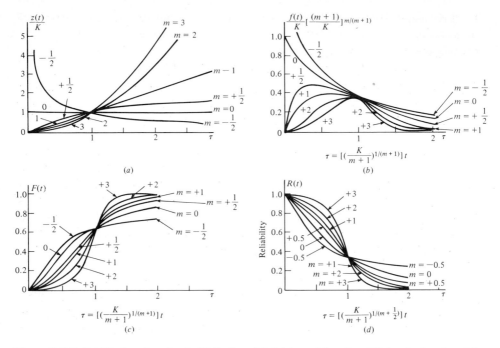

Figure B.9 Reliability functions for the Weibull model: (a) hazard function; (b) density function; (c) distribution function; (d) reliability function.

By appropriate choice of the two parameters K and m, a wide range of hazard curves can be approximated. The various functions obtained for typical values of m are shown in Fig. B.9. For fixed values of m, a change in the parameter K merely changes the vertical amplitude of the $z(t)$ curve; thus, $z(t)/K$ is plotted versus time. Changing K produces a time-scale effect on the $R(t)$ function; therefore, time is normalized so that $\tau^{m+1} = [K/(m+1)]t^{m+1}$. The amplitude of the hazard curve affects the time scale of the reliability function; consequently, the parameter K is often called the *scale parameter*. The parameter m obviously affects the shape of all the reliability functions shown and is consequently called the *shape parameter*. The curves $m = 0$ and $m = 1$ are constant-hazard and linearly-increasing-hazard models, respectively. It is clear from inspection of Fig. B.9 that a wide variety of models is possible by appropriate selection of K and m. The drawback is, of course, that this is a two-parameter model, which means a greater difficulty in sketching the results and increased difficulty in estimating the parameters. A three-parameter Weibull model can be formulated by replacing t by $t - t_0$, where t_0 is called the *location parameter*.

B.3.6 Mean Time to Failure

It is often convenient to characterize a failure model or set of failure data by a single parameter. One generally uses the mean time *to* failure or the mean time *between* failures for this purpose. If we have life-test information on a population of n items with failure times $t_1, t_2, \ldots, t_n$, then the MTTF[1] is defined by the following equation (see also Eq. (A.48)):

$$\text{MTTF} = \frac{1}{n} \sum_{i=1}^{n} t_i \tag{B.49}$$

If one is discussing a hazard model, the MTTF for the probability distribution defined by the model is given by Eq. (A.36) as

$$\text{MTTF} = E(t) = \int_0^\infty t f(t)\, dt \tag{B.50}$$

In a single-parameter distribution, specification of the MTTF fixes the parameter. In a multiple-parameter distribution, fixing the MTTF only places one constraint on the model parameters.

One can express Eq. (B.50) by a simpler computational expression involving the reliability function:[2]

$$\text{MTTF} = \int_0^\infty R(t)\, dt \tag{B.51}$$

As an example of the use of Eq. (B.51) the MTTF for several different hazards will be computed. For a single component with a constant hazard

$$\text{MTTF} = \int_0^\infty e^{-\lambda t}\, dt = \left. \frac{e^{-\lambda t}}{-\lambda} \right|_0^\infty = \frac{1}{\lambda} \tag{B.52}$$

For a linearly increasing hazard

$$\text{MTTF} = \int_0^\infty e^{-Kt^2/2}\, dt = \frac{\Gamma(\frac{1}{2})}{2\sqrt{K/2}} = \sqrt{\frac{\pi}{2K}} \tag{B.53}$$

For a Weibull distribution

$$\text{MTTF} = \int_0^\infty e^{-Kt^{(m+1)}/(m+1)}\, dt = \frac{\Gamma[(m+2)/(m+1)]}{[K/(m+1)]^{1/(m+1)}} \tag{B.54}$$

In Eq. (B.52) the MTTF is simply the reciprocal of the hazard, whereas in Eq. (B.53) it varies as the reciprocal of the square root of the hazard slope. In Eq. (B.54) the relationship between MTTF, K, and m is more complex (see Table A.1).

In many cases we assume an exponential density (constant hazard) for simplicity, and for this case we frequently hear the statement "the MTBF is the reciprocal of the failure rate." The reader should not forget the assumptions necessary for this statement to hold.

---

[1] Sometimes the term *mean time between failures* (MTBF) is used interchangeably with the term MTTF; however, strictly speaking, the MTBF has meaning only when one is discussing a renewal situation, where there is repair or replacement. See Shooman (1968), Sec. 6.10.

[2] For the derivation, see Shooman (1968), p. 197.

B.4 SYSTEM RELIABILITY

B.4.1 Introduction

The previous two sections have divided reliability into two distinct phases: a formulation of the reliability structure of the problem using combinatorial reliability, and a computation of the element probabilities in terms of hazard models. This section unites these two approaches to obtain the reliability function for the system.

When the element probabilities are independent, computations are straightforward. The only real difficulties encountered here are the complexity of the calculations in large problems.

B.4.2 The Series Configuration

The *series configuration*, also called a *chain structure*, is the most common reliability model and the simplest. Any system in which the system success depends on the success of all its components is a series reliability configuration. Unfortunately for the reliability analyst (but fortunately for the user of the product or device), not all systems have this simple structure.

A series configuration of n items is shown in Fig. B.10. The reliability of this structure is given by

$$R(t) = P(x_1, x_2, \ldots, x_n) = P(x_1)P(x_2 \,|\, x_1)P(x_3 \,|\, x_1 x_2)$$
$$\cdots P(x_n \,|\, x_1 x_2 \cdots x_{n-1}) \quad \text{(B.55)}$$

If the n items $x_1, x_2, \ldots, x_n$ are independent, then

$$R(t) = P(x_1)P(x_2) \cdots P(x_n) = \prod_{i=1}^{n} P(x_i) \quad \text{(B.56)}$$

If each component exhibits a constant hazard, then the appropriate component model is $e^{-\lambda_i t}$, and Eq. (B.56) becomes

$$R(t) = \prod_{i=1}^{n} e^{-\lambda_i t} = \exp\left(-\sum_{i=1}^{n} \lambda_i t\right) \quad \text{(B.57)}$$

Equation (B.57) is the most commonly used and the most elementary system reliability formula. In practice this formula is often misused (probably because it is so simple and does work well in many situations, people have become overconfident). The following assumptions must be true if Eq. (B.57) is to hold

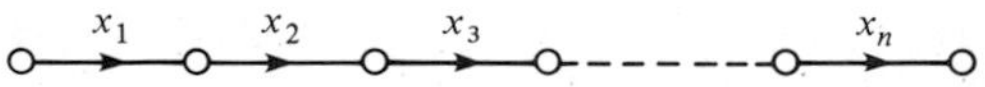

Figure B.10 Series reliability configuration.

for a system:

1. The system reliability configuration must truly be a series one.
2. The components must be independent.
3. The components must be governed by a constant-hazard model.

If assumptions 1 and 2 hold but the components have linearly increasing hazards $z_i(t) = K_i t$, Eq. (B.56) then becomes

$$R(t) = \prod_{i=1}^{n} e^{-K_i t^2/2} = \exp\left(-\sum_{i=1}^{n} \frac{K_i t^2}{2}\right) \tag{B.58}$$

If p components have a constant hazard and $n - p$ components a linearly increasing hazard, the reliability becomes

$$R(t) = \left(\prod_{i=1}^{p} e^{-\lambda_i t}\right)\left(\prod_{i=p+1}^{n} e^{-k_i t^2/2}\right) = \exp\left(-\sum_{i=1}^{p} \lambda_i t\right)\exp\left(-\sum_{i=p+1}^{n} \frac{K_i t^2}{2}\right) \tag{B.59}$$

In some cases no simple composite formula exists, and the reliability must be expressed as a product of n terms. For example, suppose each component is governed by the Weibull distribution, $z(t) = K_i t^{m_i}$. If m and K are different for each component,

$$R(t) = \prod_{i=1}^{n} \exp\left(\frac{-K_i t^{m_i+1}}{m_i + 1}\right) = \exp\left(-\sum_{i=1}^{n} \frac{K_i t^{m_i+1}}{m_i + 1}\right) \tag{B.60}$$

The series reliability structure serves as a lower-bound configuration. To illustrate this principle we pose a hypothetical problem. Given a collection of n elements, from the reliability standpoint what is the worst possible reliability structure they can assume? The intuitive answer, of course, is a series structure. (A proof is given in Shooman, 1968, p. 205; also see Sec. B.6.4.)

B.4.3 The Parallel Configuration

If a system of n elements can function properly when only one of the elements is good, a parallel configuration is indicated. A parallel configuration of n items is shown in Fig. B.11. The reliability expression for a parallel system may be

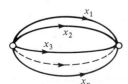

Figure B.11 Parallel reliability configuration.

expressed in terms of the probability of success of each component or, more conveniently, in terms of the probability of failure

$$R(t) = P(x_1 + x_2 + \cdots + x_n) = 1 - P(\bar{x}_1\bar{x}_2 \cdots \bar{x}_n) \qquad (\text{B.61})$$

In the case of constant-hazard components, $P_f = P(\bar{x}_i) = 1 - e^{-\lambda_i t}$, and Eq. (B.61) becomes

$$R(t) = 1 - \prod_{i=1}^{n} (1 - e^{-\lambda_i t}) \qquad (\text{B.62})$$

In the case of linearly increasing hazard, the expression becomes

$$R(t) = 1 - \prod_{i=1}^{n} \left(1 - e^{-K_i t^2/2}\right) \qquad (\text{B.63})$$

In the general case, the system reliability function is

$$R(t) = 1 - \prod_{i=1}^{n} (1 - e^{-Z_i(t)}) \qquad (\text{B.64})$$

where $Z_i(t) \equiv \int_0^t z(\xi)\, d\xi$.

In order to permit grouping of terms in Eq. (B.64) to simplify computation and/or interpretation, the equation must be expanded. The expansion results in

$$R(t) = \left(e^{-Z_1} + e^{-Z_2} + \cdots + e^{-Z_n}\right) - \left(e^{-(Z_1+Z_2)} + e^{-(Z_1+Z_3)} + \cdots\right)$$
$$+ \left(e^{-(Z_1+Z_2+Z_3)} + e^{-(Z_1+Z_2+Z_4)} + \cdots\right) - \cdots e^{-(Z_1+Z_2+Z_3+\cdots+Z_n)}$$

$$(\text{B.65})$$

Note that the signs of the terms in parentheses alternate and that in the first parentheses the exponents are all the Z's taken singly, in the second all the sums of Z's taken two at a time, and in the last term the sum of all the Z's. The rth parentheses in Eq. (B.65) contain $n!/[r!(n-r)!]$ terms.

Just as the series configuration served as a lower-bound structure, the parallel model can be thought of as an upper-bound structure.

If we have a system of n elements with information on each element reliability but little or no information on their interconnection, we can bound the reliability function from below by Eq. (B.56) and from above by Eq. (B.64). We would in general expect these bounds to be quite loose; however, they do provide some information even when we are grossly ignorant of the system structure.

B.4.4 An *r*-out-of-*n* Structure

Another simple structure which serves as a useful model for many reliability problems is an r-out-of-n structure. Such a model represents a system of n components in which r of the n items must be good for the system to succeed. Of course r is less than n. Two simple examples of an r-out-of-n system are (1) a piece of stranded wire with n strands in which at least r are necessary to pass the required current and (2) a battery composed of n series cells of E volts each where the minimum voltage for system operation[1] is rE.

We may formulate a structural model for an r-out-of-n system, but it is simpler to use the binomial distribution if applicable. The binomial distribution can be used only when the n components are independent and identical. If the components differ or are dependent, the structural-model approach must be used.[2] Success of exactly r out of n identical, independent items is given by

$$B(r:n) = \binom{n}{r} p^r (1-p)^{n-r} \tag{B.66}$$

where $r:n$ stands for r out of n, and the success of at least r out of n items is given by

$$P_s = \sum_{k=r}^{n} B(k:n) \tag{B.67}$$

For constant-hazard components Eq. (B.66) becomes

$$R(t) = \sum_{k=r}^{n} \binom{n}{k} e^{-k\lambda t} (1 - e^{-\lambda t})^{n-k} \tag{B.68}$$

Similarly for linearly increasing or Weibull components, the reliability functions are

$$R(t) = \left[\sum_{k=r}^{n} \binom{n}{k} e^{-kKt^2/2} \right] (1 - e^{-Kt^2/2})^{n-k} \tag{B.69}$$

$$R(t) = \left[\sum_{k=r}^{n} \binom{n}{k} e^{-kKt^{m+1}/(m+1)} \right] (1 - e^{-Kt^{m+1}/(m+1)})^{n-k} \tag{B.70}$$

It is of interest to note that for $r = 1$, the structure becomes a parallel system and for $r = n$ the structure becomes a series system. Thus, in a sense series and parallel systems are subclasses of an r-out-of-n structure.

B.5 ILLUSTRATIVE EXAMPLE OF SIMPLIFIED AUTO DRUM BRAKES

B.5.1 Introduction

The preceding sections have attempted to summarize the pertinent aspects of reliability theory and show the reader how analysis can be performed. This section illustrates via an example how the theory can be applied.

---

[1] Actually when one cell of a series of n cells fails, the voltage of the string does not become $(n-1)E$ unless a special circuit arrangement is used. Such a circuit is discussed in Shooman (1968), p. 2.9.

[2] The reader should refer back to the example given in Eq. (B.17) and Fig. B.3.

The example chosen for this section is actually a safety analysis. In the case of the automobile, the only dfference between a reliability and a safety analysis is in the choice of subsystems included in the analysis. In the case of safety, we concentrate on the subsystems whose failure could cause injury to the occupants, other passengers, pedestrians, etc. In the case of reliability analysis, we would include all subsystems whose failure either makes the auto inoperative or necessitates a repair (depending on our definition of success).

B.5.2 The Brake System

The example considers the braking system of a 1969 Ford, without power brakes or antiskid brakes, and excluding the parking (emergency) brake and the dash warning light. An analysis at the detailed (piece-part) level is a difficult task. The major subsystems in the braking system contain about 196 parts and assemblies as detailed in a dealer's shop manual.[1]

The major subsystems and approximate parts counts are: pressure differential valve (8 parts), self-adjusting drum brakes (4 × 15 parts), wheel cylinder (4 × 9 parts), tubing, brackets, and connectors (50 parts), dual master cylinder (22 parts), and master cylinder installation parts (20 parts). Frequently, because of lack of data, analysis is not carried out at this piece-part level. Even with scanty data, an analysis is still important, since often it will show obvious weaknesses of such a braking system which can be improved when redesigning it. In such a case, redesign is warranted, based on engineering judgment, even without statistics on frequencies of the failure modes. The example will be performed at a higher level, and will group together all failure mechanisms which cause the particular failure mode in question.

B.5.3 Failure Modes, Effects, and Criticality Analysis

An FMECA[2] for the simplified braking system is given in Table B.3. Inspection of the table shows that the modes which most seriously affect safety are modes M2, M4, and M7, and the design should be scrutinized in a design review to assure that the probability of occurrence for these modes is minimized.

B.5.4 Structural Model

The next step in analysis would be the construction of an SBD or an FT.[3] Assume that a safety failure occurs if modes M2, M4, or M7 occur singly and modes M1, M3, M5, and M6 occur in pairs. (Actually the paired modes must affect both front and rear systems to constitute a failure; but approximations are made here

---

[1] Ford (1969).

[2] Sometimes a column is added to an FMEA analysis which discusses (evaluates) the severity or *criticality* of the failure mode. In such a case, the analysis is called an FMECA.

[3] Safety block diagram or fault tree.

Table B.3 A simplified braking system FMECA

Failure mode	Mechanism	Safety criticality	Comments
M1. Differential valve failure (1/2 system)	Leakage or Blockage	Medium	Reduces braking efficiency
M2. Differential valve failure (total system)	Leakage affecting both front and back systems	High	Loss of both systems
M3. Master cylinder failure (1/2 system)	Leakage or blockage	Medium	Reduces braking efficiency
M4. Master cylinder failure (total system)	Leakage (Front and back)	High	Loss of both systems
M5. Drum brakes self-adjusting	Leakage or blockage of one assembly	Medium	Unbalance of brakes causes erratic behavior
M6. Tubing, brackets and connectors (1/2 system)	Leakage or blockage	Medium	Reduces braking efficiency
M7. Pedal and linkage	Broken or jammed	High	Loss of both systems

to simplify the analysis.) Based on the above assumptions, the SBD and FT given in Figs. B.12 and B.13, respectively, are obtained.

B.5.5 Probability Equations

Given either the SBD of Figure B.12 or the FT of Figure B.13, an equation can be written for the probability of safety (or unsafety), using probability principles. Computer programs are used in complex cases; this simplified case can be

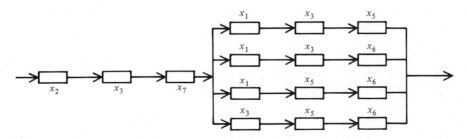

Figure B.12 Safety block diagram for simplified brake example. Presence of any x_i means failure mode i does not occur, indicating success of element i.

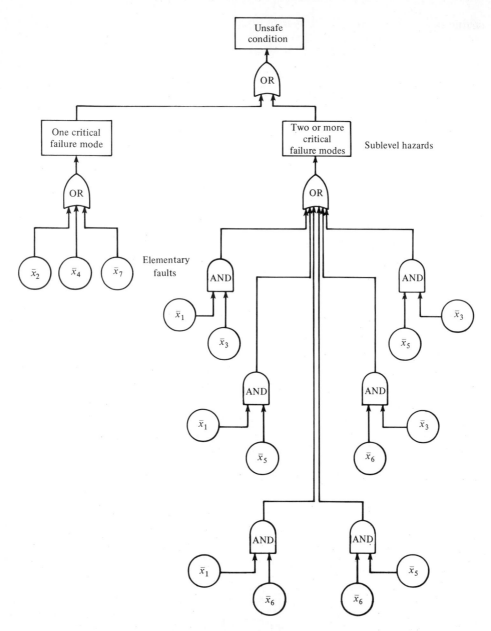

Figure B.13 Safety fault tree for simplified brake example. Presence of any $\bar{x}_i$ means failure mode i *does* occur, indicating failure of element i.

written:

$$P_s \equiv \text{probability of a safe condition from Fig. B.12}$$

$$= P[(x_2 x_3 x_7)(x_1 x_3 x_5 + x_1 x_3 x_6 + x_1 x_5 x_6 + x_3 x_5 x_6)]$$

$$P_u \equiv \text{probability of an unsafe condition from Fig. B.13}$$

$$= P[(\bar{x}_2 + \bar{x}_4 + \bar{x}_7) + (\bar{x}_1 \bar{x}_3 + \bar{x}_1 \bar{x}_5 + \bar{x}_1 \bar{x}_6 + \bar{x}_3 \bar{x}_5 + \bar{x}_3 \bar{x}_6 + \bar{x}_5 \bar{x}_6)]$$

An analysis in more depth would require more detail (and more input data). The choice of how much decomposition to lower levels of detail is required in an analysis is often determined by data availability. To continue the analysis, failure data on the modes M1, M2,..., M6 is required. If, for M3, the failure rate were constant and equal to λ_3 failures per mile, then the possibility of mode M3 occurring or not occurring in M miles would be:

$$P\left(\begin{array}{c}\text{mode M3 does not occur} \\ \text{in } M \text{ miles}\end{array}\right) = P(X_3) = e^{-\lambda_3 M}$$

$$P\left(\begin{array}{c}\text{mode M3 does occur in} \\ M \text{ miles}\end{array}\right) = P(\bar{X}_3) = 1 - e^{-\lambda_3 M}$$

To complete the analysis, the failure rate data λ_i are substituted into the equations to determine $P(X_i)$ or $P(\bar{X}_i)$; then these terms are substituted into the equations for P_s or P_u; and last, P_s or P_u is substituted into the expression for P_A.

B.5.6 Summary

The safety analysis consists of:

1. Decomposing the system into subsystems or piece-parts.
2. Drawing a safety block diagram (SBD) or fault tree (FT) (computer programs are available for this purpose).[1]
3. Computation of the probability of safety or unsafety from the SBD or FT (computer programs are also available)[1] for this purpose.
4. Determining the failure rates of each component element. This is a data collection and estimation problem.
5. Substitution of failure rates into expression of step 3 (also done by computer programs).

---

[1] The NASA-RBD computer program based upon the Messinger/Shooman algorithm (see Chap. 7 of NASA, 1968) and the AEC-FTA computer program (PREP/KITT/TREBIL) used in connection with the Rasmussen Nuclear Reactor Safety Study WASH-1400.

B.6 MARKOV RELIABILITY AND AVAILABILITY MODELS

B.6.1 Introduction

Dependent failures, repair, or standby operation complicates the direct calculation of element reliabilities. In this section we shall discuss three different approaches to reliability computations for systems involving such computations. The first technique is the use of Markov models, which works well and has much appeal as long as the failure hazards $z(t)$ and repair hazards $w(t)$ are constant. When $z(t)$ and $w(t)$ become time-dependent, the method breaks down, except in a few special cases. A second method, using joint density functions, and a third method, using convolutionlike integrations, are more difficult to set up, but they are still valid when $z(t)$ or $w(t)$ is time-dependent.[1]

B.6.2 Markov Models

The basic properties of Markov models have already been discussed in Sec. A.8. In this section we shall briefly review some of the assumptions necessary for formulation of a Markov model and show how it can be used to make reliability computations.

In order to formulate a Markov model (to be more precise we are talking about continuous-time and discrete-state models) we must first define all the mutually exclusive states of the system. For example, in a system composed of a single nonreparable element x_1 there are two possible states: $s_0 = x_1$, in which the element is good, and $s_1 = \bar{x}_1$, in which the element is bad. The states of the system at $t = 0$ are called the *initial states*, and those representing a final or equilibrium state are called *final states*. The set of Markov state equations describes the probabilistic transitions from the initial to the final states.

The transition probabilities must obey the following two rules:

1. The probability of transition in time Δt from one state to another is given by $z(t)\,\Delta t$, where $z(t)$ is the hazard associated with the two states in question. If all the $z_i(t)$'s are constant, $z_i(t) = \lambda_i$, and the model is called *homogeneous*. If any hazards are time functions, the model is called *nonhomogeneous*.
2. The probabilities of more than one transition in time Δt are infinitesimals of a higher order and can be neglected.

For the example under discussion the state-transition equations can be formulated using the above rules. The probability of being in state s_0 at time $t + \Delta t$ is written $P_{s_0}(t + \Delta t)$. This is given by the probability that the system is in state s_0 at time t, $P_{s_0}(t)$, times the probability of *no* failure in time Δt, $1 - z(t)\,\Delta t$,

---

[1]See Shooman (1968), Sec. 5.8.

Table B.4 State transition matrix for a single element

Initial states	Final states	
	s_0	s_1
s_0	$1 - z(t)\Delta t$	$z(t)\Delta t$
s_1	0	1

plus the probability of being in state s_1 at time t, $P_{s_1}(t)$, times the probability of repair in time Δt, which equals zero.

The resulting equation is

$$P_{s_0}(t + \Delta t) = [1 - z(t)\Delta t]P_{s_0}(t) + 0P_{s_1}(t) \tag{B.71}$$

Similarly, the probability of being in state s_1 at $t + \Delta t$ is given by

$$P_{s_1}(t + \Delta t) = [z(t)\Delta t]P_{s_0}(t) + 1P_{s_1}(t) \tag{B.72}$$

The transition probability $z(t)\Delta t$ is the probability of failure (change from state s_0 to s_1), and the probability of remaining in state s_1 is unity.[1] One can summarize the transition equations (B.71) and (B.72) by writing the transition matrix given in Table B.4. Note that it is a property of transition matrices that its rows must sum to unity. Rearrangement of Eqs. (B.71) and (B.72) yields

$$\frac{P_{s_0}(t + \Delta t) - P_{s_0}(t)}{\Delta t} = -z(t)P_{s_0}(t)$$

$$\frac{P_{s_1}(t + \Delta t) - P_{s_1}(t)}{\Delta t} = z(t)P_{s_0}(t)$$

Passing to a limit as Δt becomes small, we obtain

$$\frac{dP_{s_0}(t)}{dt} + z(t)P_{s_0}(t) = 0 \tag{B.73}$$

$$\frac{dP_{s_1}(t)}{dt} = z(t)P_{s_0}(t) \tag{B.74}$$

Equations (B.73) and (B.74) can be solved in conjunction with the appropriate initial conditions for $P_{s_0}(t)$ and $P_{s_1}(t)$, the probabilities of ending up in state s_0 or state s_1, respectively. The most common initial condition is that the system is good at $t = 0$, that is, $P_{s_0}(t = 0) = 1$ and $P_{s_1}(t = 0) = 0$. Equations (B.73) and (B.74) are simple first-order linear differential equations which are easily solved by classical theory. Equation (B.73) is homogeneous (no driving function), and

---

[1] Conventionally, state s_1 would be called an absorbing state since transitions out of the state are not permitted.

separation of variables yields

$$\frac{dP_{s_0}(t)}{P_{s_0}(t)} = -z(t)\, dt$$

$$\ln P_{s_0}(t) = -\int_0^t z(\xi)\, d\xi + C_1$$

$$P_{s_0}(t) = \exp\left[-\int_0^t z(\xi)\, d\xi + C_1\right] = C_2 \exp\left[-\int_0^t z(\xi)\, d\xi\right] \qquad \text{(B.75)}$$

Inserting the initial condition $P_{s_0}(t = 0) = 1$,

$$P_{s_0}(t = 0) = 1 = C_2 e^{-0}$$

$$\therefore C_2 = 1$$

and one obtains the familiar reliability function

$$R(t) = P_{s_0}(t) = \exp\left[-\int_0^t z(\xi)\, d\xi\right] \qquad \text{(B.76)}$$

Formal solution of Eq. (B.76) proceeds in a similar manner.

$$P_{s_1}(t) = 1 - \exp\left[\int_0^t z(\xi)\, d\xi\right] \qquad \text{(B.77)}$$

Of course a formal solution of Eq. (B.74) is not necessary to obtain Eq. (B.77), since it is possible to recognize at the outset that

$$P_{s_0}(t) + P_{s_1}(t) = 1$$

The role played by the initial conditions is clearly evident from Eq. (B.75). Since $C_2 = P_{s_0}(0)$, if the system was initially bad, $P_{s_0}(t) = 0$, and $R(t) = 0$. If there is a fifty-fifty chance that the system is good at $t = 0$, then $P_{s_0}(t) = \frac{1}{2}$, and

$$R(t) = \tfrac{1}{2} \exp\left[-\int_0^t z(\xi)\, d\xi\right]$$

This method of computing the system reliability function yields the same results, of course, as the techniques of Secs. B.3 to B.5. Even in a single-element problem it generates a more general model. The initial condition allows one to include the probability of initial failure before the system in question is energized.

B.6.3 Markov Graphs

It is often easier to characterize Markov models by a graph composed of nodes representing system states and branches labeled with transition probabilities. Such a Markov graph for the problem described by Eqs. (B.73) and (B.74) or Table B.4 is given in Fig. B.14. Note that the sum of transition probabilities for the branches leaving each node must be unity. Treating the nodes as signal sources and the transition probabilities as transmission coefficients, we can write Eqs. (B.73) and (B.74) by inspection. Thus, the probability of being at any node

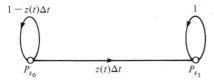

Figure B.14 Markov graph for a single nonrepairable element.

at time $t + \Delta t$ is the sum of all signals arriving at that node. All other nodes are considered probability sources at time t, and all transition probabilities serve as transmission gains. A simple algorithm for writing Eqs. (B.73) and (B.74) by inspection is to equate the derivative of the probability at any node to the sum of the transmissions coming into the node. Any unity gain factors of the self-loops must first be set to zero, and the Δt factors are dropped from the branch gains. Referring to Fig. B.14, the self-loop on P_{s_1} disappears, and the equation becomes $\dot{P}_{s_1} = zP_{s_0}$. At node P_{s_0} the self-loop gain becomes $-z$, and the equation is $\dot{P}_{s_0} = -zP_{s_0}$. The same algorithm holds at each node for more complex graphs.

B.6.4 Example—A Two-Element Model

One can illustrate dependent failures,[1] standby operation, and repair by discussing a two-element system. For simplicity repair is ignored at first. If a two-element system consisting of elements x_1 and x_2 is considered, there are four system states: $s_0 = x_1 x_2$, $s_1 = \bar{x}_1 x_2$, $s_2 = x_1 \bar{x}_2$, and $s_3 = \bar{x}_1 \bar{x}_2$. The state transition matrix is given in Table B.5 and the Markov graph in Fig. B.15.

The probability expressions for these equations can be written by inspection, using the algorithms previously stated.

$$\frac{dP_{s_0}(t)}{dt} = -[z_{01}(t) + z_{02}(t)]P_{s_0}(t) \tag{B.78}$$

$$\frac{dP_{s_1}(t)}{dt} = -[z_{13}(t)]P_{s_1}(t) + [z_{01}(t)]P_{s_0}(t) \tag{B.79}$$

$$\frac{dP_{s_2}(t)}{dt} = -[z_{23}(t)]P_{s_2}(t) + [z_{02}(t)]P_{s_0}(t) \tag{B.80}$$

$$\frac{dP_{s_3}(t)}{dt} = [z_{13}(t)]P_{s_1}(t) + [z_{23}(t)]P_{s_2}(t) \tag{B.81}$$

The initial conditions associated with this set of equations are $P_{s_0}(0)$, $P_{s_1}(0)$, $P_{s_2}(0)$, $P_{s_3}(0)$.

It is difficult to solve these equations for a general hazard function $z(t)$, but if the hazards are specified, the solution is quite simple. If all the hazards are

---

[1]For dependent failures see Shooman (1968), p. 235.

Table B.5 State transition matrix for two elements

			Final states		
Initial states		s_0	s_1	s_2	s_3
Zero failures	s_0	$1 - [z_{01}(t) + z_{02}(t)]\Delta t$	$z_{01}(t)\Delta t$	$z_{02}(t)\Delta t$	0
One failure	s_1	0	$1 - [z_{13}(t)]\Delta t$	0	$z_{13}(t)\Delta t$
	s_2	0	0	$1 - [z_{23}(t)]\Delta t$	$z_{23}(t)\Delta t$
Two failures	s_3	0	0	0	1

constant, $z_{01}(t) = \lambda_1$, $z_{02}(t) = \lambda_2$, $z_{13}(t) = \lambda_3$, and $z_{23}(t) = \lambda_4$. The solutions are

$$P_{s_0}(t) = e^{-(\lambda_1 + \lambda_2)t} \tag{B.82}$$

$$P_{s_1}(t) = \frac{\lambda_1}{\lambda_1 + \lambda_2 - \lambda_3}\left(e^{-\lambda_3 t} - e^{-(\lambda_1 + \lambda_2)t}\right) \tag{B.83}$$

$$P_{s_2}(t) = \frac{\lambda_2}{\lambda_1 + \lambda_2 - \lambda_4}\left(e^{-\lambda_4 t} - e^{-(\lambda_1 + \lambda_2)t}\right) \tag{B.84}$$

$$P_{s_3}(t) = 1 - \left[P_{s_0}(t) + P_{s_1}(t) + P_{s_2}(t)\right] \tag{B.85}$$

where

$$P_{s_0}(0) = 1 \quad \text{and} \quad P_{s_1}(0) = P_{s_2}(0) = P_{s_3}(0) = 0$$

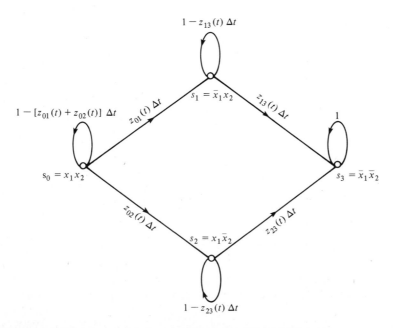

Figure B.15 Markov graph for two distinct nonrepairable elements.

Note that we have not as yet had to say anything about the configuration of the system, but only have had to specify the number of elements and the transition probabilities. Thus, when we solve for P_{s_1}, P_{s_1}, P_{s_2}, we have essentially solved for all possible two-element system configurations.[2] In a two-element system, formulation of the reliability expressions in terms of P_{s_0}, P_{s_1}, and P_{s_2} is trivial, but in a more complex problem we can always formulate the expression using the tools of Secs. B.3 to B.5.

For a series system, the only state representing success is no failures; that is, $P_{s_0}(t)$.[1] Therefore

$$R(t) = P_{s_0}(t) = e^{-(\lambda_1+\lambda_2)t} \tag{B.86}$$

If the two elements are in parallel, one failure can be tolerated, and there are three successful states, $P_{s_0}(t)$, $P_{s_1}(t)$, $P_{s_2}(t)$. Since the states are mutually exclusive,

$$R(t) = P_{s_0}(t) + P_{s_1}(t) + P_{s_2}(t) = e^{-(\lambda_1+\lambda_2)t}$$

$$+ \frac{\lambda_1}{\lambda_1+\lambda_2-\lambda_3}(e^{-\lambda_3 t} - e^{-(\lambda_1+\lambda_2)t})$$

$$+ \frac{\lambda_2}{\lambda_1+\lambda_2-\lambda_4}(e^{-\lambda_4 t} - e^{-(\lambda_1+\lambda_2)t}) \tag{B.87}$$

B.6.5 Model Complexity

The complexity of a Markov model depends on the number of system states. In general we obtain for an m-state problem a system of m first-order differential equations. The number of states is given in terms of the number of components n as

$$m = \binom{n}{0} + \binom{n}{1} + \binom{n}{2} + \cdots + \binom{n}{n} = 2^n$$

Thus, our two-element model has four states, and a four-element model 16 states. This means that an n-component system may require a solution of as many as 2^n first-order differential equations. In many cases we are interested in fewer states. Suppose we want to know only how many failed items are present in each state and not which items have failed. This would mean a model with $n + 1$ states rather than 2^n, which represents a tremendous saving. To illustrate how such simplifications affect the Markov graph we consider the collapsed flowgraph shown in Fig. B.16 for the example given in Fig. B.15. Collapsing the flowgraph is equivalent to the restriction $P_{s_1'}(t) = P_{s_1}(t) + P_{s_2}(t)$ applied to Eqs. (B.78) to (B.81). Note that this can collapse the flowgraph only if $z_{13} = z_{23}$; however, z_{01}

[1] It is easy to see why a series configuration of n components has the poorest reliability and why a parallel configuration has the best. The only successful state for a series system is where all components are good; thus, $R(t) = P_{s_0}(t)$. In the case of a parallel system all states except the one in which all components have failed is good, and $R(t) = P_{s_0}(t) + P_{s_1}(t) + P_{s_2}(t)$. It is clear that any other system configuration falls somewhere in between.

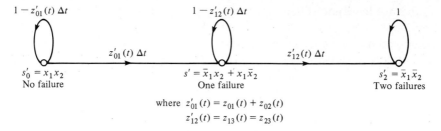

where $z'_{01}(t) = z_{01}(t) + z_{02}(t)$
$z'_{12}(t) = z_{13}(t) = z_{23}(t)$

Figure B.16 Collapsed Markov graph corresponding to Fig. B.15.

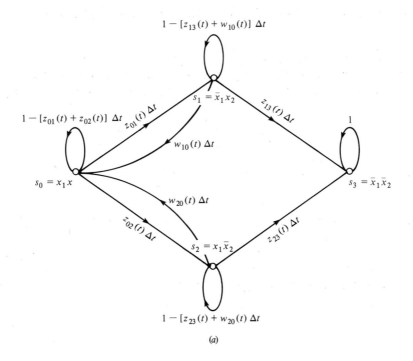

(a)

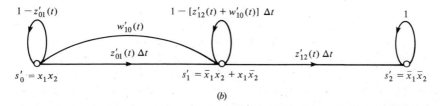

(b)

Figure B.17 Markov graphs for a system with repair: (a) general model; (b) collapsed model.

and z_{02} need not be equal. These results are obvious if Eqs. (8.79) and (8.80) are added.

Markov graphs for a system with repair are shown in Fig. B.17a and b. The graph in Fig. B.17a is a general model, and that of Fig. B.17b is a collapsed model.

The system equations can be written for Fig. B.17a by inspection using the algorithm previously discussed.

$$\dot{P}_{s_0} = -(z_{01} + z_{02})P_{s_0} + w_{10}P_{s_1} + w_{20}P_{s_2}$$
$$\dot{P}_{s_1} = -(z_{13} + w_{10})P_{s_1} + z_{01}P_{s_0}$$
$$\dot{P}_{s_2} = -(z_{23} + w_{20})P_{s_2} + z_{02}P_{s_0}$$
$$\dot{P}_{s_3} = z_{13}P_{s_1} + z_{23}P_{s_2} \tag{B.88}$$

Similarly for Fig. B.18b

$$\dot{P}_{s_0'} = -z_{01}'P_{s_0'} + w_{10}'P_{s_1'}$$
$$\dot{P}_{s_1'} = -(z_{12}' + w_{10}')P_{s_1'} + z_{01}'P_{s_0'}$$
$$\dot{P}_{s_2'} = z_{12}'P_{s_1'} \tag{B.89}$$

The solution to Eqs. (B.88) and (B.89) for various values of the z's and w's will be deferred until the next section.

B.7 REPAIRABLE SYSTEMS

B.7.1 Introduction

In general, whenever the average repair cost in time and money of a piece of equipment is a fraction of the initial equipment cost, one considers system repair. If such a system can be rapidly returned to service, the effect of the failure is minimized. Obvious examples are such equipment as a television set, an automobile, or a radar installation. In such a system the time between failures, repair time, number of failures in an interval, and percentage of operating time in an interval are figures of merit which must be considered along with the system reliability. Of course, in some systems, such as those involving life support, surveillance, or safety, any failure is probably catastrophic, and repair is of no avail.

B.7.2 Availability Function

In order to describe the beneficial features of repair in a system that tolerates shutdown times, a new system function called *availability* is introduced. The availability function $A(t)$ is defined as the probability that the system is operating *at time t.* By contrast, the reliability function $R(t)$ is the probability that the system has operated *over the interval* 0 *to t*. Thus, if $A(250) = 0.95$, then if 100 such systems are operated for 250 h on the average, 95 will be operative when 250 h is reached and 5 will be undergoing various stages of repairs. The availability function contains no information on how many (if any) failure-repair cycles have occurred prior to 250 h. On the other hand, if $R(250) = 0.95$, then if 100 such systems are operated for 250 h, on the average, 95 will have operated without failure for 250 h and 5 will have failed at some time within this interval. It is immaterial in which stage of the first or subsequent failure-repair cycles the five failed systems are. Obviously the requirement that $R(250) = 0.95$ is much more stringent than the requirement that $A(250) = 0.95$. Thus, in general, $R(t) \leq A(t)$.

If a *single unit* has no repair capability, then by definition $A(t) = R(t)$. If we allow repair, then $R(t)$ does not change, but $A(t)$ becomes greater than $R(t)$. The same conclusions hold for a *chain structure*. The situation changes for any system involving more than one tie set, i.e., systems with inherent or purposely introduced *redundancy*. In such a case, repair can beneficially alter both the $R(t)$ and $A(t)$ functions. This is best illustrated by a simple system composed of two parallel units. If a system consists of components A and B in parallel and no repairs are permitted, the system fails when both A and B have failed. In a repairable system if A fails, unit B continues to operate, and the system survives. Meanwhile, a repairer begins repair of unit A. If the repairer restores A to usefulness before B fails, the system continues to operate. The second component failure might be unit B, or unit A might fail the second time in a row. In either case there is no system failure as long as the repair time is shorter than the time between failures. In the long run, at some time a lengthy repair will be started and will be in progress when the alternate unit fails, causing system failure. It is clear that repair will improve system reliability in such a system. It seems intuitive that the increase in reliability will be a function of the mean time to repair divided by the MTTF.

To summarize, in a series system, repair will not affect the reliability expression; however, for a complete description of system operation we shall have to include measures of repair time and time between failures. If the system structure has any parallel paths, repair will improve reliability, and repair time and time between failures will be of importance. In some systems, e.g., an unmanned space vehicle, repair may be impossible or impractical.[1]

B.7.3 Reliability and Availability of Repairable Systems

As long as the failure and repair density functions are exponential, i.e., constant-hazard, we can structure Markov repair models, as done in the previous section. The reliability and availability models will differ, and we must exercise great care in assigning absorbing states in a reliability model for a repairable system.

---

[1] Technology is rapidly reaching the point where repair of an orbiting space vehicle is practical but expensive.

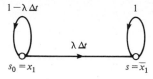

Figure B.18 Markov graph for the *reliability* of a single component with repair.

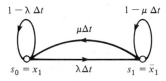

Figure B.19 Markov graph for the *availability* of a single component with repair.

The reliability of a single component x_1 with constant failure hazard λ and constant repair hazard μ can be derived easily using a Markov model. The Markov graph is given in Fig. B.18 and the differential equations and reliability function in Eqs. (B.90) and (B.91).

$$\dot{P}_{s_0} + \lambda P_{s_0} = 0$$

$$\dot{P}_{s_1} = \lambda P_{s_0} \tag{B.90}$$

$$P_{s_0}(0) = 1 \quad P_{s_1}(0) = 0$$

$$R(t) = P_{s_0}(t) = 1 - P_{s_1}(t) = e^{-\lambda t} \tag{B.91}$$

Note that repair in no way influenced the reliability computation. Element failure $\bar{x}_1$ is an absorbing state, and once it is reached, the system never returns to x_1.

If we wish the study the availability, we must make a different Markov graph. State $\bar{x}_1$ is no longer an absorbing state, since we now allow transitions from state $\bar{x}_1$ back to state x_1. The Markov graph is given in Fig. B.19 and the differential equations and state probabilities in Eqs. (B.92) and (B.93). The corresponding differential equations are

$$\dot{P}_{s_0} + \lambda P_{s_0} = \mu P_{s_1} \quad \dot{P}_{s_1} + \mu P_{s_1} = \lambda P_{s_0} \tag{B.92}$$

$$\dot{P}_{s_0}(0) = 1 \quad P_{s_1}(0) = 0$$

Solution yields the probabilities

$$P_{s_0}(t) = \frac{\mu}{\lambda + \mu} + \frac{\lambda}{\lambda + \mu} e^{-(\lambda + \mu)t}$$

$$P_{s_1}(t) = \frac{\lambda}{\lambda + \mu} - \frac{\lambda}{\lambda + \mu} e^{-(\lambda + \mu)t} \tag{B.93}$$

By definition, the availability is the probability that the system is good, $P_{s_0}(t)$:

$$A(t) = P_{s_0}(t) = \frac{\mu}{\lambda + \mu} + \frac{\lambda}{\lambda + \mu} e^{-(\lambda + \mu)t} \tag{B.94}$$

The availability function given in Eq. (B.94) is plotted in Fig. B.20.

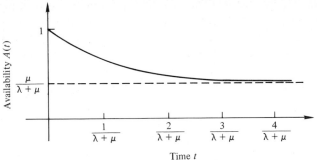

Figure B.20 Availability function for a single component.

B.7.4 Steady-State Availability

An important difference between $A(t)$ and $R(t)$ is their steady-state behavior. As t becomes large, all reliability functions approach zero, whereas availability functions reach some steady-state value. For the single component the steady-state availability

$$A_{ss}(t) = \lim_{t \to \infty} A(t) = \mu / (\lambda + \mu)$$

In the normal case, the mean repair time $1/\mu$ is much smaller than the time to failure $1/\lambda$, and we can expand the steady-state availability in a series and approximate by truncation:

$$A_{ss}(t) = A(\infty) = \frac{1}{1 + \lambda/\mu} = 1 - \frac{\lambda}{\mu} + \frac{\lambda^2}{2\mu^2} + \cdots \approx 1 - \frac{\lambda}{\mu} \qquad \text{(B.95)}$$

The transient part of the availability function decays to zero fairly rapidly. The time at which the transient term is negligible with respect to the steady-state term depends on λ and μ. As an upper bound we know that the term $e^{-\alpha t} \leq 0.02$ for $t > 4/\alpha$; therefore, we can state that the transient term is over before $t = 4/(\lambda + \mu)$. If $\mu > \lambda$, the transient is over before $t = 4/\mu$. The interaction between reliability and availability specifications is easily seen in the following example.

Suppose a system is to be designed to have a reliability of greater than 0.90 over 1000 h and a minimum availability of 0.99 over that period. The reliability specification yields

$$R(t) = e^{-\lambda t} \geq 0.90 \quad 0 < t < 1000$$

$$e^{-1000\lambda} \approx 1 - 10^3\lambda = 0.90 \quad \lambda \geq 10^{-4}$$

Assuming $A(\infty)$ for the minimum value of the availability, Eq. (B.95) yields

$$A(\infty) = 1 - \frac{\lambda}{\mu} = 0.99$$

$$\mu = 100\lambda = 10^{-2}$$

Thus, we use a component with an MTTF of 10^4 h, a little over 1 year, and a mean repair time of 100 h (about 4 days). The probability of any failure within 1000 h (about 6 weeks) is less than 10 percent. Furthermore, the probability that the system is down and under repair at any chosen time between $t = 0$ and $t = 10^3$ h is less than 1 percent. Now to check the approximations. The transient phase of the availability function lasts for $4/(10^{-2} + 10^{-4}) \approx 400$ h; thus the availability will be somewhat greater than 0.99 for 400 h and then settle down at 0.99 for the remaining 600 h. Since μ is 100λ, the approximation of Eq. (B.95) is valid. Also since $\lambda t = 10^{-4} \times 10^3 = 10^{-1}$, the two-term series expansion of the exponential is also satisfactory.

The availability function has been defined as a probability function, just as the reliability function was. There is another statistical interpretation which sheds some light on the concept. Suppose that a large number of system operating hours are accumulated. This can be done either by operating one system for a long time, so that many failure and repair cycles are obtained and recorded, or by operating a large number of identical systems (an ensemble) for a shorter period of time and combining the data. If the ratio of cumulative operating time to total test time is computed, it approaches $A(\infty)$ as $t \to \infty$. Actually the data taken during the transient period of availability should be discarded to avoid any distortions. In fact if one wished to compute the transient phase of availability from experimental data, one would be forced to use a very large number of systems over a short period of time. In analyzing the data one would break up the time scale into many small intervals and compute the ratio of cumulative operating time over the intervals divided by the length of the interval.

In a two-element nonseries system, the reliability function as well as the availability function is influenced by system repairs. The Markov reliability and availability graphs for systems with two components are given in Figs. B.21, B.22, and B.23, and their solution is discussed in Shooman (1968), p. 345.

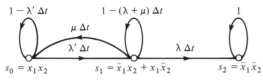

$s_0 = x_1 x_2$ $\qquad$ $s_1 = \bar{x}_1 x_2 + x_1 \bar{x}_2$ $\qquad$ $s_2 = \bar{x}_1 \bar{x}_2$

where $\lambda' = 2\lambda$ for an ordinary system
$\lambda' = \lambda$ for a standby system

Figure B.21 Markov *reliability* model for two identical parallel elements and one repairer.

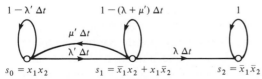

$s_0 = x_1 x_2$ $\qquad$ $s_1 = \bar{x}_1 x_2 + x_1 \bar{x}_2$ $\qquad$ $s_2 = \bar{x}_1 \bar{x}_2$

where $\lambda' = 2\lambda$ for an ordinary system
$\lambda' = \lambda$ for a standby system
$\mu' = \mu$ for one repairer
$\mu' = k_\mu$ for more than one repairer $(k > 1)$

Figure B.22 Markov *reliability* model for two identical parallel elements and k repairers.

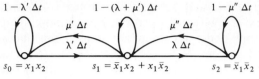

where $\lambda' = 2\lambda$ for an ordinary system $\qquad \mu'' = \mu$ for one repairer
$\qquad \lambda' = \lambda$ for a standby system $\qquad \mu'' = 2\mu$ for two repairers
$\qquad \mu' = \mu$ for one repairer $\qquad \mu'' = k_2\mu$ for more than two repairers $k_2 > 2$
$\qquad \mu' = k_1\mu$ for more than one repairer $(k_1 > 1)$

Figure B.23 Markov *availability* graph for two identical parallel elements.

B.7.5 Computation of Steady-State Availability

When only the steady-state availability is of interest, a simplified computational procedure can be used. In the steady state, all the state probabilities should approach a constant; therefore, setting the derivatives to zero yields the following:[1]

$$\dot{P}_{s_0}(t) = \dot{P}_{s_1}(t) = \dot{P}_{s_2}(t) = 0$$

This set of equations cannot be solved for the steady-state probabilities, since their determinant is zero. Any two of these equations can, however, be combined with the identity

$$P_{s_0}(\infty) + P_{s_1}(\infty) + P_{s_2}(\infty) = 1 \qquad (B.96)$$

to yield a solution.

So far we have discussed reliability and availability computations only in one- and two-element systems. Obviously we could set up and solve Markov models for a larger number of elements, but the complexity of the problem increases very rapidly as n, the number of elements, increases. (If the elements are distinct, it goes as 2^n, and if identical as $n + 1$.)

B.8 RELIABILITY IMPROVEMENT

B.8.1 Introduction

This section contains a diversity of topics, but they are bound together by the fact that each presents techniques for increasing system reliability. The first few merely preach sound design principles, most of which are suggested by common sense. Many of the early reliability studies found that a great number (sometimes half) of component failures were attributable to improper design or nonconservative choice of component ratings. Once these simple but often effective matters have been investigated, other techniques must be used for further reliability improvement.

---

[1] In the case of an *m*-state model these equations generalize in the obvious manner.

One approach is to try to procure or develop superior component parts with smaller failure rates. Much work along these lines was done in connection with the Minuteman program. Although it is often possible to trade development time, money, size, and weight to buy improved reliability obviously such an approach soon reaches limits.

Another approach to reliability improvement is to alter the system structure so as to obtain higher reliability while maintaining the basic system function. Except for certain cases of ingenious solutions, this is generally accomplished by creating additional paths and is usually termed *redundancy*. Certain simple redundancy techniques are discussed and evaluated, and then the more sophisticated schemes, such as majority voting and standby systems, are discussed. Redundancy is easy to apply and yields very effective results when there are many similar units in a system. This is just the case in digital circuitry, and therefore a specialized approach to digital reliability is included in Sec. B.9.4.

B.8.2 Proper Design and Simplicity

The title of this section implies that equipment is often poorly designed or overly complex, and unfortunately such is too frequently the case. In fact many of the early reliability studies which focused on dissection of failed components revealed that misapplication was a great source of component failure. It is probable that at least one accomplishment of reliability engineering has been to alert designers to this fact and to encourage them to reduce the number of misapplications sharply by checks and design reviews.

Any experienced designer probably knows of many cases in which a sophisticated scheme is being used to accomplish a task which could be done much more simply and reliably. Often the situation is such that a simpler design lacks a bit in performance, which can be tolerated if the benefits are large decreases in cost and increases in reliability.

B.8.3 Conservative Design and Derating

The idea of operating components below their basic ratings is fundamental to various fields of engineering design. The rated parameters can be voltages, currents, powers, force or torque loads, velocities, temperatures, humidity, etc. In the structural-engineering field the idea of a safety factor is a basic one. The electronics field has been slower to accept this as a basic tenet of design. A vivid example of the neglect of conservative design principles was brought to the author's attention many years ago when many vacuum-tube circuits were being transistorized. A standard *vacuum-tube* servo amplifier with two driving stages and a push-pull output was to be transistorized, the purpose of the change being to provide a new standard *transistor* servo amplifier which was smaller and more reliable. The new circuit was considerably reduced in volume and weight, but a preliminary reliability analysis revealed that the transistor amplifier had roughly the same reliability as the vacuum-tube version. This came as a shock, since even the very sketchy failure information on transistors revealed that they were superior to vacuum tubes. (Qualitative reasoning also predicted a great superiority of transistors over vacuum tubes.) A careful look at the problem showed that overzealousness to achieve maximum miniaturization had led to two important errors in the transistor-amplifier design. Tantalum capacitors were used at their maximum rated voltage wherever large capacitances were needed. Although reliable tantalum capacitors are now available, at that time tantalum capacitors were still new, and the early reliability data predicted sizable failure rates. In contrast, the vacuum-tube version used aluminum electrolytic capacitors, which were operated well below their maximum voltages. The transistors used were also operated near their maximum ratings, while the vacuum-tube model used tubes whose maximum plate dissipations comfortably exceeded the circuit design levels. In all fairness it should be mentioned that both tantalum capacitors and silicon transistors were very expensive at that time, and only a limited number of models were available. For example, there were two common silicon power transistors available, a medium-power one, which cost $25, and a high-power one, which cost $100.

B.8.4 Creative Design

The principles of design simplicity and conservatism stressed in the preceding sections are those which one would expect to find in any competent design. A superior job can often be done if the designer uses some thought to create a new or improved circuit with better reliability.

For example, electronic designers well know that push-pull circuits have definite advantages in terms of power output and linearity. They also provide a measure of redundancy, however, since failure of one side of the circuit generally results in continued circuit operation at a degraded level. Of course there are generally added parts in the push-pull driver stage, but the *redundancy gain* should far outweigh the *complexity loss*.

B.8.5 Component Improvement

Another approach to bettering system reliability is to improve the reliability of all the constituent components. Actually we assume that preliminary reliability studies have identified the most critical components so that effort can be focused on these components. The first attempt in this direction was the manufacture of rugged five-star tubes in the late 1940s and early 1950s. These tubes were supposed to be less sensitive to environmental stresses and have improved lifetimes. One of the first comprehensive high-reliability-parts development programs was for the Minuteman missile system. Manufacturers developed lines of high-reliability components at premium prices. This is a costly and difficult means of achieving reliability, but is quite effective up to a point. An example of Minuteman failure rates compared with ordinary parts and space qualified parts is given in Shooman (1968), Table 6.2.

B.9 REDUNDANCY

B.9.1 Redundancy Concepts

As noted earlier, the term *redundancy* in this book is used to mean, in a broad sense, the creation of new parallel paths in a system structure to improve the system reliability. The straightforward approach is to take the existing system and connect a duplicate one in parallel. For example, to increase the reliability of an automobile braking system[1] one might install a duplicate set of brake shoes and cylinders on each wheel and feed these with separate hydraulic lines attached to a second master cylinder. (One could probably assume to a good approximation that the brake pedal and linkage will not fail, and therefore these need not be duplicated.) This results in two separate systems and just about doubles the cost, weight, and volume of the braking system. An approach like this which involves paralleling the entire system or unit is called *system* or *unit redundancy*. Another technique is to parallel two master cylinders and run two parallel hydraulic lines to each wheel which connect to a parallel pair of wheel cylinders. In this case each component is individually paralleled. Such an approach is called *component redundancy*. In the early 1960s several American automobiles appeared with redundant braking systems. In some a compromise system was used. A single brake pedal activates two separate master cylinders. One master cylinder feeds a set of hydraulic lines which connects to the front-wheel brake cylinders, and the other master cylinder operates the rear-wheel brake cylinders through its own set of lines. Obviously this compromise system must operate on the principle that one set of brakes, either the front or rear, while not providing perfect operation, still yields safe operation.

B.9.2 Component and Unit Redundancy

The discussion of the previous section has shown that there are several ways in which to apply redundancy. The two techniques which are easily classified and studied are component and unit redundancy. In fact one can prove that component redundancy is superior to unit redundancy in a wide variety of situations.

Consider the three systems shown in Fig. B.24. The reliability expression for system *a* is

$$R_a(p) = P(x_1)P(x_2) = p^2 \tag{B.97}$$

where both x_1 and x_2 are independent and identical and $P(x_1) = P(x_2) = p$. The reliability for the system of *b* is given simply by

$$R_b(p) = P(x_1 x_2 + x_1' x_2')$$

---

[1]"How Effective Are Dual Brakes?" (1965).

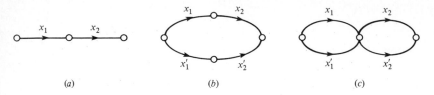

Figure B.24 Comparison of three different systems: (a) single system; (b) unit redundancy; (c) component redundancy.

For IIU[1] with individual reliabilities of p

$$R_b(p) = 2R_a - R_a^2 = p^2(2 - p^2) \qquad (\text{B.98})$$

In the case of system c one can combine each component pair in parallel to obtain

$$R_c(p) = P(x_1 + x_1')P(x_2 + x_2')$$

Assuming IIU, we obtain

$$R_c(p) = p^2(2 - p)^2 \qquad (\text{B.99})$$

One can show by algebraic manipulation (see Shooman, 1968, p. 282) that $R_c \geq R_b \geq R_a$.

A simpler proof of the above principle can be formulated by considering the system tie sets. Clearly in Fig. B.24b the tie sets are x_1x_2, $x_1'x_2'$, whereas in Fig. B.24c the tie sets are x_1x_2, $x_1'x_2'$, x_1x_2', $x_1'x_2$. Since the system reliability is the probability of the union of the tie sets, and since system c has the same two tie sets as system b as well as two additional ones, the component redundancy configuration has a larger reliability than the unit redundancy configuration. It is easy to see that this tie-set proof can be extended to the general case.

The specific result can be broadened to include a large number of structures. (See Shooman, 1968, pp. 283ff.)

B.9.3 Practical Redundancy

The previous sections on redundancy have discussed various redundancy models without regard to how such models can be realized. The main problem is that one cannot simply parallel elements without special attention to impedance levels, power and signal gains, linearity, etc.

If we try to add redundancy to the voltage-divider network shown in Fig. B.25a, some problems will be encountered. The first idea is to parallel the 90-and 10-Ω resistors. This yields a slightly different circuit (same divider ratio but twice the current drain and half the internal impedance). Also failures in any component would result in a different transformation ratio. A slight improvement over

---

[1]IIU stands for independent, identical units.

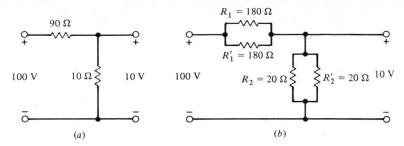

Figure B.25 Voltage divider networks: (*a*) normal voltage divider; (*b*) semiredundant voltage divider.

the above situation is obtained in the circuit of Fig. B.25*b*. The transformation ratio, current drain and internal impedances all are identical to the circuit of Fig. B.25*a* as long as all components are good. The network of Fig. B.25*a* will give an output voltage of 10 V if all components are working. If either R_1 or R_1' open-circuits, the output voltage will drop to 5.25 V, and if either R_2 or R_2' open-circuits, the output voltage will rise to 18.2 V. In most situations such a variation in output would be considered intolerable, and the reliability of circuit *b* is actually poorer than that of *a*. Thus, the reliability of Fig. B.25*a* is given by p^2, where p represents the reliability of any resistor, and that of Fig. B.25*b* is p^4. If voltage variations between 5.25 and 18.20 V are acceptable, the redundant circuit has a reliability of $(2p - p^2)^2$. In order to apply redundancy in voltage-divider circuits where tight tolerances on the voltage variations are required, other techniques must be used.

One approach is to devise some sort of switching scheme with relays or diodes to switch in the redundant element only when the primary one fails. Such a system is represented by a standby model (see the following section). It is interesting that practical application of redundancy often leads to a standby system.

B.9.4 Majority Voting

If we try to parallel digital logic gates to achieve redundancy we run into problems similar to those of the previous section. One very popular approach is to use a technique called majority voting.

If we forget about the details of how a particular digital circuit operates, we can view it merely as a device which accepts several input variables which are 0 or 1 and produces an output which is 0 or 1. Thus, if we had two parallel systems, we would compare the outputs to make a judgment on the proper answer. If the two outputs agree, we conclude that both systems are working correctly, yielding the right answer with a probability p^2, or both systems have failed, giving the wrong answer with a probability q^2. If one output is a 0 and the other output a 1, clearly one of the two circuits is in error. We cannot tell from the information provided, however, which is correct. Obviously the answer is to use an odd

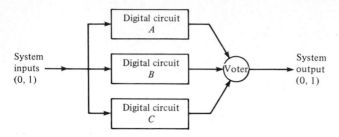

Figure B.26 Majority logic.

number of parallel circuits and side with the majority. This in essence creates a k-out-of-m system. This technique is called *majority voting* or *majority logic*.

The system shown in Fig. B.26 consists of three parallel digital circuits, A, B, and C, with the same input. The outputs of all three circuits are compared by the voter. The voter sides with the majority and gives the majority opinion as the system output. If all three circuits are operating properly, all outputs agree, and the system output is correct. If one element has failed, so that it produces an incorrect output, the voter will choose as the system output the output of the two good elements, since they agree; the system output will therefore be correct. If two elements have failed, the voter will agree with the majority, the two which have failed, and the system output will be incorrect. The system output will also be incorrect if all three circuits have failed. All the above conclusions assume that a circuit fails in such a way that it always yields the complement of the correct input. Using the above assumption, and assuming that the *voter does not fail*, the system reliability is given by

$$R = P(AB + AC + BC)$$

If all the digital circuits are independent and identical with probability of success p, then this equation can be rewritten in terms of the binomial theorem

$$R = B(3:3) + B(2:3)$$

$$= \binom{3}{3}p^3(1-p)^0 + \binom{3}{2}p^2(1-p)^1$$

$$= 3p^2 - 2p^3 = p^2(3 - 2p) \quad \text{(B.100)}$$

This is, of course, the reliability expression for a two-out-of-three system. The assumption that the digital elements fail so as to produce the complement of the correct input may not be valid. Also the voter is vulnerable to failure, and a derivation of the reliability of a majority logic circuit with an imperfect voter is discussed in Shooman, 1968, p. 300ff.

B.9.5 Standby Redundancy

Standby systems are frequently used both on their own merits and when it is difficult to connect units in parallel in the normal fashion. In such a system, the

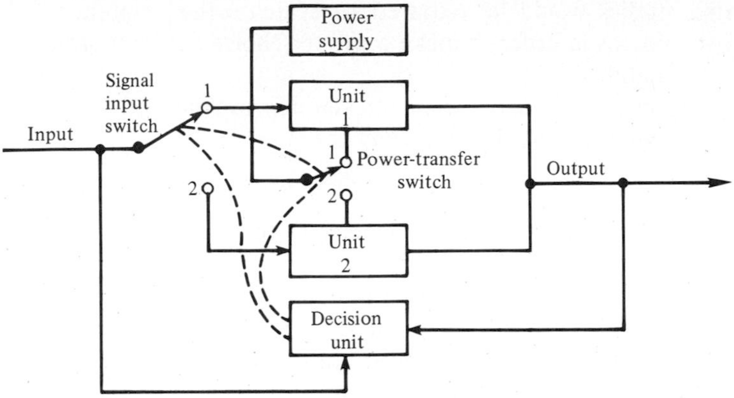

Figure B.27 A standby system.

overall reliability is very much dependent on the reliability of the standby switch. A poor switch can even yield a system which is worse than a single element. The design of such a system centers on the design of a simple and reliable switching element.

The switch in a standby system must perform three functions: (1) It must have some sort of decision element which is capable of sensing improper operation; (2) the switch must then remove the signal input[1] from unit 1 and apply it to unit 2; (3) if the element is an active one, the power must also be transferred from element 1 to element 2. These three functions are shown symbolically in Fig. B.27. Often the decision unit, input switch, and power switch can be incorporated into one unit. For example, if two electronic amplifiers are to be connected in standby, we could use a relay to perform all the decision and switching functions. If the amplifier is to operate properly, the output voltage must be equal to some amplification constant A times the input voltage. The relay could be built so as to have two opposing coils with the number of turns sized so that the force of coil 1 is equal and opposite to the force of coil 2 when e_1 volts is applied to coil 1 and Ae_1 volts to coil 2. Whenever this balance was off by too large an amount, the relay would operate. One set of relay contacts would transfer the input signal from amplifier 1 to amplifier 2, while other contacts would transfer the power. Another contact might turn on a warning light to notify the operator that the system had switched to standby.

Of course there might be transient problems when the standby unit was switched in. These could be severe enough to call for a straight parallel system in which both units were always in operation, dividing the signal between them.

---

[1] In some cases it might be better to feed both units with the same input signal and switch at the output. One could also switch at both input and output. In this section only input switching is considered; however, the results will also apply to output-switching systems and both input and output switching if the same number of states of switch failure is used.

Detailed engineering studies would be required to evaluate the reliability and feasibility of the two systems in order to make a proper choice between ordinary parallel and standby reliability.

The reliability expression for a two-element standby system with constant hazards and a perfect switch can be shown to be

$$R_{sb}(t) = e^{-\lambda t}(1 + \lambda t) \tag{B.101}$$

(See Eq. (5.86) of Shooman, 1968.) Shooman also shows that the standby system is always superior to the ordinary parallel one. This will not be the case if the switch is imperfect. The role of switching device in determining system reliability will depend on the failure model used. As a first approach we shall assume that whenever the switch fails, the system fails, even if both standby units are perfect. This is a rather simplified but conservative model.

If the switch has a constant-hazard λ, Eq. (B.101) is modified, yielding

$$R_1(t) = e^{-\lambda_s t}e^{-\lambda t}(1 + \lambda t) \tag{B.102}$$

More sophisticated standby system models are discussed in Sec. 6.9 of Shooman (1968).

PROBLEMS[1]

B.1 A series system is composed of n identical independent components. The component probability of success is p_c and $q_c = 1 - p_c$.

(a) Show that if $q_c \ll 1$, the system reliability R is approximately given by $R \approx 1 - nq_c$.

(b) If the system has 10 components and R must be 0.99, how good must the components be?

B.2 A parallel system is composed of 10 identical independent components. If the system reliability R must be 0.99, how poor can the components be?

B.3 A 10-element system is constructed of independent identical components so that 5 out of the 10 elements are necessary for system success. If the system reliability R must be 0.99, how good must the components be?

B.4 Draw reliability graphs for the following three reliability block diagrams. *Note*: The probabilities of system success for independent identical units are given below each figure.

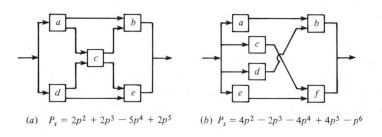

(a) $P_s = 2p^2 + 2p^3 - 5p^4 + 2p^5$ (b) $P_s = 4p^2 - 2p^3 - 4p^4 + 4p^5 - p^6$

[1]Problems B.1 through B.4, B.6, and B.10 through B.12 are taken from Shooman (1968).

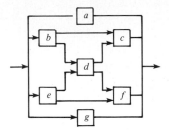

(c) $P_s = 2p + p^2 - 2p^3 - 7p^4 + 14p^5 - 9p^6 + 2p^2$

B.5 Formulate a fault-tree model for the systems given in Prob. B.4.

B.6 Find all the minimal tie sets and cut sets for the three systems in Prob. B.4.

B.7 Solve Probs. 5.2 and 5.3.

B.8 Assume numerical values for the axes of Fig. 5.1, and explain the cost trade-offs of burn-in and replacement.

B.9 Check the MTTF computation given in Eq. (B.54).

B.10 A communication system is composed of a fixed-frequency transmitter T_1 and a fixed-frequency receiver R_1. The fixed frequency is f_1, and both receiver and transmitter have constant hazards λ. In order to improve the reliability, a second receiver and transmitter operating on frequency f_2 are used to provide a redundant channel. Both channels are identical, except for frequency. Construct a reliability diagram for the system and write the reliability function. In order to improve reliability a tuning unit is added to each receiver so that it can operate at frequency f_1 or f_2. The hazard for each tuning unit is given by λ'. Draw the new reliability diagram and write the reliability function. Sketch the reliability of the improved system and the original two-channel system. Assume that $\lambda' = 0.1\lambda$ and repeat for $\lambda' = 10\lambda$. (Use series approximations, if necessary.)

B.11 Solve for the reliability expression for a three-element standby system using a Markov model. All elements are independent identical units with constant-hazard λ.

B.12 For a single component with repair, $R(t)$ and $A(t)$ are given by Eqs. (B.91) and (B.94). If we specify that $R(t_1) = 0.9$,

    (a) What can you say about $A(t_1)$?

    (b) How are λ and μ constrained if $A(t_1) \geq 0.99$?

APPENDIX
C

SUMMARY OF GRAPH THEORY

C.1 INTRODUCTION

The program graph representation is used in several sections of this book. We use some graph properties to discuss a measure of complexity in Chap. 3, and graph properties are used in the analysis of the testing process in Chap. 4. Last, we use graphs not of the program but of the development organization in Chap. 6, to discuss the effects of organization on productivity.

C.2 PROGRAM GRAPH MODELS

As we develop the salient points of graph theory which will be needed, we should keep in mind the imperfections and incompleteness of the graph model of a program. First of all, a graph model does not depict program operands or in any way represent program storage. In fact, in terms of operators, it only really treats transfer of control operators and ignores the difference between a single assignment statement and sequences of assignment statements as long as no transfer of control occurs within the sequence. Second, all programs have a sequence associated with the processing of instructions, thus the proper graph representation is a directed graph, or digraph. However, some of the results of graph theory which we will use are those which apply to ordinary graphs (undirected graphs). Last, in order to apply some of the theorems, we will need some features of the program graph modified to place it in a standard form. Notwithstanding the above problems, program graphs are a useful tool in describing programs.

C.3 DEFINITIONS

C.3.1 Introduction

Unfortunately, there is less uniformity of terms in graph theory than exists in other mathematical fields. Some of the terms used come from the theoretical studies by the pioneers in the field. Other terms come from those in common use in various fields of application, such as topology, electrical engineering, psychology, management, operations research, etc. By and large we will follow the terminology of Berge (1966; 1973), and Marshall (1971), but will include, where appropriate, some of the synonyms used in the literature.

C.3.2 A Set Model of a Graph

In general, a graph is a mathematical representation which results in a figure containing points connected by lines or arrows. In a more basic fashion, we can relate a graph to set theory if we identify the elements of the set as the collection X and define a mapping function Γ. Then, each element of X becomes a point and the mapping function Γ gives rise to the lines or arrows interconnecting the points. Examples of physical situations representable by a graph are given in Table C.1.

Each element belonging to X is represented by a point in the graph called a *vertex* or *node*. If x and y are two vertices of a graph, and if the mapping rules Γ define that y is related to x, then there is a connection between x and y in the graph. If the connection rules include orientation or sequence of succession with respect to x and y, then they are connected by a line with an arrowhead in the graph called an *arc* or a *directed branch*. If the arrow direction of the graph is from x to y, then x is called the *initial vertex* and y is called the *terminal vertex*. If *all* the branches in a graph are directed, the graph is called a *directed graph* or *digraph*. A digraph is really a special case of general graph theory; however, in this book (as is true in many other application areas), it is the case we will generally deal with. If the mapping rules Γ define the same connection between x and y as between y and x, then the orientation of the line connecting x and y is

Table C.1 Physical situations representable by a graph

X—Set elements	Γ—Set-mapping rules
1. Positions of pieces on a chess board	1. Rules for moving and capturing pieces
2. A group of relatives	2. The parenthood relationships among relatives
3. Units of electrical apparatus	3. The wires interconnecting the units
4. Instructions in a computer program	4. The rules of syntax and sequence which govern the processing of the instructions

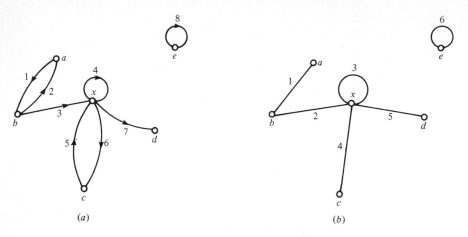

Figure C.1 Example of a directed graph (*a*) and its equivalent "regular" graph (*b*).

immaterial; it contains no arrowhead and is called an *edge* or *branch*. Not all authors assign different words to directed or undirected lines joining vertices; thus the terms *arc*, *directed arc*, *edge*, and *directed edge* are common and may cause initial confusion. Fortunately, one seldom encounters a discussion of graphs without a figure, and a quick inspection of the figure (and the lack or presence of arrowheads) generally eliminates any confusion.

An example of two graphs is given in Fig. C.1. Note in the example that the directed graph has eight arcs; however, the equivalent "regular" graph has only six edges.

C.4 PROPERTIES OF DIRECTED GRAPHS

Two *arcs* are said to be *adjacent* if they are distinct and have a vertex in common. Two *vertices* are said to be *adjacent* if they are distinct and there exists an arc between them (in either direction).

A *path* is a sequence of arcs of a graph which possess the property that the terminal vertex of each arc coincides with the initial vertex of the succeeding arc. The first vertex in the path sequence, x_1, will be called the *initial vertex* of the path, and the final vertex of the path sequence, x_k, will be called the *terminal vertex* of the path.

A path is *simple* if it does not use the same arc twice, and *composite* otherwise. We can denote paths by listing the arc sequence or the node-pair sequence (we always list the initial vertex of an arc first and its terminal vertex second). Thus, we may speak of the path 1, 3, 7 of Fig. C.1*a* or denote it by *a*, *b*, *x*, *d*. This path is a simple path. A composite path between the same initial and terminal vertices would be 1, 3, 4, 4, 7, which could be denoted as *a*, *b*, *x*, *x*, *d*. If we wished to focus our attention on the path 1, 3 we could refer to it as path *a*, *b*,

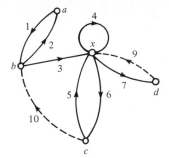

Figure C.2 Alteration of the graph of Fig. C.2*a* to produce a strongly connected graph.

x or, in more abbreviated fashion, as the simple path from a to x. If we were to use the term "the simple path from a to d", it would be ambiguous since there are several: $(1, 3, 7)$, $(1, 3, 4, 7)$, $(1, 3, 6, 5, 7)$, etc.

A path is *elementary* if it does not meet the same vertex twice. In terms of the example of Fig. C.1*a*, there are three simple paths between a and d, yet only the path 1, 3, 7 is an elementary one.

A finite arc sequence yields a *finite path*, and an infinite arc sequence yields an *infinite path*. Since we will be applying graphs to programs which terminate, we will always deal with finite paths. The one exception is the erroneous program which contains an infinite loop because of an error. This is really just a temporary state until we discover and correct the problem; thus we need say no more.

A *circuit* is a finite path in which the initial vertex x_1 coincides with the terminal vertex x_k. In essence a circuit is a path which closes on itself. We can define an *elementary circuit* as one in which no vertex is traversed more than once, except when $x_1 = x_k$. In a similar fashion we can define a *simple circuit* as a circuit in which no arc is used more than once.

The *length* of a *path* is the number of arcs in the sequence. The *length* of a *circuit* is the length of the path from which it is formed. Circuits can have a length of unity, as is illustrated by the circuits x, x and e, e in Fig. C.1*a*. Berge calls circuits of length 1 loops; however, because of common usage (in control systems and flowgraph terminology[1]) we will use the term *loop* to be synonymous with *circuit*, and we will use the term *self-loop* to refer to circuits of length 1.

A *digraph* is *complete* if every distinct node pair is connected in at least one of the two possible directions. If we examine the graph given in Fig. C.1*a*, we see that node e is not connected to the remainder of the graph; thus the graph is not complete. If we consider the two different parts of the graph—vertex e and vertices a, b, x, c, and d—we have partitioned the graph into two subgraphs. Each of these parts (components) is complete.

A *digraph* is *strongly connected* if there is a path joining every pair of vertices in the digraph. If we examine the subgraph a, b, x, c, d of Fig. C.1*a*, we see that although it is complete, it is not strongly connected, because there is no way to get from node d to node c, nor from node c to node b, etc. In Fig. C.2 we have added

---

[1] Mason (1953).

arcs 9 and 10 (shown as dashed lines), which make the new digraph strongly connected.

C.5 PROPERTIES OF NONDIRECTED GRAPHS

Most of the concepts of digraphs have direct analogs in the theory of nondirected graphs, and in fact most authors treat the nondirected case first. In many cases, the definition is identical if we replace the concept of an arc with that of an edge.

Two *edges* are said to be *adjacent* if they are distinct and have a common vertex. Two *vertices* are said to be *adjacent* if they are distinct and there exists an edge between them.

A *chain* is a sequence of edges $y_1, y_2, \ldots, y_r$ where y_1 is the first edge and y_r the last edge. For each edge y_j $(1 < j < r)$ there is one vertex in common with the preceding edge, y_{j-1}, and the other vertex is in common with the succeeding edge, y_{j+1}.

A chain is *simple* if the edges are all different, and is *composite* otherwise. A chain is *elementary* if every vertex belonging to the chain appears only once. The *length* of a chain is equal to the number of edges in the sequence. A chain can be *infinite* or *finite*.

A *cycle* is a finite chain in which the initial vertex and the terminal vertex are the same. A *simple cycle* is one containing a simple chain. An *elementary cycle* is one containing an elementary chain.

A graph is *weakly connected* if there is a *chain* joining *every* pair of vertices in the graph.

C.6 INDEPENDENCE AND BASIS PROPERTIES

In order to further explore the relationship between the physical properties of a program and its graph representation, we must first introduce the concepts of *independence* and *basis*. In the preceding sections many of the fundamental concepts of graph theory were developed from set theory. In a similar fashion, the two new terms we have introduced draw their fundamental graph theory definitions from the theory of n-dimensional vector space.[1]

If we define a set of vectors $x_1, x_2, \ldots, x_n$ to be *linearly dependent* then there exists a set of numbers $a_1, a_2, \ldots, a_n$ which are not all zero such that

$$a_1 x_1 + a_2 x_2 + \cdots + a_n x_n = 0 \qquad (C.1)$$

If no such set of numbers $a_1, a_2, \ldots, a_n$ satisfying Eq. (C.1) exists, then the set of vectors $x_1, x_2, \ldots, x_n$ are said to be *linearly independent*.

A term closely related to *independence* is *basis*.

---

[1]Gantmacher (1959), p. 50; Berge (1966), p. 28.

The concept of a *basis* is used to define the properties of fundamental sets of "building blocks" from which any vector in the space can be constructed by linear combination of the blocks. Any system of n linearly independent vectors e_1, $e_2, \ldots, e_n$ forms a *basis* in n-dimensional vector space. It is easy to show that any arbitrary vector can be made up of a linear combination of the basis vectors. Although there are many different bases, all are of dimension n.

If we associate the concept of a vector with each cycle (circuit), then we can speak of the analogous concepts of *independent cycles* (*circuits*) and a *cycle* (*circuit*) *basis*. Based upon these concepts we can define the following fundamental measures of the "cycle (circuit) complexity" of a graph or a digraph.

C.7 COMPUTATION OF THE CYCLOMATIC NUMBER

C.7.1 The Edge, Node, and Component Formula

The *cyclomatic number* $v(G)$, of graph G is equal to the maximum number of linearly independent cycles. The *cyclomatic number* $v(G)$ of a *strongly connected digraph* is equal to the maximum number of linearly independent circuits.[1]

The cyclomatic number is relatively easy to compute. We cite three techniques below for computing $v(G)$. The first method is a formula based on the m edges (arcs), the n nodes, and the p separate components. The formula is

$$v(G) = m - n + p \qquad (C.2)$$

In the graph given in Fig. C.1*b* there are six edges, six nodes, and two separate parts; thus $v(G) = 2$.

The other two methods are the *tree method* and the *face method*.

C.7.2 The Tree Method

If G is a graph, then we can define a *subgraph* G_S as any graph constructed from a subset of the vertices of G and a subset of the edges (arcs) of G. A *partial graph* G_P contains all the vertices of G and a subset of the edges (arcs). If G is a connected graph then a *tree*, G_T, is defined as a partial graph which is connected and has no cycles. It can be shown that the number of edges which must be removed from G to form a tree G_T is equal to the number of independent cycles.[2] If we use the strongly connected graph of Fig. C.2 as an example (including the dotted branches), we see that elimination of arcs 1, 10, 5, 4, and 9 reduces the graph to a tree. (Of course this is not the only tree; there are many. However, the number of deleted arcs is always the same.) Thus $v(G) = 5$ for this graph. Of

[1] For the cyclomatic number $v(G)$ of a graph with n vertices, see Berge (1966), p. 29; see also Marshall (1971), p. 42.

[2] Berge (1966), p. 155.

course the same result could have been obtained by counting the five vertices, the nine arcs, and the one part, and substituting into Eq. (C.2).

C.7.3 The Face Method

The above two methods of computing $v(G)$ work for all graphs; however, there is a third method which works for planar graphs. A planar graph is one which can be drawn on a plane with no crossing branches. Sometimes one must redraw branches to prove planarity. Although planar graphs are a special case of general graphs, this restriction causes little problem, because one can show that all structured programs can be represented as planar graphs, and in fact so can most unstructured ones (see Prob. C.6). (McCabe, 1976, uses 63 examples of graphs and subgraphs, and all except one are obviously planar. The one exception, complex nonstructured graph with $v(G) = 19$, requires the redrawing of four arcs to prove planarity.) In the case of a planar graph, each face of the graph represents a simple independent cycle; thus, the number of faces is equal to the cyclomatic number. The faces are the loops with a minimum number of branches, e.g. in Fig. C.1a, (1, 2), (4), (5, 6), (3) and in Fig. C.2 (1, 2), (3, 6, 10), (4), (7, 9). The reader should verify that the face count in the graphs of Figs. C.1b and C.2 agree with our previous computations of $v(G)$.

C.8 DIGRAPH MODELS OF PROGRAMS

We now discuss how we can model a computer program by a digraph. It is important that we represent the start point in the program by an initial graph vertex, and the stop point by a terminal graph vertex. The reason for this is that some programs can be started at various points in the program. A complicated example of this is an interrupt in a minicomputer program which returns control to an address other than the value of the program counter at the initiation of the interrupt. A simpler example is a microprocessor which is under the control of a simple Load and Go type of executive stored in the read-only memory. We can start the program at a number of different addresses by loading the start address in a particular location and typing Go. Last, the more advanced hand-held programmable calculators allow the use of alphabetic labels throughout the program, and the program can be started at any of these points by pushing the corresponding label key. If such is the case we must provide a start vertex as well as an entry vertex. Similarly, many programs have more than one stop instruction in the program. In such a program we will consider all the stop instructions as a common exit vertex and also add a stop vertex (see Fig. 3.15).

Since we have decided to use digraphs, we must ensure that the digraph is strongly connected in order to use the complexity measure. We can easily ensure that a program graph is strongly connected by adding a single arc from the exit vertex to the entry vertex, if none already exists. Since we are assuming that the program is properly constructed, the initial program digraph will possess the property that permits any other vertex to be reachable from the entry vertex. (If it is impossible to execute, i.e., reach, an instruction in a program, then the program is faulty.) Similarly, the exit vertex is reachable from any other vertex. (There must always be an end to any program without an infinite loop.) Thus, if we connect the exit vertex to the entry vertex, any vertex is reachable from any other (except the start and stop vertices), and the digraph is strongly connected. (See Fig. 3.15.)

The aforementioned rules for formulation of a digraph model of a program can be summarized as follows:

1. If the program contains multiple entries, choose one and add an arc from the start vertex to the appropriate entry point in the program.
2. If the program contains multiple stop statements, consider them to be all the same vertex.
3. If the program does not contain an arc from the stop vertex to the start vertex then insert one.
4. If after steps 1, 2, and 3 the start vertex is not a sole initial vertex, call it the entry node, and precede it by a new start node connected by an arc.
5. If after steps 1, 2, 3, and 4 the stop vertex is not a sole terminal vertex, then call it the exit vertex, and follow it by a single branch and a new stop vertex.

Examples of the computation of $v(G)$ appear in the problems at the end of this appendix.

PROBLEMS

C.1 Write a short (one- or two-sentence) definition of all the graph theoretic terms used in this appendix.

C.2 Choose three programs and draw the control graph for each. Calculate the cyclomatic complexity for each graph.

C.3 Can you find a computer program whose graph is not planar? Comment.

C.4 In electric-circuit theory the number of branches in the circuit is equal to the number of loops plus the number of nodes. Is there any relationship between this and the cyclomatic complexity theorem? Explain.

C.5 There is a formula in topology which states that the number of vertices plus the number of faces of regular polyhedrons is equal to the number of edges plus 2.

(*a*) Check this theorem for a tetrahedron (pyramid), a hexahedron (cube), an octahedron, an icosahedron, and a dodecahedron.

(*b*) Does this theorem relate to the cyclomatic complexity theorem? Explain.

C.6 Prove that the graph of a structured program is planar.

C.7 Give an example of a nonplanar program graph.

BIBLIOGRAPHY*

Abramovitz, M., and I. Stegun, eds.: *Handbook of Mathematical Functions*, National Bureau of Standards, Washington, D.C., June 1972.

Adams, E. C.: "Minimizing Cost Impact of Software Defects," RC 8228, IBM T. J. Watson Research Labs, Yorktown Heights, N.Y., Apr. 11, 1980.

Aho, A., et al.: *The Design and Analysis of Computer Algorithms*, Addison-Wesley, Reading, Mass., 1974.

Akiyama, Fumio: "An Example of Software System Debugging," *Proc. IFIP Congress '71*, Ljubljana, Yugoslavia, American Federation of Information Processing Societies, Montvale, N.J., 1971.

Amoroso, S., et al.: "Language Evaluation Coordinating Committee Report to HOLWG," National Technical Information Service Report NTIS no. AD-A037634, Jan. 14, 1977.

Amster, S. J., and M. L. Shooman: "Software Reliability: An Overview," pp. 655–685 in Barlow et al. (1975).

Amster, S. J., et al.: "An Experiment in Automatic Quality Evaluation of Software," *Proc. Polytechnic Symp. Comp. Software Eng.*, Polytechnic Press, Brooklyn, 1976, pp. 171–197.

Arguimbau, Lawrence B.: *Vacuum-Tube Circuits*, Wiley, New York, 1948.

Aron, J. D.: "Estimating Resources for Large Programming Systems," NATO Conference, Rome, Oct. 27–30, 1969, pp. 206–217 in Buxton et al. (1976). (Also reprinted in Putnam and Wolverton, 1977.)

Ashcroft, E., and Zohar Manna: "The Translation of 'GO TO' Programs to 'WHILE' Programs," *Proc. 1971 IFIP Cong.* Ljubljana, Yugoslavia, Aug. 23–28, 1971, American Elsevier, New York, 1972.

Avizienis, Algirdas: "Fault-Tolerance: The Survival Attribute of Digital Systems," *Proc. IEEE*, vol. 66, no. 10, October 1978, pp. 1109–1125.

Backus, J. W., et al.: "The FORTRAN Automatic Coding System," *Proc. Western Joint Comp. Conf.*, vol. 11, 1964, pp. 188–198.

Baggi, D. L., and Martin L. Shooman: "An Automatic Driver for Pseudo-exhaustive Software Testing," *Digest of Papers COMPCON '78*, IEEE, New York, Feb. 28, 1978, p. 278.

*Additional references follow at the end of the bibliography.

Baggi, D. L., and Martin L. Shooman: "Software Test Models and Implementation of Associated Test Drivers," report SRS-116/Poly EE 79-054, Polytechnic Institute of New York, November 1979.

Bailey, N. T. J.: "On Estimating the Size of Mobile Populations from Recapture Data," *Biometrika*, vol. 38, 1951, pp. 293–306.

Baker, F. T.: "Chief Programmer Team Management of Production Programming," *IBM Sys. J.*, vol. 11, no. 1, 1972.

Balaban, H.: "The F-16 RIW Program," *Proc. Ann. Reliability and Maintainability Symp.*, IEEE, New York, 1979.

Barlow, Richard, and Ernest M. Scheuer: "Reliability Growth during a Development Testing Program," *Technometrics*, vol. 8, no. 1, February 1966, pp. 53–60.

Barlow, Richard, et al., eds.: *Reliability and Fault Tree Analysis*, Society for Industrial and Applied Mathematics, Philadelphia, 1975.

Barnett, Michael P.: "Computer Typesetting—Experiments and Prospects," MIT Press, Cambridge, Mass., 1965.

Basili, Victor R.: "Quantitative Software Complexity Models: A Panel Summary," *Proc. Workshop Quant. Software Models for Reliability, Complexity, and Cost: An Assessment of the State of the Art*, Oct. 9–11, 1979, IEEE, New York, pp. 243–245.

Becerril, J. L., et al.: "Grammar Characterization of Flowgraphs," *IBM J. Res. and Dev.*, vol. 24, no. 6, November 1980, pp. 756–763.

Beiser, B.: *Architecture and Engineering of Digital Computer Complexes*, vol. 1, Plenum, New York, 1971, Chap. 7.

Belady, L. A.: "On Software Complexity," *Proc. Workshop Quant. Software Models for Reliability, Complexity, and Cost: An Assessment of the State of the Art*, Oct. 9–11, 1979, IEEE, New York, pp. 90–94.

Belady, L. A., and M. M. Lehman: "Programming System Dynamics of the Meta-dynamics of Systems in Maintenance and Growth," IBM research report RC-3546, Yorktown Heights, N.Y., Sept. 17, 1971.

Belady, L. A., and M. M. Lehman: "An Introduction to Growth Dynamics," pp. 503–511 in Freiberger (1972).

Belady, L. A., and M. M. Lehman: "The Evolution Dynamics of Large Programs," IBM research report RC-5615, Yorktown Heights, N.Y., Sept. 9, 1975.

Belady, L. A., and M. M. Lehman: "The Characteristics of Large Systems," IBM research report RC-6285, Yorktown Heights, N.Y., Sept. 13, 1977.

Bell, C. Gordon, and Allen Newell: *Computer Structures: Readings and Examples*, McGraw-Hill, New York, 1971.

Bell, C. Gordon, et al.: *Computer Engineering—A DEC View of Hardware System Design*, Digital Press, Bedford, Mass., 1978.

Berge, Claude: *The Theory of Graphs and Its Applications*, Wiley, New York, 1966.

Berge, Claude: *Graphs and Hypergraphs*, North-Holland Publishing Company, Amsterdam, 1973.

Bernard, H. H.: "Bubbles Take On Disks," *IEEE Spectrum*, May 1980, pp. 30–33.

Bernhard, Robert: "The 'No-Downtime' Computer," *IEEE Spectrum*, September 1980.

Bianchi, M. H., and J. L. Wood: "A User's Viewpoint on the Programmers Workbench," *Proc. 2d Int. Conf. Software Eng.*, IEEE, New York, October 1976.

Blum, B. I., and K. E. Richeson: "Inexpensive Computer Assisted Software Engineering for Moderate Sized Programs," *Digest of Papers, Spring COMPCON '77*, IEEE, New York, February 1977, pp. 202–206.

Boehm, Barry W.: "Software and Its Impact: A Quantitative Assessment," *Datamation*, May 1973.

Boehm, Barry: "The High Cost of Software," p. 4 in Horowitz (1975).

Boehm, Barry: "Software Reliability—Measurement and Management," *Abr. Proc. AIAA Software Mgmt. Conf., Los Angeles Sec.*, June 1976.

Boehm, Barry: *Software Engineering Economics*, Prentice-Hall, Englewood Cliffs, N.J., 1981. (*a*)

Boehm, Barry: *Software Life Cycle Factors*, TRW Software Series, Redondo Beach, Calif., January 1981. (*b*)

Boehm, B., et al.: "Characteristics of Software Quality," TRW report no. TRW-SS-73-09, TRW Systems, Redondo Beach, Calif., 1973.

Boehm, Barry W., et al.: "Some Experience with Automated Aids to the Design of Large-Scale Reliable Software," *Proc. 1975 Int. Conf. Reliable Software*, IEEE, New York, no. 75, CHO 940-7CSR, 1975.

Boehm, Barry W., et al.: *Characteristics of Software Quality*, North-Holland Publishing Company, New York, 1978.

Bohm, C., and G. Jacopini: "Flow Diagrams, Turing Machines and Languages with Only Two Formulation Rules," *Comm. ACM*, vol. 9, 1966, pp. 366–371.

Booth, T. L.: "Performance Analysis Techniques for Asynchronous Multiprocessor Algorithms," *IEEE Trans. Software Eng.*, vol. SE-5, no. 1, January 1979, pp. 31–44.

Borodin, A., and I. Munro: *The Computational Complexity of Algebraic and Numeric Problems*, American Elsevier, New York, 1975.

Box, George E. P., and Lars Pallesen: "Software Budgeting Model," Mathematics Research Center, University of Wisconsin, 1977. Also reprinted in Putnam and Wolverton (1977), pp. 96–112.

Brandon, Dick H., and Sidney Seligstein, Esq.: "Data Processing Contracts: Structure, Contents, and Negotiations," Van Nostrand Reinhold, New York, 1976.

Braun, Ernest, and Stewart MacDonald: *Revolution in Miniature—The History and Impact of Semiconductor Electronics*, Cambridge University Press, London, 1978.

Brooks, Fredrick P., Jr.: "How Does the Project Get to Be a Year Late?—One Day at a Time." *Datamation*, December 1974.

Brooks, Fredrick P., Jr.: *The Mythical Man-Month*, Addison-Wesley, Reading, Mass., 1975.

Brown, J. R., and E. C. Nelson: "Functional Programming," final report, contract no. F30602-76-C-0315, TRW, Redondo Beach, Calif., July 1977.

Brown, R. W.: *Basic Software Library*, Scientific Research Institute, Crofton, Md., 1976.

Brown, William L.: "Modular Programming in PL/M," *Proc. COMPSAC 77*, IEEE, New York, 1977, pp. 100–106.

Bruce, Robert C.: *Software Debugging for Microcomputers*, Reston Publishing Company, Reston, Va., 1980.

Burck, Gilbert: "On Line in Real Time," *Fortune*, April 1964.

Burton, W. A.: *CP/M BASIC Benchmark Tests*, Lifeboat Associates, New York, 1978.

Buxton, J. N., et al.: *Report on Software Engineering Techniques*, Petrocelli/Charter, New York, 1976.

Carhart, R. R.: "A Survey of the Current Status of the Reliability Problem," Rand Corporation research memorandum RM-1131, Aug. 14, 1953.

Central Computer Agency Guide No. 1, Her Majesty's Stationery Office, 1973. United States agent: Pendragon House, Inc., 2595 E. Bayshore Rd., Palo Alto, CA 94303.

Chang, H. Y.: *Software Reliability*, Infotech International Ltd., Maidenhead, England, 1977.

Chapin, Ned: *Flowcharting with ANSI Standard: A Tutorial*, ACM Computing Surveys, no. 2, 1970.

Chapin, Ned: "New Format for Flow Charts," *Software—Practice and Experience*, vol. 4, 1974, pp. 341–357.

Cherry, Colin: *On Human Communication*, 2nd ed., MIT Press, Cambridge, Mass., 1970.

Chien, Y. P., and M. D. Dreizen: "A High-Level Language for Microprocessor Applications," *Micro 77 Comp. Conf. Rec.*, IEEE, New York, 1977.

Chomsky, Noam: *Aspects of the Theory of Syntax*, MIT Press, Cambridge, Mass., 1965.

Clark, Arthur C.: *2001: A Space Odyssey*, MGM film screenplay, Signet Books, New York, 1968.

"Cobol 1961: Revised Specifications for a Common Business-Oriented Language," U.S. Government Printing Office 0-598941, 1961.

Codling, Charles: "What Diagnostics Don't Tell You," *Computer Decisions*, June 1977, pp. 68, 69.

Cohen, Harvey A., and Rhys S. Francis: "Help for Microprocessor Software Development," *Digest of Papers, COMPCON*, fall 1977, IEEE, New York, pp. 196–200.

Conrad, Marvin, et al.: "The Integration of Microcomputer Hardware and Software Development Tools and Techniques," *Digest of Papers, COMPCON 77*, IEEE, New York, September 1977, pp. 201–208.

Conway, Richard: *A Primer on Disciplined Programming Using PL/1, PL/CS, and PL/CT*, Winthrop Publishers, Cambridge, Mass., 1978.

Conway, Richard, et al.: *A Primer on PASCAL*, Winthrop Publishers, Cambridge, Mass., 1976.

Corbató, F., and Victor Vyssotsky: "Introduction and Overview of the Multics System," pp. 714–728 in Rosen (1967).

Cormier, G.: "A Quantitative Analysis of the Effect of Organizational Structure on Software Engineering Management," thesis, Department of Electrical Engineering and Computer Science, Polytechnic Institute of New York, June 1980.

Courant, R.: *Differential and Integral Calculus*, vol. 1, Interscience, New York, 1951.

Coutinho, John de S.: "Software Reliability Growth," *IEEE Symp. Comp. Software Reliability*, 1973, pp. 58–64.

Coutinho, John de S.: *Advanced Systems Development Management*, Wiley, New York, 1977.

Cowell, Wayne, ed.: *Proceedings of the Software Certification Workshop*, Argonne National Laboratory, Argonne, Illinois, Aug. 27–30, 1972.

Crow, Edwin L., et al.: *Statistics Manual*, Dover, New York, 1960.

Daly, Edmund B.: "Management of Software Development," in Putnam and Wolverton (1977).

Data and Analysis Center for Software: "A Bibliography of Software Engineering Terms," Rome Air Development Center, RADC/ISISI, Rome, N.Y., October 1979.

Davis, P. J.: "Fidelity in Mathematical Discourse: Is One and One Really Two?" *American Mathematical Monthly*, March 1972, pp. 252–263.

Deb, Rajat K.: "On Generation of Test Data and Minimal Cover of Directed Graphs," *Proc. IFIP Cong. '77*, Aug. 8–12, 1977, pp. 13–16.

Dickson, J., J. Hesse, A. Kientz, and M. Shooman: "Quantitative Analysis of Software Reliability," *Proc. Ann. Reliability and Maintainability Symp.*, IEEE, January 1972.

Digital Equipment Corporation: *Introduction to Programming*, PDP-8 Handbook Series, Maynard, Mass., 1972. (*a*)

Digital Equipment Corporation: *Programming Languages*, PDP-8 Handbook Series, Maynard, Mass., 1972. (*b*)

Digital Equipment Corporation: *Small Computer Handbook*, Maynard, Mass., 1973.

Digital Equipment Corporation: *BASIC-PLUS Language Manual*, Maynard, Mass., January 1978, Sec. 7-6, "Matrix Manipulation."

Dijkstra, E. W.: "GO TO Statement Considered Harmful," *Comm. ACM*, vol. 11, March, 1968, pp. 147–148.

Ditto, F. H., J. S. Hurley, M. M. Kessler, and H. D. Mills: "SAFEGUARD Code Certification Memo," IBM/FSD memo prepared for Bell Labs, Sept. 18, 1970.

Dolotta, T. A., and J. R. Mashey: "An Introduction to the Programmers Workbench," *Proc. 2d Int. Conf. Software Eng.*, IEEE, New York, October 1976, pp. 164–199.

Dolotta, T. A., et al.: "The LEAP Load and Test Driver," *Proc. 2d Int. Conf. Software Eng.*, IEEE, New York, October 1976.

Donovan, John J.: *Systems Programming*, McGraw-Hill, New York, 1972, Chap. 7.

Doty Associates, Inc.: "Software Cost Estimation Study," RADC TR-77-220, Rome Air Development Center, Rome, N.Y., August 1977.

Drake, A.: *Fundamentals of Applied Probability Theory*, McGraw-Hill, New York, 1967.

Ellingson, O. E.: Supplement to "A Prediction Tool for Estimating the Confidence Level of a Computer Program Subsystem in the Space Systems Department," technical memorandum TM-L-3335/001/00, System Development Corporation, May 18, 1967.

Ellingson, O. E.: "Computer Program and Change Control," *Rec. 1973 IEEE Symp. Comp. Software Reliability*, IEEE, New York, pp. 80–89.

Elliott, I. B.: SPTRAN: "A Fortran-Compatible Structured Programming Language Converter," in *Computer Software Engineering*, Proceedings of the Apr. 20–22 1976, Symposium, Polytechnic Press, Brooklyn, 1976, pp. 331–352.

Elmendorf, W. R.: "Cause-Effect Graphs in Functional Testing," report TR-00.2487, IBM Systems Development Division, Poughkeepsie, N.Y., 1973.

Enders, Albert: "An Analysis of Errors and Their Causes in System Programs," *Proc. 1975 Int. Conf. Reliable Software*, IEEE, New York, no. 75 CHO 940-7CSR, 1975.

Engineering Management in the Computer Age, Proc. IEEE 26th Ann. Joint Eng. Mgmt. Conf., Oct. 1978.

Estes, George: "An Investigation of Alternative Hypotheses in Halstead's Software Science Metrics," research memorandum, Polytechnic Institute of New York, June 1981.

Fairley, Richard E.: "Modern Software Design Techniques," *Proc. Symp. Comp. Software Eng.*, Polytechnic Press, New York, 1976, pp. 111-131.

Feller, W.: *An Introduction to Probability Theory and Its Applications*, 2d. ed., vol. 1, Wiley, New York, 1957.

Fergerson, Donald F., and Albert J. Gibbons: "A High-Level Microprocessor Programming Language," *Digest of Papers, COMPCON*, fall 1977, IEEE, New York, pp. 185-188.

Ferrari, Domenico: *Computer System Performance Evaluation*, Prentice-Hall, Englewood Cliffs, N.J., 1978.

Fleishman, T.: "Current Results from the Analysis of Cost Data for Computer Programming," technical memorandum TM-3026/000/01, System Development Corporation, July 1966.

Fletcher, Dennis: "Users Love It [PASCAL], Vendors Are Getting the Message, and Standards Are on the Way," *Datamation*, July 1979, pp. 142-145.

Ford Motor Company: Car Shop Manual, vol. 1, 1969, a Ford Service Publication.

Franklin, Philip: *A Treatise on Advanced Calculus*, Dover, New York, 1964.

Freeman, David N.: "Error Correction in CORC, the Cornell Computing Language," *Fall Joint Comp. Conf.*, AFIPS, 1964, pp. 15-34.

Freeman, Harold: *Introduction to Statistical Inference*, Addison-Wesley, Reading, Mass., 1963.

Freiberger, Walter, ed.: *Statistical Computer Performance Evaluation*, Academic Press, New York, 1972.

Freiman, Frank R., and Robert E. Park: "Price Software Model—Overview," internal paper, Price Systems, RCA, Cherry Hill, N.J., February 1979.

Freund, John E.: *Mathematical Statistics*, Prentice-Hall, Englewood Cliffs, N.J., 1962.

Friedman, F. L.: "Decompilation and the Transfer of Assembly-Coded Minicomputer Systems Programs," *Proc. Symp. Comp. Software Eng.*, Polytechnic Press, Brooklyn, April 1976, pp. 301-330.

Frielink, A. B., ed.: *Proceedings of the International Symposium on Economics of Automatic Data Processing*, North-Holland Publishing Company, Amsterdam, 1965. Papers presented at the international symposium organized by the International Computation Center, Rome, Oct. 19-22, 1965.

Funami, Y., and M. Halstead: "A Software Physics Analysis of Akiyama's Debugging Data," *Proc. 1976 Symp. Software Eng.*, Polytechnic Press, Brooklyn, 1976, pp. 133-138.

Gannon, J. D.: "Data Types and Programming Reliability: Some Preliminary Evidence," *Proc. Symp. Comp. Software Eng.*, Polytechnic Press, Brooklyn, 1976, pp. 367-376.

Gannon, J. D., and J. J. Horning: "The Impact of Language Design on the Production of Reliable Software," *Proc. Int. Conf. Reliable Software*, IEEE, New York, 1975, pp. 10-22.

Gansler, J. S.: "Keynote: Software Management," *Proc. Symp. Comp. Software Eng.*, Polytechnic Press, New York, 1976, pp. 1-9.

Gantmacher, F. R.: *Theory of Matrices*, Chelsea Publishing Company, New York, 1959.

Gault, John K., R. E. Horner, B. McMillan, F. R. Naka, M. L. Shooman, and W. H. Ware: *Reliability in Avionics Equipment: A Report of the Air Force Technological Tradeoff Panel*, National Academy of Sciences, Washington, D.C., 1975.

Geller, Dennis P., and Daniel P. Freedman: *Structured Programming in APL*, Winthrop, Cambridge, Mass., 1976.

General Motors Corporation, Delco Electronics Division, *Apollo 15 Guidance and Navigation Summary Handbook*, Milwaukee, 1971.

Gilb, Tom: *Software Metrics*, Winthrop, Cambridge, Mass., 1977.

Gilb, Tom, and Gerald M. Weinberg: *Humanized Input—Techniques for Reliable Keyed Input*, Winthrop, Cambridge, Mass., 1977.

Giloty, D. R., et al.: "System Testing and Early Field Experience," *Bell Sys. Tech. J.*, vol. 49, December 1970.

Girard, E., and J. C. Rault: "A Programming Technique for Software Reliability," *Rec. 1973 IEEE Symp. Comp. Software Reliability*, New York, Apr. 30, 1973, pp. 44–50.

Glass, Robert L.: "From PASCAL to Pebbleman... and Beyond," *Datamation*, July 1979, pp. 146–150.

Glasser, Alan L.: "The Evolution of a Source Code Control System," *Proc. Software Quality and Assurance Workshop*, ACM, New York, November 1978, pp. 122–125.

Goel, A. L., and K. Okumoto: "Bayesian Software Prediction Models," RADC TR-78-155, July 1978.

Goldberg, Jack: "A Survey of the Design and Analysis of Fault-Tolerant Computers," in Barlow et al. (1975), pp. 687–731.

Good, I. J.: *The Estimation of Probabilities: An Essay on Modern Bayesian Methods*, MIT Press, Cambridge, Mass., 1965.

Goode, H., and R. Machol: *System Engineering*, McGraw-Hill, New York, 1957.

Goodenough, John B., and Douglas T. Ross: "The Effects of Software Structure on Software Reliability, Modifiability, Reusability, and Efficiency: A Preliminary Analysis," Softech, Inc., Waltham, Mass., 1973, NTIS-AD 780 841.

Godwin, H. J.: "On Generalizations of Chebycheff's Inequality," *J. Amer. Stat. Assoc.*, vol. 50, 1955, pp. 923–945.

Graham, R. M.: *Performance Prediction*, Advanced Course on Software Engineering, no. 81, Springer-Verlag, New York, 1973, Chap. 4.

Grant, E. Eugene, and H. Sackman: "An Exploratory Investigation of Programmer Performance under On-line and Off-line Conditions," *IEEE Trans. Human Factors in Electronics*, vol. HFE-8, no. 1, March 1967, pp. 33–48.

Grochow, Jerrold M.: "A Utility Theoretic Approach to Evaluation of a Time-Sharing System," pp. 25–50 in Freiberger (1972).

Hajek, Victor G.: *Management of Engineering Projects*, McGraw-Hill, New York, 1977.

Halstead, Maurice: "Software Physics: Basic Principles," IBM research report RJ1582, IBM Research Laboratory, Yorktown Heights, N.Y., May 20, 1975.

Halstead, Maurice H.: *Elements of Software Science*, Elsevier North-Holland, Inc., New York, 1977. (*a*)

Halstead, Maurice H.: "A Quantitative Connection between Computer Programs and Technical Prose," *Digest of Papers, COMPCON '77*, IEEE, New York, Sept. 6–9, 1977, pp. 332–335. (*b*)

Halstead, Maurice, and Rudolf Bayer: "Algorithm Dynamics," *Proc. 1973 Ann. ACM Conf.*, p. 126.

Hamilton, Patricia A., and John D. Musa: "Measuring Reliability of Computation Center Hardware," *Proc. 3d Int. Conf. Software Eng.*, IEEE, New York, May 10, 1978, pp. 29–30.

Hammersley, J. M., and D. C. Handscomb: *Monte Carlo Methods*, Methuen, London, 1975.

Hassett, R. P., and E. H. Miller: "Multithreading Design of a Reliable Aerospace Computer," *IEEE Trans. Aerospace and Electronic Sys. (Suppl.)*, vol. AES-2, November 1966, pp. 147–158.

Hecht, Herbert: "Software Standards—with Hints of Their Relation to Computer Architecture," *National Computer Conference*, 1978, pp. 927–929.

Heller, K. A., et al.: "System Testing," *Bell Sys. Tech. J.*, vol. 49, no. 10, December 1970, p. 2711.

Heniger, Kathryn L.: "Specifying Software Requirements for Complex Systems," *Proc. Specifications of Reliable Software*, IEEE catalog no. 79 CH-1401-91, 1979, p. 3.

Hetzel, William C., ed.: *Program Test Methods*, Prentice-Hall, Englewood Cliffs, N.J., 1973.

Higgins, David A.: "Structured Program Design," *Byte*, October 1977, pp. 146–151. (*a*)

Higgins, David A.: "Structured Program with Warnier-Orr Diagrams—Part 1: Design Methodology," *Byte*, December 1977. (*b*)

Higgins, David A.: "Structured Program with Warnier-Orr Diagrams—Part 2: Coding the Program," *Byte*, January 1978.

Hilbing, Francis J.: "Software Engineering for Microprocessors," *Digest of Papers, COMPCON*, fall 1977, IEEE, New York, pp. 180–184.

Hilburn, John L., and Paul M. Julich: *Microcomputers/Microprocessors: Hardware, Software, and Applications*, Prentice-Hall, Englewood Cliffs, N.J., 1976, Chap. 5.

616 SOFTWARE ENGINEERING: DESIGN, RELIABILITY, AND MANAGEMENT

Hiller, Frederick S., and Gerald J. Lieberman: *Operations Research*, 2d ed., Holden-Day, San Francisco, 1974.

Hnatek, E.: "Semiconductor Memory Update," *Computer Design*, December 1979, p. 69.

Hoel, Paul G.: *Introduction to Mathematical Statistics*, Wiley, New York, 1954.

Hoffman, Lance J.: *Security and Privacy in Computer Systems*, Wiley, New York, 1973.

Holthouse, M. A., and J. B. Cohen: "High-Level Language Programming for Mini- and Micro-Computer Systems." *Micro 77 Comp. Conf. Rec.*, IEEE, New York, 1977, pp. 26–29.

Horowitz, Ellis, et al.: *Practical Strategies for Developing Large Software Systems*, Addison-Wesley, Reading, Mass., 1975.

"How Effective Are Dual Brakes?" *Consumer Reports*, August 1965, p. 410.

Hudson, G. R.: "Program Errors as a Birth-and-Death Process," report SP-3011, System Development Corporation, Dec. 4, 1967.

Hyman, Mort: Private communication, 1973.

IBM: "Electronic Circuit Analysis Program," ECAP 1620-EE-02X, IBM Technical Publications Department, 112 E. Post Rd., White Plains, NY 10601, 1965.

IBM: "1130 Continuous System Modeling Program," CSMP 1130-CX-16X, IBM Technical Publications Department, 112 E. Post Rd., White Plains, NY 10601, 1967. (*a*)

IBM: "General Purpose Simulation System/360," GPSS H20-0326-0, IBM Technical Publications Department, 112 E. Post Rd., White Plains, NY 10601, 1967. (*b*)

IBM: "System/360 Scientific Subroutine Package (PL/1), (360A-CM-07X), Program Description and Operations Manual," IBM Technical Publications Department, 1133 Westchester Ave., White Plains, NY 10604, July 25, 1969.

IBM: "Improved Programming Technologies—An Overview," GC20-1850-0, IBM Corporation, White Plains, N.Y., 1974.

IBM: "HIPO—A Design Aid and Documentation Technique," GC20-1851-1, IBM Corporation, White Plains, N.Y., 1975.

IEEE Computer Society Technical Committee on Software Engineering: *Software Engineering Terminology*, New York, 1979.

Isaacson, Portia: "Personal Computing—1984's Information Appliances," *Datamation*, February 1979, pp. 215–218.

Itoh, Daiju, and Takao Izutani: "FADEBUG-I: A New Tool for Program Debugging," *1973 IEEE Symp. Comp. Software Reliability*, IEEE, New York, catalog no. 73 CHO 741-9-CSR, pp. 38–43.

Jackson, Michael A.: *Principles of Program Design*, Academic Press, New York, 1975.

Jelinski, Z., and P. Moranda: "Software Reliability Research," pp. 465–484 in Freiberger (1972).

Jensen, Kathleen, and Niklaus Wirth: *PASCAL User Manual and Report*, Lecture Notes in Computer Science, Springer-Verlag, New York, 1974.

Jensen, Randell W., and Charles C. Tonies: *Software Engineering*, Prentice-Hall, Englewood Cliffs, N.J., 1979.

Jolley, L.: *Summation of Series*, Dover, New York, 1961.

Jones, Capers: "A Survey of Programming Design and Specification Techniques," *Proc. Specifications of Reliable Software Conf.*, IEEE, New York, 1979, pp. 91–103.

Jones, T. C.: "Measuring Programming Quality and Productivity," *IBM Sys. J.*, vol. 17, no. 2, 1978.

Katzen, Harry, Jr.: *Systems Design and Documentation: An Introduction to the HIPO Method*, Van Nostrand Reinhold, New York, 1976.

Kernighan, Brian W.: "A Tutorial Introduction to the UNIX Text Editor," in *UNIX Programmers Manual*, Bell Laboratories, Murray Hill, N.J., Sept. 30, 1978.

Kernighan, Brian W., and P. J. Plauger: *Software Tools*, Addison-Wesley, Reading, Mass., 1976.

Kernighan, Brian W., and P. J. Plauger: *The Elements of Programming Style*, McGraw-Hill, New York, 1974; 2d ed., 1978.

Kernighan, Brian W., and Dennis M. Ritchie: *The C Programming Language*, Prentice-Hall, Englewood Cliffs, N.J., 1978.

Kettlen, A. W., et al.: "Operational Programs, Sec. VI: Audit Programs," *Bell Sys. Tech. J.*, special issue on TSPS, no. 1, vol. 49, no. 10, December 1970, pp. 2668–2675.

Kidall, Gary A.: "High Level Language Simplifies Microcomputer Programming," pp. 80–86 in Laurence Altman, *Microprocessors*, McGraw-Hill, New York, 1975.

Knudsen, D. B., et al.: "A Modification Request Control System," *Proc. 2d Int. Conf. Software Eng.*, IEEE, New York, October 1976.

Knuth, Donald E.: *The Art of Computer Programming*, Addison-Wesley, Reading, Mass., 1968.

Knuth, Donald E.: "An Empirical Study of Fortran Programs," Computer Science Department report no. CS-186, Stanford University, 1970.

Knuth, Donald E.: "Structured Programming with GO TO Statements," Stanford University report no. STAN-CS-74-416, May 1974.

Knuth, Donald E.: "TAU EPSILON CHI: A System for Technical Text," report no. STAN-CS-78-675.1, Computer Science Department, Stanford University, November 1978.

Knuth, Donald E.: *TEX and METAFONT—New Directions in Typesetting*, Digital Press, Bedford, Mass., 1979.

Knuth, Donald E., and Francis R. Stevenson: "Optimal Measurement Points for Program Frequency Counts," *BIT 13*, 1973, pp. 313–322.

Koffman, Elliot B., and Frank L. Friedman: *Problem Solving and Structured Programming in BASIC*, Addison-Wesley, Reading, Mass., 1979.

Kohavi, Zvi: *Switching and Finite Automata Theory*, McGraw-Hill, New York, 1970; 2d ed., 1978.

Kreitzberg, C. B., and Ben Shneiderman: *The Elements of Fortran Style*, Harcourt Brace Jovanovich, New York, 1972.

LaBolle, Victor: "Cost Estimating for Computer Programming," *IEEE Int. Conv.*, March 20–23, 1972.

Laemmel, Arthur E.: "Final Report on Research Study in Digital Communication Codes," report PIB MRI-1298, Polytechnic Institute of Brooklyn, February 1966, App. A, "Path Enumerating Functions."

Laemmel, Arthur: "Study of General Digital Codes with Emphasis on Signal Compression," report no. PIBEP-73-125, Polytechnic Institute of Brooklyn, Apr. 16, 1973.

Laemmel, Arthur: "Dillworth's Theorem and Program Testing," unpublished memorandum, Polytechnic Institute of New York, Dec. 9, 1975. (*a*)

Laemmel, Arthur: "Notes on Digraphs and Programming," unpublished memorandum, Polytechnic Institute of New York, August 1975. (*b*)

Laemmel, Arthur: "Testing Flow Charts with Loops," unpublished memorandum, Polytechnic Institute of New York, Dec. 10, 1975. (*c*)

Laemmel, Arthur: "Zipf's Law and Program Information Content," unpublished memorandum, Polytechnic Institute of New York, August 1976.

Laemmel, Arthur: "A Statistical Theory of Computer Program Testing," report no. SRS 119/POLY EE 80-004, Polytechnic Institute of New York, June 1980.

Laemmel, Arthur, and B. Rudner: "Study of the Application of Coding Theory," PIBEP-69-034, Polytechnic Institute of Brooklyn, June 1969.

Laemmel, Arthur, and Martin Shooman: "Statistical (Natural) Language Theory and Computer Program Complexity," Polytechnic Institute of New York, report no. POLY-EE/EP-76-020, Aug. 15, 1977.

Landes, Michael: "RADC Development Specification," *Joint Eng. Mgmt. Conf.—Engineering Management in the Computer Age*, IEEE no. 78CH1359-9EM, New York, Oct. 16, 1978, pp. 88–91.

Lawler, E. L.: "The Complexity of Combinatorial Computations: A Survey," *Proc. Symp. Computers and Automata*, Polytechnic Press, Brooklyn, 1971, p. 305.

Ledgard, H. F.: *Programming Proverbs*, Hayden Book Company, Rochelle Park, N.J., 1975.

Leeman, George B., Jr.: "PREP2: A Program to Simplify the Typing of Manuscripts," research report RC 6948, IBM Research Center, Yorktown Heights, N.Y., Jan. 18, 1978.

Lewis, Larry E., and J. Lynn Saunders: "Using High Level Languages to Produce Load Modules for ROM in Medium (2000) Quantities," *Digest of Papers, COMPCON*, fall 1977, IEEE, New York, pp. 189–194.

Lients, B. P., et al.: "Characteristics of Application Software Maintenance," UCLA report AD/A-034-085, December 1976.

Linger, R. C., and H. D. Mills: "Definitional Texts in Structured Programming," *Tutorial on Structured Programming*, IEEE Computer Society, New York, 1975, pp. 178–183.

Linger, R., H. Mills, and B. Witt: *Structured Programming Theory and Practice*, Addison-Wesley, Reading, Mass., 1979.

Littlewood, B.: "Theories of Software Reliability: How Good Are They and How Can They Be Improved?" *IEEE Trans. Software Eng.*, vol. SE-6, no. 5, September 1980, pp. 489–500.

Littlewood, B., and J. L. Verrall: "A Bayesian Reliability Model with a Stochastically Monotone Failure Rate," *IEEE Trans. Reliability*, vol. R-23, July 1974, pp. 108–164.

Lloyd, David K., and Myron Lipow: *Reliability: Management, Methods, and Mathematics*, Prentice-Hall, Englewood Cliffs, N.J., 1962; 2d ed. published by the authors, 201 Calle Miramar, Redondo Beach, CA, 90277, 1977.

Lucas, Henry C.: *Why Information Systems Fail*, Columbia University Press, New York, 1975.

Lycklama, H.: *UNIX on a Microprocessor*, Special Issue on UNIX timesharing system, *Bell Sys. Tech. J.*, vol. 57, no. 6, pt. 2, 1978, pp. 2087–2102.

Mackie, R. R., ed.: "Vigilance: Theory, Operational Performance, and Psychological Correlates," vol. 4, *Human Factors*, NATO Conference Series, Plenum Press, New York, 1977.

Maisel, Herbert: *Introduction to Electronic Digital Computers*, McGraw-Hill, New York, 1969.

Mandelbrot, B.: "On Recurrent Noise Limiting Coding," *Proc. Symp. Information Networks*, Polytechnic Press, Brooklyn, 1954.

Mandelbrot, B.: "On the Theory of Word Frequencies and on Related Markovian Models of Discourse," *Proceedings of Symposia in Applied Mathematics*, vol. XII, American Mathematical Society, Providence, 1961, p. 190.

Maples, Michael D., and Eugene R. Fisher: "Basic for Intel's 8080," *Micro 77 Comput. Conf. Rec.*, IEEE, New York, 1977, pp. 60–63.

Marshall, Clifford W.: "Quantification of Contractor Risk," *Naval Research Logistics Quarterly*, vol. 16, no. 4, December 1969.

Marshall, C. W.: *Applied Graph Theory*, Wiley, New York, 1971.

Marshall, Clifford W.: "Structural Models of Award Fee Contract," *Naval Research Logistics Quarterly*, vol. 21, no. 2, June 1974.

Mashey, J. R.: "Using a Command Language as a High-Level Programming Language," *Proc. 2d Int. Conf. Software Eng.*, IEEE, New York, October 1976.

Mashey, J. R., and D. W. Smith: "Documentation Tools and Techniques," *Proc. 2d Int. Conf. Software Eng.*, IEEE, New York, October 1976.

Mason, Samuel J.: "Feedback Theory—Some Properties of Signal Flow Graphs," *Proc. IRE*, September 1953, pp. 1144–1156.

Mason, S. J., and M. J. Zimmerman: *Electronic Circuits, Signals, and Systems*, Wiley, New York, 1960.

Matejka, Jerry W., and Gerald Sandler: "Project Management and Control in a Structured Programming Environment," *Joint Eng. Mgmt. Conf.*, catalog no. 7:CH1335999-9E3, IEEE, New York, Oct. 16, 1978, pp. 69–73.

McCabe, Thomas J: "Notes on Software Engineering," 5380 Mad River Lane, Columbia, Md. 21044, 1975.

McCammon, S.: "Applied Software Engineering: A Real-Time Simulator Case History," *IEEE Trans. Software Eng.*, December 1975, p. 377.

McCracken, Daniel D.: *A Guide to FORTRAN Programming*, Wiley, New York, 1961.

McCracken, Daniel D.: *Guide to PL/M Programming for Microcomputer Applications*, Addison-Wesley, Reading, Mass., 1978.

McIntire, Thomas C.: *Software Interpreters for Microcomputers*, Wiley, New York, 1978.

Messinger, M., and M. Shooman: "Approximations for Complex Structures," *Proc. 1967 Ann. Symp. Reliability*, IEEE, New York.

Meyer, Paul L.: *Introductory Probability and Statistical Applications*, Addison-Wesley, Reading, Mass., 1965; 2d ed., 1970.

Miller, E. H.: "Reliability Aspects of the Variable Instruction Computer," *IEEE Trans. Electronic Computers*, vol. EC-16, no. 5, October 1967, pp. 596–602.

Miller, George A.: *Language and Communication*, McGraw-Hill, New York, 1951.

Miller, George A.: "Human Memory and the Storage of Information," *IRE Trans. Information Theory*, vol. IT-2, no. 3, 1956, pp. 129–137.

Mills, Harlan D.: "Chief Programmer Teams, Principles, and Procedures," IBM Federal Systems Division report FSC 71-5108, Gaithersburg, Md., 1971.

Mills, Harlan D.: "Mathematical Foundations of Structured Programming," IBM Federal Systems Division document FSC72-6012, Gaithersburg, Md., February 1972.

Mills, Harlan D.: "Software Development," *Proc. 2d Int. Conf. Software Eng.*, IEEE, New York, Oct. 13–15, 1976, vol. II, p. 79.

Miyamoto, Isao: "Software Reliability in Online Real Time Environment," *Proc. 1975 Int. Conf. Reliable Software*, IEEE, New York, no. 75 CHO 940-7CSR, 1975, p. 194.

Mohanty, S. N.: "Automatic Program Testing," Ph.D. thesis, Polytechnic Institute of New York, Department of Electrical Engineering and Computer Science, June 1976.

Musa, John D.: "A Theory of Software Reliability and Its Application," *IEEE Trans. Software Eng.*, vol. SE-1, no. 3, September 1975, pp. 312–327.

Musa, John D.: "An Exploratory Experiment with 'FOREIGN' Debugging of Programs," *Proc. Symp. Comp. Software Eng.*, Polytechnic Press, April 1976.

Musa, John: "The Use of Software Reliability Measures in Project Management," *Proc. COMPSAC '78*, IEEE, New York, 1978, pp. 493–498.

Musa, John D.: "Validity of Execution-Time Theory of Software Reliability," *IEEE Trans. Reliability*, vol. R-28, no. 3, August 1979, pp. 181–191. (*a*)

Musa, John D.: "Software Reliability Data," DACS Center, Rome Air Development Center, Rome, N.Y., 1979. (*b*)

Myers, Glenford J.: *Software Reliability Principles and Practice*, Wiley, New York, 1976.

Myers, Glenford J.: "An Extension to the Cyclomatic Measure of Program Complexity," *SIGPLAN Notices*, October 1977, pp. 61–64.

Myers, Glenford J.: *Composite/Structured Design*, Van Nostrand Reinhold, New York, 1978.

Myers, Glenford J.: *The Art of Software Testing*, Wiley, New York, 1979.

NASA: "Practical Reliability," NASA CR-1129, Chap. 7, August 1968.

Nathan, Irwin: "A Deterministic Model to Predict Error-Free Status of Complex Software Development," *Proc. Workshop on Quantitative Software Models*, Kiamesha Lake, N.Y., IEEE, New York, Oct. 9, 1979, pp. 159–169.

Naur, Peter: "Revised Report on the Algorithmic Language ALGOL 60," in Rosen (1967), p. 109.

Naur, Peter, et al.: *Software Engineering Concepts and Techniques*, Petrocelli/Charter, New York, 1976.

Nelson, Richard: "Software Data Collection and Analysis," draft report, Rome Air Development Center, Rome, N.Y., September 1978.

Neuhold, E., and H. Lawson, Jr.: *The PL/1 Machine: An Introduction to Programming*, Addison-Wesley, Reading, Mass., 1971.

Nicholls, J. E.: *The Structure and Design of Programming Languages*, Addison-Wesley, Reading, Mass., 1975.

Nolos, E. J., and R. B. Schultz: "Reliability and Cost of Avionics," *IEEE Trans. Reliability*, October 1965.

Norden, Peter V.: "Useful Tools for Project Management," in B. V. Dean, ed., *Operations Research and Development*, Wiley, New York, 1963.

Noyce, Robert N.: "Microelectronics," *Scientific American*, September 1977, pp. 62–69.

Ogdin, Carol A.: *Software Design for Microcomputers*, Prentice-Hall, Englewood Cliffs, N.J., 1978.

Opler, Ascher: "Is Assembly Language Passé?" *Data Processing Digest*, October 1968. Reprinted in Edwin O. Joslin, *Software for Computer Systems* (readings), College Readings, Inc., P.O. Box 2323, Arlington, VA 22202, 1970.

Orr, K.: *Structured System Design*, Yourdon Press, New York, 1978.

Papoulis, A.: *Probability, Random Variables, and Stochastic Processes*, McGraw-Hill, New York, 1965.

Parker, Donn B.: *Crime by Computer*, Scribners, New York, 1976.

Parker, R. W.: "The SABRE System," *Datamation*, September 1965, pp. 49–52.

Parker-Rhodes, A., and J. Joyce: "A Theory of Word-Frequency Distribution," *Nature*, Dec. 8, 1956, p. 1308.

Parnas, D. L.: "A Technique for Software Module Specification with Examples," *Comm. ACM*, May 1972.

Penney, George: *Managing Computers: Data Processing Case Histories*, Hayden, Rochelle Park, N.J., 1975.

Peters, L. J., and L. L. Tripp: "Software Design Representation Schemes," *Proc. Symp. Comp. Software Eng.*, Polytechnic Press, New York, 1976, pp. 31–56.

Petrick, Stanley R.: "On Natural Language Based Query Systems," report no. RC 5577, IBM T. J. Watson Research Center, Yorktown Heights, N.Y., Aug. 13, 1975.

Pferd, W., and K. Ramachandran: "Computer Aided Automatic Digitizing of Engineering Drawings," *Proc. COMPSAC 78*, IEEE, New York, November 1979, pp. 630–635.

Phister, Montgomery, Jr.: *Data Processing Technology and Economics*, Santa Monica Publishing Company, Santa Monica, Calif., 1976; 2d ed., Digital Press, Bedford, Mass., 1979.

Pierce, J. R.: *An Introduction to Information Theory: Symbols, Signals, and Noise*, Harper & Row, New York, 1965; 2d rev. ed., Dover, New York, 1980.

Poole, Lon, and Mary Borchers: *Payroll with Cost Accounting—In BASIC*, Adam Osborne and Associates, Berkeley, Calif., 1977.

Popkin, G. S., and Martin L. Shooman: "On the Number of Tests Necessary to Verify a Computer Program," report SRS-113/Poly EE 78-047, Polytechnic Institute of New York, June 1978.

Premo, A. F., Jr.: "Computer Software: Estimating Guidelines," *COMPCON Dig. of Papers*, IEEE, New York, fall 1976, pp. 146–151.

Presson, P. Edward: "A Software Error Data Study—In Progress," Minnowbrook Workshop on Software Engineering Models, Syracuse University, Syracuse, N.Y., 1980.

Project MAC: "Progress Report X," July 1972–July 1973, MIT, Cambridge, Mass.

Putnam, Lawrence H., and Ray W. Wolverton: "Quantitative Management: Software Cost Estimating," Tutorial Notes, no. EHO-129-7, IEEE, New York, Nov. 8, 1977.

Randell, Brian, ed.: *The Origins of Digital Computers*, Springer-Verlag, New York, 1975.

"RCA's Uncanny System for Estimating Costs," *Business Week*, June 7, 1976.

Reddien, C. H.: "Legal Aspects of Software Development," in Jensen and Tonies, Prentice-Hall, Englewood Cliffs, N.J., 1979, Chap. 7.

Reifer, Donald J., and Stephen Tratter: "A Glossary of Software Tools and Techniques," *Computer*, July 1977.

Repsher, William G.: "BELLFLOW Draws Flow Diagrams Automatically," *Bell Labs Record*, vol. 39, no. 49, August 1971, pp. 209–215.

Reynolds, C. H., and J. E. Van Kinsbergen: "Tracking Reliability and Availability," *Datamation*, November 1975, pp. 106–116.

Ritchie, D. M., and K. Thompson: "The UNIX Time-Sharing System," *Comm. ACM*, vol. 17, no. 7, July 1974, pp. 365–375.

Robinson, Richard A.: "National Software Works—Status Report No. 1," RADC-TR-76-276, vol. 1, Rome Air Development Center, Rome, N.Y., September 1976.

Robinson, Richard A.: "National Software Works: Overview and Status," *Digest of Papers, COMPCON 77*, IEEE, New York, September 1977, pp. 270–273.

Rosen, Saul: *Programming Systems and Languages*, McGraw-Hill, New York, 1967.

Rosen, Saul: "Programming Systems and Languages 1965–1975," *Comm. ACM*, July 1972, pp. 597–598.

Rosengard, Phil: "Software Quality Assurance Standards under Development," *Computer*, February 1979, pp. 84, 85.

Rothenbuescher, Oscar H.: "The Top 50 Companies in the Data Processing Industry," *Datamation*, June 1978, pp. 85–110.

Rothstein, Marvin: "American Airlines 'SABRE': The Analyst's Viewpoint," unpublished paper, American Airlines, Jan. 1, 1965.

Rubey, J.: "Quantitative Aspects of Software Validation," *Int. Conf. Reliable Software*, IEEE, New York, 1975, p. 246.

Rudkin, Ralph, I., and Kenneth D. Sphere: "Structured Decomposition Diagram: A New Technique for System Analysis," *Datamation*, October 1979, pp. 130–146.

Rudner, B.: "Seeding/Tagging Estimates of the Number of Software Errors: Models and Estimates," report POLY EE/EP 76-019 Smart 104, Polytechnic Institute of New York, November 1976.

Ruston, Henry: *Programming with PL/1*, McGraw-Hill, New York, 1978.

Ruston, Henry: "The Polynomial Measure of Complexity," vol. II, report no. POLY EE 79-057/SRS 117, Polytechnic Institute of New York, June 1980.

Sabean, Ruth M., et al.: "Critical Path Analysis," *Creative Computing*, November–December 1978, pp. 86–93.

Sackman, Harold: *Computers, System Science, and Evolving Society*, Wiley, New York, 1967. (An account of the SAGE air defense system.)

Sackman, Harold: *Man-Computer Problem Solving—Experimental Evaluation of Time-Sharing and Batch Processing*, Auerbach Publishers, Philadelphia, 1970.

SAFEGUARD Data Processing System, 1975, Bell Sys. Tech. J., special supplement, 1975.

Sammet, Jean E.: *Programming Languages: History and Fundamentals*, Prentice-Hall, Englewood Cliffs, N.J., 1969.

Savage, I. R.: "Probability Inequalities of the Chebycheff Type," *Journal of Research*, National Bureau of Standards, vol. 65B, no. 3, July–September 1961, pp. 7–18.

Scherr, A. L.: "Developing and Testing a Large Programming System, OS/360 Time Sharing Option," in Hetzel (1973).

Schick, G. J., and R. W. Wolverton: "Assessment of Software Reliability," 11th Annual Meeting, German Operations Research Society, Hamburg, September 1972.

Schick, G. J., and R. W. Wolverton: "Analysis of Competing Software Reliability Models," *IEEE Trans. Software Eng.*, vol. SE-4, no. 2, pp. 104–120, March 1978.

Schmall, Theresa M., ed.: "Conference Record for 1979 IEEE Standards Workshop on Human Factors and Nuclear Safety," IEEE catalog no. TH0075-2, New York, 1979.

Schnable et al.: "Reliability of CMOS Integrated Circuits," *Computer*, October 1978, pp. 6–13.

Schneider, Ben: *Travels in Computerland or Incompatibilities and Interfaces*, Addison-Wesley, Reading, Mass. 1974.

Schneiderman et al.: "Experimental Investigation of the Utility of Detailed Flow Charts in Programming," *Comm. ACM*, vol. 20, no. 6, June 1977.

Schneiderman, Ben: *Software Psychology—Human Factors in Computer Information Systems*, Winthrop, Cambridge, Mass., 1980.

Schwartz, Jacob T.: "An Overview of Bugs," in Randall Rustin, ed., *Debugging Techniques in Large Systems*, Prentice-Hall, Englewood Cliffs, N.J., 1971.

Schwartz, Mischa: *Information Transmission, Modulation, and Noise*, McGraw-Hill, New York, 1959.

Shannon, C., and W. Weaver: *The Mathematical Theory of Communication*, University of Illinois Press, Urbana, 1975.

Shaw, C. J.: "JOVIAL—A Programming Language for Real-Time Command Systems," *Annual Review of Automatic Programming*, vol. 3, R. Goodman, ed., Pergamon Press, New York, 1963, pp. 53–119.

Sheridan, T. B., and W. R. Ferrell: *Man-Machine Systems: Information, Control, and Decision Models of Human Performance*, MIT Press, Cambridge, Mass., 1976.

Shillington, Keith: "Structure: The Key to PASCAL's Problem-Solving Power," *Datamation*, July 1979, pp. 151–152.

Sholl, H., and T. Booth: "Software Performance Modeling Using Control Structures," *IEEE Trans. Software Eng.*, December 1975, p. 414.

Shooman, Martin L.: *Probabilistic Reliability: An Engineering Approach*, McGraw-Hill, New York, 1968.

Shooman, Martin L.: "Estimation of Software Reliability from Debugging and Operational Test Data," unpublished Bell Labs memorandum, Spring 1972. (*a*)

Shooman, Martin L.: "Notes on Computer Hardware, Software, and Systems Reliability," IAP course on computer architecture, MIT Department of Electrical Engineering, January 1972. (*b*)

Shooman, Martin L.: "Probabilistic Models for Software Reliability Prediction," pp. 485–502 in Freiberger (1972). (*c*)

Shooman, Martin L.: "Error Generation Models," unpublished memorandum, Bell Laboratories, March 1973. (*a*)

Shooman, Martin L.: "Operational Testing and Software Reliability Estimation during Program Development," *Rec. 1973 IEEE Symp. Comp. Software Reliability*, catalog no. 73 CHO741-9 CSR, New York, Apr. 30, 1973, pp. 51–57. (*b*)

Shooman, Martin L.: "Seeding Model for Determining the Number of Bugs in a Computer Program," unpublished memorandum, Polytechnic Institute of New York, Dec. 14, 1973. (*c*)

Shooman, Martin L.: "Software Reliability: Analysis and Prediction," *Proc. NATO Conf. System Reliability*, University of Liverpool, July 1973, published in H. J. Henley and J. W. Lynn, eds. *Generic Techniques in System Reliability Assessment*, Noordhoff International, Reading, Mass., 1976. (*d*)

Shooman, Martin L.: "Analytic Generation of Test Data," unpublished memorandum, Polytechnic Institute of New York, December 1974. (*a*)

Shooman, Martin L.: "Analytic Models for Software Testing," unpublished memorandum, Polytechnic Institute of New York, Dec. 17, 1974. (*b*)

Shooman, Martin L.: "Meaning of Exhaustive Testing," research report EE/EP 74-006/EER 105, Jan. 2, 1974. (*c*)

Shooman, Martin L.: "Structural Models for Software Reliability Prediction," *2d Int. Conf. Software Eng.*, IEEE Computer Society, October 1976, pp. 268–280.

Shooman, Martin L.: "Software Engineering," notes for course CS606, Polytechnic Institute of New York, 1978.

Shooman, Martin L.: 1979: "Software Reliability," Chap. 9 in T. Anderson and B. Randell, eds., *Computing Systems Reliability*, Cambridge University Press, New York, pp. 389–406. (*a*)

Shooman, Martin L.: "Software Reliability Data Analysis and Model Fitting," *Proc. Workshop on Quantitative Software Models for Reliability, Complexity, and Cost: An Assessment of the State of the Art*, IEEE, catalog no. IM 0067-9, New York, Oct. 9, 1979, pp. 182–189. (*b*)

Shooman, Martin L.: "Tutorial on Software Cost Models," *Proc. Workshop on Quantitative Software Models for Reliability, Complexity, and Cost: An Assessment of the State of the Art*, IEEE, catalog no. IM 0067-9, New York, Oct. 9, 1979, pp. 1–19. (*c*)

Shooman, Martin L., and Morris Bolsky: "Types, Distribution, and Test and Correction Times for Programming Errors," *Proc. 1975 Int. Conf. Reliable Software*, IEEE, New York, catalog no. 75 CHO 940-7CSR, p. 347.

Shooman, Martin L., and Arthur Laemmel: "Statistical Theory of Computer Programs—Information Content and Complexity," *Digest of Papers, Fall COMPCON '77*, IEEE, New York, Sept. 6–9, 1977, pp. 341–347.

Shooman, Martin L., and Srinivasan Natarajan: "Effect of Manpower Deployment and Bug Generation on Software Error Models," *Proc. Symp. Software Eng.*, Polytechnic Press, New York, 1976, pp. 155–170. (*a*)

Shooman, Martin L., and Srinivasan Natarajan: "Effect of Manpower Deployment and Bug Generation on Software Error Models," report no. POLY EE/EP 76-007, SMART 102, Polytechnic Institute of New York, May 1976. (*b*)

Shooman, Martin L., and Henry Ruston: "Final Report Software Modeling Studies," report no. SRS 119/POLY EE 80-006, vol. I, Polytechnic Institute of New York, Dec. 31, 1979.

Shooman, M. L., and R. W. Schmidt: "Fitting of Software Error and Reliability Models to Field Failure Data," *Conf. App. Probability—Comp. Sci.*, The Interface, Boca Raton, Fla., Jan. 5–7, 1981.

Shooman, M. L., and S. Sinkar: "Generation of Reliability and Safety Data by Analysis of Expert Opinion," *Proc. 1977 Ann. Reliability and Maintainability Symp.*, IEEE, New York, pp. 186–193.

Shooman, Martin, et al.: "PLAGO on the PDP-11," proposal, Department of Electrical Engineering, Polytechnic Institute of New York, March 1970.

Sontz, C.: "Quality Assurance for the Data Processing Industry," *Proc. 1973 Ann. Reliability and Maintainability Symp.*, 1973, p. 136.

"Space Shuttle Software," *Datamation*, July 1978, pp. 128–140.

"Speaking of Chip Shortages—New Compiler Can Be Used on Any 8 or 16-Bit Micro—Now or to Come," *Datamation*, January 1980, pp. 81, 82.

Spiegel, Murray R.: *Probability and Statistics*, Schaum's Outline Series, McGraw-Hill, New York, 1975.

Stenning, Vic, et al.: "The Ada Environment," *Computer*, June 1981, pp. 26–36.

Stephenson, W. E.: "An Analysis of the Resources Used in the SAFEGUARD System Software Development," pp. 303–312 in Putnam and Wolverton, 1977.

Straeter, Terry A., et al.: "Research Flight Software Engineering and MUST, An Integrated System of Support Tools," *Proc. COMSAC 77 Comp. Software and Applications Conf.*, IEEE, New York, November 1977, pp. 392–396.

Stroud, J. M.: "The Fine Structure of Psychological Time," Annals of the New York Academy of Sciences, 1966, pp. 623–631.

Strunk, W. S., Jr., and E. B. White: *The Elements of Style*, 2d ed., Macmillan, New York, 1972; 3d ed., 1979.

Sukert, A. N.: "An Investigation of Software Reliability Models," *Proc. Ann. Reliability and Maintainability Symp.*, IEEE, New York, Jan. 18–20, 1977.

Swain, A. O., and H. E. Goffman: *Handbook of Human Reliability Analysis with Emphasis on Nuclear Power Plant Applications*, U.S. Nuclear Regulatory Commission, NUREG/CR-12788, April 1980.

Tanenbaum, Andrew S.: *Structured Computer Organization*, Prentice-Hall, Englewood Cliffs, N.J., 1976, pp. 34–35.

Tausworthe, Robert C.: *Standardized Development of Computer Software*, Prentice-Hall, Englewood Cliffs, N.J., Part I, 1977, Part II, 1979.

Teichroew, Daniel: "ISDOS and Recent Extensions," *Proc. Symp. Comp. Software Eng.*, Polytechnic Press, Brooklyn, 1976, pp. 75–81.

Teichroew, Daniel: *Computer-Aided Software Development*, Infotech State of the Art Tutorial, Maidenhead, England, Mar. 3–4, 1977.

Texas Instruments: *SR-52 Statistics Library*, programs ST 1-09 and ST 1-10.

Thayer, Thomas A., et al.: *Software Reliability: A Study of a Large Project Reality*, North-Holland Publishing Company, New York, 1978.

Thompson, K. L., and Dennis M. Ritchie: "The UNIX Time-Sharing System," *Comm. ACM*, vol. 17, no. 7, July 1974, pp. 365–375.

Thompson, K., and D. M. Ritchie: *UNIX Time-Sharing System*, special issue, *Bell Sys. Tech. J.*, July–August 1978, pp. 1928–1948.

Thornton, J. E.: *Design of a Computer—The Control Data 6600*, Scott, Foresman, Glenview, Ill., 1970.

Trakhtenbrot, B. A.: *Algorithms and Automatic Computing Machines*, Heath, Boston, 1963.

Trivedi, Ashok K., and Martin L. Shooman: "Computer Software Reliability: Many-State Markov Modeling Techniques," report no. POLY-EE/EP-75-005-EER 116, Polytechnic Institute of New York, March 1975.

Turn, Rein: *Computers in the 1980's*, Columbia University Press, New York, 1974.

UNIX Programmers Workbench: a series of six papers presented at the Second International Conference on Software Engineering, IEEE catalog no. CHI 125-4C, New York, 1976.

U.S. Air Force: "Information Processing/Data Automation Implications of Air Force Command and Control Requirements in the 1980's," CCIP-85, USAF SAMSO XRS-71-1, AD 900031L, April 1972.

U.S. Department of Defense: "Interim List of DOD Higher Order Programming Languages (HOL)," DOD directive 5000.31, Nov. 24, 1976. (*a*)

U.S. Department of Defense: "Management of Computer Resources in Major Defense Systems," DOD directive 5000.29, Apr. 26, 1976. (*b*)

U.S. Department of Defense: "Reference Manual for the Ada Programming Language," DOD Management Steering Committee for Embedded Computer Resources, Room 2a318, The Pentagon, Washington, D.C., 20301, July 1980.

"U.S. Department of Defense Common High Order Language Effort," U.S. Defense Advanced Research Projects Agency, 1400 Wilson Blvd., Arlington, Va. 22209.

Vesley, W. E., et al.: "PREP and KITT: Computer Codes for the Automatic Evaluation of a Fault Tree," Idaho Nuclear Corporation, Idaho Falls, Idaho, August, 1970; available from NTIS, Springfield, Va.

Vold, H., and B. H. Sjogren: "Optimal Backup of Data Bases: A Statistical Investigation," *BIT*, no. 13, 1973, pp. 233–241.

Volk, Eugene R.: "Project Control—Yesterday's Dream—Tomorrow's Reality," *Proc. 26th Ann. Joint Eng. Mgmt. Conf—Engineering Management in the Computer Age*, IEEE, New York, pp. 2–6.

Wadsworth, George P., and Joseph G. Bryan: *Introduction to Probability and Random Variables*, McGraw-Hill, New York, 1960.

Walston, C. E., and C. P. Felix: "A Method of Programming Measurement and Estimation," *IBM Sys. J.*, vol. 16, no. 1, 1977. (Also reprinted in Putnam and Wolverton, 1977.)

Warnier, Jean D.: *Logical Construction of Programs*, Van Nostrand Reinhold, New York, 1976; French 3d ed., Les Editions d'Organization, Paris, 1974.

Wegner, Peter: *Programming with Ada: An Introduction by Means of Graduated Examples*, Prentice-Hall, Englewood Cliffs, N.J., 1980.

Weibull, W.: "A Statistical Distribution Function of Wide Application," *J. Appl. Mech.*, vol. 18, 1951, pp. 293–297.

Weinberg, Gerald M.: *The Psychology of Computer Programming*, Van Nostrand Reinhold, New York, 1971.

Weinberg, Victor: *Structured Analysis*, Yourdon Press, New York, 1978.

Weinwurm, George: "Economics of Automatic Data Processing, pp. 109–126 in A. Frielink, ed., *Proceedings of the International Symposium on Economics of Automatic Data Processing*, North-Holland Publishing Company, Amsterdam, 1965.

White, J., and T. Booth: "Towards an Engineering Approach to Software Design," *Proc. 2d Int. Conf. Software Eng.*, IEEE, New York, October 1976, p. 220.

Williams, T. L., and R. W. Smith: "A High-Level Language and Interpreter for 8 BIT Machines," *Micro 77 Comp. Conf. Rec.*, IEEE, New York, 1977, p. 981.

Wirth, Niklaus: *Algorithms + Data Structures = Programs*, Prentice-Hall, Englewood Cliffs, N.J., 1976.

Witty, Robert W.: "Dimensional Flowcharting," *Software—Practice and Experience*, vol. 7, 1977, pp. 553–584.

Wolverton, Ray W.: "The Cost of Developing Large-Scale Software," *IEEE Trans. Comp.*, June 1974. (Also reprinted in Putnam and Wolverton, 1977.)

Woodward, Martin R., et al.: "A Measure of Control Flow Complexity in Program Test," *IEEE Trans. Software Eng.*, vol. SE-5, no. 1, January 1977, p. 981.

Wooldridge, Susan: *Software Selection*, Auerbach Publishers, Philadelphia, 1973.

Wooldridge, Susan: *Systems and Programming Standards*, Petrocelli/Charter, New York, 1977.

Workshop on the Attainment of Reliable Software, University of Toronto, June 17–18, 1974.

Yourdon, Edward: *Techniques of Program Structure and Design*, Prentice-Hall, Englewood Cliffs, N.J., 1975.

Yourdon, Edward, and Larry L. Constantine: *Structured Design*, Prentice-Hall, Englewood Cliffs, N.J., 1979.

Zelkowitz, Marvin: "Automatic Program Analysis and Evaluation," *Proc. 2d Int. Conf. Software Eng.*, IEEE, New York, October 1976.

Zelkowitz, Marvin V., et al.: *Principles of Software Engineering and Design*, Prentice-Hall, Englewood Cliffs, N.J., 1979.

Zenith Radio Corporation: *Service Manual, Television Receivers*, N-6 Series, Chicago, 1966.

Zipf, George K.: *National Unity and Disunity*, Principin Press, Bloomington, Ind., 1941.

Zipf, George K.: *Human Behavior and the Principle of Least Effort: An Introduction to Human Ecology*, Addison-Wesley, Reading, Mass., 1949.

Zipf, George K.: *The Psycho-biology of Language: An Introduction to Dynamic Philology*, Houghton Mifflin, Boston, 1935; paperback, MIT Press, Cambridge, Mass., 1965.

Zolnowski, J. A., and D. B. Simmons: 1977: "Measuring Program Complexity," *Digest of Papers COMPCON '77*, IEEE, New York, 1977, pp. 335–340.

Zweiben, J., and Maurice Halstead: "The Frequency Distribution of Operators in PL/1 Programs," *IEEE Trans. Software Eng.*, vol. SE-5, no. 2, March 1979.

Additional References

Berg, K. K., et al.: *Formal Methods of Program Verification and Specification*, Prentice-Hall, Englewood Cliffs, N.J., 1982.

Bloch, Arthur: *Murphy's Law and Other Reasons Why Things Go Wrong!*, Price/Steven/Sloan Publishers, Inc., Los Angeles, Ca., 1977.

Deutsch, Michael S.: *Software Verification and Validation—Realistic Project Approaches*, Prentice-Hall, Englewood Cliffs, N.J., 1982.

Freedman, Roy S.: *Programming Concepts with the ADA Language*, Petrocelli Books, Princeton, N.J., 1982.

Garman, John R.: "The Bug Heard 'Round the World" (Discussion of the software problem which delayed the first shuttle orbital flight), *Software Engineering Notes*, vol. 6. no. 5, October 1981, pp. 3–10.

Glass, Robert L., and Ronald A. Noiseux: *Software Maintenance Guidebook*, Prentice-Hall, Englewood Cliffs, N.J., 1981.

Goos, G., and J. Hartmanis: *Advanced Course on Software Engineering*, Springer-Verlag, New York, 1973.

Hamilton, H., and S. Zeldin: "The Relationship Between Design and Verification," *J. Sys. and Software*, vol. 1, Elsevier North-Holland, Inc., New York, 1979, pp. 29–56.

Higher Order Software, Inc.: *The FAME Configuration Reference Manual*, HOS, Cambridge, Mass., Dec. 1981.

IEEE: *Proc. Specs. of Reliable Software Conf.*, IEEE Cat. No. 79CM-1401-91, 1979.

Joint Engineering Management Conference: "Engineering Management in the Computer Age," *IEEE*, Oct. 1978.

Kernighan, Brian W., and P. J. Plauger: *Software Tools in Pascal*, Addison-Wesley, Reading, Mass., 1981.

McCabe, Tom J.: "A Complexity Measure," *IEEE Trans. on Software Engineering*, Dec. 1976, p. 308.

Mehlmann, Marilyn: *When People Use Computers*, Prentice-Hall, Englewood Cliffs, N.J., 1981.

Naur, P.: "Software Reliability Invited Papers," pp. 243–251. Infotech International Limited, Nicholson House, Maidenhead, Berkshire, England, 1977.

Perlis, Alan T., et. al.: *Software Metrics*, MIT Press, Cambridge, Mass., 1981.

Pyle, I. C.: *The ADA Programming Language*, Prentice-Hall, Englewood Cliffs, N.J., 1981.

Rauch-Hindin, Wendy: "Software Tools: New Ways to Chip Software Into Shape," *Data Communications*, April 1982, pp. 83–113.

Reifer, Donald T.: "Tutorial: Software Management," IEEE Computer Society, Cat. No. EMO 146-1, 1979.

Richeson, George: "Software Reliability Data Analysis and Model Fitting for the Shuttle Data Processing Complex Real-Time Applications," Johnson Space Center, unpublished memo, 1981.

Schindler, Max: "Code Generator Delivers Fortran in Minutes, Not Months," *Electronic Design*, Nov. 12, 1981.

Vyssotsky, Victor A.: "Common Sense in Designing Testable Software," Chap. 6 in Hetzel (1973).

ANSWERS TO SELECTED PROBLEMS

The following solutions have been compiled by the author for several of the problems which appear at the end of the chapters. Many of these have been prepared as solutions to exam problems or homework assignments; thus, some may be terse, while others may try to extend the ideas introduced in the problems or present alternative solutions. In cases in which design is involved, there may be alternate solutions and opinions.

Chapter 1

1.1 (*a*) Unless Bowman could have analyzed the faulty component himself, it is unlikely that he could have anticipated the ensuing problems.

(*b*) Hal could have been designed to have stored problems available for periodic test. By comparing the known solutions with Hal's solution it might have been possible to anticipate the problem. In any case, there always should be a manual override mode which can never be countermanded by the computer.

1.7 The data in Table 1.1 consists of memory words for aircraft computer systems. In Table 1.3, the total size of support software is given for a typical mainframe computer. Clearly, aircraft computers are smaller than typical mainframe computers. There is also much support software written for a typical aircraft computer, but none of it is included in Table 1.1. Also, it is quite common to develop software for a real-time computer system on a larger development system or on a mainframe computer simulating the target computer.

Chapter 2

2.9 (1) Hierarchy charts:

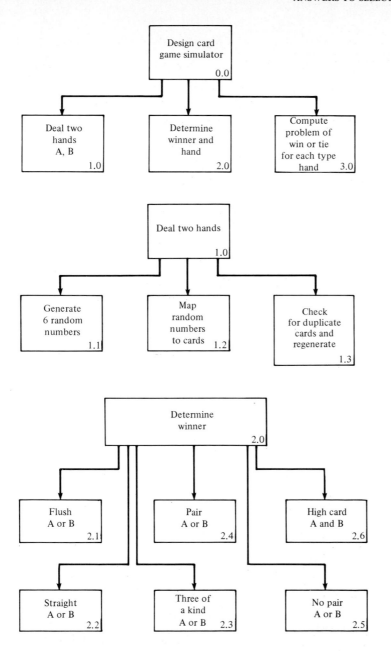

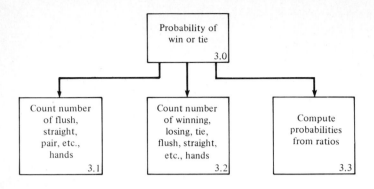

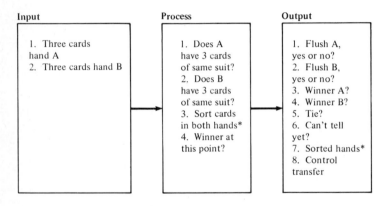

(2) Sample IPO chart for level 2.1 (other similar charts for 1.1, 1.2, 1.3, 2.1, etc.)

(3) *Comments*: At the levels shown or at the next lowest level we will have to resolve certain design issues and alternatives which will be well characterized by the HIPO charts.

a. Should we sort first? (∗)

b. Should we process A and B first, rank them, and then determine the winner?

c. Should we process A and B together and determine the winner?

2.13 (*a*) and (*b*) Control structure graphs and pseudo-code

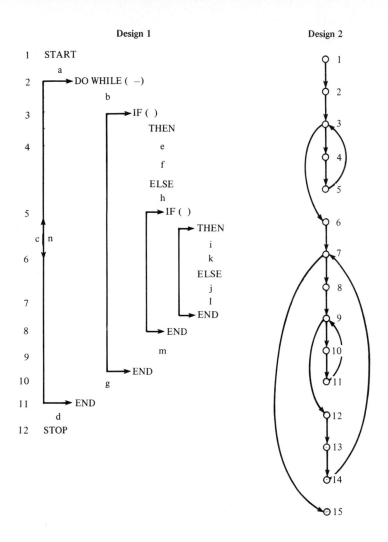

Design 3

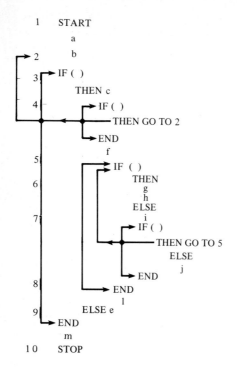

```
1    START
        a
 2      b
 3    IF ( )
          THEN c
 4          IF ( )
              THEN GO TO 2
            END
          f
 5          IF ( )
              THEN
                g
                h
              ELSE
                i
 7            IF ( )
                THEN GO TO 5
                ELSE
                  j
              END
 8          END
              l
 9      ELSE e
      END
        m
10   STOP
```

Design 1	Design 2	Design 3
(*c*) Structured: Only IF THEN ELSE and DO WHILE	Structured: Only IF THEN ELSE and DO WHILE	Unstructured: GO TO 2 and GO TO 5 transfer control out of IF THEN ELSE constructs, causing multiple exits

(*d*) Each pseudo-code has a unique graph; however, the converse is not true. As an example, consider the pseudo-code given above for design 1. An alternate pseudo-code could have been written where 2 IF ( ) GO TO 11; 10 g; 10-11 GO TO 2; 11 d. All other statements remain the same. This alternate pseudo-code represents a structured program with GO TOs because it still maintains a single-input–single-output structure.

2.18 (*a*) Top-level *H* diagram; (*b*) Second-level *H* diagram:

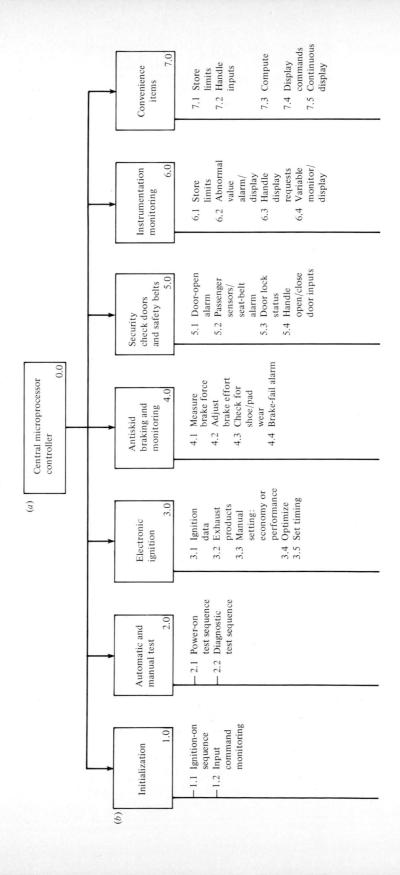

(a)

Central microprocessor controller 0.0

| Initialization 1.0 | Automatic and manual test 2.0 | Electronic ignition 3.0 | Antiskid braking and monitoring 4.0 | Security check doors and safety belts 5.0 | Instrumentation monitoring 6.0 | Convenience items 7.0 |

1.1 Ignition-on sequence
1.2 Input command monitoring

2.1 Power-on test sequence
2.2 Diagnostic test sequence

3.1 Ignition data
3.2 Exhaust products
3.3 Manual setting: economy or performance
3.4 Optimize
3.5 Set timing

4.1 Measure brake force
4.2 Adjust brake effort
4.3 Check for shoe/pad wear
4.4 Brake-fail alarm

5.1 Door-open alarm
5.2 Passenger sensors/ seat-belt alarm
5.3 Door lock status
5.4 Handle open/close door inputs

6.1 Store limits
6.2 Abnormal value alarm/ display
6.3 Handle display requests
6.4 Variable monitor/ display

7.1 Store limits
7.2 Handle inputs
7.3 Compute
7.4 Display commands
7.5 Continuous display

(b)

(*c*) IPO diagram for the electronic ignition function of the system.

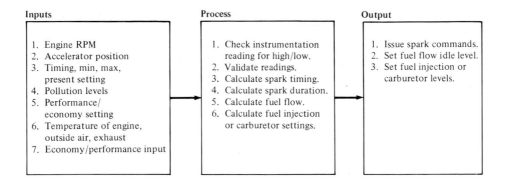

Inputs	Process	Output
1. Engine RPM 2. Accelerator position 3. Timing, min, max, present setting 4. Pollution levels 5. Performance/ economy setting 6. Temperature of engine, outside air, exhaust 7. Economy/performance input	1. Check instrumentation reading for high/low. 2. Validate readings. 3. Calculate spark timing. 4. Calculate spark duration. 5. Calculate fuel flow. 6. Calculate fuel injection or carburetor settings.	1. Issue spark commands. 2. Set fuel flow idle level. 3. Set fuel injection or carburetor levels.

2.19 To be simulated:

```
IF X
    THEN A
    ELSE B

END
```

Solution 1: Two DO WHILEs, FLAG, and compound test:

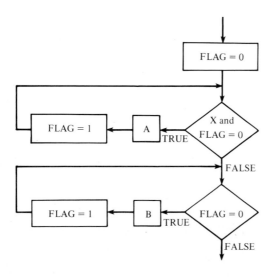

Solution 2: Two DO WHILEs, FLAG, and simple test:

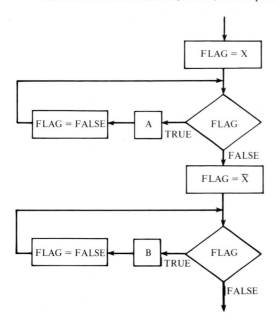

2.20 No practical solution is possible unless we also use a GO TO which has not been allowed. Two nonpractical solutions as well as the GO TO solution are presented below:

1. Unwrap the loop:

To be simulated

```
  ┌──► DO WHILE Z > 0
  │          X = A + B
  └──► END
```

This solution only works if we can determine or bound the number of loop repetitions, N.

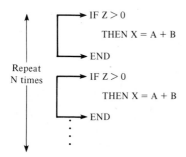

2. We can use the fact that many computer architectures address location 0 when we apply a sequence to an instruction at the bottom of memory. This creates a loop which uses all of memory.

3. The solution with a GO TO is

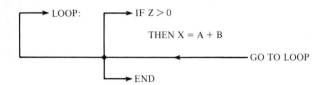

Note: The crossing of control lines clearly indicates an unstructured program.

2.30 (*a*) The program is unstructured because there are *two* exits from the loop at T and W.
(*b*) and (*c*)

Solution 1–With flags	Solution 2–Without flags

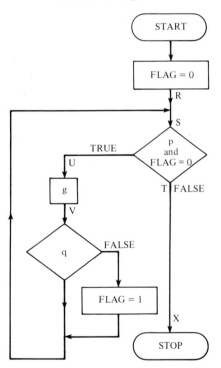

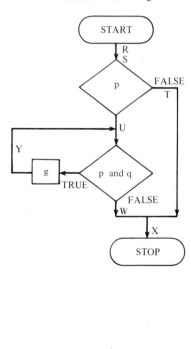

Software system:	Cost	Risk	Difficult portions	Time to first working model	Overall recommendation
(a) Upgraded air traffic control system	The top-down design would have a higher initial cost but a lower maintenance cost.	Probably equal for both approaches since a system already exists and only an *upgrade* is desired.	Radar interface (Why is the system being upgraded? What will be the increased capacity? New processor? What are the logic or code defects?)	Could be shorter than usual in both cases if portions of the previous system are used initially.	Use a top-down design for lower life-cycle cost.
(b) Pascal compiler for an M6800 system	Should be high for a reliable system because several versions and some significant changes in specifications may be needed.	High, since this is basically a large difficult problem for a microprocessor.* It is best to use a bottom-up design first to prove feasibility.	Long running time and large core usage. (An interpreter would be easier.)	Shorter for a bottom-up design.	Use bottom-up for the first design followed by top-down for the final design.
(c) An expanded payroll system for an IBM 360/65 computer	There will be modest additional costs which will be mainly in the testing area. We cannot rely on old tests except for unit tests on unchanged modules.	There should be no surprises here. If an old system is modular, perhaps we can mostly change and add modules.	Interfaces with an existing system if new modules are to be added.	Should be short.	Basically a bottom-up approach is not really indicated.
(d) Graphics editor for 3-D holographic movie	Hard to judge. Thus, not too much should be spent on the first version.	The entire concept is very risky. It is best to adopt an existing system and plan for replacement.	We may lack an adequate description of some of the hardware or special effects which are still under investigation.	It had better be quick, to explore feasability early.	Do something reasonably fast and put your effort into a follow-on effort for a good system if the concept is shown to be feasible.

*Note: For the increased power of the M6800 this difficulty would disappear.

2.39 (*a*) Original design, binary search program:

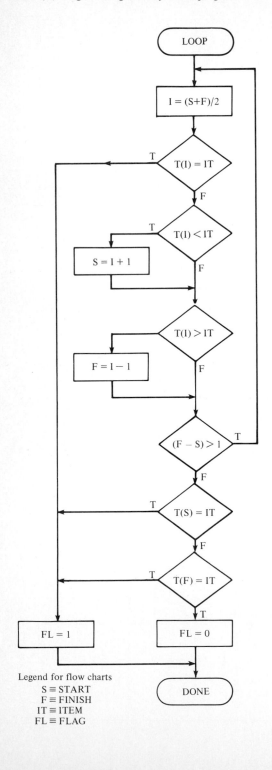

Legend for flow charts
$S \equiv$ START
$F \equiv$ FINISH
$IT \equiv$ ITEM
$FL \equiv$ FLAG

(*b*) The program is unstructured; see multiple exits and entrances shown below.

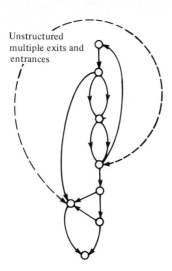

Unstructured
multiple exits and
entrances

(*c*) Structured redesign (*Note*: Flowcharts for module 1 and 2 are on the next page):

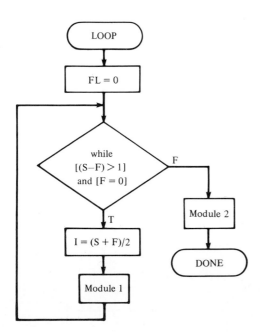

Alternative Module 1 Designs

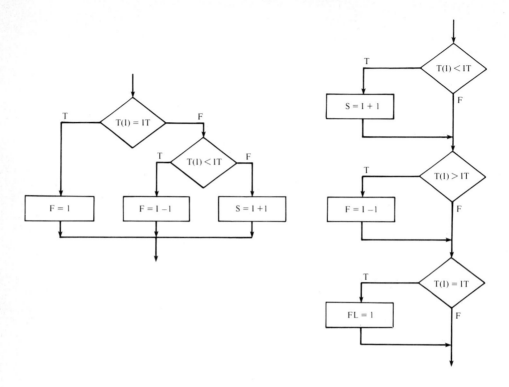

Alternative Module 2 Designs

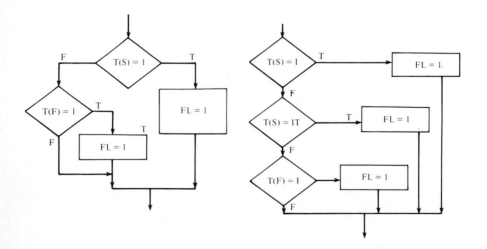

(*d*) The program performs a binary search to find the given item stored in a table.

2.43 (*a*) Design 1—Unstructured:

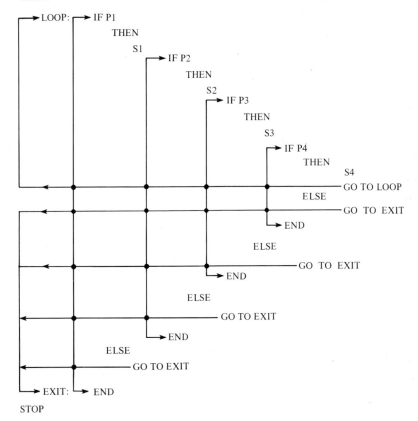

Note: The crossing of control lines shown above due to the GO TOs clearly indicates an unstructured design.

(*b*) Design 2—Structured, with flags:

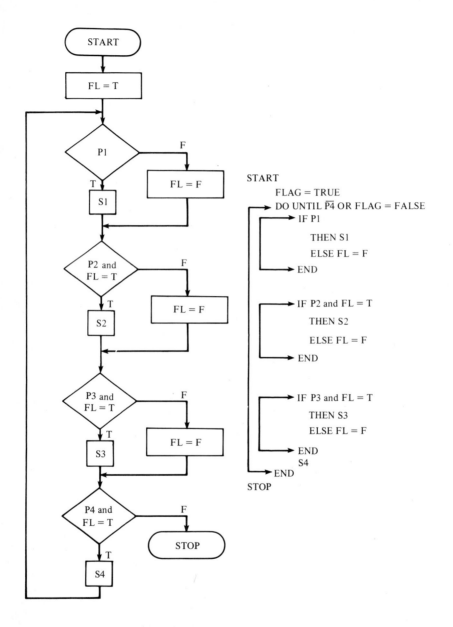

START
    FLAG = TRUE
    DO UNTIL $\overline{P4}$ OR FLAG = FALSE
        IF P1
            THEN S1
            ELSE FL = F
        END

        IF P2 and FL = T
            THEN S2
            ELSE FL = F
        END

        IF P3 and FL = T
            THEN S3
            ELSE FL = F
        END
        S4
    END
STOP

Note: FLAG = TRUE ≡ FL = T
        FLAG = FALSE ≡ FL = F

(*c*) Design 3—Structured, no flags but compound IF predicates:

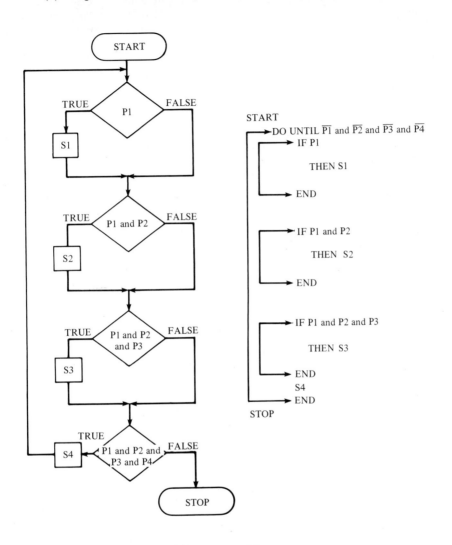

START
    DO UNTIL $\overline{P1}$ and $\overline{P2}$ and $\overline{P3}$ and $\overline{P4}$
        IF P1

            THEN S1

        END

        IF P1 and P2

            THEN S2

        END

        IF P1 and P2 and P3

            THEN S3

        END
        S4
        END
STOP

Note: Several other valid solutions are possible:

1. Using DO CASE construct
2. Using DO WHILE FLAG = TRUE
3. Nested DO WHILE P1, DO WHILE P2,...DO WHILE P4

(*d*)

Design	Efficiency	Clarity of the pseudo-code	Clarity of the flowcharts
(*a*) Unstructured	Best by small factor	4 nest levels	All easily understood
(*b*) Structured with flags	Extra flag tests	2 nest levels	*"*
(*c*) Structured—No flags but compound IF predicates	Compound predicate tests	2 nest levels	*"*

2.44 (*a*) The transfer via GO TO from the middle of loop B creates two exits to loop B.
 (*b*) FLAG = 0

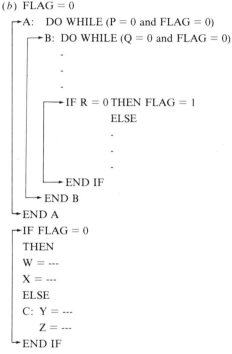

```
A:   DO WHILE (P = 0 and FLAG = 0)
  B: DO WHILE (Q = 0 and FLAG = 0)
        -
        -
        -
        IF R = 0 THEN FLAG = 1
                 ELSE
                      -
                      -
                      -
        END IF
  END B
END A
IF FLAG = 0
THEN
W = ---
X = ---
ELSE
C: Y = ---
   Z = ---
END IF
```

 (*c*) Remove all references to FLAG in the above design, insert IF R = 0 THEN BREAK in loop B in place of IF R = 0 THEN FLAG = 1; and similarly in loop A.
 (*d*) Go back to the original design and substitute IF R = 0 THEN LEAVE in loop A.
 (*e*) Any other solutions? All of the author's are given above.
 (*f*) Since all the above programs are short, the main effect of eliminating the GO TO is to cause a small decrease in clarity due to the compound IF and DO WHILE conditions, and a small increase in running time and storage requirements.

2.45 (*a*) The primary deciding factor in deciding on bottom-up versus top-down would be risk and cost. The only hardware item which is not "off the shelf" is an electronic scanner or a TV camera tube to convert optical to electronic images. (In the late 1960s one American TV manufacturer made such a device which was later discontinued.) All the other functions seem straightforward. (1) Thus, first investigate why the previous optical to electronic image device was withdrawn. Was it because of performance? Cost? Reliability? Lack of sales? (2) In a bottom-up fashion, investigate the hardware and software feasibility and cost of the image converter. Design the system (should (1) and (2) prove to be okay) in a top-down fashion.

(*b*) The timer function could use a clock (either mechanical or IC chip) or microprocessor and software. One would have to weigh the cost versus the novelty and sales appeal. If digital tuning were to be used for the FM and TV, then a keyboard and display would be already available to serve for the timer setting.

(*c*)

Functions to be implemented	Devices
Play only	AM radio
Playback only	FM radio
Record only	TV receiver
Play and record	records; mike
Timer for playback and recording	TV camera
Search mode	Scanner
Edit mode	Audio tape; videotape

H diagram—Design 1:

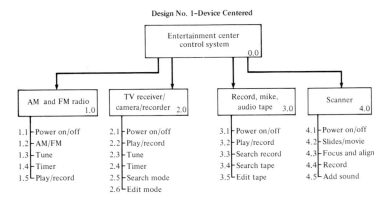

Design No. 1–Device Centered

H diagram—Design 2:

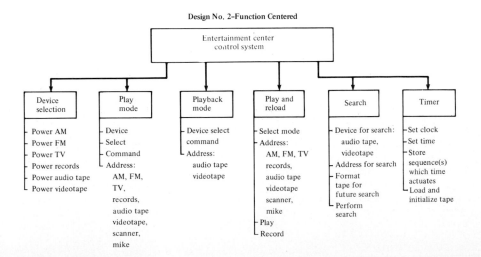

Design No. 2–Function Centered

(*d*) IPO diagram—Design 2:

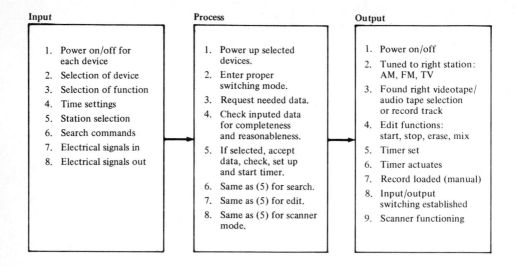

Input	Process	Output
1. Power on/off for each device	1. Power up selected devices.	1. Power on/off
2. Selection of device	2. Enter proper switching mode.	2. Tuned to right station: AM, FM, TV
3. Selection of function	3. Request needed data.	3. Found right videotape/audio tape selection or record track
4. Time settings	4. Check inputed data for completeness and reasonableness.	4. Edit functions: start, stop, erase, mix
5. Station selection	5. If selected, accept data, check, set up and start timer.	5. Timer set
6. Search commands	6. Same as (5) for search.	6. Timer actuates
7. Electrical signals in	7. Same as (5) for edit.	7. Record loaded (manual)
8. Electrical signals out	8. Same as (5) for scanner mode.	8. Input/output switching established
		9. Scanner functioning

Comments:

1. The clock is always powered up. Any other power signal automatically turns on the audio amplifier as well.
2. A sound mixing facility could be added.
3. It is not clear whether design 1, design 2, or a conventional design (with switches, control knobs, and cables) would be best. Further analysis is needed comparing

    a. Costs
    b. Buyer appeal (gimmick, prestige?)
    c. Flexibility to future changes and the impact on the cost of redesign (less important for many high-volume items)
    d. Ease of consumer use

Note: Comparison of design 1 and design 2.

The following computation is for design 1:

Inputs		Outputs	Operators
Power on	AM (8)	Power on AM (8)	
		Operation FM	
Command	FM	TV	
	TV		
	records	·	
	mike	·	
	videotape	·	
	audio tape	·	
	scanner	scanner	

ANSWERS TO SELECTED PROBLEMS 645

Power off	AM (8)	Power off AM (8)	D/A
	FM	FM	Outputs to switching (2)
	.	.	
	.	.	
	.	.	
	scanner	scanner	
Play	AM	Connect to AM (7)	
	FM	Amplifier FM	
	.	Input TV	
	.	Records	
	.		
	scanner	Mike	
Record videotape (2)		Audio from videotape	
audio tape		Audio tape	
Record and play TV (2)		Connect to TV–TV (2)	
		Videotape	
Amplifier		Scanner	
Edit tape audio (2)		Tape write audio, video (2)	STORE
Tape video		Tape erase audio, video (2)	MUL
Search start (1)		Fast forward audio (2)	SUB
		video	ADD
Track number (1)		Found track audio (2)	COMPARE
		video	JUMP
Timer set (1)		Stop search audio (2)	GO TO
		video	Constants
			Locations tape? (5)
	33	36	14
Tune AM (2)			
station			
Tune FM			
station (2)		Scan tune AM, FM, TV (6)	
Tune TV		Frequency match	
station (2)		Lock tune	
	39	42	

Note: If design 2 is used, there may be fewer inputs and outputs. Also many of the functions such as power probably would be analog.

(*e*) Addition of a home computer option: A home computer could use the same central processing unit as the system but would need an addition of much more memory, keyboard (unless the entertainment center design included one), and peripheral devices; thus, not too much would be saved by combining the microprocessor-controlled home entertainment center with this feature. Also, what sort of conflicts would occur between one family member who wished to watch videotapes and another who wished to program?

2.46 (*a*)

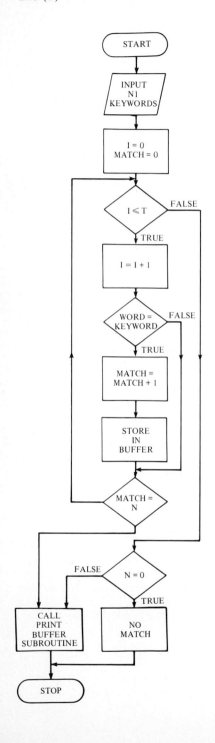

(*b*) The program is not structured because of outputs for MATCH = N and N = 0, that is, two inputs to call print buffer subroutine.

(*c*) Solution A:

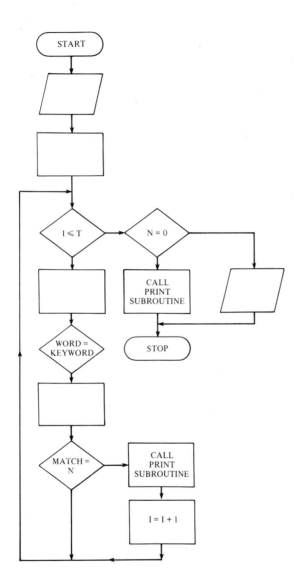

Solution B:

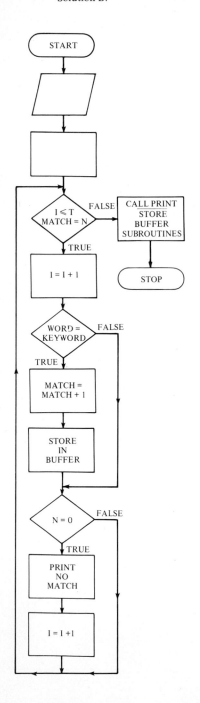

Pseudo-code for design 2:

```
START
INPUT  N
INPUT KEYWORD(S) FOR TOPIC
I = 0
MATCH = 0
DO WHILE (I ≤ T) and (MATCH ≠ N)
    I = I + 1
    IF WORD = KEYWORD
        THEN MATCH = MATCH + 1
            STORE IN BUFFER.
    END
    IF N = 0
        THEN PRINT NO MATCH
            I = T + 1
    END
END
CALL PRINT BUFFER SUBROUTINE
STOP
```

(*d*) Shouldn't program read (see third and fourth line from bottom):

$$\text{IF } \textbf{MATCH} = 0$$
$$\text{THEN PRINT "NO MATCH"}$$

The only change is that the expression in the IF statement changes.

Chapter 3

3.7 Denote operators by X and operands by O. Comments are ignored.

Example 1		**Example 2**	

```
    X
START

    X                   OXOXO          C     EXAMPLE
INPUT               (A, B, C)
                                        O        X        OXO
                                   LOOP:  DO WHILE 270

                                       O X O X O
                                       A = B + 1

    X  O X O                        X  O X O
    IF A > 5                        IF A > 10

            O X O                          O X O
        THEN X = 10                    THEN X = A

            O X O                          O X O
        ELSE X = 1                     ELSE Y = Z

        END                            END IF
    X  O X O                        X  O X O
    IF  B > 10                      IF  Y < 5
```

Example 1 (*continued*)

```
        O X O
THEN Y = 20

       O X O
ELSE Y = 2




        END
  X O X O
IF  X > 15

        O X O
THEN Z = 30

      O X O
ELSE Z = 3



        END


   X        OXOXO
PRINT    (X, Y, Z)

   X
STOP
```

Character string of alternating
operators and operands:

XXOXOXOXOXOOXOOXOXOXOOXOOXO

XOXOOXOOXOXOXOXOX

There are 44 symbols, 43 pairings,
and 7 reversals.

Percentagewise $\dfrac{7}{43} \times 100\% = 16\%$

Example 2 (*continued*)

```
      X     OXO
THEN PRINT  X, Y

     X  O X O
ELSE IF  Y = 2

              X         O
         THEN GO TO  LOOP

            O X O
         ELSE C = 3

         END IF

      END IF

   O X O X O
   G = H + R

   END DO

      O X O
   IF  F > 0

           X      O
      THEN PRINT  G

           X      O
      ELSE PRINT  K

   END IF

   X
STOP
```

Character string of alternating
operators and operands:

OXOXOOXOXOXOXOO

XOOXOXOXO XOXOXOXOXOO

XOOXOXOOXOXOXOX

There are 50 symbols, 49 pairings,
and 6 reversals.

Percentagewise $\dfrac{6}{49} \times 100\% = 12\%$

Conclusion: The alternating hypothesis is approximately correct.

3.34 (*a*) Estimate of token length: Start by estimating variables and operators.

Problem specification	Input variables	Output variables	Intermediate variables and constants	Operands
(1)	(Employee data)	(Paycheck and weekly averages)	?	READ PRINT
(2)	Name Social security number Pay rate Hours worked per week Number of employees	—	—	READ
(3)	—	Name Social security number Net pay	—	PRINT (We assume check has preprinted headings.)
(4)	—		Net pay Gross pay Social security tax Tax 0.04 0.0175	* — =
(5)	—	Average total hours	"Weekly average number of hours"	+ PRINT
Unique Numbers:	5	2	6	6

Thus types (unique operands + unique operators) = 5 + 2 + 6 + 6 = 19.
Using Zipf's formula $n = 19(0.5772 + \ln(19)) = 66.9 \approx 67$.
Using Halstead's formula $n = 6 \log_2 6 + 13 \log_2 13 = 63.6 \approx 64$.
   Note: The following PL/I program performs the payroll computation.

	Program	Operands	Operators	Total number
Payroll:	PROC:	Payroll	:PROC;	4
	Declare (all variables)	0	0	0
	T hours = 0;	T hours, 0	= ;	4
	Get list (N employees);	N employees	GET LIST;	3
		I, N employees	DO TO;	6
	DO I = 1 to N employees;		=	
	Get list (Name, social security number, pay rate, hours);	Name Social security number Pay rate Hours	GET LIST;	6
	T hours = T hours + hours;	T hours T hours Hours	= +;	6

PL/I program (*Continued*)

Program	Operands	Operators	Total numbe
Gross pay = Pay rate * hours;	Gross pay Pay rate Hours	= * ;	6
Net pay = Gross pay * (1 − .04 − .0175);	Net pay Gross pay 1, .04, .0175	= * ( );	9
Put list (Name, social security number, Net pay);	Name Social security number Net pay	PUT LIST;	5
END;		END;	2
Put skip list ("Weekly Avg. Hours = ,"		PUT LIST SKIP	7
T hours/N em- ployees)	"Weekly Avg. Hours = " T hours N employees	/;	
End payroll;	Payroll	End;	3
		Total	61

Note: 1. Close agreement to token estimates of 67 and 64.
        2. The 12 line PL/I program has 12 statements rather than the 8 estimated.
        3. The Fortran solution in Ledgard's book is 16 statements long, not counting declare, format, and comment statements.

(*b*) Assume that one line of assembly code has one operator and one operand. Thus

$$67 \text{ (tokens)}/2 \text{ (assembly code lines/token)} = 33 \text{ assembly code lines}$$

(*c*) Assuming that a Fortran statement is equivalent to 4 assembly statements.

$$33 \text{ (assembly code lines)}/4 \text{ (assembly/Fortran)} = 8 \text{ Fortran lines}$$

(*d*) To estimate the total time to specify, design, code, and test, we use the productivity coefficient from Table 3.17 for Akiyama's data = 25 tokens/man-day for assembly code.

$$67 \text{ tokens}/25 \text{ (tokens/man-day)} = 2.68 \approx 2.5 \text{ days for 1 man}$$

Note: If we refer to Table 6.13, we see that a medium difficulty project of 6 to 12 months duration (ours is much shorter) can be designed, coded, tested, and documented at the rate of 10 instructions per day. For the 12-statement PL/I program we estimate the total time to be 1 1/2 days.

3.35 (*a*) See Prob. 2.13 and its solution for flowgraphs.

Design 1

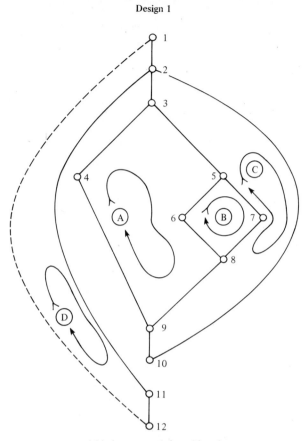

Add phantom path from 12 to 1

Faces: A, B, C, D
$v(G_1) = 4$

Design 2

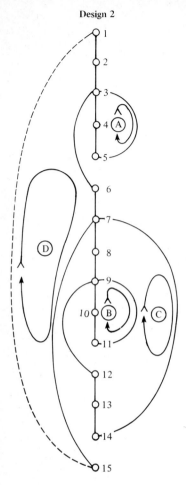

Design 3

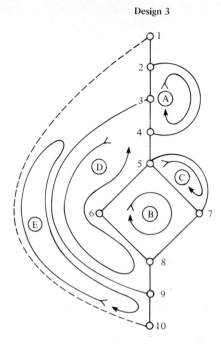

Add phantom path from 10 to 1

Faces: A, B, C, D, E
$v(G_3) = 5$

Add phantom path from 15 to 1

Faces: A, B, C, D
$v(G_2) = 4$

(*b*) $v(G)$ from branch and edge count

$$e = 15$$
$$n = 12$$
$$v(G_1) = e - n + p$$
$$= 15 - 12 + 1$$
$$= 4$$

$$e = 18$$
$$n = 15$$
$$v(G_2) = e - n + p$$
$$= 18 - 15 + 1$$
$$= 4$$

$$e = 14$$
$$n = 10$$
$$v(G_3) = e - n + p$$
$$= 14 - 10 + 1$$
$$= 5$$

3.42 If we choose as our three programs those given in Prob. 2.13, we find the necessary diagrams in the problem statement along with solutions to Prob. 2.13 and Prob. 3.35.

Design 1	Design 2	Design 3
From the solution to Prob. 3.35 $v(G_1) = 4$ From the solution to Prob. 2.13 we see no crossing of control lines since all structures are nested thus: knot complexity = 0	$v(G_2) = 4$ From the statement of Prob. 2.13 we again see a structured design with nesting thus: knot complexity = 0	$v(G_3) = 5$ From the solution to Prob. 2.13 we see three control lines crossing due to nonstructured GO TOs thus: knot complexity = 3

Conclusion: There is no particular relationship between knot and cyclomatic complexity.

3.43 All structured programs are composed only of SEQUENCE, IF THEN ELSE, and DO WHILE, and none of these individual structures have crossing control lines. In a structured program we must nest all control structures so that no control lines cross. Thus, we conclude that a structured program has a knot complexity of zero.

Note: This observation leads to the conclusion that knot complexity is not a very useful measure if all structured programs have the same complexity measure, that is, zero.

3.49 (*a*) Estimate of number of unique operators and operands:

Part of program	Operators	Operands
Inputs	INPUT	A, B, C, D
Real root	$/, +, -, *$	OLDR, NEWR, ROOT
Extraction	IF, DO, =	SLOPE, ERROR
Quadratic equation	SQRT	REAL 1, IMAJ 2
		REAL 2, IMAJ 2
		DISC
Output	PRINT	
Unique Number	10	14

(*b*) Program length:

t = operator types + operand types = $10 + 14 = 24$

$n = 24(0.5772 + \ln 24) = 90.1$

Note: $\log_2 x = 3.3219 \log x$

(*c*) Volume:

V = volume = $N \log_2(\eta_1 + \eta_2) = 90.1 \log_2 24 = 90.1 \times 3.3219 \log 24 = 413.1$

V^* = volume min = $(2 + \eta_2^*)\log_2(2 + \eta_2^*)$

η_2^* = input + output variables = A, B, C, D, REAL 1, IMAJ 1, REAL 2*, IMAJ 2, ROOT = 9 total.

$V^* = (2 + 9)\log_2(2 + 9) = 11 \times 3.3219 \log 11 = 38.05$

Level:

Level $l = \dfrac{V^*}{V} = \dfrac{38.05}{413.1} = .092$

Effort:

Effort $= \dfrac{V^2}{V^*} = \dfrac{V}{l} = 4490.2$ bits

(*d*) If a human processes 10 bits in 1 s, it takes 449 s $\times \dfrac{1}{60} = 4.48$ min. The time estimate seems too short. If we use a length estimate of 90.1 tokens and use 25 tokens per day (see Table 3.17), we obtain 3.6 days, which is more reasonable. Can you explain the inconsistency?

Note: Since the complex roots have the same real part, one could eliminate Real 2 if desired.

3.50 All the tests are IF tests; thus, there are no additional operators. Additional operands are the character string constants: "all negative real," "all real one or more positive," "complex negative real," "complex positive real." Thus

$$t = 10 + 14 + 4 = 28$$
$$n = 28(0.5772 + \ln 28) = 109.46$$
$$V = 109.46 \log_2 28 = 109.46 \times 3.3219 \log 28 = 526.2$$
$$V^* = (2 + 4)\log_2(2 + 4) = 15 \times 3.3219 \log 15 = 58.6$$
$$l = \frac{V^*}{V} = \frac{58.6}{526.2} = 0.111$$
$$E = \frac{V}{l} = \frac{526.2}{0.111} = 4724.8 \text{ bits}$$
$$\text{Time} = \frac{4725}{10} = 472.5 \text{ s} \frac{1}{60} = 7.87 \text{ min}$$

Alternate estimate 109.46 tokens ÷ 25 tokens per day = 4.4 days. Can you explain the inconsistency?

Since the level stays about the same, the effort increase is due to the increase in V.

Chapter 4

4.18 (*a*) Module Testing: A module is a small block of code (50 lines or less of a fixed control complexity) which performs one function. Once the code is written and compiled successfully, the first tests of the module itself without interconnections to other modules are performed; they are called module or unit tests.

Integration Testing: When two or more modules are tested together (or if a module is tested with the control program) then such a test is called integration testing. Such testing concentrates on module (control program) interfaces.

Module testing	Integration testing
1. Up to 50 lines of code.	The size varies depending on how much of the system has already been integrated.
2. Occurs early in bottom-up designs and later in top-down designs.	Occurs later in bottom-up designs and early in top-down designs.
3. The total number of errors removed is approximately the same in either test.	
4. The designer generally does the module test.	The designer or separate tester does the integration test.
5. Needs test drivers in bottom-up development.	Needs test stubs in top-down development.

(*b*) Estimated number of errors = 0.01% of machine instructions

Number of errors = $0.01 \times I_T$

Estimated $I_T = 5 \times I_T' = 5,000$

Number of errors = $0.01 \times 5,000 = 50$

I_T = Number of lines of machine code

I_T' = Number of lines of higher level code

(*c*)

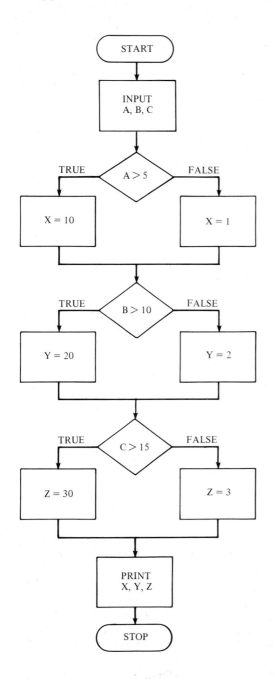

1. For a type 0 test we must test each line of code at least once. A test which performs this is

$$A = 100, B = 100, C = 100$$
$$\text{and}$$
$$A = 1, B = 1, C = 1$$

2. A type 3 test is an exhaustive test. This must transverse each path for every combination of input data.

$$
\begin{array}{llll}
\text{Paths:} & A < 5, & B < 10, & C < 15 \quad 000 \\
& A < 5, & B < 10, & C > 15 \quad 001 \\
& A < 5, & B > 10, & C < 15 \quad 010 \\
& A > 5, & B < 10, & C < 15 \quad 100 \\
& A < 5, & B > 10, & C > 15 \quad 011 \\
& A > 5, & B < 10, & C > 15 \quad 101 \\
& A > 5, & B > 10, & C < 15 \quad 110 \\
& A > 5, & B > 10, & C > 15 \quad 111
\end{array}
$$

(Each digit of a binary number represents a different decider; where 0 = False and 1 = True.) Assume this is on a 16-bit machine in which A, B, C are integers in the range $+2^{15}$ to -2^{15}. Thus $A < 5$ involves a little less than 2^{15} values and $A > 5$ involves a little more than 2^{15}. Assume for each path $2^{15} \times 2^{15} \times 2^{15} = 2^{45}$ tests. For all eight paths $= 2^3 \times 2^{45} = 2^{48} \approx 2^{10} \times 2^{10} \times 2^{10} \times 2^8 \cong 500 \times 10^9 = \boxed{5 \times 10^{11}}$.

4.19

(a) Normal operations:
Normal sequence 1

	yields	
b (RELIABILITY)	$\Rightarrow$	1. Reliability, equipment
		2. Reliability, mathematics
		3. Reliability, probabilistic
		4. Reliability, software
		5. Reliability, theory
s (4)	$\Rightarrow$	Reliability, software
		1. Author 1
		2. Author 2
		3. Report 1
		4. Report 2
		5. Paper 1
		6. Paper 2
d (2)	$\Rightarrow$	2. Tom Smith, "All There Is to Know about Software Reliability," Polytechnic Press, Brooklyn, N.Y., 1977, 212 pp.

Normal sequence 2

f (Tom Smith)		1. Tom Smith (book)
d (1)		1. Tom Smith, "All There Is to Know about Software Reliability," Polytechnic Press, Brooklyn, N.Y., 1977, 212 pp.

Other normal sequences:
Check to see if they are listed under keywords Software Reliability

---

For repetitive testing of normal data one could select an additional *n* sets of test data from the following sources

1. The library card catalog
2. The listing of "All the Books in Print"
3. A listing of government documents

(*b*) Abnormal Operation:

1. See what happens with too many keywords

    b (Reliability software and hardware combined)

    (Should truncate to reliability software)

2. See what happens with unknown keyword

    b (AARDVARK)

    Either it should have been designed to return no entries or perhaps the best match possible, e.g. AARON, JULES (book)
3. Select a number greater than one on the list and see what happens. It should give back a message not on the list.
4. Use numerals and punctuation for arguments of b and f commands and characters for arguments of s and d commands.
5. Use numeral 0 and negative numbers for s and d commands. Try decimals and floating point numbers.
6. Try wrong sequences

    s without a browse

    d without a select, etc.

7. Try wrong syntax: omit command, leave out parentheses.
8. Leave out arguments of commands to see if there are default options.
9. Try misspellings of author's name on a find command.
10. Try numerical arguments of commands which are outside valid range for s and d commands.

4.23 (*a*) and (*b*) Definition of digital watch control buttons and modes:

Control buttons		
Button	Notation	Function
Lamp	BL	Push in, lamp on; release, lamp off.
Mode	BM(M1–M5 defined below)	Each push of the button advances sequentially from mode 1 to 5 and back to mode 1. If the select and/or adjust button is pushed one or more times, the next push of the mode button resets to mode 1.
Select	BS	The function depends on mode as defined below. (Basically it selects submodes.)
Adjust	BA	The function depends on mode as defined below. (Basically it makes adjustments in each submode.)

(*b*) Detailed functions of BS and BA:

Mode	Pressing BS	Pressing BA	Comments
M1— Normal time	Push in displays the alarm setting in hours, minutes, and a.m. or p.m. Release returns the setting to time display. Pushing BS and BA together either disables or sets the alarm depending on the initial state.	Push in displays the date instead of seconds. Another push restores the second counter. If the alarm is beeping (it lasts for 60 s) it can be turned on and off by successive pushes of BA.	All functions are unaffected; only the display is changed. Display also shows the day of the week and the alarm set indication.
M2— Chronograph	If the chronograph is running, it enters the lap mode where the time display is frozen for 6 seconds; however, the chronograph continues, and after the freeze the display jumps ahead 6 s. If the chronograph is stopped, pressing the button resets it to zero.	The first press starts the chronograph. The second press stops the chronograph and holds the display. Alternate starts and stops accumulate time on the display.	This mode implements the normal two-button stopwatch function S. The display shows h, min, s, and 1/10 s.
M3— Alarm set	Upon entry, the hour setting is blinking. Pressing BS stops the hour setting from blinking and starts the minute setting blinking. Further pushes repeat the sequence.	Pressing BA advances the blinking display by one. Pushing BA all the way in hard advances the display.	The alarm always triggers at 00 seconds; thus, there is no alarm seconds setting. The alarm can be triggered by either the normal time or dual time mode.
M4— Dual time mode	Same functions as normal time mode.	Same functions as normal time mode.	All time and date functions are independently adjustable, except minutes and seconds are slaved to the setting of the normal time mode.
M5— Setting submodes:			
M51— Seconds	Pushing of BS switches to mode M52. and sets the hours blinking.	Pushing BA sets second counter to 00.	In M51 when M5 is entered with seconds blinking.
M52— Hours	Pushing BS switches to mode M53 with minutes blinking.	Pushing BA advances the hour setting by 1 for each push.	
M53— Minutes	Pushing BS switches to mode M54 with the month blinking.	Pushing BA advances the minutes by 1.	
M54— Month	Pushing BS switches to mode M55 with date blinking.	Pushing BA advances the month by 1.	
M55— Date	Pushing BS switches to mode M56 with day blinking.	Pushing BA advances the date by 1.	
M56— Day of week	Pushing BS switches to mode M57. (Start of dual time)	Pushing BA advances the setting by one day of the week.	

(*b*) *Continued*

Mode	Pressing BS	Pressing BA	Comments
M57— Hour (Dual time)	Pushing BS switches to mode M58.	Same as M52.	
M58— Month (dual time)	Pushing BS switches to mode M59.	Same as M54.	
M59— Date (dual time)	Pushing BS switches to mode M60.	Same as M55.	
M60— Day of the week (dual time)	Pushing BS switches to mode M51. (Cycle resets.)	Same as M56.	

(*c*) and (*d*) M1—Inputs: BS, BS + BA, BA, alarm + BA, no alarm + BA, silent alarm + BA, BM, BL, BL + BS, BL + BA = ⑩

M2—Inputs: No chronograph + BA, chronograph running + BA, chronograph stopped + BA, no chronograph + BS, chronograph + BS, BL, BM = ⑦

M3—Inputs: BS + BA (1–24 times, hold in), BS + BS + BA (1–60 times, hold in) BL, BM = 1 + 25 + 61 + 2 = ⑧⑨

M4—Dual time—Same as M1 = ⑩

M5—BS, BS + BS + BA (1–24 times, hold in), BS + BS + BS + BA (1–60 times, hold in), BS + BS + BS + BS + BA (1–12 times, hold in), BS (5 times) + BA (1–31 times, hold in), BS (6 times) + BA (1–7 times, hold in) , BS (7 times) + BA (1–24 times, hold in), BS (8 times) + BA (1–60 times, hold in), BS (⑨ times) + BA (1–12 times, hold in), BS (10 times) + BA (1–31 times, hold in), BS (11 times) reset, BM, BL

$$1 + 25 + 61 + 13 + 32 + 8 + 25 + 61 + 13 + 32 + 1 + 1 + 1 = 274$$

Total tests: $10 + 7 + 89 + 10 + 274 = 390$

Conclusion: It is also difficult to test complex hardware with many operating modes.

4.24

Flowchart

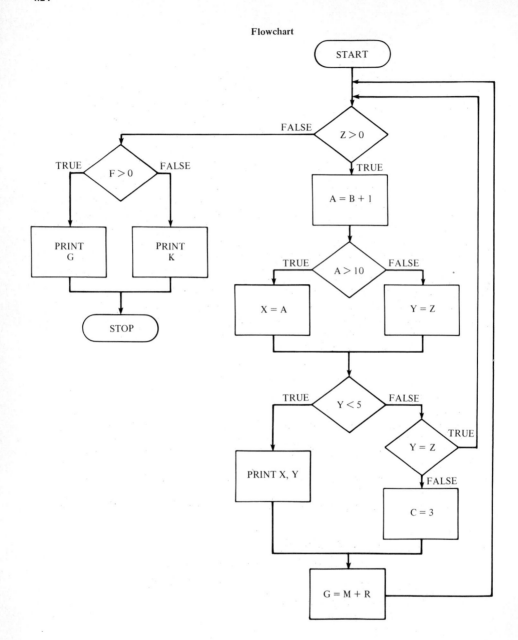

4.24 (Cont.)

Graph

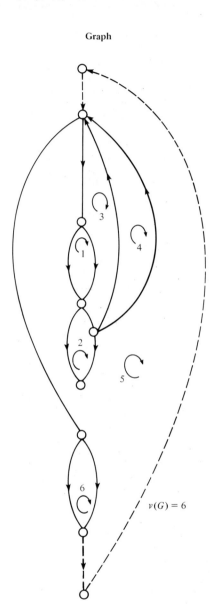

$v(G) = 6$

4.25 The acceptance test will be composed of nominal input data as well as exceptional input data.

Nominal input data

---

1 Departure, destination, five position-check points, altitude, speed, and aircraft type are entered for one set of end points.

2 Repeat of test #1 for five different end points (destination–departure).

Iterated normal input data

Test	Departure	Destination	Five position-check points	Altitude	Speed	Aircraft type
3	Fixed	Fixed	Fixed	Fixed	Fixed	Vary 3–5
4	"	"	"	"	Vary 3–5	Fixed
5	"	"	"	Vary 3–5	Fixed	"
6	"	"	Vary 3–5	Fixed	"	"
7	"	Vary 3–5	Fixed	"	"	"
8	Vary 3–5	Fixed	"	"	"	"
9	Vary parameters in pairs.					
10	Vary parameters in triplets.					
10a	Vary weather in an appropriate way.					

Extremes of range

---

11 Input destination and departure points very close and very far.
12 Input unusual configurations at check points if they aren't fixed.
13 Input extreme high and low altitude.
14 Input extreme high and low speeds.
15 Input any unusual plane types.

Bad input data

---

16 Input ridiculous data—garbled mixture of alphanumerics and control characters.
17 Input zero values for all parameters.
18 Input negative values of altitude and speed.

4.26 An H diagram for the basic system is given below

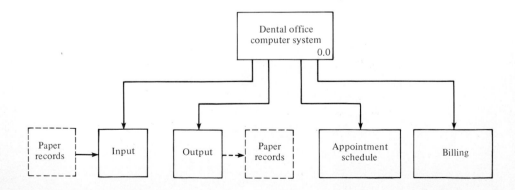

Note: As costs of disk storage units decrease, it may be feasible to eliminate paper records for all but backup purposes.

(*a*) *Module test*—Choose input cases which exercise each function of the module at least once and test them.

Integration test—Develop sets of test data for normal and extreme cases. Be sure to include special cases such as one or more people being absent (up to all absent) on a particular day. Test what happens if from one to all of the patients cancel on one day. Also include overload conditions, nonsense input, operator errors, and so on.

Simulation test—See field test.

Field test—In this case the simulation and field test would be identical. One would use the manual appointment books being presently kept and enter past monthly data. Run both systems parallel for three months and compare results and correct any errors.

Regression test—One should store past test data and correct answers on disk. As new errors are fixed, go back and rerun a subset of past tests.

(*b*) Since this will be a two-stage development—first a bottom-up prototype, then a top-down final design—both drivers and stubs will be needed. The prototype design should concentrate on input and output formats and develop these modules first. Then a driver can be written to link these modules to the appointment and billing modules. A modest amount of module and integration tests will be performed on the prototype system. The office staff will be given the prototype system to use for 2 to 4 weeks in parallel with the paper system. After a thorough review of the prototype performance, the final system will be planned. If any of the prototype modules survive largely intact they can be used in the final top-down development to test the control structure which is written first. Modules which must be largely or completely rewritten cannot be used in testing the control structure, and test stubs must be substituted.

(*c*) Estimation of program size:

Variable names						
Patient i	Hygienist 1	Technician	X ray 1	Checkup	Finance	Delete
Old	Hygienist 2	Cavity	X ray 2	Bill 1	Extension	Add
New	Assistant 1	Clean	X ray 3	Bill 2	Payment	Correct
Dentist 1	Assistant 2	Plate	Bridge	Bill 3	Appointment 1	Search
Dentist 2	Assistant 3	Extract	Followup	Overdue	Appointment 2	Insert
Dentist 3		Cap		Collection	Appointment 3	Clean
List i	Constant cost for,			Appointment Date		
List all	say, 25 procedures			Appointment Time		

69 variables above plus, say, 31 more which further analysis and design will designate.

Operators		
$+,-,/,*$	IF THEN	ON ERROR
$>,<,=,\neq$	DO WHILE	COMMENT
,;:	PRINT	SUBSTRING
GO SUB, RETURN	INPUT	STRING CONCATENATE

21 operators plus, say, 9 we have forgotten $= 30$

$t = 30 + 100 = 130$

$n = 130(0.5772 + \ln 130) = 708$ tokens

1. If the development is to be done in assembly language, we estimate 2 tokens per instruction or ≈ 354 lines of assembly code. From Fig. 4.2 we obtain about 4 to 5 man-months to that time. Assume that you will need 40 percent of this or 2 months for testing and debugging. Assume 1 month for module testing, two weeks for integration testing, and 2 weeks for field testing.

2. As an alternate estimate, assume that the FORTRAN code yields 4 lines of machine code of 2 tokens each or 8 tokens per line of code. Thus, the program would require 89 lines of FORTRAN code. If a programmer can work at the rate of 10 lines a day, it should take 9 days. Obviously, there is a gross disagreement here with the manual modifications even if we throw in a factor of, say, 2 for the higher efficiency of a higher level language.

Chapter 5

5.2 Density and hazard functions for the data. (a) Data failure density function; (b) data hazard rate; (c) data failure distribution function; and (d) data success function.

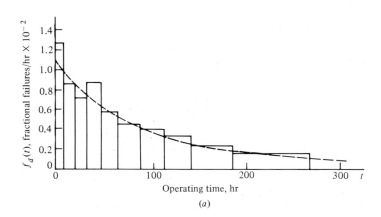

(a)

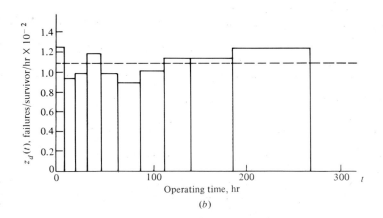

(b)

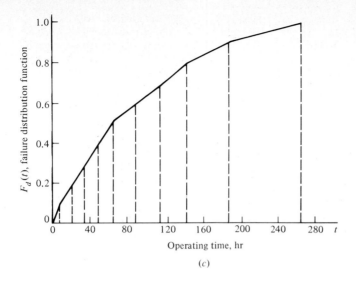

(c)

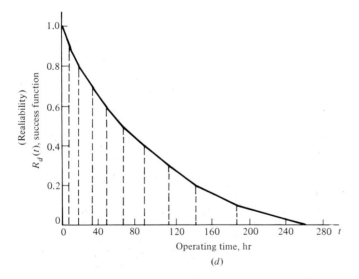

(d)

5.3 Reliability functions for the example (a) $f_d(t)$ and $z_d(t)$; (b) $F_d(t)$ and $R_d(t)$.

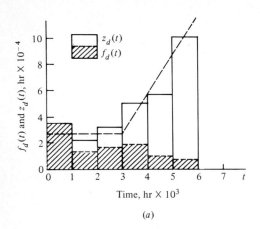

(a)

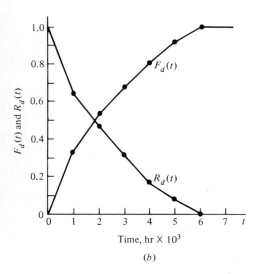

(b)

5.14 Use constant hazard model.
(a)

$$\text{MTBF}(\tau) = \frac{1}{\dfrac{K}{I_T}[E_T - E_C(\tau)]}$$

after 1 month

$$10 = \frac{1}{\dfrac{K}{10^4}[E_T - 15]}$$

after 2 months

$$15 = \frac{1}{\dfrac{K}{10^4}[E_T - 25]}$$

Dividing

$$\frac{10}{15} \approx \frac{E_T - 25}{E_T - 15} \qquad \text{solving } E_T = 45$$

$$\text{Substituting } 10 = \frac{1}{\frac{K}{10^4}[45 - 15]} \qquad \text{solving } K = 1/3 \times 10^2$$

Model is

$$\text{MTBF}(\tau) = \frac{1}{\frac{\frac{1}{3} \times 10^2}{10^4}[45 - E_C(\tau)]} = \frac{3 \times 10^2}{[45 - E_C(\tau)]}$$

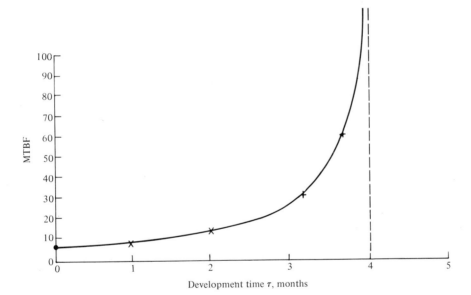

Development time τ, months

Legend for Figure:
× Data points
· Calculated at $\tau = 0$ assuming $E_C(\tau = 0) = 0$ yielding $\text{MTBF}(\tau = 0) = 6.7$
+ Assuming the error removal rate continues at 10 per month.
(*b*) Note that the estimate of 3 3/4 months depends strongly on what the error removal rate is during months 3 and 4, which has been assumed to be 10 errors per month. Interpreting the model exactly, 42 errors would be removed, 3 would be left, and it would take 3.7 months, or leaving a little safety factor, 4 months, to achieve a 100-h MTBF.

5.17 (*a*)

1. If we use the fact that the number of errors $\approx 0.01 \, I_T$, we obtain a very rough estimate of $E_T = 0.01 \times 24{,}000 = 240$ errors

2. To obtain better estimates, match the MTBF expression at the two data points

$$1 \text{ month} - \text{MTBF} = 10 = \frac{1}{K\left[\dfrac{E_T}{I_T} - \epsilon_C^{(1)}\right]} = \frac{1}{K\left[\dfrac{E_T}{24,000} - \dfrac{20}{24,000}\right]}$$

$$2 \text{ months} - \text{MTBF} = 20 = \frac{1}{K\left[\dfrac{E_0}{I_T} - \epsilon_C^{(2)}\right]} = \frac{1}{K\left[\dfrac{E_T}{24,000} - \dfrac{50}{24,000}\right]}$$

Taking ratios of the two equations

$$\frac{10}{20} = \frac{\cancel{K}\left[\dfrac{E_T}{\cancel{24,000}} - \dfrac{50}{\cancel{24,000}}\right]}{\cancel{K}\left[\dfrac{E_T}{\cancel{24,000}} - \dfrac{20}{\cancel{24,000}}\right]}$$

Solving for E_T yields $E_T = 80$
Substitution into either original equation yields $K = 40$.

(b) $60 = \dfrac{1}{40\left[\dfrac{80 - X}{24,000}\right]}$ solving $X = 70$.

(c) We must make assumptions about the future error removal rate

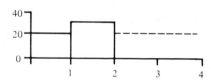

Estimate of future:
  1 more month to reach 70
  corrected errors, that is,
  3 months testing time.
  Note: At $\tau = 0$, MTBF $= \dfrac{600}{80} = 7.5$

(d) MTBF $= \dfrac{600}{80 - \epsilon_C(\tau)}$ (e) Reliability

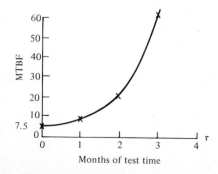

Months of test time

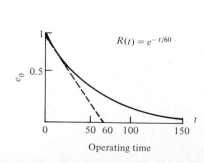

Operating time

(f)

$$R(t) = e^{-t/60} \approx 1 - \frac{t}{60} \text{ for small } t$$

$$0.9 = 1 - \frac{t}{60}, t \approx 6$$

5.26* Use exponential reliability model

$$R(t) = e^{-K[E_T - E_C(\tau)]t}$$

$$\text{MTBF} = \frac{1}{K[E_T - E_C(\tau)]}$$

Use least squares method to determine K and E_t for all three sets (assumptions) of data*

$$z = K[E_T - E_C(\tau)]$$

$$\frac{z}{K} = E_T - E_C(\tau)$$

$$E_C(\tau) = E_T - \frac{1}{K}z$$

Plot $E_C(\tau)$ versus z; fit best straight line "by eye."

Assumption 1

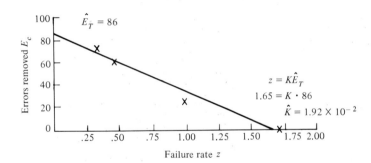

Assumption 2

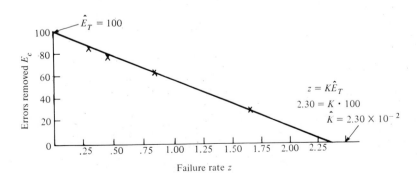

*For a complete analysis of this data, see technical paper: Shooman (1979b).

Assumption 3

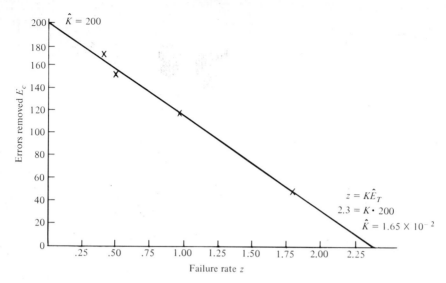

$R(t)$:

$$R_1(t) = e^{-1.92 \times 10^{-2}[86 - 74]t} = e^{-0.23t}$$

$$R_2(t) = e^{-2.3 \times 10^{-2}[100 - 81]t} = e^{-0.44t}$$

$$R_3(t) = e^{-1.65 \times 10^{-2}[200 - 162]t} = e^{-0.63t}$$

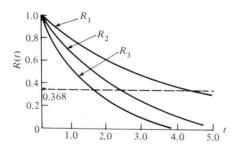

MTBF:

$$\text{MTBF}_1 = \frac{1}{1.92 \times 10^{-2}\left[86 - E_C(\tau)\right]}$$

$$\text{MTBF}_2 = \frac{1}{2.30 \times 10^{-2}\left[100 - E_C(\tau)\right]}$$

$$\text{MTBF}_3 = \frac{1}{1.65 \times 10^{-2}\left[200 - E_C(\tau)\right]}$$

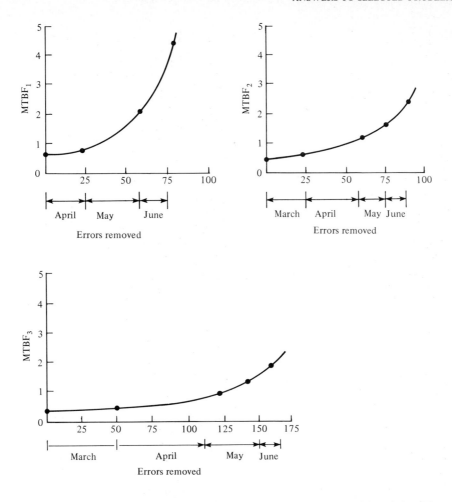

Note: Regardless of the assumption, the MTBF ≈ 2 to 5 hours, which is very low. The software must be in an early stage of integration testing.

Chapter 6

6.1	Document	Author	Vehicle	Purpose
	Needs	Customer	Memorandum result-ing from an internal or external study	To outline the purpose of the system and what it must do (WHY).
	Requirements	Customer	Memoranda, technical reports, studies	To record the quanti-tative parameter val-ues which must be satisfied (WHAT).
	Specification	Customer, or third party, or contrac-tor	Prose document, specification language, pseudo-code, algo-rithms	Show details of HOW to proceed in the pre-liminary design.
	Preliminary design	Contractor	Pseudo-code, high-level flow charts,	First attempt at the design. HIPO diagrams, and narrative on design.

6.2 (c) Design of a home records system for a homeowner with a home office.

Needs: To provide timely records each month which are suitable for income tax and accounting purposes.

Requirements: To provide the information required for invoices, accounts receivable, accounts payable, all income and deductions on itemized income tax form 1040, schedules A, B, C.

Specifications: Use an existing software system such as VISUCALC to expedite the production of the needed software. A complete set of monthly matrices, yearly matrices, and cumulative totals will be produced. The format will be stored in a given file so that each matrix is created by reading of the file. Each monthly matrix is stored in a seperate file, and a cumulative total is kept.

Preliminary Design: The rows of the matrix will represent each individual transaction and the columns will represent receivables, payables, deductable car expenses, deductable business expenses, and so on.

6.16 (c) Estimate of total development time 2 weeks, half time, or 40 hours.

```
          0                        5                        10 days
          !            !           !            !           !
Specs.    XXXXXXXXXXXXX                                      3 days
Design                 XXXXXXXX                              2 days
Test                        XXXXXXXXXXXXXXXXXXXX             4 days
Document                                         XXXX 1 day
```

6.24 (c) This is a small project and not too many reviews are needed. The crucial stages are when the specifications have been drawn, when the design is complete, and after the system has been tested. The key features of each review are given below. Since this is a small project, the number of participants in each review should be small.

Stage	Questions to be asked	Participants
End of specifications	Are they complete? Are they correct?	User and designer should discuss with accountant.
End of design	Is the implementation correct? Is the design simple and direct?	User and designer should show to another potential user.
End of project	Try out the finished product in a month.	User and second user should test.

6.26 According to the model, the development force, D, will shrink, and the maintenance force, M, will grow for the chosen example, $X = 0.2$, $D = 0.8^k$, $M = 1 - D$

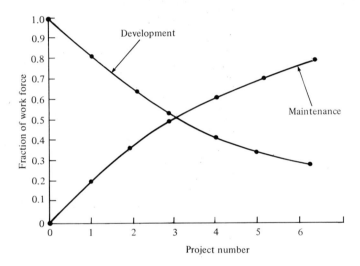

NAME INDEX

Abramovitz, M., 528
ACM (Association for Computing Machinery), 121, 130
Adams, E. C., 353
Aho, A., 207, 211, 212, 214
Akiyama, F., 188–193, 196, 327
Amoroso, S., 125
Amster, S. J., 313, 328, 359, 433, 434, 467
ANSI (American National Standards Institute), 17, 91, 130, 131
Arguimbau, L. B., 207
Aron, J. D., 444, 445
Ashcroft, E., 83, 84
Avizienis, A., 306

Babbage, C., 122
Backus, J. W., 66
Baggi, D. L., 257, 287
Bailey, N. T. J., 335, 338
Baker, F. T., 464–466
Balaban, H., 456
Barlow, R., 361
Barnett, M. P., 509
Basili, V. R., 150
Bayer, R., 175, 180
Becerril, J. L., 53
Beidler, J., 48
Beiser, B., 218
Belady, L. A., 155, 203, 489–491
Bell, C. G., 28, 29, 67, 121, 208, 217, 218, 428, 429
Bell Laboratories, 20, 91, 123, 233, 506
Berg, H. K., 92
Berge, C., 603, 606, 607
Bernard, H. H., 205
Bernhard, R., 306
Bianchi, M. H., 134
Bloch, A., 116
Blum, B. I., 134
Boehm, B. W., 3, 4, 10, 11, 13–15, 19, 209, 313, 315, 432, 435–437
Bohm, C., 66, 83
Bolsky, M., 236, 237, 315, 318, 439
Booth, T. L., 218
Borchers, M., 99, 100

Borodin, A., 214
Box, G. E. P., 474
Brandon, D. H., 416, 417
Braun, E., 5
Brooks, F. P., Jr., 47, 131, 313, 321, 322, 349, 413, 457, 464, 477
Brown, J. R., 200
Brown, R. W., 176
Brown, W. L., 127
Bruce, R. C., 248
Bryan, J. G., 376, 379, 513, 522
Burck, G., 494
Burks, A. W., 121
Burton, W. A., 217
Buxton, J. N., 31
Byron, A. A., 122

California, University of, Berkeley, 91
Carhart, R. R., 564
Central Computer Agency, 111
Chang, H. Y., 120
Chapin, N., 49, 50, 53
Cherry, C., 168, 183
Chien, Y. P., 129
Chomsky, N., 159
Clark, A. C., 27
Clark, R. W., 297
Codling, C., 253
Cohen, H. A., 127
Cohen, J. B., 128, 129
Conrad, M., 134
Constantine, L. L., 102, 106
Conway, R., 74, 80
Copps, S., 311
Corbató, F., 20, 123, 503–505
Cormier, G., 479
Courant, R., 162
Coutinho, J. de S., 340, 457, 468
Cowell, W., 16, 17
Crow, E. L., 29

DACS (Data and Analysis Center for Software), 31, 233, 363, 395

676

SUBJECT INDEX

Note: The symbol "prob." refers to a designated problem number.

Acceptance testing, 232, 482, 483
Ada (U.S. Department of Defense language), 20–22, 91, 93, 122*n.*, 123, 125, 126
Algol (programming language), 74*n.*, 93
Algorithmic complexity, 210–215
APL (programming language), 90, 93
Ashcroft-Manna technique, 83, 84, 86, 148–149 (prob. 2.48)
Assembly language programming, 122–129
Assertion (*see* Program proofs)
Automatic flowcharting, 53
Automatic programming, 23
Availability, 587–592
  steady-state, 590–592
  (*See also* Markov models; Software availability)

Backtracking (*see* Debugging)
Basic (programming language), 93
Bathtub curve, 303, 304
Benchmark programs, 217, 427
Big bang testing, 243
Binomial distribution, 521–523, 530
Bottom-up design, 38–43
BREAK construct (*see* LEAVE construct)
Breakpoints (*see* Debugging)
Bug (*see* Error)
Burn-in period, 304

C (programming language), 93
CASE statement, 72, 74, 76, 78–80
Certification, 232
Chief programmer teams, 464–467
Cobol (programming language), 93, 121
Code reading, 225–227
Coding (*see* Programming)
Comments (*see* Documentation)
Compiler diagnostics, 253, 254
Complement, 86*n.*
Complexity:
  algorithmic, 210–215
  code, 158
  concepts of, 150, 154–157

Complexity (*Cont.*):
  versus errors, 188–194
  graph theoretic, 196–203, 263, 264, 607, 608
    (*See also* Effort measure; Information content of program; Operator-operand length)
  knot, 200–203
  problem, 25, 476
  versus test difficulty, 226
Confidence interval, 542, 543
Cost estimation:
  classification of techniques, 438–443
  comparison of methods, 449, 457
  models for, 443–449
  penalty-incentive and warranty contracts, 454–456
  (*See also* Software cost)
Coupling among modules, 108
Cyclomatic complexity (*see* Complexity, graph theoretic)

Data-directed design, 97, 98
Data flowgraphs, 98–107
  definitions of symbols for, 101
Debugging:
  concepts of, 248–251
  deductive method of, 249, 252, 253
  definition of, 232
  inductive method of, 249, 252
Debugging plan (test plan), 485
Debugging tools, 131–134
Defensive programming, 78, 116–120
Demonstration test, 482–483
Design:
  bottom-up, 38–43
  concepts of, 24, 34–38, 230, 231
    (*See also* Software development)
  examples of, 43–47, 426
  modular, 107–108
  reviews of, 228, 479–482
  top-down, 38–43
  two-stage, 38–43
Design representation, 47–49, 61–65, 106, 107
  (*See also* Flowcharts; HIPO diagrams; Pseudo-code)
Development life cycle (*see* Software development)